Douglas Jay

Change and Fortune

A POLITICAL RECORD

Hutchinson

London Melbourne Sydney Auckland Johannesburg

Hutchinson & Co. (Publishers) Ltd

An imprint of the Hutchinson Publishing Group

3 Fitzroy Square, London W1P 6JD

Hutchinson Group (Australia) Pty Ltd
30–32 Cremorne Street, Richmond South, Victoria 3121
PO Box 151, Broadway, New South Wales 2007

Hutchinson Group (NZ) Ltd
32–34 View Road, PO Box 40–086, Glenfield, Auckland 10

Hutchinson Group (SA) (Pty) Ltd
PO Box 337, Bergvlei 2012, South Africa

First published 1980

© Douglas Jay 1980

Set in Monotype Imprint

Printed in Great Britain by The Anchor Press Ltd,
and bound by Wm Brendon & Son Ltd,
both of Tiptree, Essex

British Library Cataloguing in Publication Data

Jay, Douglas
     Change and fortune.
     1. Jay, Douglas
     2. Statesmen – Great Britain – Biography
     I. Title
     941.085′092′4   DA591.J/

ISBN 0 09 139530 5

to H. G. J. & M. L. J.
with love and gratitude

Contents

List of Illustrations

Foreword

This is not a history, but a personal record of events as seen by one single observer. Except for the background of childhood, school and university, it is a record of working rather than private or family life; and the latter is glanced at only when to omit it would seem unreal. What follows here is a mixture of narrative and argument, because life is like that, and because the narrative seems to me to illustrate the argument and the argument better to explain the narrative. I have compiled it partly from private records, partly from public sources, and partly from memory; and fallible as is memory, I hope inaccuracy has been cut to the minimum. Diaries I did keep for long periods, but only intermittently, because the pressure of working life, particularly in the war years, was too strong to allow time for any such respite. Where I have drawn here on these private sources, I have in most cases explicitly said so. I have used official Cabinet records to check facts and dates, not to add further information. After I had written this book, but before publication, Philip Williams's admirable biography *Hugh Gaitskell* appeared, covering many of the same years. The two accounts are thus independent, except where he has used information supplied by me.

I am most grateful to Professor H. L. A. Hart for reading the typescript of this book and correcting inaccuracies, though any that remain and opinions expressed are of course mine. I should also like to thank Dr Elizabeth Durbin for advice on pre-war Labour Party affairs, the House of Commons Library for their always invaluable services, the Cabinet Secretary for guidance on official records, my sister Mary for typing help, and Messrs Hutchinson for all sorts of assistance. Above all, I would like to thank my wife for unflagging support over a very long period in composing this book.

January 1980   D.P.T.J.

When summer's end is nighing
　　And skies at evening cloud,
I muse on change and fortune
　　And all the feats I vowed
　　When I was young and proud.

A. E. HOUSMAN, *Last Poems*

I was born at Tower House, Woolwich, at the top of Shooters Hill, on 23 March 1907. My father, Edward Aubrey Hastings Jay, represented Woolwich on the London County Council as a Municipal Reformer (as the Conservatives then called themselves) and duly became Chairman of the Education Committee. His family, whose records he preserved with much care, were Huguenot refugees from France, called 'Jaye' or 'le Jaye', who settled in East Anglia and devoted themselves to the wool trade. My father was born in Putney in 1869. He went to a prep school, St George's, Ascot, where he was later joined by a boy five years younger than himself: Winston Churchill. In his own later writings Churchill painted a rather sinister picture of this school which he regarded as oppressive and excessively disciplinarian. My father recorded quite different memories, put most of the blame on the mutinous young Winston and remained an admirer of the headmaster, Mr Kynnersley. The clearest personal memory which my father had of the young Winston was of his lurid language, reputedly picked up from the stable boys at Blenheim. My mother, who married my father in 1898, was the daughter of a Scotsman from Perth, Patrick Craigie, a civil servant and statistician who pioneered the foundation of the Ministry of Agriculture, and became one of its senior officials as well as a President of the Royal Statistical Society.

So fortune planted me at Tower House (which my father inherited from his aunt, Lady Teynham) in pre-1914 years with my elder brother, Alan, and two younger sisters, Mary and Helen. There were six acres of grounds, covering two fields, a cricket pitch, tennis court, a greenhouse, vegetable garden, two Jersey cows and a nomadic herd of chickens. Seven or eight servants, including nurses and two gardeners, made up the complement. But the garden was the paradise in which up to the chilling arrival of schooldays we could wander, explore, play, rest or just disappear. I soon developed a deep but amateur passion for flowers which never weakened, though the scope for it steadily contracted.

In the years before 1914 my father and mother devoted themselves almost entirely to social work in Plumstead, Woolwich and the East End of London. My father concentrated on the LCC, the Charity Organisation Society in Poplar and other parts of the East End, and the St Alban Boys' Club which had the free run of the Tower House fields for cricket and football. The sound of bat on ball would send me to sleep on summer evenings. My mother specialized in bible classes and guilds for girls from Plumstead. As children, however, we were very conscious of the military activities down the hill. We were frequently taken to church on Sunday via the Royal Artillery parade ground; so that the military bands, the British Grenadiers, and memorials to General Gordon got somewhat mingled in my mind with the hymns, prayers and psalms.

Besides his work on the LCC and in the East End, my father in 1912 took on the chairmanship of the Woolwich Juvenile Employment Committee set up under the Labour Exchange Act of 1909. The aim of this early effort was to find suitable jobs for school-leavers. Throughout the period up to 1914 he had been occupied full-time in voluntary unpaid work. He was nominally a Conservative. He wrote characteristically in 1947 in his unpublished memoirs about the LCC elections in Woolwich in which he was defeated in 1904: 'I was by conviction an individualist, and regarded the Socialist schemes of our Labour opponents as being a real menace to freedom. At the same time I was uncomfortably aware that the attitude of many of my supporters was a purely selfish one.' But his daily efforts to mitigate the poverty around him led him into contact and sympathy with the early Labour leaders of those days. Will Thorne, Will Crooks, Harry Gosling and George Lansbury were names I learnt very early. With George Lansbury my father remained friends for nearly thirty years. The friendship had already begun in March 1907 when my father stood in Woolwich successfully as Municipal Reform candidate for the LCC and defeated his Labour opponent, George Lansbury. And it still prospered when my father and I visited Lansbury, then suffering from a broken leg in the Manor House Hospital, Hampstead, in the mid-1930s.

In June of 1911 I was taken by my father to watch the Coronation of George V from the balcony of LCC Headquarters, Spring Gardens, alongside the Admiralty Arch. My father handed me over to Sir John Benn, LCC Liberal ('Progressive') leader, and father of Ernest Benn and Lord Stansgate, and grandfather of Tony Benn. He shepherded me on to the outside balcony as the imperial coach with the King-Emperor appeared under the Arch.

A little later, probably 1912 or 1913, I was walking with my nurse outside the 'elementary' school in Plum Lane, just below the brow of Shooters Hill, when the schoolchildren came streaming out on their way home. I noticed for the first time that they were nearly all bare-footed. I asked my nurse: 'Why do I wear shoes and socks and all these children none?' 'Because they are poor,' she said, 'and their parents cannot afford to buy boots and shoes for them.'

In June 1914 my father took me to a Naval training ship in the Thames Estuary to hear Prince Louis of Battenberg (distinguished by his royal beard as well as full Admiral's uniform), the First Sea Lord and father of Louis Mountbatten, present the prizes to the cadets in that ship. This was the Prince Louis who later, after the declaration of war, was forced to resign by a foolish public clamour stirred by his German name. Over fifty years afterwards, as President of the Board of Trade in May 1967, I was asked to visit the National Sea Training School on the Thames near Gravesend, and enquired from the Admiralty the exact date of my encounter with Prince Louis. It was 27 June 1914, the day before the assassination at Sarajevo.

On the morning of 5 August 1914 I carried *The Times* up to my father before breakfast at Tower House and read on the staircase that Britain had declared war on Germany on the previous evening. The picture in my mind was of British troops marching across Belgium with bands playing and Union Jack flying. It did not then occur to me that these stirring events could ever impinge on the calm world inside the Tower House garden. We took our normal summer holiday in late August 1914 at Woolacombe, where I had already formed what turned out to be a life-time attachment to the West Country. Each morning I picked up the papers from the village shop and brought my parents the news that the Germans had captured what the press called 'fortresses' at Namur, Lieges, Ghent, Brussels. But also in the early war years, the first blow fell. The more vigorous of our two gardeners left to join the forces, and I was recruited as part-time volunteer gardener.

At about the same time my father felt rather suddenly and harshly the economic wind of change. Income tax was jumping rapidly from a pre-war one shilling and eightpence in the pound towards four shillings. The cost of living, by the criteria of those days, was rising fast. And there were four children to support and educate. Having been comfortably off in 1905, even by Edwardian professional class standards, my father found himself by 1915 and 1916 hard put to it to maintain the Tower House establishment.

One evening in 1916 Tower House was literally shaken by the explosion of a TNT factory at Silvertown just across the river. My father had a fairly narrow escape in Charlton coming back on the 53 bus. After the war we learnt that it was an accident; but at the time at Woolwich it was taken very seriously because the Greenwich gas-works was hit by burning fragments from the explosion and itself went up in flames.

Then in early 1917 the real blow fell. Our not very fit second gardener was called up for military service – leaving, as my elder brother was at school, only myself, aged nearly ten, and my father in spare moments to look after several acres of garden. I rather relished the challenge and resolved that a mass display of pansies would be the centre-piece in the spring of 1917. But in May of that year I was due to join my brother at a boarding prep school, New Beacon, near Sevenoaks.

There was probably nothing wrong with New Beacon as a school, or much different from many other fee-paying prep schools for boarders in that era. But the sheer shock of sudden separation from home, mother, family and garden, and total immersion in a strange world of stone staircases, unknown people and unintelligible lessons, was to me shattering. Ironically, it had been made worse by my parents' well-meant decision to take me some weeks beforehand to a psychologist in North London because I was persistently afraid of the dark. This no doubt conscientious but foolish man (who would nowadays presumably be called a psychiatrist) gave me the impression that I was quite a different sort of creature from normal human beings.

At New Beacon my brother helped greatly with sympathetic common sense. Indeed I feared he might suffer from doing so. Looking back dispassionately years afterwards, one could easily understand that an instantaneous translation of a nine- or ten-year-old child from a family to a wholly alien scene is to some, though not to many others, unendurable. I was just one of the unlucky minority. At times the strain was so great that I devised stratagems for escape. But somehow I fought it out, right through to the end of July when the promised day came, and my brother and I found ourselves in the Tower House garden once again. That afternoon I told my mother I could not ever return to New Beacon, and I hoped without full confidence she would understand. It was a lovely, long, late July evening. When I went to bed, my mother said that she and my father had decided I would not go back to New Beacon. To my surprise, the whole experience of the past three months then seemed to burst a dam inside me, and tears of uncontrollable relief poured through the gap for several hours before I could put my gratitude into words. Happiness as deep has come to me since, but never as violent as on that July evening.

Only a few weeks, however, were left at Tower House. My father could no longer maintain even the reduced Tower House complement, and we must move. He had now taken a full-time job in the new Ministry of Food under Lord Rhondda. He worked in the Rationing Department of this pioneering venture and amongst his colleagues were William Beveridge, Victor Gollancz and Walter de la Mare. So we moved in August 1917 to Hampstead, which was intimately known by my mother who had been born and had lived there until 1898. And in Hampstead my family and I have remained on and off for sixty years. The move cut the complement of servants from eight to two; and I was, naturally, to be the only unpaid gardener. My father's financial struggles, of which I now became very conscious, were for the moment eased.

I was to attend, thank heaven, a day school and a suitable one was found in Shepherd's Walk, Hampstead, now a post office depot. I loved the system in force at this school, by which we all sat in an order and the first boy who answered a question correctly went to the top place and everyone else moved one down. This system greatly appealed to most of us, because it turned lessons into a sporting event. It incidentally awakened my hitherto unsuspected powers of learning. After two terms, however, St John's closed down and my parents cautiously compromised by moving me to a boarding school at Northwood between Harrow and Watford where a Broadstairs school, Wellesley House, had evacuated itself because of the war. Here just before lunch on 11 November 1918 the news spread round the school grapevine that the Germans had signed an armistice and the war was over. But the full reality and horror of that war was still wholly hidden from all of us in my generation.

By the summer of 1919 my father's job at the Ministry of Food was in doubt and the general atmosphere was that of the Geddes Axe. Faced with a bleak financial prospect, my father reluctantly decided that the family could not afford a summer holiday in Devon that year for the first and almost last time in our lives. My disappointment was acute, but I chanced to discover at this moment that nine out of ten of the children born in this country normally had no summer holiday at all. This discovery made all the more unforgettable an impression on me because of the intensity of my grief at the cancellation of our own holiday. From this moment onwards I was keenly conscious of the family's need to save money, and felt an abiding sympathy with all those who were short of it and a corresponding contempt for those who splashed money about as though it did not matter.

Earlier in the summer of 1919 Wellesley House had moved back to its normal home close to the chalky cliffs in Broadstairs. For the first time, now twelve, I found school not merely manageable but at times almost a pleasure. We were each allowed a garden. In my last year, 1919–20, at Wellesley House I surprised myself by emerging at the top of the school in work, still spurred on by the gaming system. Early in 1920 the headmaster suggested I should compete for a scholarship at Eton. My father, who had been at Winchester in the 1880s, was not too keen on this, for all his loyalties were to Winchester. I agreed to do the Eton scholarship exam as a long shot, and arrived to stay in Windsor with my mother, in June of 1920. But immediately I saw the dingy, red-brick forbidding buildings of the college and its surroundings at Eton, I took a strong dislike to the whole place. I did not try very hard to make the best of my Latin and even more defective Greek, but did strike up a fleeting acquaintance with my next-door neighbour at the exam desk: Quintin Hogg. He got the top scholarship, and I got none, but was soon accepted at my father's old House at Winchester instead.

As a family we stayed in our first Hampstead house in East Heath Road until 1922, when economy drove us to a still smaller house a hundred yards away, 13 Well Road, where my mother lived till her death in 1965. In 1919 and 1920 there lived next door to us in East Heath Road a family called Millar. My brother (then a Naval cadet) and I used to play tennis with their eighteen-year-old daughter, Vi Millar. One day in early 1919 we met Vi outside our gate accompanied by a smallish military man just back from the wars, in full officer's uniform, complete with leather belt and cane, peak cap and other Army insignia. Rather embarrassed, Vi muttered: 'May I introduce my friend, Major Attlee?' 'Hullo,' we responded in lame schoolboy fashion. The major clicked heels, sprang to attention and replied in sharp parade-ground tones: 'Good After *NOON!*' Vi Millar became his wife not long afterwards, but I did not meet the major again for some sixteen years.

In September 1920 I arrived at Winchester. Dick Crossman, my exact contemporary for six years at Winchester, writing thirty years afterwards, described life there as 'five years' struggle for survival and one year's struggle for success'. This was one of the truest things he ever said. The living unit at Winchester to which he belonged was in practice not the school, but the House, a group of forty boys and a rather remote housemaster; and here we ate, slept, worked on our own, argued, fought and played such games as were possible indoors or in a small concrete yard. And from the House one made forays several times a day to school classrooms, playing fields and the medieval buildings of the chapel and the College proper. After the first fortnight it was a free-for-all in the House, with no holds barred (other than biting, which was regarded as not done). I was relieved to find that school work at any rate was based clearly on merit and performance.

The contemporary hero, however, in the House was not Sir Edward Grey, or H. A. L. Fisher, or A. P. Herbert, or the poet Robert Nichols, all of whom had been inmates, but Douglas Jardine, who had left the term before. He had led the school to victory at cricket over Eton, had won the House Cricket Cup, and – I was given to understand – had virtually never lost a game, though on some occasions as school captain he had found it necessary to alter the score in House matches after the play was over in order to be sure of winning. When he became captain of the English side playing Australia nearly ten years later, I felt sure England would win.

Winchester, however, was not all cricket. There was the winter. Heating was unknown in the 'galleries' (dormitories) and not much anywhere till December. Food was scarce, allegedly due to the aftermath of the 1914–18 war, but really, as we suspected, to the effort of the housemaster to make a profit. Except in the spring term, we suffered a horrible penance known as 'Morning Lines' – a forty-five minutes' working period at 7.30 a.m. in the school buildings seven minutes' walk away, followed by chapel, before we returned to the House for breakfast. As I like many others lived on sugar, there was a wild rush after chapel back to our House to grab some sugar for breakfast before it was all gone. Victory went to the fleetest, of whom I was not at first one. Also dreaded by most of us were OTC (Officers' Training Corps) parades, which involved dressing up in khaki with brass buttons, leather belts and puttees. The 'corps' was nominally voluntary, but the alternative to joining was to learn German. Faced with this, everybody chose, and cursed, the corps.

The best moments at Winchester were the summer half-holidays – Tuesdays, Thursdays and Saturdays – when from noon to 7.30 we were free from compulsory work. The beauty of the Itchen valley, the medieval buildings, river, water meadows and rolling downs, came first fully alive for me in the summer afternoons in those years. By my fifth and sixth year, I devised a happy compromise with the imperious necessity of working. Bicycling from the House at about 1.30, fully equipped with school books, chocolate, fruit, rug and cushion, I escaped alone to a high railway embankment in the full sunshine which commanded a splendid view of Winchester and the Itchen valley and St Catherine's Hill. In five hours a great deal of work was done. For work and academic success had now become a pressing obligation. My family were making major sacrifices to educate me, and somehow this had to be requited. At this moment I was lucky. Spencer Leeson, later headmaster and thereafter Bishop of Peterborough, but at this time a young enthusiastic junior master with a single-minded – some said simple-minded – attachment to medieval architecture, history and English literature, decided that I had a hidden talent for the English if not for the Greek and Latin languages.

Spurred on by Leeson's architectural zeal, a group of us visited Romsey, Chichester and Salisbury, and in the spring holiday of 1925 Rouen, Chartres, Paris and Amiens. The latter party was a huge success and included William Hayter, Dick Crossman, and Roger Cooke from my House.[1] It gave me a lifelong admiration for Chartres to which I returned with Hayter and my son Peter in 1952. At Winchester in 1925 we also produced a history of the College; and among the authors were Roger Cooke, William Hayter, John Sparrow and myself. Crossman refused to participate on the ground that it was an 'unscholarly' exercise.

Roger Cooke had also at this stage taken up with the League of Nations Union, and he and I preached the message of internationalism. The need for an international authority to enforce a world rule of law became my political creed thereafter. At the same time Ian Parsons (prefect in charge of our 'gallery' and eventually chairman of Chatto and Windus) used his prefect's light to read contemporary English poetry every evening to those of us who chose to stay awake. Rupert Brooke, Wilfred Owen, Housman, Flecker, de la Mare, Masefield and many others of the 1914–18 generation entered our consciousness in those evenings.

In the summer of 1925 faced with the necessity of earning a living and repaying my family, I told my father that I meant to take a paid job and not go to a university. This ultimatum led to a compromise plan. I should stay on next term, and take the New College scholarship exam, in which a special history paper would be set for me, to make up for my lamentable failure to

[1] Later a Conservative MP.

remember the Greek irregular verbs by heart. If I failed, I would leave then and there, and earn my own living somehow. So I resolved to work morning, noon and night, and seized gratefully on the hours of personal tutoring which both Leeson and A. T. P. Williams (the headmaster, afterwards Bishop of Durham and Winchester) offered me. Williams' dry scepticism I now found particularly stimulating. Medieval history and the English eighteenth and nineteenth century were the subjects he chose for me; and I ended the term with as warm, if rather less erudite, an enthusiasm for British parliamentary democracy as his own. When the scholarship results were announced, I could not face looking at the list and had to ask a friend to report it to me. Wilberforce and Crossman were naturally first and second, and I was – by the skin of my teeth – sixth and last, but on it.

The new prospect opened up was intoxicating indeed. The scholarship would repay and reward my father for the heavy sacrifices he had made; and suddenly I was free from all school restrictions and duties, and could read, play, walk, swim, or recite poetry just as I chose, for two whole terms. Crossman, now a regular companion of mine, took a very poor view of my defeating him one term later in the English Poetry prize. He had written, of course, an elaborate and rather unintelligible composition in the latest fashionable style of T. S. Eliot, whom he loudly admired; while I had played safe with a series of sonnets in the manner of Matthew Arnold, Wordsworth and Keats. It just showed, Crossman thought, how out of touch the examiners were with contemporary post-romantic poetry. He was probably right this time.

In the same month, May 1926, the start of our last term, I found myself confronting Crossman again, but this time in the debate on the General Strike in the school Debating Society with the headmaster presiding. Crossman made the leading speech for the Baldwin Government, and I for the TUC, and my memory is that the vote went to the Government. The miners' strike, dragging on month by month throughout that summer, as an outright cut in wages was forced on them, aroused my political feelings and left me by the autumn an ardently convinced supporter of the Labour Movement. I therefore set myself the rather formidable programme for the rest of my academic years of studying in the following order: first history, second philosophy, third economics and fourth politics. Already in the previous five weeks' spring holiday I had made a brave start on this odyssey by reading, while laid flat in bed by a dislodged cartilage, the whole of Gibbon and Macaulay's *History of England*. Gibbon unfolded for me altogether unsuspected horizons and thereafter remained the most enjoyable single literary experience I can remember. He also led me to a philosophical revolution. My mother had always been a scrupulous observer of Anglo-Catholic duties and principles. For years her Christianity had meant much to me; for if it were all true, what could be more important? But at nineteen I asked myself how did I know it was true? In the last resort it was evidently I who had to choose between those who thought it was and those like Gibbon and Shelley who apparently did not. And the obstinate conclusion forced itself on me that if I had to decide this as rationally as I could, I also had no less and no more power to decide the direct question of the truth of the beliefs themselves. So in the heady atmosphere of high summer in the Hampshire countryside, this last term at Winchester left me a Shelleyan, an internationalist and a would-be champion of both social justice and personal freedom.

In the House itself toleration was now in fashion. The five of us who ran it had, with reasonable harmony, converted the previous arbitrary despotism into a sort of benevolent anarchy. It remained, of course, a wholly male society, where half-realized erotic impulses did not turn out to be nearly so disturbing to mental balance as critics of the system would no doubt assume. We did, however, as the midsummer 'Eton Match' weekend of 1926 approached, embark on an audacious adventure never before attempted in the House – a dance on the premises to which sisters and female cousins would be freely invited. Next evening, still flushed with pride at our successful daring, I climbed Saint Catherine's Hill with my closest friend to look down before sunset on our precious little world. It was one of those shining evenings that come rarely and unpredictably at midsummer. Never again, I said out loud, can I be as carefree as this, and never again have no worries at all.

But there was still one month to go till the final school formalities known as 'Medal speaking'. At this ceremony my father sat next at dinner to Mr Justice Crossman, a most upright Victorian Christian, classical scholar and so conscientious a judge that he was said to find great difficulty in bringing any case to an end. Next morning my father told me that Judge Crossman had said to him on the way home: 'Do you understand your son? I cannot understand mine.' Dick's mother, as I found staying with the family in the holidays at Buckhurst Hill, was half-German and one maternal grandparent wholly German; a fact which contributed, I realized in later years, to a fair understanding of Dick. In my last year at school I was a firm admirer of his scholastic virtuosity. But I had already noticed that those who had known him longest tended to be his unkindest critics. When I was one day warmly extolling his powers to one of his College contemporaries, the latter replied with a comment I never quite forgot: 'Yes, you are right. Dick has every intellectual faculty known to man, except the power of distinguishing between truth and falsehood.'

Romantic interludes have a way of ending in near-farce. At the end of this summer term those of us in the OTC at Winchester went to an OTC camp at Tidworth near Salisbury. Having damaged my cartilage again in an improvised rugger scramble, I was forced to go home early and was driven away in full khaki and puttees in the school corps commander's car, (together with my best friend, who was being given a lift elsewhere) across the parade ground amid ironic cheers to Tidworth station. So this was the end. Hobbling on one khaki-leg on the platform, I could think of no more appropriate gesture than shaking hands with my friend and saying a banal 'good-bye'. We must have looked foolish, though that was not what I felt. So it turned out that I always thought of Tidworth station when I later read the verse, not then known to me:

> He would not stay for me; and who can wonder?
> He would not stay for me to stand and gaze.
> I shook his hand and tore my heart in sunder
> And went with half my life about my ways.[2]

After Winchester, Oxford for two years at least was something of a disappointment to me. At Winchester you were never lonely. Leisure and freedom were usually brief respites from the ever-running routine. At New College there was no routine from which to be relieved. You found yourself alone in a fairly spacious room for most of the day with a number of books you might or might not read. No daily automatic games were provided to recharge the mind. I bravely spent my first vacant week reading through the whole of Shakespeare's historical plays, and this was perhaps the best spent week of that term. Worse still was the intensely felt absence of one's best friends left at school with whom one had half-consciously counted on being reunited. Years afterwards I discovered that both Byron and Rupert Brooke in their very different epochs had hated their first few barren weeks at Cambridge because of the loneliness; and if one had known at the time that even they had suffered in this way, it might have been some solace to us smaller fry. Oxford also plunged one unexpectedly into a class society. At Winchester at least all those in the school lived in the same way, and one knew little of their parents' income. At Oxford in the 1920s we were rich or poor. Despite my scholarship, my father was still covering two-thirds of my living and tuition costs, and for this reason I decided on an austerity regime with only two serious meals a day, little heating in my rooms and no costly holidays abroad. Lack of money also cut one off from the lunch-party, sherry-drinking circuit linked with popular young dons like Maurice Bowra, whose celebrated aphorisms were, however, freely gossiped around the university. One suddenly discovered that some of one's old associates from school were possessed of surprising wealth and entertained freely in Christ Church. There were limits to the hospitality that one could accept, if nothing but tea and biscuits could be offered in return. I had no option anyway but to concentrate on two objectives: spending as little money as possible, and achieving a First in Greats.

Wykehamists started at New College in my time with one guiding principle firmly implanted in their minds. They must not form an Old Wykehamist clique at Oxford. So earnestly did some of us take this at first that we hardly dared be seen talking to one another in public. But of course after a few

[2] A. E. Housman, *Additional poems*, no. VII.

weeks human nature broke through. John Sparrow lived above me for two years on the same staircase, but he had left Winchester, with a great reputation, one year before the rest of us; and a difference of one year in generation was at Oxford in those days a considerable gulf. Hugh Gaitskell had reached New College two years before me; and though I knew him by sight both at school and at New College, I cannot remember ever speaking to him at either.

Very early in my first term, however, walking back from a lecture in Balliol, I was joined by another New College freshman whose comments on the lecture and whose marked Yorkshire pronunciation both much attracted me. This was Herbert Hart, straight from Bradford Grammar School. We worked frequently together for much of the next three years at Oxford and remained lifelong friends thereafter. He practised as a barrister in the 1930s, but after the war became a philosophy tutor at Oxford, then Professor of Jurisprudence and eventually Principal of Brasenose. Another new discovery who enlivened New College for me was John Witt, whose reputation for excessive Etonian polish was redeemed in my eyes by his enthusiasm both for tennis and for my long-distance walking ventures. Thirty years later John Witt duly became Chairman of the National Gallery. During the vacations in the 1920s, thanks to him and his mother I spent some extremely harmonious working weeks at their National Trust cottage at Alfriston among the Sussex Downs. A little later in my first year I came to know an equally talented undergraduate who also became a long-standing friend, Arnold Pilkington of the St Helens Pilkington family. Besides being well off (which at New College meant having a car) and good-looking, he was equally proficient at music, rugger, athletics, foreign languages, rock-climbing and economics. He introduced me to both economics and serious rock-climbing. Last but not least, still at New College that year, was Frank Pakenham, later Lord Longford, whose rather elephantine form I first encountered on the soccer field. There were times when the New College forwards included John Sparrow, Frank Pakenham, myself and Goronwy Rees, who arrived at New College from Cardiff two years later. We were not notably successful as a forward line.

My generation reached Oxford in 1926 just after the heyday of the professional aesthetes, many of them writers and a few mere pleasure-seekers, who had flourished there in the earlier 1920s. Those were the years of Cyril Connolly, Harold Acton, Graham Greene, Evelyn Waugh, Richard Hughes, Kenneth Clark and Peter Quennell. Most of them were gone by 1926. Of Harold Acton, usually represented as a sort of post-war Oscar Wilde, I heard as many stories in my first term at Oxford as I did of Jardine in my first term at Winchester. Though the frivolous extravagance and alleged riotous parties of the Acton epoch had worn off by 1926 and 1927, the conventional morality of the intellectuals was still violently antipathetic to politics or indeed to serious interest in anything other than philosophy, literature and the arts. We were constantly warned against 'careerism' which was regarded as the unforgivable sin. I remember Dick Crossman, who became my closest confidant in these years, giving me to understand that anyone who joined the Union, or talked about politics, was really falling below the minimum standard expected of an educated man. Intensely agitated as I was about the treatment of the miners in 1926, and therefore the fortunes of the Labour Party, I judged it best not to argue with him about all this. Almost all the ambitious intellectuals around me, apart from those few bent on a special profession, were determined to become novelists or poets. And, strangely enough, some of them did; notably from my years, Auden, Day-Lewis, Louis MacNeice and Stephen Spender. Of these, Stephen Spender was the only one I finally knew at all well, and that in my last year at Oxford. Though at his invitation I occasionally, like many others, contributed to *Oxford Poetry*, I very soon discovered that, much as I loved English poetry and imaginative literature of many kinds, I certainly could not write it myself.

One day in my second term Crossman stamped into my room, and told me he was entering for the Chancellor's English Essay prize and he thought I ought to compete as well. I laboured hard for some weeks and went back to London to get the finished product properly typed. The night before it was due to be delivered to the University authorities, I called on Crossman and asked if he had his essay ready. 'What essay?' he enquired. I reminded him and he replied: 'That! I gave up the idea weeks ago.' Undeterred I handed in my typescript and was frankly exceedingly pleased as well as surprised later to hear that I had won the prize, because it presented me with the altogether magnificent sum of £25.

Oxford in the late as well as the early 1920s was, for the ordinary undergraduate, almost entirely without female company. Only on special traditional occasions, such as the Commem. Balls or Eights Weeks were women seen in the presence of the rest of us. Association with them was tacitly regarded by most of my friends as eccentric, perverse, and rather uncivilized. This was, I suspect, why so many of my contemporaries married foreign girls whom they had met after leaving Oxford away from the vigilant eye of their friends – for instance John Witt an American and Crossman a German. Almost the only female undergraduate whom I can remember meeting, and that only at Greats lectures, was Elizabeth Harman, known throughout much of the University as the Zuleika Dobson of the day. Her fabulous charm, one found on meeting her, had not been overrated. Just a few chinks existed in the iron curtain; for Elizabeth and Hugh Gaitskell, I afterwards heard, were close friends. He introduced her to Frank Pakenham whom she married a few years later. But, Elizabeth apart, we scarcely met a girl; romantic moments were rarer than they had been even at school; and such erotic life as came our way tended to remain airily suspended on a high platonic and literary plane.

Philosophy was what mattered to me. I was not one of those who, perhaps to avoid the trouble of thinking, regarded philosophy as a dialectical exercise or a 'technique of thought'. I wanted to find the answers to the ultimate questions. What did human beings know, and how? What was the meaning of good and evil? Was human free will an illusion or a reality? Naturally I started with all sorts of irrational, adolescent notions picked up semi-consciously from the fashionable intellectual perversities of the day – at that time pragmatism, behaviourism and of course Freud. But all these cobwebs were soon blown away by the reigning New College philosopher, H. W. B. Joseph, with whom I was exceedingly lucky to have been thrown into immediate contact. He had married in middle age the daughter of Robert Bridges, the Poet Laureate; but she had died in childbirth some months before my generation came to Oxford. All humbug, muddle and ambiguity were mercilessly annihilated in dialogue with Joseph. A follower at Oxford of the logician, John Cook Wilson, Joseph possessed the most penetrating and honest mind I ever encountered. My first tutorial with him, supposed to be one hour, lasted for four hours; and it was characteristic that with all his attainments he was cheerfully ready to devote all this attention to an ignorant and loquacious young man of nineteen. Joseph was naturally criticized, because some of his victims resented the treatment and took refuge in abusing either him or philosophy itself. Yet he was in many ways when you knew him, an intellectually humble man, who frequently confessed he did not know the answers to the questions put to him. I was rebuked at reading parties by his colleague, A. H. Smith, for putting to Joseph such ill-judged questions as 'Do animals think?' – to which he answered: 'I don't know.'

If one was prepared as an undergraduate to persevere as rigorously as Joseph himself, he offered one a marvellous opportunity. By the end of my first year I found most of my preconceived beliefs in ruins and was overwhelmed in addition by the task of mastering Plato and Aristotle (in Greek) and a selection of the eighteenth- and nineteenth-century European philosophers as well. It was not till my third year that the clues began gradually to fall into place, and I at last felt that the whole exhausting exercise was going to be worth while. In ethics, at least, I became convinced that there was firm, hard ground; though the problem of sense perception and the real nature of the physical world baffled me till the end.

Professional philosophy since the nineteenth century has of course bravely explored new country and has arguably revived some old fallacies. It has now by the 1970s, like many subjects, become virtually impossible for any but the professional to follow. Looking back myself over half a century, I believe that the two thinkers I found in the end most illuminating and liberating were Plato and in our own time G. E. Moore. In later years, when forced out of contact with academic philosophy, my mind would revert to Plato's Republic more often than any other philosophical work. Kant and

Hegelianism were still much in fashion in my years at Oxford. But in the short time available to us after translating the Greeks I could not pretend to make up my mind which of their portentous writings were profound and which unintelligible. I finished Greats with the tentative suspicion that the former preponderated in the works of Kant and the latter in those of Hegel.

Our other philosophy tutor was A. H. Smith, later Warden of New College, as different a character from Joseph as could be found. A naturally benevolent and likeable bachelor, he was supposed to be a Kantian expert, but his real interest was in the visual arts. Smith took over the Wardenship of New College soon after H. A. L. Fisher's death in 1940. In my years, Fisher had appeared to undergraduates a remote figure, who occasionally asked one to lunch to meet celebrities such as J. L. Garvin, Editor of the *Observer* (the first and worst compulsive talker I ever met). Within New College, Fisher, for all his impressive academic record was, I fear, most remembered for his habit of interspersing his conversation with the words: 'When I was in the Cabinet', or 'As Lloyd George used to say to me', lit up with a rather mirthless smile. Smith (himself a New College undergraduate from 1903 until 1906 was still Warden in 1958 when a few months before his death he related to me, as he stood pensively in New College Front Quad, the following story of how the news of Mafeking came to New College. Before Fisher as Warden came Spooner of the notorious 'Spoonerisms', and before Spooner reigned Warden Sewell till 1903. A few years earlier, when the report of the victory at Ladysmith (so Smith recounted) reached Oxford, bells were rung and flags were flown in all Oxford Colleges except New College where, to the indignation of the undergraduates, Sewell ruled against any such excesses. Later, when in May 1900 news broke of the even more glorious triumph at Mafeking, New College undergraduates decided that no further slur on their patriotism would be tolerated. A deputation of five was nominated and an appointment made for later that afternoon with Warden Sewell, for which a major oration was prepared by the undergraduate spokesman, *requesting* the Warden that the bells be rung and the flags flown that evening. The Warden, according to Smith, replied as follows: 'Young men, you may not realize that I have known not merely Oxford, but New College, for a very long time. I well remember, at the age of five, being stopped by my aunt in New College Lane and told the news of the victory – at Waterloo. No bells were rung that evening in New College, and I see no reason why they should be on this lesser occasion.' Warden Sewell, an inscription in New College cloister records, was born in 1810 and died in 1903.

Third among our Greats tutors in the 1920s was Christopher Cox, himself only five or six years older than our generation of undergraduates. He later became Educational Adviser to the Colonial Office; and, as Sir Christopher Cox, helped in the founding of a series of universities throughout the Commonwealth. In the 1920s he was formally teaching Greek and Roman history; but very soon became, to many undergraduates, not merely a tutor but their most valued adviser, personal friend and moral support in the whole shifting sands of the university – and for me, among others, a lifelong friend. In those days Joseph, Smith and Cox were available at almost any hour of the day and night, with invariable patience, to be visited and persecuted with questions from inquisitive undergraduates. To Christopher Cox, counting personal and intellectual sustenance together, I owed more than to any other individual in university or school.

His understanding support was especially precious in my second year in New College when, till the summer came, depression and discouragement tended to bear down upon me. In the first year the expectation of close friends from school rejoining me a year later had upheld the hope that the idyll of that last summer at Winchester would be restored. But it was not to be. The discovery that old friends had made new friends, and that our interests had diverged, mine to philosophy, theirs to athletics, made the disillusion all the keener, and the long hours sitting in my room, trying to translate Herodotus, all the more desolating.

But there were consolations. These were years when a new novel, play or book of verse from an established author was a major event in one's life; and I shared with my contemporaries the excitement of discovering Hardy, Yeats, D. H. Lawrence, T. S. Eliot, Aldous Huxley, and the playwrights then favoured at the Oxford Playhouse: Ibsen, Chekhov, Strindberg and Shaw. D. H. Lawrence and *The Waste Land* attained almost the status of cults in Oxford at this time, though my own lifelong distaste for fashion led me, I fear, somewhat to undervalue them. It was Hardy, Yeats, Matthew Arnold, Housman and above all Shakespeare's Sonnets which to me rang truest and struck deepest.

My other constant reading in these years was shared with most of my colleagues also: the sudden outburst of descriptive novels about real life in the First War. They began with Remarque's *All Quiet on the Western Front*, soon succeeded by Robert Graves' *Goodbye to All That*, Siegfried Sassoon's *Memoirs of an Infantry Officer*, Edmund Blunden's *Undertones of War*, and, most memorable to me, Hemingway's *A Farewell to Arms* in 1929. These personal records left an immense impression on my generation at Oxford. My own fervent internationalism was hardened into a conviction that the main purpose of politics in future should be to prevent another major war. Not yet were we compelled to face the question whether, if threatened by force, a nation should defend itself with similar force. But one of the very first events which opened my eyes to the real nature of the Nazi movement was their attempt by violence to prevent the film of *All Quiet on the Western Front* from being shown at all.

My third year was an almost continuous grind right up to the final Greats exam, and respites were few and far between. One was the discovery of the Cotswold country in spring and summer with its distinctive colours and unique architecture, which remained for me Oxford's most precious virtue. Another diversion was breakfast on Sunday mornings at the OUDS,[3] which was partly run as a club and contained many non-acting members. The star occasion of the OUDS year was the annual 'smoker' when Osbert Lancaster, dressed as an Anglo-Indian colonel in shorts and sun hat, accompanied by a troop of undergraduates disguised as chorus girls, gave the annual address to the Girl's High School, and led the singing of traditional verses ending with the refrain:

> The days before the war
> When men were men,
> And girls were then
> Just girls and nothing more.

High-speed long distance walking, though a peculiar taste, proved in my case one other effective antidote to the tedium of over-concentrated work. Crossman and I managed the fifty-two miles from Oxford to Winchester most enjoyably in fourteen hours; and I cut one hour off this in a mainly solo walk, from New College to the Witt's house in Portman Square, after John Witt had been struck with muscle trouble soon after leaving Oxford. Later, when I was working at Hampstead, a benevolent lady who lived a few doors from us and specialized in hospitality for eccentric young men, appealed to me to take her then tenant, Richard Hughes, for a curative walk. He had, she told me, just suffered a nervous shock after deserting his intended bride at the church gate and was now writing a serious novel. The bride later married another writer, and the novel turned out to be *A High Wind in Jamaica*. I suggested a Metropolitan train from Finchley Road into the Chilterns and a walk towards Oxford. We finished that night at the Spread Eagle, Thame, after Richard Hughes had frequently protested he could go no further. But his conversation had easily overpowered his weariness as well as mine throughout the day, and I was delighted later by the success of *A High Wind*.

In Oxford itself, my other main periodic respite was provided by 'Sligger' Urquhart, the Dean of Balliol, who maintained evening sessions in his room for anyone who chose to drop in. Though despised by super-intellectuals, because he could not compete with Maurice Bowra in malice of speech or scale of hospitality, Sligger was a highly cultivated and essentially kindly character who delighted in conversation with the young and was, within his means, endearingly generous. To escape from work one evening a week for an hour or two, to Sligger's room over the Balliol gateway, was, for many of us, both refreshing and undemanding. Sligger used to complain with mock nostalgia that in his youth young men talked about Botticelli but now they all talked about unemployment. In his room I met the seventeen-year-old Randolph Churchill, who struck me as the most physically attractive and mentally incoherent character I had yet encountered. He used to denounce

[3] Oxford University Dramatic Society.

Stanley Baldwin (this was in 1928/9) with a ferocity that made me realize for the first time how little love was lost between Baldwin and his then Cabinet colleague, Winston Churchill.

In this third year I also fell in with the celebrated Father d'Arcy of the Jesuit establishment, Campion Hall. Far more intellectually acute, if less indiscriminately hospitable, than Sligger – only less acute than Joseph – Father d'Arcy somehow radiated warmth through a sharp, frosty, mocking manner. He loved unrelenting, merciless logic as avidly as I did; and we spent many evening hours arguing for and against the existence of God without either, I fear, converting the other. Father d'Arcy (who lived till 1977) had in some circles a reputation for mild snobbery, and the current Oxford doggerel ran in my day as follows.

> Are you rich and highly born?
> Is your soul by anguish torn?
> Come to me, I'll cure it all,
> Martin d'Arcy, Campion Hall.

But I never myself saw any evidence of this weakness.

Such were the temporary diversions. Most of that last year for me, however, was uninterrupted Herodotus, Thucydides, Plato, Aristotle, Cicero and Tacitus. Fear of collapse at the last hurdle haunted me for months. Joseph, Cox and Smith gave never-flagging help. But I owed even more to sporadic dialogues with Herbert Hart, which, whether on philosophy ancient or modern, or history Greek or Roman, possessed the charm of frequently ending in hilarity as well as enlightenment.

In May 1929, ten days before the Greats exam began, I was deeply though privately stirred by the general election of that month, which I hoped would give the first real chance for the mass of the population to strike back at the unavenged injustices of 1926. I persuaded a particularly sombre New College don, Dr Poole, who had a wireless, to let me sit up in his room after midnight and hear the results. At 3 a.m. or thereabouts it was clear the Labour Party was winning, and I went to bed happy. But Dr Poole anxiously remarked: 'See you in the morning if our throats are not cut first' – by which he meant that the election result presaged, in his view, a reign of terror. This picture of Ramsay MacDonald, Sidney Webb and Philip Snowden, running riot with long knives among the Oxford dons, never failed to entertain me throughout the rest of MacDonald's timid reign.

The next week actually brought not revolution, but the Greats exam of June 1929. The night before, John Sparrow thoughtfully invited all of us competing from New College, including William Hayter, Herbert Hart, Edmund Compton, and myself to a sherry party in his rooms. I could not have felt nearer panic if it had been the Last Judgement which impended. Indeed so acute was the inner tension that total silence fell on the assembled company, till Sparrow effectively broke it by remarking: 'Let us be honest,

and admit what we're all afraid of is getting a Second.' The exam itself was
followed three weeks afterwards by a viva, which was for me prolonged –
an accepted sign of failure. Luckily the philosophy examiner, MacMurray
made a slip in asking me a question (he mistranslated a Greek word), and I
pounced on this and would not let go until he admitted after some time that
he was mistaken. I believe it was this slip of his which saved me and affected
much of my later life; for a week later my mother handed me a telegram on
the tennis court in Hampstead saying that they had given me a First after
all. We achieved seven Firsts in Greats that year from New College, including Sparrow, Hart, and Compton. Of these, Hart's was adjudged the best.
Three of those competing (Sparrow, Hayter and Hart) afterwards became
Heads of Oxford Colleges.

But Joseph had the last word. In case any young man became too pleased
with any academic success, he always added a terse comment by letter after
the results for each candidate. For me, just as I began at last to pride myself
as a philosopher, the Josephian verdict ran: 'It was a narrow shave. His
philosophy was helped out by his history. His mark in Green history was
β–' – words which fifty years have not erased from my memory. For these
ordeals meant desperately much to most of us at this aspiring age. No six
months have passed in half a century since then without my experiencing
the dream that I am unaccountably, inexplicably, but all too inexorably,
taking the Greats exam all over again – sometimes for the third time.

In July 1929, however, the ecstatic relief that it was all over soon gave
way to the obstinate question: what should one do next? My only firm conviction was that as almost all Old Wykehamists became civil servants, lawyers or dons, these three professions at least were firmly ruled out. I had
some idea that I ought to go into business or industry. But it is a curious
comment on our educational system that, though I had done tolerably well
at school and Oxford, nobody seemed able to advise me how to set about
so eccentric a career. My father, therefore, consulted H. A. L. Fisher,
Warden of New College, who suggested that as I was supposed to be good at
writing essays, I might perhaps become a journalist, and added that he was
very willing to consult his good friend, Geoffrey Dawson, Editor of *The
Times*. He did. And Dawson offered me a job as a sub-editor on two years'
probation at £5 per week, which I gratefully accepted. I clocked in at
Printing House Square on 21 October 1929, in the same week precisely as
the start of the great Wall Street crash, which ushered in – some said
started – the Great Depression of the thirties.

The Wall Street crash also coincided with the stage in my planned academic voyage when I was to change tacks from philosophy to economics.
What was the cause of the Wall Street collapse? What was the cure for unemployment? Since sub-editing at Printing House Square only occupied
one – even nominally – from 4 p.m. to 11.30 p.m. or so, I embarked on
economics, unsupervised except by Arnold Pilkington, with simple text

books like Hubert Henderson's *Supply and Demand* and more boldly with Bernard Shaw's just published *Intelligent Woman's Guide to Socialism and Capitalism*. But my main occupation in November and December 1929 was neither journalism nor economics, but assisting my younger sister Helen, now eighteen, to win a scholarship to Oxford. Helen, I very soon realized, though indifferently taught at school, possessed intellectual, imaginative and creative talents far exceeding those of any other member of the family. She shared my devotion to history, and added an appetite for knowledge of all kinds, as well as an intense and deepening attachment to the visual arts and to English poetry. She was already regularly writing verse of her own with far greater range and originality than I would have thought possible at her age. For the Oxford exam I gave what help I could, and passed on the accepted tricks of the examination trade which, at least, I had by this time accumulated. We worked together almost daily with rewarding enthusiasm and rehearsed the answers to all the main likely questions. When the Lady Margaret Hall scholarship exam came in December, I rang Helen anxiously each evening from *The Times* office, and she repeated the questions and the papers and her answers to them. So when news arrived just before Christmas that she had indeed won the LMH scholarship, Helen's joy and gratitude knew no limits and the family celebrated the most truly happy Christmas that I could then remember. So began 1930, the climactic year of my life.

In early 1930 I wondered increasingly how I could effectively study serious economics without Oxford tutors and libraries, and how long life was to be bounded by Room 2 at Printing House Square. Christopher Cox as always supplied the answer. Why not take the All Souls Fellowship exam in October 1930 and persuade Geoffrey Dawson, himself a lifelong Fellow of All Souls, to give me just two terms' leave of absence from *The Times* to attack economics and prepare for the Fellowship? I considered an All Souls Fellowship, regarded then as a sort of summit in academic Oxford, as far beyond my reach and the whole plan as an excuse for another summer of freedom. But Geoffrey Dawson thought it an excellent idea, and by mid January I was back at Oxford in digs with eight other close New College friends at 92 High Street, including Pilkington. Crossman was to have been one of the party, but in the previous summer term had been asked to become Steward of the Junior Common Room, or senior undergraduate (which prevented one going into digs), and had forgotten to tell the rest of us. When he casually did, it was almost too late for us to reconstruct the long-agreed compacts involved. Crossman was quite entitled to alter the arrangement. But as he had been, I thought, my closest confidant since Winchester days, his forgetting even to tell us was to me, simple-minded as I was, a stunning shock. We did not speak again for some years.

Lionel Robbins, teaching at this time at New College, was my informal tutor and immediately launched me on Alfred Marshall, Pigou and Marx's

B

Das Kapital. But struggle as I might, I soon found that the blessed freedom from the tyranny of lectures and essays, which I thought would enable me to work more, meant in fact that I worked less. Robbins, fresh from the LSE and devoted to his subject, though in later life regarded as an 'establishment' figure *par excellence*, suffered somewhat at this time from a belief that the 'older universities' looked down on him. This was totally false, as his colleagues assured me. But it still showed itself in the 1931–2 period in his quarrel with Keynes. To me, however, his advice could not have been more timely. Wrestling accordingly with Marx and Marshall in the spring of 1930 from a philosophical standpoint, I was steadily moved to the conclusion that rationality was not on the side of Marx. Marshall, so it seemed to me, offered the secret of the whole controversy in lucidly explaining that in a purely *laissez-faire* system, despite its genuine merits, the demand represented by the rich man's pound would tend to be over-weighted in terms of need as compared with the poor man's pound – a basic truth which fully explained the worst human consequences of unrestrained *laissez-faire*, but whose significance was often neglected both by some Marxists and the orthodox followers of Adam Smith.[4] So Marx, I came to think, was in effect willing to cast away the whole precious British tradition of political tolerance and personal freedom on grounds which could not be rationally defended. It was perhaps the good luck of being introduced more or less simultaneously to Marx and Marshall which helped me to skip the temporary immersion in the Marxist labyrinth which was commonly experienced by those who grew up seeking, first and foremost, greater social justice in the world of the 1920s and 1930s. Some of my contemporaries, notably Hugh Gaitskell and Evan Durbin, whom I did not at this time know well, reached substantially the same conclusion as I. Others some years later, like Denis Healey and Tony Crosland, whose university years coincided with the horrors of the Spanish Civil War and the spectacle of Hitler, found the Marxist version understandably more persuasive for a time, until they also more decisively rejected it.

For me the prospect of one more summer at Oxford was brightened still further by the burning enthusiasm of my sister, Helen, for her university life due to start that autumn. Her talents seemed ideally adapted to profit by Oxford to the full; and her spontaneous impulse to write verse was in these months so strong that the always critical university atmosphere would, I thought, strengthen rather than kill it. On her nineteenth birthday, 22 March 1930, as we walked over Hampstead Heath in spring sunshine, she confided in me all her aspirations, convictions and ardent hopes for the future. A few days later I left for Crackington Haven on the North Cornish

---

[4] See Marshall's *Principles of Economics* (7th edition, London, 1916), p. 471, where he states that free exchange and perfect competition achieve a situation where nobody can improve his condition by free exchange, but not 'one of maximum aggregate satisfaction in the full sense of the term'.

coast, where Christopher Cox had organized a three weeks' reading party of mainly New College undergraduates and tutors, including himself and Joseph, Herbert Hart, Arnold Pilkington, Crossman, and Bill Wentworth, an eccentric millionaire Australian athlete (who in the 1960s became an Australian minister), and Stephen Spender whom I had recently got to know and persuaded to join us. Two camps did tend to develop, as between those like Hart, Pilkington and myself who had finished our final schools and felt carefree, and those like Crossman and Spender who were a little more edgy because their ordeal was still to come. But the Cornish spring and the ample opportunity for rock-climbing exercises (in which Pilkington excelled and Hart did not), racing, walking and swimming effectively smoothed all friction.

On a Saturday, a week or so after our arrival, a letter arrived for me saying that my sister Helen had been taken ill, and on the following Monday morning, 14 April, a telegram from my mother asked me to return home. Reaching London by train that evening, I was told that Helen had polio, for which at that time, though everything was tried, there was no effective remedy known to medical science. She recognized me, but could not speak, and died on the Wednesday morning.

At the end of April 1930 Stephen Spender, realizing that I would feel unable to face the new Oxford term, generously suggested that we should first
spend ten days in the Cotswolds together. This I most gratefully accepted;
and we stayed at a hotel in Winchcombe in the western Cotswolds. Stephen's
support was unsparing. In the intervals of walking on the hills we both did
our best to work. Paradoxically he was striving hard to understand Ricardo,
and I for the last time to express my feelings in verse. Both of us failed. His
performance in economics in the Schools two months later was not distinguished, and I proved to myself that the talent my sister possessed in
such early abundance was wholly denied to me; though the love and pride
which I felt for the English language never faded. I was already a keen
admirer of Spender's poetry, and I now owed him a heartfelt personal
debt when we returned to Oxford together at the beginning of May. This
was nevertheless for me a baffling period in which I knew I had gained six
months' leave to work as I pleased at Oxford, which should have been a
precious privilege, but in which my ability to work systematically was
paralysed by the memory of April. It was also a beautiful summer and many
May and June days were spent walking in the country. But I still found
myself unable to resolve the sharpening dilemma: should I take the All
Souls exam and fail, or should I ignominiously confess to Geoffrey Dawson
and New College that I was incapable of even trying?

At the end of September, with ten days to go before the exam deadline,
I was by chance invited to a knock-out tennis competition in Hampstead. I
loved tennis, and so this seemed the appropriate Rubicon. If I won, I would
face the exam; if not, I would give up. My partner was Peggy Garnett, aged
seventeen, a close neighbour. She fitted endearingly into my tactics, and we
won. That evening, with her warm and much-valued support, I travelled to
New College equipped with all the notebooks I had ever accumulated, feeling that anything was now possible. Sure enough in New College I found
Herbert Hart, the most enlivening and chivalrous of competitors, already
installed; and we each worked round the clock for nine days. Just before the

deadline we had to visit Warden Pember of All Souls to register ourselves as candidates. Pember was a cultured but somewhat inactive ex-barrister, radiating old-world courtesy and benevolence, who owned a large house in the Housman country near Clee Hill, Shropshire. He asked me whether I wished to take the 'political philosophy' or 'political economy' paper. Priding myself on each of these subjects, I said 'both'. That, Pember said, is impossible, because they are taken simultaneously. Bewildered, I asked him to choose, and he firmly refused. So reluctantly tossing up, as it were, in my head, I said 'political economy'; and this twist of fortune launched me unknowingly into lifelong wedlock with that austere science.

Immediately the exam became a gamble on my picking a question in the 'political economy' paper which would enable me to write my long-prepared essay on Marshall and his followers. I found one which quaintly included the phrase 'neo-classical economies' (*sic*), presumably a misprint for 'economics'. But in my ignorance I was not sure which were the 'neo-classical' economists. So tossing the dice again, I guessed, and guessed right. Knowing, however, that only two fellowships were on offer out of twenty or so candidates, I returned to London the following week and to *The Times*, rating my chances so low that I bought a three-month season ticket from Hampstead to Blackfriars, and settled in again to the sub-editor's 4 p.m. to 11.30 p.m. routine at Printing House Square. Three weeks later, at lunch-time on All Souls Day, Christopher Cox rang up to say that I had been elected a fellow together with Ian Bowen from Christchurch. My first thought was thankfulness to Peggy Garnett and Herbert Hart who had sustained my flagging resolution; my second that it was a very long step from that first miserable term at Sevenoaks; and my third that Hart deserved success much more than I. But he had attempted to become an academic lawyer in one year, and this was acknowledged to be impossible.

The luck of the draw had thus again launched me on a new life: four weeks each term living in All Souls, the rest of the year working in Printing House Square, and £300 a year for two years from the College on top of my £5 a week from *The Times*. This was affluence indeed. But finding myself elected as an economist, I felt bound to make an all-out assault on this subject; and within a few weeks was asked to review in two columns in *The Times Literary Supplement* Keynes's two-volume *Treatise on Money*, just published. On this I laboured for two months with an assiduity never again quite repeated, I fear, in book reviewing. Feeling it absurd to criticize Keynes in my review (which appeared on 19 February 1931) I confined myself to setting out what Keynes was saying. My unspoken criticism of the *Treatise* at the time was this: Keynes gave the impression that an excess of saving could only be countered by more capital expenditure, when in fact, so far as employment goes, consumer spending would do just as well.

Before the review of Keynes's *Treatise* appeared, however, I was back at Printing House Square, apart from week-ends at All Souls. Room 2, at *The*

Times, where I had started in October 1929, contained about a dozen of us sitting round a large table and sub-editing exclusively Home News. Chief sub-editor was George Anderson, who maintained the Fleet Street tradition of shirt-sleeves and an eye-shade, and spoke rarely, but with a slightly cynical humour when provoked. His deputy, Colonel Maude, was an ex-military man, immaculately dressed, and meticulous both in his courtesy and his verbal precision. In 1977, forty-eight years later, I learnt that he was still living, and was the father of Angus Maude, Conservative MP. A third Room 2 stalwart, Mansfield, took great pride in his high office as President of the NUJ. Another good sub-editor was Russell, a dry, frosty and laconic Scotsman. In the canteen, where we repaired via the compositors' room for steak and kidney pudding and apple tart for eleven pence between 8 p.m. and 9 p.m., he once opened his mouth to the surprise of his colleagues, and remarked out of the blue: 'The first seventeen years of marriage are the worst.' 'How long have you been married?' someone asked. 'Eighteen years,' he replied and relapsed into his customary silence.

The younger generation, fed straight from Oxford into Room 2 by Geoffrey Dawson, included besides myself John Hood, an Australian Rhodes scholar, and Ivor Thomas, highly gifted and fresh from a double-first and running blue at Oxford, a native of South Wales and strong supporter of the Labour Party. And nightly in the canteen we met Graham Greene, who had recently after a spell in Room 2 graduated to Room 1, where a more select group sub-edited the news from abroad. It was typical of *The Times* and the ingrained snobbery of the diplomatic world that Foreign News qualified for Room 1, and merely British news was down-graded to Room 2. So though there was a great gulf fixed between Graham Greene and us second-class citizens, we did meet for supper and occasionally on the Hampstead tube on the way home. Looking rather hungry and cadaverous, sometimes even tormented, Greene was already passionately devoted to the writing of fiction. In the intervals of copy descending in front of us – often one third of the evening – I read economics, mainly review copies of books for *The Times* or the *TLS*. Some of our colleagues preferred *Who's Who*, *Debrett* or even, in the case of the celebrated Colonel Pirie-Gordon in Room 1, the *Almanach de Gotha*. Graham Greene read fiction. By the time I returned to *The Times* in November 1930, he had resigned in order to concentrate on his next novel; a step which he tells us in his autobiography[1] he for a time greatly regretted. In 1966, nearly forty years later, when as President of the Board of Trade, I had the duty to bless or ban the transfer of *The Times* to Lord Thomson, Greene wrote a letter from Paris to its columns generously volunteering the opinion that, as an ex sub-editor there, I was not unfitted for the task.

In 1929–30, however, we sub-editors were very small fry in the daunting hierarchy of Printing House Square. Far above and beyond, legendary figures, hardly ever visible to the common herd, were the great men of *The*

[1] Graham Greene, *A Sort of Life* (London, 1971), p. 195.

Times. Geoffrey Dawson, Editor before 1914, who had been thrown out by the usurper Lord Northcliffe, and had then returned in the Restoration of 1922 after Northcliffe's downfall; Lint-Smith, the Manager, whose reign according to legend also went back well before 1914 and survived both Northcliffe and the Restoration. It was said that Lint-Smith had been sacked by Northcliffe by telegram on a Friday evening, when the latter's mental health broke down on his last journey to Australia. But on the following Monday morning, when Northcliffe's mental collapse had been confirmed, Lint-Smith returned to his desk and was still there in 1929. Mill, the City Editor, reputed to date back even before Lint-Smith, inserted in the 1931 crisis in his City column the immortal words: 'The phrase "equality of sacrifice" has an ominous sound for the investing classes.' Finally, Brumwell, the Deputy Editor, Mill's contemporary, groaned aloud when he heard that the pound sterling had (as we then called it) 'gone off the gold standard' in September 1931. A rather different and more human, if equally well-established *Times* institution was Richmond, Editor of the *TLS*, whose kindness in offering me economics books to review was almost unlimited and, I suspected, conveniently got these dull, uncultured volumes off his shelves.

All these grand old men were still thundering from Printing House Square in 1929 – and some of them for many years afterwards. Dawson who lasted, unfortunately for *The Times* and the nation, till 1941 was the driving force of the whole formidable machine. Quick and fluent as a writer, highly intelligent, active, persuasive and engaging as a man, stimulating and often encouraging to younger colleagues at *The Times* or All Souls, he tended however to be limited in his vision to the Yorkshire Moors, Eton, All Souls common room, the private rooms at No. 10 and of course, as the centre of the world, Printing House Square. Halifax, Stanley Baldwin and Archbishop Lang were his heroes. If ever a man believed sincerely in the establishment of Church, State, Eton and Empire as they existed in the 1920s and 1930s, it was Geoffrey Dawson. Unfortunately neither Hitler nor unemployment fitted into the picture and so they were both blithely disregarded. It was only the prospect of the King marrying a divorced woman that stirred the full depths of his political faith and aroused the thunderous eloquence of which he was surprisingly capable.

All this, however, was not yet apparent to me as I in turn moved up in 1931 from Room 2 to Room 1, where I stayed throughout that year and 1932, watching – and sub-editing – the record of the rise of the Nazis in Germany, the disastrous increase in unemployment throughout the western world, and the even more calamitous slump in the United States. My particular field was the deepening depression and its political consequences in the US and Germany; and I found myself now treated rather unexpectedly as an expert on American and Continental politics. Those years, 1931 and 1932, were publicly periods of almost unrelieved gloom. Two morals struck deepest in my mind. First that the Labour Government of 1929, from which naturally I had hoped so much, had failed because its leaders simply did not understand the economic forces that hit them so brutally in 1931. It should surely therefore be the job of us in the younger generation to understand these forces and see that such a surrender never happened again. I was enormously impressed by an article of Keynes in the *Evening Standard* in the autumn of 1931 in which he described the new 'National' Government's Budget and Economy Bill as being 'replete with folly and injustice'.

Secondly the news from Germany in the daily telegrams from *The Times* correspondents, Norman Ebbutt and Douglas Reed, filled me with mounting pessimism – all the more so because it did not seem to me that the full import of what they were saying was being allowed to percolate through to the readers of *The Times*. (Ebbutt was later expelled by the Nazis.) In 1931 and 1932 also, I watched, as I sub-edited these messages from Berlin, two myths grow gradually into British conventional wisdom; one of which took nearly ten years to expel, and the other which even lives on in the 1970s. The first was that major concessions must be made to the Nazis, as being normal extremist politicians leading a natural revulsion against the Treaty of Versailles. It was largely the dispatches of Ebbut and Reed from Berlin which convinced me, before I left *The Times* in 1933, that Hitler and Goering were not so much political extremists as desperate maniacs who would shrink from no sort of violence or duplicity to achieve their criminal aims. Not merely was this implicit in the telegrams which *The Times* Berlin correspondent sent for publication during the Chancellorships of Schleicher and von Papen after Brüning's resignation in 1932. But it was even clearer in the background memoranda which they offered for the guidance for those of us in the office.

Even more long-lived has been the second myth propagated naturally by deflationist economists, that the German hyper-inflation of 1922–3 was a prime cause of Hitler's accession to power. This belief is based on a confusion of dates, which should deceive nobody who had followed events in Germany day-by-day in 1929–33. The great German inflation had been overcome by the Shachtian currency reforms in 1924; and there followed five years of reasonably stable money values and reasonably low unemployment in Germany. Hitler and his party were winning few if any more votes in 1929 than after their first Munich *putsch* six years before; and the much abused Weimar Republic had in fact overcome its economic problems remarkably successfully, when in October 1929 the Wall Street crash launched the slide which threw the whole world into economic chaos. From that moment unemployment in Germany rose uncontrollably reaching six millions at the end of 1932, and the Nazi vote rose with it. Hitler's first real electoral success was not till September 1930. Walter Layton, a friend and adviser of Brüning, told me a few years later (when I had joined the *Economist*) that he had repeatedly implored Brüning in 1931 and 1932 to desist from his extreme deflationary policies, but that Brüning, a devout Catholic, replied that he believed Germany must find salvation 'through suffering'. The figures, when later published, showed that the actual real income of the German wage-earner (employed and unemployed) was cut by the order of 50 per cent between June 1929 and January 1933 when Hitler came to power – a cut probably greater than has occurred in peace-time in any other major country in the present century. It was deflation, not inflation, which brought the Nazis to power. Certainly Germans long retained most bitter memories of the inflation of 1922–3. But the history of the Nazi vote shows that to attribute Hitler's rise mainly to that inflation is the reverse of the truth.

Week-ends at All Souls in those years – and a compulsory month each term in the first year – were for me a welcome relief from the gloomy experience of observing from Printing House Square the gathering menace in Germany. At least at All Souls one could read, argue and question the causes of the deepening world slump, and do so in a rational atmosphere. I was myself ever-grateful for the fertile opportunities which the College offered to any young man who at this stage of life wanted to think the economic problem right through. All Souls was at that time nearly unique in admitting no undergraduates. Its academic members concentrated on research and teaching. Those who entered by the annual Fellowship Exam (one, two or three a year) had to choose after two years of a £300 a year income between an academic life in Oxford or elsewhere or a career in the outside world, often in law, the Civil Service, journalism, business or politics. Normally dons predominated, and a quota of university professors lived and worked, as they still do, in the College. But a sizeable minority of practising lawyers, civil servants and politicians turned up fairly regularly for week-ends, College meetings and gaudies. Like most of Oxford after the decadent habits of the eighteenth century, All Souls had of course been reformed in the Gladstone epoch so as to ensure that entrance was by competitive merit, and that academic fellows were actively engaged in research or university teaching. Indeed the GOM himself in 1890 had spent a period of opposition in All Souls studying Homer and the Old Testament. To any young fellow in his early twenties the time, facilities and contacts were so obviously precious that my generation, as I remember those years, were actively conscious of the obligation to use them fully and preserve the traditional standards. Was this a justifiable and valuable institution, or a system of 'meritocracy'? Half a century later, in a world of falling or at least uncertain standards, I would defend it with much greater conviction than in the Oxford of the 1930s.

My first acquaintance with the inner life of the College, however, was somewhat disconcerting. Seated at the high table for dinner on the night of my arrival, my neighbour on my right who had a long beard and a sort of periscope attached to his eye (his name turned out to be Spencer-Wilkinson), told me he had spent forty years working on the *Morning Post* and sixty years on *The Times*. Was he, I wondered, an eccentric or intoxicated, or perhaps pulling my leg? It emerged later on that he had worked for forty years on both papers at once. Next my neighbour on my left remarked that as a new fellow like myself he had on his first night in College taken a sheet of All Souls notepaper, written a letter to a girl proposing marriage, and had regretted it ever since. This was Kenneth Bell, a respected historian at Balliol. I moved on to the port room wondering just what sort of institution I had joined. But I then found myself sitting next to A. L. Rowse, whose intense love of Cornwall and naive interest in economics, both immediately exhibited, were agreeably reassuring after the rather strange behaviour of his two senior colleagues.

As it turned out, I was exceedingly fortunate in the younger fellows of my generation. To Rowse I was at once sympathetic partly because he was an avowed supporter of the Labour Party – then not so common in Oxford – and indeed Labour Candidate for Penryn and Falmouth, where he stood and lost in the 1931 Election. He even published in this period a booklet, with a Marxist flavour, called *Politics and the Younger Generation*. Much more abiding were his knowledge and love of the Elizabethan Age and of Shakespeare. His Shakespeare books I later valued extremely highly. He sometimes suffered perhaps from Celtic effervescence, as did Nye Bevan, which misled both into extravagant outbursts, to the frequent amusement of their friends, but to the scandal of the simple Anglo-Saxon mind. These excesses in both cases tended to obscure solid attainments.

The two young fellows who immediately preceded me, being elected in 1929, were John Sparrow and Denis Rickett. Sparrow's main interests were literature and law; but his needling type of wit, newly sharpened by the Josephan dialectic at New College, would always enliven and often illumine any topic which came along. Rickett, by contrast, an acute philosopher from Balliol, had turned his mind at just about the same time as I, to economics. He told me one day he had just decided not to spend the rest of his life sitting in a panelled room in Oxford wondering whether he existed. Thereafter, I formed the habit of trying out my own amateurish economic ideas and arguments on him and was very well rewarded. The economists Hubert Henderson and Arthur Salter both also became senior fellows of All Souls in these years, and another convert to economics was Ian Bowen, elected with me in 1930 as a historian. Argument with these four, as well as the economic books, pouring down on me to review for *The Times* and the *TLS*, filled a large part of my All Souls week-ends. Henderson, later Warden, and Salter, Gladstone Professor of Political Theory and Institutions and MP for Oxford University, were both particularly tolerant and free with assistance to us budding, ignorant, and no doubt opinionated would-be economists. Salter, though a war-time minister, somehow never found his feet as a postwar MP, since he appeared in the Commons as needlessly pompous and was unkindly nicknamed Uriah Heep. But at All Souls he was another man – full of wisdom, humour and experience.

Next year, 1931, two very dissimilar new fellows were elected: Quintin Hogg and Goronwy Rees. Quintin was the established public school and Oxford success story, son of a Lord Chancellor, scholar of Eton and Christ Church, double first and President of the Union. Goronwy Rees, son of a Cardiff minister, had forced his way through sheer talent by means of a scholarship to New College. Being a writer by nature, full of charm and fluency, and devoted to the arts, rather than serious philosophy or economics, but interested if rather mockingly in almost everything, Rees usually kept his Celtic fervour under firmer discipline than did Rowse. By contrast Hogg was always loyal to his father's orthodox conservatism and Victorian standards. Sometimes in later life I heard him attacked as a poseur, or even cynic or humbug. This was wildly far from the truth. In fact, not far beneath his legal professionalism and debating exuberance, he harboured the strongest emotions and sincerest convictions (on the sanctity of marriage, for instance) which on occasions – as when he was questioned in later years on the radio about the Profumo scandal – uncontrollably exploded. I was once honourably bracketed with Hogg by Sparrow who, when asked whether All Souls examination fellows were really chosen for their smart clothes and polished manners rather than their intellectual merits, replied that if this was so, Hogg and Jay would never have been elected.

In 1932 three new fellows were, exceptionally, elected: Wilberforce, Reilly and Berlin. Wilberforce and Reilly had the reputations at Winchester – not always welcomed by their colleagues – of hardly ever making a mistake, but unlike Berlin were not prone to conversational extravagance. Wilberforce, a descendant of the opponent of the slave trade, noiselessly ascended in later years the legal ladder to become a senior Law Lord in the 1970s; and Reilly similarly climbed the diplomatic greasy pole to the British Embassy in Paris. Berlin was indeed a law – and a philosophy, history and literature – unto himself. I had first been introduced to him by Stephen Spender when we were all three undergraduates. By the time Berlin reached All Souls, he had mastered nearly all subjects known to Oxford as well as most European languages, including his native Russian. His conversation scintillated far into the night; and some of his brightest jewels would be squandered on the one sleepy colleague or two, surviving into the early hours. His lectures became before and after the war the most popular in Oxford; and his despatches during the war from the British Embassy in Washington reputedly attracted the eager curiosity of Churchill. Happily his later eminence as Sir Isaiah Berlin, University Professor and Head of Wolfson College, only slightly moderated his volubility.

Two other younger fellows of the 1930s stand out clearly in my memory: John Foster and Richard Pares. After the war, Salter used to point proudly to the fact that four fellows of the College – Halifax, Salter himself,

Berlin and Foster – had been among those representing this country in Washington in the crucial war years. In pre-war days John Foster, who combined for much of his life law tutoring at Oxford with the practical work of a barrister, was Berlin's only serious conversational rival – less turbulent but not less witty. I most enjoyed his rendering in many languages, appropriately intoned, of the rituals of a number of the best known European and Asian religions. Richard Pares, history tutor and researcher and close friend of Rowse, poured a steady flow of cold water and sanity on his colleagues' verbal excesses. He was universally respected, and in the later war-time years at the Board of Trade, I found him, together with Hugh Gaitskell, a highly talented civil servant. On his return to Oxford after the war, Pares would by common consent have made an admirable Warden of the College had he not been tragically struck down at an early age by a fatal illness and died not many years later.

Among our elder colleagues were a number of professors, a few bishops, and in addition the much-publicized 'Milner's Kindergarten', later the appeasers, known to themselves as 'The Establishment': Geoffrey Dawson, Dougal Malcolm, Lionel Curtis, and more loosely associated Bob Brand, Halifax and John Simon. Of these, Dawson, Malcolm, Curtis and Brand had actually worked as young men with Milner in South Africa in the hopeful days after the Boer War. But Brand in the 1930s differed from the other three in being strongly anti-Nazi and anti-appeasement, just as after 1945 he was strongly anti-apartheid and not afraid to say so. By the 1930s Dawson was Editor of *The Times*, Brand a Managing Director of Lazards, Malcolm Chairman of the Chartered Company, and Curtis a semi-academician at Oxford, periodically engaged in devising constitutions for India and ideal but sadly unrealistic blueprints for the Empire as a whole.

Robert Boothby, a lifelong anti-appeaser, gave currency in the post-1945 era, by the use of a famous phrase, to the notion that appeasement had been virtually conceived and launched by these men at 'that fatal dinner table' in All Souls in the 1930s. This is far from the truth, which is seldom so simple or picturesque. There was no such All Souls conspiracy. Still less were Chamberlain's views forced on him by Oxford appeasers. Though only a week-end visitor myself, like other non-academic fellows, I would have been conscious of any concerted campaign of this kind, and can in fact recall no occasion even in the late 1930s, when this group were using All Souls to promote their plans. It was, I believe, true that they periodically met in College, maintained their association in this way, and doubtless exchanged views in private both in Oxford and elsewhere. It was certainly also true that the whole issue was constantly debated by the younger fellows, and that we became increasingly conscious of the line-up between those for and against appeasement. But this line-up by no means coincided with the division between left and right. Among the younger fellows, Rowse, Pares, Rees, Bowen, Berlin and I were strong anti-appeasers. But so were

Sparrow, not generally regarded as a radical, and from the middle generation, Salter, Henderson and Brand. Amery, another fellow but not a member of the Milner group, passionately opposed Munich. Hogg was almost
alone among the younger generation in being explicitly pro-appeasement.
It often seemed to me uncharacteristic of Hogg, with his sharp mind and
pugnacious character, to have accepted so defeatist a point of view. I concluded in the end that the reason was partly his loyalty to his father and the
conventional Conservative wisdom and partly genuine ignorance even in
1938 (when he stood as pro-Chamberlain candidate in the Oxford by-
election) of the true nature of Nazi Germany.

Though All Souls, however, was not the source of appeasement, the
attachment to it of most of the Milner group was beyond doubt. The question which puzzled me then and for years thereafter was this: how did it
come about that these clever, highly experienced and undoubtedly patriotic
men could not merely embrace, but relentlessly pursue a policy which was
not only threatening the interests of this country and the Empire, but
rendering almost certain a world war in which we should start at a crippling
disadvantage? The conventional answer, which I believe was partly true of
Chamberlain, and perhaps of Dawson, Halifax and Simon, was that
Communism and Soviet Russia meant to them the destruction of so much
of their cherished world as to be an even worse menace than Hitler. Nevertheless, I felt then and have continued to feel since, that this hardly explained the tenacity with which they pursued their ill-fated policy.[2] There
always seemed to be some missing clue to the puzzle. Could part of it be
this? Various biographies of Milner[3] show that in the immediate years after
1918 (before his death in 1924), he had been a strong critic of the Treaty of
Versailles, and believed that Germany had been unjustly treated. A German
by birth himself, Milner, who failed as a parliamentary candidate in this
country in the 1885 Election, certainly held these views in his last years. He
also remained a strong influence on men like Dawson, Malcolm and Curtis,
as was often impressed on me at All Souls. Milner, according to Marlowe's
biography,[4] ever since the Russian Revolution of 1917 'had held that the
real enemy was Communism and that the Allied war aim should be to get
themselves into a position of sufficient strength to negotiate with Germany
"a draw in our favour" which would leave both West and Central Europe
sufficiently strong to combat the menace of Communism'. You could not
have a better description of what I believe was the basic attitude of Dawson,
Halifax and Chamberlain just twenty years later in 1938 and 1939. A recent
study of Milner by an American, A. M. Gollin, reinforces the point in
saying:[5] 'Before the War [the 1914 War] the extreme Conservatives in

[2] The lengths to which they went are described in A. L. Rowse's *All Souls and Appeasement*
(London, 1961).
[3] e.g. John Marlowe, *Milner, Apostle of Empire* (London, 1976), pp. 314–18.
[4] Marlowe, p. 314.
[5] A. M. Gollin, *Proconsul in Politics* (London, 1964), p. 577.

Britain, who placed their faith in Milner, feared and suspected the Germans. After the war some of them – Dawson, Astor and Lothian, for example – were prepared to work with the Germans.' This was 'the background for any understanding of their motives and aspirations in the age of appeasement.' Speaking of Milner's proposals for a negotiated peace with Germany in October 1918, Mr Gollin also says:[6] 'Although they were not immediately accepted, these proposals, and the ideas which lay behind them, created a legacy that dominated the outlook of Milner's disciples in the 1930s, the age of appeasement.'

Another influence on the appeasers certainly was the general revulsion, felt in all parties and schools of thought, against the horrors of the First War. This was strongly felt by Robin Barrington-Ward, Dawson's chief editorial assistant at *The Times*. It might even explain the disastrous advocacy by *The Times* just before Munich of territorial concessions by Czechoslovakia. But it would not in itself have accounted for the persistent opposition of such men as Chamberlain and Dawson to the building up of a collective and defensive alliance which could have deterred Nazi Germany from risking war. I suspect – and can no more than suspect from numerous impressions rather than positive evidence – that Milner's enduring influence may have been the main missing link that kept this highly influential group and *The Times* on their fatal course.

Even this grim controversy, however, had its moments of light relief in All Souls. One of these, not quite accurately told in Hugh Dalton's autobiography, concerns Sir John Simon's appointment in November 1931 as Foreign Secretary. Early in that month, just after the defeat of the Labour Party in the October election, I was working late at *The Times* when I learnt from a colleague that an obligatory All Souls College meeting occurred next morning at 10 a.m. in the College at Oxford. I caught a midnight train and arrived at Oxford at 2.40 a.m. I then occupied a panelled room over the front lodge belonging to Simon, who rarely used it. Reaching the bedroom door, I was about to follow my usual habit of swinging my large heavy case full of books on to the pillow before turning on the lights, when I saw a small piece of paper on my table. Should I read it before crashing down the suitcase or not? I did. It read: 'Sir John is sleeping in his own bed tonight. Mr Jay will sleep in Mr Rickett's room.' Sir John was offered by Ramsay MacDonald later that week-end the post of Foreign Secretary and accepted it. It was said he had come to Oxford so as not to appear too expectant. My anti-appeasement friends, when told this story in the years following, found it entertaining to suggest that had I deposited the suitcase before reading the message, Simon might have never become Foreign Secretary and the long tale of disaster in Manchuria, Abyssinia and Western Europe might have been avoided. This I regard as a pardonably colourful exaggeration.

[6] Gollin, p. 568.

One advantage for younger All Souls fellows was that they met there at week-ends guests, distinguished or otherwise, as well as fellows. One reputed guest I never saw was Guy Burgess. He cannot have been quite as frequent a visitor as some subsequent writings have implied. I never met him till 1940 when he arranged for the BBC a programme of sound radio talks on war production which I was giving. Two guests whom I do vividly remember were Harold Laski and H. G. Wells. To Laski's lively monologue I listened with fascination. His anecdotes – mainly about Roosevelt and the US Supreme Court – seemed to me, though doubtless not fabrications, nevertheless distinctly imaginative. H. G. Wells was more restrained. Having described a recent dinner party, he was asked what the women said, and replied: 'They made holes in the conversation.'

An even more welcome if short-lived relief from both economics and Printing House Square were the summer week-ends of 1931. From the moment just before the All Souls exam in October 1930 when Peggy Garnett had restored my morale and capacity to face the ordeal, she and I became fast friends. A few weeks later she introduced me to Shiela Grant-Duff, her closest school friend, and several other contemporaries at St Paul's School. Relying on my £5 a week from *The Times*, plus £6 a week from All Souls, I bought a second-hand round-nosed Morris Cowley for £25; and now that we could drive as well as walk, spent the summer week-ends in the Cotswolds, at Burford, Salisbury, Stratford or on the south coast on the then-unspoiled Seven Sisters. After ten years of monastic segregation of the sexes at Winchester and Oxford, female society burst upon me with a revolutionary flash which would seem wholly absurd to a twenty-four-year-old young man of the present generation. But it was then as intoxicating as the summer itself and the All Souls port. Peggy Garnett and Shiela Grant-Duff, both eighteen, came up to Somerville and Lady Margaret Hall respectively in the autumn of 1931 and got quickly to know a number of my male contemporaries at New College and All Souls. In the two years from 1930 to 1932 Oxford had startlingly changed. Segregation of the sexes had faded; and it sometimes seemed to us as if our little group had almost instigated the revolution. The truth no doubt was that the same sudden social intermingling was being generated all over the university by the same sort of people at the same time. The Oxford University Labour Club, which in 1929 consisted of three or four eccentric Wykehamists meeting in New College garden (including Colin Clark, later the celebrated statistician, and E. A. Radice, in 1931–3 Secretary of the New Fabian Research Bureau, had by the mid 1930s swollen to a membership of five or six hundred, holding frequent dances and social gatherings of both sexes and all university types.

Back at *The Times* in 1932, I was firmly ensconced on weekday evenings at Printing House Square in the superior and scholarly atmosphere of Room 1, sub-editing the foreign news. Meticulous care was then exercised by *Times* sub-editors not merely to abbreviate down to the bone, to check every fact, date and spelling, but to exorcize every form of grammatical or linguistic solecism. One could not 'emphasize that', but only 'emphasize the fact that'. One could not 'stress' something, but only 'lay stress on'. One spoke 'about' something and never 'in connection with' or 'in regard to'. Split infinitives were as unheard of as an insult to the Royal Family. Personally I welcomed all this and enjoyed the competition to uphold the purity of the language. But after a time I came to wonder whether it was my destiny and duty in life to continue this ritual indefinitely, and delete 'in connection with' not 10,000, but perhaps 50,000 or even 100,000 times. For most of 1932 I compromised by also writing periodically one of the then so-called 'third' or light leaders in which *The Times* indulged; and by contributing to the 'Court Page' longer articles on such subjects as Salisbury Cathedral, Burford Church or the Chiltern woods in the moonlight. (The article on Salisbury Cathedral actually led to the return from many places, including the United States, of some of the Cathedral's long-lost medieval glass.)

From Germany, meanwhile, the stream of news became ever more gloomy, and intensified my frustration at the failure of *The Times* fully to pass on to the public the warnings conveyed to us by our correspondents in Berlin. One evening, when this mood was heavy on me, Reggie Harris, another fellow of All Souls and leader-writer on *The Times*, walked into Room 1 and characteristically asked me whether I felt that:

> Shades of the Printing House begin to close
> About the growing boy.

I replied that I sometimes did. Why not then, said Harris, join the *Economist*? Harris was in the old classical-scholar, All Souls tradition, and could recite long passages of Homer by heart. I said the idea of the *Economist* much appealed to me; and he benevolently arranged with Walter Layton, then Editor of the *Economist* and Chairman of the *News Chronicle*, for me to be offered a job on the former at the huge salary of £9 a week. Here was a chance, not just to manipulate words, but to write – perhaps even to propagate my strengthening convictions on fighting unemployment, and above all on the true character of the Nazis. I accepted, and started work on the *Economist* in the first week of March 1933, the very week in which all the banks closed in the US and Roosevelt took over as President; and in which Hitler (Chancellor since January) seized absolute power after the Reichstag fire. But in my last few days at *The Times* I was able to read the messages from Ebbutt and Reed on the Reichstag fire (27 February 1933), which left me with the belief that it had been started not by the half-witted Dutch boy, van der Lubbe, as the Nazis claimed, but by the Nazis themselves.

Before arriving at the *Economist*, I had been asked by them to review a book of Roosevelt's campaign speeches, published under the title *Looking*

Forward; and reading all these I formed for the first time the opinion that here was a remarkable mind, strong and independent, and far removed from the ordinary run of American politicians. One other unexpected bridge carried me across the gap between *The Times* and the *Economist*. *The Times* correspondent in Ottawa, named Stephenson, used regularly to infuriate Room 1 by sending telegrams literally three, four or five feet long (usually speeches by Mr R. B. Bennett or Mr Mackenzie King), which then had to be abbreviated to two or perhaps three inches. One of the minor impulses which inclined me to leave *The Times* for the *Economist* was the desire to be rid of Stephenson once and for all. On my first morning at the *Economist*, full of enthusiasm for the new venture, I found I was regarded as an expert on overseas news and politics, and the first task I was given was to edit a telegram from their Ottawa correspondent. It was from Stephenson, and was three feet long.

The *Economist*
and the Labour Party

Geoffrey Crowther, Graham Hutton and I all started work on the *Economist* at about the same time in the spring of 1933. Hutton and I were the only full-time members of the staff, apart from one statistician and those in the stock exchange section. The *Economist*, as we found it in March 1933, was largely a City paper. Its circulation was barely 5000; and its front page consisted of an index in gothic type, followed by the first sentence of 'The Money Market' section, which almost invariably read: 'Conditions in the money market this week remained unchanged.' The paper was old-fashioned Liberal in doctrine. Walter Layton, the Editor, was also Chairman of the *News Chronicle*, and spent most of his time trying to keep the *News Chronicle* afloat. With his background as a Cambridge statistician, and war-time assistant and still close friend of Lloyd George and Churchill, his prestige was considerable. He presided benevolently at a weekly conference each Monday, and looked in on Wednesday and Thursday to approve leaders and read proofs. If Layton felt at a late hour on Thursday, when proof-reading went on till midnight, that the young leader-writers were too emphatic, and there was not much time or space to correct them, he used simply to add the words at the end: 'Time alone will show.' 'Will Hitler desist from further aggression?' we would ask. 'Time alone will show,' added Layton altering the entire tone of the article.

Next senior on the *Economist* came Aylmer Vallance, trusted confidant of Layton, and also part-time leader-writer and assistant on the *News Chronicle*. A most accomplished journalist and highly entertaining companion, Vallance greatly impressed us novices by his ability to appear in the office, write a polished leader in forty-five minutes on any subject, economic or political, with a few apt literary allusions, and disappear as rapidly across Bouverie Street. It was a good deal later still when our ultra-patient and conscientious statistician, Walter Hill, discovered that Vallance had been in the habit sometimes, when acutely short of time, of guessing the figures for the then famous *Economist* index of wholesale prices instead of working it out. Geoffrey Crowther, later Editor for many years, but in 1933 still under thirty, brought a high reputation from Cambridge as an economist and statistician. In the 1930s he was a self-confessed radical and was fertile in ideas for reforming and modernizing the *Economist*, as he successfully did.

The third newcomer, near the same age as Crowther and myself was Graham Hutton, a product of the London School of Economics and expert on Central European affairs. What he really enjoyed was writing articles about Hungary; but these had to be rationed. Another of our Thursday late-night proof-reading party was Nicholas Davenport. A devoted follower of Keynes, Davenport combined two specialized talents, seldom found together: knowledge of the Stock Exchange and a rare capacity for writing good English. At this time he wrote weekly one Stock Exchange article for the *New Statesman* and one for the *Economist*; and continued to write such an article for either the *Economist*, *New Statesman* or *Spectator* for at least fifty years. Since Hutton shared a flat at this time with Kingsley Martin, the personal link between the *Economist* and *New Statesman* was somewhat close, almost incestuous – but policies differed. Davenport, an incomparably lively and amusing colleague, and supporter – though somewhat critically – of the Labour Party, and generous host at his Berkshire country house, Hinton Manor, remained from 1933 onward a long-standing friend. Our formal Stock Exchange Editor, Hargreaves Parkinson, a dour Northcountryman, and accountant by training and temperament, took finance very seriously, and no doubt gratified Layton by off-setting what some City readers regarded as Davenport's frivolous attitude to the Stock Exchange.

One evening at his flat in Mecklenburgh Square (Bloomsbury was favoured by economists at this period) Hutton introduced me to Thomas Balogh, then working in the City as a protégé of Keynes, Nicholas Kaldor of the LSE, and George Tugendhat, also a refugee from central Europe, and father of Christopher Tugendhat, Conservative MP and EEC Commissioner in the 1970s. Balogh and Kaldor became regular and welcome intruders into our room at the *Economist*. They were both fertile and provocative: Kaldor mainly with original economic ideas, and Balogh with both ideas and equally original stories about what was allegedly going on – often something sinister – in the City or Whitehall. Kaldor, I remember, advised (I think in 1934) as a remedy for the depression a major income-tax relief for each person employed by the taxpayer. It seemed to me that this would certainly reduce unemployment, but I had to tell him I was sure it would never be adopted. Balogh's ideas and reports, I found both at the *Economist*, and later at the *Daily Herald* City office, required critical scrutiny; but I reckoned after some experience that a good few of them were well-founded. He was also fairly free with his attacks on various worthy public figures. Crowther once remarked after one of Balogh's visits: 'Tommy will never understand that in this country we don't hang a man for making a slight mistake.' Nevertheless, when Balogh did not appear in Bouverie Street, we missed him.

The *Economist*'s most distinguished regular outside contributor was Arnold Toynbee, who wrote almost weekly on international issues, and invariably delivered a hand-written manuscript, perfectly legible, which required the amendment of no syllable or comma before proceeding to the printer – the only writer I ever knew of whom this could be said, except Geoffrey Hudson of All Souls whom I had persuaded to write for us on China and the Far East. An equally eminent and of course anonymous – we were all anonymous – occasional contributor was our Italian correspondent Luigi Einaudi, then a professor of economics, orthodox free-trader, and critic of Mussolini. I was particularly enjoined by Layton not to alter a single word of the rather odd English in Einaudi's Italian letters, since any change might land him in serious trouble with Mussolini. Though therefore I took great pains in translating all other overseas letters into plain English, I was forced to leave Einaudi's in all their semi-grammatical oddity. Some readers must have been puzzled. But twenty years later, in the post-war world, when Einaudi became President of Italy, Head of State, having survived Mussolini and the war, I met him on a visit to this country, and he cordially thanked the *Economist* staff for their help in enabling him to out-live Mussolini and preserve his economic conscience at the same time.

In the years 1933–7, the bulk of the *Economist* was written by Crowther, Hutton and myself. Three or four full-timers were sufficient to maintain the paper, in rather marked contrast to the 1960s and 1970s, when the staff had vastly expanded (and new activities had of course been added and circulation greatly multiplied). But even in my four years, the printing and layout were radically modernized and the circulation doubled from a modest 5000 to about 10,000. The *Economist* in those years under Walter Layton had principles, purposes and serious political ideals. We fought three major battles: first, in the tradition of Bagehot and F. W. Hirst for free trade, and above all free import into the UK of food and raw materials; secondly, defence of the League of Nations and the doctrine of collective security; and thirdly in favour of an internal expansionist policy to bring down the unemployment figures, which stood at their peak of nearly three millions when I joined the *Economist*. It was a great liberation to move from *The Times* and be working for causes in which one firmly believed. Layton was as convinced a supporter of the traditional free trade cause as Bagehot or F. W. Hirst. The *Economist* often pointed out in 1933–5 that it was the fall in import prices of food and materials which made possible a cheap money policy and so the recovery in house-building and the steady drop in unemployment which began in 1933. It was in these years that I fully understood the fundamental wisdom of free importation of primary products for this country – as was again proved after 1951 – and was thus able in the 1960s and 1970s to foresee rather sooner than some people the disastrous consequences of the Common Agricultural Policy of the Common Market.

In its second crusade, in support of collective security under the League of Nations against Mussolini and Hitler, the main inspiration sprang from Layton and Toynbee. This was the period of Mussolini's attack on Abyssinia, and the final débâcle of the Hoare–Laval Plan of December 1935. So incensed was I by the Hoare–Laval betrayal, that I stood on the pavement outside the Houses of Parliament on a particularly grim and foggy afternoon of that December to protest, while Baldwin announced the dénouement and the resignation of Hoare. Not surprisingly the *Economist*'s crusade for collective security, and resistance to dictators, excited the criticism in the City that the paper was becoming unduly 'political'. Layton won even greater respect from the rest of us by ignoring all such complaints.

In the *Economist*'s third campaign, for expansionism, the driving force came from the post-1918 generation – Aylmer Vallance, Geoffrey Crowther and me. Layton was a moderate, but did not oppose reflationary moves, provided they operated in harmony with liberal imports. Crowther and I were even permitted to introduce the phrase 'full employment'. Here I believe that the backing of Arthur Salter and Josiah Stamp for cautious reflation influenced Layton. The *Economist*'s support for reflation in 1933–5, before Keynes's 'General Theory' was published in 1936, helped a little, I believe, to make reflation respectable in those years.

But my first major journalistic adventure was launched on the anti-Nazi front, and came within six months of my joining the *Economist*. In August of 1933, a few weeks before Peggy Garnett and I were due to be married on 30 September, Layton went on holiday to Cornwall, leaving Crowther, Hutton and me in virtual charge of the paper. Into my hands at the *Economist* came a very startling volume, *The Brown Book of the Hitler Terror*, anonymous, sponsored by a committee of which Einstein was President and published by Gollancz, exposing the Nazis' methods with a mass of evidence, and accusing them of having started the Reichstag fire as an excuse for suppressing the German Parliament. The whole book, including the treatment of the Reichstag fire, only confirmed in my mind the view of the Nazi leaders, which I had derived from *The Times*'s Berlin correspondents. I therefore wrote a full *Economist* leader which appeared on 2 September 1933, reviewing the *Brown Book*. I reproduce some of this below; for in post-war years when apologists for Baldwin and Chamberlain have argued that nobody could have understood the Nazis' intentions fully before 1938 and 1939, I have noticed that these apologists become sceptical when I reply that it was all perfectly clear in 1933.

THE HITLER TERROR

The orgy of barbarism and brutality which heralded Herr Hitler's regime was at first only known to the outside world through stray newspaper reports and un-verified rumours. Lately, however, the process of investigation and verification by reliable inquirers has been carried a long way; and the main facts may now be regarded as established beyond all reasonable doubt. A substantial part of the work of investigation has been performed by an International Committee under the Presidency of Professor Einstein, and in a book prepared by his Committee, published yesterday,[1] the history of the Terror is fully and systematically set out. The book is avowedly polemical, and is written with a Ciceronian vigour and realism; but since the events it has to describe are reminiscent of the age of the conspiracy of Cataline rather than of 20th century Europe, its manner would seem to be no more than appropriate to its matter. As guarantees of the reliability of the information collected, we have the name of Professor Einstein, President of the International Committee which collected it, as well as a foreword by Lord Marley, chairman of the Committee. In this foreword Lord Marley explains that all the documents and statements laid before the Committee have been carefully verified before publication; and that all the events related are typical cases, the most sensational individual incidents having been omitted, even though well-authenticated.

In substance, however, and in virtue of the evidence that follows, the book remains a terrible and damning indictment of the aims, methods and spirit of the Nazi movement.

In the second part of the book a well-authenticated and well-documented account is given, with photographs, of the 'concentration camps' and other forms of Nazi brutality which are now generally familiar outside Germany. It is pointed out that these methods are not mere sporadic outbreaks, but the direct conse-quences of incitement by Nazi leaders ('I would rather shoot a few times too short and too wide, but at any rate I would shoot' – Goering at Essen, 11 March 1933). The Committee estimate that 60,000 people have been subjected to violence since 27 February, and that over 35,000 were in concentration camps in July. Unlike some of the original atrocities, the concentration camps are permanent instru-ments of cruelty where the opportunity for mental and physical sadism will pre-sumably continue as long as the Nazi regime. A recent writer in *The Times*, who is unlikely to have had 'Marxist' leanings, concludes a description of a Nazi con-centration camp with the following remark:

'The visitor left the camp with a feeling of repulsion. He felt guilty of something approaching indecency . . . in having been permitted to witness such inhuman treatment imposed by ruthless men on their own flesh and blood.'

Definite information is also in the Committee's possession of 500 murders carried out by Nazis since 3 March; at least forty-three Jews having been murdered for no other reason than that they were Jews. We are reminded that Professor Einstein's works have been publicly burnt – not to mention those of André Gide, Proust, Zola, Emil Ludwig, Thomas Mann and a host of others.

[1] *The Brown Book of the Hitler Terror and the Burning of the Reichstag.* Prepared by an International Committee under the presidency of Albert Einstein. Gollancz [London, 1933], 5s.

The article ended with these words:

The confirmation by full and reliable evidence of the worst suspicions that have been felt about the Reichstag Fire and the Hitler Terror is bound to produce a shock of revulsion and horror throughout the civilised world. It will also raise the question whether the right to equality of status among the nations can be claimed by a Government which disregards the ordinary canons of justice and humanity in revenging itself on its own fellow-countrymen.

That the Nazis lied in attributing the fire to the Communists, there is not much doubt. Subsequent research has suggested that the fire started by accident, and that the Nazis then blamed the Communists. This may well be true, just as Tolstoy argues in *War and Peace* that the Moscow fire was an accident, and not a conspiracy by the Russians.

A few days after my article appeared, a letter arrived addressed to Layton from Von Krosigk, Finance Minister in the first Nazi Government, protesting violently against it. Von Krosigk was not a Nazi, but one of the few Nationalist members of the first Nazi Cabinet, and as an economist he had previously met Layton. He accused the *Economist* of lending itself to Communist propaganda and demanded an apology. Layton informed of this, hurried home from Cornwall. Instead of rebuking us young men, and me in particular, for our impetuous and rather illiberal invective, he examined the book and replied to Von Krosigk saying he understood that those charged with starting the Reichstag fire would receive a fair trial in open Court, and that the *Economist* would send a reporter to the trial who would give an impartial account in the paper of the proceedings. Von Krosigk replied that no such correspondent of the *Economist* would be allowed into Germany. This went far to convince Layton that my view of the Nazis was the right one after all; and he asked me to write a weekly summary in the *Economist* of the Reichstag fire trial, which I accepted with the greatest relish. Before the trial opened, however, came our wedding on 30 September and an intended honeymoon in Germany, Austria and Italy. Layton strongly advised me not to enter Germany and I willingly contented myself with surveying the German frontier from Salzburg, before staying in the Austrian Tyrol and later with William Hayter, who was then working in the British Embassy in Vienna. As a result of the *Economist* article, I never visited Germany till after 1945.

When I returned to the *Economist* at the end of October, the Reichstag fire trial opened, and for me the fun began. Layton had not realized, when committing himself to a report each week, that the trial would continue until Christmas Eve. As I expected, with each week that went by, the Nazi case became less convincing; and the Bulgarian Communist, Dimitroff, delighted the British public by defying Goering in open Court. When Goering finally lost control, and shouted at Dimitroff: 'You wait till I get you out of this Court,' I managed to obtain special extra space for my weekly exposure. By Christmas, when the trial ended, not merely Layton but a good number of *Economist* readers, were, I believe, no longer in much doubt about the real character of the Nazi leaders.

In these last months of 1933, I fought out in my own mind a political battle which was soon to face the whole country and torment the Labour Movement. If Hitler, as I was now convinced, could only be stopped by force, was it right to use force against him even if this provoked another European war? All my internationalism learned at school, and my reading of the war memoirs at Oxford, had left me an unavowed pacifist. I had unconsciously assumed that monsters like Hitler could not exist in the real world. Now there was no escape from the hideous fact, unless one surrendered to self-deception, that they did. So I resignedly accepted the inescapable conclusion that, if necessary, force must be used against the Nazis even at the risk of another Great War. To clear my mind I wrote an article headed 'Pacifism'; and though it was really a personal confession of faith, Layton, with his usual tolerance, agreed to print it as a normal anonymous *Economist* leader in the issue of 2 December 1933. The key words were:

It is certain that if all those who hate war refuse to sanction or support the use of force in any circumstances, the nascent international system of to-day will crack, the world will relapse into chaos, and ultimately there will be war. For the idea that permanent peace can be preserved by the refusal of every individual to fight is a mere piece of Utopian folly.

If, instead of indulging all such illusions, extremisms and categorical imperatives, every believer in peace would unite to support and improve by every means that may be necessary, including, above all, a scrupulous observation of Treaty obligations, the tottering but positive peace organisation that actually exists, there would still be some genuine hope of the final abolition of war.

This declaration – if not very momentous to my colleagues and the *Economist*'s readers – was for me a revolution, and from this moment for twelve years the resistance to Nazism by any means necessary became my overriding political aim.

Meanwhile the *Economist* preserved another honourable tradition. As an information service in the 1930s, it carried regular articles on the spread of UK trade between different countries and products, shifts in the terms of trade, and so forth. Some who remember those articles must have been struck in the 1960s and 1970s by the decline in general knowledge of these basic facts, particularly about British international trade. How far, however, this decline was connected with the later disappearance of these articles in the *Economist*, and how far this growing ignorance contributed to the miscalculations leading to the UK joining the EEC, must be a matter of opinion.

It was also in the winter of 1933-4 that I progressed from being a supporter to being an active member of the Labour Party. Here again it was contemplation of the Nazis which convinced me that the life of a writer or an academic was not enough. The spectacle of German Liberal and Social-

Democratic professors, authors and journalists being picked up after a midnight knock on the door and then disappearing, was not to be ignored. If one was going to resist, better to do so as part of an organized political movement which could influence and arm the country and not as a helpless academic confronted by thugs. So I was recruited into the Paddington Labour Party, as we had moved there from Hampstead after our wedding. Secondly I got in touch with Hugh Gaitskell, and we lunched together in late 1934 or early 1935 at University College, Gower Street.[2] Having virtually never spoken to Gaitskell at Winchester or New College, where he was two years my senior, I had been immensely impressed reading in 1933 G. D. H. Cole's symposium *What Everybody Wants to Know About Money*, by the lucidity of Gaitskell's chapter on the 'Social Credit' theories of Major C. H. Douglas. And when we lunched together I discovered that Gaitskell's feelings about the Nazis were as intense as my own. While working in Vienna previously he had seen at close quarters the attack by the Dolffuss regime on the Socialist-built Karl Marx Hof flats; and this experience dominated his mind. Instead of telling me, as some friends and colleagues understandably did, that I was suffering from an obsession about Hitler, he wholeheartedly agreed. We decided then and there to work together; and so began the closest working friendship of my life, which continued almost without a break and without disagreement, for close on thirty years till Gaitskell's death in January 1963.

In the general election of 1935, fought on the issue of Abyssinia and collective security, I joined Gaitskell and Evan Durbin in Chatham and Gillingham, where respectively they were standing – unsuccessfully – as Labour candidates. Durbin had been a contemporary of ours at New College, had since become an academic economist, had joined the Labour Party, and was a close friend of Gaitskell. My wife and I stayed in Chatham and had our first taste of days spent in Party rooms addressing envelopes and folding up 'literature'. In the same year Gaitskell, Durbin and I went together to a meeting at the Friends' House in Euston Road to hear the result of the election of the new leader of the Labour Party, following George Lansbury's resignation. The candidates were Morrison, Attlee and Greenwood. We were all three passionately in favour of Morrison, who had heartened the whole Party by winning the LCC election the year before. When we heard that Attlee had won, we three went home filled with deep gloom. To us at this stage he seemed an unglamorous, routine member of the Parliamentary Labour Party. How wrong we all were; and what a justification this election was of the system of the choice of a leader by Members of Parliament only, who happen to know the man they are selecting! Attlee's rare qualities were never on show, and it took the outside world some years to perceive what his immediate colleagues had already seen in 1935. But at least one non-MP had spotted them even in that year – Ernie Bevin. The story is

[2] As I have related in Douglas Jay, *Hugh Gaitskell*, ed. W. T. Rodgers (London, 1964), p. 78.

well-known of Bevin's denunciation at the 1935 Party Conference of Lansbury's impractical pacifism. Less well-known is a tale told me forty years later by a member of the Hampstead Labour Party, Mark Bass, who claimed to have been present at a meeting in Transport House in 1935. I cannot vouch for its authenticity; but it struck me as true in spirit. Bevin was criticizing Lansbury, and someone asked him what alternative leader was available. Bevin, pointing at Attlee, replied: 'Do you see that little man in the corner who smokes a pipe and says nothing? I don't know much about him. But he'd do.'

Also in my first years at the *Economist* I was brought into contact with the Labour Party machine through several separate channels. First Graham Hutton suggested to Harold Laski that he might propose me as an economic adviser on some of the network of sub-committees formed by the National Executive Committee of the Labour Party, in particular its International and Finance and Trade sub-committees. I served on one or another of these committees right up to 1939, starting on a sub-committee[3] studying the activities of 'imperialist' powers. In this sub-committee I found myself sitting next to Attlee, whom I had not met since our encounter outside our front gate in Hampstead sixteen years before. The second meeting impressed itself sharply on my mind, because Attlee – briefly, of course – queried all the weak points in a paper I had rather hurriedly written. Another member of this sub-committee was Leonard Woolf. At first contact he appeared a grave and gloomy figure, and his great Bloomsbury reputation was not then fully known to me. Philip Noel-Baker, also a member, equally assiduous, but much more enthusiastic than Attlee or Woolf, excited my admiration by his almost boyish enthusiasm for the League of Nations. As a fervent supporter of the League, I greatly valued the link with Woolf and Noel-Baker right through into the war years when Woolf sponsored an unofficial group designed to ensure that a strengthened United Nations emerged after the war.

Formally, it was when working for these various committees of the Labour Party that Gaitskell, Durbin and I became accepted advisers to the Party on financial and economic policies in the 1930s. In June 1936, we circulated an ambitious twenty-page paper, complete with statistical appendices, under the signature of Colin Clark, Durbin, Gaitskell and myself, setting out a detailed programme for achieving full employment by an expansionist, lower interest-rate and public investment policy.[4] Rural electrification, public housing and a vigorous depressed area programme were all included.

My second link with the Labour Party formed at this time was the New Fabian Research Bureau. Set going mainly by G. D. H. Cole, the NFRB

[3] The Ottawa Agreements and Trade Questions Advisory Committee.
[4] Labour Party Finance and Trade Committee: Memorandum of the Economic Group, Research Paper no. 311.

was partly a protest at the inertia of the old Fabian Society, but also one of the numerous responses of the Labour Movement to the debacle of 1931, and a surprisingly lively and successful one. Gaitskell, Evan Durbin and I plunged enthusiastically into NFRB activities. We three became known as 'the young economists'. Secretary of the NFRB after 1933 was John Parker, who was elected in 1935 as the first MP of our generation and held his Dagenham seat right through to the 1970s. Attlee was the first Chairman. The NFRB, which merged with the Fabian Society in 1938, operated through publishing pamphlets and holding periodic conferences. Its first recorded Executive Committee meeting (according to the files preserved at Nuffield College, Oxford) was in March 1931. A regular series of conferences followed right through to 19 February 1939. Two NFRB conferences I always remembered as particularly lively were one at Maidstone on 18–19 May 1935 on 'Banking and Financial Policy' and one on 27–8 June 1936 at Cambridge on 'Labour's Foreign Policy'. At Maidstone I met Francis Williams, the City Editor of the *Daily Herald*, and Robert Fraser, the *Daily Herald* leader-writer. Their common-sense ideas about Labour Party propaganda greatly appealed to me. At the Cambridge conferences Stafford Cripps was the star turn, and the main issue was the Labour Party's attitude to a possible war between this country and Nazi Germany. Cripps was still arguing that this would be an 'imperialist' war, and that the trade union movement should strike against it. I boldly stood up and asked him: 'If this country, with Soviet Russia as an ally, were to be at war with a Nazi Germany, would you oppose the war effort?' To this he replied: 'Those were the arguments used in 1914.' I long remembered this reply because, at the time of my next visit to Cambridge, as a Ministry of Supply official organizing war production in September 1941 (only five years later), Cripps was our Ambassador in Moscow actively supervising the supply of munitions to Russia.

It is often forgotten, by those who in later post-war years professed alarm about the 'Marxism' of the so-called 'left' in the Labour Party as if it were a new phenomenon, that the existence of a quasi-Marxist minority usually with major support from Scotland and Wales, has been an enduring element in the British Labour Party from its foundation – and also that the individuals who form it mostly grow in wisdom as the years go by. In the 1920s and later it was the ILP. In January 1933 Attlee and Cripps submitted a paper to the Finance and Trade Committee of the Labour Party under the title of 'The Joint Stock Banks', in which they advocated the nationalization of the banks as a necessary and immediate move by a Labour Government. The paper reads as if drafted by Cripps. Dalton, in his copy, preserved with his papers, marks it 'feverish'. But Attlee signed it. In 1935–7, Cripps, supported by Bevan and George Strauss, was organizing the 'Socialist League', which was in fact a rival political party that held, for instance, a rival party conference in Bournemouth in 1937, alongside the official Labour Party Conference which I attended there. In the 1950s, after Cripps and George Strauss had long forsworn such deviations, we still had the 'Bevanites', and in the 1960s and 1970s the Tribune Group, by the end of which time Michael Foot had also faced realities.

My third activity with the Labour Party, dating from the mid 1930s, was XYZ. This started as a purely unofficial and individual attempt by a few Party supporters or sympathizers in the City or financial journalism to bridge the gulf between the City and the Labour Party, and to ensure that Party policy-makers were rather better informed about finance and economics in the future. The original pioneer and moving spirit was Vaughan Berry (later Sir Vaughan Berry), an assistant manager of the Union Discount Company. On 8 January 1932, Berry arranged the first XYZ gathering at Lambs, a restaurant in Mitre Street in the City. The name XYZ was adopted to preserve anonymity, and the aim was to 'provide the Labour leaders with advice on administrative and financial problems'. Early in 1932 a meeting was arranged through George Middleton, Secretary of the Labour Party, at Transport House with Arthur Greenwood, Pethwick-Lawrence and Hugh Dalton to see how far an unofficial advisory service could be supplied to the Party in this way. Dalton became the principal liaison, and often attended XYZ meetings himself and circulated its papers to Labour Party committees. From 1932 onwards, regular XYZ meetings were held right up to 1940, usually in the evening at one or another member's flat. I was recruited, I think in 1934, by either Gaitskell or Dalton and attended regularly thereafter. Dalton,[5] Davenport[6] and Francis Williams[7] have recalled early days of XYZ. Berry himself recorded, in a note written for XYZ's thirtieth birthday in 1962, that 'among the earliest to join and attend regularly' were: Francis Williams, City Editor of *Daily Herald*; George Strauss, Strauss & Co. Metal Merchants; C. F. Chance, Stockbroker; John Wilmot, of the firm of C. F. Chance; Charles Latham, Chairman, LCC Finance Committee; George Wansborough, Robert Benson; J. H. Lawrie, National Bank, New Zealand; Evan Durbin, LSE; Douglas Jay, the *Economist*; Hugh Gaitskell, University College. XYZ guests in the 1930s included Attlee, Pethwick-Lawrence, Lees-Smith and Cripps as well as Dalton.

XYZ had no constitution, no chairman, secretary or rules. The only assumption was that members were broadly supporters of the Labour Party or Fabian Society. Most of us in 1934 and 1935 expected it to last a few months. Yet, as I write, it is still in active existence forty-five years later. After the initial effort to re-educate the Labour Party out of its 1931 failures, some of us – including Gaitskell and me – being certain that resistance to Nazism was the overriding future issue, got the discussion shifted

[5] Hugh Dalton, *The Fateful Years : Memoirs 1931–45* (London, 1957), pp. 23–4.
[6] E. H. Davenport, *Memoirs of a City Radical* (London, 1974), p. 76.
[7] Francis Williams, *Nothing So Strange, an Autobiography* (London, 1970), pp. 111–13.

in the 1936–9 period to the technique of running an all-out controlled war economy. With this idea, we recruited some of those who had successfully organized the 1914–18 war economy: notably Bill Piercy (later Lord Piercy), then an expert on timber and other raw materials; Ted Lloyd, Manager of Food Supplies for the 1916–18 Ministry of Food; and Coates (Treasurer of ICI in the 1930s and an XYZ guest rather than member). These talks continued intensively right up to September 1939; and it turned out that most of us were occupied full-time in the economic and industrial war effort after 1939.

The XYZ meetings of the 1930s were exceedingly valuable to me. Particularly rewarding was the constant contact with Gaitskell and Durbin. Indeed it was at one of these evening gatherings (as I related in my chapter in *Hugh Gaitskell*[8]) in George Wansborough's flat that I first became explicitly conscious of Gaitskell's unique combination of intellectual lucidity, balance and vigour of mind, which marked him as outstanding among his contemporaries. When 1940 came and I found myself in the Ministry of Supply, Gaitskell with Dalton at the Ministry of Economic Warfare, Durbin in No. 11 Downing Street with Attlee and others elsewhere, we felt so strongly the need to continue the contact that we lunched regularly together from 1940 to 1945 in the Griffin public house in Villiers Street close by the Ministry of Supply. Any members of XYZ present in London might come; and Oliver Franks, my immediate superior at the Ministry, sometimes joined us as a sort of benevolent assessor. After the 1945 election, however, with Gaitskell and Durbin in the House of Commons, we were compelled by division duties to transfer to dining once a fortnight at the House. New blood was recruited in the 1940s and 1950s. It included Jack Diamond, Frank Pakenham, Jim Callaghan, Harold Wilson, Douglas Houghton, Bill Rodgers, Nicholas Kaldor, James Meade, Patrick Gordon-Walker, Anthony Crosland, Roy Jenkins, Len Murray and Robert Neild. But XYZ was never quite the same after Hugh Gaitskell's death. It remained a forum, but lost something of the cohesion, spirit and purpose that he always instilled. It was even occasionally accused by those ignorant of its proceedings of being a conspiracy or even a 'Party within a Party'. This was very far from the truth. From 1939 onwards, when it ceased formally to advise the Labour Party, XYZ never had a policy, never reached conclusions and never exerted pressure on anybody.

My first meeting with Hugh Dalton occurred when I was staying a weekend (I think in 1934) with Nicholas Davenport at his very fine and hospitable country home, Hinton Manor, Hinton Waldrist, Berkshire. The party were to meet Dalton and his wife for a Sunday picnic beneath the Swindon White Horse Hill. After lunch Dalton challenged the rest of us to a walking race up the three miles to the summit of White Horse Hill, and loudly

[8] Jay, p. 81.

denounced the sloth and decadence of the women and younger generation generally. I did not mention to him that I was in the habit of racing up mountains and was in fair training from a recent visit to the Lakes. As Dalton boomed ahead of the ladies, wasting breath on words, at a mere four m.p.h., I professed exhaustion until we finished the first mile; whereupon I quietly accelerated and reached the summit some hundreds of yards ahead of Dalton, who led the rest of the party by about as much.[9] He was so deeply impressed by this little ruse as to insist then and there that I should become an active worker for the Labour Party in every possible capacity. From that moment I never lost touch with him, and found his ever loyal and reliable, if hearty, encouragement, of enormous value. The help Dalton gave to young members of the Labour Party was unsparing and generous to a fault. His exuberant partisanship and sonorous indiscretions, which sometimes exasperated others, were to me irresistibly entertaining.

In 1935 I embarked on a much more ambitious venture: a full-scale book on the major economic controversies of the period, which I proposed to call *The Socialist Case*. Having read economics books, and argued with economists in London and Oxford for five years since the All Souls exam, it seemed time to reach some conclusions and set them down. Three main theses were argued in my book. First that the case for greater social justice rested on Alfred Marshall's 'broad proposition'[10] that 'aggregate satisfaction can *prima facie* be increased by re-distribution of wealth, whether voluntarily or compulsorily, of some of the property of the rich among the poor', and had been sadly distorted by Marx's obsession with ownership and outdated theory of value. Secondly that there was no rational ground for believing re-distribution could not be peacefully and democratically achieved. Thirdly that unemployment and cyclical depression were monetary phenomena which could be overcome by intelligent management of what I boldly labelled 'total effective demand'. I called the book *The Socialist Case* to emphasize the extent to which Marx was a revisionist, whose dogmatism and stridency were not shared by earlier socialists such as Robert Owen. More relevant to the hour was my insistence that 'total effective demand', or the flow of money demand, and not the crude 'quantity of money' or anything else, determined the level of employment and production. I had largely written this section of the book when, fortunately for me, in 1936 came Keynes's famous *General Theory of Employment, Interest and Money*. I was thus lucky in being able to ensure that my doctrine of effective demand was at least consistent with Keynes's argument. My book was also a defence of personal freedom as an equal value with social justice, and not incompatible with it. The main weakness in the book, not fully apparent to me till the 1970s, was my failure to see that, given vigorous collective bargaining on pay, the effort to manage demand without managing labour

[9] This incident is also recounted in Dalton, p. 417, and Davenport, p. 103.
[10] *Principles of Economics* (seventh edition, London, 1916), p. 471.

costs (pay rates) could generate cost-push inflation. But this facet of the problem did not become actual for nearly forty years because the collective bargaining power of labour grew only slowly.

I was forced to work on *The Socialist Case* virtually every evening and week-end for three years and during our Cornish holiday in 1936. Such virtues as the book had I largely owe to two people, Hugh Gaitskell and James Meade. I asked Gaitskell to read and criticize the typescript; and this he did with great care and perspicacity. To James Meade's own book, *An Introduction to Economic Analysis and Policy*,[11] I owed more than to any other printed work. The reception of *The Socialist Case*, when it was finally published in September of 1937, was unexpectedly heartening. It was reviewed at length (as was possible in those days) by J. A. Hobson, who came so near the truth in his earlier doctrines of deficient purchasing power, Lionel Robbins, Hugh Dalton in the *Daily Herald*, Opie of Magdalen, Oxford, and Keither Feiling, Conservative historian at All Souls and Neville Chamberlain's biographer. *The Socialist Case* was translated into Swedish a year later, and I published a revised and up-to-date edition in 1947 just after becoming an MP. Any influence which the book had in 1937–9 lay probably in countering – together with Hugh Dalton's *Practical Socialism for Britain*[12] – the flood of quasi-Marxist volumes pouring forth in the 1930s from Gollancz's Left Book Club and proclaiming the imminent collapse of capitalism. John Strachey, however, stood out among these. He wrote me a letter in 1938 expressing keen interest in my argument, which led to a valuable correspondence[13] and thereby to a lasting friendship between us. Distant echoes of *The Socialist Case* still occasionally reached me in post-war years. Dr Kreisky, Austrian Minister, and later Austrian Chancellor, told me at an EFTA meeting in 1965 that it helped to sustain his faith in social-democracy in his youth.

In the latter part of 1936 changes began at the *Economist*. Layton formally resigned as Editor so as to concentrate on the Chairmanship of the *News Chronicle*, and took Aylmer Vallance with him as *News Chronicle* Editor. Hargreaves Parkinson was promoted from Stock Exchange Editor to Editor of the *Economist*. All this sharply affected the morale of the *Economist* staff, particularly us three thirty-year-olds: Crowther, Hutton and myself. We had been for three years an unusually harmonious team, glad to work with Layton, Toynbee and Vallance. Layton had that singular quality, so necessary to the head of an organization, which I encountered in him, for the first time, of being respected by all. But we did not feel the same about Parkinson. At this moment Bill Aitken, Beaverbrook's nephew, later a Conservative MP after 1945, approached me and asked me if I would like a job on the *Evening Standard* City page. He arranged a meeting for me

---

[11] James Meade, *An Introduction to Economic Analysis and Policy* (Oxford, 1936).
[12] Hugh Dalton, *Practical Socialism for Britain* (London, 1935).
[13] Quoted in Hugh Thomas, *Biography of John Strachey* (London, 1973), p. 175.

with Percy Cudlipp, eldest of the three Cudlipp brothers, who had been appointed as Editor of the *Evening Standard* at the age of twenty-eight. Percy Cudlipp some years later became a much valued colleague and friend to me; but at the first meeting I regarded him with some suspicion. He offered me a job then and there at £1000 a year, just double what I was getting from the *Economist*. At the time the whole Beaverbrook press were fighting a campaign against the League of Nations, against collective resistance to the dictators, and in favour of appeasement. I was beginning to regard the whole Beaverbrook organization as little better than Hitler and Mussolini themselves. So I turned the offer down, feeling I had perhaps behaved churlishly to Aitken and Cudlipp who were disarmingly cordial. When I duly related the whole story to Layton, he received it with characteristically thoughtful silence.

Soon after this, to my even greater surprise, Francis Williams asked me to call on him in his *Daily Herald* City office in Old Broad Street. I hoped he might be going to offer me a job of assistant to him as City Editor. I was delighted at this prospect. I had formed the strongly held conviction that the popular press dominated twentieth-century elections, that a near-100 per cent Tory press monopoly could distort the whole democratic process, and that the parliamentary system could only be vindicated against the Communists by building up a strong, mass circulation paper supporting the Labour Party. So to work on the *Daily Herald* for Francis Williams, who had won a remarkable reputation for himself as journalist, City writer and Labour Party propagandist, seemed to me to be almost too good to be true. When I met him in his office at the old Victorian Palmerston House in Old Broad Street, he told me he was to become Editor of the *Herald*, and he was asking me to succeed him as City Editor at a salary of £1000 a year. This was one of the few moments in my life when, as soon as I grasped that he meant it seriously, I felt myself walking on air. But could I do the job? At the age of twenty-nine one accepts such offers without waiting for answers.

Twenty-five years later Percy Cudlipp told me his version of what occurred at the *Daily Herald* Board meeting at which my appointment was approved. Elias (later in 1937 Lord Southwood) was Chairman of the *Daily Herald*, and Ernie Bevin was Deputy Chairman. I had apparently been proposed not by Francis Williams but by John Dunbar, an old-style Scottish puritan and Odham's director, who always referred to the Labour Party as 'The Comrades', but apparently read my articles in the *Economist*. Bevin, as it happened, had a son-in-law working in Francis Williams's City office, and thought this son-in-law and not myself should have become City Editor. When finally overruled by the rest of the board, Bevin remarked, according to Cudlipp: 'Well, I call this man Jay's appointment just a piece of nepotism.'

The *Daily Herald* and
the Years of Appeasement 4

I started work in the *Daily Herald* City office at the end of January 1937 just about a week before our eldest child, Peter, was born on 7 February 1937. I cared deeply from the start about the *Herald*'s success. The old *Daily Herald* of pre-1930 had been an amateurish, small-circulation, semi-bankrupt propaganda sheet, gallantly kept alive by George Lansbury and others, but hardly capable of influencing national political swings. The new 1930 *Herald*, conceived like so much else by Ernie Bevin on the grand scale, was a joint venture with Bevin and Elias (himself once a Long Acre messenger boy) as the moving spirits. The political policy of the paper was to be determined by the Labour Party (the Party Conference and Parliamentary Party) and the journalistic enterprise supplied by Odhams. Between 1930 and 1937 the new *Herald* had plunged into frantic competition with the *Daily Express*, to be the first paper to reach the two million mark. Southwood's main idea for winning the battle was to give away more and more free copies of Dickens, the Bible, Shakespeare, etc., to those who bought the requisite numbers of *Herald* issues. The Beaverbrook interests naturally retaliated. The *Daily Herald* just passed the two million mile-post first, while this extravagant rake's progress still prevailed. By 1937 it had been by common consent abandoned. Our task, therefore, was to hold a circulation of over two million by journalistic merit instead of mass bribery.

It was one thing to prize the *Daily Herald* as a safeguard of political democracy. It was another to arrive at the office in Old Broad Street in the morning with the daunting knowledge that a whole page, and sometimes more, must be ready by 5 p.m. which would stand up to criticism by the City, the Labour Party and the Odhams libel lawyers. Francis Williams had contrived to combine left-wing criticism of the City and of Montagu Norman (Governor of the Bank) with exposure of scandals, advice to small savers, and finally revelations of the Nazi Government's industrial re-armament plans and consumption of key metals in particular. This latter attracted Churchill's notice. Knowing myself that what I cared for most was Labour Party propaganda rather than City scoops, I resolved to play

c

for safety and devote our page on at least three days out of four to strictly financial or economic stories, starting on my very first day with a disquisition on the future of gilt-edged prices. One precious asset, however, was worth all the rest put together: I did acquire for the first time a room of my own and a first-class secretary, Sally Weiner, who knew all the tricks of this trade, and to whom one could dictate straight on to the typewriter, with virtually no need for correction, no delays, no drafts or tapes – a practice which I sought to follow for much of the rest of my working life in Fleet Street, the government machine and the City.

Meanwhile, at the *Daily Herald* head office, adjoining Odhams in Long Acre, Francis Williams was the dominating personality. My sympathies were wholly with him, because at root he cared far more about the Labour Party and opposing the Nazis and appeasement than he did about Odhams' circulation, scoops or any other of Fleet Street's gods. This naturally made him somewhat suspect to Elias and Dunbar. Dunbar – 'J.D.' to the staff – had long laboured together with Elias in the Odhams machine which also published *John Bull* and the *People*; and by 1937, like Elias himself, he offered advice in long telephone soliloquies to all and sundry on the staff from the Editor downwards. Being rather deaf, he did not listen to any reply. My next closest friend after Williams at head office was Robert Fraser, full-time leader-writer and also well-known to Gaitskell and me through the New Fabian Research Bureau. Fraser was at the time Labour candidate for Wellingborough and took a coolly rational view of politics generally. Another colleague whom I met on the paper for the first time was W. N. Ewer, diplomatic correspondent on the *Daily Herald* from the 1920s to the 1950s. His experience of the Communists had left him with a near-obsession about them and with an attitude almost approaching sympathy with appeasement and Chamberlain. Gaitskell and Dalton were often suspicious in 1937–40 that Ewer was inhibiting the *Daily Herald*'s anti-appeasement campaign, and they urged me to outwit his alleged nefarious influence with Francis Williams. Nor shall I ever forget the 'Industrial' (really Trade Union) Editor, George Thomas. He looked exactly like Walter Citrine, and Citrine was in all things his hero and the fount of all wisdom and truth. George Thomas also had no patience with Communists – or with current Fleet Street fads or fashions either. He gave the news, briefly and frankly, and if you didn't like it (even if you were 'J. D.' himself) you had to lump it.

In the City itself, I was lucky to start with a list of valuable contacts and sources of information furnished to me either by Williams or Vaughan Berry (himself still walking around in a top hat for the Union Discount Company) through XYZ. It was one of the attractions of the City to me that all these collaborators worked within five minutes' walk of my City office and of each other. With some City colleagues I soon built up a close relationship. John Wilmot, then working with C. F. Chance, had founded

with Charles Latham of the LCC an organization called the Shareholders
Protection Association which defended investors against unscrupulous
company directors. More memorably Wilmot had won the famous Fulham
by-election of 1933 for the Labour Party and for collective security. We
had a fruitful arrangement by which I supplied him with Parliamentary
Questions to the Chancellor of the Exchequer; announced on my page that
he was asking them; and later published the answers with suitable comments. Wilmot was also a close ally of Dalton and Gaitskell in these years in
trying to convert the Labour Party from pacifism. Tommy Balogh maintained for me the plentiful stream of ideas and stories, some of them well-
founded, which had assisted me at the *Economist*. Edwin Plowden, then an
expert on potash on the staff of C. Tennant Sons & Co., and a personal
friend since *Economist* days, was no professed supporter of the Labour
Party, and more cautious in his dealings with a popular Labour paper than
with the *Economist*. But you could always rely on what he did say.

With my fellow financial journalists relations were slightly more delicate.
The convention in those days was that as competitors we did not discuss
the day's news with other journalists before publication. Nicholas Davenport,
as a weekly journalist, was a special case; and as a partner in the Stock
Exchange firm of Chase, Henderson and Tennant, was always willing to
talk on Stock Exchange affairs. He introduced me to an unusual City
figure, also a partner in this firm, John Cadogan, brother of Alexander
Cadogan, later Permanent Secretary of the Foreign Office. John Cadogan
was at once a model of old-world courtesy and old Etonian polish, and a
strong supporter of the Labour Party. He delighted, for some reason, to
entertain me to lunch at the Trollopian City Club next to Lazard's also in
Old Broad Street; and, over excellent port, he launched into the most
powerful attacks on Neville Chamberlain I heard from anyone other
than Gaitskell. Thank heaven there are such men in England, I used to say
to myself. Paul Einzig, then money market and foreign exchange specialist
on the old *Financial News*, and a passionate campaigner against appeasement, was the best-informed financial journalist in the City. Being always
one step ahead, he could be unconventionally free with news or comment
even among his fellow writers.

But my closest professional commerce was with R. W. B. (Otto) Clarke,
then 'Lex' of the *Financial News*. Otto, as he was always known, was not only
a Fabian, author of a New Fabian Research Bureau pamphlet signed
'Ingot', advocating nationalization of iron and steel, but also a first-class
Cambridge mathematician, a brilliant chess player, and one inventor of the
famous FN (eventually FT) index of equity share prices. Otto and I
lunched together more or less weekly throughout my four years at the
Daily Herald in Pimms Red House in Bishopsgate. We had a private arrangement by which if either of us felt in need of special advice (usually I did)
we conversed confidentially before the event. I vividly remember Otto

once, when I was too importunate, retorting sharply: 'Look here, I'm a statistician, not a ready reckoner.' Our working lives seemed always to converge thereafter: in the Ministry of Supply throughout the war, in Whitehall and the Treasury from 1945 to 1951, in Economic Ministries in the 1960s, and, curiously, both doing a spell as non-executive directors of Courtaulds even after that. Otto finished, as Sir Richard Clarke, a most distinguished career in the Treasury and Ministry of Technology.

Contacts between the *Daily Herald* and the Bank of England were in those days unorganized and few and far between. I occasionally had telephone talks with Humphrey Mynors, then Economic Adviser and eventually Deputy-Governor. Once one of my news stories about the Bank, written for page 1 of the paper, had been given such an appallingly misleading heading by our head office sub-editors that I exploded at home reading it at breakfast. Later that morning Mynors on the telephone used the very same expression about this heading; and when I told him I had made the identical comment myself, I fear he did not believe me. At one point the Bank asked me to cease publishing some regular figures of gold movements, which were undoubtedly correct, but which the Bank said hampered their job of defending the currency. Little as I liked scoop journalism, I was slightly reluctant to abandon one of our exclusive stories. I consulted Francis Williams on this awkward point of newspaper ethics, and he ruled that if the Bank firmly believed the information to be nationally damaging, we should not publish it. I accepted this, and believe now he was right, though such standards have admittedly fallen since. The Bank at one time designated Ruby Holland-Martin, who came of a fine old banking family, to speak to the press. But though a most affable character, he turned out to know more about horsemanship than public relations and looked as if he was more at home in the Cotswolds than Threadneedle Street. C. F. Cobbold, twenty years later Governor of the post-war Bank, was tried instead and made a very much better job of it.

We in the *Daily Herald* were of course persistent critics of the Bank's deflationary policies and Montagu Norman in particular. Norman was then at the zenith of his career, and was constantly meeting and conferring with the notorious Dr Schacht, head of Hitler's Reichsbank. Over my desk in the City office was a photograph of Norman and Schacht in grave converse with a chess board hung behind their profiles. I only met Norman once, in due circumstances of mystery. I was shown first into his inmost sanctum at the Bank, and he then emerged from a side door with his famous beard enhancing the general air of wizardry which surrounded him. He said little, and I attempted no serious argument. As I left, I was reminded of Thomas Gray's owl, who complained

> ... Of such as, wand'ring near her secret bow'r
> Molest her ancient solitary reign....

But I was no nearer to understanding then or afterwards how Norman maintained his unprecedented twenty years' regal sway.

My major themes in the *Daily Herald* in 1937 and 1938, on days when campaigning seemed possible, were the success of the New Deal, the need for expansionist policies as the mini-boom of 1937 dipped into the 'recession' – the word was invented in that year – of 1938, and the stagnation of the Continental 'gold bloc' where deflationary policies were still being continued. One of my heroes was Paul van Zeeland, Prime Minister of Belgium, who had rescued that country by devaluing the Belgian franc in 1935. From his experience and that of the Blum 'Popular front' devaluation of 1936, I coined the maxim: 'Devaluation always succeeds.' But we also ran on the *Daily Herald* City page a good few individual serial stories of our own, which had the merit of serving the Labour cause, and which the Tory papers did not like to touch. My biggest coup was the successful demand for the Profits Tax as a tax on company profits additional to income tax, in the summer of 1937, my first year on the *Daily Herald*. In the Budget of 1937 Chamberlain as Chancellor of the Exchequer had proposed the 'National Defence Contribution', a special tax on so-called excess profits assessed at a percentage of nominal capital. This was almost universally attacked by the City and accountancy profession as unfair and unworkable. I could not but agree with this; but had long been calling for a special tax on profits. I therefore proposed a straightforward extra 5 per cent tax on company profits as assessed for income tax, and I estimated – it was only a guess – that it might yield about £15 millions, a large sum in 1937. Dalton and Wilmot seized on this idea, and pressed it strongly in the committee stage of the Finance Bill in the House in June. At this moment Chamberlain succeeded Baldwin as Prime Minister, and Simon took over as Chancellor. Simon capitulated and introduced instead of NDC a tax very similar to what I proposed – and estimated to raise about £15 millions. This was the Profits Tax, which survived and raised large sums until 1965.

Another *Daily Herald* City page campaign in these years was in support of Sir William Firth's battle as Chairman of Richard Thomas to build that company's modern steel works at Ebbw Vale instead of in the Midlands. Largely for the sake of employment, Firth decided to press ahead with the scheme, relying on Richard Thomas's resources alone and ignoring his rivals. Unfortunately he ran out of funds, and construction came to a grinding halt, spreading an atmosphere of disaster in South Wales. Ernie Bevin, as Deputy Chairman of the *Daily Herald* (now forgetting his charge of 'nepotism'!) sent for me and asked me to see his friend William Firth and launch a campaign in the *Daily Herald* demanding that the strip mill should be saved. This was my earliest meeting face to face with Bevin. I naturally leapt at the story. Elias (now Southwood) and 'J.D.' could not obstruct if Bevin was behind it, and I called on Firth in his office in the Adelphi, Strand. Firth was, I thought, slightly doubtful whether the *Daily Herald*'s support would recommend him to Montagu Norman; but he did not wish to deter me if Bevin was the guiding hand. So the *Daily Herald* campaigned vigorously over a period of months for Bank of England help, with support from Labour MPs in Parliament. In the end Norman pledged the funds – it was of the order of £5 millions, astonishing as that seems today – on condition that a consortium of rival steel firms joined in the enterprise. Firth's independence was clipped; but the steelworks was built. In the war years we thanked God for it. And a few of us thanked the *Daily Herald* also.

After Hitler's invasion of Austria in 1938, and as the ghastly drama leading up to Munich was enacted, I used my page on one pretext or another more and more as part of the campaign to discredit Chamberlain and the appeasers. In the summer of 1938 Walter Runciman was sent on a mission to Czechoslovakia nominally to investigate the alleged grievances of the German minority but really, we anti-appeasers feared, to soften up resistance. I happened to discover from City sources that Runciman, though a minister, had retained a number of directorships in private companies in defiance of the rule that ministers must not do so. Challenged in the House, the Prime Minister had to admit the truth of this; Runciman had to resign the directorships; and a strengthened rule on ministers' directorships was formally laid down. Our most successful anti-appeasement story, however, emerged later after the full-scale invasion of Czechoslovakia by Hitler on 15 March 1939. As soon as the Nazi Government had established control of the Bank of Czechoslovakia, they requested the Bank for International Settlements at Basle to transfer to Prague £6 millions of gold owned by the Czech Bank but actually located in Basle and London. The BIS Board, including Norman, meeting in Basle agreed without waiting to consult the governments of the countries involved. Paul Einzig commented: 'BIS *dat qui cito dat*.' We in the *Daily Herald*, starting on the City page, raised a storm over this, demanding to know whether Montagu Norman was acting as Governor of the Bank of England or Director of the BIS, and whether he consulted the British Government before presenting Hitler with a valuable tranche of gold. Sir John Simon, then Chancellor, was very hard put to answer the Parliamentary Questions from Wilmot and others, and to explain whether Norman had the right to ignore the British Government's foreign policy. This story ran for weeks, and we felt we had really found a financial theme which struck a powerful blow for the anti-Nazi cause.

But that was only one tiny corner of the battle against appeasement. On the wider political front, 1938 and 1939 were baffling and stifling years. At times I found it hard to share Gaitskell's confident faith that eventually appeasement would be defeated and reversed, and that this country would unite and lead an alliance against Hitler. Week by week – this became forgotten in later years – almost the entire press poured forth articles and twisted news stories designed to prove that Hitler meant little harm, and that warnings of danger were bad for business anyway. The *Daily Express* went only a little further than the rest. Even on 7 August 1939, the *Daily Express* front page heading said: 'No war this year,' and the sub-heading added: 'Berlin emphatic: Hitler is not ready.' On the *Express* front page on 11 August 1939 we read: 'No war says Lord Beaverbrook, Ottawa, Thursday. I would not be out here if I did believe that war was imminent.' In the *Daily Herald* City office in these years I was acutely conscious of the insistent pressure from the City establishment and the press advertising interests in favour of appeasement, and above all against any suggestion in the press that we perhaps ought to prepare for war. Francis Williams and I became aware that Southwood and 'J.D.' in their lairs in Long Acre regarded us as political extremists who were endangering the circulation and worse still the advertising revenue of the paper. I could see that this pressure was being exerted less discreetly and much more successfully on most of the rest of the press, particularly in the Beaverbrook empire.

The advertisers believed that the public would not buy if they thought a war was coming. One grotesque manifestation of this pressure was exhibited by the Odhams group itself. The *Daily Herald* was of course regarded by Southwood and 'J.D.' as a problem child led astray by 'the comrades'. Their real pride and joy were the *People* and *John Bull* (which had somehow survived its unhappy adventures with Horatio Bottomley). *John Bull* was normally printed three or four days before publication in order to reduce costs; and the number due for publication on 18 March 1939 was written five or six days beforehand. It included a political leader faithfully recording the Southwood 'party line', declaring that the alarmists and troublemakers had been proved wrong in their prediction that Hitler would invade Czechoslovakia; that the Ides of March had come; that no tank or gun had moved; and that the moaners and mischiefmakers should now pipe down. The article contained these words:

The International Know-Alls said everything was going to happen. . . . It seems they didn't know anything. . . . For Hitler didn't do anything. In fact no one did anything. . . . They said Europe would be in turmoil. . . . But it was just another pleasant day.

But the Ides of March had not gone. Unluckily for Southwood on 15 March, after printing but before publication, Hitler marched on Prague. The unfortunate editor of *John Bull*, I was told, asked Southwood next day whether publication should go ahead. 'Of course,' Southwood replied, 'Why not?' And on 18 March it did.

The pressure of the advertisers on Fleet Street was, I believe, the additional driving force, reinforcing the anti-Communist obsession and the other motives I have attributed (chapter 2) to Halifax, Geoffrey Dawson and the rest of the Milner group. For those of us however humbly resisting this, the atmosphere of self-deception was choking. All good men supported Chamberlain, and anyone who did not was outside the pale of decent society. All those who wanted to get on, be promoted and make money, must naturally bow to the idol of appeasement. I never forgot the suffocating pressure for a false orthodoxy in those years, and could not fail to notice the grim fidelity with which it was all repeated in the Common Market controversy of the 1960s and 1970s. To anyone who lived through both periods the parallel was grotesquely close;[1] the basic motives of the Conservative majority; the confusion on the Left; and the rallying of all the vested interests in the City, the press and the advertising world to the establishment party line of the moment.

Yet in two respects at least the 1930s did present a more honourable picture than the 1960s and 1970s. First, a few national newspapers – the *Daily Herald*, the *Daily Telegraph*, the *Yorkshire Post* and rather fitfully the *News Chronicle* – stood out against the tide of self-deception in the 1930s; whereas in the 1960s and 1970s, a mysterious, but almost total press monopoly supported the pro-marketeers. Secondly, Churchill in the ardent admiration for him, warts and all, in these years which never left me. But Hugh Dalton also (whom Churchill unfortunately, if characteristically, did not much like) deserves more credit than he has perhaps yet received for almost single-handedly at first, persistently and successfully in the end, bringing the Parliamentary Labour Party round to full opposition to appeasement and eventually full support for re-armament. No doubt events helped Dalton's campaign; for when the Nazi armies marched into Prague, even Chamberlain could not still pretend, though he tried, that Hitler was a nice peaceful man who wanted only to do a business deal. But without Dalton's efforts, all-Party unity might not have been achieved even in 1939, and the Labour Party would have been exposed to even more damning criticism of wanting to stop Hitler and cut our own defences at the same time.

Gaitskell and I, meeting regularly at XYZ and elsewhere, despite our puny resources attempted to exert influence on two fronts: the *Daily Herald* and the Parliamentary Labour Party. Our chief ally on the *Herald* front was Francis Williams, backed by Bevin in the boardroom. By this means and by constant argument, the *Daily Herald* was kept reasonably firmly on the anti-appeasement side. But there were worries and wobbles, and the persistence of the Parliamentary Labour Party in voting against the Defence Estimates right into 1938 did not make things easier. Robert Fraser, a close friend and ally of ours on all other issues, felt so deeply about the appalling realities of European war, as to be doubtful whether resistance to the Nazis was really necessary or possible. Even Evan Durbin shared some of these doubts. His hesitation caused the greatest anxiety and disappointment to Gaitskell, his closest friend, and nearly, but never completely, cooled the personal bond between them.[2] In fairness to Evan Durbin, it should be said that his continued insistence at this time on the tyrannical nature of the

[1] See pages 424 and 433–4 for this comparison.
[2] I write this after reading, by courtesy of Durbin's daughter, Miss Lizzie Durbin, the correspondence between him and Gaitskell which followed Munich.

Stalin regime, which earned him much criticism and which both Gaitskell and I then thought exaggerated, was wholly vindicated by the evidence which came to light after Stalin's death. Secondly, Gaitskell and I did all we could to back Dalton in his long struggle to persuade the Parliamentary Labour Party to stop voting against the Defence Estimates. Bevin supported Dalton from an early stage, but Attlee and Morrison were only gradually converted. Dalton has himself told the story in his autobiography[3] where he states that support from the younger generation 'encouraged' him in his campaign. In all this, though those of us who agreed with Dalton and Gaitskell had long been convinced that war with Hitler was nearly certain, and Chamberlain's policy disastrous, we did not know, because it was concealed from the public, the appalling magnitude of the blunders Chamberlain was making. Now, however, the full truth has been recorded in particular in Anthony Eden's autobiography[4] and elsewhere.

On 11 January 1938, Mr Sumner Welles, Roosevelt's Secretary of State, approached the British Ambassador in Washington, Sir Ronald Lindsay. He told Sir Ronald that the President intended to make a highly important speech on 22 January, and that Britain alone was being consulted about this beforehand. The speech would only be made if the plan had the 'cordial approval and wholehearted support of HMG.' Sumner Welles added privately that the intention was to do all the US could to check Hitler and Mussolini; and everyone, including Chamberlain, assumed that this was the real purpose. Sir Ronald Lindsay advised 'quick and cordial acceptance', and the FO officially agreed. Eden, as it happened, was out of the country; and Chamberlain without first consulting him or any member of the Cabinet sent a message to Roosevelt in effect turning the offer down. Sumner Welles described Chamberlain's response as 'a douche of cold water'. Lindsay reported that Roosevelt himself was 'disappointed', and Eden recorded his opinion that this ended 'close confidential Anglo–US consultation' on the overriding issue facing both countries and the world. The view of Eden, Cranborne, Sir Alexander Cadogan and Lindsay (Eden makes clear) was definite that Roosevelt intended, so far as he judged US opinion would allow, to support Britain and France in any action needed to stop the dictators. Yet at an eventual meeting of the Foreign Affairs Committee of the Cabinet on 19 January,[5] Chamberlain, Halifax, Simon and Inskip rejected Eden's arguments and turned down Roosevelt's offer. Eden and Cranborne resigned and Eden makes this considered comment:[6] 'The truth was that some of my seniors in the Cabinet, like Inskip, could not believe that Mussolini and Hitler were as untrustworthy as I painted them. After all, had not Mussolini defeated the Reds and made the trains run time? They instinctively regarded Roosevelt as something of a demagogue.'

[3] Hugh Dalton, *The Fateful Years*, Vol. 2, Chapter VIII, especially p. 140.
[4] Anthony Eden, *Facing the Dictators* (London, 1962), Chapter XII, 'Roosevelt Makes a Move'.
[5] [6] Eden, p. 560.

Chamberlain's incredible response to Roosevelt in January 1938, all the more catastrophic because wholly hidden at the time from the entire political world even after the event, apart from a few ministers, can be seen in retrospect as the real turning point in the inter-war years, and the worst blunder by any British Government in recent times; together with the rejection by the Wilson Government in 1969 of de Gaulle's offer to the UK of a free-trade-area linked with the EEC.[7] (Here again there was a sombre parallel between the two periods, with only the ironic difference that the FO's advice was right and rejected in 1938 and wrong and accepted in 1969.) If Roosevelt's 1938 offer had been accepted, and the British Government had supported the effort to create a US-backed defensive alliance of ourselves, France, the Soviet Union and Czechoslovakia, with even half the obstinate energy with which Chamberlain sought his deal with Hitler, it is possible if not probable that war would have been avoided. This country would not then have been bankrupted and exhausted by the effort; the Soviet Union would not have advanced into Eastern Europe; and the whole second half of the twentieth century might have turned out very differently both for Britain and for many other countries. Chamberlain's rejection of Roosevelt's crucial offer can only be explained on the assumption that he was first and last determined to avoid any sort of alliance with Russia, even at the cost of losing the support of the US.

If all this had been fully known at the time, it is probable that the resulting explosion would have engulfed Chamberlain then and there. But Eden and Cranborne out of gentlemanly reticence, it seems – though resigning ministers have a dispensation from the Official Secrets Act – never disclosed the full disastrous reason for their resignation. It was thus hidden as much from Dalton and the leaders of the Labour Party as from small fry like Gaitskell and myself. We assumed that Eden and Cranborne were protesting against the general drift of Chamberlain's policies; and when Hitler invaded Austria in March 1938 only a few weeks later, we naturally took this as only confirming our assumptions.

Gloom continued throughout the summer months of 1938, as the struggle went on, within the Labour Party as well as outside it, against Chamberlain. When Geoffrey Dawson had his finest hour and *The Times* wrote its notorious leader of 7 September 1938, advocating territorial concessions to Hitler in Czechoslovakia, I was on holiday in North Cornwall with my family, and reading it feared the worst.[8] Back at the *Herald* in mid September, as Chamberlain was flying to and from Germany, Tommy Balogh warned me in characteristically lurid terms that a ghastly sell-out was impending. Immediately before Chamberlain's journey to Berchtesgaden on 15 September, I by chance met Hugh Dalton that day lunching with Francis Williams. Dalton told me he had just seen Chamberlain on behalf of the Labour op-

[7] See pages 431–4 for the comparison.
[8] R. A. Butler has recorded his belief that Halifax knew of this leader beforehand and had discussed it with Dawson. See his *The Art of the Possible* (London, 1971), p. 69.

position, and Chamberlain had assured him he was going to Germany to inform Hitler that if he made any further aggressive moves, we should be ready to fight. Dalton – who was nothing if not sceptical – evidently believed this, and I was somewhat reassured. Surely he must be a better judge than the shrewd but erratic Balogh. A few days later, when Chamberlain had flown to Godesberg, my wife and I spent the week-end with Sheila Grant-Duff at a cottage adjoining the Avebury home, High Elms, Farnborough, Kent; and Shiela's excellent Penguin book *Europe and the Czechs* was just on the point of publication. Since working in Czechoslovakia from 1936 to 1938, Shiela had kept in touch with Ripka (a friend of Benes) in Prague and Churchill in London. As Mrs Churchill was a relative and friend of hers, Shiela rang up the Churchills at neighbouring Chartwell, and boldly from a telephone kiosk in the lane asked Churchill what he thought was going on in Germany. He replied down the telephone: 'I don't know, but I suspect it is something shameful.' I came home rather less reassured from this week-end. On the Monday or Tuesday of the following week we all went to the City, prepared for war, and practised the use of gas masks and underground shelters at the office. In the afternoon of Wednesday 28 September, while on my usual round of City offices in the afternoon, on the refuge in the middle of the road at the junction of Threadneedle Street and Bishopsgate, I met Paul Einzig and Otto Clarke. Einzig, always half an hour ahead of everyone, told me as we stood on the island that Chamberlain had surrendered and announced in Parliament he was going to Munich. I could for a moment hardly believe it. Clarke asked me: 'Which is worse, fear or shame?' We all three answered: 'Shame.'

Naturally Munich struck confusion into our wing of the Labour Party who were trying to nerve the pacifist elements to accept the need for resistance and re-armament. To stop the rot Dalton arranged a meeting on 19 October 1938 of a group at his flat to see if we could agree on what the next step should be in this wholly new situation.[9] Besides Dalton, among those present were Philip Noel-Baker, Kingsley Martin, Evan Durbin, Hugh Gaitskell, Robert Fraser, John Wilmot, Leonard Woolf and myself. Dalton asked each of us in turn what policy should now be pursued. Unqualified support for Dalton's insistence on all-out resistance to Hitler, even if it meant war, came from only Gaitskell, Noel-Baker and me. Robert Fraser in a letter to me on 27 November 1963 commented on this evening as follows: 'Evan and I took the view that nothing had so far happened to prove that war was inevitable . . . and were in the majority. . . . It was the march on Prague that seemed to Evan and me the first absolute proof that we should have to fight.' Returning home with Gaitskell in the underground after the meeting at Dalton's flat, I confessed to him that I was filled with deepest gloom. If this were the demoralized mood of the non-pacifist wing

[9] Leonard Woolf in a letter to me of 7 October 1963 confirmed my memory of this meeting as being held at Dalton's flat in Carlisle Mansions, Victoria, on 19 October. See also *Hugh Gaitskell*, ed. W. T. Rodgers (London, 1964), pp. 82–4.

of the Labour Party, what hope of the Opposition stiffening Chamberlain?
And what remote chance of Chamberlain stiffening the vacillating French?
It was at this moment that Gaitskell replied with the utmost confidence
that in effect Dalton, with the help of some of us, would soon convert the
Labour Party, that they and Churchill would overturn and supplant
Chamberlain, and that in the end Roosevelt would be drawn in to help us.
Gaitskell then of course knew nothing of Roosevelt's offer of January 1938.
For this conversation we had only the underground journey from Victoria
to Charing Cross. But for me it was doubly a watershed in this long struggle.
First, it revived my conviction that Hitler could be defeated. Secondly, it
impressed me with a fuller understanding than ever before of the underlying strength which Gaitskell normally hid beneath his straightforward,
almost commonplace, manner.

Those of us who at the time opposed Munich root and branch always
argued that the British Government should have actively organized a firm
and collective plan of resistance by ourselves, France, Czechoslovakia, and
if possible Russia; that a convincing collective warning might have deterred
Hitler or even led to his removal; but that if it led to war, we should have
fought with the strongest possible moral case, and with the considerable
Czech and possibly some Russian military resources added to our own and
those of France. Have these assumptions been undermined or confirmed by
the mass of evidence accumulated in the subsequent years?

John Wheeler-Bennett, in his *Munich : A Prologue to Tragedy*, attempted
a dispassionate judgement. R. A. Butler quotes Wheeler-Bennett's verdict
on Munich 'that it was inescapable; that faced with the lack of preparedness
in Britain's armaments and defences; with the lack of unity at home and in
the Commonwealth; with the collapse of French morale; and with the
uncertainty of Russian capacity to fight, Mr Chamberlain had no alternative to do other than he did . . . but let us not omit the shame and humili-
ation which were ours'.[10] And this, in R. A. Butler's eyes, establishes the
'historic inevitability' of Munich.[11] But he does not quote Wheeler-Bennett's
final judgement:[12]

The apologists for Munich cannot have it both ways. Either Britain was so ill-
armed and undefended that she was forced with great reluctance to a certain
course of action in order to ensure peace, or else she was in a position to fight and
of her own free will chose not to do so. In neither case is there cause for self-
approbation . . . in any case, whichever claim is made for Munich, it was a failure.
It brought neither peace with honour, nor for our time.[13]

With all the advantage of hindsight, therefore, I still see no reason to doubt

[10] John Wheeler-Bennett, *Munich : A Prologue to Tragedy* (London, 1948), p. 433.
[11] Butler, p. 67.
[12] Wheeler-Bennett, pp. 434-5.
[13] The excuse that Munich gave Britain time to re-arm has no force because the figures
show that Germany increased arms production correspondingly in 1938-9. See M. M.
Postan, *British War Production* (London, 1952), pp. 471, 484. Czech war production was
also transferred to Hitler.

that those of us were right who vehemently opposed Munich at the time. Of course the anti-defence wing of the Labour Party must bear a share of the blame for making re-armament more difficult by voting against Defence Estimates until late in the 1930s. It was indeed the latter lesson, never forgotten, which led Hugh Gaitskell to accept perhaps a little too easily the re-armament programme of 1951.

The one comforting comment which can truly be made about Munich is that as a result, when war came a year later, there was nobody left in Britain of any school of thought, bar a few eccentrics and some Communists, who believed that it was not necessary. But this is no defence or excuse for the appeasers of 1938, because it was not what they planned either publicly or privately.

To say so much about Munich after forty years will not seem excessive to those of my generation on whom its impact was so profound. My own anger at what seemed at the time an appalling betrayal was so inflamed that various juvenile impulses filled my mind for a few days: such as throwing bricks through the windows of No. 10 or somehow violently demonstrating in Parliament Square. I calmed down when I read there was to be a Munich debate in the Commons, and that Churchill as well as the Labour Opposition leaders, including Morrison, would put the case for condemning the Agreement. Better perhaps in the end to argue the issue this way than to break harmless people's limbs in the streets. So I threw no bricks; and this abiding memory led me to understand very starkly that one of the functions of Parliament, and particularly of Opposition, is to voice the deeply held beliefs and grievances of the ordinary citizen.

It is part of the conventional history of the Munich period to assume that in the immediate weeks after the Agreement, a majority of the British public supported Chamberlain and believed that he had truly brought home 'Peace in Our Time'. I have always doubted this. Certainly there was relief – how could it be otherwise? – that immediate war had been avoided. But such relief is very different from reasoned approval of what had been done in Britain's name. Quintin Hogg's victory in the Oxford City by-election in late October 1938 is sometimes quoted as evidence that a general majority supported Chamberlain for a few weeks. But Oxford was always a Conservative seat, not merely at this time, but even in 1945, and the hastily contrived non-Party candidature of Lindsay no doubt suffered from the usual handicaps of all such electoral improvisations. And Vernon Bartlett won the Bridgewater by-election in November 1938 as an independent anti-appeasement candidate. It must remain unproven whether Chamberlain could have won a general election in October 1938.

What struck me, however, at the time as the real decisive turning point in British opinion, now seldom emphasized, was Goebbels's anti-semitic campaign of November and December 1938. Despite Hitler's triumph at Munich, discontent grew in Germany as an exceptionally cold winter aggravated the food shortages, high prices and other discomforts caused by his ever-expanding war machine. Goebbels conceived an anti-semitic pogrom as the easiest diversion. But it misfired. Prominently and luridly reported in the British and other non-German press, it excited indignation which boomeranged powerfully against the Nazi Government. I felt myself in November 1938 that the battle was won, and that it was only a matter of time till action followed. Dalton and those working with him, like Gaitskell and our other friends, found Goebbels's new campaign to be the most per-suasive weapon we had yet held for convincing the doubters within the Labour Party that resistance by force was the only possible policy. And so, when Hitler invaded Czechoslovakia on 15 March 1939, and tore even the Munich Agreement to shreds, there was hardly any rational dispute that we must prepare for war. It was now that doubters in the Labour Party like Evan Durbin and Robert Fraser became convinced that Hitler could only be stopped by force. But Chamberlain still wavered, and could only bring himself to say in the Commons, when challenged about the invasion: 'I cannot regard the manner and method by which these changes have been brought about as in accord with the spirit of Munich.'[14]

By April, it seemed probable that even the Chamberlain Government would introduce military conscription. Gaitskell and I now feared that the Parliamentary Labour Party would make a fool of itself by demanding resistance to Hitler and voting against conscription at the same time. So, together with Durbin, we devised a scheme to avert this, and successfully sold it to Dalton. Our proposal was that the Labour Party should accept military conscription if the Government in turn would simultaneously accept 'conscription of wealth'; and to convert the latter from a slogan into a practical plan, we advocated an annual capital tax (now called a 'wealth tax') such as I had been suggesting in my *Daily Herald* City column.[15] We set out this combined proposal in a formal paper, drafted by Gaitskell and myself, and presented in the name of all three of us, to Attlee as Leader of the Party and the Shadow Cabinet. It was headed 'The Conscription of Wealth', 24 April 1939, and began as follows: 'Some eighteen months ago a small group of Labour Party supporters, three of whom are members of the Finance and Trade Committee, began a series of discussions on the subject of war finance.' The 'group' was XYZ; the three were Gaitskell, Durbin and myself; and the Finance and Trade Committee was a sub-committee of the Labour Party National Executive. Our paper included these words:

Our general object has been to try and work out the kind of economic and financial policy for which the Labour Party ought to press in the event of war. Already there is probably a majority of Conservative members who would like to introduce military conscription, and as time goes on the pressure in favour is likely to in-crease. It is in our opinion very doubtful indeed whether the country as a whole is really in such violent opposition to it as is sometimes represented. We ourselves

[14] Hansard, 15 March 1939, col. 440.
[15] I had also advocated this in a formal Labour Party pamphlet called *The Nation's Wealth at the Nation's Service*, published in November 1938.

feel, too, that from the point of view of foreign policy certain forms of compulsion might be an important step towards deterring the aggressor states. We believe, therefore, that circumstances may arise in which it would be unwise for the Party to adopt a purely negative attitude towards any and every form of conscription.

The Policy of the Party should be rather to insist on certain conditions before withdrawing its opposition. These conditions must be 'the conscription of wealth'. The phrase has already been used fairly widely in speeches and resolutions and as such is generally acceptable to the supporters of conscripting man power. We therefore propose:

1 That the gap between total expenditure and current revenue should not be met any longer by borrowing, i.e. that the national debt must not be increased any further.

2 That the gap should be filled by a special defence levy on capital, so long at least as conscription continues. The Levy will therefore be an annual one, and take the place of borrowing as a method of finance.

3 The Levy must be paid either in cash or to the extent of 75% in Trustee Securities, and the remaining 25% in any securities quoted on the Stock Exchange.

4 The Levy will be paid by individual British citizens, and will be graduated on much the same scale as Death Duties.

Dalton arranged that the three of us, as authors of this paper, should meet Attlee, Morrison, Shinwell, Greenwood, A. V. Alexander and Dalton himself, in the Leader of the Opposition's room in the House, and discuss our plan. Dalton strongly supported us. Attlee and all the others were converted, and agreed to recommend it to the Parliamentary Labour Party. Shinwell remarked, I remember, as we left: 'I don't know if it is good economics, but it certainly sounds good politics to me.' Attlee and Dalton duly recommended it in the name of the Shadow Cabinet to the full meeting of the PLP. But the latter body, still moved by old-fashioned pacifism even in April and May of 1939, turned it down by a clear majority – on the ground that military conscription could never be accepted by the Labour Party. We were deeply disappointed. It seemed hardly credible that, even after the march on Prague, the Labour Party should be willing the end but still afraid to will the means. But there was little more that Gaitskell, Durbin and I could do for the moment, other than work out (through XYZ as already recorded)[16] the details of our plans for war-time financial and economic policy.

In the *Daily Herald* in April/May 1939 I found some relief from appeasement, and felt I was helping the cause even on my City page, by denouncing day in and day out the conduct of Montagu Norman already described[17] in allowing the Czech gold to fall into Nazi hands. In these months, however, I had privately become impatient and weary of Fleet Street values, the subordination of all in heaven and earth to increasing the circulation and advertising revenue of one's own paper. Much as I believed in the *Daily*

[16] In Chapter 3. XYZ documents of the spring and summer of 1939 included papers by Berry on war-time interest rates, and banking control, and by Piercy on the limitation of profits.
[17] On p. 70.

Herald, I frankly longed to be working in the public service. Dunbar and the Odhams faction in the *Daily Herald*, I was sure, regarded me as a crypto-politician who was keener on my 'political' propaganda against Hitler, Chamberlain and Montagu Norman than on my proper job of increasing the advertising revenue. I was exceedingly grateful nevertheless in these tense months to Francis Williams, the Editor, who was wholly sympathetic, and was fighting the same battle himself. There were other independent spirits in City journalism who gladdened my heart, including Otto Clarke, Paul Einzig, already mentioned, and Oscar Hobson, City Editor of the *News Chronicle*. Hobson was a traditional *laissez-faire* Liberal who understood and admired the established City institutions. But like Walter Layton he also scrupulously upheld old-fashioned journalistic standards of accuracy and integrity. I met Hobson, one afternoon, a few days after Munich, in a stockbroker's office; and the stockbroker in question quoted *The Times* as having written that morning 'The whole country must unite behind Mr Chamberlain.' 'The trouble is,' Hobson replied, 'that the whole country is united in front of him.'

It was in May 1939 that our son Peter, aged 2¼, contracted what three doctors diagnosed as pneumonia. At the very last moment, my wife, to whose resource we owe his life, called in another specialist who found it was appendicitis and operated within the hour.

When the news came first of the Ribbentrop/Molotov Pact and then on 1 September of Hitler's invasion of Poland, I was staying at Crackington Haven, North Cornwall, with my family (my second son Martin having been born in the inauspicious month of July 1939). A friend of ours, also staying there, wife of a Central European refugee, who told me the news, then took my breath away by saying that she would emigrate with her small son to America because of petrol rationing in Britain. This was a sharp lesson to me about the different attitudes of some people to this country. Having arranged for the family to stay in Devon, I returned via Oxford where I was to join Herbert Hart, Christopher Cox, Isaiah Berlin and Arnold Pilkington for a week in mid-Wales. This was cancelled, and Hart and I drove back to Hampstead in the glorious evening of September 3 with hundreds of silver barrage balloons for the first time shining in the intense blue sky over London. There were more cars entering London after the week-end than leaving it in the great panic exodus which so many had feared. We camped in my mother's house, together with Dick Crossman and Tommy Balogh, both of whom wanted temporary lodging in London. Crossman, I learnt, had been transferred by the national registration scheme automatically into the new Ministry of Information. So had Otto Clarke from the *Financial News* and Robert Fraser from the *Daily Herald*. Gaitskell had gone to the Ministry of Economic Warfare, together with Edwin Plowden, David Eccles, Gladwyn Jebb and others from the City and universities.

I found myself left on the *Daily Herald* partly because the press was considered essential as a 'reserved' occupation, and partly for a reason which emerged later. Not content, however, with a mere City life in war-time, I persuaded Francis Williams, who readily agreed, that in Fraser's absence I should write the daily political leaders as well as a shortened City column. It was an immense relief to be at last sharing directly in the political and propaganda war effort; and we spent the months of the phoney war in the winter of 1939–40 campaigning for far greater government effort on the war production front and exposing the British Communist Party's virtual propaganda alliance with the Nazis which followed the Ribbentrop/Molotov Pact. My new position as leader-writer entitled me to attend as a silent observer the weekly meetings of the Parliamentary Labour Party in Committee Room 14 at the House, and I regularly did so from the start of the war up to the end of 1940. The idea was that the *Daily Herald* leader-writer should know the mind of the Labour Party. At the end of these meetings I normally returned with Attlee to his rooms in the House and sought to extract a few laconic words of advice from him, sometimes unsuccessfully.

Francis Williams has frankly described in his autobiography the strength of his feeling for this country, as the defender of civilized values and the leader of the anti-Hitler world coalition in the early months of the war: 'and then suddenly the war exploded and I found that what I most cared about was England. . . . I was astonished at the strength of my feelings, for they seemed to deny many of the things in which I had formerly thought I believed.'[18] He did not talk to me as emotionally as this at the time; but I shared his feelings. How little do some of us value this country until its very existence is threatened!

Now that war was declared, newsprint was rationed, and circulation mattered little, it might have seemed that Southwood would have eased off in his opposition to Williams's campaign in the *Daily Herald* for a more vigorous prosecution of the war. But no. Even now the incongruous remnant of the Cliveden Set and others – Nancy Astor, Bernard Shaw, even Lloyd George, and the insufferable American ambassador, Joseph Kennedy – were still hankering after appeasement. Southwood, as Francis Williams records, sympathized with them. His idea seemed to be that if we didn't press the war too far, Hitler might still be induced to call the whole thing off. When Williams and I pushed the argument beyond a point with articles calling for stronger action, the old obstruction and interference from Southwood and Dunbar began to operate.

The first clash came over a proposed feature page which was intended, rather oddly, to be written half by Keynes and half by myself. It was Williams's idea. Keynes had been advocating the scheme for 'post-war credits' afterwards put into force. You paid income-tax during the war and got a portion back afterwards. I had been proposing instead the annual

[18] Francis Williams, *Nothing So Strange, an Autobiography* (London, 1970), p. 157.

capital tax as expounded in our 'Conscription of Wealth' paper of 1939. Williams's suggestion was for each scheme to be argued side by side on a single page; and Keynes, having agreed, duly turned up at my City office to correct the proofs. It was the first time I had met him, and I was frankly overawed by the occasion. But the articles went ahead – only to be struck out late at night by Southwood and Dunbar. They felt that we were now really going too far with this ultra-highbrow stuff. Williams protested violently next morning, and this time the articles were duly re-instated on the following day.

By the early weeks of 1940, however, Southwood had judiciously recruited on to the *Daily Herald*, as chief assistant to Williams, Percy Cudlipp, ex-Editor of the *Evening Standard*. Percy Cudlipp was the oldest and most serious-minded of the three Cudlipp brothers, and in later years became a close friend of mine. He had a cutting wit as well as a generous ration of the Celtic fluency with which his family were so lavishly endowed. But at this stage I still regarded him with suspicion as a counter seized upon by Southwood to help in the removal of Francis Williams. And so it turned out. Not much later, in early 1940, Williams wrote a signed article suggesting the organization of underground resistance movements in Hitler-occupied countries. Cudlipp removed the article overnight on orders from Southwood; and when Williams protested next day and threatened resignation, Southwood and Dunbar succeeded in outvoting Walter Citrine on the *Daily Herald* board. Williams's resignation was accepted, and before long he became Chief Press Officer at the Ministry of Information. Cudlipp began a fourteen-year reign as Editor of the *Herald*. I was myself so disgusted with this episode as to be disillusioned with Fleet Street and journalism generally; and was from this moment more anxious than ever to be assigned to some active branch of the war effort.

Before it came, however, Hitler unleashed his war machine first on Norway and Denmark in April, and then in May on the Western Front; and at last the British public and even the ex-appeasers understood what we were fighting. To the immense relief and delight of Gaitskell, myself and our friends, the Churchill Government was formed and Labour ministers entered it in force. It is hard now to describe adequately the lightening of the heart and the lifting of the spirit which we felt at the knowledge that the country for the first time for twenty years had a Government which one could wholeheartedly respect and support. Having evacuated my wife and two children and my parents (my father was still working full-time for the Red Cross at seventy-one) to Beaconsfield, which I judged, rightly, would be just outside the range of the coming air attacks; I spent the nights of the weeks following Dunkirk on Home Guard patrols on the Chiltern Hills round Penn, waiting for German parachutists, and the days on the *Herald* mainly campaigning for the use of Tube stations as air-raid shelters. We were a favoured Home Guard area, as the military took the parachutist threat seriously, and we patrolled the fields with several rounds of ammunition – unlike some Home Guard units – as well as rifles. (Only after the war did I discover that Bomber Command HQ was in near-by High Wycombe.) The hideous unpreparedness of the Forces after Dunkirk was brought home to me by a visiting officer from the South Coast defences, who told us that if we saw any tank anywhere in the next few weeks, we could assume it was German. At about the same time I heard A. V. Alexander, as First Lord of the Admiralty, tell a meeting of the Parliamentary Labour Party that following Dunkirk over fifty British destoyers and other small naval craft were under repair and out of action – a statement which seemed to me distinctly indiscreet as made at this moment to this notoriously leaky gathering.

The worst moment was the last week of June, after the fall of France, and before the destruction of the French fleet at Oran. In that week, for a moment, as has not always been remembered since, the prospect of Hitler gaining naval superiority by seizing the French fleet was seriously threatened. Wondering whether I should send my small children to America, I asked a few close colleagues what they honestly expected to happen. 'Do you think,' one replied, 'that twenty-one miles of shallow sea can alter the course of history?' I then tried Tommy Balogh, who had become a British subject a week or two before, and whom I had always regarded as the arch-pessimist among my friends. '*We* shall win,' he said, 'it will be a long and horrible business, but *we* shall win in the end.' Perversely, perhaps, I was much cheered by this pronouncement, believing that if even Balogh retained hope and confidence, then certainly so should I. But should I keep my family at home within reach of the invasion we all expected, or send them to the US or Canada at the risk of submarine attack on the voyage? It is perhaps worth recording today, in a far more comfortable but perhaps more discontented society, the dilemmas that some of us then faced. My wife and I decided that we would all stay in this country, and we never regretted that decision.

As September 1940 came, and the blitz broke on London, the day staff on the *Herald* worked until the air raid sirens sounded usually at about 8 p.m., and we then moved as rapidly as possible down Long Acre to Leicester Square Tube Station, hoping to get there before missiles started falling. It was a matter of pride to walk and not run, and one soon found that the danger of injury from falling over sandbags in the black-out was much greater than that of being hit by bombs. The least pleasant moments of my day were spent sitting in darkness in the train at Marylebone waiting for it to start. Conversation tended to lag until the train moved safely into the tunnel. At night in the Home Guard on the hills above Beaconsfield we could both see and hear the battle over London, with a continuous rumble of guns and flashes of bursting shells in the sky. It was undoubtedly a comfort at this and some later stages of the war to know that those still in civilian jobs were sharing almost equal physical dangers with the Forces. One member of my Home Guard platoon was working a twelve-hour day in an aircraft factory at Slough, and patrolling the fields with his rifle for four hours at night.

By this time my impatient wish to enter the active war effort, and if possible the now crucial industrial war machine, was very strong. And in early December one evening at the *Daily Herald* I was rung up and offered a job as an assistant secretary in the Ministry of Supply. The cause of the delay, I discovered years later, was this. A very close friend of mine, when he joined MI5 early in the war, found a secret file which cast doubt on my loyalty and patriotism, because I was known to have attended many Fabian conferences and was apparently reported by some City source to have sinister 'foreign contacts', and was therefore in the eyes of the pre-1939 MI5 a suspicious character. There was certainly some irony in a situation in which I was simultaneously suspected by Southwood of harbouring greater zeal for winning the war than increasing the circulation of the *Daily Herald*, and by MI5 of disloyalty to the country. Thirty years later in the Common Market controversy I also used to be privately entertained by the thought that in 1940 I was regarded as subversive by MI5 because of my close foreign connections, while in 1970 I was reputed by people of a similar level of intelligence to be inspired by a dislike of all foreigners. However in 1940, unknown to me until after the war, my friend secured the destruction of the absurd file; and so the authorities in their next desperate trawl round the register to find efficient recruits for the industrial war effort were no longer confronted with it. Knowing nothing of this at the time, I immediately accepted the offer, and found that my job would be organizing the supply of labour of all kinds for the whole Ministry of Supply effort. So great was the hurry that in the last few days of December 1940 I worked in the Ministry of Supply at the Adelphi in the morning and at the *Daily Herald* on the other side of the Strand until the bombs began falling in the evening.

My last night on the *Daily Herald* was December 29, the evening of the great fire blitz on the City, when almost the whole area from St Paul's to Moorgate was burnt down. I felt on that afternoon that after four years in the City I should write a farewell piece on my signed City page recording how almost all the reforms I had advocated there such as exchange control, low interest rates, investment control, banning of outright speculation 'on margins' on the Stock Exchange and so forth, had now been put into force. I gave this farewell piece the ambitious heading: 'Socialism comes to the City'. Next morning I was not there. But any City worker who read that heading would have observed that a large part of the City around him was disintegrating in flames, smoke and rubble. Probably, however, nobody saw this particular joke except myself.

I thus started full-time at the Ministry of Supply in the Adelphi just off the Strand on December 30 with the City burning and the equipment of the British Forces at an even lower ebb than I or the public realized at the time. Having campaigned in my small way ever since 1933 for all-out resistance to Hitler, I felt under an overriding obligation to devote every ounce of energy and hour of time to the job until it was all over. I was exceedingly lucky once again, not merely in starting as an assistant secretary but in being immediately responsible to Oliver Franks. On being first offered the job, I had enquired about Franks from a close Oxford friend, and had been given a somewhat ambiguous answer. But there was nothing ambiguous about the reputation which Franks acquired as the most competent temporary civil servant in the war machine. At the end of 1940 he headed the whole Labour Department of the Ministry of Supply, which included welfare, training, hostels, etc., as well as my own straight task of recruiting the vast labour force needed for the munitions effort.

My keenest regret on leaving the *Daily Herald* was the severance from my secretary, the invaluable Sally Weiner. I now found myself installed in a room at the Adelphi with a well-meaning but unfortunate girl who could not type at all, had never worked in an office, and had been recruited straight from looking after dogs in a veterinary establishment in the country. I suggested she should learn typing as we worked. But tears were so frequent that it proved kinder to make a change, and I was allocated another girl, who, though she also could not type, was bursting with zest for the war effort. I refused all suggestions for typing 'pools' and 'drafts' as time-wasting, and in another few weeks my new assistant, Mrs Cairns, had learnt all my time-saving clerical devices and served me with ever-increasing efficiency for the next three years.

On only my second day at the Ministry of Supply, however, I narrowly escaped disaster. My *Daily Herald* City office had presented me two days before with a brief-case which I much valued and used for the rest of my working life. Just after leaving at Trafalgar Square the 24 bus in which I had travelled from Hampstead, I realized that I had left on top of it my new brief-case full of secret Ministry of Supply papers. And details of our munition war effort really were secret in 1940–41. Hailing a taxi and following the bus to Victoria, I caught it in Wilton Road and found the brief-case still on top before paying the taxi fare. I never forgot this chase, and never again in twelve years' work in the government service in war or peace as official or minister let go of my brief-case in bus, underground or taxi or lost an official paper except once temporarily (as related later) in the summer of 1951.

Also in the first weeks at the Adelphi in January 1941, I was invited to attend for the Ministry of Supply, with Franks and Geoffrey Crowther, a very superior meeting of the official Manpower Requirements Committee. Crowther, together with Walter Layton, had joined the Ministry of Supply Statistical Department. The Manpower Requirements Committee was presided over by Sir William Beveridge in person. Franks also told me that Beveridge, now Master of University College, Oxford, had brought in as secretary of the Committee a very young and very clever statistician from Oxford called Harold Wilson. There they both were across the table in a large Whitehall committee room, rather like an owl and a sparrow: Beveridge, august, white-haired, venerable and dogmatic; and Wilson diminutive, chubby and chirpy. The meeting was a mass one, of the sort severely discouraged as the wartime machine got fully into gear in 1941. I was not much impressed by it as a method of doing business and making decisions; and was not surprised to hear soon afterwards that this Beveridge Committee, having presented its report, was to be abolished, and that Beveridge was not to be appointed, as some thought he wished, Director-General of Manpower. Instead, the job of mobilizing manpower was placed firmly on the shoulders of Ernie Bevin at the Ministry of Labour and the executive departments, including my own, of the three production ministries: Ministry of Supply, Admiralty and Ministry of Aircraft Production. This decision, which led to the appointment of Godfrey Ince as Director-General of Manpower within Bevin's Ministry for the next three crucial years, was certainly one of the most vital and wisest of the internal war effort. Beveridge had many great qualities, but he was widely felt by potential colleagues to be unduly autocratic. Prima-donnas were not suffered gladly in the wartime Ministries. Two other indirect consequences of this decision were, first, to divert Wilson from the manpower world for the rest of the war, and secondly to launch Beveridge in due course on his famous report on the future of the social services.

What struck any newcomer to the Ministry of Supply in January 1941 was the appalling lack of equipment of the Armed Forces, particularly the Army, after Dunkirk, and the grievously low level of crucial munitions output. I learnt to my private astonishment in my first week that, even at the January 1941 rate of output of rifles, the re-equipment of the British and Indian Armies with rifles would take seventy years. It was equally sobering to discover that rifle production was far from a simple engineering process, and that apart from Woolwich Arsenal and BSA virtually no capacity for it existed in the British Isles. Had it not been for the million second-hand rifles supplied by Roosevelt, the extreme shortage would have persisted right through 1941; and in the first six months of that year we all expected a renewed attempt at invasion of this country by Hitler. Sweeping priority had been given to fighter aircraft in the summer of 1940. Herbert Morrison, appointed Minister of Supply in May 1940, had been forced to contend with this excessive priority, had proved only a partial success, and had been transferred in the autumn to the Home Office and Ministry of Home Security, for which his talents were far more aptly fitted. Sir Andrew Duncan succeeded him and was Minister when I joined the Ministry of Supply. But all that had really been achieved in the industrial war effort by the end of 1940 was the building of the aircraft 'shadow factories', and a number of Ministry of Supply 'Royal Ordnance Factories' – the latter mainly in areas of pre-war unemployment. Few of the existing factories were fully manned up for two or three shifts: many of those needed were not yet built; and major unemployment still existed. At the end of 1940[1] production of rifles was only one third of the level reached by the end of 1941, of tanks one quarter, of twenty-five-pounder guns one third, of smaller guns one seventh, of filled shells one third, and of small arms ammunition less than half. It was perfectly clear to all of us at the Ministry of Supply in January 1941 that the building of a vast war production machine and the mobilization of manpower and womanpower on a scale not previously known would be the heart of the war effort in that year.

The task was so immense, the time so short and the effort so unprecedented, as to imbue at any rate all the active spirits at the wartime Ministry of Supply with a determination not to be defeated by anything short of physical impossibility. In sustaining this spirit Churchill's speeches were certainly decisive, and I have never forgotten the effect on me of: 'We shall fight on the beaches, we shall never surrender.' But it was organization and hard effort to which we all applied ourselves; the industrialists (who called themselves 'practical men'), permanent civil servants, ex-servicemen, technicians, and amateurs like myself from journalism, the universities and professions, in a vast complex at its peak of nearly 100,000 persons, who settled down somehow after a few months into a tolerably smooth-running machine. It was a joy to be a member of so essential a dynamo of the national effort after years of Fleet Street. The HQ of the Ministry of Supply occupied most of Shell-Mex House and the Adelphi and about ten other major London office blocks. Hours of work lasted from 9.30 to 7.30 on weekdays, 9.30 to 4.00 on Saturdays, and every other Sunday.

Some heads of departments took virtually no week-ends off or holidays throughout 1941 and 1942; and quick decisions and despatch of business

[1] See M. M. Postan, *British War Production* (London, 1952), p. 176.

became a matter of pride, and were with some exceptions pushed to a higher pitch than I ever encountered in any organization, public or private, apart from the Treasury, before or since. Decisions agreed between departments were usually taken by telephone, minutes of meetings were dictated and circulated immediately after they had finished; messages to regional and other outlying offices went by teleprinter; and most of us liked to answer when asked to do something: 'I did that yesterday.' Unexpectedly but fortunately I found that the problem of organization in itself had all the absorbing fascination of an art or game. My best training for it, I sometimes felt, was 'racing demon' as played on holidays in youth. Improvisation was at a premium among us amateurs; but the crises and muddles which inevitably did occur were usually settled or patched up with far less expenditure of time and energy than would have been possible in the blaze of publicity considered necessary in peacetime politics. I often spurred on my own staff with the reminder that we were not only doing a job but running a race with our opposite numbers in Germany; only to be surprised to learn after the war (e.g. from Albert Speer's autobiography) that the Germans in many spheres never pushed industrial mobilization as far as we did.

My own small 'Labour Supply' department at HQ consisted (apart from clerical grades) of only twelve or fifteen, mainly old men and young women, and our job was to recruit all the labour needed for Ministry of Supply munition industries and the whole range of controlled 'raw material' industries, as they were called, including iron and steel, non-ferrous metals, chemicals, explosives, cotton, wool and timber. We were an essential link with the Ministry of Labour for two purposes: first to be the sole source of requests for labour from the Ministry of Supply to the Ministry of Labour; and secondly to advise the Ministry of Labour on the comparative importance of the different claims. Up till this time that Ministry had been beset by a babel of conflicting approaches from numerous Ministry of Supply departments, each professing its own product to be of supreme and unique priority. My department gained greatly by establishing confidence in the Ministry of Labour that when we said labour was needed it really was, and that the priorities we specified were those of the Ministry of Supply as a whole.

This confidence was grounded on our candid acceptance of two principles: first that to justify the demand for labour not merely did the product have to be of high priority, but the number and type of workers claimed had to be genuinely essential for production; and secondly that labour was a mainly geographical resource and could not be rapidly moved about the country like a machine tool or a ton of steel. The latter truth implied that the more capacity we developed in areas where potential workers already lived, the faster would output expand. A great deal of the success of manpower mobilization in 1941 and 1942 was due to our whole-hearted grasp of these two facts; and the lesser success of the Ministry of Aircraft

Production in these years, after their initial frantic efforts in the summer of
1940, was due to their unwillingness at first to acknowledge them. Very
early at the Ministry of Supply I had been struck by the absurdity of the
competing production departments (ourselves, the Ministry of Aircraft
Production and the Admiralty) all crowding their labour demands into a
few notoriously congested areas like Birmingham, Coventry and Luton,
and leaving hundreds of thousands of workers unemployed elsewhere; and
also by the ease with which any department could pick up labour if it had
the sense to put its new orders and factories in places where thousands of
people were asking for work

Another soon-learnt lesson was that, despite all the wartime powers of
so-called 'direction' of labour, and the Essential Work Order supposedly
holding people in existing industries, it was in fact pay differentials that
were more effective than any other single weapon in moving large blocks of
labour quickly, as we had to, from one form of production to another. The
secret here was to realize that – as is true in war and peace – 'mobility'
between jobs can be very large if people stay in their own homes, but that
'mobility' between homes is insignificant. Bevin understood all this perfectly, as if by instinct. When a large and rapid shift of labour was needed, he
contrived by what was politely called 'collective bargaining' to uprate the
pay in the units that had to expand. I remember in my early weeks in 1941
travelling to a day's meeting in Manchester to request our Regional
Controller there and cotton magnates like Sir Frank Platt and Sir Raymond
Streat to arrange the transfer of 90,000 workers in six months or so from
cotton spinning and weaving into the Lancashire ROFs, notably Chorley,
Kirkby and Risley. Unanimously, apart from our own Controller (an admirably vigorous retired admiral) they said it could not be done. But Bevin
contrived that the wages for women in ROFs should be set at fifty shillings
a week compared with the prevailing rate of thirty shillings in the cotton
industry. As a result the 'impossible' shift was achieved. Here incidentally
is a profound lesson for incomes policy in peacetime.

Effective mobilization, however, in wartime needed not merely an understanding of the mechanics of labour supply, but effective levers of control.
The actual machine organized in our Labour Supply department for
recruiting labour was essentially simple. One individual was responsible for
each section of industry covered by the Ministry of Supply, from home
timber production to ball-bearings. We worked through 'labour supply
officers' in the regional offices of the Ministry, who were formally on the
staff of the Regional Controller but were responsible to us on labour
supply policy. I was thus constantly in contact with virtually all the Ministry
of Supply programmes, and a huge range of industry, in every part of the
British Isles. One general lesson we also learnt from bitter experiences was
that you could seldom absolutely rely on promises from anyone that such
and such would be done by a certain day unless you checked, checked and

checked again. For this reason a growing horde of 'progress chasers' grew up in our own and the other wartime economic ministries.

The particular mechanism, however, which achieved much more than any other in solving the wartime labour problem was the Preference Committee. In the summer of 1940, the War Cabinet, at the height of the Dunkirk crisis, and in immediate fear of mass air attack, had made an understandable false start in the attempt to see that the most essential war production got scarce labour first. On 31 May 1940, the 'Priority of Production Direction' laid down crudely that aircraft production and a few ancillaries were to receive priority for all purposes over virtually everything else. To quote the official history of British War Production:[2] 'As long as it was in force, this Direction threatened to play havoc with the whole munition programme in general and with the tank programme in particular and led other departments to place their orders as far ahead as possible, thus adding to the general congestion.' The absurdity of this was so glaring that it had been modified in September 1940, and the more refined principle of 'allocation' – which meant in effect a fair share for all genuine needs – was introduced. But I found in the early weeks of 1941 that no rational or effective system for allocating labour really existed, and that each department was fighting furiously against the others. At this stage Sir George Turner, the colourful and formidable Second Secretary of the Ministry of Supply, retorted to some challenge from the Ministry of Aircraft Production with the words: 'We in the Ministry of Supply believe in the rule of law; but if you don't, we have a better machine than you have.'

The solution to this crucial conflict at the heart of the war effort was found, not by an all-wise decision handed down by the Cabinet from on high, but by an informal meeting between the four of us at that moment engaged in an internecine war with each other: the Ministry of Supply, the Ministry of Aircraft Production, the Admiralty, and the Ministry of Labour. Ronnie Edwards for the MAP, Le Maitre for the Admiralty, Alan Hitchman for the Ministry of Labour and I were these four. Ronnie Edwards, little known at this time, had when a young man in the City taught himself economics out of working hours at the LSE; and after the war became Chairman of the Electricity Council, Chairman of Beechams and finally Chairman of British Leyland just before his early death. Starting as my chief adversary in the struggle for labour, he became during the war one of my few most trusted confidential colleagues, and a good friend thereafter. He was not the only example of a lasting friend whom I first met as a professional antagonist; but he was one of the best. Le Maitre of the Admiralty was the minor claimant for labour in quantity, but a crucial one; and possessed a never-failing talent for racy speech which much enlivened our proceedings, and always stopped short of unduly prolonging them. Hitchman was one of the very best of permanent civil servants suddenly

[2] Postan, p. 153.

plunged into the wartime Whitehall convulsion. Shrewd, intelligent, and quite conspicuously fair-minded between us three ravenous claimants, he was the prime-mover of the mechanics of the system. After 1945 he served in the Treasury during the Cripps period, and later became Permanent Secretary of the Ministry of Agriculture in its happiest days before the Common Agricultural Policy downgraded it.

We four decided, without any authority as yet from on high, to compile a list to be revised fortnightly, of first-priority labour demands. Each demand was to be absolutely precise: e.g. fifty women a week for ten weeks for ROF Bridgend; or twelve fitters for Skefco at Luton. Each had to be justified *both* by the urgency and importance of the product, and the demonstrated need for the labour. Every decision had to be unanimous: i.e. we had a right to challenge each other's demands. The list did not claim absolute priority, in the sense that nobody off it got any labour at all; but it was a guide to local officials to apply it first, and use their common sense and local knowledge on quantities and timing. For this reason, and so as not to conflict openly with the Cabinet's notorious and now semi-defunct Priority Direction, beloved of Beaverbrook as Minister of Aircraft Production, we sedulously avoided the word 'priority', and spoke instead of 'preference' and 'allocation'. The fortnightly meeting we set up with Hitchman as chairman became known as the 'Preference Committee', and was afterwards legitimized by the influence of Oliver Franks and Godfrey Ince.

Our Preference Committee met every other Friday morning at 9.30 a.m. from the summer of 1941 until near the end of the war, and issued a secret list of preference vacancies teleprinted an hour after its conclusion to every Ministry of Labour office in the land. It became known as PAL or 'Preference in the Allocation of Labour'. It normally took four hours to complete the fortnightly business, and for the first year or so the original four of us, together with a secretary, A. V. Judges of the Ministry of Labour, were the only attenders. We scarcely ever failed to reach agreement on each demand by the time limit of 1.30 p.m. – partly through a give-and-take spirit, and partly through an unwritten agreement to let Hitchman act as umpire if the deadlock was absolute. Another unwritten principle was that the list must not be allowed to grow, and that any ministry which added to it must at the same time take something off it. It was also the invariable rule that no demand – even for three fitters for ball bearings – would be admitted unless it had been agreed jointly on the spot between a regional technical official of the Ministry of Labour and one of the production department. Altogether this machine saved an infinity of time and exchange of ministerial letters in futile controversy.

An ample share of the credit was due to Ronnie Edwards, who was pushed from behind by more unreasonable production chiefs and a much more unreasonable minister than mine; but contrived nevertheless to exercise just enough restraint to maintain the integrity of the system. He never quite managed, as I fortunately did, to establish the principle in his own ministry that no request for preference from that ministry should go forward to the Ministry of Labour except through himself. But he retained the goodwill of the rest of us throughout by adding a saving grace of rationality to the aggressiveness required of every MAP official. We both reserved the right to say to the other: 'You know this is an absurd and exaggerated demand: please come off it and leave it over till today fortnight.' In my own Labour Supply Department in the Ministry of Supply we henceforth built up our operations round the fortnightly rhythm of the Preference Committee. Naturally, as the secret got around Whitehall, both within and without the three war production Ministries, that a mysterious secret list was being used, demands came forward thick and fast for membership of the Committee. These were only gradually accepted; and not till late in 1943 did the committee of four become a quasi-public meeting and a babel of voices. Sometime before this happened Ernie Bevin, in a secret debate in the House of Commons, had praised the work of this Committee as more or less his personal creation, while mis-stating most of its practical mechanics.

At the end of twelve years spent in the government service by 1967, the Preference Committee still seemed to me the most efficient and successful organizing machine in which I ever had the luck to work – barring some sections of the Treasury in Cripps's and Gaitskell's days. It started at the time when a desperate struggle for labour between competing demands might have deadlocked the whole munition-production effort; and it maintained a rational and flexible control until the production problem was largely solved – in 1943 and 1944. But even so it was of course only one part of the complete labour mobilization campaign. We were supposed, for instance, to be operating from 1942 onwards, under a so-called 'Manpower Budget' ordained by the Cabinet and by Sir John Anderson, the Lord President, as the supreme umpire. This was a laudable attempt to relate the demands of the Services and munitions departments to the total manpower and womanpower available in the country; and it at least ensured that if a department had substantially exceeded or fallen short of its ration, suitable general pressure could be applied. In July 1942, for instance, the War Cabinet approved a global allocation of labour to the Admiralty, the Ministry of Aircraft Production and Ministry of Supply. The net increase for the munitions industries as a whole was to be about 200,000[3] less than these three Ministries had asked for. The Manpower Budget was a blunt instrument, dealing in annual movements, and hundreds of thousands of persons; whereas what mattered for the purpose of winning the war were ten die-sinkers next week at Smethwick Drop Forgings, or four tool-setters forthwith for rifle production at ROF Fazakerley. Being sceptical of blunt instruments, therefore, I bent my efforts to the concrete demands, and left

[3] H. M. D. Parker, *Manpower* (London, 1957), ch. XII.

my excellent and wholly reliable statistician, R. L. Davies, to juggle on paper with thousands and hundreds of thousands.

Such was the machine. But in the last resort, as always, success depended even more on personalities than on procedure. Oliver Franks, luckily my immediate superior, had been a young professor of philosophy at Glasgow University in 1939. Not the ideal choice, some might have thought, for the higher direction of an unparalleled wartime industrial mobilization. But Franks possessed not merely an outstanding talent for manipulating a huge organization, but a rare intuition into the psychology of colleagues, high or low, and not least of those in the business world. In what was known as the First Drop-Forging Crisis – into which I was immediately plunged in January 1941 – I was required to visit Birmingham and appeal to the assembled drop-forging employers to take on large numbers of additional workers quickly, including the extremely scarce die-sinkers; to pay much higher wages; and to man up their plants very rapidly on double shifts. I carried a special appeal from Sir Andrew Duncan, Minister of Supply, to them which explained that aircraft engine production, tank production and much else was threatened by an appalling bottleneck in output of drop-forgings and that the whole war effort was at risk. The meeting – in the Old Queen's Hotel in New Street – was an almost total failure. The massed drop-forging employers certainly frightened me. Some appeared not merely threatening but still unaware there was a war on.

Near-panic followed at the Ministry of Supply; and the inevitable decision was reached: the drop-forgers must be invited to the Adelphi and addressed in person by Mr Franks. They came and – one is tempted to say – saw Mr Franks, and he conquered. He addressed them for fifteen minutes, after which they unanimously agreed to carry out all the requests of the Government, including the outrageous proposal nearly to double there and then the rate of pay of die-sinkers. At the end of this meeting, which took barely one hour, several of the drop-forgers present approached me quietly and asked whether I could introduce them to Mr Franks, because they would be only too glad to do anything in their power which he wished. In the next few weeks all our other still imperfect levers were pulled full out; and so by the late spring of 1941, the Drop-Forging Crisis was, for the moment, solved.

From the spring of 1941 onwards, when faced with what appeared insuperable obstacles, we regularly appealed to Franks, who moved every few months on to a higher bureaucratic rank. In time the shift of priorities had swung right round again and by the winter of 1942–3 the Second Drop-Forging Crisis loomed up. This time suitable labour could only be secured by closing down, in advance of the official 'concentration' scheme, a number of iron foundries mainly located, strangely enough, in north London. But the official Iron & Steel Control resisted all pressure to do this. The struggle was forced up to Sir Charles Wright himself, Iron & Steel Controller, in both the First and Second World Wars, and now Chairman of Baldwins. He flatly refused to move. So he was invited with his second, George Briggs, an able and affable, if adventurous, character, to Franks' office where the four of us sat down to a final trial of strength. Sir Charles looked to me more like a pirate chief than a leading industrialist. To all entreaties he answered: 'It can't be done,' duly echoed by Briggs. After forty minutes I noticed beads of perspiration on Franks' forehead; and as I had never seen such a thing before, I feared he was at last going to fail. But no. Raising his lofty brow to its full moral altitude, as if from a pulpit, Franks directed to Sir Charles a stirring appeal to his personal patriotism, and then instantly broke into one of the most charming and disarming smiles I have seen: 'Don't you think, Sir Charles?' The double shaft was invincible. 'All right,' said Sir Charles: and the Second Drop-Forging Crisis was overcome.

Another equally forceful character in the Ministry of Supply was George Turner, permanent civil servant, and twin Second Secretary with Franks in the later war years. George Turner had joined the War Office before 1914 as a boy in the lowest possible grade; and fought through the First War as a private. By 1939 he was an established assistant secretary in the War Office, and was moved to the Ministry of Supply as soon as it was set up. He was reputed to remain in the office night and day, throughout the week and week-ends; and any decision taken by others which he did not approve was likely to be reversed sometime between 8 p.m. and 8 a.m. Everyone liked to have George Turner on their side. His pointed and bracing utterances were much quoted round the Ministry. One which I never forgot was: 'Minutes should be used to record decisions and not conduct conversations.' At one stage my arrangements for employing prisoners of war on suitable Ministry of Supply work such as timber production were threatened with interference by our two Parliamentary Secretaries, Duncan Sandys and Harold Macmillan. They wrote minutes to me suggesting that prisoners might be used for tank production. This was so absurd that I refrained from answering. The international Geneva Convention, which even the Nazis honoured, forbade the use of prisoners on direct munitions production. Thereupon Sandys and Macmillan wrote minutes to one another, and appealed to Turner. Next morning Franks and I were summoned early to Turner's office and he began by remarking: 'Our two parliamentary liabilities downstairs' (Macmillan and Sandys) 'have, I hear, been writing minutes to the least responsible members of the secretariat' (me). Attempting to continue the discussions on this level, I added: 'Worse still, they have been writing minutes to one another.' 'Nearest thing to masturbation I ever heard of,' said Turner; and even Franks's lofty forehead almost dissolved into an involuntary smile.

The other most talented of all my wartime colleagues was Christopher Hinton, responsible at the time for Filling and Explosives ROFs. A

Cambridge mathematician, turned chemical engineer in ICI during the 1930s, Hinton was equally brilliant as a chemist, a statistician or an engineer. He alone, of all whom I ever met in public or private industry, together with Frank Kearton of Courtaulds (a colleague twenty-five years later), combined the gifts of wide scientific knowledge, first-class organizing capacity, and a generous share of human understanding. Edwin Plowden, wartime Chief Executive of the Ministry of Aircraft Production, and afterwards a mainstay of Cripps in the Treasury, possessed the latter two, and business experience as well, but would not have claimed to be a scientist. Hinton also greatly attracted me by his complete reliability. Since he was responsible for the production side of the Filling and Explosives ROFs, which were large employers of labour (the ROFs as a whole at the peak in 1943 employed 300,000 people), this was a godsent quality. Just as I could always accept Hinton's word on what could or could not be produced where, so he accepted mine on where labour could or could not be found. I greatly valued our three-year partnership. After the war Hinton, of course, achieved even more brilliant success in devising the first electricity generating plant based on nuclear energy.

It was also in these war years that I first met Norman Brook, then principal private secretary to Sir John Anderson, Lord President. Once again prisoners of war were the bone of contention. Robert Hudson, the wartime Minister of Agriculture, had obtained early in the war, before priorities and allocations were properly managed, a prescriptive right for his department to employ all available prisoners of war. It was a grossly uneconomic practice, that thousands of prisoners of war, for whom agriculture had for the time no use, should remain without work, even though the Ministry of Supply work such as tree-felling or limestone quarries was acutely short of labour. We in the Ministry of Supply attacked this restrictive practice; Sir John Anderson was asked to adjudicate; and his alter ego, Norman Brook, invited me to explain our case. Anderson ruled that prisoners of war not needed for agriculture should be used for other essential work, and that disputes should be sent to him. Norman Brook, whom I got to know much better after 1945 when he was Secretary of the Cabinet, was probably, with Edward Bridges, the most accomplished permanent civil servant of my years in the government service. He blended suavity with sagacity in a way which somehow made work pleasant, and seemed to possess a hardly ever failing instinct for a compromise or a procedural device which would resolve the worst ministerial deadlocks. He adjudicated with charm. Nobody could draft a more masterly minute, letter or parliamentary answer.

The best parliamentary secretary in the wartime Ministry of Supply, as seen from the labour-supply world, was not Macmillan or Sandys, but Ralph Assheton, later Financial Secretary to the Treasury – eventually Lord Clitheroe. It was not easy to be a junior minister in a war-production department, because the department's job was organization not politics. But Assheton managed to combine an intelligent interest in the real issues with help and encouragement when needed, and without foolish interference. For one piece of help I was always thankful. In 1942–3, when the Northern convoys to Murmansk and Archangel were desperately short of oerlikon ammunition (as I knew incidentally from my brother Alan who was commanding frigates in these convoys), the Ministry of Supply, because of earlier mistakes, had only one factory for filling such ammunition. This was near Reading in an area of acute labour scarcity; and the only possible way of manning up the factory was to bring over hundreds of women from Eire, whose transport and hostel needs we had already organized. At the last moment a director of Imperial Tobacco, who were to manage the factory, announced that his company would not accept Irish girls because of the lice in their hair. As the first group of girls were already on their way, I appealed to Assheton who immediately summoned the recalcitrant director to his room; and as he was admitted by one door, I left through the other. Thanks to Assheton's persuasive skill, the director completely caved in, and an hour later was standing on Reading Station in person to meet the Irish girls. The flow continued; and only a few weeks behind time the Northern convoys received their oerlikon shells.

Among senior ministers of Supply during the war Herbert Morrison, much as I admired him in many ways, was not the best. But he was an excellent Home Secretary and Minister for Home Security. At the Ministry of Supply, he was miscast. Lawyers and policemen do not make good economic ministers, though they may be good Home Secretaries or Leaders of the House of Commons. John Simon, Herbert Morrison and Selwyn Lloyd are all examples. The reason is simple. Broadly, there are two sorts of administrative minds: the one which likes order, discipline and a rigid machine; the other which understands that economic processes are more like plants which grow or wither in the right or wrong conditions, and in their own time, but cannot be manipulated by pulling levers or issuing orders. Morrison was of the former; Andrew Duncan an admirable, and Bevin a superlative, example of the latter. Duncan and Bevin understood equally well what made an industry move, how fast production of this or that could be increased, and what the labour force would stand. This insight made Duncan the best wartime Minister of Supply and Bevin the twin genius, with Churchill, of the war effort. It gave Duncan and Bevin a keen respect for one another, which made co-operation easy. When the war effort hung on the possibility of finding fifty die-sinkers, both Bevin and Duncan knew equally well what a die-sinker was and what he did. Duncan's method of working was a quick-fire, prickly Scottish diatribe. At my first encounter he told his very august Permanent Secretary that it was 'not his business to think', and asked me after my first timid intervention why I was 'making trouble' – all said with frosty good humour. Unlike Beaverbrook, he knew how to steer the whole vast complex of the Ministry of Supply's production programmes moving forward in more or less the right balance.

Beaverbrook was a bad Minister of Supply. His arrival there in place of Duncan (in 1941) was greeted in the Department with alarm; he only narrowly escaped doing real damage; and his departure (in 1942) and the return of Duncan were celebrated by all of us with immense relief. This was not Beaverbrook's fault, any more than it was Morrison's. It was due in both cases, not to lack of zeal, but to his own make-up and experience. All his life Beaverbrook had steered moderate-sized enterprises to success – the *Daily Express*, the *Sunday Express*, the MAP – by pushing other people ruthlessly out of the way. It is arguable that this was necessary in MAP in the summer of 1940. But tank production was damaged and hardly ever recovered. When Beaverbrook, however, became head of the vast Ministry of Supply machine, covering most industries in the country, he found for the first time in his life that he was pushing not somebody else but himself out of the way, and he did not know how to respond to such an unfamiliar predicament.

On Beaverbrook's first day at the Ministry of Supply, a Sunday, Franks had the characteristic prescience to arrive at the office at, I think, 8 a.m. Beaverbrook entered about twenty minutes later, and asked which of his senior officials were already on duty. He was told, Mr Franks; who was accordingly closeted with Beaverbrook for a major part of that morning, and most fortunately for all of us gained his confidence and skilfully made sense of some of his more disruptive ideas. Beaverbrook not unnaturally wanted rapidly to boost output of tanks, tank-guns and anti-tank guns, and proposed to do this by diverting nearly all obtainable skilled labour to these particular weapons. Franks ingeniously devised a system of telegrams which he knew could be fitted into our now smooth-running preference machine without actually wrecking other programmes. Even so, we heard that six director-generals from other programmes had vehemently protested to Beaverbrook within a week.

A little later, knowing that Beaverbrook would never be a match for Bevin, Franks had to go rather further in resisting hare-brained manoeuvres. One day Beaverbrook, with no advice from those of us responsible, confronted Bevin in a Cabinet Committee with some figures of alleged labour needs for the Filling ROFs, which he said Bevin had failed to meet. The figures were totally at variance with those carefully agreed in regular sessions between Hinton and myself and accepted by the Ministry of Labour. Bevin said bluntly that he did not believe the figures were genuine, and that he was prepared to accept figures from Mr Franks but not from Lord Beaverbrook. The Committee decided that Mr Franks and Mr Ince of the Ministry of Labour should jointly present agreed figures to Churchill himself at Chequers on the following Sunday. I was asked by Franks whether

D

any sense could be made of Beaverbrook's figures; and R. L. Davies, my statistician, concocted a sort of mock justification for them – which Franks immediately described as 'chicanery'. So he and Ince duly conveyed the real figures from us to Chequers on the Sunday, and Churchill received them in person. But the incident left Beaverbrook's reputation much impaired in the Ministry of Supply and in Cabinet circles, and did not create the best of blood between him and Bevin.

Ernie Bevin himself was a more massive character, in both mind and will, than any other I ever encountered; and the only one – apart from Hugh Gaitskell, poles apart as they were – for whom I felt unbounded admiration, from the heart as well as the head. He was an essentially English character, with a vein of Celtic warmth, deriving perhaps from his West Country origins, which gave him an irresistibly rustic sense of humour; as well as a perception approaching genius for what was going on and would go on in the minds of his companions; and an intuitive grasp of hard realities. The Duke of Wellington was credited by a colleague with 'boundless sagacity'; and the phrase is with equal justice applicable to Bevin. Certainly he was loved and respected in his own Ministry during the war with a fervour I never knew aroused by any other minister; and by common consent he transformed and galvanized his Ministry. Equally certainly, he was both a pillar of the war effort and an architect of victory.

We only appealed to Bevin in 1941–3 when we were forced to. This happened, for instance, in the case of the wool industry, which should have been releasing labour in thousands, as the other textile industries were doing, for munitions. But Sir Harry Shackleton, the Wool Controller, stubbornly obstructed all measures to slim the industry. Richard Pares (whom I knew well from All Souls), now a principal assistant secretary at the Board of Trade, tacitly agreed with me that as the only remedy we would refrain from applying the Essential Work Order to the wool industry unless and until Sir Harry came to heel. That Order retained labour in an existing industry. This provoked Sir Harry to appeal to Bevin; and to my surprise, and no doubt to Sir Harry's, Bevin invited him to a near-public meeting in the largest committee room in the Ministry of Labour in St James's Square, with twenty-five or thirty people present including the leaders of the cotton industry and high-level delegations from every ministry remotely concerned. Bevin opened the proceedings with the words: 'What's all this, Sir 'Arry?'; and Sir Harry replied with a none too brief catalogue of his grievances. In the dignified and deferential silence which followed, Bevin turned his huge head full face to Sir Harry, and observed: 'If many people had behaved like you, Sir 'Arry, we should have lost this war by now.' Not accustomed to being thus addressed before such a distinguished company, the Wool Controller was speechless. 'What you've got to do,' added Bevin, 'is as follows. . . . That concludes the meeting. Thank you.' It had lasted less than half an hour, and Bevin had spoken in all for about two minutes. We had no further trouble from the wool industry.

On an earlier occasion it was one of the Ministry of Supply's minor misfortunes – for of course misfortunes and failures occurred as well as successes – which drove us to consult Bevin. At the end of 1940 I was allocated as one of my assistants, Monica Felton, a young woman of marked ability, unhappily half crippled by polio. Her disability naturally excited the sympathy of all of us; and when I was told most confidentially that she was the mistress of the then Chairman of the House of Commons Select Committee on National Expenditure, I ignored this as wholly irrelevant. Unfortunately some weeks later, Monica Felton was found to be inexcusably ignoring her job. I transferred her elsewhere, only to find later that this happened a second and third time; so that Franks and I agreed she must be dismissed from the Department. We were somewhat surprised when after a few weeks she was appointed as a clerk to the Select Committee on National Expenditure; and even more surprised when some weeks later the Committee published a report on the Ministry of Supply Filling Factories. Next we were told there was to be a secret debate in the House on this Report, in which Duncan and Bevin would speak for the Government. Duncan, it was felt, must be told of the curious relationship involved. But should Bevin be told also? This question was regarded as so delicate and confidential that it was referred even higher than Franks and George Turner, to Sir William Douglas himself, a full-blooded old-time civil servant and now super-Permanent Secretary and umpire-in-chief. He ruled that Bevin should be told. But who should tell him? Answer of course: Mr Franks. With much careful stage-management, it was contrived that Franks should meet Bevin absolutely alone in the latter's own personal office, and confide in him, with due solemnity, in the greatest privacy, the terrible secret. On hearing it, Bevin replied: ' 'Undreds of people have told me that.'

But Bevin had many other capacities. Late in 1939, in the 'phoney war' period, at one of a number of so-called 'National Defence' lunches organized in Grosvenor House by Arthur Salter and Colonel Nathan, and laudably intended to support Churchill, Bevin was addressing the polite company as prosaically as others (including John Simon) had done in the series. Suddenly, as he spoke of the Nazi persecution of Jews and trade unionists, his great head swung this way and that, his fist struck the air like a steam hammer, and his voice rose to a roar. The words were no more than pedestrian: 'I'm not going to have my people treated like this.' But his highly respectable audience were astonished and enthralled, and sprang to their feet with unrestrained applause. Heavens, I said to myself, we shall win this war after all. And perhaps, as a pendant to that, the last words I heard Bevin say should be recorded. In March of 1951, Attlee reluctantly appointed Herbert Morrison as Foreign Secretary, as Bevin's health was visibly failing, and gave Bevin as Lord Privy Seal many of Morrison's home-front duties instead. One of these was to be Chairman of the Cabinet 'SIM'

Committee (Socialization of Industries, Ministerial), of which Norman Brook was the Secretary and I happened to be the Treasury member. At Bevin's first meeting we discussed the Committee's standing dilemma: how to persuade Walter Citrine, now Chairman of the Central Electricity Authority, to follow the Government's policies instead of attacking them in public speeches. The official minutes doubtless recorded in Brook's impeccable language that 'the Committee invited the Lord Privy Seal [Bevin] to consult further with the Chairman of the CEA on the matters raised in the previous paragraph'. But as we broke up for lunch, Brook, mindful naturally of Bevin's twenty-year association with Citrine at Transport House, remarked *sotto voce* to Bevin: 'Perhaps, Lord Privy Seal, you might care to have a personal word with Walter Citrine.' ' 'Im,' replied Bevin, 'I'd rather negotiate with Molotov.' Exactly a week later Bevin died.

Without Bevin and Duncan, and some of those others mentioned, I do not believe the immense war production effort could have succeeded. For the industrial conflict was in some ways like the military struggle: a series of hard-fought campaigns against new and stubborn adversaries. The two Drop-Forging Crises I have mentioned already. The other most menacing and persistent was the shortage of ball-bearings. Only manufactured by private industry, not by ROFs, difficult to produce and desperately short in 1940 and 1941, ball-bearings repeatedly became the super-bottleneck holding back aero-engines, tank production and shipbuilding. They were only manufactured in any quantities by Skefco at Luton, Ransome & Marles at Newark, Hoffmans at Chelmsford, and British Timken in Birmingham, all areas of acute labour shortage. With a few others, I daily nursed the grim secret in these years that if the Germans cared to drop on Luton, Newark, and Chelmsford one half of the bombs they dropped in a single night in London in the autumn of 1940, we should be knocked out of the war – or at least become wholly dependent on Sweden (as a producer of ball-bearings) and the US.[4] They never did. The struggle for labour was most acute and most prolonged at Luton, since Skefco persistently paid lower wages than Vauxhall. One crisis meeting after another was held at the Skefco works; and the atmosphere was not helped by an underlying suspicion that the Swedish authorities, who controlled Skefco and were also supplying the Germans from Swedish plants, might not be too keen on the British war effort. Inch by painful inch the Skefco labour force was raised to the required level, and somehow held there. But if any words were written on my heart at the end of the war, they were 'Skefco, Luton'.

Another memorable campaign was the hectic battle for 'jerricans' in 1942 and 1943. Rather typically of the British habit of losing every battle but the

---

[4] We sometimes asked whether the same might not be true of Germany; it was fascinating after the war to find Albert Speer recording: 'The ball-bearing facilities at Schweinfurt were crucial to our whole effort.... The war could largely have been decided in 1943 if instead of vast but pointless area bombing the planes had concentrated on centres of armament production.' Albert Speer, *Inside the Third Reich* (London, 1970), p. 280.

last, it had turned out that the British petrol can used to supply petrol to the tanks in North Africa leaked two thirds or more of its contents before it was even emptied. After the usual attempts at improvement had failed, the War Office and the Ministry of Supply suddenly decided to make a Chinese copy of the captured German can – swastika and all – which the troops called 'jerricans'. Millions were required in a few months; and the job was naturally given to the Ministry of Supply. The motor-body press shops of Pressed Steel (Cowley), Fisher & Ludlow (Birmingham), Briggs Bodies (Eastleigh), Williams & Williams (Chester) and other firms were mobilized with great speed, and my department was required at the peak of labour shortage to find thousands of women in a few weeks. We pulled out all the stops, including hundreds of Irish women; and in the case of Pressed Steel I was able to take over Cuddesdon Theological College only a few miles from Cowley as a hostel for the Irish girls. In the second half of 1943 half a million jerricans a week were being produced throughout the country, and at the end of the war fifty million had been supplied to the Armed Forces.[5]

By 1943 the prospect of 'D' Day was already beginning to cast its shadow before us. First heard of under the mysterious names of 'Overlord', 'Mulberry', 'Phoenix', 'Whale', etc., many of the construction programmes were entrusted in 1943 to the Ministry of Supply. The building of equipment for the proposed embarkation and landing operation was an almost wholly new type of production, and required new types of labour by fixed dates in areas like the London Docks, the Thames Estuary, Margate, Portsmouth, Southampton and Goole. Large as the labour demands were, fortunately the labour supply machine was so comparatively efficient by this time that it was able to meet them.

Simultaneously with these and other campaigns, we in the Ministry of Supply were continuously assisting the Ministry of Labour in tapping new sources of labour wherever it was physically possible. Prisoners of war were useful, but could not be used for direct war production. Despite some doubts among colleagues, I turned to Irish labour, both from Northern and Southern Ireland, since there were tens of thousands of unemployed in Eire, and the wage we offered of fifty shillings a week for women and ninety shillings for men was a powerful attraction. In addition, by organizing the journey and the hostels or billets, we could steer these workers at short notice to whatever vacancy was most acute. A British Ministry of Labour 'Liaison Office' was established in Dublin by arrangement with the Eire Government, who were faced with heavy unemployment, and quietly welcomed what we were doing. At first recruitment was carried out by private firms. But after a time direct employees of my own department began to operate in Eire under such names as British Metals, British Factories, British Foundries, British Products, etc., which in fact had no legal existence. It was naturally feared that German spies and saboteurs would be

[5] Postan, p. 356.

planted in our munition factories under the guise of Irish labour, and an attempt was made by the security authorities to vet every single application – mainly on the basis of 'nothing known against'. But no evidence ever emerged, much to my relief, that the Germans even attempted this obvious ruse. For many months the flow of Irish labour remained almost a Ministry of Supply monopoly (apart from traditional building and farm labour); until after a time Ronnie Edwards from the Ministry of Aircraft Production asked to be shown how to join in.[6] Altogether the Ministry of Supply alone recruited from Eire in the four years 1942–5 some 28,593 workers, over 11,000 of them women. This was not a huge number, but at the precise time and place needed it was invaluable – and in effect released a comparable number of British personnel for the Armed Forces. One of my private hopes in these months was that the contact established between the thousands of Irish recruits and the working English public might help a little to assuage the ancient and irrational feud harboured by the Irish. How wrong I was.

My Irish activities also led to my having to attend a body called the Security Executive, which was supposed to be the highest wartime co-ordinating authority in Whitehall for security. It met in an office at the lower end of the Haymarket, and usually numbered thirty or more, most of them in uniform. One had to sign one's name at the door; but nobody seemed to care, least of all the aged commissionaire. After a few weeks, to test the Security Executive's security, I took to signing myself 'Joseph Goebbels'. Nothing happened. So I thought it was wise to inform George Turner, and suggest that the Security Executive should examine its own security.

Less melodramatic than the Irish recruitment campaign, but even more productive of munitions labour, was the employment of women in part-time shifts. Early in 1942, my department strongly backed the Ministry of Labour in arguing that a large reserve of potential women workers existed if both government and private factories would organize two four-hour shifts instead of one eight-hour shift. Resisted at first by many factory managers, this proved highly successful: and at the peak of mobilization at the end of 1943 some 200,000 part-time women workers were employed in the engineering, chemical, explosive and shipbuilding industries, as against only 20,000 at the start of 1942.[7]

Another crucially important device in the near-total mobilization of man-power was based on the principle mentioned on pages 88–9 of locating production where the labour could be found. The country was divided into scarlet, red, amber and green areas – changed from time to time as conditions changed. The 'scarlet' were areas of extreme labour shortage, where no new production was permitted and into which 'mobile' labour was im-

[6] P. Inman, *Labour in the Munitions Industries* (London, 1957), p. 173.
[7] Inman, p. 177.

ported. 'Red' were areas of rather less acute shortage, with new production not permitted, but labour not imported. In 'amber' new production was allowed, but labour neither imported nor exported; and in 'green' new production was encouraged and mobile labour was exported. The 'green' of course included the depressed areas of pre-war days. I strongly pressed all Ministry of Supply production departments to co-operate – in their own interests – by expanding if conceivably possible in the green and amber areas. For instance, by 1944 Dundee became almost a Ministry of Supply preserve. The lesson was also indelibly impressed on my mind that what was true of wartime was equally true of peacetime. You could not have full national production, any more than full employment, unless the production was located where the workers lived.

By mid-1943 the feeling spread through the Ministry of Supply that we were winning our battle, that seemingly impossible targets were being achieved, and that the munitions programmes would be met. The stark official figures show that between June 1939 and the peak in June 1943 – a time during which millions were also being drawn into the Armed Forces – the total of all workers employed in the metal and chemical industries rose from 3,106,000 to 5,223,000 or by 68·5 per cent. By 1943 also, the munition factories had shaken down into far more smooth-running organizations, and output per man and per woman was rising even faster than the labour force. Ministry of Supply statisticians (including Walter Layton and Geoffrey Crowther) had devised a simple index of the volume of output of all Ministry of Supply 'warlike stores'. Starting at 100 in December 1939, it rose to 239 by December 1940, 431 by December 1941, 780 by December 1942, and reached a peak at 821 in the spring of 1943 – an eightfold increase in total output[8]. For guns the index (Sep–Dec 1939 = 100) reached 793 by the spring of 1943, for small arms, and filled shells and bombs over 1000, for small arms ammunition 4800 (and over 5000 in late 1943) and for 'armoured fighting vehicles' nearly 2000. Tank production remained till near the end the Ministry of Supply's most difficult and weakest performance, and was often criticized in press and Parliament. The quantity very substantially improved, but until late in the war the quality was alleged by the critics to lag behind. Meanwhile aircraft production of all types had risen from about 750 a month in the last month of 1939 to 1665 in July 1940; but did not touch 2000 till May of 1942, and reached a peak of 2715 in March 1944.[9]

By the summer months of 1943 the Ministry of Supply's programmes were almost all well in hand, but the MAPs still lagging. The Cabinet, therefore, decided that a further shift of labour should be made, and that some production programmes could now be eased off. The Ministry of Supply's greater success on the labour supply-front was mainly due, I

[8] Postan, pp. 174 and 354.
[9] Postan, pp. 484 and 485.

believe, to two factors: first the wholehearted co-operation already mentioned with Bevin's Department's policy of geographically taking the work to the workers; and second on our settled strategy of generally working hand-in-glove with Ministry of Labour officials. The MAP's attitude by contrast was normally criticism and protest. In 1942–3 the Ministry of Supply instituted a new procedure known as 'programme reviews', by which when any production programme had to be cut, the cuts were made, if at all possible, in 'red' and 'scarlet' areas where the labour was certainly needed for other programmes and would not simply become unemployed. The full details of the relevant programme were set out on paper with the existing labour force at each factory; and I could advise at once where the cut should be made. Numerous production chiefs used to attend these gatherings. The new superman on the production scene, Sir Graham Cunningham, previously Chairman of Triplex, sat in the chair at the end of the table with, inevitably, George Turner reclining beside him in an armchair. Cunningham prided himself on rapid, firm decisions, after a few minutes' discussion. 'My decision in this case,' he would say, 'is No.' 'Yes,' Turner would whisper from beside him. 'I mean Yes,' Cunningham would add. As long as he could pronounce, he seemed not greatly to care what the decision was. Turner was well content to whisper, as long as his word went. They worked admirably together.

One main reason for the over-emphasis on aircraft in 1943–4 was the raucous demand from Bomber Command and 'Bomber Harris' for Lancaster aircraft for night-bombing of German towns. My own belief at the time was that the concentration on the Lancaster was excessive, and was not contributing to the war effort on a scale in any way comparable to the extent to which resources were being devoured by this single aircraft. I naturally was much too junior to argue this formally, because it was an issue for the Chiefs of Staff and indeed the PM. But I did argue it informally with colleagues within the official machine. The Lancaster was an aircraft which carried a heavy load of bombs, but little defence against fighter attack, and could therefore usually only be used at night. It thus could not take a major part in the invasion, and had to be confined to night bombing of civilian towns. This could only be justified by the argument that German war production was being crippled. But there was no evidence that it was being crippled to anything like the extent that labour in Britain was being diverted from other British war production. At times in 1943 nearly one-third of British munition labour was employed not just on aircraft, but on Lancasters alone; and it could not possibly be argued, I maintained, that anything like one-third of German war production was being knocked out by the night raids.

Certainly American production had to be considered too, by 1943; but the information from the post-war autobiography of Albert Speer strongly suggests that Bomber Harris's night bombing had very little lasting effect on German munition output until after the Allied Forces had landed in France in 1944. In the 1942–3 period, according to Speer:[10] 'Neither did the bombings and the hardships that resulted from them weaken the morale of the populace. On the contrary, from my visits to armaments plants, and my contacts with the man in the street, I carried away the impression of growing toughness. It may well be that the loss of 9 per cent of our own production capacity was amply balanced out by increased effort.' Speer adds, however, that further resources had to be diverted to anti-aircraft defences as a result of the raids. Post-war information has also shown convincingly[11] that the figures with which Professor Lindemann (Lord Cherwell) justified Bomber Harris's mass bombing were ten times too high. Snow quotes Sir Henry Tizard summing it up after the war: 'The actual effort in manpower and resources that was expended in bombing Germany was greater in value than the value in manpower of the damage caused.' The main blame must rest on Cherwell.

Though over-concentration on the night bombers was probably the greatest mistake in the British war production programmes, the record as a whole was certainly a wonderful achievement. Christopher Hinton remarked to me, in a conversation thirty years later, that he believed our success in those days was due to two things: that we were a group of young men and had one common objective. Of the powers of youth I am not so sure, though in terms of crude energy and hours of work this was no doubt precious. Churchill's speeches, as I have said, genuinely counted for a lot; and so did indignation against the long list of Nazi atrocities, and the sheer national will to survive. Morale was also powerfully sustained by the knowledge that in the second war the chair-borne bureaucrats in London were at times under as immediate a threat of bombing attack as the troops in camp or overseas; such as the night of 16 April 1941, when after an all-night raid we arrived next morning at the Adelphi to find our offices shattered and no glass left in the windows. Work began after lunch.

But there were nevertheless times of despondency; especially in early 1941, when it seemed that every battle was still being lost. I remember the electrifying effect in the Ministry of Supply of the news at the start of June 1941 that the *Bismarck* had been sunk. Here was suddenly a victory, which made people feel that the whole vast machine could certainly deliver the goods. Even more heartening of course was the knowledge at the end of December 1941 that the United States was at war with Germany. I remember reading the *Evening News* at lunchtime in the Strand and finding on the *second* most important story in the lunchtime edition the heading: 'Germany and Italy declare war on the United States'. People years afterwards, I thought, would not believe that a German declaration of war on the United

[10] Speer, p. 278.
[11] C. P. Snow, *Science and Government* (London), 1961), p. 51. See also Max Hastings *Bomber Command* (London, 1979), which reaches a similar conclusion.

States was considered that day to be the second story in an evening news-paper. The first was the sinking at Pearl Harbour of about ten major American warships. Already before the United States entered the war, I had heard Harry Hopkins, visiting London on a special mission from Roosevelt, finish a talk on the BBC with the words: 'People of Britain, you are not fighting alone.' As I had always had faith that Roosevelt would see us through, and admired him more than any other political leader in this century in any country, this statement left me for the first time wholly con-vinced that the war would be won in the end.

Certainly also success in 1941–5 was partly due to the speed with which things could be done and decisions made – in marked contrast with the post-war years, and almost frightening contrast with the 1960s and 1970s. I give one instance. In my last months with the Ministry of Supply, I was asked to attend a meeting at the Air Ministry to decide on a site for a post-war civil airport, and protested at first that this was no business of mine at this stage of the war. But I was ordered to go, and about six of us assembled at assistant secretary level. The meeting lasted forty minutes, and we decided on Heathrow. In the 1960s and 1970s the Government and Parliament discussed for fifteen years the location of a third London Airport, spent several millions on public inquiries, and by the late 1970s we had no decision and no new airport.[12]

All these facts help to explain the success of the wartime Government. But if one asks why the British government machine achieved such out-standing results in 1941–5, compared to its performance thereafter, I believe Hinton was right and that the common objective was crucial. From the moment when the three main parties joined the Government in May 1940, the government machine in London and throughout the country was transformed. From 1941 onwards, the right people in a remarkable number of cases had somehow moved into the right jobs, from Churchill, Bevin and Montgomery at the top, down to those I met around me at all sorts of middle and lower levels. The war effort simply showed how much this country can achieve when virtually all the most talented people combine with a single purpose. The party system is a price overwhelmingly worth paying to ensure civil liberties and genuine political freedom. But it is a substantial price all the same.

Work in the wartime Ministry of Supply left us with exceedingly little time for private life. I had only a few respites: week-ends with my family evacuated to Beaconsfield or Oxford; evenings in the blackout at Hampstead, where I shared my pre-war house with Herbert Hart of the intelligence services, Jenifer Williams of the Home Office (later his wife) and Chris-topher Cox of the Colonial Office. Thirdly I seized the chance of reading something other than official papers on constant Ministry of Supply train journeys to Birmingham, Manchester, Leeds, Nottingham and elsewhere.

[12] See pp. 396–402.

I made three godsent literary discoveries, which I had somehow missed within the academic grind of university years. The first was *War and Peace*, my most memorable literary experience since Gibbon, and by pure chance it was in the third week of June 1941, when Hitler invaded Russia, that I reached in *War and Peace* Napoleon's crossing of the Niemen and Vistula in the same week of 1812. The coincidence persuaded me that Hitler had chosen this date, not as the current propaganda asserted, because the British invasion of Greece had upset his timetable, but because as in Napoleon's time the Russian plains had not dried out from melting snows until mid-June. Secondly, when the late summer and autumn came, *War and Peace* gave an inner conviction, which I kept to myself as it might have invited ridicule, that the Russians would finally come out on top. My next train-reading diversion was *Barchester Towers*, hitherto left on its shelf. It came to me as a joy and revelation, and Trollope remained thereafter a constant delight and refreshment. My third piece of wartime literary luck was the exhilarating discovery of 'Don Juan'. Reading on a train journey Peter Quennell's admirable volume *Byron in Italy*,[13] I noted his view that 'Don Juan' was Byron's greatest poem. Starting it on my next journey, I could only suppose that my failure to read it at school – though I had thought I had read all Byron – must have been due to the reluctance of even the liberal-minded Winchester dons to bring it too soon to the notice of the growing boy. However, it transformed the rest of my wartime train journeys, and a good few dark evenings, and left me a Byron enthusiast for life. Perhaps the dons were right, and 'Don Juan' is best read after the age of thirty.

My other welcome respite from wartime office life was the brief (nominally XYZ) lunches every Monday at the Griffin public house in Villiers Street off the Strand.[14] Conversation tended naturally to concentrate on the effectiveness of the war effort, though departmental secrets were scrupulously kept. These lunches lasted throughout the war, as the Griffin was cheap, and because Gaitskell, Durbin and I found it a valuable method of keeping contact. At this stage the Gaitskells had not moved to Hampstead, as they did later in the war. Hugh himself had been delighted to work as Private Secretary (together with Gladwyn Jebb) to Dalton in the first few months after 1940. But in the course of 1941 he began to feel, when the rest of us were being promoted to more responsible jobs, that he also should move to more demanding work. He asked me if the Ministry of Supply had any such job available at assistant secretary level. I recommended him strongly at once for a new such post being created parallel to my own in our labour department. But he was practically unknown in the Ministry of Supply and was not accepted. The job went to one of my own staff who had not a fraction of Gaitskell's abilities.

[13] Peter Quennell, *Byron in Italy* (London, 1941).
[14] See p. 61.

Not long after this, however, Dalton moved to the Board of Trade as President in February 1942 in the Government reshuffle following the Pearl Harbour and Malaya disasters; and Gaitskell, transferred with him, became a general personal aide with the rank of assistant secretary. In this position in 1942 Gaitskell pressed me repeatedly on Dalton's behalf to leave the Ministry of Supply and join them at the Board of Trade. But it was clear to me in 1942 that the Ministry of Supply was much closer to the heart of the war effort than the Board of Trade. So I declined. But by the late summer of 1943 the balance had shifted. The Ministry of Supply was releasing labour overall through the Programme Reviews, and the machine both for recruitment and release had been built up and was working smoothly. The remaining job on this front was simply to manage the rapid shifts of labour this way and that which the invasion of the Continent would require. But broadly manpower would move away from industry and into the armed forces. Secondly I was increasingly anxious to use all that I had learned about the location of labour and mobility of industry during the war in the service of a new full-employment policy which would prevent the curse of the depressed areas arising after the war.

Our wartime experience at the Ministry of Supply and Ministry of Labour had taught how this could be achieved. But I was acutely worried that not enough would be done to prevent huge unemployment appearing in the old areas. For instance, in late 1943 and early 1944, partly due to my constant pressure for wartime employment in South Wales, the Ministry of Supply was actually employing 250,000 workers in South Wales on ammunition, explosives and filling alone. It so happened that when visiting C. A. Parsons factory at Newcastle in July 1943 (in the week Mussolini fell) with D. E. W. Gibb, a Ministry of Supply Director-General, and later Chairman of Parsons', I fell ill with wartime jaundice. While lying in bed at home with this horridly protracted disease, and reading Trollope, I received an even more pressing invitation from Dalton to become his personal assistant at the Board of Trade and special adviser on post-war industrial reconstruction and employment. This time I accepted. It was agreed that I should move to the Board of Trade as soon as the jaundice was overcome, which turned out to be September 1943. I left the Ministry of Supply with heartfelt regret at parting from so many highly valued colleagues with whom I had shared so many strenuous battles, and also with the feeling that I should never have the chance of doing a more crucial job.

Development Areas

My aim in going to the Board of Trade was to forestall post-war unemployment in the old distressed areas by steering in new industry on a major scale. But I found myself at first in the anomalous position of a 'personal assistant' to Dalton, standing outside the official machine, and deprived of all the executive powers I had exercised for three years. The intensity of the change was a shock. It convinced me that it is not very useful to be a member of the government machine unless one is part of the working hierarchy with executive authority, and that the whole idea of semi-political advisers to ministers standing half outside the official machine is a misguided one which tends to friction. You soon discover in this twilight that papers do not come to you unless you ask for them; and that you cannot ask for them unless you know of their existence. Churchill once damned the whole idea, when describing the function of 'overlord' ministers, as 'brooding in ignorance on the work of others'. I resolved at the Board of Trade in 1943 to make the best of it for the time, but not to be led into this trap again. At its worst I spent lonely hours in my room, whereas my room at the Ministry of Supply had been the centre of furious activity all day. Gaitskell had had exactly the same experience as 'personal assistant' to Dalton, and had now got himself appointed a full principal assistant secretary (a rank, later abolished, between assistant secretary and under secretary), responsible at this time for price control and the film industry.

My own terms of reference were post-war 'reconstruction' including 'industrial re-conversion' on Dalton's behalf, but under the supervision of Lord Woolton, who had become Minister for Reconstruction and was most happily served by Norman Brook as his chief official. This interlude did at least allow me a little time to resume contact with the outside world. I even lunched with Dunbar of the *Daily Herald* occasionally as well as Percy Cudlipp. I felt we were making peace after our pre-war struggles at the *Herald*, and I suppose Dunbar thought he was in contact with the government machine and indirectly with Dalton. Lunch with Percy Cudlipp was an unfailing pleasure. He was another memorable example of those whom I first met in professional conflict, later to become fast friends. Unlike many

men and most journalists, Cudlipp had become less and not more cynical
as his fourteen years of editorship wore on. He had clearly now developed
sincere principles, and wanted as much as I did to see a post-war Labour
Government. His descriptions of the follies of Fleet Street and Odhams in
particular were endlessly entertaining, and he seemed almost as amused by
what I could relate of the oddities of Whitehall. Bevin, Cudlipp said, used
to ring him up frequently, forgetting he himself was no longer Deputy
Chairman of the *Herald*, and always addressed him as 'Cuncliffe'. The
object of these phone calls was to incite the *Herald* to some campaign or to
protest at its failings. Once, when even Bevin's own Ministry had been
criticized, Bevin had retorted over the phone: 'Your *Herald*, Cuncliffe, is a
miserable, nagging, quisling paper.' Meanwhile, Lord Southwood and
other Odhams directors, Cudlipp maintained, shared Hannen Swaffer's
addiction to spiritualism and guidance from on high was on occasion
sought and received at board meetings.

At the Board of Trade working with Dalton was very different from working with Franks. I profoundly shared Dalton's two guiding passions: to
defeat the Nazis and to bring new employment to the old distressed areas,
particularly in his case Durham and the North East Coast. Also Dalton's
views and sympathies were beautifully simple and clear. He was in favour
of miners, the young, white men, socialists, New Zealand, Australia and
dwellers in Durham and Northumberland. He was against the Germans,
reactionaries, the elderly and the rich. But he tended to shout at all junior
or senior officials, visiting industrialists, or myself and John Wilmot, his
very assiduous PPS. Attlee once described Dalton's voice as a 'confidential
whisper which echoes round the lobbies'. He had an excellent private
secretary in 1943–5, a young permanent civil servant called George Preston,
who was about one foot shorter than Dalton. When abuse was shouted at
him by Dalton beyond a point, Preston used to stand on tiptoe and shout
abuse back nearly as loudly; whereat Dalton, we found, used to subside
into hearty good humour. Both useful and agreeable was Dalton's habit of
inviting one to his room (the ICI Chairman's room high up in ICI House,
Millbank), at 7 p.m. or so for a general talk about the state of the Government, the war, and the Labour Party. These sessions, often attended
by Wilmot, tended to finish up with dinner in the office (Dalton slept
there), or else in a Soho restaurant. I preferred the office. For in Joseph's
restaurant in Greek Street, where we sometimes went, he tended to observe
suddenly in his booming whisper: 'Winston told me today. . . .' As D-Day
approached, I was forced to threaten to walk out if this continued, and
once did so. Also useful was the more confidential regular talk which
Dalton wisely maintained with Walter Citrine to keep the TUC consulted
on post-war industrial plans. Citrine reclined in an armchair, while his
assistant, George Woodcock, and I sat silently on upright chairs. Dalton
thundered away and Citrine made pithy and pertinent comments.

With the other personalities in the Board of Trade, I was again fortunate. Parallel with Gaitskell as a principal assistant secretary was Richard Pares, who was popular with everyone. My closest associates, however, were two established civil servants also concerned with post-war reconstruction plans: Laurence Watkinson and Alex Kilroy. Both might well have resented my sudden invasion of their field, but in fact were wholly co-operative. Watkinson, an under-secretary, was perhaps the less bureaucratic of the two; but Alex Kilroy, the leading woman civil servant of those days together with Evelyn Sharp, radiated courtesy and charm. Accidentally, as it happened, my good relations with both were firmly cemented by one of Dalton's outbursts. Addressing the three of us one day, he suddenly and rashly declared: 'I believe some of my officials are disloyal to me.' Watkinson was compelled to retort: 'I hope, President, you are not referring to anyone present.' Dalton replied, putting his feet even further into it: 'I have chosen my words carefully.' Realizing that A.K. and Watkinson were bound to suspect me of this wholly unfounded canard, I told Dalton as emphatically as I could that from personal experience I knew what he said to be wholly untrue of those present. Salvation was thus luckily snatched from the jaws of disaster. Two other close colleagues in the Board were the established knights, Sir Arnold Overton and Sir William Palmer. Overton, the Permanent Secretary, was a straightforward example of the old-type, Wykehamist, classical scholar and liberal pre-war Board of Trade official. He looked with distinct mistrust on any suggestion for innovation, and his brief and negative minutes once provoked me into composing some couplets, which amused Dalton, ending with the refrain: 'No, no, no, signed A.E.O.' Sir William Palmer could hardly have been more different. Jovial, benevolent, loving compromise and the middle way, he was now called 'Chief Industrial Adviser' to the Board of Trade, and would swallow – not quite – anything. So when I wanted to do something, I approached Sir William, and when I did not, Sir Arnold.

The main drive in the Reconstruction Department of the Board of Trade in these last wartime months was to prepare the country for a forbidding balance of payments problem and a determined export campaign as soon as the war ended. So far from being starry-eyed or complacent about this, the officials and economists concerned were pessimistic and insistent that we had to achieve in a few years an export volume about 70 per cent above pre-war. But my specific job in my nine months as personal assistant to Dalton from September 1943 to June 1944 was to persuade the Board of Trade and the rest of Whitehall to prepare for putting into effect, as soon as the European war ended, my plans for rejuvenating the pre-war distressed areas. This involved three stages: first to insert in the projected White Paper on 'Employment Policy' (popularly called the 'Full Employment White Paper') a passage which would authorize our ambitious programme; secondly to draft and help in passing through Parliament a Bill which would give the Board of Trade legal powers to carry all this out; and thirdly, to set up in the Board of Trade itself the necessary department and regional organization, similar in some ways to the wartime machine at the Ministry of Supply. In all this Dalton gave me the unflagging ministerial support needed, and Bevin backed it up staunchly from the Ministry of Labour. Dalton knew clearly what he wanted, but he did not know clearly how to get it; and thanks to the last three years at the Ministry of Supply, I believed I did. The plan in essence was to enlarge the pre-war industrial estates, Team Valley at Gateshead, Hillington outside Glasgow, and Treforest, South Wales; to add many new estates to them; to build government-owned factories to let or sell to private firms in these areas; to convert the great wartime ROFs like Aycliffe and Bridgend into new industrial estates; to sell wartime government factories for production in the areas needing employment and for storage elsewhere; to take powers for government lending to firms producing in these districts; and to control new industrial building in the then congested areas like the Midlands and London. I was convinced that this strategy would work. Two successful experiments persuaded me of this; the wartime location of new capacity in accordance with labour supply, and the rapid growth of the pre-war Team Valley, Treforest and Hillington estates as viable partnerships between public and private enterprise. The central idea was that the Government would choose the site, own the land and put up the buildings, and the private firm would organize production and sales and take the normal risk and earn the profit.

The first task in the winter of 1943 was to get the required paragraph inserted in the White Paper on Employment Policy. This was being prepared by the official inter-departmental Reconstruction Committee of which – fortunately again – Norman Brook was Chairman. He was particularly sympathetic to our ideas on location. The general drafting of this White Paper was shared by the leading economists in the government service, including of course Keynes and other radicals like James Meade, as well as the *laissez-faire* traditionalists such as Lionel Robbins and John Jewkes. In the Board of Trade itself, I encountered mercifully little doctrinaire opposition to the idea of some government steering of the location of industry – we always used Dalton's word 'steering'. The myth dies remarkably hard that the Board of Trade was or even is dominated by nineteenth-century-minded, *laissez-faire* adherents of Adam Smith, still opposed to all government intervention in trade and industry. This (despite Overton) was not even true in 1944–5. The serious opposition which Dalton's policise encountered even then was from Beaverbrook and Bracken when the White Paper and the Bill came to the Cabinet. But with the decisive backing of Bevin both passed the Cabinet in the spring of 1944, after Churchill had remarked on the wonders of modern thought: 'It used to be said,' he commented according to Dalton's version given to me at the time, 'that in difficult times you pull in your horns. In future, in difficult times, we shall push out our horns.' In May 1944 the White Paper was published, and the crucial paragraph on Distribution of Industry – this was Bevin's characteristic phrase substituted for 'location' – read to our entire satisfaction as follows:

It will be an object of Government policy to secure a balanced industrial development in areas which have in the past been unduly dependent on industries specially vulnerable to unemployment. The Government will encourage the establishment of new enterprises in these 'Development Areas' by the following means. . . .

This White Paper was a remarkable document. It did not, as has sometimes been supposed since, argue that full employment could be assured by expanding demand without income restraint. On the contrary, it prophetically stated that pay restraint was a condition of full employment: 'Action by the Government to maintain expenditure will be fruitless unless wages and prices are kept reasonably stable.' Keynes, as one of the sponsors of this White Paper, clearly did not think that without income restraint full employment could be assured and inflation avoided.

For us in the Board of Trade in May 1944, the next part of the whole venture was to build up a department to steer industry into the areas of threatened unemployment and to draft the Bill. We decided – it was Dalton's phrase – to call the areas 'Development Areas' and the Bill, the 'Distribution of Industry Bill'. Organizing the department was more controversial. I myself, having waited quite long enough in my ambiguous advisory position, wanted full executive authority, and believed that my contacts with the Ministry of Supply, the Ministry of Labour and with industry would very greatly help. Overton, on the other hand, feared that I was 'too positive'. Dalton hesitated. But at the crucial point in the first week of June 1944 (the week of D-Day) John Wilmot pressed him and a splendid English compromise was devised. There were to be twin heads of the new department: Sir Philip Warter (Chairman of Associated British Pictures and wartime Controller of Factories and Storage) for the business side of our operations, and myself as a principal assistant secretary and head of the civil service side. This decision gave me the opportunity and the means to do a job on which I was desperately keen, which was far more welcome than pouring out munitions of war, and to do it at the moment when post-war industrial and employment plans were highly fluid and their development for many years ahead could be decisively influenced in a few months.

The duplication of Warter and myself as joint heads of the department may have looked very odd and illogical. But it worked. We operated in rooms next door to one another, and never had a serious clash in the following fifteen months. Warter concentrated on negotiations with major firms on their post-war plans, and I on Whitehall dealings and on the building up of the Board of Trade regional machine and the industrial estate companies in the three main Development Areas: South Wales, Scotland and the North East. But in talks with the biggest firms we usually acted together. The wartime building licence system funnelled to our section at the Board of Trade all applications for post-war industrial building sites, and we could 'steer' these to our regional officers in the proposed Development Areas. Secondly the Board of Trade took over the Team Valley, Treforest and Hillington Estate Companies, gave them the job and the finance for building new factories on their old estates and new ones to be constructed. I felt sure myself that the idea of the industrial estate would catch on, and spread naturally in the post-war world. When I first called in our three excellent new Regional Controllers from the Development Areas, as well as the three industrial estate Chairmen, they were so astonished to hear of our ambitious plans that they hardly believed we meant them seriously. They were so used to urging London to do this or that, and having it turned down, that they almost thought that there must be a catch in it when I said clearly and loudly: please go ahead from now on. Lord Bilsland, the Chairman of the Scottish Industrial Estate was particularly sceptical, but did splendid work over the whole period as soon as he grasped that we actually meant what we said.

The response from large-scale industry was extremely cheering over the following months. Remembering all too well the agonizing pre-war story of Ebbw Vale and Sir William Firth, I was naturally most anxious about the steel industry's plans for locating post-war steel and tin-plate mills. Everyone knew that the old 'hand' tin-plate mills, largely sited round Swansea, could not continue. Fortunately, Sir Sam Beale, in 1945 Chairman of Guest Keen, was also an industrial adviser to the Board of Trade. After some weeks of mystification, he told me in much secrecy that Guest Keen, Richard Thomas and Baldwins planned a massive strip mill project operated by a joint company: the Steel Company of Wales, and that he would let me know their proposed location, if I could keep it confidential even from Dalton (whose garrulity he suspected) for three months. I willingly agreed: and when Beale told me that the site was Margam between Port Talbot and Bridgend, I was so thankful as to offer to keep it secret as long as he liked. Dalton (who was born in Neath) was of course equally delighted when he was told. He had been exerting much pressure on the steel companies to put their huge plant in Wales and indeed was so enthusiastic that he almost came to believe he had selected the Margam site himself.

Next ICI asked to consult Warter and me on their biggest post-war project. We called on Sir John Nicholson, the Deputy Chairman, in Nobel House, since to secure this prize for the new Development Areas it seemed abundantly worth the mountain visiting Mohammed. Sir John had a map, and said he would put his finger on the proposed location if we would say 'yes' or 'no' verbally, and keep the secret to ourselves until the land was bought. We agreed. Sir John put his finger on the south bank of the Tees near to the mouth and I said: 'Yes'. That was the origin of ICI Wilton, and that was how such matters were settled between the Government and industry in 1944–5. Then came BP – or the Anglo-Iranian Oil Company, as they were then still called. Word reached me that they were planning a huge-scale post-war refinery and petro-chemical complex, and I feared it might be designed for the Thames Estuary or Southampton Water. However, to our immense relief the proposed site turned out to be Grangemouth on the Firth of Forth. At the end of our negotiations on this, I asked the Anglo-Iranian representative why the company suggested Grangemouth when the water in the Clyde was so much deeper and more suitable for large tankers than the Forth. He answered that Sir William Fraser,[1] Chairman of the Company, who had joined it in early youth in pre-1914 days, had come from Stirling and the central Scotland shale-oil area. It was of course pure chance that the vast complex of Grangemouth today, employing thousands, is so happily placed for processing the flow of North Sea oil which was wholly unforeseen in 1944–5.

These great companies were no doubt influenced by the knowledge that the Government strongly favoured developments in these areas, and wisely proposed them themselves so as to avoid conflict and delay. But others had to be pushed a good deal harder. Pressed Steel put in an application for a major expansion at Cowley, where they already employed over 10,000. This would have been exceedingly unwelcome in Oxford. By chance at this same moment I was told that the Ministry of Supply's large wartime factory at Linwood near Paisley was surplus and could be re-allocated. I suggested that Pressed Steel might take Linwood instead, regarding this privately as a very forlorn hope. But they agreed, and manufactured steel rail wagons at Linwood for the coal industry in the immediate post-war years. Over ten years later Rootes agreed with Pressed Steel to build a full car manufacturing plant alongside the first Pressed Steel factory: and later still Chrysler and eventually Peugeot took over the whole complex. Thus did the car industry come to Scotland: and if it had been left to purely Scottish enterprise, there would have been no car industry there today.

Even greater difficulties had to be overcome in the case of British Nylon Spinners at Pontypool. BNS was a joint subsidiary of Courtaulds and ICI (now ICI Fibres and wholly ICI-owned), and after being refused a licence at Banbury, was steered by the Board of Trade to a site which the firm found suitable at Pontypool on the fringe of the South Wales mining area, where unemployment had been so grievous before the war. ICI and Courtaulds in the later months of 1944 pressed to be allowed to start building in January 1945, as a condition of accepting the site. But the Ministry of Supply Glascoed ROF hostels (by 1945 no longer needed, as I knew) occu-

[1] Later Lord Strathalmond.

pied part of the site, and BNS would not build unless they were sure they could dismantle the hostels when they reached them. The Ministry of Supply (George Turner in person) flatly refused to give any such promise until the war was over. As January approached, and the project was nearing collapse, I resorted to what some may call sharp practice. I told BNS that the Ministry of Supply would agree to the hostels being demolished in May 1945, and George Turner that BNS would not demolish them till the European war was over. This was a gamble on the European war ending by May 1945. It did. BNS started building in January and demolishing the hostels in May. And neither they nor George Turner, nor the thousands who have since found jobs in BNS Pontypool, ever knew that this pious fraud had been perpetrated.

Next step after the formation of our 'Distribution of Industry' Department at HQ, as it was called for many years, was for me to visit the proposed Development Areas to hear everybody's views. Dalton was extremely keen on what later became fashionable as 'participation'. Left to myself, I should probably have concentrated on pushing the new enterprises from London, because I had learnt so much about the geography of the areas and sentiments of the people – they wanted work – that I doubted whether prolonged tours, though I enjoyed them, were worthwhile. But Dalton was right, and the weeks spent with our Regional Controllers in South Wales, the North East Coast, West Cumberland, and Scotland, taught me a great deal more, and ensured that firms sent there would find someone to welcome them. Dalton was insistent that we should meet the local authorities as well as government officials, trade unionists and industrialists. Religiously carrying this out in Durham one Saturday afternoon with the Board of Trade Controller, Sadler Forster – who did an immense amount for the North East – I arrived in good time for our meeting with the Crook & Willington Council in west Durham. The municipal buildings appeared to be surrounded by a field of long grass; and when we walked in through the imposing entrance, nobody could be found. Persevering conscientiously upstairs, we discovered two old gentlemen sleeping soundly in two armchairs. On being woken up, they turned out to be the Mayor and Town Clerk, and our consultations proceeded. In Scotland, it was on one of these visits that Robert McLean, the Board of Trade Scottish Controller and later Chairman of the Estates Company, and I selected the site of Newhouse, halfway between Edinburgh and Glasgow, for an entirely new post-war estate which later attracted Honeywell to Scotland and now employs thousands. We also at this time decided to launch the Dundee industrial estate which, with the help of National Cash Register, transformed that city's post-war fortunes. The much criticized American 'multi-nationals', quite contrary to the popular myth, deserve indeed a very large share of the credit for saving Scotland from much heavier post-war unemployment.

In South Wales the unemployment prospect was formidable. Our statisticians at HQ could see no immediate prospect of re-employing the hundreds of thousands who were working for the Ministry of Supply in ammunition and explosives alone. I started my first visit for the new Board of Trade department to South Wales in July 1944 by staying with Arthur Jenkins, ex-miner, MP for Pontypool, PPS to Attlee, and Roy Jenkin's father, at his house in Pontypool, and was able to tell him of our hopes for the BNS project. I found Arthur Jenkins a most effective propagandist for the employment claims of Blaenavon and Pontypool. At the extreme west end of the Development Area, at Llanelly, I stayed with Jim Griffiths, a close ally of Dalton and an exceedingly valuable adviser on the whole Welsh operation. Jim Griffiths was almost unique in possessing all the Celtic oratorical gifts at their best and in full measure, and a high degree of practical common sense at the same time. He also represented admirably the old non-conformist conscience of the Labour Movement, which was still strong in 1945.

I was not entirely prepared, however, for the torrent of Welsh oratory awaiting me in the Valleys. My job was to explain our plans, and ask for practical suggestions large or small. The reply was almost invariably in the past tense: 'My father used to say . . .', 'Fifty years ago in this town. . . .' The scene at Maesteg, in the Ogmore Valley near Bridgend, always stuck out in my memory. For nearly two hours the assembled municipal dignitaries vividly described the history of the area for the past fifty years, and scarcely one single practical suggestion was offered. On return to London I consulted Hilary Marquand, then in the Ministry of Production, whose pre-war 'Plan for Wales' had much impressed me, and related some of my adventures. 'Oh yes,' he said: 'there is nobody in South Wales who can't make a wonderful speech, and there's nobody who can do anything else' – an exaggerated piece of cynicism of course.

Fortunately, Brunning, our Board of Trade Regional Controller in South Wales, who worked hand in glove with the Ministry of Labour Controller, was a hard-headed Lancashire businessman who did not suffer Celtic oratory gladly. It was people like Brunning who did the effective work at the crucial stage of the 'industrial re-conversion' in 1945-6. Visiting with him in my July 1944 trip the Bridgend ROF, where the Ministry of Supply was still employing over 25,000 workers, I told the Superintendent there, Corbett, an ex-rugger international, of my plan for turning Bridgend into a post-war industrial estate. But I had to add that the Ministry of Supply HQ would not allow this news to be passed on to anys one else at Bridgend, because the Ministry feared talk of post-war plan- would damage morale in the factory. 'On the contrary,' said Corbett, 'the one thing that would raise morale sky high in this factory would be to tell them the Government has a plan for employing them after the war is over.'

At this time also the idea of the 'standard' or 'advance' factory was developed. It originated first with Norman Kipping at the Ministry of

Production and emerged in 1944 as a plan to build some twelve major factories (about 100,000 sq. ft each) in the areas of the worst potential unemployment, and to allocate them to firms which would produce war stores in the last years of the war, and then when the war ended change over to peacetime goods in the same factory. By a quick decision in February 1944 these factories went to Merthyr Tydfil, Swansea, Sunderland, Hartlepool, and the Lanarkshire coalfield, and major firms took them over. This gave much quicker employment in the immediate post-war months than would have been possible from factories still to be built. Although we at the Ministry of Supply had had our conflicts during the war with Norman Kipping (who was in the Ministry of Production), I always felt warm gratitude for his steadfast support of this crucial 1944 programme. By the 1970's some hundreds of originally 'standard' or 'advance' factories had been built and were operating in Development Areas.

The centre-piece, however, of my plan was to convert the huge-scale ROFs in Development Areas into new industrial estates and to build new estates in other parts of the Areas. Most crucial were the ROFs at Aycliffe in Durham, and Bridgend and Hirwaun in South Wales – the latter located 1000 ft above sea level just north of the Rhondda mountain. In 1944 the Ministry of Supply were employing 11,000 people at Hirwaun mainly drawn from the Rhondda and Aberdare Valleys. Setbacks and crises beset my obstinate efforts to get these three converted to industrial estates. Here Christopher Hinton came to my rescue. He used his already great prestige as an engineer to insist that conversion was perfectly feasible for many of the buildings. Next Aycliffe was very nearly imperilled by a well-meaning town-planner and professor of geography at Durham University, Professor Daysh, a member of the Northern Regional Board. He argued that Aycliffe was in the wrong place, and that a major new estate should be wholly built from scratch somewhere else. This would have meant leaving up to 20,000 people unemployed for five years or more. As the whole plan was at risk, I appealed to Dalton, who exploded in a manner highly uncomplimentary to the unfortunate professor, and directed in stentorian tones that Board of Trade officials in London and Newcastle should push Aycliffe forward with all speed. After a few years, a full-scale New Town was built at Aycliffe to compliment the already flourishing industrial estate.

Since, however, Aycliffe, Bridgend and Hirwaun could not stop filling and manufacturing ammunition until the war ended, the aim of getting peacetime firms and new work into these estates quickly after VE day was extremely difficult to achieve. My admirable statistician R. L. Davies, who had come over from the Ministry of Supply, discovered early in 1945 the hideous fact that both Bridgend and Aycliffe were geographically just outside the bounds of the old Special Areas laid down by the 1934 Act, and that it would therefore be illegal for the Government Estate Companies to operate them, as I intended, till our new Bill became law. I told him to keep quiet and tell no-one. And nobody found out – not even Sir Arnold Overton. But unfortunately by the first week of May 1945, the Bill was still firmly embedded in its Committee stage. It was now clear to us that the European War would end in a few days, and the Ministry of Supply mass production of ammunition at Aycliffe, Bridgend and Hirwaun, must stop instantly. We had been unable to get full authority from any Cabinet committee to transfer the three ROF's to the Development Area Estate Companies. But employment for about 50,000 people in these highly vulnerable areas was now at stake.

On the day the European war ended, I telephoned Christopher Hinton to ask if he would write forthwith on Ministry of Supply notepaper to the ROF authorities at Aycliffe, Bridgend and Hirwaun, if I did the same on Board of Trade paper to the Board's regional officials and to the Estate Companies, saying that the three ROF's were to be transferred to Board of Trade ownership and to be converted at once into peacetime estates. He agreed. We both sent out all the necessary letters that day on official notepaper, saying 'it has been decided'. Nobody in fact other than we two had decided anything. But the authorities in Durham and South Wales were delighted and immediately acted on our instructions. I expected an explosion from George Turner or someone higher up for this gross irregularity. But none came, and by the end of May Parliament had approved the Bill. Though I worked later on as a minister in two governments for seven years, I often wondered whether that day's swift operation was not the most worthwhile service of my lifetime to the British public. By the 1960s and 1970s, Aycliffe, Bridgend and Hirwaun were all employing many thousands in a variety of industries. Bridgend was very substantially expanded in my second term at the Board of Trade – 1964–7 – and the enlarged area became the centre of the huge-scale £180 million Ford engine plant announced in 1977.

These three estates were of course only a part, though a major part, of our whole programme for the main Development Areas. My conception for South Wales was that, in addition to those already mentioned, we should develop Fforest Fach (now the Swansea Estate) on the west fringe of Swansea. Fforest Fach was one of the major constructive ideas which came from Wales and not from London. The Swansea local authority had already conceived the plan and bought the land; and it was agreed with the Board of Trade in 1945 that the Board should develop it in partnership with Swansea. By the 1960's this estate also was employing over 5000. On the North East Coast, Team Valley was to be supplemented by full-scale estates at Jarrow, at West Chirton on North Tyneside, Sunderland, Hartlepool and West Auckland. It was, I confess, an exciting moment to stand with Sadler Forster in the summer of 1944 on 'Jarrow Slake', amidst the ruin of derelict chemical works and take the effective decision that this ugly wilderness should be transformed into a major new industrial venture (the Bede Estate). In Scotland, besides Hillington, the very large and growing estate including the major Rolls-Royce wartime complex, the most ambitious new estates were to be at Dundee and Newhouse, supplemented by smaller projects in the Lanarkshire coalfield.

In the whole of our plan for the distribution of industry policy, as I conceived it in 1944-5, there was to be very little outright government expenditure involved at all. In the Development Areas themselves, apart from minor grants for 'basic services', the principle would be public investment: purchase and construction of estates, land and factories which the government would hold in the long term. Financial aid for firms would almost invariably come in the form of loans rather than grants, and would overall also prove a sound investment for the taxpayer, as indeed happened in the long and successful history of DATAC (Development Areas Treasury Advisory Committee) introduced by the 1945 Act. Pressure on firms to move to the Development Areas would derive principally from the advantages to be gained there – the immediate offer of a factory or site. I have always believed that the policy could have succeeded on this basis, as it did for the first ten years, without the introduction of huge 'regional grants'.

In 1944 however, when the whole idea was novel, the remaining move in the campaign was to carry through Parliament a Bill which would give the Board of Trade the powers needed. In the summer of that year, I felt myself as unfitted to prepare an Act of Parliament as I felt fitted for the industrial side of the job. Since a building licence system was in force, there was no need at this stage to introduce the Industrial Development Certificate (IDC) which was later included by the post-war Labour Government in the Town and Country Planning Act of 1947. We did include a clause in the 1945 Distribution of Industry Bill as drafted, which would have declared a list of 'congested areas', where specific permission to build a factory would have been needed. This was something of a pious hoax, which we inserted in the Bill partly in order to allow Dalton, if necessary (as in fact was done) to show moderation later by dropping the clause and getting the rest of the Bill through. On the surface the clause appeared to be draconian because it would have banned factory-building in certain areas without permission. But in fact it would have limited the negative power to those areas. For a general power otherwise existed through the building licences and later through the IDC's. So successful was the hoax, however, that for years afterwards it was an established left-wing myth that the Government had dropped 'direction of industry' from the Bill.

Before starting on my tour of the Development Areas in the summer of 1944, I asked for a qualified legal expert who would take responsibility for the Bill. On returning from one of these visits, and finding I had been assigned a young woman from Oxford, twenty-three years old, Christine Reynolds (later Bicknell) who, I feared, knew no more than I did about legal mumbo-jumbo, I protested strongly, but in vain. Within a few weeks she had proved exceedingly competent, took entire charge of the Bill for the rest of the year, and became the most efficient assistant I ever had in the civil service, and went on to a flourishing career. One other salutary lesson I learnt from the fortunes of this Bill: the immense time, effort and argument it needs to get a major bill through the Whitehall and Cabinet machine before it gets to Parliament at all – six months even in 1944–5, and sometimes twelve months in peacetime. This experience left me sceptical about those who argue that Parliament gives inadequate time and scrutiny to Bills. The truth is that if it gave very much more, the effort and labour of legislating at all would become almost impossible. Parliament is essential, and well qualified, to approve or disapprove the principles, voice the objections and ideas of all the interests affected, and correct mistakes, but not in most cases to re-examine and re-fashion for the tenth time the minute details and phraseology of a Bill.

In the case of the Distribution of Industry Bill, in particular, Christine Reynolds and I had by great efforts steered it through the Whitehall machine and up to the Cabinet by the last few weeks of 1944. Little time remained if it was to become law before the end of the war and so legitimize the industrial deals on which we had already embarked. Yet the employment for several years of hundreds of thousands of people hung on this issue. Dalton was rightly becoming impatient. At this moment Beaverbrook and Brendan Bracken, the still kicking old-fashioned reactionary limb in the Cabinet, suddenly showed signs of unwelcome life and opposition to the Bill as an interference in the peacetime right of private industry. Woolton, Minister for Reconstruction, was wriggling and ambivalent, and it seemed doubtful on which side Churchill would come down. Before the final Cabinet discussion on the Bill, Dalton, with his usual gusto, composed a formal letter to Churchill saying he would resign from the Government unless the Bill was in substance approved. He rehearsed this letter to me several times, and explained that if Beaverbrook won in the Cabinet, and he, Dalton, had to resign, he would publish it as his political creed.[2] In the end, as Churchill was out of the country, he sent his letter to Attlee on 6 February 1945. We were saved by Ernie Bevin. Whatever effect Dalton's letter would have produced on its own, Bevin's intervention was decisive. He made clear in the Cabinet that he was not going to have the Distribution of Industry Bill abandoned or emasculated. That was that. John Anderson supported the Bill, and Beaverbrook was heavily defeated. Without Dalton and Bevin we should have had no post-war Development Area policy. But the prime credit must of course go to Dalton.

In the spring of 1945, the Bill was introduced into Parliament, and received much support in the press; but then the next stage in the battle

[2] His letter is recorded in Hugh Dalton, *The Fateful Years: Memoirs 1931–45* (London 1957), pp. 449–50.

began. It was my job, in the intervals of negotiating with large firms on their post-war developments, to sit beside Dalton and advise him during the Committee Stage of the Bill. In the course of one of these sessions it occurred to me for the first time that perhaps I might become a Member of Parliament myself. This was a new idea for me, as I was no good at making speeches. But listening to the quality of the contributions by the Committee on the Bill, I privately asked myself whether Members of Parliament were not just ordinary human beings. The Bill, however, wound on its slow way until in May 1945 the European war finished, Churchill ended the wartime Coalition and the prospect suddenly loomed before us of a general election and the dissolution of Parliament before the Bill became law. With the resignation of the Labour ministers on 23 May, Dalton had of course gone from the Board of Trade, and Oliver Lyttleton, until then Minister of Production, took over. In this crisis, Dalton, though no longer in office, appealed privately to Charles Waterhouse, orthodox old-style Tory MP, but still remaining Parliamentary Secretary to the Board of Trade, to stand by the Bill which they had both espoused. I suggested that this was the moment to drop the largely phoney Clause 9 (for scheduling congested areas) in return for the rest of the Bill.

To our delight Waterhouse – known in the wartime Board of Trade as 'Parly Charley' – put his loyalty to Dalton, the Department and the Bill, above any personal political views he may have had. He made the best of the meaningless concession on Clause 9 and persuaded the Tory majority on the Committee that you could not abandon the whole Bill now. There was precious little time. Indeed, we found that we had one parliamentary morning – 4 June 1945 – in which to finish the Committee Stage, Report Stage and Third Reading in the Commons. 'Parly Charley' performed splendidly, assuring all his Tory colleagues briskly and briefly that they need have no fears of revolution. For the Lords, it was the job of Christine Reynolds and myself to see Lord Woolton and explain the Bill. His only explicit comment was: 'No other country in the world would stand it.' But in the Lords soon afterwards (then in the diminutive Royal Robing Room, as the Commons occupied the Lords' Chamber proper), Lord Woolton rose at all the appropriate moments, murmured inaudibly and listened to ritual responses from the Clerk of the Lords – and the Bill had survived all stages in the Upper House. The proceedings there lasted about ten minutes; and I could not help whispering to Christine Reynolds in the box:

> The House of Peers throughout the War
> Did nothing in particular,
> And did it very well.

So all our ambitious, and now irrevocable transactions with the industrial estates, and financial operations had been legitimized after the event, but with only minutes to spare.

These last months of the war, like those at the Ministry of Supply, had left precious few moments of respite for any private life. Herbert Morrison's draconian 'compulsory fire-watching' regulations obliterated almost any off-moments one might have had. In my case instead of fire-watching amid the fragile Hampstead buildings, where one's neighbours and family needed protection, I was forced to spend nights in the invulnerable stone fortress of ICI House, Millbank, where I could not sleep and no protection was needed. Fortunately on the night in mid-June 1944 when the first Flying Bomb fell on north London – in Camden Town – I was fire-watching in the Hampstead streets at night with Hugh Gaitskell who had moved near to us. We observed a curious explosion in the Camden Town area. I knew from previous Ministry of Supply information that attack by 'pilotless planes', as they were then known, was threatened, but felt bound to say nothing to Gaitskell. We then met an ARP colleague, long known to me as the gardener of a neighbouring public garden: 'It's one of them pilotless planes,' he said. Thus sometimes does the popular grapevine work even in wartime.

In the office in working hours, we devised a regular system of retreating for ten or fifteen seconds into a glass-free passage while flying bombs 'cut off' and descended. I had been profoundly relieved myself when a few days after the first flying bomb I was able to evacuate my own family first to Wiltshire, then to Oxford; and on the nights when spared from compulsory fire-watching, slept under a table at home in the basement of our lonely house, and grew used to the flying bomb explosions. Despite the popular grapevine, the secret of D Day itself was astonishingly somehow kept. Living close by were my naval brother, Alan, who was responsible for the crucial minesweeping vanguard of the Armada, and Herbert Hart, whose job made him aware of the successful scheme for planting on the Germans the false plan of a landing in the Dieppe area. I had only indirect knowledge of the 'Mulberry' 'Phoenix' etc. strands in the vast operation. None of us spoke to the other about the plan, except for one minor indiscretion of mine, when walking with my brother on Hampstead Heath on the Saturday before the invasion, I carelessly remarked that the north-west wind seemed a bit too strong. He showed complete indifference.

Somehow, however, in late 1944 and early 1945, despite all this, I did contrive to attend in the late evenings a series of meetings, under Leonard Woolf, intended to ensure that an improved League of Nations was set up after the war. This informal group, which usually met in Leonard Woolf's flat in Victoria, was linked with the Labour Party's 'Advisory Committee on International Questions' of which Woolf was chairman. Members of the group included, besides Woolf, Philip Noel-Baker, Arthur Creech Jones, Ivor Thomas and Conni Zilliacus. We were regarded by some as unworldly idealists and wild internationalists. But in my firm opinion it was not much use fighting the war, if we finished up with a more and not less defective League of Nations. We bravely kept up these talks for some months and exerted pressure on Attlee via Durbin. Not till Durbin assured us in the spring of 1945 that plans for the San Francisco Conference on setting up the UN were going forward, did we disband.

Also outside office hours in the winter of 1944–5 and spring of 1945, I had many conversations with Dalton about the Labour manifesto for the general election which we all expected in 1945. After at ime we joined Herbert Morrison for these talks, and occasionally lunched or dined together. I was also at this time receiving copies from 11 Downing Street of prolific minutes written by Evan Durbin for Attlee on post-war policies, and was a member of an Economic Committee of the Fabian Society which discussed the post-war programme and included – when they could attend – Evan Durbin, Otto Clarke, David Worswick, Harold Wilson and Austen Albu. In my talks with Dalton and Morrison, following the basic arguments of my book *The Socialist Case*, with which Dalton sympathized, I argued for inclusion in 'Let us Face the Future' of a pledge on the Beveridge national insurance plan, suitably improved; a big space for Full Employment and the Development Area policy; and public ownership for the Bank of England, the coal industry, railways, electricity, gas and civil aviation, but not iron and steel. Iron and steel was the marginal issue; and having dealt throughout the war with the iron and steel industry, I was a bit shocked at the ignorance shown by both Dalton and Morrison about its complexities. My aim was at least to warn them how immensely varied and complicated this so-called 'industry' was. At one lunch in early 1945, I appeared to have persuaded both; but later on that day at a meeting of the Labour National Executive Committee this was reversed, and iron and steel went in after all. This appears to be what Dalton describes when he says: 'On April 11 we [he and Morrison] had a row. Morrison proposed, supported by Greenwood, to back down on iron and steel, and leave it out of the Policy Declaration. He had been lunching, he said, with some friends of ours in the City, who had told him that it was too ambitious to talk of any Public Board "owning" that complicated and troublesome industry. I strongly resisted this and won.'[3] The inclusion or exclusion of steel was legitimately arguable in 1945. On balance, I still hold the view that great trouble would have been avoided if it had been omitted from 'Let us Face the Future', and the 1945 Labour Government had concentrated on those industries like coal and railways, where the labour force itself demanded nationalization; and electrictiy and gas where there was a proved technical case. But in any case the concentration of 'Let us Face the Future' on Full Employment and the improved Beveridge Plan were unquestionably right.

On 8 May 1945, the day of the final German surrender, I dined at St Ermin's Hotel, Westminister, after the day's work with Dalton, Wilmot, Bill Piercy and Will Henderson. After dinner floodlights were lit, the blackout was gone and crowds gathered in Whitehall, St. James's Park, and out-

[3] Dalton, p. 432.

side Buckingham Palace. Churchill spoke from a balcony in Whitehall. We joined the crowd, whose mood was one of thankfulness, deep but not loud, and in clear contrast with the hysteria which greeted the news of the Armistice on 11 November 1918. Dalton and I met once or twice privately during the election campaign, both taking it for granted that the election would be an easy victory for Churchill. We dined at his then favourite restaurant, the Akropolis in Percy Street, on the night on which Attlee replied on the sound radio to Churchill's national broadcast predicting that a Labour Government would set up a Gestapo in Britain. We repaired to an upper room above the restaurant after dinner to hear Attlee's response, which was, predictably, dry and terse. 'No flame, no flair,' said Dalton, more sure than ever that the election would be lost. He still under-rated Attlee and Attlee's understanding of the mind of the British public. Nobody was more surprised than I when Christine Reynolds put her head round my office door one rainy July evening, and told me that the Labour Party had won the election by a huge majority.

This brought another sudden reversal of the situation in that hectic summer. Stafford Cripps came to the Board of Trade as President. Within a few days, I found myself, rather over-awed by the occasion, walking, though an official, into Palace Yard with Cripps at the opening in August of the first day of the 1945 Parliament. It was still raining very hard; and A. P. Herbert, whom we passed at the gate of New Palace Yard remarked to Cripps (they were contemporaries at Winchester): 'Our wettest hour, I suppose.' But now under a Labour Government, with Dalton as Chancellor, the Development Area policy would be safe whether I stayed there or not. Stafford Cripps, as it happened, came to the Board of Trade with many good, but in my sphere some crazy, ideas. He wanted to launch an industrial estate for some irrelevant reason in Walsall, of all places. I managed to snatch some sense out of confusion here by proposing that if he would drop this, we should now – as we had the power – schedule Wrexham, Wigan and St Helens, Lancashire, as extra Development Areas. They had always had a strong claim. Cripps fortunately agreed: and this was how these two areas came to enjoy Development Area status for many of the post-war years.

The prospect now opened up for me of continuing indefinitely as a temporary civil servant in peacetime – neither established nor yet free to write and speak my political views – even though the policy I had launched was now safe. This, it seemed, would lead nowhere, and on reflection I found that the desire to resume the freedom to write and champion causes publicly was now my dominant motive. So in September, I approached Percy Cudlipp, and suggested that as we had foreseen, I should return to the *Daily Herald*, not as City Editor again, but purely as political leader writer. Cudlipp agreed. But a day or two after I had received final confirmation from the *Daily Herald*, and was proposing to leave the Board of

Trade, a note arrived from Attlee inviting me to become his personal assistant and adviser on economic policy thenceforth at No. 10 Downing Street. I soon learnt that this suggestion had been recommended to Attlee by Dalton and by Durbin, now an MP, who had so acted for Attlee as Deputy Prime Minister in wartime. My first impulse was to refuse. Temporary civil servants in peacetime seemed to me hybrid animals. I knew I could not serve a Conservative Government. After five years, I also hankered after the freedom and propaganda opportunities of the *Daily Herald*. But as against this, could I refuse an invitation from the Leader of my Party, now Prime Minister, at a crucial moment in history, to assist him at the very heart of the Government? I decided I could not. Naturally I had keen regrets in leaving the Distribution of Industry Department of the Board of Trade after only fifteen months. Dalton wrote in his diary on 15 June 1945, the day the Distribution of Industry Bill became law: 'This is the best thing I have done at the Board of Trade.'[4] In after years I was never sure whether my three years at the Ministry of Supply or two years at the Board of Trade were the more fruitful. But certainly the latter were the more exhilarating; because we were working for peace and against unemployment, and because so much was done so quickly, and such lasting foundations laid for the future. The spirit of those months was hardly ever recaptured.

The election result of 1945 had meanwhile confirmed my long-held conviction of the power of the press in determining the result of elections, and thereby re-kindled my enthusiasm for the *Daily Herald*. According to the conventional wisdom of 1945 and since, the election result of that year was determined by the activities of ABCA[5] in the armed forces, the WEA and other semi-educational bodies on the home front, and by propaganda associated with the Beveridge Report and so forth. This explanation has never seemed to me convincing. Certainly revulsion against the Chamberlain appeasement policy and pre-war unemployment were still strong in the electorate's mind in 1945. But the main explanation of the election result, I suggest, is that the British electorate in the 20th century has usually been basically Left Centre, but has been influenced by a preponderently Conservative press normally to vote Right Centre. From September 1939 to May 1945, party propaganda vanished in effect from the national newspapers. And when the electorate – unbrainwashed for six years – had the chance to vote after this interlude, it responded precisely as the hypothesis advanced above would have predicted – by the largest Left-Centre majority for forty years. A mere five weeks' outburst of mainly pro-Conservative propaganda in May and June 1945 was not long enough to undo the effect of six years of non-indoctrination. In addition, if this explanation were true, you would expect that as the normal preponderantly Conservative press resumed its drip-drip propaganda in the post-war years, election results

4 Dalton, p. 454.
5 Army Bureau of Current Affairs.

would move steadily further away from that of 1945. And so they did: in 1950, 1951, 1955 and 1959. Nor is it hard to see that if this explanation were broadly correct, the result of the Common Market referendum of 1975 would have been precisely what it was. As I already inclined to this view in 1945, I became increasingly convinced then that, though I must accept the immediate job at No. 10, journalism if not politics must be my peacetime vocation.

I arrived at No. 10 as economic adviser in September 1945 at a moment when Lend-Lease had been abruptly terminated by Truman; the demobilization of five million service personnel on the age-and-length-of-service principle, and at the rate of 100,000 a week, had to be achieved; and the programme 'Let us Face the Future' had to be steered through Parliament. My first job, as something of a fifth wheel to the No. 10 coach, was to get a good working understanding with the officials in the private office. Fortunately my five years in the government machine had taught me that the best way to approach an established organization is to assume that if one treats one's colleagues as reasonable and straightforward beings, they are more than likely to behave as such in return. The way not to approach the senior civil service is to assume *a priori* that they are a sinister and hostile conspiracy, to treat them as such, and then to adduce the resentment one has oneself created as evidence that one's suspicions were justified. This inferiority obsession is not unknown in the Labour Party;[1] and it was one of Bevin's many endearing qualities that he was wholly free from it (and indeed often equated himself with the Government and sometimes with the nation). The principal Private Secretary at No. 10 in 1945 was Leslie Rowan, a highly efficient civil servant, who had served Winston Churchill in the same job. Stalin indeed at Potsdam had expressed great surprise that the Opposition Leader should return after the election with the same private secretary. We had a momentary difference over my request to see Cabinet papers on economic issues within my field. A compromise was agreed in a few days by which one copy circulated round the office and was returned to him; and all went smoothly thereafter – particularly as I was myself added to Cabinet committees on major subjects such as food and coal. Francis Williams was installed in the next room to me as Press Officer, and joined in the arrangements with Rowan. When Williams had walked out of the *Daily Herald* in January 1940, we never thought we would next meet as tolleagues at No. 10 Downing Street. In those days No. 10 got along with one press officer, one economic adviser, three or four private secretaries and one part-time PPS (Parliamentary Private Secretary) – no think-tank, and

[1] For an instance see Marcia Williams, *Inside No. 10* (London, 1972), p. 27.

no special 'political advisers'. Since Williams and I shared an interest both in economics and the press, he used to pass on visiting pressmen to me when the load on him was too great; and Hugh Massingham of the *Observer* was one regular client. My other main ally was Norman Brook, then Secretary of the Cabinet together with Edward Bridges, and Attlee's main official assistant. Our wartime collaboration came in handy, and at his suggestion I called on the permanent secretaries of the main economic departments to explain modestly what I was trying to do.

The second Private Secretary with whom I had most dealings was Joe Burke, also a temporary civil servant, who later became a professor in Melbourne University. He gave me one very categorical piece of inform-ation, which I was bound for a long time not to repeat. It is well-known that immediately after becoming PM on 26 July 1945, Attlee intended Bevin to become Chancellor and Dalton Foreign Secretary, but changed his mind twenty-four hours later and switched them round. What or who induced him to change? According to prevalent gossip then and since, it was the King himself. Dalton, in his memoirs, *High Tide and After*,[2] reviews the evidence available to him. The official biography of George VI by Sir John Wheeler-Bennett[3] says that the King in his diary recommended Bevin for the Foreign Office, and that, in effect, Attlee accepted. Attlee[4] himself, on the other hand, says that the official biography 'makes rather too much' of this incident; that the King 'seemed inclined to prefer Mr Bevin as Foreign Secretary'; but that this was 'not a decisive factor'; and that Attlee later made up his own mind. Morrison also in his autobiography[5] claims to have favoured Bevin for the FO. In face of all this, Dalton concludes that the King probably expressed a preference, but that this may not have been the decisive factor in changing Attlee's mind. Dalton advances complicated reasons for the King's preference, going years back, which I suspect are imaginary.

Joe Burke told me emphatically only a few weeks after the appointments that it was Edward Bridges (then Secretary to the Cabinet, Head of the Civil Services and Permanent Secretary of the Treasury) who persuaded Attlee. I checked this again with Burke some years later and he was quite positive. Bridges' reasons, according to Burke, were that Bevin and Morrison were notoriously a bad team, and that if they were both working on the home front, conflict and indecision would be probable. This sounded con-vincing to me, since I knew myself that high civil servants feared the Bevin-Morrison feud; and in fact the separation worked well from 1945 to 1951. Also Attlee himself in the *Observer* article mentions as a reason for his change of mind that Morrison 'did not get on very well with Mr Bevin'.

[2] Hugh Dalton, *High Tide and After* (London, 1962), vol. 2, ch. II.
[3] John Wheeler-Bennett, *George VI, His Life and Reign* (London, 1958), pp. 636–9.
[4] *Observer*, 23 August, 1959.
[5] Herbert Morrison, *Autobiography* (London, 1960), pp. 246–8.

E

Bridges would have been quite entitled to put the point to Attlee, who would have recognized the truth. On the other hand Attlee would never have named the source, but would have taken responsibility himself, as he did; and the real story would never have been known to Dalton, Bevin or Morrison. It is quite possible that the King's view happened to coincide with that of Bridges and others, and that Bridges conveyed his view to the Palace via Sir Alan Lascelles, the King's secretary. I believe, myself, on the evidence that it was Bridges who exerted the crucial influence; and even more certainly that it was the Bevin-Morrison incompatibility that was decisive in Attlee's mind. Attlee himself in his autobiography[6] is typically uncommunicative, and says: 'Various reasons impelled me to my final decision, which was, I think, justified by events.' But in a conversation with Dalton in February 1952, Attlee said: 'I thought of it myself,' but significantly added: 'Ernie and Herbert would not have worked well together on the Home Front.'[7]

I gleaned also in my first weeks at No. 10 two other reports from the private secretaries about the early days of Attlee's Premiership. It is known that on 26 July, Morrison, supported by Laski of the National Executive, tried to persuade Attlee not to form a Government until the new Parliamentary Labour Party had the chance to elect a new leader. According to the account accepted in No. 10 in that autumn, Attlee had consulted Bevin about this; and Bevin had said 'leave him to me,' and telephoned Morrison with the remark: 'If you don't stop monkeying about, you won't be in the Government at all.'[8] Morrison denies in his autobiography[9] that this conversation occurred, and the evidence of it is therefore conflicting. But certainly Attlee decided to ignore the Morrison-Laski proposal; and certainly Bevin did not want Morrison as PM. The second report which I heard from Rowan, concerned the Attlee-Laski correspondence of these early days. The first letter from Laski, Rowan said, suggesting that Attlee should give way to Morrison, arrived in the first few days of the new Government. Feeling unable to propose the usual draft reply himself, Rowan showed the letter to Attlee, who scribbled forthwith: 'Thank you for your letter' (of the relevant date) 'the contents of which I have noted.' The second arrived a week or two later, and was both lengthy and learned; and it was to this that Attlee replied with the oft-quoted words: 'A period of silence on your part would be welcome.' I did not see these letters, but the reported wording remained very clear in my mind.

Next to the Cabinet Room, where the PM normally works, and linked to it by a connecting door is the No. 10 private office. Here sat the private secretaries; from here papers were circulated; and here in my time we

[6] C. Attlee, *As It Happened* (London, 1954), p. 153.
[7] Hugh Dalton, *The Fateful Years: Memoirs 1931-45* (London, 1957), p. 473.
[8] This is the report as I heard it at No. 10. Dalton has an only slightly different version, *The Fateful Years*, p. 468.
[9] Morrison, p. 246.

usually all foregathered at 4.30 for a stand-up tea and cakes, when a great deal of information could be exchanged. Francis Williams and I, the private secretaries, and Geoffrey de Freitas, the PPS, made up the party. A PPS is always a slight anomaly in the British system as being part-time, and neither a minister nor an official. Attlee mainly used de Freitas for replying to insulting letters from Sir Waldron Smithers (Tory MP) and other cranks accusing the PM of treason and similar offences. The PPS did not see official papers. Security was achieved by confining such papers to the ground floor, and party-political and press-secretarial work to the first floor, and by channelling journalists normally to Francis Williams's passage and away from the private office. The odd man out was the patronage secretary, whose time was largely occupied, apparently, selecting bishops and deans. Only once in my ten months at No. 10 did my liaison with the official secretaries break down. One of the secretaries, one day, off his own bat persuaded the PM to sign a minute to the President of the Board of Trade (Cripps) calling in question the whole Development Area policy. I was frankly horrified when this naturally came back to me from my ex-colleagues at the Board of Trade, who must have first thought I had gone off my head. The secretary responsible, who had no idea I was in any way connected with Development Area policy, abjectly apologized.

Another valued colleague of mine in Downing Street was Burke Trend, senior Private Secretary to Dalton at No. 11. Unlike Cripps, who later preferred Gt George Street, Dalton liked to work in the traditional Chancellor's study on the ground floor of No. 11 under Gladstone's portrait; and so Trend's private office was only half-a-minute's walk away from mine through the inner connecting door. By this method I could exchange messages and co-ordinate ideas with Dalton, and incidentally started a close working arrangement with Trend.

Such were the externals of our daily working life in Downing Street. But the realities in the ten months after September 1945 were three menacing and intractable economic strains: the dollar and balance of payments crisis, following the sharp ending of Lend-Lease in August; the world food scarcity caused by the war; and the coal and fuel shortage remorselessly building up in the UK itself. The country had voted for social reform. But the shortages of dollars, food and coal were no less stubborn because nobody had voted for them. My most vivid impression of all in these months at No. 10 was the falsity of the illusion, harboured by journalists, academics, and others that something called 'power' resides in the hands of a Prime Minister. The picture drawn, or imagined, is of a great man, sitting down in his office, pulling great levers, issuing edicts, and shaping events. Nothing could be further from the truth in the real life of No. 10 as I knew it. So far from pulling great levers, the PM at this time found himself hemmed in by relentless economic or physical forces, and faced with problems which had to be solved, but which could not be solved; unable to do this because

Parliament had not yet legislated, or that because it cost too many dollars, or the other because the Americans would not agree, or something else because an obstinate minister objected. Of course there was some little latitude for action here and there and, by persistent effort and ingenuity, inch by painful inch still might be gained. But too often at No. 10 in that winter the outlook seemed one of deadlock, impotence and threatened checkmate next move; and the position of the PM more that of a cornered animal, or a climber on a rock face unable to go up or down, than that of a general ordering his troops wherever he wished around the landscape. 'Power' tends to be something believed in mainly by those who have never worked near the putative centre of it.

My own understanding and estimate of Attlee changed dramatically during the ten months I worked with him at No. 10. I went there, I must confess, with the picture uppermost in my mind of the little military man, just back from the First War, springing to attention on the pavement in Hampstead, supplemented a little by his sharp comments in Transport House committees in the 1930s. I feared he might not be able to do the job of PM, and shared the feeling of Gaitskell, Durbin and others that we all had to rally round vigorously and help. I left in July 1946 with the conviction that he was fully in command of the job and more likely than anyone else to steer the Government through four or five years of crises. He was extremely well served by his three chief civil service advisers: Edward Bridges, Norman Brook and Leslie Rowan. Certainly at first they were – Rowan in particular – a bit surprised at his methods. One day in October 1945, when Lend-Lease had been cancelled, an atomic energy policy had to be agreed with Truman, Parliament was meeting, and the whole Labour Party programme was to be launched; Rowan asked Attlee in his room at the House after a meeting if he would like a cup of tea. 'I'll get it in the Tea Room,' said Attlee. Rowan assured him that a messenger could bring it. 'He's probably busy,' said Attlee, and tripped off down the passage. Rowan, who had spent many months with Churchill, was left speechless.

But we soon got used to his working habits. My normal method was to send a reasonably brief typed comment on leading Cabinet papers within my field, to reply to his terse requests, and to launch initiatives of my own where I saw a need. I usually suggested a precise course of action, to which he need merely reply 'Yes'; so that I could write to some minister, saying 'The PM has asked me to suggest. . . .'. But every so often he would write 'No'. Sometimes we used to try a moment or two's conversation in the Cabinet Room, where (unlike an interview with most ministers, company chairmen and such, in which one sits in an armchair beside a desk), one was awkwardly perched alongside Attlee at the Cabinet table, and his silence implied he had only four or five seconds to spare. Among the longest comments I ever extracted from him was this: 'Wouldn't serve any useful purpose.' It was much harder to draft parliamentary speeches for Attlee than for Dalton. I was asked one morning after breakfast to draft an opening speech for the introduction of the National Insurance Bill embodying the improved Beveridge scheme for that afternoon, 6 February 1946. I did my best with relays of typists on the 'garden floor' level at No. 10, and referred to Beveridge, Lloyd George, Churchill, the Means Test, etc.; and being a lover myself of rational grammar and punctuation made it literate. It was a failure. 'Notes, not a lecture,' he said, and my grammar and punctuation sank without trace in the delivery. More successfully, when Churchill in December 1945 put down a vote of censure on the Government for failure to demobilize the troops faster than 100,000 a week, I built some staccato notes round the theme: 'Would Churchill depart from the age-and-length-of-service plan or not?' Attlee stuck to this and, offering to sit down, challenged Churchill to answer. This time he scored a real debating success over Churchill on a clearly substantial issue. Though nobody, least of all Attlee himself, would have claimed that he was a great parliamentary speaker, this debate strengthened his authority in a way which was valuable for a good time afterwards. He was at his most effective at Question Time, for these were years when both ministers and backbenchers understood the merits of brevity. Once Henry Strauss (later Lord Conesford), an amiable but pedantic Cambridge academic, asked by way of a supplementary question if the Prime Minister could explain 'whether nationalization and socialization are the same thing'. 'Very much the same,' said Attlee, to the House's great pleasure. A Prime Minister in the 1970s would have taken forty or fifty words to reply.

In the spring of 1946, Dick Crossman came back into my life. Now an MP, and fresh from the Anglo-American Commission on Palestine, he intimated to us at No. 10 that he must be granted a thirty-minute private interview with the PM on Palestine. Eyebrows were raised at this, as the Chancellor of the Exchequer and Chief of the Imperial General Staff would normally require less than thirty minutes. But it was conceded; Crossman came; spent half an hour alone with Attlee; and then joined me for a talk in my own room. He did not describe to me his thirty-minute interview, and the following account of it was given to me five or six years later by a Dutch journalist, who was not present: 'Crossman arrived punctually and was sat, as usual, with those received by Attlee uneasily alongside the latter, who remained silent. So Crossman expatiated on the Haifa Refinery, the pipeline, the Holy Places and the Stern Gang and so forth, and paused after nine-and-a-half minutes. Silence for about fifteen seconds. Crossman then moved over to the Jordan Valley, the potash, and the Gulf of Aqaba, and after nineteen-and-a-half minutes paused again. Silence for twenty seconds. Somewhat nettled, Crossman passed on via the Suez Canal and the tanker fleets back to the Haifa Refinery, and after twenty-nine and a half minutes obstinately fell silent. After nearly half a minute's pause, Attlee commented: 'I saw your mother last week.' That was the precise version of the story as told to me, though it has since assumed various forms. I naturally cannot in any way vouch for its truth.[10]

Several other characteristic incidents, however, one involving Crossman as well as Attlee, I can relate from direct knowledge. Some years later, when Attlee was still Leader of the Opposition after 1951, Crossman approached me in a corridor of the House and complained that Attlee still rebuffed all his efforts to be friendly. Crossman by his own account had said to Attlee in the Tea Room of the House that he agreed with a Labour Party statement on foreign policy made that day: but Attlee made no reply. Crossman persisted and remarked: 'I said, Clem, that I agreed with the Party's statement today on foreign affairs.' And all Attlee said in reply (Crossman told me in tones of protest) was: 'Did you?' But perhaps my own most vivid memory of Attlee concerned an incident in 1954, when he was also still Leader of the Party, and the controversy was running about the issue then called 'German re-armament'. There was to be a debate next day in the House on this and Attlee was to make the leading speech for the Labour Opposition expounding the 'Five Attlee Conditions', which were official Party policy. But a party meeting was to be held at 9 p.m. – a most inconvenient hour – as the dissidents wanted to move a motion binding the Party to total opposition against 'German re-armament'. It was moved by Harold Wilson. The meeting was crowded with over 200 excited Labour MPs, and Room 14 was so full that Roy Jenkins and I had to sit on a window sill. So much hysteria was aroused about 'giving guns to Nazis', etc., etc., that it looked as if the rebel motion would be carried and Attlee defeated. What would happen then? He certainly could not voice views in the House next day which he did not hold. Would he resign? Nobody knew.

Amid much confusion and suspense a vote was taken in which bewildered minor Party officials attempted to count hands; and a small piece of paper was handed to Attlee. In a tense silence he rose to his feet and said: 'For the motion 109. Against 111. Motion Lost. Meeting adjourned' – and walked out of the room. As most of the 200 members present relapsed into gossip and speculation, and discussed whatever Attlee would have done if he had lost, I followed my usual habit and, since the business of the House had ended, walked straight out to Westminster Underground station. Beside me, descending the steps to the platform, was Attlee; but knowing his distaste for conversation, I merely nodded. He responded, however, with the just audible remark: 'My wife's been left a little money; how should I invest it?' Was this really what was uppermost in his mind that evening? I do not know.

Back in No. 10 in 1946, however, we once had a sharp reminder of the sternness of his standards. Francis Williams managed his most successful

[10] Later it emerged, unknown to me at the time, that Crossman was performing rather special s rvices for the extreme Zionists, according to Hugh Thomas, *John Strachey*, p. 229.

press work there with little assistance other than one secretary, a girl of exceptional charm, who was safely ensconced on the first floor where no Cabinet papers were seen. He and I were also visited frequently by a well-known and friendly American scoop journalist, whose main reputation was concerned with his ability to extract exceedingly sensitive secrets from the heart of various government machines, and publish them to the world. One day Francis Williams discovered to his consternation that his girl secretary was sharing a flat in the West End with this journalist. He reported it to Attlee, who at once replied: 'She must go.' Williams asked when this would have to take effect. 'Now,' said the PM, and the lady left within ten minutes, never to be seen again at No. 10. How different standards were in the Attlee years from those that prevailed at No. 10 a generation later!

More complicated characters than Attlee, including Herbert Morrison and Nye Bevan – and even Michael Foot[11] – have found it incomprehensible that such a man could have attained the position he did, and held it for twenty years. 'No one,' says Michael Foot, 'has ever unravelled the riddle.'[12] 'It was quite impossible,' said Morrison[13] in his autobiography, 'to approach near enough to get into his mind and know what he was really thinking.' The truth, my experience would incline me to judge, was simpler. Attlee was a straightforward Victorian Christian, who believed one should do one's job and one's duty, whether as an Army officer or Member of Parliament or Prime Minister. My own father, though lacking Attlee's capacities, was in character a similar type, and sprang from a similar background; so that the characteristics were not unrecognizable to me. Nor should one suppose that, because this type may now be extinct, it therefore never existed. But secondly Attlee combined in a rare measure the three qualities of honesty, common sense and intelligence: the first two to an outstanding degree and the third on a much higher level than many recognized.

None of Attlee's colleagues in the Government, apart from Bevin, so manifestly possessed all three qualities together; and it was these, as it seemed to me, which enabled him to retain authority over such diverse and explosive individuals as Morrison, Bevin, Dalton, Cripps and Bevan. Attlee's reliability inspired ever-increasing confidence among colleagues. Above all, it endeared him to Bevin. As reported to me at the time, Bevin, after a three-hour barrage from Dalton on a drive back from Durham on 26 July 1947, in support of the foolish Cripps/Dalton plan to replace Attlee by Bevin as PM, responded with the brief words: 'I'm sticking to little Clem.' Bevin had no difficulty in 'unravelling the riddle'. Attlee made no claim to understand technical fields such as economics, which he engagingly regarded as a subject similar to medicine, in which one consulted qualified

[11] To judge from comments on Attlee in Chapter 1 of Michael Foot, *Life of Bevan*, vol. 2, *1945–60* (London, 1962).
[12] Foot, p. 27.
[13] Morrison, p. 295.

experts and if necessary took a second or third opinion. But his pre-eminent virtue of mind was his clear knowledge of what he understood and what he did not. If ever there was a wholly English character, it was Attlee.

I did not fully realize all this in my ten months at No. 10. But later on, for instance when Dalton resigned after the 1947 Budget leak, and out-standingly when the Lynskey Tribunal investigated the misfortunes of the unhappy John Belcher, a junior Minister, at the end of 1948, the reputation of Attlee and Cripps for Victorian standards was priceless to the Government and the Labour Party.[14] The trust and affection inspired by Attlee's straightforwardness partly explains, I am sure, the strength of the Labour Party in the country in these years, the record of no by-elections lost between 1945 and 1950, despite economic convulsions, and the all-time high Labour vote in 1951. It has become conventional in recent years to speak of Attlee's occasional 'ruthlessness', as though he hid some sort of dark cunning beneath a simple manner. This strikes me as another mis-understanding. When Attlee accepted Dalton's resignation after the Budget leak, or told a colleague (reputedly John Wilmot) that he did not 'measure up to a minister', and above all when he had to move Bevin from the Foreign Office in 1951, I see no reason to doubt that he was carrying out what, as he saw it, was a public duty.

It was also a public duty when in the winter of 1945–6 during an un-official Communist-inspired dock strike, which threatened London's food supply, he broadcast an appeal to the dockers to go back to work. This was preceded by a telephone conversation between Sir William Haley of the BBC who argued that in the name of free speech the unofficial strike leaders should have the right of reply, and the PM who said this was carry-ing 'balance' on the air to absurd lengths. Haley insisted, and Attlee agreed that it was Haley's decision, though he thought it wrong. But the strike was called off. Attlee's idea of public duty, however, did not prevent him per-ceiving the qualities and failings of his colleagues with a sometimes un-expectedly cold clarity. Once as Financial Secretary to the Treasury, I said to him in a conversation à deux at No. 10 that Cripps as Chancellor was opposed to some suggested action, and was startled to be told in reply: 'He's no judge of politics.'

My immediate first job at No. 10 in September 1945 was to join in the daily discussions on the American Loan. For virtually every weekday evening at No. 10 from mid-September to mid-December, Attlee, Bevin, Dalton, Morrison and Cripps met in the Cabinet Room from 9 p.m. till about midnight with Edward Bridges, Wilfred Eady of the Treasury Overseas Finance Section and myself. This was a slightly over-awing experience for me at first. In Washington, meanwhile, Halifax, the Ambassador, Keynes, Lionel Robbins and others were negotiating for us; and shoals of telegrams passed to and fro daily which I sought to sift and

14 See p. 180.

summarize for Attlee and add my comments, as Bridges and Eady did for Dalton. The plethora of telegrams did not always make for clarity. On one occasion quoting from one of them, Dalton said peremptorily to Bevin: 'Foreign Secretary, have you got the telegram?' 'I've got 'undreds,' replied Bevin, and Bridges trotted round the table to reshuffle the cards for him. Bevin, like many of us, started the negotiation with a strong distaste for accepting any help from the Americans or any conditions imposed by them. He used to march down the corridor to the Cabinet Room at No. 10 each evening remarking loudly with a broad grin: 'Any danger of a settlement tonight?' But the stark realities of the situation steadily impinged on his mind, and in the end the very fact that he had started from this viewpoint gave him greater conviction and authority in his defence of the inevitability of the loan.

The negotiation did not show the Americans in an altogether happy light. If Roosevelt had lived, I do not believe we should ever have been left so critically in the lurch or asked to accept terms which we could not carry out. President Truman cut off Lend-Lease from all European countries on 21 August, just seven days after the war with Japan ended. He was persuaded[15] by the Foreign Economic Administrator, Leo Crowley, an Irish-American lawyer who had previously induced him on May 8 to sign a similar order without reading it. This first order Truman rescinded, but signed the further order in August without fully grasping its consequences for Britain. Clayton, the American Assistant Secretary of State, who was in London at the time, was furious when he heard of it. Britain almost alone of the belligerents was left in 1945 with enormous war debts because we had both mounted an immense war effort, and borrowed abroad to pay for it on a large scale. Germany had commandereed everything from occupied countries and was left with few debts. Keynes calculated that on optimistic assumptions this country could not achieve an overseas payments balance before 1949, and that in the meantime we should incur a further total deficit of £1700 millions. He proposed therefore that we should try to raise £1250 millions ($5 billion at that date), or perhaps £1500 millions from the American Treasury somehow.

The talks began in Washington on September 11th in the same week that I started work at No. 10. On the American side the chief negotiators were Vinson, Secretary of the Treasury, a rather narrow-minded small-town politician, who could not follow Keynes's brilliant exposition, and Clayton who was far more sympathetic. The details of the three months' argument have been clearly set out in Dalton's autobiography.[16] Keynes and the British Ministers started much too optimistically with the belief that £1250 millions or £1500 millions could be obtained, without strings or interest, as a free gift or 'grant-in-aid'. There were to be 'no strings' according to

[15] H. Truman, *Year of Decisions* (London, 1955), p. 145.
[16] Hugh Dalton, *High Tide and After*, ch. VIII.

the brave slogans exchanged among each other by the negotiators in London. But unfortunately London badly under-estimated the speed at which the spirit of Roosevelt had evaporated in Washington. When we studied the telegrams, and as ministers argued it out every evening at No. 10, it steadily became more obvious that though we might indulge in brave talk, our bargaining position was hopelessly weak. We must have the foreign exchange very soon (the gold and dollar reserve was then only about £500 millions): and there was nowhere else from which we could get it. These weeks would again have been a salutary lesson to anyone who believes that something called 'power' resides in No. 10. By the end of September it was clear that a 'grant-in-aid' was unobtainable, but there was still hope of an interest-free loan. The Americans, however, had begun to talk about 'liberalizing the sterling area', cancelling the sterling debts, and an Anglo-American economic concordat – i.e. strings.

By the end of October the split was also widening between our negotiating group at No. 10 and Keynes in Washington. He felt we were out of touch with reality, and we wondered whether he was not too sympathetic to the American 'liberal' view, and too inclined to put the other Government's views to us rather than ours to them. After a full Cabinet meeting in which ministers like Bevan, Alexander and Shinwell outside the negotiating team very naturally voiced all the objections we ourselves had advanced two months before, a compromise offer was sent to Washington on 6 November. By this time Bevin, as well as the other negotiating ministers, was convinced that we had to compromise. But by the end of November, the American attitude had hardened still further, and Keynes and Robbins in Washington appeared, very understandably, to be nearly exhausted. So on 30 November, Edward Bridges, who had attended every nightly meeting at No. 10 in the previous ten weeks, flew to Washington to clinch the deal or else accept breakdown.

The team at No. 10 met for the last time on 3 and 4 December in an atmosphere of crisis. By this time the main details of the 'Line of Credit' was agreed. The total would be $3·75 billions carrying interest at 2 per cent and repayable over fifty years from 1951. But there were to be political strings to the credit. The first was that this country was to seek to 'cancel' a part of our large war debt to countries like Egypt and India who had helped us during the war. It always seemed to me intolerable that we should enter into a public agreement with our richest creditor, the US, to default on our debts to our poorest creditors, India and Egypt. I therefore proposed that we should alter the word 'cancel' to 'adjust', and this was agreed: my one specific contribution to the whole deal. By accident it fell to me two years later at the Treasury to open with Ceylon the first post-war 'sterling balance' discussion, and it immediately became clear that cancellation was out of the question. We gave up the proposal, and in the end paid every penny to each of these poor countries – the first 'aid' to developing countries in the post-war years. The second 'string' was more serious, not merely a general commitment to GATT, but a firm one to convertibility of sterling within twelve months of the ratification of the deal by the US Senate. This was the climax which nearly broke the negotiations in December. The Americans had wanted convertibility at the date of the ratification of the agreement; which we flatly refused, but compromised on twelve months later (in the event, July 1947). Virtually none of us in London believed that convertibility would be possible at any rate for five years; and we thought that to accept it meant a sterling crisis at the moment when it came into force. Here, I fear, Keynes allowed himself to be drawn into excessive optimism by his fundamental belief in a free liberal system of international payments and trade, backed by the IMF and World Bank. It was a noble vision; but its nobility did not prove that we could stand convertibility in eighteen months.

However, the agreement was signed in Washington on 6 December, with the final commitment to convertibility one year after US ratification. At the last meeting before this, I had advised Attlee to refuse the convertibility commitment, to accept the resulting extreme austerity at home, and to seek what help we could from elsewhere – Canada, Australia, New Zealand and friendly American private banks. The alternatives were either this, or to accept a convertibility undertaking we could not carry out, and let the Americans learn from experience, if they would not from argument, that it would not work. Attlee turned down this piece of advice out of hand. And not long afterwards I realized he was right. He understood better than I did then that the resulting drop in living standards here and check to our whole recovery would soon have been attributed by the Opposition and the press not to a fine assertion of British pride and independence, but to the incompetence of the Government. Much more important than this, the blow to industrial recovery, exports, investment and full employment would in the end have been far worse than our having to undertake – under *force majeure* – a commitment we probably could not honour. The whole later story of Marshall Aid and of our stubborn post-war difficulties confirmed this conclusion and showed how essential the Loan Agreement was. And despite the defiance of some heroic souls, including Bob Boothby, the Agreement was of course accepted by the British Parliament very quickly and by a large majority.

Shortly after the end of the negotiations, Dalton gave a private dinner at the Savoy to Keynes and those of us who had negotiated in London. Keynes's health had been so impaired by his efforts that, to our distress, he was forced to lie on a sofa and rest throughout most of the evening. Not many weeks later he died. Nevertheless, the Loan Agreement gave a fine start both to the country's industrial recovery and to the Government's legislative programme in 1946. But in the summer of 1947, when convertibility collapsed in six weeks, the crisis struck a blow from which the Attlee

Government never fully recovered, and lastingly damaged Dalton's health, morale and reputation.

The second major problem which dominated life at No. 10 in the winter of 1945–6, was world shortage of food, and threatened famine in Germany, India, Malaya and elsewhere in the Far East. It was again a sharp lesson for those who believe in 'power'. While ministers and economists juggled on paper in Washington with billions of dollars and pounds sterling, the grimmest of economic facts reasserted itself: that dollars and pounds will not enable people to eat if there is not enough wheat, rice and maize in the world. The Minister of Food, Sir Ben Smith, an ex-T&GW official, was not the strongest card in the Attlee pack. Yet the basic facts were simple. The 1945 summer crop of wheat and rice had been disrupted or ravaged in northern Europe, Russia, China, Burma and other large areas of Asia. Would supplies last out until the new Northern Hemisphere harvest of late summer 1946? Intense efforts and repeated calculations of the world prospects were made, reviewed and constantly revised in the Ministry of Food, the Central Statistical Office, by Herbert Morrison's officials under Max Nicholson and by ourselves at No. 10. Norman Brook wisely took responsibility at once for co-ordinating these forecasting exercises into a team, so that ministers could be at least presented with agreed figures. But these calculations were interrupted every few days in the winter months by desperate telegrams from Germany, India and Malaya in particular, sometimes predicting total exhaustion of supplies within a few days and large-scale death from starvation. From the signing of the American Loan Agreement in December, wheat, rice and maize filled my working hours. My past years at the *Economist* helped, as I at least knew where the grain came from.

Early in 1946 Attlee, on Norman Brook's advice, formed a Food Committee of the Cabinet, which met frequently, including Bevin, Morrison and Ben Smith, with Attlee himself as Chairman and Brook as Secretary. Brook also became Chairman of an official Committee formed to sort out figures and alternative proposals. I was a member of both Committees. This device at once transformed the Whitehall effort, and made quick decisions possible. It soon emerged – since neither we nor the US Government had the power to make wheat or maize grow in the winter in the Northern Hemisphere – that there were basically only two immediate remedies: first to manipulate grain shipments at sea, so as to divert the grain at short notice to where it was most desperately needed; and secondly to raise the 'extraction rate' for milling, so as to obtain a larger amount of food out of each ton of wheat.

Naturally there were psychological and political difficulties as well. Dalton did not take kindly to the idea of feeding Germans, if it was at the expense of the British. Bevin had some sympathy with this, until he remembered that his Foreign Office was responsible for the British Zone of West

Germany. But he also unfortunately held strongly the opinion that the British working man liked white bread; while raising the extraction rate meant making the bread browner. I took the simple view – perhaps an official was not entitled to – that it was morally impossible to allow mass starvation to develop in countries within our responsibility, and that we must direct and divert all the supplies within our control, even at the expense of further sacrifice by the British public. (And maybe I was excessively starry-eyed in believing that rescue measures might even earn us gratitude in post-war Germany.) My attitude was regarded in some parts of Whitehall, not only by Dalton, as internationalism run mad. But it also gained some strong friends and allies. Sir Herbert Broadley, Deputy Secretary of the Ministry of Food and an experienced grain expert, who understood the facts and practicalities far better than I, shared my aim and was silling to fight stubbornly to achieve it. I soon established a close working agreement with Broadley, and occasionally authorized him on No. 10's behalf to divert supplies to avoid some immediate disaster. Hugh Thomas, in his life of John Strachey[17] records how on one occasion Broadley and I diverted a large Australian wheat shipment to India on our own responsibility. Frank Pakenham, then junior Minister at the Foreign Office, also proved a staunch ally. Moved by his life-long principles, he refused to contemplate mass starvation of Germans. My own pre-war friendship with Pakenham was strengthened by our strenuous alliance in these critical months.

Much of the credit, however, for avoiding the extreme disasters which threatened in 1946, though little publicly realized at the time, should be given to Norman Brook. By patience, ingenuity and much good humour, he continued to steer the strongly held and conflicting Whitehall views, and the confusing statistical estimates, into a coherent programme of action. How different he was from the fictitious stereotype of the strait-laced bureaucratic official, which still lives on in the world of caricature! Two other valuable allies were Max Nicholson, Chief Adviser to Herbert Morrison on economic policy and a member of the official Food Committee, and James Meade, head of the Economic Section. Herbert Morrison at this period, as Lord President, possessed a rather shadowy general co-ordinating responsibility for economic policy. Nicholson and Meade worked together with Broadley and myself, and with Brook's help we were normally able to ensure that agreed advice was given to Attlee, Morrison and Bevin.

Bevin took a great interest in the Food Committee, dominated the proceedings and showed an impressive knowledge of the world grain trade. He somehow knew for instance just how rice is sown and harvested in Thailand (Siam as it then was). At one meeting the Minister of Food was demanding a cut in the margarine ration. The argument was taken out of the mouth of

17 Thomas, p. 233.

Ben Smith by Jasper Knight, the Ministry's Controller of Fats, and in private life a director of Unilever. Knight was a very big man with a loud voice, a sort of capitalist Bevin. He interrupted Attlee, who looked distinctly surprised at this treatment from an official in the Cabinet Room, but said nothing. Morrison took up the opposition case, and Knight loudly interrupted again. Bevin then joined in; and as Knight opened his mouth to intervene, Bevin bared his teeth, leant over the table to where Knight and I were sitting and roared like a full-grown lion. Those threatened, including Knight, more or less sank under the table, and I felt as one does when a lion roars at one through the bars at a zoo, and one's faith in the bars is not sufficient to prevent one cowering backwards. Bevin then affirmed that the cut in margarine ration was unnecessary and he 'would not have it'. It was never made.

Despite these diversions, and setbacks, Broadley, Brook, Nicholson and I managed to raise the 'extraction rate' in the UK gradually towards 100 per cent thus getting the utmost food value out of the available grain, and also contrived to switch supplies to wherever in the world famine seemed most imminent. In the end, though food was acutely short in West Germany, in the Indian sub-continent and Malaya in particular, little or no outright starvation occurred. Whether it would have occurred but for the efforts of No. 10 that winter cannot be proved; but certainly many grain experts believed in the early winter months that it was inevitable. In the spring of 1946 John Strachey took over as Minister of Food from Ben Smith, when the weeks of extreme shortage were still to come. I welcomed this greatly, remembering our economic discussions of the 1930s, and saw much of Strachey and his officials, including Broadley and Strachey's Private Secretary, George Bishop (who later had a successful City career) in the later stages of the grain battle. But by July 1946, in the final weeks before the European and North American grain harvest, when Strachey became involved in the crisis over bread rationing, I had left No. 10, and was fighting a by-election. Strachey was much criticized, and evidently annoyed Attlee and Dalton as a result of several sharp changes of mind on rationing in July. On balance, rightly I believe, Attlee refused to cancel at the last moment a Cabinet decision in favour of rationing, and it went ahead at the end of that July – the first time in British history that bread had been rationed. The fact remains that the country got through 1946 without famine in British-protected areas overseas or undue hardship at home.

The third battle at No. 10 in 1945–6 was against coal shortage and fuel crisis in the second winter after the war. It occupied rather less of our time than food in the first winter, 1945–6, and it ended not in success but in failure. The reason why it occupied less time, and why it failed, were substantially the same. The food crisis had to be faced immediately, and ministerial decisions had to be made, because starvation threatened in some parts of the world within days. But in the case of coal, decisions taken in December 1945 and January 1946 would determine coal supplies and stocks twelve months or eighteen months later. What was needed immediately was much greater weekly recruitment into the coalmines. This would affect the labour force, which would then affect production, and so stocks in the autumn of 1946, and eventually stocks and supplies in the crucial first three months of the year, when they always reach a low point, in 1947. This was clear to many of us, and to me from my experience of repeated production and labour crises at the Ministry of Supply. The remedies were the same. All the figures for the coal industry were available; weekly recruitment, wastage, strength, production and stocks. One could easily, therefore, calculate on any reasonable assumption what rate of recruitment was necessary in the first half of 1946 to prevent a fall in stocks by the spring of 1947 below the level of about four million tons, at which a general fuel crisis would occur. I did so, as did various others, and it was plain by Christmas 1945 that unless very vigorous action was taken at once, a breakdown was highly probable in February and March 1947, and with very cold weather inevitable. I was fully supported in this by Max Nicholson in Morrison's office, James Meade at the Economic Section, the statisticians at the Ministry of Fuel and Power and by Hugh Gaitskell privately after he became Parliamentary Secretary there in April 1946. But Shinwell, almost alone in the Government, resisted the demand for a vigorous new recruitment effort; and the National Union of Mineworkers outside was reluctant to agree to exceptional forms of recruitment such as the engagement of Polish ex-miners, of whom large numbers released from the Polish armed forces were available in this country

As early as 26 November 1945, in a Minute to the PM on the Coal Mines Nationalization Bill due to come before the Cabinet, I argued that we might in a crisis need to subsidize coal wages and prices and used these words: 'I think there is some danger of drifting into nationalization while averting our eyes from this awkward problem. At least we should be sure that the Bill does not commit ourselves statutorily against any sort of subsidy direct or indirect.' (I noted on a copy of this Minute: 'Section extracted and sent to Mr Harold Wilson MP, Ministry of Works', who was the Parliamentary Secretary there and had recently published a valuable book on the coal industry.) Next on 30 January 1946 since astion seemed to me still inadequate, I wrote this Minute to Attlee:

PRIME MINISTER 30.1.46

You will probably wish to know how the coal production and labour outlook has developed since my minute of November 26th, in which I suggested that new steps would have to be taken to make the industry more attractive if we were to have any material coal export trade in 1946 and 1947.

The actual winter crisis over shortage of stocks seems in a fair way to being overcome, thanks to the emergency measures taken to employ military labour, etc. Provided very cold weather does not return, it should be possible to get through the winter; but stocks are extremely low and production, though no worse than in October, is much below last year. It is the long term outlook which is so disturbing. I pointed out in my note of November 26th that the Ministry of Fuel and Power were aiming at a production in the year June 1946 to June 1947 of 200,000,000 tons; that this allowed practically nothing for export; and that it assumed a labour force restored to, and held at, 700,000 persons. In fact, the labour force, having stood at 713,000 in June, has since moved as follows:

Men on Colliery Books (thousands)

	September	702·3
	October	698·7
	November	697·3
	December	697·6
week ending	5th January	697·3
week ending	12th January	698·0
week ending	19th January	698·6

This means that we have just been able to hold the strength steady at rather under 700,000 in a period when the flow of ex-miners from the Forces and from munitions has been near its greatest. For instance, some 8,000 ex-miners from the Forces returned to the pits in the last quarter of 1945, compared with 800 in the second quarter. Thus it has required a large windfall to keep strength where it is.

All the probabilities thus are that a decline will again set in when demobilisation and the outflow from munitions diminish, i.e., in the Spring. In these circumstances, if no other action is taken soon, we shall find ourselves next Autumn with virtually no exports, and an even greater shortage of coal at home, just at the time when the National Coal Board has taken ever. As you know the lack of coal exports is already depriving us of Swedish timber for housing and acutely needed Argentine wheat. It will also be a counsel of despair to have to face the critical foreign exchange year of 1947 without coal exports. The probability of a further fall in the industry's labour force thus seems to me the bleakest prospect on the whole home front.

The basic trouble is the failure to attract young men in coal-mining areas into the pits. In 1936–9 the annual intake of juveniles averaged 25,600 (which just sufficed to *maintain* the total strength). In 1945 it was about 9,600. New factories providing alternative work are now being built in the coal mining areas; and it seems to me crystal clear from these two figures that some really substantial change in the attractiveness of the coal industry must be made quickly if the situation is not to get out of hand. The Ministry are of course running a publicity campaign. But experience of such campaigns shows that they can be very successful if they have something to sell, but not otherwise.

I still think myself that a further rise in earnings, financed if necessary by a subsidy (as in agriculture and housing), is likely to be the only lasting solution. Assuming, however, that this is not practical politics at the moment (though I cannot help regretting that Mr Shinwell keeps committing the Government publicly against it); there remains the possibility of improving conditions, while leaving earnings where they are. Two possible ways of doing this suggest themselves:

1 *The National Union of Mine Workers Charter*

This, a copy of which I attach, suggests a number of improvements, including greater safety measures, health and welfare services, 40-hour week, holidays, pensions, etc. It may be argued that shorter hours and existing wages may only aggravate the manpower problem at the time; but I believe we should be wise on balance to take this risk in the hope of attracting more labour....

2 *An increase in food rations*

It seems to me that this suggestion, often as it has been looked at and turned down during the war, ought to be examined again. The TUC and, I believe, the Foreign Secretary are not very favourable to it. Mr Shinwell himself would welcome it.

... I wonder if you would care to invite the Minister of Fuel and Power and perhaps the Minister of Labour to discuss these possibilities, or any others they can suggest.

D.J.

30 January, 1946

This Minute led to renewed prodding of Shinwell by Attlee. There was a great deal of discussion, and inch by inch decisions were taken, but prolonged delays ensued. NUM reluctance for emergency measures continued understandably; but less understandably Shinwell did not appear to take seriously the threat of a crisis in early 1947. So far as one could divine his inner mind, he seemed to regard predictions of what might happen twelve months later as being remote from reality. After April 1946, when Gaitskell went to the Ministry of Fuel and Power as Parliamentary Secretary, I could at last confide in him about all this, as I could not, despite our close friendship, when he was only a private MP. He entirely accepted my view and backed it fully within Whitehall, but maintained an extreme loyalty to Shinwell as his senior Minister, and refrained from giving any hint outside of the risks the Government was running.

By June 1946 I was convinced that, despite some vigorous recruitment efforts, not enough had been done, and that we had reached the last weeks in which a crisis in 1947 could be avoided. I therefore wrote the following *cri de cœur* to Attlee on 6 June 1946:

PRIME MINISTER   6.6.46

The Coal Position

Since your talk with Mr Shinwell on May 22nd, I have been following up the suggestion made that recruitment of available Poles into the industry should go ahead. Basic arrangements for this have been made on the Foreign Labour Committee, and are being discussed with the NUM. A working party has been set up by the Foreign Labour Committee, under Mr Gaitskell, to supervise further practical arrangements. It is proposed to start with English-speaking ex-miners among the Poles already in this country, and to proceed by stages in the hope of absorbing numbers of Poles now abroad if all goes smoothly.

Meanwhile, the situation remains substantially as described in my minute of 16 May. The labour force since then has remained practically stationary at

699,000; and as output per head has not changed, production has been stationary also. . . . It therefore remains at a level insufficient to build up during the summer the stocks which we need for the winter.

Conversation in the last few days with the Permanent Secretaries of the Ministry of Labour and the Ministry of Fuel and Power has convinced me that the effort by the Ministry of Labour machine to increase intake into the Coal Industry could be greatly intensified. It is the Ministry of Labour view that their Exchange officials are at the moment working on the assumption that the housing and building material industries have a higher priority than coal, and that a bigger effort could be made to man-up coal if it were clearly placed on the same priority. This seems to me contrary to national need and the Government's intentions, since by common consent a coal shortage next winter is likely to hold up the building industries as well as others. In the Ministry of Labour view, a greater effort could be made if a high level directive on the general importance of coal were issued. The Ministry of Fuel and Power would naturally welcome this also.

In these circumstances, you may wish to consider addressing some such directive to the Minister of Labour. It would be best, I think, simply to refer to the prime importance of coal generally, without implying that other industries are to be put specifically on a lower level. I am not sure whether it would be necessary to discuss this first with the Minister of Labour, the Minister of Fuel and Power and perhaps the Lord President. The Minister of Fuel and Power would presumably welcome it in any case; and I know that the Lord President's advisers regard coal as at present the most acute home front problem. I believe that a directive such as the above, as a supplement to the other measures being taken by the Minister of Fuel and Power by way of recruiting campaigns, absorption of Poles, etc., would be of definite practical value.

D.J.

6 June, 1946

This move led Attlee to send the suggested Minute to the Minister of Labour, George Isaacs, and it was followed by a paper circulated by Shinwell at the request of Morrison to the Lord President's Committee. As a comment on this paper, I again commented to Attlee on 19 June in these words:

PRIME MINISTER 19.6.46

You will see C.P.(46)232 by the Minister of Fuel and Power is to come before the Lord President's Committee on Friday. This paper summarises the coal prospect as Mr Shinwell sees it, and proposes in effect to promise the National Union of Mineworkers

(a) a five-day week at an unspecified date;

(b) special concessions on holiday pay.

I think these steps are desirable and necessary as far as they go, but are quite inadequate to correct the present dangerous trend. In a further note on the coal prospect (which I attach) I have summed up the latest situation, as I see it, in less optimistic terms than Mr Shinwell, and suggested some further action which might be considered by way of supplementing your minute to the Minister of

Labour on recruitment. I have forwarded a copy of my note attached to the Lord President, since I know he is concerned about the coal situation and C.P. (46)232 comes before his Committee on Friday.

You may like to ask for a report from the Lord President on the decisions taken at Friday's meeting.

D.J.

19 June 1946

Coal Crisis

1 Mr Shinwell's paper, C.P.(46)232, shows that a serious situation faces the country, owing to the low level of coal stocks, and inadequacy of the present output to up sufficient stocks to face the winter (see para. 2 and annex para. 10). If anything C.P.(46)232 is too optimistic and the statement that 'the worst is over' really cannot be substantiated. In fact, as things are going at present, industry, transport and domestic consumption are bound to be dislocated on a wide and uncontrollable scale by December or a little later.

2 Stocks normally reach a minimum in April or May, and are built up to a maximum in October. In 1945 distributed stocks were considered dangerously low at 13,778,000 tons in October, and they fell seasonally to 6,810,000 tons in April. Present production, at a fairly stable level not much higher than a year ago, is at present only achieving a summer increase in stocks at the rate of about 1,000,000 tons a month. This even if all goes well, would only give us about 11,000,000 tons distributed stocks in October. The normal seasonal fall (which is likely to be sharper this year with increased industrial and other consumption) *will thus reduce stocks to the impossible level of 3,000,000 or 4,000,000 tons by next spring. This clearly means uncontrollable dislocation before then.*

3 *This easily predictable and avoidable disaster is likely to occur at exactly the moment when the National Coal Board takes over the first great nationalised industry in this country.* The discredit to the Government would be as devastating as the dislocation to industry.

4 *The cause of all this is the failure to build up the labour force in the industry,* and the tendency to diffuse effort and attention on long-term red herrings such as mechanisation, output per head, absenteeism, etc. These are no doubt important; but we must have far more men recruited per week into the industry in the immediately coming weeks if disaster is to be avoided.

5 About 1,250 persons a week leave the coal industry even under the Essential Work Order; and it is idle to suppose that this can be materially reduced. Therefore we must put into the industry something like 2,000 a week if the increase in labour force and production required is to be secured before the autumn. At present less than 2,000 persons per week are entering the industry, and of these about 600 are demobilised men from the Forces. This group of 600 will fall rapidly from now on; and this is the dangerous factor in the situation, which at present is not being adequately recognised or countered. The increase in juvenile recruitment mentioned in C.P.(46)232 is trivial (from 200 to 250 a week since a year ago).

6 All the above assumes that we virtually abandon the effort to export coal, which is itself a lamentable confession of defeat and a blow to European recovery generally.

Action required

1 C.P.(46)232 proposes in effect the offer of a five-day week and a concession on holiday pay to the NUM. These roundabout methods of raising wages are desirable and should be adopted. But they are not nearly enough; and further action as suggested below should be taken.

2 The Prime Minister's recent minute asking the Ministry of Labour to give the maximum attention to labour supply for coal mining should now be followed by a decision to give an emergency first priority to the coal industry over all other industries, including house building and building materials. A definite target of 2,000 a week gross intake should be laid down. If these steps are not taken, it is certain that the building industries, as well as exports, food production, etc, will be forced partially to close down and throw labour into unemployment for lack of coal next winter.

3 All unemployed men in coal mining districts (particularly in Development Areas) should be personally interviewed by the Ministry of Labour, and urged pointedly to go into the coal industry.

4 All possible support should be given to the recruiting and publicity campaign now being run by the Ministry of Fuel and Power throughout the country, with support from the Ministry of Labour. . . .

5 Recruitment of male labour from Eire, now being conducted by the Ministry of Labour, should be concentrated virtually entirely on the coal industry for six months. This might be a definite direction to the Ministry of Labour. . . .

6 The absorption of Poles in the mines should be pressed as speedily and as extensively as it possibly can be, naturally with the co-operation of the NUM. The five-day week should only be granted on this condition.

7 Employment of German prisoners for open-cast mining surface and ancillary work should be adopted on an increased scale energetically.

8 A further special priority allocation of prefabricated houses to mining areas should be made, if necessary as a first priority on supplies of prefabs.

9 The proposed bread ration scheme should ensure a differential in favour of coal miners at least as great as that given to other heavy workers. . . .

10 The necessary first priorities should be given to the secondary needs of the Coal Industry, such as materials for mining machinery, and to oil, fuel burning appliances, etc, . . .

The words italicized here were underlined in the Minute as addressed to Attlee. It predicted 'the impossible level of stocks of three to four million tons by next spring' (the actual level reached in April 1947 was four millions).

By the end of June 1946, the possibility had surfaced of my being selected as the Labour candidate for North Battersea in the impending by-election. As I might be leaving No. 10 within a week or two, I decided to leave nothing undone or unsaid which might avert the crisis I foresaw. I therefore wrote yet another minute to Attlee on 22 June, with the prospective figures of four million tons of stocks in March 1947 underlined in red ink, and spoke of this again as 'an impossibly low stock level'. This minute persuaded Attlee to play our last card: an invitation to Shinwell to discuss it *à trois* with Attlee at No. 10. At this meeting a few days later, which I attended, Attlee put his finger on my figure of four million tons in 1947 marked in red ink, and asked whether Shinwell disputed this and what he proposed to do. Shinwell looked out of the window of the Cabinet Room at the Horseguards Parade, and replied in words that I never forgot: 'Prime Minister, you should not let yourself be led up the garden path by the statistics. You should look at the imponderables,' and continued with a twenty-minute soliloquy which had no relation to fact. When I heard this soliloquy I realized the game was up, unless Attlee immediately removed Shinwell. Ten days later on 6 July, when I knew I should be leaving No. 10, and plunging into the by-election, I allowed myself a last note at No. 10 and indeed in my life as an official:

PRIME MINISTER   6/7/46

Coal Prospects
In my note of June 22nd, I set out the weekly recruitment of ex-miners from the Forces to the Coal Industry; and I think you will like to have the further weeks' figures now available, since it emphasises the downward trend which has been long predicted. The number of ex-miners from the Forces entering the coal mines has been as follows:

Week ending 25 May   570
Week ending 1 June   540
Week ending 8 June   415
Week ending 15 June   376

Ex-miners entering the coal industry from other industries – i.e. mainly from War Production – have been as follows:

Week ending 25 May   337
Week ending 1 June   262
Week ending 8 June   260
Week ending 15 June   219

It is true that 8 June was the Whitsun week-end; but the declining trend is unmistakeable. Since this time, your minute on priority for coal mining labour has been sent to the Minister of Labour, and the Lord President has authorised Mr Gaitskell's Working Party to pursue all possible lines of action. These are steps forward; but on the other hand the NUM is becoming less and less co-operative, and has now refused to agree to any Polish workers being placed in return for all the conditions laid down.

In spite of the efforts which Mr Gaitskell's working party are making within their capacity, I still must record my opinion that we are moving steadily into a disastrous coal situation in the early winter, and that the matter is still not being tackled with the overriding grasp and energy which the national interest requires.

6 July, 1946

The last words could be taken as a hint that the situation would only be saved if Shinwell were moved elsewhere. But the hint was not taken; and I left No. 10 with no comfort on coal other than the hope that Gaitskell might be able to achieve something as Chairman of a working party on recruitment. He did his best; and outside his Ministry remained scrupulously loyal to Shinwell. On Black Friday, 7 February 1947,[18] however, Shinwell was forced to announce the fuel collapse in a debate in the House – having in October remarked prophetically in public that: 'Everyone knows there is a coal crisis except the Minister of Fuel and Power.' Later Shinwell's friends tried to defend him by putting it about in the House and elsewhere that Gaitskell had been disloyal and that Dalton, as Chairman of a Fuel and Power Committee in late 1946, must bear a share of the blame. Dalton asked me, though by then only a private Member of Parliament, for an account of what had really gone on at No. 10; and as Dalton was Chancellor, I was entitled to tell him and did so in the following letter:

February 14th, 1947

PERSONAL & CONFIDENTIAL

My dear Hugh,

Following my note yesterday on the future coal problem, I am letting you have now some facts about the past. May I emphasise in particular that it was perfectly obvious on the figures ever since the spring of last year that the stock position would become impossible this winter. As evidence that this was so quite regardless of the weather, I enclose two among many minutes of mine dated 22 June and 6 July respectively. You will notice that in the first . . . I said that 'We are faced next winter even on the assumption of a maintained labour force and production, with an impossibly low stock level.' Please note that the sheet which was attached to this minute gave figures of stocks as I foresaw them for October, 1946 and April, 1947. These have turned out almost exactly correct. . . .

It was this minute which led to a meeting à trois which began by attention being called by the Chairman to the last two of these figures. The reply was 'You should not let yourself be led up the garden path by the statistics. You should look at the imponderables,' (followed by a twenty-minute oration at no point relating to reality).

The next minute (July 6) states (last paragraph) that 'We are moving steadily into a disastrous coal situation in the early winter.' In my speech in the coal debate on October 16 I pointed out that we would be down to one week's consumption by the end of the winter. I quote these statements simply as evidence that it was obvious to anyone with a superficial knowledge of the facts that the present situation must arise regardless of the weather.

The whole Economic Section at the Cabinet Offices were entirely in agreement with me on this, and drew attention to the fact and the remedies required again and again. These warnings were continuously blocked by the reply from the responsible quarter that all was well and nothing need be done.

As one example of this, a great effort was made to get the Foreign Labour Committee set up as a means of getting Poles into the industry, at the first meeting of this which I attended (I think about April, but the files will show) the dis-

[18] See later p. 162.

cussion ended with the statement (repeated twice with thumps on the table) 'I will not have Poles in this industry, except over my dead body.'

It was, I think, in June that the Cabinet gave a mandate to the member responsible to negotiate at the Bridlington conference of the NUM for the immediate introduction of Poles, in return for the five-day week. Instead, the NUM were informed that it was quite unnecessary to have Poles. I have very good reason to believe, that the NUM, given a little Government pressure, were ready to agree there and then. These facts and dates can easily be checked; but in my considered opinion at the time, a Cabinet decision was directly disregarded.

At the end of June, I succeeded with the help of H.M., H.G. and others in getting a series of practical decisions, including the recruitment of Irish, about which nothing had been done up to them. A target of 2,000 a week gross intake was laid down (as you can see on the papers); and in my opinion, if these decisions had been followed up with real drive, the situation could still have been saved. They were not followed up, and I know from a very high authority in the M. of L. that they were informed late in September by the other department that 'more labour was not needed in the industry'.

On October 24 the famous public statement was made 'Everybody knows there is a coal crisis except the Minister of Fuel and Power.' Was this made in ignorance of the figures of stocks? Or not? About the same time a public speech was made to the effect that 'We do not need more manpower in the industry.' This directly sabotaged the very brave efforts being made by M. of L. and M. of F. and P. officials to encourage recruitment. I do not quote the other numerous public statements.

Finally, it was, I think, in June that the suggestion was made that a minute be sent from Number 10 to the M. of L. instructing that Department to give an over-riding priority to the coal industry for suitable male labour (which I knew was not being done) it was nine or ten days before agreement could be extracted with great difficulty from Smith Square, and the minute sent....

Yours Douglas

The Right Hon. Hugh Dalton MP,
Chancellor of the Exchequer.

('H.M.' and 'H.G.' in this letter were Herbert Morrison and Hugh Gaitskell. Smith Square was the Ministry of Fuel and Power. The 'member responsible' was of course Shinwell.)

It is easy to see that Shinwell's later attacks on Gaitskell (and the feud against him lasted for years) and on Dalton were the conventional reflexes of an uneasy memory. But why did he behave in this way, neglect all warnings, and refuse to take timely action? And why did Attlee not remove him sooner? For it was not till October 1947 that Gaitskell replaced him. Attlee cannot, I think, escape criticism for weakness in not transferring Shinwell earlier to a department where he could do no harm. His only motive, as it seemed to me then and still seems now, must have been partly some feeling for an old comrade of the 1923 and 1929 governments, but mainly a fear of Shinwell's mischief-making talents. The fuel crisis, however, caused immensely greater trouble to the whole Government. And what of Shinwell?

His fatal obstruction, one must suppose, was first generated by his natural fellow-feeling for the Durham miners and the NUM, and so indirectly by the normal impulse towards the restrictive practice of keeping unaccustomed labour out of the industry. Probably this became still further aggravated by his congenital dislike of long-haired statisticians who 'led one up the garden path' by making unwelcome predictions. Cripps once said to me in this period that Shinwell's way with hard figures was to 'sweep them off the table'. In much later years, at the time of the prolonged EEC controversy, I formed a great respect for Shinwell's courage, perspicacity, vigour – and indeed longevity. But despite all these tentative explanations, there remains an element in Shinwell's disastrous, bone-headed perversity during 1946 which is still to me inexplicable.

Apart from these three crises, a great deal of time was devoted in the first post-war year at No. 10 to what was known as the 'Production Campaign'. A myth has grown up since that the Attlee Government after 1945 plunged into vast expensive welfare schemes and ignored the hard economic base of production and exports which could alone support them. This is almost the reverse of the truth. The pathetic old-age pension was only raised from ten shillings to twenty-six shillings in 1946 and not even to thirty shillings until 1951. Meanwhile, right from the start much of our time and energy in Downing Street was concentrated on preaching the message, as Government and not Party propaganda – and Morrison always kept the two sharply separate – that the country had to repair the immense damage of the war and pay back huge debts, including the American Loan, and that the only way to do this was by the steady, unromantic slog of production and exports. I composed, in *Daily Herald* language, what was known as the 'Master Document' preaching this austere theme. I first wanted us to be at least cheerful enough to call the whole enterprise the 'Prosperity Campaign'. But even this was banned as being too frivolous, and 'Production Campaign' it was. I did manage, however, to get 'A Fair Day's Work for a Fair Day's Pay' accepted as the leading slogan. The message was then propagated throughout the country, through leaflets, industrial conferences, ministerial speeches, and the whole 'information' machine that had already been used so successfully in the war. Robert Fraser, my old *Daily Herald* ally and now Permanent Secretary at the Central Office of Information, had a major hand in all this, as well as Francis Williams; so that we three were united again. When Cripps later became Chancellor, the whole effort was redoubled. Looking back thirty years later, I am inclined to believe that our success in these years in holding down the rate of price and pay increases, and expanding exports and investment much faster than consumer spending, was partly due to these campaigns.

Attlee and Dalton were also very alert in the immediate post-war months to the need to demobilize the Forces at the fastest possible rate – in order to supply labour to industry, as well as to satisfy servicemen themselves and meet parliamentary pressure. We kept up a demobilization rate of 100,000 a week, released strictly according to the promised 'age-and-length-of-service' system – right through the winter of 1945–6. But the question what should be the target figure for the Forces at the end of 1946 compared with almost five millions in May 1945, provoked a fierce battle in Whitehall. The economists wanted a low figure and the Services a higher one. Finally Edward Bridges, the summit of all official pyramids, held a meeting in his room to decide on a figure to recommend to the PM. At this meeting I found most of my closest colleagues of the previous ten years for once assembled together; Oliver Franks, now official head of the Ministry of Supply, Godfrey Ince, the same from the Ministry of Labour, Francis Williams from No. 10, Norman Brook, James Meade from the Economic Section, and Ian Jacob, Secretary of the Defence Committee. What a wealth of talent, I thought. Jacob suggested 1,100,000 as a compromise figure. We agreed, and so did Attlee and so did the Defence Committee. But when Attlee announced it in my hearing in the House a few days later (4 March 1946), a clear voice from the Labour backbenches called out: 'Not low enough'. It was James Callaghan, not long since demobilized from the Navy; and his instant reaction was clearly very popular with his colleagues on the back benches.

Meanwhile during my ten months at No. 10 between September 1945 and July 1946 I came ever more firmly to the conclusion already mentioned that someone with strong party-political convictions should not work as a civil servant, temporary or permanent, in peacetime. A senior public servant should either be a minister and member of Parliament, openly responsible for his views and actions to Parliament and his constituency; or he should be a permanent civil servant without disclosed partisan opinions. The position of a hybrid 'political' official or adviser to a minister may be temporarily defensible in wartime or exceptional circumstances. But, as I found out in these three years, a political official is in an anomalous and ambiguous predicament in normal peacetime. For, first, a civil servant with openly declared partisan views cannot be fully trusted by a minister of the opposite party. Secondly, any public servant who holds partisan views one way or the other, which are rejected by a large section of the electorate, ought to be accountable to the electorate.

Being increasingly conscious of this, despite my excellent working relations with Leslie Rowan, Norman Brook, Herbert Broadley and others in the winter of 1945–6, I decided I ought honestly to take the plunge, like Gaitskell, Durbin, Crossman and others, and go into Parliament myself. So though I had hardly made a public speech in my life, and knew that my aptitudes were for organization, for economics and for journalism, I told Attlee that I was really only masquerading as a civil servant and wanted to make an honest man of myself as soon as possible. He wished me to stay for a time and promised to let me know which by-election I should hazard.

Smethwick he advised against; and it went to Patrick Gordon Walker. Rossendale he also deprecated on the ground that Lancashire was politically fickle, and it went to Tony Greenwood.

But when North Battersea became vacant in June 1946 because Attlee had made the previous Labour Member Governor of Malta, he strongly recommended me to go ahead. It had previously been held by, among others, John Burns and Saklatvala, the latter of whom had turned Communist after being elected as a member of the Labour Party. John Wilmot, now Minister of Supply and a power in the London Labour Party, arranged for me to be proposed as a candidate. As this by-election was likely, together with two others, at Bexleyheath and Pontypool, to amount to a sort of mini-general election in the midst of the Government's bread-rationing troubles, I was extremely anxious that all the proprieties should be observed. I therefore consulted Edward Bridges on the delicate question just when I had to resign from No. 10 and the civil service. Not till I was actually selected as candidate, he said, to my surprise; and I therefore went through the constituency double-selection procedure (Executive Committee and General Management Committee) while still attending Cabinet Committees at No. 10. Fortunately no press gossip columns made trouble out of this, and I was left to muse in private at the contrast between the beautifully smooth-running machine of No. 10 and the happy-go-lucky scramble of a local Party office.

My competitors for the job included Charlie Dukes, an ex-President of the TUC, Norman Pritchard, a respected nonconformist local leader and councillor, and Fred Wingrove, a Battersea railwayman and NUR member, who later became an excellent chairman of the local Party. While waiting to make our rival speeches, we were crammed together in a small wet room adjoining the Latchmere Baths, which was oddly enough full of young girls' *left* shoes. Every minute or two a girl aged nine or ten in a dripping bathing dress came and extracted one left shoe from the pile. Asked by the ex-President of the TUC why they did this, one girl replied that each shoe of a pair had to be stowed in a different room, while they bathed, to avoid theft. At this stage of the selection I was most careful not to claim any link with Attlee, as it was thought that nothing might harm me so much with a local Party as the appearance of being foisted on them by the Party's leader. I believe that what actually told in my favour was the memory of my name in the pre-war *Daily Herald* and the fact that my age, thirty-nine, was the fashionable one at that moment in selection committees. (Dalton always said that thirty-nine was the latest age to enter Parliament; both he and Attlee were near that age when they did so.)

However, in the first week of July, I found myself the by-election Labour candidate, and took my leave of No. 10, and of the civil service, after five-and-a-half eventful years. I should also have taken leave of all income for four weeks, but for the timely help of Percy Cudlipp who welcomed me back on the *Daily Herald* as part-time leader-writer from the day of the selection. This was exceedingly fortunate. In my first period at the Ministry of Supply, by a marvellous dispensation of the Inland Revenue, I was charged two years' income-tax in one year, as PAYE came into force, and only by courtesy of my bank manager was I able to continue both working for the government and supporting my evacuated family in the war years. In 1946 I was still catching up, and the prospects of four weeks with a wife and four children and no income was distinctly discouraging. So, with much gratitude to Cudlipp and the *Daily Herald*, I embarked on my first bout of practical electioneering since I had addressed envelopes for Gaitskell and Durbin in Chatham and Gillingham in 1935.

These were the days when parliamentary elections were still uproariously rowdy, when street-corner and 'factory-gate' meetings were in demand, when window-bills appeared in almost every window of countless streets, and 'committee-rooms' were opened in every ward. As this particular contest was a by-election, agents were thick on the ground. I was perturbed at first by the startling inefficiency, as I thought, all around me, not realizing that this is traditional electioneering and has little effect on the result. My excellent agent, Bert Amey, who later became a fast friend over many years, taught me that electioneering is a matter of Muddling Through, with equal emphasis on each word. It was Bert Amey who asked me to send him a brief rhyming North Battersea slogan. I suggested: 'Fair Shares for All, is Labour's Call'; and from this by-election 'Fair Shares for All' spread in a few years round the country.

One of my other anxieties, novice as I was, concerned the ILP candidate. He called himself 'Independent Labour'. Whatever chance was there, I asked myself, as I encountered innumerable housewives, pensioners and council tenants on innumerable doorsteps, of most of these voters' distinguishing between 'Labour' and 'Independent Labour'? If they voted fifty-fifty between us two, the Tories might well win and I would have lost a long-established Labour seat. But when the votes were counted, I received 11,000 and the ILP 200: a salutary lesson that the electorate are not so ill-informed as they sometimes seem on the traditional doorstep. Another worry was the threat of bread-rationing which Strachey was being forced to introduce, though I naturally did not then know that the Cabinet was being torn by indecision and reversals of policy this way and that. In the end bread-rationing was announced a few days before the election polling day, 25 July, and had no perceptible effect on the result. Before this Strachey had come to address a huge meeting also at the Latchmere Baths to defend his policies and won immense applause. Memorable also was a magnificent oration by Jim Griffiths in a local school (Culvert Road) in which he praised the Government's National Insurance scheme and then answered questions from all and sundry. One questioner was Mary Churchill, afterwards married to Christopher Soames, and known to me through my Oxford friend Shiela Grant-Duff. Mary had most loyally come to put in a word for the Tories. When she rose to ask a question, one of my supporters sat on her chair while she was speaking, which, as there were more people present than chairs, left the poor girl helplessly standing thereafter. A harmless, and as I thought, distinctly British, form of political warfare. When in the end the result was declared from the balcony of the Battersea Town Hall, the figures were these:

Jay (Labour)	11,329
Shattlock (Conservative)	4,858
Dewer (ILP)	240

After the announcement of the result at near midnight, three Members of Parliament whom I had never met before appeared at the Town Hall; introduced themselves amid the mêlée of Labour supporters; and drove me back to the Palace of Westminster. They were Sir Will Y. Darling, Tory MP for Edinburgh, dressed like Mr Gladstone, Ian Mikardo and Jim Callaghan.

The Battersea Labour Party was, has been, and is, one of the best local parties in the country. I was exceedingly fortunate in 1946 and have been since in the chance that brought me into alliance with it. It has always been markedly and blessedly free from extremists, cranks and theorists, and has drawn its main membership and strength from ordinary working people more interested in housing, pensions, wages and living standards, than in doctrine. One main reason for this has been, I believe, the Party's long record, going back to the beginning of the century and John Burns's time, of controlling first the old 'Vestry' and then the Battersea Borough Council. Many of the more active Party members had been councillors for a number of years, a good few also chairmen of Council Committees, leaders of the Council, and mayors of the Borough. A little responsibility in a public authority, which forces one sometimes to say certain things cannot be done, or cannot be afforded, has a wonderful effect in turning political extremists into reasonable spirits. In Battersea not a few families had a long history over several generations of service to Party and Council. Best known perhaps was Jimmie Lane, Senior, who served on the Vestry and Council together for close on seventy years and claimed to have given Winston Churchill his bricklayer's union card. His son became mayor of the Borough also. Another historical reason was the genuine local community spirit that prevails in Battersea – as for instance also in Woolwich and Hampstead – a spirit which survived even the swallowing up of the local authority in the vast amorphous jellyfish of 'Wandsworth'.

As the 1940s gave way to the 1950s and 1960s, naturally the original preponderence in the Battersea Party of railwaymen, factory workers, London Transport staff and other trade unionists, was reduced by a steady stream of young men and women who had recently come down from universities, new or old. But in Battersea at any rate, partly due to the ever-pressing need to get on with the job at the Town Hall, these new recruits fused rather than feuded with the old. The avoidance of faction fights, splits between young and old, 'left' or 'right', was greatly assisted by the splendid cockney common sense of Bert Amey, agent for many years. Only once in the thirty years after 1946 was this basic harmony disturbed by a discordant voice of serious nuisance value. This was a character who embraced all the fashionable fellow-traveller slogans of the moment, moved resolutions in a conspiratorial manner, and was accused of breaking sundry Party rules. Several times motions for his expulsion were moved at General Management Committee (GMC) meetings. And several times they were rejected after eloquent pleas for tolerance, free speech, second chances and so forth. But in the end, he went too far. He was alleged to have addressed the Mayor in full Council in most unparliamentary language, in front of officials, the public, the press and – what was worse – the Tories. This time a motion for expulsion was clearly going to be carried by a huge majority; and so the offender left in a would-be-dignified protest against the whole GMC procedure; but unfortunately went through the wrong door into a small dark cupboard and not into the street. One of his only two extremist supporters was orating loudly about the iniquity of condemning a man in his absence, when the cause of the trouble decided to emerge from the cupboard and become visible to everyone in the Hall except the speaker, who continued to declare how monstrous it was to convict a man who was not there to defend himself. All eyes turned on the defendant sheepishly reappearing from the cupboard, and the resulting explosion of mirth brought to a fitting end both his political adventures and the prospect of trouble in the Battersea Labour Party.

Thanks also partly to the importance of the Council's work, it soon became clear to me that what the local Party wanted was support, not interference. They wanted me very naturally to assist them in their struggles with government departments, to carry out a regular 'surgery' in the constituency for all comers, and to answer and follow up every bona fide letter from a constituent. So we achieved in time a tacit understanding by which I always came when possible, listened to all that was said at GMCs and elsewhere, but usually did not speak myself unless asked, and did not interfere with the Party or expect others to interfere with me. Members of the Party, however, welcomed my saying in Parliament what I genuinely thought about national issues. This regular contact, combined with non-interference is perhaps the secret of the right relationship between an MP and a local party. He should more often listen than talk.

Far the most important and exacting part of the job, I soon found, was responding to the huge number of personal problems which ordinary people expect MPs to solve. Attlee advised me not to take on what was clearly local councillors' work. From the beginning I decided not to act on this advice. For since councillors often have almost no secretarial resources, it would have amounted to saying: I will not help. But this decision loaded on me a substantial and growing amount of work, starting with twenty or twenty-five constituency letters a week in 1946 and rising to more than double that number by the 1970s. In Battersea for many years, until immigration became a pressing problem in the 1970s, some nineteen out of twenty of these letters were consistently concerned with bad housing. A major part of my working time over the whole period was devoted to these troubled households. I did occasionally succeed in getting an unhappy family re-housed, and when I received thanks for it, it made the whole job seem worthwhile. Despite an immense rebuilding effort over twenty-five years in Battersea, the problem still remained far from solved in the 1960s and 1970s, and the situation grew worse still under the Thatcher Govern-ment of 1979. One certainly learnt thereby as a Member of Parliament that housing remains, especially in the cities, far the most grievous human evil of the age.

This indeed is the most vivid single lesson borne in upon me as a Member; though I never felt I was able to convey it convincingly enough either to Parliament or to the government machine. But the whole ex-perience was at any rate just one further proof, if any were needed, of the permanent value of a genuinely free and representative Parliament, in which the legislators are personally exposed week by week to the reality of ordinary people's lives. This lesson alone would also have made it incon-ceivable for me to support any party other than the Labour Party. Real life seemed so different, as one listened in one's surgery to the distressed family histories, from the blurred picture prevailing in White Papers and Westminster committee rooms.

In Parliament itself in 1946, I found the end of July a very lucky time to become a Member. It offered me a week or so in which to begin studying the place, and then two months of recess in which to recover from the by-election and begin work again seriously on the *Daily Herald*. In this August, I enjoyed the precious respite of two weeks on Dartmoor and the North Devon coast at Hartland with my sons, Peter and Martin, now nine and seven, which began a life-giving series lasting for nearly twenty years, until they left Oxford in the 1960s. Back at the *Daily Herald* working with Percy Cudlipp was a much greater pleasure than in 1940, because he had added serious views to his ever diverting conversation. In 1946–7 on the *Daily Herald*, one could still write solid, though not solemn, leaders of 200 or even 300 words on the dollar shortage, or the case for nationalizing electricity supply, without fear of them being mutilated into a caricature of the *Daily Mirror*.

After a few weeks of this, Strachey as Minister of Food, told me he wanted either Wilson (then Parliamentary Secretary at the Ministry of Works) or myself to attend for three months at a Food & Agriculture Organisation (FAO) Conference in New York. What Attlee called a 'trained economist' was needed. I demurred at this, feeling that in my first three months in the House of Commons I really could not totally remove myself elsewhere; whereupon Strachey and Attlee hatched the curious plan that Wilson should go to New York and I should spend half of each day doing his work, unpaid, at the Ministry of Dorks. This seemed to me a hardly defensible regime, even if I scrupulously separated in my mind everything that happened in the Ministry from anything I wrote in the *Daily Herald*; and I told Strachey I could not accept unless formally authorized by the Prime Minister and the head of the civil service. Perhaps I was too fastidious. Bridges saw me and said it was quite acceptable as a temporary plan, provided I kept all secrets to myself. So for my first three months as an MP, I carried on a very odd life in the morning as a crypto-junior Minister in the Ministry of Works, most afternoons as a back-bench MP in the House, and many evenings writing leaders at the *Herald*. My liberation from the bureaucratic life had, so far, lasted only about ten weeks. In January of 1947, I insisted on giving up my dubious Ministry of Works assignment, even before Harold Wilson returned.

This time my thoughts were concentrated on the House of Commons, its working habits and rules, and the fortunes of the new Government, about which I cared deeply. I was not one of those Members who, as soon as they arrive in the House, feel sure they know how it should be 'reformed'. It seemed to me probable that practices which had been evolved by trial and error over seven centuries, which had survived and been copied by not a few countries, might have something to be said for them, and anyway could hardly be learnt out of a book or understood in a few weeks. Quite apart from my clandestine Ministry of Works activities, a certain shadow of unreality dogged me in these months, because I knew from the figures that a shattering fuel crisis in the winter or coming spring could only now be avoided by exceptional weather. I therefore had to walk something of a tightrope in making a maiden speech on 16 October 1946, in a coal debate.[1] I had meant to devote my maiden speech to the influence of the advertisers and to the Beaverbrook press's pro-appeasement propaganda in 1938–9. But this had to wait. Instead I set out the figures of coal stocks and the acutely urgent action required if a crisis in the spring was to be avoided. I learnt in this debate the salutary moral that a single speech usually has a very limited impact.

In the new session of November 1946, the notorious 'Crossman amendment' in the debate on the King's Speech was put down by him and other dissidents. This was the beginning of the end of the enthusiastic harmony between Government and Party which had glowed so brightly after the 1945 election. Almost all governments find their honeymoons ending after twelve or eighteen months, as some group of their supporters discovers that the Government is not doing, usually because it cannot, all that they had hoped. But I did not at first realize – nor, I suspect, did Crossman – how serious a political crime an anti-Government amendment in the Debate on the Address is traditionally held to be. In this case, much bad blood was spilt. No doubt one can see in retrospect that Attlee would have been wiser

[1] Hansard, 16 October 1946, col. 937.

to have given Crossman a tough ministerial post at the start, or at least in April 1946 when Gaitskell became a junior minister. Crossman felt excluded, and being nothing if not active, reacted loudly and wildly, lapsing into a personal feud against Attlee and Bevin. But in 1946 Attlee and Bevin had little to rely on, other than Crossman's dogmatic views on Palestine; and so his reckless decision to move his amendment to the Address, attacking Bevin's whole foreign policy, on 18 November 1946, and then not even daring to vote for it, no doubt finished his chances with them. What would loyal Members think, if he was rewarded for this?

It was of course this fatal Crossman sortie which Bevin had in mind when he made his famous 'stab-in-the-back' speech at the Margate Party Conference in 1947. I heard it. Bevin was Foreign Secretary and not a member of the Party National Executive Committee, and by all the Party rules he should have spoken for five minutes from the rostrum, not the platform. Instead, he spoke from the platform for fifty minutes or more. He was describing his still-continuing fight to extract wheat from the United States to save starving Indians, when suddenly and illogically he hissed in a parenthetical stage whisper, audible throughout the whole packed assembly: 'That was the moment they chose to stab me in the back.' It brought the house down. Near me were sitting some of the guilty men who had supported the rebel amendment – for instance Ben Levy and Geoffrey Byng. They looked at each other in impotent fury, as wave after wave of applause surged round the crowded hall.

Early in the 1946–7 session, I joined the Finance Group of the Parliamentary Labour Party, then a lively and active body. Normally the 'subject' groups are rather unsatisfactory, though necessary, links in the Party machinery. Since they meet when the House is sitting, the attendance is ever-fluctuating; decisions can seldom be taken; and very short-term views – such as next week's business – usually preponderate. But the Finance Group in 1945–50 was much more coherent and effective. It often met in the Chancellor's room, instead of a committee room. In return Dalton understandably hoped we would support him in financial debates. Somehow he had also acquired the power (this would never have been allowed after 1951) to select its members, and these in 1946 included Gaitskell, Durbin, Jack Diamond, and Christopher Mayhew. The Chairman was the studious George Benson of Chesterfield, who had hoped to be Financial Secretary to the Treasury. Instead Dalton chose Willie Glenvil Hall, another mild unassuming character, for this, and got Benson made Chairman of the Parliamentary Finance Group. Naturally I seized on what was in effect the chance to continue an updated version of the XYZ arguments of the past ten years, particularly with Gaitskell and Durbin. At the end of one of our more vigorous discussions, I found myself locked in argument with a most pugnacious protagonist, whom I had never met before. For verbal bellicosity he reminded me of Quintin Hogg. But as I still suffered from my

F

youthful inability to extricate myself from a disputation with someone who seemed to me in error, I persisted, and so did he. This was George Brown, then PPS to Dalton. I was distinctly attracted.

As the weeks of December 1946 and January 1947 wore on, I watched the published figures of coal stocks falling inexorably to the four million ton mark, which was bound to ignite the crisis. The weather in mid-January was exceptionally mild. Then, literally, the storm broke. On 20–21 January, the wind moved into the north-east, and stayed there, with the temperature continuously below freezing point, for just eight weeks. Within a few days the gale also prevented colliers from the Tyne bringing coal to power stations in the Thames and the south of England. Oddly it so happened that on 7 February, I was attending a normally thin Friday debate in the House on coal, and had not decided whether to speak or not, as I was waiting for Shinwell to rise. Up he got in the middle of the debate and announced to a stunned House[2] (rather as did Ted Heath twenty-seven years later on 13 December 1973, at the start of the three-day week) that numerous power stations had run out of coal, that colliers could not put to sea, that much of industry would have to close down for lack of power, and that domestic consumers would have no electricity for large parts of each day. Dalton describes the news,[3] when given to the Cabinet a few hours earlier, as 'a thunderclap' even to them. Uncertain after this thunderclap whether to speak myself in the debate or not, I rose indecisively a little later – a mistake I never made again – and was unexpectedly called by the Speaker. I took refuge in recording what had actually been done by the Government to ward off the crisis, in calling for a good deal more action, and in reminding Shinwell that in my 16 October speech in the House I had predicted a fatal level of stocks in March 1947.[4]

From this disaster the Attlee Government never fully recovered in reputation, though it substantially did so in policy. It was never glad, confident morning again. The Opposition moved relentlessly in to the attack and the slogan invented by someone: 'Shiver with Shinwell and Starve with Strachey' had an irresistible vogue. For the next three months together with fifty or so colleagues, I was incarcerated, or rather refrigerated, in Committee Room 14 for the Committee Stage of the Transport Nationalization Bill. Room 14 faces eastwards; there was no heating; and the sessions lasted from 10 a.m. till 1 p.m. most weekday mornings. We wore overcoats, woollen jerseys and scarves and several pairs of socks. It did not need the Whips to point out to Labour backbenchers that they were there to *vote* and that speeches from the Government side merely prolonged the freeze. But from that Committee I learnt much, and remembered much; the jovial figure of the Minister's PPS, young Alfred Robens, bustling here and there

[2] Hansard, 7 February 1947, col. 2178.
[3] Hugh Dalton, *High Tide and After*, p. 203.
[4] Hansard, 7 February 1947, col. 2185.

as if we were all quite warm; the Minister himself, Alf Barnes of the Co-op Party, every one of whose speeches included the phrase 'matters of that description' like a text in a sermon; the admirable Chairman, Sir Charles McAndrew, pronouncing with true Scottish frigidity the words 'order, order' punctually at 1 o'clock to enormous cheers; and last, but not least, the monotonously sepulchral tones of the Opposition leader, David Maxwell-Fyfe, which inspired a long-suffering Labour member of the Committee to pen, or at least revive, the apt couplet:

> The nearest thing to death in life
> is David Patrick Maxwell-Fyfe.

Not till nearly mid-March did the wind change, and the Committee itself ended on 2 April. Despite freezing feet and fingers, however, I did succeed in achieving one serious aim in this Committee. Alf Barnes, the Minister, had proposed before the Transport Nationalization Bill had reached the Cabinet, to prohibit the so-called 'C licensees' – lorry-owners carrying their own goods – from operating more than forty miles from their base. This was of course favoured by the railway unions as it was intended to retain traffic for the railways. It seemed to me far too restrictive and illiberal, just the kind of restrictionism likely to make public ownership unpopular. I had argued this strongly while at No. 10, and in particular at a meeting there with Attlee, Barnes, Sir Cyril Hurcomb, his extremely distinguished Permanent Secretary, and Stephen Wilson the Under-Secretary responsible at the Ministry of Transport and a personal friend of mine. Barnes refused to give way, and the Bill appeared with the threatened restriction. It would, I feared, have severely affected new Development Area projects where firms wanted to move their own goods rapidly from a parent to an associated factory. In the Parliamentary Committee on the Bill, I found I had an enthusiastic ally in Tom MacPherson, a prickly but pertinacious Scottish Labour MP. We jointly drafted an amendment to give freedom to the C licensees (but not to lorries plying for hire). This split the Labour majority on the Committee. But the Opposition naturally supported it; and the Minister, fearing defeat, gave way. That was my main contribution to the national welfare in my first year in Parliament. But at least the House of Commons had succeeded where No. 10 had failed. This early lesson taught me also that the Commons is not necessarily a legislative rubber stamp, and that ministers can be induced to give way if a serious mistake is threatened or public opinion aroused – contrary to the popular belief that everything is fixed up by the Whips.

In the spring and summer of 1947, though the Government and Labour Party were both shaken by the fuel crisis, most of my colleagues in the House did not share the other horrid secret, which I carried as a legacy from No. 10, that though 'convertibility' had been promised to the Americans by July, sterling was unlikely to be able to stand the strain. I was partly reassured, but I fear misled, by reports reaching me of confidence at the Bank of England. Lunching in the spring of 1947 with Otto Clarke, who was now a member of the Treasury Overseas Finance Department, I learnt that the Bank of England did not expect a serious run on the pound when convertibility was announced. Clarke pointed out that at the rate of consumption of dollars up to the time of our talk, the loan would last till 1949. Being asked at this point to write a new pamphlet for Transport House defending the Government's economic policy, I included the cautious sentence in the pamphlet that at the rate of spending hitherto the loan would last till 1949. But I relied too innocently on the Bank's superior knowledge; and when the convertibility collapse came in August 1947, the anti-Government press misquoted me by omitting the words 'at the rate of spending hitherto', and pretended I had said unconditionally that the loan would last till 1949. From this episode I learnt that politicians do not enjoy the glorious irresponsibility of journalists, and must avoid, not merely firm statements about the future, but also any which can easily be cut out of context and misquoted. Secondly I noted that the Bank of England, just because it traditionally stood for liberal policies and sterling convertibility, was allowing its policy preferences to distort its practical judgement. It was the same intellectual weakness which misled Keynes into believing that the UK could stand liberal currency and trade policies within a few years after the war. Clever men are just as surely prone to wish fulfilment as stupid men.

Dalton himself was of course receiving at this time exactly the same advice from the Bank of England, and hence the Treasury, as was vouchsafed to me by Clarke. And it was not inconsistent with Keynes's attitude in the last stages of the loan negotiation, though by 1947 he had died. Dalton cannot therefore be seriously blamed for paying some attention to these advisers. Sterling became formally convertible on 15 July 1947. In the next two weeks Parliament and the public did not know what was happening; though the dollars were in fact melting like snow. On August 6 a debate in the House on the state of the nation began in an atmosphere of tension and anxiety. Speeches by Attlee and Dalton were tired and uninspiring. But Cripps to everyone's surprise, and despite his bread-and-butter language, rose to real heights of oratory which stirred deep feelings. The young Peter Thorneycroft came up to me immediately afterwards behind the Speaker's Chair and blurted out: 'That was a really *great* speech.' It was the finest I ever heard in Parliament, apart from Gaitskell's on the Suez crisis, and perhaps one or two of Bevan's. Cripps ended with these words:

It is no part of the British character to resign ourselves to such difficulties or fail to take the measures, however hard, to overcome them. It is by our faith in ourselves, in our country, in the free democratic traditions for which the people of this country have for centuries fought and battled; it is by our faith in the deep spiritual values that we acknowledge in our Christian faith, that we shall be enabled and inspired to move the present mountain of our difficulties and so emerge onto that serene, fertile plain of prosperity which we shall travel in happiness as a result of our efforts and our vision.[5]

Reading it in cold print, one cannot easily believe thirty years later that a minister could have thus declared his deepest personal convictions in the House of Commons in 1947, and been sincerely cheered by virtually every Member of the House. But he did, and he was. This speech on August 7 made the reputation which sustained Cripps's super-human efforts over the next three years. It did indeed move political mountains.

On August 17, the Cabinet decided to suspend convertibility; but this could not be announced, because of negotiations with the Americans, until August 20. On August 19, I was working in the *Daily Herald* office, and heard rumours in the City and Fleet Street of an impending decision. I telephoned Dalton at Downing Street to ask what he would like us to say. He told me that a statement would be made next day, but he sounded to me tired, tense and near exhaustion. He had then been a senior minister, almost without a pause, since May 1940. Next day the end of convertibility was announced by him in a broadcast, and the public was told that much of the American Loan had been dissipated in six weeks. So far as I could, I explained this in the *Daily Herald* to Labour Party supporters, and left myself for a holiday with my family in exceptionally glorious weather, which always seemed to accompany national crises

Despite Cripps's speech, however, the convertibility collapse, coming only six months after the fuel crisis, left the Government's economic policy and its reputation for the moment in ruins. There followed in September 1947 the celebrated attempt of Cripps, backed by Dalton, to replace Attlee by Bevin as Prime Minister, and remove Morrison from his shadowy role as economic co-ordinator in favour of Cripps. This was unknown to most of us outside the Government at the time, but has since been fully described.[6] The upshot was that Cripps forgot to discover whether Bevin wanted to be PM and was non-plussed when Attlee told him he had asked Bevin, and Bevin 'didn't want the job – but would Cripps himself like to be the chief co-ordinator of economic policy?' And so on September 29 the new set-up was announced: Cripps to be Minister for Economic Affairs, Dalton to stay as Chancellor, Morrison to take command of parliamentary legislation and Party affairs as Lord President and Leader of the House of Commons, and an Economic Policy Committee under the Prime Minister as Chairman, including Bevin, to assume the final authority.

This was the first turning point in the fortunes of the Attlee Cabinet, and it fashioned a machine of government which was humanly speaking nearly, but not yet quite, ideal for the job. The essential need of post-war economic management was for all final authority to be concentrated in one senior

[5] Hansard, 7 August 1947, col. 1766.
[6] e.g. Dalton, ch. XXIX, and Bernard Donoughue and G. W. Jones, *Herbert Morrison, Portrait of a Politician*. ch. 31.

economic minister, and for that minister to be plainly responsible for the balance of payments. This was not realized in the first two years after the war, because it had not been grasped that dollar shortage and the balance of payments would be the over-riding problem. During the war the Ministry of Production and Ministry of Supply could make decisions and place orders because the bill was simply sent to Washington, and the Treasury could be regarded as merely accounting. But as soon as Lend-Lease was cancelled, finance – foreign exchange – was no longer just accounting, but became the crucial limiting factor on the national effort. You could no longer, therefore, work with an economic department as a rival to the Treasury; since one of them must be responsible for the balance of payments, and that one must also be responsible for the rest of economic policy. This was at last beginning to be understood in 1947.

Much nonsense has been talked about it since, however, because it is popularly believed that something unchangeable exists called 'the Treasury', and that the relevant question is whether this body should or should not have the effective power. In truth it does not matter what name you give to the supreme authority; Cripps was first called Minister of Economic Affairs, and later Chancellor and Minister of Economic Affairs. What matters is that central authority should rest in competent hands. In fact this must mean in British conditions, first adding the required personnel and resources to the existing Treasury, as the Treasury already commands much greater expertise than any other department; and secondly, giving the necessary authority to its head. If he is to be responsible for the country paying its way, you cannot have rival authorities spending what they choose. This was the principle on which the Attlee Government was organized from 1947 to 1951, and this was the secret of the recovery from 1947. The same principle was foolishly defied in 1964[7] by the setting up of a rival 'Department of Economic Affairs' which, precisely as in 1945–7, led to duplication and the crises of 1966 and 1967. Both Morrison and Dalton were blamed for the failures of 1947, and similarly, in 1964–6, nobody knew whether Brown or Callaghan was responsible for the balance of payments. Yet there was less excuse in 1964 than in 1945. To be wise before the event is perhaps difficult. But to be unwise after the event is surely foolish.

The continued dualism of Cripps and Dalton after September 1947 was still in principle wrong. But it would probably have worked in practice for a period, because they were on close terms at this time, and were experienced economic Ministers, and operated only a few doors distant from each other in the same corridor. But in the next scene of the drama it was fortune which disposed where Attlee had proposed, and fortune which found the solution. In the September reshuffle of the Government, Durbin had become Parliamentary Secretary to the Ministry of Works, following Harold Wilson, and so ceased to be Dalton's PPS. In October Dalton

[7] See pp. 295–8.

accordingly asked me to be his new PPS: and knowing something by this time about Whitehall scrambles for rooms, I moved rapidly into a room adjoining Stafford Cripps's private office on the second floor of Great George Street. Dalton was preparing an extremely disinflationary budget to be introduced in November.

On 12 November, Budget Day, Dalton asked me as PPS to lunch with him alone at No. 11 to be told about the Budget in great secrecy an hour or two before the speech. He said this was the custom and privilege of a PPS, though I had never known it. I swore myself to heroic secrecy (I was after all still on the *Daily Herald* staff). The Budget was one of calvinistic austerity, with a surplus of over £700 millions – greater than any introduced later by Cripps. No 'public sector borrowing requirement' in those days! Dalton has never had the credit for his courage in tough budgeting. After lunch we drove to the House and continued our discussion of the Budget in the Chancellor's room, while Question Time proceeded, as the Budget Speech was not due till 3.30 p.m. My very clear memory of what then happened is as follows. The Commons was in 1947 still meeting in the Lords Chamber; and so at about 3.20 p.m. we walked together the whole length of the Library corridor to the Members' Lobby of the House of Lords, getting there about 3.25 p.m. Dalton asked me to go into the House and see that the Whip placed a glass of water by the dispatch box for him. I did so, and returned to the lobby about half a minute later. Dalton was speaking in the lobby to someone I did not know, and I took him by the arm and said 'Come on,' as it was by then about 3.26 p.m. or 3.27 p.m. Dalton in his Statement to the subsequent Select Committee says that the fatal conversation 'must have taken place between 3 p.m. and 3.15 p.m. I am pretty sure that I was in the Chamber and on the front bench by 3.20 p.m.' According to my memory, the conversation did not take place till 3.26 p.m. or 3.27 p.m.;[8] and though the difference may seem immaterial, nevertheless if the latter is correct, the risk of any damaging effect of the conversation was even more minimal than Dalton suggested. I knew nothing of course of the content of the conversation.

Next day, November 13, I joined Dalton in his room at the House just after lunch and before the Budget debate opened. 'Here is a bit of fun,' he said: and told me a Tory MP, Victor Raikes, had put down a Private Notice Question asking 'Whether the Chancellor has considered the accurate forecast of the Budget proposals in newspapers sold at 3.45 p.m. yesterday?' Dalton proposed to answer that in the lobby before the speech 'in reply to questions put to me by the lobby correspondent of the *Star* [John Carvel], I indicated to him the subject matter contained in the publication in question.' I was staggered. I appealed to him to stop and think. Was it really necessary to drag down all the pillars of the temple for a minimal technical

[8] Lord Cockfield, who was in the lobby at the time as an Inland Revenue official, confirmed my memory thirty years afterwards (in 1977) that the conversation was at 3.27 p.m.

error, which could have done no harm and which nobody else would reveal? 'One must always own up,' Dalton said, and we moved into the House to wait for the PNQ at the end of normal Questions. When it came and Dalton gave his answer, the House gasped in astonishment and incredulity. Raikes asked a friendly supplementary and Churchill then rose. In a characteristically sympathetic and almost sentimental tone (there but for the grace of God) he asked: 'May I acknowledge on the part of the Opposition the very frank manner in which the Right Honourable Gentleman has expressed himself to the House and our sympathy with him at the misuse of his confidence which has occurred.' To my intense relief, as I sat just behind Dalton, the whole House murmured approval of Churchill and sympathy with Dalton. But at about 6 p.m. that day I met Burke Trend, still Dalton's Private Secretary, looking extremely glum in the passage behind the Speaker's Chair, and I asked him what was happening. He implied that things were not too good. Later that evening I heard that, despite the sympathy of the House, Dalton had felt bound to offer his resignation, Attlee had felt bound to accept it, and Cripps had been appointed Chancellor of the Exchequer and Minister of Economic Affairs with full authority over all strands of economic policy.

So the right solution had been reached, and the foundation laid for restoring the Government's fortunes, not as the result of deep calculation, but of human error, personal tragedy and a million-to-one chance. Such is the way things actually happen. I have constantly noticed, when close to the centre of government, that events are precipitated by error, misfortune or coincidence, and are very soon attributed by press, popular and academic comment to design or conspiracy. Already legends have grown up about the Budget Leak of November 1947. (I expect one day a book will be written to prove that Dalton did it on purpose because he wanted a rest.) One legend is that Attlee accepted the resignation because he secretly wanted to remove Dalton and give the whole job to Cripps. I do not believe this. Being fairly close to both men at the time, I have no doubt that Dalton resigned because he believed this was required by the prevailing ethics of British public life, and Attlee accepted it because he believed that a Chancellor of the Exchequer, as the guardian of the civil service's standards and conscience (as indeed he said in his letter to Dalton), must be above suspicion – not just of malpractice, which was not in question – but also of loquacity or indiscretion. Dalton himself was desperately tired, worn out finally by the convertibility crisis, and so imagined when he was talking to Carvel for barely one minute that the latter was a daily journalist who could not publish anything till next morning anyway. A few seconds' indiscretion cost Dalton a position built up over forty years. Evan Durbin said to me truly, a few days afterwards, that the error was characteristic of Dalton's one great weakness: he could not resist a good story or a good joke. Durbin added the pertinent comment to me: 'When I was PPS, we lost all the gold; and when you were PPS, we lost the Chancellor.'

Nevertheless, the personal tragedy was great. Dalton had done great service to the country and Labour Party in wartime and peace. He, more than any other single person, had by his own personal efforts, rescued the old Distressed Areas from the threat of heavy unemployment after the war, and strengthened the economy of the country by doing so. Secondly he gave more disinterested help to young recruits in his own department and in Parliament than anyone else in his generation. Thirdly, he did as much as any single individual to swing the Labour Party in support of re-armament and resistance to Hitler in the 1930s. His weaknesses – apart from indiscretion – were an exaggeration of the benefits of cheap money, which he shared with Keynes, and a comparative lack of expertise in international as opposed to domestic economics, which he shared with almost all British economists. The virtues vastly outweighed the frailties; but the indis-cretion damaged his career.

Years afterwards Walter Layton, who was still chairman of the *News Chronicle* and *Star* in 1947, told me the full irony of the story. John Carvel, on hearing the details of the Budget from Dalton a few minutes before 3.30 p.m. on 12 November, stepped straight into a telephone box. The call went straight through, and the stop-press section of the next edition was held up waiting for a racing result. Instead the *Star* inserted the Budget news. It was on sale in Fleet Street by 3.45 p.m. and on the desk of the Editor of the *Evening Standard* a few minutes later. It was a million-to-one chance that a conversation at Westminster after 3.20 p.m. should be on sale in a news-paper at 3.45 p.m., and has probably seldom if ever happened before or since. Percy Cudlipp's comment to me a few days after Dalton's resign-ation was as follows: 'What a profession journalism is when it is one's pro-fessional duty to trap someone else into a breach of their professional duty.' He well expressed my own increasing distaste for the whole scoop aspect of journalism.

In mid-December, four weeks after Dalton's resignation, Attlee offered me, and I accepted, the job of Economic Secretary to the Treasury, a new post, as second junior Minister to the Chancellor. (Up till then there had been only one and we managed with two till 1951.) The change of Chancellor had enabled the whole machine to be rationalized. A new Economic Department of the Treasury was set up; but the mistake of 1945 and 1964 in making this a separate Ministry duplicating and conflicting with 'the Treasury' was avoided. Instead the new department became – together with the old Treasury Budget, taxation and overseas departments – part of a single, but larger organization responsible to Cripps as 'Chancellor and Minister of Economic Affairs'. And though I should naturally have preferred it not to happen this way, the Dalton tragedy had ended by affording me as Economic Secretary a remarkable opportunity and piece of good fortune. My chief fear was that my parliamentary inexperience might land Cripps and the Department in some form of trouble. In January I had to make my first Front Bench speech in moving a minor Treasury Order, and my heartfelt relief and surprise at surmounting this hurdle without disaster led me into one of those rare and brief moments of elation – such as I suppose we all experience – and so to a late-night walk in St James's Park to calm myself down.

The Treasury as refashioned and re-inforced at the end of 1947 contained not merely a Chancellor whose prestige and moral authority, thanks to his August speech in the House, were unique, but also the most efficient organization and strongest office team in the post-war years. Certainly the task was stiff enough: to re-build the country's shattered economic strength after the war, the end of Lend-Lease and the convertibility crisis, and to maintain national solvency while a vast programme of social reform was launched by Parliament. At the heart of the new economic wing, where my responsibility lay, was the new Central Economic Planning Staff already started by Cripps as Minister of Economic Affairs, and headed by Edwin Plowden. Added to this were the Economic Section of the Treasury, directed by Robert Hall; the Central Statistical Office; the headquarters of the

Regional Boards now being switched on to the Production and Exports Campaign, and the Economic Information Unit, under Clem Leslie, whose job was to publish factual economic information and convince the country that production and exports had to come before higher consumption. The overseas side of the Treasury (Overseas Finance or OF), which had been the weakest in Dalton's time, was completely re-organized. Wilfred Eady, who had headed OF under Dalton and was unhappily inexpert in foreign exchange issues, was transferred to home policy. At a private conversation at No. 11, when I was still a PPS in November 1947, as a post-mortem on the convertibility fiasco, I had been alarmed by Eady's imprecision. Instead Otto Clarke and Leslie Rowan were now put in charge of a greatly strengthened department, and the situation was transformed.

I was also exceedingly fortunate, on arriving at the Treasury, not merely in the remarkably high level of abilities of the new team, but because so many of the leading characters in it had been previous close colleagues of mine. It was far the ablest group with whom I ever had the chance to work before or since. Bridges and Norman Brook, the latter not formally a member of the Treasury, but very close to it, I knew well from the years at No. 10. Edwin Plowden,[1] who exerted great influence throughout these years, had been a regular lunch companion of mine in Fleet Street in *Economist* days during the early 1930s. As Chief Executive of the Ministry of Aircraft Production in the war, he had gained an impressive reputation as a practical organizer, and his sympathy with Cripps's religious beliefs gave him great persuasive power with the Chancellor. Sometimes it seemed to some of us that Plowden's inclination to share Cripps's faith in strength through sacrifice might push this moral maxim too far. But in 1947–51, as we have all learnt since, it was certainly a fault on the right side. Robert Hall[2] had been an Oxford Socialist in the 1930s and a colleague of mine at the Ministry of Supply throughout the war. As an economist his pre-eminent quality was common sense – the most valuable for an economist in Whitehall. He was brief, and we could all understand what he said. His long sustained and harmonious partnership with Plowden forestalled any conflict between the Economic Section and the Planning Staff, and was one main key to the success of the whole team. On the overseas side, which was clearly to be crucial, Otto Clarke[3] and Lelsie Rowan[4] formed an equally effective partnership. Clarke was a brilliant statistician and economist and now an experienced civil servant. His understanding of foreign trade and foreign exchange issues was as clear as Eady's and Dalton's had been fallible. Rowan's skill and energy in using the government machine to produce firm decisions and quick action were unrivalled in Whitehall at this time. He

[1] Later Lord Plowden, Chairman of Tube Investments and many public Committees of Inquiry.
[2] Later Lord Roberthall.
[3] See also p. 67.
[4] Later Managing Director of Vickers.

worked as Chairman of a committee, the ONC (Overseas Negotiations Committee). The ONC, representing all departments, met almost daily, marshalled the facts, and managed the UK's trading and financial dealings in these years with almost every separate country in the world. Some ministers did at moments ask me whether the ONC was not taking over the functions of the Cabinet. But unquestionably it played a decisive part in extracting us from the fearful payments deficit of 1947.

Among the rest of the new Treasury team, Denis Rickett, economist colleague of mine at All Souls in the early 1930s, became Plowden's deputy on the Planning Staff and later moved over to Overseas Finance. Also working at first on the Planning Staff were Alan Hitchman, my closest Ministry of Labour contact in wartime days, and Austin Robinson, the Cambridge economist, who designed the four-year plan prepared as the basis for Marshall Aid. He made remarkably accurate forecasts of the future decline in the British percentage – then over 20 per cent – of world exports of manufactures (despite a rise in the absolute total) as other great industrial nations such as Germany, Japan and Russia recovered from the war. These forecasts were thought to be pessimistic at the time. In later years I read frequent press articles deploring this 'decline', which was in fact perfectly predictable in 1948 as general recovery from the war progressed. Cripps's private office was managed by Burke Trend and later by William Armstrong, both of whom I found had, besides other talents, the best qualities of a father confessor with whom one could discuss one's toughest problems. Clem Leslie, Head of the Economic Information Unit, had moved from the old North Thames Gas Board in the 1930s, to organize publicity for Herbert Morrison's wartime Ministry of Supply and Home Security, and possessed an admirable flair for distinguishing between economic information which was his province, and political propaganda which was not.

In all this the old school of Treasury officials may appear to have been wholly swamped. But not entirely. Sir Bernard Gilbert, a stalwart life-time Treasury servant, manfully kept up the tradition. He shared my responsibility for the future finances of the nationalized industries and used to observe that the Government's policy, supported by the electorate, must go forward. But he ventured to predict that in time salaries and wages in these industries would rise, prices would be held down, and deficits would mount; and that in the end the Exchequer would have to bear the losses. Once when we were striving vainly to keep some department's expenditure under control, Gilbert said to me: 'I've always found that with the female members of my own family, the only way to stop people spending money is to see they don't have it.' Occasionally, the unworthy thought crept into my mind that there might be as much truth in his outmoded wisdom as in the advanced thought of the Keynesian economists surrounding me. But the old Treasury, strictly in this case the Inland Revenue, contributed brilliant young men as well, notably Arthur Cockfield, later Chairman of the Price Commission in the 1970s,[5] but in Cripps's time head of the Inland Revenue's statistical department. With a first-class mathematical brain, Cockfield, aged barely thirty, knew nearly the whole direct tax system in his head, and in Budget discussions would flatly contradict – and silence – Stafford Cripps and Edward Bridges with a self-confidence that took my breath away. 'No Chancellor,' he would say, 'that is quite wrong. It works like this...' and we all humbly listened.

Every weekday morning throughout my four years in the Treasury (and we all worked on Saturdays in those years) Cripps held a 'morning meeting' at 9.30 a.m. in his room. Cripps had wanted it to start at 9 a.m. every day, but agreed to a compromise on 9.30 a.m. and 10 a.m. on Monday as an act of clemency to those who lived some way from Westminster. He himself had always done at least three hours' work before this gathering. In those days we all set a stern example of public economy (which faded in the later Conservative years), and there were no official cars for Permanent Secretaries or Parliamentary Secretaries like myself. Bridges, Head of the Civil Service and the Treasury, lived in Epsom, and at times could be seen running down the pavement of Great George Street so as to reach the Chancellor's room at 9.30. My journey from Hampstead by Underground involved one change. But it was my pride never in three years with Cripps and one with Gaitskell, to have reached the Chancellor's private office after 9.29½. Once, Hilary Marquand entered the Chancellor's room at 9.30½. Cripps addressed him icily: 'Good afternoon,' and Marquand was not amused. The meeting lasted usually only fifteen to twenty minutes, and by the time I reached my own office later I often felt too exhausted by the race in the Underground to do anything useful for some time. For all too often we had been kept in the House till midnight or after on the previous evening. Those present at 9.30 consisted, besides Cripps, of the blameless Glenvil Hall as Financial Secretary, Bridges, Gilbert, Plowden, Robert Hall, Wilfred Eady, Leslie and myself. The idea was that anyone, starting with Cripps, could raise any point, or ask any question he wished – briefly – and others could comment. Formal decisions were not taken, but initiatives were often launched. The session gave one a daily chance to find out what was going on, and if necessary to ask. Certainly it saved much time in circulation of papers and two-sided conversations. Gaitskell, when he took over in 1950, continued these meetings without change.

Meanwhile, a fairly simple structure of ministerial committees maintained the necessary co-ordination with departments outside the Treasury and the proprieties of ministerial responsibility. It was rather more stable than the hastily improvised Food and Fuel Committees of the hectic two years 1945–7. At the top was the Economic Policy Committee, formed in the 1947 reorganization, with the Prime Minister as Chairman, and the Foreign Secretary and Defence Minister represented as well as economic

[5] And as Lord Cockfield a Treasury Minister in the 1979 Tory Government.

ministers. But the real work was done by the Production Committee under Cripps as Chairman, including the main spending, as well as economic ministers. I was allowed to be an additional Treasury member. Here conflicts between Cripps, Bevan, Gaitskell and Strachey in particular were fought out almost weekly. The rows over food, coal, oil, power stations, housing, etc., which had tended in 1945–7 to explode in the Cabinet (if not the press), were normally ironed out after 1947 in the Production Committee. Cripps, like Attlee, was an admirable Chairman. Repetition of a paper laid before the committee was vetoed. Cripps usually started by asking: 'Does anyone disagree with this paper?' Neither indecision nor loquacity were suffered gladly. Bevan, for whom Cripps always had a soft spot, was allowed a few more verbal frolics than others, but even he shut up if Cripps insisted.

Once, to everyone's surprise, when Cripps was at the height of his reputation and authority, Gaitskell challenged on constitutional grounds the right of Plowden's Planning Staff to purport to take decisions on fuel investment programmes for which he, Gaitskell, as Minister of Fuel and Power, was responsible. As Minister, he reminded us, he was accountable to Parliament, not to the Chancellor or the Cabinet or the Prime Minister. Cripps looked down his nose with a rather glacial expression, and said he would consult the Head of the Civil Service on the constitutional issue. But Gaitskell was not contradicted or rebuked, and the Investment Programme was reconsidered. At another meeting in 1948 Gaitskell had circulated a paper proposing the abandonment of open-cast coal-mining in view of the success of the Coal Board in raising deep-mined output since 1947. Since most ministers present were senior to me, I did not say much at these meetings; but this time was bold enough to suggest that there were so many changes, chances and risks in the future fuel prospects that it might be better to keep open-cast mining as one practical insurance. Gaitskell replied that he would think again and decided to let open-cast continue. In the 1970s it still survived. This incident I used to quote to those who occasionally accused Gaitskell of unreasonable obstinacy.

Servicing these ministerial committees, a few, but not too many, official committees co-ordinated different departments' policies. In the early war years, confusion was caused by conflicts between departments, but by the end of the war, co-ordination had been carried to a fine art. By the 1960s it had been carried so far that decisions were inordinately delayed to get approval from yet one more committee or consult one more public body. Under the Cripps régime, apart from Rowan's Overseas Negotiations Committee already mentioned, Plowden presided over an official Investments Programme Committee. This was useful in tailoring the programmes for coal, electricity, oil, factory-building and housing, road building, etc., to the resources available. It also suggested alternative mixes so that ministers, as they should, could rationally decide that within the limits practicable housing, for instance, should receive a little more and power stations a little less – a function which Parliament should perform for public spending as a whole if some procedure as efficient as the 1948 Investments Programmes Committee could be devised.

Another crucial cog in the Cripps machine was the Import Programme Committee under Otto Clarke which decided, period by period, how much of each type of imports could be allowed in. For one of the great secrets of the success of the Cripps régime was the almost complete exclusion by import quota of manufactured consumer goods. I was myself conscripted as chairman of the Raw Materials Committee, which survived from the war and 'allocated' almost every material from newsprint to softwood and copper. It consisted of a marathon meeting every three months of about fifty people – all officials apart from myself – lasting seven or eight hours of one day, reaching by a sort of Dutch auction what were in theory 'unanimous' decisions on the rations of everything to everybody – e.g. timber to the Ministry of Agriculture for constructing hen-houses. I never thought it a notably efficient or orderly mechanism; but nobody could devise a better. And nobody wanted to take it over from me; so that I bore it out almost to the edge of doom – actually till I moved from Economic Secretary to Financial Secretary in February 1950, after which Jim Callaghan shouldered this cross.

Then there was the Budget Committee – so hallowed and secret in 1945–51, that, like the mysteries of the Vestal Virgins in classical Rome, it was not allowed by tradition to be even mentioned to the uninitiated. It consisted of all the chief officials within the Treasury, Inland Revenue and Customs, who prepared the Budget all the year round; and it was supposed to be unknown even to the rest of the Treasury, let alone to lesser breeds. But as the alternatives and dilemmas became apparent in the winter each year, Treasury Ministers had to be brought in and decisions taken in meetings stretching right up to the Budget. Cripps characteristically instituted a system by which we adjourned for at least one Budget working week-end from Friday evening to Monday morning in some secret hide-out in the country. Most favoured rendezvous was a home for rehabilitating nervous invalids in deepest Sussex near Horsham, and plenty of innocent mirth was excited among the participants at the thought of public reactions to the news that the annual Budget was being constructed in a rest-home for nervous wrecks. In sober fact the opportunity of all-day discussion with all concerned, in total seclusion in the light of all the known facts, was a thoroughly business-like method of weighing up all Budget possibilities. In the few odd moments in which Cripps allowed us off work I used to play chess with William Armstrong; but we never finished a game.

Certainly the Economic Information Unit under Clem Leslie, was an essential organ in the whole Cripps enterprise. It expounded to the public in pamphlets, leaflets, popular editions of the annual Economic Survey, and in 'Production Conferences' (which I had to address) all over the country, the unwelcome message that the nation had to build up industrial and social capital and pay our debts, and export on a huge scale, before we could raise living standards. All this could of course be easily caricatured as austerity, Crippsian puritanism, etc.; and when critics could think of no more original theme, so it was. (Actually, the word 'austerity' in its modern sense was instituted by Oliver Lyttleton, a very unpuritan character, when he rationed clothes during the war.) In Cripps's time I sometimes doubted the value of the information effort. But in the retrospect of thirty years I suspect that, like the Production Campaign of 1945–6,[6] it was more effective than we realized at the time. What government, what Chancellor would not have been thankful in the 1960s or 1970s to have achieved ever-growing export volume, a rising pay rate of 4 or 5 per cent a year and of living costs of little more. Yet in the Cripps era when wage-earners, particularly the miners, could have easily held the country up to any ransom, this level of comparative price and pay stability was maintained.

The information campaign of that period could claim one other outstanding virtue. It was grounded on a clear distinction between political propaganda and hard information. Public money, according to the principles then followed, could only be used for the spread of information or arguments which were not seriously in dispute between any major sections of public opinion. Government policy, if the Opposition or any major group disagreed, did not qualify. Road safety or national saving passed the test. Nationalization did not. Herbert Morrison stuck to this doctrine. It is a notable sign of the decline in public standards between the 1940s and the 1970s that both the Heath and Wilson Governments of the latter years used government funds – e.g. in the 1975 referendum – to propagate Government policy even though it was repudiated by a large section of public opinion.

And what of Cripps himself? He was a changed man since his Marxist phase in the 1930s, when he replied to me at a Fabian conference that arguments for armed resistance to Hitler were 'the arguments used in 1914'. The opportunity of a man's job at the Ministry of Aircraft Production had turned him from a doctrinaire into a practical organizer of immense ability. Or rather, his remarkable intellectual capacity was now, apart from his work in the courts, fully used for the first time. His August 1947 speech had completed the transformation by both raising his political reputation and strengthening his own confidence that the national job he was doing was the most crucial in the Government. As a result the flesh was driven to the last ounce of exhaustion – and indeed literally to his premature retirement and death. After that August 1947 speech, in the late evening when almost any other minister or MP would have paused for a drink, Cripps walked straight

[6] See page 152.

back to his room and opened his Red Boxes. He often attended late-night sessions in the House; and if they went through the night, carried on with the next day's work without a break. I remember one Budget week-end at the home for nervous wrecks in Sussex at which he proposed Sunday breakfast at 8 a.m. and only reluctantly agreed to 8.15 a.m. as a compromise. When we all arrived, barely shaved at this hour, he received us beaming and had already been to church, done one hour's work and walked round the estate. Attlee used to tell with schoolboy glee how a caller had arrived at 5 a.m. at No. 10, saying that he had an appointment with the Chancellor of the Exchequer. The policeman, assuming him to be a lunatic, played for time. But when the visitor insisted: 'Sir Stafford Cripps asked me to come at this hour,' the policeman replied: 'Oh, him. Yes, please come in.'

Strangely enough, Cripps, though he had managed a munition factory in the First War, did not possess that inborn flair for economic and industrial policy, which was second nature to Bevin and Andrew Duncan in wartime and Hugh Gaitskell later. He never wholly rid himself of the static lawyer-like approach. Indeed he never fully understood in the crisis of 1949 the arguments for and against devaluation, though he could of course have recited them all with great lucidity. Why was it, I often asked myself at the Treasury, that despite this, he was able to give such distinguished leadership to the whole team? The answer was, I believe, twofold: first that he used the outstanding powers he had to the very limit of his capacity; and secondly that he was served by an exceptionally qualified and talented group of advisers. In particular, if Bridges and Plowden both took a different view from him, he was disposed to believe that he might be wrong. (He regarded me, I suspect, though he treated me with the utmost kindness and courtesy, as still something of a dangerous radical.) Later he placed an ever-growing trust in Gaitskell.

One aspect, however, of Cripps's method of reaching decisions was sometimes disconcerting to the rest of us. He tended, after having formed his decision, to imply that it had been imparted to him by some higher wisdom; and that those who argued against it were allying themselves with the forces of evil. At times the rest of us would suspect that the Higher Power was really Nye Bevan, or Plowden, or someone else who had happened to get in first. This might possibly have prompted a certain scramble by different members of the team – though the 9.30 a.m. meetings helped to forestall this – to speak first and be identified with the higher wisdom; had not a spirit of restraint prevailed. One could not work closely with Cripps for long, however, without becoming convinced that his religious convictions were profoundly genuine and sincere, and that he believed they could be translated directly into political action. This had both its advantages and disadvantages. Precisely as Sir Philip Magnus[7] has said of

[7] Philip Magnus, *Gladstone* (London, 1954), p. 256.

Gladstone: 'It is a great strength to any man once he has embarked on a course of action to believe that he is executing God's will. It is, however, difficult in such circumstances to do justice to the motives of opponents.' Exactly so with Cripps. Oliver Stanley, the wittiest member of the 1945 House of Commons, and one of those rare old-fashioned aristocratic Tories, too well off to need City directorships, was regarded by Cripps as a mere frivolous cynic if not an agent of the devil. Once when I had to explain to the House that Cripps had not, as Hansard said, 'indicated assent' to some proposition, but had 'indicated dissent', Stanley asked: 'How would the present Chancellor indicate assent to anything?'

The parallel between Gladstone and Cripps in this respect (though in others of course they sharply differed) only became apparent to me when I read Sir Philip Magnus's biography some time after my three years' close working with Cripps.[8] One evening at the Treasury in these years, after a day's work, Trend, who had by then served Cripps daily for a good time as Private Secretary, was debating with me how we could restrain him from ruining his health and strength by overwork. We concluded, reluctantly, that nothing could be done. 'The fact is,' said Trend, 'that the things of this world mean nothing to him.' Later I read Magnus's description of the impression made by Gladstone on his Private Secretary, Sir Edward Hamilton. Magnus speaks of Gladstone's 'habitual unworldliness',[9] and records that his 'innocence, simplicity and candour made the most profound impression upon Hamilton.' Naturally the facile cynic will attribute a high degree of hypocrisy or at least self-deception to both Gladstone and Cripps. Self-deception, perhaps. But from my three years' contact with Cripps, and the evidence given by Magnus, I would surmise that cynics discovering hypocrisy are here wide of the mark, and that both Gladstone and Cripps were examples of that eccentric type of English politician who believes that the will of God can be immediately translated into political decisions. No doubt this caused much perturbation to their colleagues and led at times to avoidable errors. And it was Cripps's misfortune that to many people (such as Disraeli, if not Oliver Stanley) the very existence of such characters, particularly in politics, is well-nigh incredible. Churchill was supposed to have remarked at this time, seeing Cripps stalking down a Commons passage; 'There, but for the grace of God, goes God.' Whether authentic or not, there was some truth in this jest, but not the whole truth.

Yet Cripps had another side less seen by the public or even Parliament. Despite his ferocious hours of work, he was a great believer in personal contact with colleagues high and low and in personal encouragement and particularly in occasional meetings between ministers without officials present. He several times addressed the entire London staff of the Treasury, Inland Revenue and Customs headquarters – several thousand people – in

[8] It was first published in 1954.
[9] Magnus, pp. 306 and 109.

the Central Hall, Westminster, to explain what the department was trying to do. He wrote a number of us warm personal notes at Christmas, wishing us (at least in my case) not merely health and happiness but 'deep satisfaction in your work'. He also arranged, and paid for, a fortnightly private dinner in the House of Commons of hand-picked economic ministers which lasted throughout his three years as Chancellor, at which we could all talk freely. He had noticed the odd feature of the Westminster political system by which officials meet together in private and concert their ideas and projects, and ministers meet with officials present, but ministers virtually never meet on their own. Present at these fortnightly dinners were: Cripps, Bevan, Gaitskell, Strachey, Wilson, Strauss, Marquand and myself. As XYZ had moved to the House and met on alternate Wednesday evenings, I had the most welcome chance of a meeting with Gaitskell and others and a free political discussion once a week.

Needless to say, Nye Bevan dominated the conversation during the Cripps dinners and not seldom poured forth a stream of mischievous gibes about most of his other senior colleagues. Bevin and Morrison were his favourite targets. Once one of us protested gently that Bevin did perhaps possess a few modest merits. 'Yes,' Bevan conceded: 'He does at least have the courage of his own bad grammar.' But Bevan would always stop dead when Cripps, usually putting a hand on his arm, told him to be quiet, as serious economic debate was now to begin. For nobody else other than Attlee in Cabinet would Bevan check the flow. Cripps had a direct and abiding personal accord with Bevan, which was based, one assumed, on their joint 'Socialist League' aberrations of the 1930s. As two poachers turned gamekeepers, they were drawn together. Cripps used to ask me frequently to go and talk to Bevan (his room as Minister of Health was only a few minutes' walk from the Chancellor's in Great George Street where Cripps always worked) in order to avoid friction. I normally found Bevan at this stage remarkably co-operative (my familiarity with A. L. Rowse enabled me to ignore the outrageous verbal antics). Bevan would always listen to a message from Cripps. Indeed, throughout these years Cripps went to great personal pains to restrain Bevan from causing conflict and getting himself into trouble. Sometimes Cripps approached him through Lady Cripps, Jenny Lee or Bevan's old mother in Tredegar. Once Cripps travelled himself all the way to Tredegar at a week-end to invoke Mrs Bevan's help in inducing Nye (in Dean Swift's words) to 'curb his tongue and pen'. On his return, I asked Cripps what luck he had had with Mrs Bevan. 'She said,' Cripps replied: 'If only I could get that boy's tongue between my teeth.'

Only Cripps could have claimed the right, without any formal authority, to invite to these fortnightly dinners those economic ministers whom he chose and exclude others. We found there debates on economic policy most valuable. They varied between general economic disquisitions from Strachey and factual reports on the world cereal, timber or metal markets from Harold

Wilson. Only once was acrimony narrowly averted. I had noticed that Bevan's immediate smoking-room circle, where he normally appeared in the evenings, were almost all without children, and sometimes wondered if there were truth in the famous words attributed by Thucydides[10] to Pericles in his Funeral Speech: 'Those without children cannot give fair and honest counsel to the State.' Bevan was denouncing with surprising vitriol a current proposal to give special anaesthetics to women in childbirth. Gaitskell, Wilson and I rashly ventured to disagree. Bevan turned on us: 'Your wives,' he said, 'are nothing but middle-class neurotics.' Always believing in self-defence, I ill-advisedly retorted: 'They are not childless ones anyway.' Cripps sternly and briskly switched the conversation to the Bank Rate and dollar drain, and peace was restored. Bevan, however explosive his vocabulary, never bore any grudge for this sort of exchange.

Though economics was not really Cripps's strong point, his intellectual and forensic capacity were too great for this ever to be apparent to Parliament and the public. Once in 1948 I spent most of the morning studying the answers to Treasury Questions which I had to give in the House that afternoon in his absence. A minute or two before Questions were due, he unexpectedly turned up, put the question book under his arm, did not open it till the first question was due, and gave the most impressive series of supplementary answers I had heard for a long time. Incidentally Cripps, like Attlee, by brevity and cutting out waffle, would get through two or three times as many questions in a given time as became usual in the slipshod habits of the 1970s. Yet his moral authority, which the Opposition unintentionally enhanced by their constant attacks on his 'austerity', 'asceticism' and so on, was an even greater strength. Once at Question Time he was rashly accused of dishonesty by a Tory backbencher, Godfrey Nicholson. Called on by Cripps to withdraw, Nicholson said he meant 'political' not 'personal' dishonesty. 'I do not recognize the distinction,' Cripps replied.

This moral authority was invaluable in holding together the team of economic ministers, including Bevan, just as Attlee's alone composed the wider group of potential prima donnas in the Cabinet. The crucial value of the Attlee/Cripps reputation for scrupulous standards became clear to us immature politicians when the Lynskey Tribunal (already mentioned)[11] was set up in the autumn of 1948. As the Tribunal proceeded, the egregrious Sydney Stanley, finding he enjoyed complete legal immunity, poured out a stream of wild fabrications about one after another member of the Government. I found my name one day in the headlines of the *Evening Standard*; and in the text this turned out to be another Jay, a journalist, whom the inventive Mr Stanley claimed to have invited to a dinner which in fact never took place. I asked Cripps if I had any legal remedy against this misuse of names and he said: 'None.' A day or two later Stanley tried to drag

[10] Book 2, para. 44.
[11] See page 136.

the names of Attlee and Cripps into his romances, and all his other utterances were thenceforth drowned in an atmosphere of general mirth. The reputations of Attlee and Cripps were the Government's greatest asset.

Earlier than this, in February 1948, an almost equally strange incident occurred which might have ruined my relations with Cripps and indeed much else. It was only a month or two after Dalton's resignation following the notorious Budget leak, and my own arrival at the Treasury; but we had already discussed the forthcoming April 1948 Budget. On emerging from the House after answering Treasury Questions, I was approached by Hugh Massingham of the *Observer*, who used to call on Francis Williams and myself regularly at No. 10; and he suggested to me a cup of tea in the strangers' dining room. I was just about to sit at the one vacant table, when I saw, eyeing us hard from the next table, Harold Macmillan, Lord Winterton (also of the Tory Front Bench) and James Margach, Massingham's opposite number at the *Sunday Times*. I hesitated, and then realized I must sit down. We talked, and as soon as Massingham said anything remotely relating to the Budget, I said that if he continued I would walk out. He desisted, and I left as soon as possible, but with the eyes of Macmillan, Winterton and Margach hard upon me.

The following Sunday, to my alarm, Massingham's column was largely devoted to the coming Budget, and one or two of his guesses – not surprisingly – were near the truth. Margach could not fail to notice this, and the horrible prospect loomed of a Private Notice Question six weeks later on the day after the Budget (as with Dalton) about the *Observer* article. I had said nothing, but how could I prove it? For these were the days when Budget secrecy was the prime criterion of the integrity of a government. I saw visions of another Tribunal and Hartley Shawcross asking me all sorts of clever questions. To avoid six weeks' mounting suspense, my first impulse was to tell Cripps the whole story. But might he not ask himself why, if I had said nothing, did I trouble him with so trivial an incident? What ought one to do? I meditated for forty-eight hours, and decided to say nothing. But then I had to wait and work for six anxious weeks till Question Time the day after the Budget, when – nothing happened. Thereafter, I resolved that, as long as I was a minister, I would keep at a fair distance from Fleet Street and all its works.

Another unexpected incident in this period confirmed my faith in the importance of Question Time in the House, which I came greatly to value both in government and opposition, quite contrary to the contemporary fashion of deprecating its effectiveness. To a question by a Scottish Tory MP, Lord William Scott, about a candidate alleged to have cheated in the Civil Service exam, I gave the official answer that the Civil Service Commission had no doubt he had cheated. Scott wrote a letter to me and said he was unconvinced, and after further enquiries came to see me before putting down another Question. Eventually the Commissioner set up a special committee of enquiry which probed all the evidence, decided the candidate had made a mistake and not cheated, and reinstated him in the civil service. At another time an employee of the Stationery Office, handling top-secret documents, was found to be a Communist, and many hours of ministerial and official Treasury time were spent in discovering for him another job in the Stationery Office within reach of his home which did not involve secret papers. A waste of time in both cases, or a crucially worthwhile safeguard of civil liberties? The latter, I believe.

A likewise special but different job which fell to me as Economic Secretary was to be Chairman of a combined ministerial and official working party on food distribution, on which the Ministry of Food was represented by Edith Summerskill and the Ministry of Agriculture by George Brown. George Brown, overcome by indignation at the heresies of the Ministry of Food, expressed himself frequently with a passion hitherto unknown in Whitehall, which astonished the officials and scandalized Edith Summerskill. It became normal for me to apologize personally by telephone after each meeting for my colleague's verbal fertility. The experiment was not repeated.

Such were some of the less normal and more picturesque incidents of working life at the Treasury in the years after 1947. But the aim and object of the whole operation was to steer the country back into payments surplus, and negotiate with the US an agreement for Marshall Aid and a four-year plan for ourselves and the rest of Western Europe. If we had then known the subsequent years' economic history, we should have been more daunted by the task than we were, and more pleased with our early successes. The tide of success and failure repeatedly ebbed and flowed from 1947 to 1951. Throughout 1948, with the Marshall Aid Agreement signed in July, recovery was remarkable; till in the spring of 1949 sterling swung again into retreat and forced the 1949 devaluation. From September 1949 till nearly midsummer of 1951 we achieved an almost continuous surplus and an inflow of dollars; but at midsummer 1951 the tide suddenly turned again. Marshall Aid was perhaps (till this day as I write in the 1970s) the most far-sighted and constructive initiative since the Second World War. General Marshall's speech in June 1947 was instantly seized on by Bevin with both hands, and Oliver Franks was despatched to Paris to negotiate the arrangements which later became the OEEC (Organization for European Economic Co-operation). The final Marshall Aid Agreement was signed by Bevin, Cripps and Lew Douglas, US Ambassador in London, on 6 July 1948, and the operation of it for the UK handed over to the Treasury. Our 'Long-term Programme of the UK', prepared by the new Treasury, was presented to the OEEC and Marshall Aid authorities in October 1948, and published as a White Paper in December (Cmd 7572). Our relations with the US Marshall Aid team in London were one of the happiest parts of the whole operation

It was one of the still little realized ironies of the post-war years that while Germany, France and other Continental countries were able to use their Marshall Aid payments to invest in public and private industry, we were compelled simultaneously to pay off our huge war debts to India, Egypt and other Commonwealth countries. Only Canada, Australia and New Zealand agreed to remit part of the debt. It was another of my Treasury jobs to negotiate on these 'sterling balances'. We started with the Ceylon Government represented by Mr Jayawardene, a charming and highly sophisticated political leader, who eventually became Prime Minister in 1977. Not surprisingly he refused to contemplate repudiation of the debt. The whole idea that we could, as the Americans thought, 'cancel' or 'write off' these debts was an illusion; just as was the idea revived by such as Roy Jenkins in the next twenty years that we could somehow 'liquidate the sterling balances'. The simple truth was, and is, that if people wish to hold sterling you normally neither want to, nor can, prevent them. After repayment of all our wartime sterling debts by 1952, the sterling balances were higher than in 1945; and by 1977 and 1978, after all sorts of efforts at 'adjustment' and 'liquidation', they were higher than at any time in the post-war years. Meanwhile Marshall Aid generated economic recovery among its Continental recipients, notably Germany, where growth progressed more rapidly in the 1950s before the formation of the Common Market than it did afterwards. Germany had no war debts this time.

However, in the UK in 1948 all went well. The most successful post-war price and pay restraint policy was introduced by a Cripps White Paper of January 1948. In the four years 1947–51[12] payrates and the cost of living rose only 21 and 25 per cent respectively (i.e. only a few per cent per year). The most dramatic turn-around between 1947 and 1948 occurred in the balance of payments. The deficit on the current payments balance which had been £630 million in 1947 fell to only £30 million in 1948, and in both 1949 and 1950 we were in surplus. Production, in real – not just money-terms, also rose rapidly.[13]

In these years a vast deal of my time, together with that of Glenvil Hall as Financial Secretary and Frank Soskice as Solicitor-General, was consumed by the Budget and Finance Bill debates. The Committee as well as the Report Stage of the Finance Bill was in those days debated on the floor of the House, and frequent late night and all-night sittings with numerous divisions were normal. Soskice was the mainstay of the Government throughout these ordeals, and the more complex and legalistic the debate became, the more inexhaustible his stamina appeared to be. Glenvil Hall and I used to have to beg him to take a rest and allow us at any rate to reply to one amendment in five – often without success. Two other almost as pressing claims on one's time were reading and signing letters from MPs,

[12] See figures on page 211.
[13] See figures on page 211.

and receiving deputations largely about taxation from vested interests of all kinds. I had once to write to the stage Tory right-wing MP of the day, Sir Waldron Smithers, telling him on behalf of the Stationery Office that Hansard could not republish a speech of his in the House calling Attlee and Herbert Morrison 'traitors', because this would render both him and the Stationery Office liable to damages for defamation. I expected in reply a loud denunciation of the Treasury for suppressing free speech. Instead Sir Waldron wrote and thanked me cordially for saving him from heavy damages. The trouble about the tax deputations was that one almost always knew before they came precisely what they would say. I was impressed, however, by one most persuasive plea for easing the Purchase Tax on cars from a young motor-manufacturer, Donald Stokes, and an even more splendid appeal, which I did not accept, for a major cut in the whisky tax from Bob Boothby. But it was as a result of these deputations that I boldly decided to exempt the Land Rover, as not being an ordinary passenger car, from Purchase Tax; a concession which long survived and may have contributed something to the world success of the Land Rover.

In Budget policy I pressed Cripps strongly and had the private support of Dalton, to include in his April 1948 Budget a once-for-all 'annual property tax', such as I had advocated at the start of the war. He adopted this in the form of the 'Special Contribution', a once-for-all capital levy or wealth tax of 1 per cent on personal capital fortune as defined for Death Duties. We also in this period raised the Death Duties on fortunes of £1,000,000 and over to 80 per cent where it stood for many years. These measures were partly a short-term support for the successful pay restraint policy of 1947–51, but they also followed from the argument of my 1937 *The Socialist Case* that large inherited fortunes should be the prime object of direct taxation. Secondly, the job at the Treasury also gave me the chance to promote the Development Area policy I helped to initiate at the Board of Trade. I was also Chairman of a combined ministerial and official Distribution of Industry Committee. Harold Wilson as President of the Board of Trade, vigorously sustained the policy, and as a result in the years 1944–8, some 50 per cent of all new factory space built in the country was in Development Areas, as compared with less than 10 per cent in the same areas under *laissez-faire* policies before 1939. This gave heartfelt pleasure to all of us; and it was about this form of expenditure that Dalton said he had 'a song in his heart'.

One issue on which I felt forced to fight a running battle with the official Treasury and Cripps himself in 1948 and 1949 was the food subsidies. Earlier, while Dalton was still Chancellor, I had suggested to him a compromise by which food subsidies were not indefinitely increased so as to stop any rise in food prices, but were stabilized at the existing figure of about £400 million a year. I argued with Cripps that we should stick to the Dalton compromise and in the end this was substantially agreed. Here again the subsidy policy was justified, I thought, both by the short-term need for price restraint and the fundamental long-term argument set out in *The Socialist Case* for holding down the price of necessities. But this particular fight behind the scenes was exhausting. I remember one long night in a room in the House, when the Finance Bill Committee was dragging on downstairs, and my three-year-old daughter Catherine was seriously ill in hospital, writing a perhaps over-emotional appeal to Cripps not to give way. One comfort in that tormenting summer night was the great sympathy and kindness shown me by Bevan as Minister of Health earlier in the evening when I confided in him about my daughter's illness. In the event, she rapidly recovered and Cripps held firm. Indeed, as a complement of the subsidy policy, we soon removed virtually all remaining taxes on food.

Another special initiative which cost a lot of time and trouble, was a Treasury and Bank of England committee intended to restrain excessive credit inflation by the banks. In the 1970s the so-called 'monetarists' fell into the old fallacy of regarding an increase in the stock of money as virtually the only source of inflation. In 1948 I had to argue in the face of much dispute, that profit-seeking expansion of credit by the banks was at least one potential source of demand inflation, and indeed that the banks' drive to increase advances might offset much of the effect of the Government's unpopular and disinflationary Budgets. Humphrey Mynors represented the Bank of England on this committee and Robert Hall and Wilfred Eady, the Economic Section and the Treasury. I hope that on balance we held back a potential bank-led inflation. A more moderate attitude from the bankers then, and the monetarists in the 1970s, would have been salutary in both cases.

It was on 3 September 1948 that Evan Durbin, who was staying with his family near us in North Cornwall, was drowned while rescuing one of his daughters and another girl who were bathing with him. My family were in a neighbouring bay that day, and I only heard of the tragedy one and a half hours later. There was nothing I could do when I got to the place where he was last seen. I knew this spot extremely well; and though there was a very strong westerly gale blowing, I never fully understood what occurred. Evan's death was a grievous loss to the Labour Party and to Parliament. I had to ring Gaitskell, his closest friend, that evening and tell him what had happened.

The year 1949 was the second turning point for the Attlee Government. The decision over devaluation in the summer of 1949 revived the country's economic fortunes and enabled the election of 1950 to be just won; but it also determined the succession to Cripps as Chancellor, gave rise indirectly to the so-called 'Bevanite' schism and so eventually to the succession to Attlee as Leader also. In the spring of 1949, after the remarkable success of

1948, the economic tide again turned against the Sterling Area countries. As we learnt after the year was over, the UK itself paradoxically showed in the end a near surplus on its current balance of payments even in 1949. But the Sterling Area was hit by the first post-war US recession, which slowed down US purchases of raw materials from all over the Commonwealth. The 'dollar drain', which we had to restrain somehow, depended on the whole Sterling Area and not just the UK. By the early summer of 1949 a steady weekly deficit was being shown in the (unpublished) 'dollar drain' figures, which were my guiding light, and which had been instituted at the start of the Cripps régime so that we would at least (unlike in 1947) know almost at once what was happening. Keen controversy grew up in the Treasury as to what should be done to stop the new drain.

Some naturally began to suggest devaluation of the pound, which then stood at $4.03 where it had been fixed in September 1939. We were much embarrassed by public hints about this from the United States. Cripps was dead against devaluation, on what appeared to be moral rather than economic grounds, and I was unconvinced until the Commonwealth Finance Ministers gathered in London at the end of June 1949. At this conference Edgar Whitehead, Finance Minister of Southern Rhodesia, as it was then called, and later Prime Minister, made an outstanding contribution (though stone-deaf and conversing through notes) by producing figures for the price of leading American and British exports, which showed clearly that British exports were almost all relatively too dear. The logical conclusion, which Whitehead did not draw, was that the exchange rate should be changed. Naturally this implication was not lost on Plowden, Robert Hall and others in the Treasury, and it was apparent to me that though before 1949 devaluation would have been pointless because physically we could not produce more exports, now surplus capacity was beginning to emerge.

Early in July the US Secretary of the Treasury, Mr Snyder, came to London to confer with Cripps, and we seized on this chance to persuade Snyder – we hoped – to stop uttering public hints about devaluation. Snyder, supported by Lew Douglas, the extremely friendly US Ambassador in London, was received in a Committee Room in Great George Street by Cripps, Edward Bridges, Oliver Franks, now British Ambassador in Washington, and myself. The meeting started frostily. Cripps, who was by this time exceedingly tired, tried to say diplomatically that he hoped the Americans would keep quiet and give us a little time. Snyder, no financial genius, made some wooden reply, and Lew Douglas failed to warm things up. Then Oliver Franks remarked that none of us were quite saying what we really meant, and that bluntly he thought the British meant this, and the Americans that; and he suggested that we both said so plainly. He had as usual judged the atmosphere exactly right, and good humour broke out all round. Snyder undertook to offer us his advice in private in future, and Cripps promised that our decisions would be given in absolute confidence to him. No further complications from the American side troubled us thereafter.

It was now clear that Cripps's health was failing and that he must leave at the end of July for a long respite in the Zürich clinic which provided a health régime in which he believed. Some of us had doubts about Cripps's special health ideas, which he shared with his wife. But it did not seem possible for us to question them. However, Cripps was leaving at the end of the month, and our dollars were draining away. Attlee then circulated an official minute that, subject to himself, Gaitskell, Wilson and I would be responsible for Treasury policy in the Chancellor's absence. On Sunday 17 July 1949, meditating on the whole horrid situation on my usual Sunday walk round Hampstead Heath, I came home with my mind firmly made up that we must devalue the pound, if no alternative remedy had been suggested; and that we must get Cabinet authority for it before ministers dispersed at the end of July. Next morning I called on Gaitskell alone in his Ministry of Fuel and Power office in Smith Square and told him what I thought. He replied that he had reached the same conclusion on the day before for exactly the same reasons, and we decided there and then to talk with Wilson *à trois* on the Thursday. Before this there was just time for me to see Cripps before he left for Switzerland and tell him I favoured devaluation. 'What, unilaterally?' he said, and left it at that. Wilson, at our meeting, agreed (as we thought) to support our view and to recommend it to Attleee and Morrison at a meeting before the end of that week. At this, however, with Bridges and Henry Wilson-Smith of the Treasury also present, Gaitskell expounded our view and Attlee asked Wilson for his; whereupon Wilson argued against devaluation.

Astonished at this, Gaitskell and I arranged to see Wilson a second time and again thought we had all three agreed; only to discover at the second meeting with Attlee and Morrison early in the next week that he took refuge in ambiguity. Attlee ruled that at a further meeting before the last Cabinet on 29 July we must make a decision; and by the time this later meeting was held Bridges had clearly reached the view that there was now no alternative to devaluation, and that the only question was when, by how much, and how should the authority of Cripps and the Cabinet be secured. At this meeting (Attlee, Morrison, Wilson, Gaitskell, Bridges and myself) Wilson announced that he was holidaying in the South of France and suggested he should call on Cripps at Zürich as an apparent courtesy visit, and get his agreement to our plan. Attlee, however, directed that a minute from himself to Cripps should be drafted by Gaitskell and myself, naturally with Bridges's help, brought to Chequers for him to sign in the following weekend and conveyed to Cripps in Zürich by Wilson's Board of Trade Private Secretary, Max Brown. As I walked across Palace Yard with Morrison after this discussion, he used some unsympathetic expressions about Wilson. It had also been decided at my suggestion in the meeting with

Attlee that the Cabinet next day should simply be asked to refrain from all public reference to the pound sterling during the recess and to give the Prime Minister authority to take whatever action he thought necessary. When Attlee proposed this at the Cabinet, it was greeted not merely with agreement but with an audible sigh of relief.

By this time, the discussion in the Treasury was no longer about whether we should devalue, but how the operation should be managed. Gaitskell and I drafted the following minute (addressed to Cripps for Attlee to sign), and took it down to Chequers on a beautiful August day, Friday 5 August 1949:

TOP SECRET   5.8.49

Though most reluctant to inflict official business on you at this time, I feel compelled to seek your views on certain vital issues arising out of the dollar situation. I have been considering further, together with those of my colleagues most closely concerned, and the officials charged with responsibility for preparing materials for the Washington talks, the question of devaluation. All of us are now agreed, including the responsible officials, that this is a necessary step (though not of course the only step) if we are to stop the present dollar drain before our reserves fall to a level so dangerous as to impair the Government's ability to handle the situation. Although the weekly dollar drain since you left London has not exceeded expectations, we have all been strengthened in this conviction by three main considerations: 1. The ever-accumulating evidence that universal expectation of devaluation is holding back purchases of British exports day by day and discouraging the holding of sterling all over the world. 2. The now evident fact that the United States and Canada are not likely to take short-term action which will materially affect the dollar drain in the next few weeks. 3. The clearly emerging probability, confirmed by Sir Oliver Franks, that substantial help by the Americans is not likely to be forthcoming as a result of the talks in Washington in September sufficiently early to prevent the reserves falling to a dangerously low level.

At the same time the official advice unanimously tendered to us is that if we are to obtain any lasting benefit from devaluation the inflationary pressures which are hampering us at the moment must be speedily reduced. It is suggested that the situation requires above all a reduction in Government expenditure. Certain supporting action in the monetary field might also be appropriate. The Cabinet have held a general discussion on Government expenditure, and I am proposing to issue a strongly worded directive to my colleagues on it. The view, however, of my colleagues whom I have consulted is that devaluation, if desirable at a certain date on other grounds, should not be delayed in order to await further decisions on Government expenditure.

I have therefore been considering the vital question of timing. All those concerned are agreed that, because of the injury to our reserves and the general uncertainty it is not now possible to contemplate waiting later than mid-September. The choice therefore seems to lie between some date early in September during the Washington talks, and a still earlier date; and I am most anxious to have your opinion on this vital point. I agree with my advisers here that a decision must be taken before you and the Foreign Secretary go to Washington, and if possible a date fixed. Sir Oliver Franks is clear in his view that we should not gain, but lose, with the Americans, if we appear to be trading an offer of devaluation for concessions on their part, or even if we had failed to make up our own minds. His view is that the Americans will expect us to have taken a decision ourselves on this crucial point of British policy; and I think we must accept his judgment. All my advisers, therefore, agree that the idea of postponing a decision until the Washington talks for the express purpose of gaining reciprocal concessions, should be abandoned. At least a week must of course elapse between the decision and the announcement, owing to the need for consultation with the US Treasury, the IMF and the appropriate Commonwealth and certain European governments.

There are accordingly three alternative dates which (on the assumption that we must choose a Sunday) suggest themselves – August 28, September 4 and September 18. September 11th is excluded, because on that day many Finance Ministers and governors of Central Banks will be en route to the annual meeting of the international Bank and Fund which is due to open in Washington on September 13th. We could not decently act at that particular moment. . . .

A detailed discussion of dates followed, and the minute continued:

I must be acquainted with your view and that of the Foreign Secretary before any decision can be taken; and if possible the final Cabinet decision on this should be taken with you and the Foreign Secretary present. In any case, I regard it as essential to make it quite clear that any decision, when it is taken, has been taken by yourself together with others here in London.

The Cabinet has given me authority, together with such colleagues as may be available, to take any decision necessary to deal with the situation during August. If either of the earlier dates were chosen, the necessary Cabinet decision could be taken in your absence, your views being given to them. I do not anticipate any opposition. This Cabinet would be composed of those available, as any endeavour to recall absentees might blow the gaff. An early return on your part would also of course inevitably excite comment. Clearly, however, you must be here before any announcement is made.

There is also the possibility that on the announcement the Opposition might ask for the immediate recall of Parliament; but I am inclined to hope that they would be willing to postpone this until you and the Foreign Secretary return.

I have asked Harold Wilson to obtain the views of the Foreign Secretary as well as your own on the whole matter and report both to me.

This explosive piece was duly signed by Attlee that day, encased in many official envelopes and conveyed by Max Brown, with Wilson's help in Zürich, to Cripps there. He reluctantly agreed; but the date of 18 September for devaluation was selected mainly in order that he might be able to attend the necessary Cabinet meeting, and announce the news himself in a broadcast on that Sunday evening. Meanwhile Plowden and Robert Hall, after much consultation with the economists, came out with $2.80 as the best new rate for the pound. This seemed to me at first sight too drastic;

but they argued that if we devalued at all we must do it properly: and in retrospect I am sure they were right. Up till this moment the dollar–sterling rate had not been changed since September 1939; yet the relative strength of the two economies had basically altered. Wilson did in fact call on Cripps with the minute but their conversation was not known to me. This left us in the Treasury with six weeks in which to organize the whole operation and maintain absolute secrecy. The international 'gnomes' were of course agog everywhere to guess what was going to happen, with hundreds of millions at stake. A 'D-Day' programme was devised with great skill by the two or three Treasury officials necessarily concerned (including Edward Playfair in particular) which involved courtesy notification to key authorities overseas, varying from forty-eight hours' notice to the US Secretary to the Treasury to about one hour to the French Finance Minister.

Absolute secrecy was in fact maintained. On holiday at Postbridge, Dartmoor, at the end of August, I had to exchange one or two handwritten letters in cryptic terms with Gaitskell, but for double security burnt his after reading them. My wife asked why I had suddenly started burning Gaitskell's letters; and pressed by this question while picnicking on the moor (it was a very fine summer), I was provoked to the brink of replying: 'There are some things even more secret than Budgets.' Before I *spoke* these words, my eyes fell on the *News Chronicle* spread on the heather in front of us and the heading: 'Is devaluation coming?' by Paul Bareau.

Returning to London in early September, I was anxious somehow to mollify the shock which loyal supporters of the Labour Party and Government would feel at this sudden change of policy. Naturally ministers were compelled to deny any suggestion of devaluation before it occurred. The crucial Cabinet meeting was held on Saturday 17 September, and ministers percolated through to No. 10 through diverse doors other than the normal entrance from Downing Street. There was some surprise among those who came, but no opposition. Scrupulously observing all the proprieties, I telephoned Percy Cudlipp, still Editor of the *Daily Herald*, at 8.30 that Sunday night, half an hour before Cripps's broadcast, advising him to listen to the broadcast and adding that I would call on him at the *Daily Herald* at 9.15 after it was finished. I did so, and handed him two prepared typewritten documents: a leader of the right length, explaining the decision, for Monday morning; and a question-and-answer feature piece between the *Daily Herald* and myself for Tuesday morning. Cudlipp seized gratefully on both. Here I was going beyond my ministerial book; but the scheme was well within the proprieties of the time, and achieved the twin objectives of allaying Government supporters' anxieties and helping the *Daily Herald*, which was in turn doing so much for the Government and the Labour Party.

The immediate sequels to devaluation were not precisely what we had foreseen. First the Americans were greatly relieved and almost delighted and the financial tide immediately swung round. The dollar drain ceased. By November 1949 everybody was agreed that devaluation was a major success, and some strange people began to claim the credit. The *Evening Standard* and the *Daily Telegraph* then published in the same week a curious gossip story, saying that the true history of devaluation could now be told: Harold Wilson had conducted a campaign resisted by Gaitskell in favour of devaluation and won the victory by persuading Cripps to agree in a visit to Zürich, during August. I happened to remark next day in Cripps's private office, before the 9.30 a.m. meeting, that this was a very odd story to appear twice; and Clem Leslie, as Press Officer, offered to ascertain the source. A day or two later he volunteered the information that the source of this story appeared to be the President of the Board of Trade. William Armstrong (then chief private secretary to Cripps) asked me whether I would pass this on to Cripps, and I replied that it was mere gossip and I certainly would not. 'Then I shall,' Armstrong remarked.

Naively perhaps, I was mystified at the time by Wilson's attitude to these events. One colleague suggested to me that he was conscious of Cripps's failing health, had set his heart on succeeding him as Chancellor; and believed in July that Bridges, who would greatly influence the choice, was at this time opposed to devaluation. This suggestion I rejected as unworthy. But there was no doubt in my mind by the end of 1949 that if Cripps's health failed, Attlee, Morrison and Cripps himself would certainly select Gaitskell as his successor. I relate the record of 1949 in some detail because it determined the succession to Cripps. Gaitskell's strength and clarity of mind in this crisis enormously and visibly impressed both Atlee and Cripps.

Another wholly different, and slightly comic, if touching, repercussion ensued after 18 September 1949: a personal rift between Cripps and Churchill. Before 18 September, Cripps courteously invited Churchill, as Leader of the Opposition, and ex-Prime Minister, to a confidential talk on the Sunday afternoon of 18 September, at which he would be told in advance of Cripps's broadcast. Churchill, Cripps told me, showed little interest in the pound or the dollar, but broke into a mood of romantic nostalgia about their wartime comradeship, when all good and patriotic men had worked together for the common cause; and affirmed how he would always share these glorious memories with his wartime ministers. Cripps could be emotional too, and was clearly touched by this quite unscheduled response. But a little later Churchill came out with a violent public speech accusing Cripps of deceiving the nation, political dishonesty and so forth, because he had previously denied any intention to devalue. To Churchill, who well knew Cripps could have done nothing else, this was just party-political combat as he had learnt it in his youth. But Cripps was deeply hurt and could not be reconciled. It so happened that a few weeks later as a Bristol MP, Cripps was due to receive from Churchill (Chancellor of Bristol University) an honorary degree. Cripps refused to attend, and the ceremony had to be publicly postponed. Churchill this time was also deeply offended, and in his turn regarded Cripps's refusal as carrying political warfare too far.

By December 1949, following the success of devaluation, the Government had carried through 'the consequential measures', designed to prevent inflationary effects, and consisting mainly of a rise in Profits Tax which I had to pilot through the House. In the weeks before Christmas talk of a general election, due by mid-1950, had become persistent in the press, in the House and within the Government. It was clear to most of us by December that the economy would be firmly on the upgrade by the summer of 1950, and that by May or June this would be generally felt through the country. Gaitskell and I strongly favoured an election in May 1950, by which time the devaluation crisis of the previous summer would be fading from memory, and the Lynskey Tribunal of the end of 1948 would be fading even further. Herbert Morrison agreed with us.

At this moment, however, Cripps, totally unpredictably, delivered a blow which was disastrous for the Government and the post-war Labour Party for a very long time. At about Christmas, he reached the personal decision, inspired apparently from on high with Gladstonian certainty of conviction, that the general election must come before the Budget. The reason he gave for this was that any Budget introduced *before* an election was an 'Election Budget' and that any such Budget was immoral. In vain we pointed out that we were proposing he should introduce a tough Budget in April, with tax increases on petrol and a vehicle tax on lorries, and that nobody could say this was an immoral 'Election Budget'. Indeed, I suggested the main lines of the Budget which he in fact introduced in April as the Budget he should be introducing in 1950 *before or after* an election. I addressed a formal minute to Cripps in January 1950 which eventually led to a petrol tax increase in the April Budget, and which opened with these words:

I have come increasingly to the conclusion recently that we have been throughout the last few years seriously under-taxing motor transport and as a result – though not intentionally – encouraging a very rapid increase in our road vehicle fleet of all kinds, which is most uneconomic. Great and increasing amounts of steel and oil, which either cost dollars or could earn dollars, are being devoted to the building up of a road fleet, which to a great extent is duplicating already existing transport. Here is a case where rates of taxation have failed to keep pace with economic forces, and with the change in the value of money; and where as a result, in my view, we could obtain substantial extra revenue not merely without doing economic harm but actually to the advantage of the economy. I suggest that possibilities should be studied by the Budget Committee, with a view to practical proposals.

Tower House, Shooters
Hill, about 1914

Winchester College
Archaeological Society
visit to Chichester, 1925.
Standing, from the left:
the author, William
Hayter, John Sparrow,
P. C. Eccles, the Bishop.
*Standing, third from
right:* Dick Crossman.
Standing, fifth from right:
Spencer Leeson.
Sitting, left: Roger
Cooke

Campaigning in Battersea by–election, July 1946, outside Morgan Crucible factory

Signing the Marshall Aid agreement, 1948. *Seated, from left:* Stafford Cripps, Ernest Bevin and US Ambassador Lew Douglas. *Standing:* on the left the author, in the centre Harold Wilson, and officials

Production conference in Swansea, 1948. *In the centre front,* the Lord Mayor; *on right* Sir Percy Thomas, Chairman of Wales Regional Board; *on left* the author; with officials, industrialists and trade unionists

On a Dartmoor summit with
Helen, Martin and Peter,
in 1955

Opposite President of the
Board of Trade, 1964

Below Leaving for India with
John Strachey (top) and
George Thomson (centre),
1963

With Chou en Lai in
Peking, 1964

Opening a British
industrial exhibition,
Moscow, July 1966.
Front row, right,
Soviet Trade
Minister Patolichev

Британская
шленноя Выст
8 - 24   1966г

With Harold Wilson at
EFTA Conference,
Vienna, May 1965

With Catherine (left)
and Helen (right) on
their graduation, July
1966, Brighton Pavilion

General Election October 1974; right with Mary, and below with elector and power station

When I wrote this, the total yield of the oil duties was £63 millions. By 1978 it had reached £2500 millions.

Both Attlee and Morrison favoured the May election date. But Cripps flatly refused to agree, still believing that an 'Election Budget' would be contrary to the guidance received from an even higher authority than the Prime Minister. He made it clear he would resign as Chancellor if the election was postponed until after the Budget in April. Attlee could not accept Cripps's resignation, as at this time it would have been shattering for the Government. So, contrary to the firm view of Attlee and Morrison, and many others in the Government, the election was announced for February. It was at this moment that Attlee made to me in private the remark about Cripps that 'He's no judge of politics.' The Government and Labour Party were thus forced into an election on a most awkward wicket, only a few months after devaluation. This accident had profound consequences for the entire post-war history of the country. Opinion polls in May 1950, after petrol had been de-rationed, suggest that in that month the Labour Government would probably have won a majority of forty or fifty in the House of Commons. In this case there need have been no 1951 election.

Cripps's single-mindedness – if this is the right word – ensured, however, that this was not to be. We were plunged ill-prepared into the February 1950 election. George Strauss has recently[14] recalled to me a dinner at this point at which Cripps, Bevan, Strauss and others of our colleagues (I think, our regular fortnightly dinner) were present. Cripps asked each of us in turn what result we expected at the election, and everyone except myself (according to Strauss's account) predicted a clear Labour victory, while I said it would be a near thing. I cannot recall this conversation, but this was my view at the time. In the few months preceding this, I had also, as a member of a Labour Party committee, including Herbert Morrison, Jim Griffiths, Morgan Phillips and others, been trying to devise a sensible Labour Manifesto for the 1950 election. I had some responsibility, I fear, drawing on my Stock Exchange knowledge of the immediate pre-war years, in suggesting certain near-monopoly firms for public ownership rather than whole 'industries'. This was a mistake, and the whole idea of a 'shopping list' was later wisely dropped. We were in a much greater difficulty in framing a programme in 1949–50 than in 1945, because the Government of 1945–50 had done so much so quickly. I did compile a pamphlet for Transport House documenting the success of the Development Area policy since 1945, which was one of our strong cards. But fundamentally we were caught in the same difficulty as any reforming government which has run out of obvious and desirable reforms.

The 1950 election was my first experience of fighting one as a serving minister, because though of course Parliament was suspended, the

[14] In 1978.

G

government was not. Mornings were spent as usual at my Treasury office reading learned Inland Revenue memoranda, afternoons walking the streets of Battersea in the rain, and evenings making speeches in Council schools mainly in some part of London. So cynical and trivial had been the Tory grumble-propaganda about the Attlee Government in these years, that I found myself more passionately and uncompromisingly devoted than ever to the cause of the Government and the Labour Party and resolved to expend the last ounce of energy I possessed in winning this election. In my local Party the same spirit prevailed. For nearly four weeks from 2 p.m. to 6 p.m. (it always seemed to start raining at 2 p.m.) I tramped the streets imagining I was somehow influencing the result. Having luckily enjoyed excellent health all my life, I never felt quite the same after those four weeks. But I was much cheered at this time by discovering in Trollope's *The Duke's Children* (1880) the story of Lord Silverbridge's adventures in an Election in 'Polperro' in Cornwall:

On the next day, after breakfast, it was found to be raining heavily . . . About four, when it was beginning to be dusk, they were very tired, and Silverbridge had ventured to suggest that, as they were all wet through, and as there was to be another meeting in the Assembly Room that night, and that nobody in that part of the town seemed to be at home, they might perhaps be allowed to adjourn for the present . . . But the philosophers [i.e. the agents] received the proposition with stern disdain. Was His Lordship aware that Mr Carbottle [their opponent] had been out all day from eight in the morning and was still at work?

T'was ever thus.

The evening meetings in 1950 did not lack humorous interludes. Once at Islington, when Herbert Morrison was to be the star speaker, I arrived to find the 'Meetings Officer' being asked by the agent if he had phoned Morrison that day to confirm the time. The Meetings Officer, it turned out, had never approached Morrison at all, but thought it sufficient to put notices all over Islington announcing that Morrison would be there. So I was told, with a minute or two to go, and drenched with rain like poor Lord Silverbridge, that I must make the main speech and explain that Morrison had been taken ill. Unfortunately he was reported next morning as having spoken to at least one meeting in London that evening. A few days later in Battersea, Cripps did turn up to a packed overflow meeting at which he attacked the 'Radio Doctor', Charlie Hill, to joyous cheers from our numerous supporters. For years afterwards Labour supporters in Battersea were to recall this meeting as fulfilling their idea of what real politics ought to be. For a few days I was sent on a West Country tour during which Churchill called for an end to petrol rationing. Both Callaghan, also a junior Minister, and I responded to this independently next day with the orthodox Government case that we must still economize on imports of oil. To my surprise the day after, Gaitskell, as Minister of Fuel and Power, replied that the

Government itself might well de-ration petrol before long. Here Gaitskell showed much more foresight and political sense than we did, because petrol was in fact de-rationed that spring.

On Friday 24 February, the results of the election were declared. At mid-day and in the early afternoon it was uncertain, as the few late results came in, whether Labour would just gain an overall lead. I cared about it all so much, and was so exhausted, that I lay on the floor at home, listening to the radio, and waving arms and even legs in the air at each crucial result, until Labour finally went one seat ahead at 8.20 p.m. Labour finished with an overall majority of six, and a few more if the Irish Nationalists did not vote (assuming a Conservative Speaker). The actual result was:

Labour	315
Conservative	299
Liberal	9
Irish Nationalist	2

In terms of votes, the result was:

Labour	13,266,592
Conservative	12,502,567
Liberal	2,621,548

Many people asked why the Labour Party, which had not lost a bye-election since 1945, should have suffered so large a drop in its overall majority. Seen in retrospect, the truth about the 1950 election was probably more understandable. First, though, the Labour majority would almost certainly have been higher in mid-1949 or mid-1950, the devaluation crisis was still depressing the vote in February 1950, and the beneficial effects had not yet had time to show themselves. As against this, and as compared with 1951, the large number of Liberal candidates standing in 1950 drew away some Conservative votes which came back to the Conservative candidates in 1951. The second major force telling against Labour must have been the steady revival of the Conservative predominance in the press mentioned in earlier chapters of this book. Thirdly, as compared with 1945, the Government's policy, certainly right nationally, of giving priority throughout to exports and investment rather than raising living standards, inevitably disappointed long-deferred popular hopes of an easier life. The final handicap was the redistribution of parliamentary seats, scrupulously carried out by the Labour Government itself, which lost a number of Labour seats to the Conservatives. Churchill himself estimated this loss at thirty-five, and the Annual Register put it at thirty.[15]

In all this period the Government and Labour Party owed much to Herbert Morrison. His weakness in economic policy and his ill-judged

[15] Hugh Dalton, *High Tide and After*, p. 347.

attempt to supplant Attlee in July 1945 have been allowed to obscure somewhat his hard work and immense powers of parliamentary and popular persuasion. From 1945 right through to 1951 Morrison was a wonderful solace and help to bewildered junior ministers. From the moment I went to the Treasury, direct talks with Attlee or Bevin became naturally rare; and though I saw Cripps almost daily, he was never quite the sort of colleague to whom one would bare one's thoughts, let alone one's heart, or pour out uninhibited comments on life and politics. But Morrison, also working just down the same passage at Great George Street, would always readily receive one, however junior in the hierarchy, and resolve or at least debate one's doubts and difficulties in his cheery, enlivening fashion. He was, without question, the best Leader of the House of Commons in the thirty years after the war. When for a few weeks Arthur Greenwood had to stand in for Morrison, who was ill, as Leader of the House, one Labour backbencher, after the Thursday 'Children's Hour' exchanges with Churchill, sighed to me with deep feeling:

> ... But O for the touch of a vanish'd hand
> And the sound of a voice that is still. ...

Lloyd George was reputed once to have said: 'Great statesmen are very common, but great politicians are very rare.' The best epitaph on Herbert Morrison is that he was a great politician.

The February 1950 election changed the whole climate of the Government, and in particular the life of us Treasury Ministers. Henceforward it was no longer a struggle to push through major legislation and unpopular budgets, but rather to hold the line and avoid defeats in the House which would provoke another general election. In those days, any defeat on a Committee or Report Stage amendment to the Finance Bill was supposed to involve the Government's resignation. Few people thought that we could long survive the hundred or more divisions on the floor of the House which the Finance Bill provoked. Churchill, indeed, privately told Chuter Ede, the Home Secretary – who passed the remark on to me – that he did not think the Government could last many months. Immediately after the election, Attlee brought Gaitskell over to the Treasury as Minister of State in the justified belief that the Treasury would now bear the main parliamentary as well as policy burdens of the Government, and with the private assumption (I now felt sure) that if Cripps's health collapsed Gaitskell would become Chancellor. It was made clear that Gaitskell still ranked as a senior minister, as at the Ministry of Fuel and Power. I was delighted to be reunited with him as a close daily colleague again, even more so after the events of July and August 1949. This meant my transfer to become Financial Secretary of the Treasury, nominally more responsible for the legal and budgetary side of Treasury affairs, on which I was far weaker than on economic policy. When I pointed this out to Cripps, he did not comfort me greatly by saying that it would be 'good for' me to tackle problems I did not understand. But Frank Soskice had lost his seat at the election, which deprived us of at least 50 per cent of the Treasury's House of Commons debating strength. Without waiting for Cripps, I bearded Morrison and pointed out that we must have Soskice back in the House by the time the Budget debates began. Somehow Morrison managed it by finding him another seat, and got him there well on time. Probably Soskice was at that moment more indispensable than any other member of the Government.

Gaitskell and I then turned our minds to the coming April Budget; and he supported the ideas, including higher petrol taxes, that I had been urging on Cripps. But Gaitskell also agreed that, as the balance of payments was dramatically improving, we could ease up a little on new house-building. He and I devised an amiable conspiracy by which I would suggest to Bevan that if he would approach the Chancellor and press for an increase from 175,000 to 200,000 in the new house-building programme for 1950, we would both tell Cripps we strongly supported it. My Battersea experiences had already deeply impressed on me the fact that bad housing remained far our greatest social evil. In 1950 building 200,000 new houses was the most which softwood supplies would permit. Bevan, however, was much less enthusiastic than I had expected at this private nudge from the Treasury towards an increase in one of his own key programmes. He almost had to be pushed; but in the end he agreed, and the increase was announced in the Budget Speech. Bevan made no mention of the origin of this increase in his resignation speech a year later, though the 175,000 figured in it; and Michael Foot in his biography of Bevan naturally did not know how the increase came about. It surprised me that Gaitskell was actually more keen on this improvement than Bevan. The reason was, perhaps, an element in Bevan's character that I often noticed. He normally cared more about quality than quantity. He felt more strongly about each house being up to a certain standard than about the number of houses being enough to meet the demand; and he was reluctant to admit that there might be a choice. It was this deep concern with quality, which genuinely appeared to him as a principle, which partly explained why he cared even more about the Health Service than about housing. But I was delighted to have secured the 200,000 houses and this time to have helped steer Cripps, Bevan and Gaitskell all harmoniously into line.

In April/May 1950 all except our voting strength in the House of Commons seemed set fair at last. The current UK balance of payments in 1949, partly due to devaluation, had shown a small surplus and the rise in living costs and pay rates was still moving only a few per cent a year. Gold and dollars were flowing into the reserve. Unemployment remained under 2 per cent. For ten months after devaluation in September 1949 the cost of living was actually held stable, which would appear almost incredible in the

1970s. Petrol and clothes rationing were abolished by the summer. It was my job as Financial Secretary, as was the firm tradition in those days, to move on 16 May the Second Reading of the Finance Bill. My father, aged eighty, sat in the Gallery, and recounted to me afterwards how he had listened to Gladstone in the 1890s. Only three weeks later, on June 6, my father died, having collapsed after a swim at Lyme Regis where he had spent holidays as a boy.

Throughout that summer the Government's majority in the Finance Bill, despite endless debates and innumerable divisions, never fell below two. Frank Soskice was ever present, inexhaustible and almost omniscient. A minor mishap did occur in one of these Finance Bill debates. We thought it natural for Jim Callaghan, as an Admiralty junior Minister, to answer an amendment proposing some concession for naval ex-Service men. Callaghan, as an ex-Inland Revenue official, was always keen to join in tax debates. Unfortunately the speech was taken to mean that the Government would grant the concession. Cripps, who had not intended this, disagreed and laid it down that only Treasury Ministers and Soskice should speak in future on the Finance Bill.

In May 1950 in the midst of these debates, there suddenly became audible the first rumbling of disasters to come: the unveiling of the supranational Schumann Coal and Steel Plan which was the precursor of the Common Market. The circumstances of this have been so distorted by propaganda, like so much in this controversy, that I relate precisely what happened at the start. On 9 May the French Ambassador told the British Foreign Secretary in London that the French Government was proposing an apparently supra-national coal and steel plan, and that the UK must decide at once whether it wished to join, even though the main details were not known. On the same day, the French announced the plan publicly in Paris. Discussions followed between the British and French Governments, and the British Government repeatedly expressed willingness to join in a serious examination of the plan. Cripps welcomed the idea of such a joint effort; and Bevin met Schumann, the French Foreign Minister, on 11 May. Telegrams[16] were exchanged throughout May in which the British Government said they would like to 'participate'. On the evening of Thursday 1 June, however, my Private Secretary told me that the French had sent an ultimatum, expiring at 8 p.m. that evening and stating that if we had not by then decided to accept the plan, we would be excluded from all further participation. I said I could not believe that the French Government had sent such a message, and that we had better go back to the Embassy in Paris and ascertain the true facts. My Secretary said that the FO and other Departments concerned had responded in the same way, that telegrams were being sent, and that a meeting at 10 Downing Street

[16] The documents were published later by the Government as Cmnd 7970 *Anglo-French Discussions*.

was to be held next day, 2 June, which, in the absence of Cripps, I must attend. By 9 a.m. next morning telegrams had been received in the Treasury saying that there was no mistake, and that Britain would be excluded from the plan unless unconditional agreement was given that day.

Together with Bridges and Plowden, I went to No. 10 where Morrison presided, and McNeill and Younger represented the Foreign Office. Naturally there was no debate as to whether we could accept an unknown plan or not, but merely bewilderment as to what such an 'ultimatum' (the word was used in the record) could mean. It was decided to reply again that we welcomed the idea of a joint co-operation over steel and coal;[17] that we could not commit ourselves to supra-national control without knowing any details; and that we proposed a high-level working party with French and other representatives to see if an agreed plan could be worked out. Cripps, when he heard of these exchanges, was enthusiastic about the idea of some joint plan. But the French replied on 3 June that since we had not unconditionally accepted the terms, we were now excluded. The fact that the French publicly announced the Plan on the same day as we heard of it, 9 May, shows pretty plainly that the whole operation had been so devised that the British Government was bound initially to decline. The reference in the French public statement to 'Franco-German production' of coal and steel also suggests that it had always been their intention to exclude the British.

As soon as the exchanges of the telegrams began, propaganda started to seep out from Paris to the effect that the British had been invited to join a great coal and steel plan and had refused the offer. So persistent was the propaganda that it came to be believed by even responsible, if ill-informed, people in this country, and for years afterwards it could still be heard. This was the first major incident in the post-war years of what later became common, but was hardly known in other countries: the British media swallowing what was basically propaganda designed to weaken this country. For, of course, no British Government – certainly no Churchill Government – could have acted otherwise than we did, and no Cabinet could have seriously considered sending any other reply to the French ultimatum. This was confirmed by the debate in Parliament on 26 and 27 June. Eden admitted on 26 June in this debate that the French had sought to 'impose conditions before conversations opened'. Cripps said in the same debate that we must at least know whether the suggested supra-national 'authority' would have the power to close down a British coalfield or steelworks, and made clear that the French were excluding us from further talks.[18] Churchill said on 27 June: 'I cannot conceive that Britain would be an ordinary member of a federal union limited to Europe in any period that can be foreseen.' Throughout the debate both Churchill and Eden care-

[17] Attlee said this in the House on 11 May.
[18] Hansard, 26 June 1950, col. 1933.

fully refrained from saying that they would have accepted the supra-national 'authority'. But Cripps for the Government made it perfectly clear that we were ready to negotiate on any reasonable terms by moving a motion which was accepted by the House, in these words: 'This House approves the declared willingness of HMG to take a constructive part in conversations with the hope that they may be able to join in, or associate with, this common effort.'

I was myself amazed at first by the French ultimatum and general con-duct of this affair. But, in the light of after events, and the persistent propa-ganda campaign, I was forced to the conclusion that the whole episode was a political manoeuvre. The ultimatum is not explicable except on the as-sumption that the French were determined to keep future moves for so-called 'European unity' under French control, and exclude the British at least until such time as the whole arrangement had been so devised as to promote French interests and where possible to damage this country. If the French Government had seriously wished this country to join a supra-national scheme, they would have invited us to discuss this over a reason-able period and would have set out the main details. It was, however, con-sidered necessary by the French first to make an offer which could not be accepted by any British Government, and then propagate the fiction that a reasonable offer had been made and turned down out of insularity, etc., etc. In later years it has constantly been asserted that, though the ensuing developments of the EEC were damaging to Britain, if only we had accep-ted the 1950 offer we could have fashioned it all differently. This is a com-plete mis-representation of what actually happened; unless it is seriously maintained that a British Government should have accepted, in advance, with hardly any notice, a supra-national authority with unknown powers.

In the same week of June 1950 as the Schumann Plan debate in the House, the Korean war broke out. Nobody foresaw at first the far-reaching and damaging economic consequences that the war would have for Britain. The immediate thought was for the vindication of the United Nations by Anglo-American military resistance, and Attlee won general applause by at once launching this policy. But the crucial consequence for Britain was the huge rise in the prices of imported raw materials due to the American Government's decision to stockpile on a massive scale on account of the war. Economic indices for Britain were set so fair in June 1950 that excessive stockpiling was not foreseeable. All eyes were on the military side of the operation. By chance, when the invasion occurred, I had just received a letter from my naval brother, Alan, then serving in a frigate in the Far East, telling me that his and a number of other small warships were stationed in Japanese waters. On the day when Attlee was to announce the British decision to support the UN, I was officiating as usual on the front bench replying to technical amendments on the Finance Bill. Shortly before 5 p.m. on 28 June I was told the debate would be suspended at that hour for a short time to enable Attlee to speak. After Attlee's announcement,[19] Churchill, who applauded it, asked if there were any British warships in Korean waters. Attlee scrutinized his notes, looked surprised, but rose to say that there were larger British than American naval forces in these waters. Attlee had the expression of not believing what he had said. Churchill started to rise, presumably to ask whether this really could be true, but visibly changed his mind, and reflecting presumably that the Admiralty must have given Attlee the facts – as they had – sat down. I watched this drama with distinct amusement since, thanks to my brother's letter, I happened to be more sure Attlee was right about the naval situation than were either Attlee or Churchill.

As the summer wore on, and our first Finance Bill supported by a minute majority was steered into port by August, it became indisputably clear that Cripps's health was failing. I used to discuss with William Armstrong, now principal Private Secretary to the Chancellor, whether we could somehow obtain additional medical opinion; but both Cripps and his wife had deep feelings about treatment, and we could do nothing. On 19 October 1950, he retired. He died in April 1952. The greatest grief was felt at his death by all who had been working with him; and respect for his character and achievement was unbounded among those most closely associated with him since 1947. The economic recovery accomplished after August 1947 was remarkable, as is best seen by the fact that Britain was able to dispense with Marshall Aid in December 1950, only two months after Cripps's retirement, before any of the sixteen other recipients, and two years ahead of the target date. Cripps in his way deserved as well of his country as did Churchill in the war years. He certainly worked himself to the point of exhaustion, and to his death eighteen months later. The extreme burdens he laid on himself were excessive by ordinary human standards. Lacking only the pre-eminent common sense of Attlee and Morrison, he was capable of errors of judgement. But his uncompromising devotion to his own standards and to the public interest was a lasting inspiration to those who worked with him.

As I had assumed ever since July 1949 to be inevitable, Attlee at once chose Gaitskell to succeed Cripps as Chancellor. Dalton (though he did not know at first-hand the events of July–September 1949) was at one with Cripps in proposing Gaitskell as his successor. But Attlee needed no pressure, as Dalton recalls:[20] 'I found that I was pushing an open door.' On Gaitskell's first day at the Treasury as Chancellor, with myself as Financial Secretary, we could not help remembering all our pre-war debates about Labour policy and the need to avoid another 1931 collapse. 'We never expected,' he said, 'to find ourselves in this position.' I realized that the appointment would cause some resentment in the mind of Wilson, but I had not expected the violent explosion which hit me from Nye Bevan. He

[19] Hansard, 28 June 1950, col. 2319.
[20] Dalton, p. 352.

descended on me a day or two later in the rather special passage of the House known as 'behind the Speaker's Chair', which divides the Chamber from the Chancellor's and Prime Minister's rooms. There, in front of the policeman, and any other official or MP who happened to be passing, he began to pour forth with uncontrolled passion a torrent of vitriolic abuse on the head of Attlee for daring to make such an appointment. For Bevan's sake as much as anyone else's, I pushed him physically down the passage into the empty Chancellor's room a few yards away, shut the door, stood against it myself, and said 'Now carry on': which he did, for some time but now happily in private.

It was a sad exhibition of egomania, and it swamped for the moment all Bevan's attractive and brilliant qualities. It was manifest to me then that the appointment of Gaitskell had provoked a violent revolt in Bevan's mind against the whole leadership of the Labour Party, which rankled and simmered on and in time flared up into what was known as 'Bevanism'. Bevan even told some people, according to Dalton,[21] that Cripps had promised him the Chancellorship. This was a wild distortion. I recorded at the time (January 1953) a story then related to me by Graham Spry, Agent-General of Saskatchewan, but also a long-standing friend of Cripps since the 1930s. Cripps had told Spry that he, Cripps, had once asked Bevan whether the Chancellorship was a job he wanted. Bevan, on Spry's account, had answered: 'No. I couldn't go about making speeches on figures. I prefer the Colonial Office.' Perhaps this was the question which in Bevan's mind had become a 'promise'. In fact, the events of July 1949 led to Gaitskell's selection as Chancellor, and that selection in turn led to the controversy on the 1951 Budget, and to the long and unhappy story of 'Bevanism'.

Publicly, however, in the autumn of 1950 all seemed reasonably under control, and the triumphant announcement of the suspension of Marshall Aid was made on 13 December. The UK current balance of payments showed the huge surplus of £244 millions in 1950.[22] Marshall Aid had proved the happiest of post-war international experiments. Promises were kept by both sides and targets achieved. Our own relations with the US Marshall Aid delegation in London were extremely friendly, particularly with Thomas Finletter, later American Secretary for Air, and Lincoln Gordon of Harvard, as well as Marjolin, one of the chief French negotiators. International economic policy was in these years conducted on economic grounds, and with success, by the enlarged Treasury and not the Foreign Office.

There was still no sign by the end of 1950 of any major ill effects of the Korean war on the UK balance of payments. But it had become obvious that the defence budget, continually cut since the war, would have to be increased again if we were to make an effective contribution to the UN

[21] Dalton, p. 358.
[22] *Economic Surveys*, 1950–2.

effort in Korea. Many in later years have forgotten that at this time we did not know whether that war would be won, or whether Russia, which had organized the Berlin Blockade, and was still ruled by Stalin, might join in the Korean campaign on the Northern side. The British Government therefore realized by the turn of the year 1950-1 that we faced a major increase in defence expenditure; as well as an imperatively necessary increase in old-age pensions (the single pension had stood at twenty-six shillings since 1946); and an already mounting bill for other social services, particularly the Health Service. For these reasons very thorough and prolonged thought was given to the 1951 Budget by the whole Treasury team and others outside between December 1950 and March 1951. I had already in that December experienced my first Treasury economy campaign as Financial Secretary. We assiduously examined the estimates and demanded explanations wherever major increases were shown. Very soon the conviction was forced on me that 'power' was an even greater myth at the Treasury than at 10 Downing Street. We thought, for instance, we had at last made a useful economy on university grants. But the Minister, George Tomlinson, and the Permanent Secretary, Sir John Maude (later Lord Redcliffe-Maude) arrived in my room and made a case against it that was irresistible. Almost all forms of public spending will increase all the time automatically, if the Treasury does not curb them, because everyone else wants them to increase. The minister or official in the Treasury who has to say 'No' is naturally the most unpopular man in the Government. In these months I felt like the father of a family – which I was.

However, Gaitskell was determined to battle on. He had, I believe, two overriding motives at this time. The first was his memory of appeasement in the 1930s and the discredit that fell on the Labour Party because of their failure until almost too late to recognize the need to re-arm against Hitler. Some may think we exaggerated this in 1950-1. It may be that there was never any danger of further major Communist aggression despite the Berlin Blockade and Korean attack. But it equally may be that the formation of NATO, and the quick UN response to the Korean invasion forestalled it and gave us thirty years of comparative peace. The Soviet invasion of Afghanistan in 1979-80 supports the latter view. Secondly, Gaitskell was determined that a Labour Government should not again drift into the error and disrepute of 1931 by becoming the victim of economic forces. He thus set himself the stiff assignment of both increasing defence expenditure by arrangement with the Americans and maintaining a stern Budget policy. My own particular contribution was to aim at an increase in the real resources available to us, which would ease the pressure all round by tapping, as we did in the war, extra sources of productive manpower. In particular it was absurd in an age when the health of the population was improving, and the length of life increasing, that people anxious to work should be forcibly retired and paid to do nothing from the age of sixty onwards. In preparation for the 1951 Budget after a long Whitehall struggle, I got it agreed that the compulsory retirement age at sixty in the Civil Service should be abolished, and that an individual could go on working up to sixty-five if both he and his Department wished it. Not a great revolution. But it was thought so at the time, and was my most lasting contribution to this side of the Treasury. When it was all settled, we discovered that the Foreign Office had somehow stood aside and maintained the right to throw everyone out at sixty.

These events set Gaitskell and Bevan unhappily on a collision course. Though Bevan in a Defence debate on 15 February 1951 defended the proposed £4700 millions re-armament programme, it was not known publicly at the time that Shinwell, the new Defence Minister, had without Cabinet authority virtually agreed in Washington to a £6000 million programme and that Gaitskell firmly rejected this and held the bill down to £4700 millions. Bevan was now Minister of Labour, and had been succeeded by Hilary Marquand as Minister of Health, and so the Cabinet Committee reviewing the Health Service did not include Bevan. When Bevan approached me again in a Commons passage in March 1951 and asked what was proposed about the Health Service, I had to say (truly) that I did not know. The dilemma over the Health Service came at the worst possible moment. Cripps had gone, and Bevin's health had finally given way. He died on 14 April 1951, after sitting loyally on the Treasury Bench to support Gaitskell throughout his Budget Speech of 10 April. Bevin's death thus came between Gaitskell's Budget Speech and Bevan's resignation. Attlee was also unwell at the time of the final Cabinet deadlock between Bevan and Gaitskell, and Bevin's death was a crushing blow to him. If Attlee, Bevin and Cripps had all been in full health and approved whatever the Cabinet decided on the Health Service, I believe Bevan, however reluctantly, would have accepted it.

The upshot of the long debate on Health Service economy had been the proposal for charges on false teeth and spectacles. This was the marginal, disputed economy, and only worth about £13 millions (£25 millions in a full year). But Bevan, of course, with all his passion for quality and principle, did not care much for quantity. To him the Health Service was his child and creation. I sympathized with this feeling, because I felt exactly the same about the Development Area policy. This was my favourite son; and if anyone had tried to dismantle it, I would have thrown away everything to save it. Gaitskell, on the other hand, believed that he must maintain financial control, and that it was unfair for other Ministers to have to accept economies if the Health Service was to be exempted from the economies approved by the Cabinet as a whole.

Having ascertained all the facts as the Budget approached, I saw Gaitskell and told him that I agreed on merit with the economy proposed, though without much enthusiasm, but that I did not think £13 millions would be worth the trouble caused. Recalling Bevan's explosion in the corridor in October, I was sure he would erupt again. I also believed that the appointment of Morrison as Foreign Secretary in March, only a week or two before, had enraged Bevan even further. He thought he should have had this too.[23] But Gaitskell in our talks felt he would not keep faith with the rest of the Cabinet if he gave way now. It was an impossible and uncivilized procedure if one minister, and one minister alone, exercised a veto on majority decisions by threatening to create a crisis whenever he wished. This was hard to answer: though it was the first material disagreement I had with Gaitskell for nearly twenty years. Having told him my view, and found he disagreed, I had of course thereafter to defend the Government's decision loyally in public throughout this difficult summer. The final compromise was that teeth and spectacles would be charged, but that there would be no charge for prescriptions, although a legal power to impose these had existed since 1949 and had been accepted by Bevan.

Having failed with Gaitskell, I set myself to try to work for a compromise by helping Bevan's friends to persuade him to accept what was after all a Cabinet decision reached by a large majority. The days leading up to the Budget Speech on April 10 were tense, as reports of inner dispute had naturally echoed round. Dalton wrote Bevan a friendly note on 7 April, appealing to him not to resign.[24] John Freeman, a junior Minister, one day in the Tea Room of the House, asked me if it was true that Bevan and Gaitskell were involved in a clash which might lead to resignations. I said I feared it might, though it was a Budget secret and I could not therefore tell him the issue. He said that if Bevan resigned, he would do so; and when I pointed out that he did not yet even know the issue, he said this made no difference, as it was a matter of personal loyalty. I was astonished at this feminine attitude to politics, but he could not be moved.[25] Much more helpful at this time was John Strachey, who like myself did not feel strongly one way or the other about teeth and spectacles. As Bevan was more likely to listen to Strachey than to me (I was part of the wicked 'Treasury'), he and others tried persistently, for a time successfully, both before and after the Budget Speech to dissuade Bevan from resigning. Indeed on the day after the Budget Speech Bevan told a Parliamentary Labour Party meeting that he had decided against 'a certain step'. There was much applause for this. The Party as a whole was pleased by the major rise in retirement pension from twenty-six shillings to thirty shillings and increase in other social benefits, and a majority was prepared to accept health charges. Social Service expenditure as a whole rose by £50 million.

[23] Dalton, p. 362, sees this, I fear rightly, as one major motiv e of Bevan's resignation. Dalton also thinks in retrospect it would have been better if Bevan had succeeded Bevin.
[24] Dalton, p. 367.
[25] In fairness to John Freeman, it should be said that immediately after the Budget Speech he wrote to Bevan asking him not to resign. M. Foot, *Aneurin Bevan* (London, 1962), vol. II, *1945–60*, p. 326.

Strachey continued his efforts to maintain peace and dissuade Bevan from resigning. At this time and others I found Strachey helpful, sympathetic, always highly intelligent and so far as I could see, dependable. He genuinely admired Gaitskell. His only possible ministerial fault was a tendency to write long chatty papers and letters about general economics. These did not worry me, but others professed to find him devious. Dalton indeed maintained he had to have a typist present to record ministerial conversations with Strachey, and used to add, with a baleful look, one of his favourite dicta: 'Once a Communist, always a crook.' Though seeing Dalton's point here, I never found it applicable to Strachey. I am sure he did his best with Bevan; but he failed.

On 21 April Bevan wrote his letter of resignation to Attlee, followed by Wilson and Freeman. Bevan's letter went beyond teeth and spectacles, and opposed the re-armament programme, though he had defended it in the debate of 15 February. The statement in Attlee's reply: 'I note that you have extended the area of disagreement a long way beyond the specific matter to which I understood you had taken objection,' shows that Attlee at any rate believed that teeth and spectacles were up till then the issue at stake. The general opinion among Bevan's colleagues was that Wilson had originally supported Bevan on the assumption that the dual threat of resignation would force Gaitskell to give way; but that when he found this was not so, he realized that teeth and spectacles would not appear to the Labour Party or the public a sufficient reason for so drastic a step. He therefore urged the inclusion of defence expenditure as among the reasons for resignation; and it became a staple theme in the 'Bevanite' party line thereafter.

Bevan made his resignation speech in the House on 23 April, just thirteen days after the Budget. There was much sympathy for him, as there always is for a man in the midst of this ordeal, until, describing the disagreement about housing, he announced: 'I had to manoeuvre, and I did manoeuvre.' It was a classical demonstration that the Celt is sometimes as unable to understand the Anglo-Saxon as the Anglo-Saxon to understand the Celt. To Bevan this meant: 'How clever I was in outwitting these stupid English.' To the Anglo-Saxon two-thirds of the House of Commons, he appeared to be saying: 'I deceived my colleagues, and I am proud of it.' Norman Brook – the coolest and fairest of men – who was then in the Gallery as Secretary of the Cabinet, told me afterwards he lost sympathy when Bevan appeared to be actually boasting that he had deceived his colleagues. To me this remark was particularly ironic, because it referred to his supposed resistance to the cut in the housing programme from 200,000 to 175,000: and I knew that in fact, with Gaitskell's agreement, I had to prod Bevan into asking for this to be restored. Nevertheless the whole episode was for me acutely disturbing, because I did not believe 'the specific matter', as Attlee called it, of the teeth and spectacles was worthy of these deep feelings either way, and I could not but remember Wilson's record in the devaluation controversy of July 1949 and Bevan's explosion on hearing of Gaitskell's appointment as Chancellor.

Though the great majority of the Parliamentary Labour Party backed Gaitskell, we now faced an appallingly gruelling summer in piloting the Finance Bill with a tiny paper majority, a dissident 'Bevanite' group and a Tory Opposition seeing a heaven-sent chance to defeat the Government. Bob Boothby called on his colleagues to 'harry' the Government night after night throughout the summer. Few thought the Government would survive. But it did. The task of parliamentary defence in the prolonged Committee and Report Stages of the Finance Bill fell overwhelmingly again on Frank Soskice, who was equal to every ordeal, backed by Gaitskell, myself, and John Edwards, who had joined the Treasury team. Throughout much of May and June we spent many continuous hours of the day and night answering innumerable questions and amendments from aspiring young Tories like David Eccles, John Boyd-Carpenter, Freddie Errol, Peter Thorneycroft, John Foster (of All Souls), now a Tory MP, and Quintin Hogg. Of these, Peter Thorneycroft usually impressed me most as a debater. Soskice had an utterly disarming way of responding to all this. He gave the right answer – at some length. Almost nobody understood it except the Inland Revenue pundits trying to keep awake in the official box. I occasionally asked them quietly whether his erudite replies were really correct, or improvised mumbo-jumbo. 'Absolutely correct,' they always answered.

The Government never lost a division. Eventually, on 11 and 12 June 1951, the argument went right through one day and night and the next day till 10 p.m. – the longest session since the days of the Lloyd George Budget in 1909, and not so many hours less than the Irish Nationalists' record obstruction of the 1880s. Occasionally, during the night, Churchill would emerge from repose of some sort and embark on an irrelevant, wandering and knockabout speech. It was curious how hesitating and faltering he could be when he had no script and was genuinely improvising. At breakfast on one morning after these nightly ordeals, I saw him served by his Chief Whip with bacon and eggs and coffee and two large whiskies in either hand. Some twenty-five years later, Soskice told me that Churchill met him in a Commons passage on the day after the marathon of 11 and 12 June and asked: 'Have you had some sleep, young man?' Soskice replied that he had managed two or three hours; and Churchill, pondering deeply, remarked: 'Unconsciousness is the greatest of human blessings.'

At the time I used to think it an odd way of carrying on the Government of the country that those entrusted with the burdens and intricacies of economic policy should be subjected at the same time to prolonged physical endurance tests. Could not Parliament be more efficient? Most observers start with this notion. And of course there is some truth in it, but only part of the truth. As time went on and as I remembered the Münich Debate and the relief of knowing that one's furious feelings were being voiced in Parliament, I came to realize that Parliament is not just an efficient or inefficient legislative machine, or debating chamber, but among other things a political safety valve. R. A. Butler once expressed it well in a debate on procedure when he said: 'This is not a debating society; it is a struggle for power.' It is better that a genuinely aggrieved Opposition – as Suez again showed – should be able to talk and argue to the physical limit, even if a few ministers are worn out, than that the resentful minority should take to the streets, as is not exactly rare in much of the rest of the world. Conceivably the war of attrition in 1950 and 1951 wore out Cripps and affected Gaitskell's health. But even the exhaustion of a few individuals, who after all voluntarily choose this life, is not too high a price to pay for a system which resolves the fiercest conflicts by talking for however long, and voting however narrowly, rather than by alternative methods in which hundreds or thousands of wholly innocent victims suffer much worse penalties.

Yet even in that summer parliamentary debates did not wholly fill a Treasury minister's life. Amid these debates a chance incident occurred which I found briefly more harrowing than anything since the efforts of Hugh Massingham to extract Budget secrets from me in the spring of 1948. Gaitskell and I in the summer of 1951 were troubled, like all post-war governments, with a threatened upsurge in pay rates, and we both believed that statutory dividend limitation was a fair quid pro quo for pay restraint. We had prepared a draft White Paper with an elaborate statutory limitation scheme which was being discussed in Cabinet Committees. Its details were more explosive, if revealed, for Stock Exchange prices, than most budgets. One day I went over from the Treasury to a series of ministerial meetings in the House with this draft in a sealed envelope. When I returned to the Treasury three hours later, my Secretary, Derek Mitchell, found it was gone from my papers. We together retraced my steps to each Committee Room in the House and found nothing. (He told me many years afterwards that I had remarked to him in the middle of Parliament Square: 'This is my fault, not yours.') Trying to keep calm, I rehearsed in my mind each movement of the previous few hours and suddenly remembered I had gone to the Commons Library and checked a train time. And on the relevant table in the Library I found the explosive envelope untouched and unopened. Derek Mitchell was throughout this testing summer of the greatest possible value and help to me, and the best private secretary I had at the Treasury among an exceedingly competent series. He was later (1964) Principal Private Secretary to the Prime Minister, Sir Alec Douglas-Home; and I strongly advised Harold Wilson, when he took over in 1964, to keep Mitchell on. He accepted this advice, if hesitantly at first; but after a time Mitchell's attempt to preserve his idea of the proprieties of the system apparently proved unacceptable.

Another much longer-lasting worry, however, unknown to the public for a time, thrust itself on us in June 1951. The weekly 'dollar drain' figures turned again into deficit for the first time since September 1949. For eighteen months after the 1949 devaluation the weekly surplus had been almost continuous, and the transformation since 1947 had been so great that even informed people were slow to believe that the tide could turn again. Indeed, in later years when 1951 came to be recalled as a crisis year, it was seldom remembered that the dollar surplus lasted well into June. What had really happened was that the huge US stockpiling of raw materials, provoked by the Korean war, had raised their prices by an average 40 per cent in a year, and this had – despite higher earnings by the sterling area – turned the UK current balance into deficit. For the first few weeks of July Treasury officials were naturally inclined to argue that a fortnight's small deficit in dollar inflows or outflows should not cause us to panic. The prospect of another 1947 or 1949 crisis could hardly have been more unwelcome, and there is always of course a tendency to avert one's eyes from warning signals. John Edwards, to give him full credit, had urged in the spring an even more disinflationary Budget than that of April 1951 in case such trouble was coming; and I had resisted this. We should occasionally listen, I thought, to the Party rather than the statisticians. But, as it turned out, he was right and I was wrong.

By the end of July, when Gaitskell was away resting to avoid total exhaustion, I was convinced that a major tightening of import quotas for inessential imports was necessary if a new sterling crisis was to be avoided. I had a long discussion with Otto Clarke, now the supreme commander of all import policy (it was known as the 'Ottoman Empire'), in which I urged a major cut in import quotas for manufactures all along the line. Clarke was dubious; and I knew that officials might attribute my wish for action to my suspected disposition for over-hasty initiatives. But I persisted. Before I left on holiday for the South-West with the family in mid-August, Clarke had agreed that some import cuts would be made. Years afterwards, when the usual Party argument was proceeding in the House about the 1951 crisis, and I was in Opposition and Reggie Maudling at the Treasury, I recalled how these cuts had been made. Maudling replied that he had made a search among the records and that he could discover no effective import cuts except in such minor items as pineapples. If this were true, the official action did not measure up to what I believed in August was being done. By the time when I returned from holiday in September 1951 to the Treasury, the general election of that autumn was upon us. The prospect for the election was not helped by the echoes of the Bevan resignation at the Labour Party Conference at Scarborough on 1–6 October, where Bevan came first in the vote for the National Executive. Dalton and Morrison for the moment survived, though Shinwell dropped out. Attlee had already announced on 19 September that the election would be held on 25 October.

It seemed to me at the time that the 1951 election, which had such lasting results, was unnecessary and undesirable from the point of view of both the country and the Labour Party. Those who advocated it argued that it was impossible to carry on for another year with so tiny a minority. My reply to this was that we had been told in February 1950 we could not survive one Finance Bill, and in fact we had survived two. To launch an election in the autumn of 1951 appeared to me to be choosing nearly the worst possible moment. As always, I put this strongly to Gaitskell, saying that I felt it amounted to 'abdication'. To my surprise, Gaitskell was not nearly so strongly convinced of this, though he inclined on balance to agree with me. George Brown and I actually went on a two-man deputation to Attlee, and pressed our views on him. It is a pleasure to recall years later that I was wholly at one with Brown at this time. But we made no impression. Morrison was opposed to the election, but he was in Washington. Dalton, on the other hand, favoured it, arguing that if Labour lost, it would only be by a few seats, and that if we waited longer, the loss would have been heavier. I do not believe that events bore this out. Although 1951–2 was a difficult year economically, the years 1953 and 1954 were the easiest years for the UK in the post-war epoch, as prices of imported materials and food fell after the Korean boom. I still believe the decision was wrong, and that the main motive for it was that senior Labour ministers, apart from Morrison, after eleven years in high office, and with Bevin and Cripps both lost to the Government, felt too exhausted to carry the burden any longer. The clinching motive in Attlee's mind was probably the attitude of the King, who was due to visit Australia that autumn and was worried at the prospect of a dissolution of Parliament and general election, and perhaps change of government, in his absence. Attlee took his duties to the monarchy, like his other duties, very seriously, and has told us himself that 'the King was worrying a good deal about the election'.[26]

It was the most fiercely fought, passionate, neck-and-neck, exhausting parliamentary election I ever contested (out of eleven). I also cared more about the result of this election, together with 1950 and 1959, than any other, pushing myself again to the physical limit. But the Labour Party had almost everything in 1951 against it: the redistribution of seats, the Bevanite quarrel only six months before, the loss of Bevin and Cripps, the Korean war burden, and the steady swing back of votes due to the revival of anti-Labour propaganda in the post-1945 press. Even on top of all this, the withdrawal of a large number of Liberal candidates, as compared with 1950, undoubtedly favoured the Conservatives. As polling day was 25 October, St Crispin's Day, I risked at our final crowded Battersea eve-of-the-poll meeting the night before, reciting: 'Tomorrow is St Crispian', from *Henry, V* (carefully omitting the words 'we few, we happy few') and was not actually shouted down.

In all the circumstances the result was as surprising as it was ironic. It was

[26] See Dalton, p. 377, and Wheeler-Bennett, *King George VI*, pp. 790–4.

indeed a close-run thing. Labour won more votes than ever before, or since, more than the Conservatives, and more than any political Party ever had. But the Conservatives won more seats in the Commons. The result was:

In seats		*In votes*	
Conservatives	321	Conservatives	13,717,538
Labour	295	Labour	13,948,605
Liberals	6	Liberals	730,556
Irish Nationalists	3		

There was thus a Conservative majority of seventeen seats over all others. On the evening of the Friday on which these results were known, my wife and I dined with Frank and Elizabeth Pakenham at the White Tower Restaurant, Percy Street, and no company could have been a more refreshing relief from total exhaustion. Rab Butler, who was to take over from Gaitskell as Chancellor, most amicably invited us to spend Saturday and Sunday at the Treasury, if we wished, and clear up the debris of (in my case) four years in Great George Street.

The outstanding fact about the record of the 1945–51 Government is this: that it not merely accomplished more than any other Government since 1914 in peacetime in six years; but it accomplished so much that many people even among those who lived through those years find it hard to remember and compile the complete list even of major measures. First undoubtedly, seen in retrospect from the 1970s, was the economic recovery achieved, in real terms, and the intensity of full employment maintained. As already recorded, from a current balance of payments deficit of £630 million in 1947, surpluses or small deficits were achieved in 1948, 1949 and a surplus of £244 million in 1950, before the Korean war drove us back into the temporary deficit of £398 million in 1951. But the really remarkable success in these years was the growth in volume of production and exports, and the very slow rise in living costs and pay rates, despite unemployment of around 1·5 per cent. Though this book is far from being an economic history, the story would not be complete without just one statistical table to commemorate the national effort in these years: [27]

	1947	1948	1949	1950	1951
Industrial production: (1946=100)	108	121	129	140	144
Manufacturing production: (1946=100)	109	123	132	146	150
Export volume	100	127	140	162	167
Weekly wage rates	100	106	109	111	120
Retail prices	100	108	111	114	125

[27] *Economic Surveys* 1951, 1952 and 1953 and *Annual Abstract of Statistics*, 1955.

If we had known in 1951 the history of the next twenty-five years, we should have felt very much more satisfied with the record of these early years than we did at the time.

Naturally in the first years of recovery from the war, one would expect a fairly rapid increase in the volume of output and exports. But it *was* achieved. And what would not any government have given, in any other years since the war, to have achieved a 50 per cent rise in the volume of manufacturing output in five years, and 67 per cent in the volume of export in four years? Even more impressive, because here wartime shortages were working against moderation, was the rise of only 25 per cent in four years in living costs, and 21 per cent in weekly wage rates. In 1949 and 1950 the rise in retail cost and wage rates was held to not more than 3 or 4 per cent a year; which thirty years later would have been regarded as a triumph. Production and employment in 1947–50 were so high that earnings may well have kept pace with living costs, and real standards of the mass of the population not actually have fallen. But certainly real income generally scarcely rose. The 40 to 50 per cent rise in national production in these years was absorbed almost entirely by greater exports, re-payment of overseas debts, repair of wartime damage and investment in industry. The first majority Labour Government thus built for the future and put higher consumption sternly at the end of the queue. The immediate effect, of this long-term policy was to swing political support away from the Government. Political popularity meant nothing to Cripps. Despite all this, more Labour than Conservative votes were cast in 1951, must surely be explained by continuing public support for the Government's record of reforms.

What naturally meant most to me in 1951 was the visible success of my own child, the Development Area policy. It was only a hope for the future in 1944–5, but the achievement could be measured in hard figures by 1951; and Labour candidates in 1951 in Scotland, Wales, the North East coast, West Cumberland and Lancashire had unanswerable arguments which were well understood by the electorate. In spite of the sudden ending of war production in these areas in 1945, the new policy had exerted a dramatic effect on employment. The quick switch-over of wartime factories, the launching of new industrial estates and the mounting programme of Government factory-building, gave these areas in a few years a bigger share than they had ever had before of new industry in this country. In 1935, for instance, of 488 new factories opened in England and Wales, 213 were actually in Greater London, and only two in the 'Special Areas' as they were then called. Yet in the years 1944–8, about 50 per cent of all new factories were built in the new Development Areas, including Scotland. By the end of 1948, some 218 new factory buildings had been completed in Scotland, 181 in the North East coast, and 132 in South Wales. As a result, within three years of the end of the war, employment in the Development Areas was far higher than in any previous peacetime years. By the end of

1948, some 250,000 more people were at work in these areas than in 1939, 400,000 more than in 1937, and 800,000 more than in 1932 – a substantial gain in itself to the nation's productive capacity. The unemployment figures give the sharpest picture of the post-1945 revolution:

	Unemployment % 1932	1948–9
North East Coast	38	3
Industrial Scotland	35	$4\frac{1}{2}$
South Wales	41	$5\frac{1}{2}$
West Cumberland	46	$3\frac{1}{2}$

By 1951 the unemployment percentage of the Development Areas had in some cases fallen even further: to 1·5 per cent in the North East Coast, for instance in June 1951. The industrial estates and the 'advance factories' were in the long run the main single secret of success. No doubt, even if there had been no Development Area policy at all after 1945, unemployment would have been lower in these areas than in the worst years of the 1930s, due to the general expansionist policy being followed in this and other countries. But the result of *laissez-faire* in industrial location in 1945–50 would have been intense congestion in new building and labour shortage in London and the Midlands, and a major upsurge of unemployment in the Development Areas, as war production shut down. Probably unemployment in the Development Areas, instead of reaching about 100,000 as it did in 1949–50, would have touched 300,000 or 400,000. What the Development Area policy achieved, apart from the human regeneration, was the proof of what had so often been denied in the 1930s, that deliberate policy could influence the geographical spread of new industry and employment: so successfully indeed that thirty years later it could reasonably be argued that the policy should be halted. But whatever might have happened otherwise, the facts of employment, unemployment and location in 1950–1 were hard and visible and could not be denied. I could not help taking some pride in this. Perhaps most of us do our best work before we are forty.

Yet economic policy was only one strand in the complete story of the 1945–51 Labour Government. Even if full employment was the main achievement, and if the founding of the UN, the World Bank, the International Monetary Fund and other UN Agencies are credited to the wartime Coalition, the list is long:

Formation of NATO, in which Britain took the initiative
Formation of the OEEC,[28] led by Bevin, which channelled Marshall Aid and revived Western Europe
Grant of independence to India, Pakistan, Burma and Ceylon

[28] Organization for European Economic Co-operation.

National Insurance Act 1946 embodying improved Beveridge Plan and doubling
   of old-age pension
Public Assistance transformed into National Assistance
Family Allowances
Revival of British Agriculture through guaranteed prices without protection
National Health Service
Raising of school-leaving age and grants for university students
Building of over one million new houses
Town and Country Planning Act of 1947
New Towns
Legal Aid
National Parks
Public ownership of coal, electricity, gas, civil aviation and railways
Generation of nuclear power
Higher taxation of inherited wealth and greater redistribution of incomes and
   property generally
Re-payment of the greater part of our wartime debts overseas
Colombo Plan, the first major step towards international aid to poorer countries.

Nobody could say that the 1945 Government was inactive or its programme
narrow. Perhaps the best verdict on it is that of Harold Macmillan that it
was 'one of the most able governments of modern times'.[29]

Yet the statistical accident of the 1951 result, by which the Party with
the most votes failed to get the most seats, determined the course of British
politics for more than twelve years afterwards. The Government that won
in 1951 was destined to coast along into the economically easy years of 1952,
1953 and 1954, when, after the Korean war boom, the balance of trade fell
back naturally in favour of this country, and we had the wit to continue the
policy of buying food and materials from the world's most efficient producers. This made possible, thanks to the tough policies followed up till
1951, the first rise in real living standards since 1939 and a relaxation of
controls and restrictions. That in turn was bound to gain support for whatever government was in power after 1952, as the Conservatives found in the
elections of 1955 and 1959. Yet the chance to reap these rewards derived
from the paradoxical 1951 result, and this result in turn stemmed from
Cripps's refusal to allow the 1950 election to be postponed until after the
April 1950 Budget.[30] Had it been so postponed, it is highly probable that
Labour would have won in 1950 by a rather larger margin, and Attlee
would have felt no compulsion to call another election in 1951. In that case
the post-war Labour Government would itself in all human probability
have coasted through to the easy years.

[29] Harold Macmillan, *Tides of Fortune* (London, 1979), p. 49.
[30] See p. 192.

When I ceased to be a Treasury Minister in October 1951, I had worked in the Government service, with only a few months' break in 1946–7, for eleven years. After that length of time, one tends to value the bureaucratic life at its lowest, and political freedom very highly. But loss of ministerial office also confronts most politicians, unless they are lucky enough to have private resources, with a sudden and sharp drop in income. Much as I should have liked in October 1951 to devote myself wholly from then on to Parliament and politics, the halving of one's income overnight, with five other members of the family to support, concentrates the mind wonderfully. Percy Cudlipp saved the situation immediately by offering me my old job as part-time leader-writer on the *Daily Herald*. Michael Foot was the other, and we normally took turn-and-turn about. I volunteered for the unpopular Sunday stint, as on Sundays one was free of Parliament. Frankly I was delighted. Though it was now the third time I had joined the *Daily Herald* (after 1937 and 1946), I believed that the old crusading spirit would prevail, and that the paper was doing a national job in giving the British public a genuinely democratic choice of newspapers. Cudlipp, now a sincere but sceptical Labour Party supporter, was one of the most loyal as well as stimulating and spirited colleagues with whom I ever worked. He made work almost enjoyable. Nor could one have wanted a more co-operative fellow leader-writer than Michael Foot, whom I found to be as laconic in conversation as he was eloquent on paper and on the platform.

Before, however, I had barely a week in which to reconstruct this new double life, I nearly involved myself in a parliamentary catastrophe. In the first few days of Debate on the Address, under the new Churchill Government, I was asked by Attlee to open the economic day on November 8, as Gaitskell and I were the two surviving ex-Treasury Ministers. This was a fairly formidable prospect with Attlee, Morrison and Gaitskell beside me, and Churchill, Eden, Lyttleton, Butler and John Anderson facing us across the Dispatch Box. In the morning at the *Daily Herald* office, I composed a speech. It had, I hoped, one good joke. As there was still no sign of the 'red meat' Woolton had promised the electorate, I proposed to say that 'Lord Woolton's red meat has gone the way of all flesh'. Encouraged by this, I blithely lunched with Lord Piercy in the City – and remembered at 2.15 that the Debate on the Address starts, not at 3.30 like other major debates, but at 2.30. Leaping into a taxi, I found I had left my speech at the *Daily Herald* office. My heart sank deeper than I could recall since schooldays. There was ten minutes to go. Should I divert the taxi to Long Acre and recover the speech? Or go straight to the House and try to speak without notes? The spectacle of Churchill glaring across the table loomed before my mind. Then, overcoming panic, and searching again in my brief case, I found the speech, and arrived on the Front Bench between an anxious Attlee and relieved Gaitskell with two minutes to spare.

My normal day after 1951 was a constant shuffle to and fro by bus or Underground between the House and the *Herald* offices off Long Acre. One room in a cottage in the Odham's complex was generously allocated to me by the *Herald*, where a willing girl typist, even more generously, helped with constituency correspondence as I could not afford a paid secretary. The morning I normally spent at the *Herald*; Question Time in the House after lunch; much of the rest of the afternoon at the *Herald* on days when I was responsible for leaders; and one or two evenings a week in Battersea until the normal division in the House at 10 p.m. Not having a car myself till 1960, I found the late journeys to and from Battersea on public transport the most exhausting part of the week. Sundays were left for the *Daily Herald*. Seldom have I known human life more gloomy than on a wet Sunday afternoon in Long Acre in late November.

The really threatening problem in these years was to earn enough to support a growing family without taking too much time away from Parliament. I am sure that many other MPs in the 1950s would also have wished to devote more time to Parliament and their constituencies, but were forcibly diverted to other pursuits simply to make ends meet. I was invited in 1951 as an ex-Financial Secretary to the Treasury, to become Chairman of the Public Accounts Committee, an ancient, honourable, and laborious office. I would have dearly loved to accept, but felt bound to decline, as it was of course unpaid, and I did not believe I could give a fair amount of time to the *Daily Herald* if I took this on also. These years left me with the firm conviction that MPs should set an example by being paid less than those outside doing comparable jobs, but not so much less that members with families are compelled to neglect their parliamentary duties. The salary should be enough for those who wish to be whole-time members to be so, though permitting others, if they prefer, to do other work outside. At times in the 1950s the parliamentary salary fell below this limit; the full-timers were in great difficulty and anxiety, and the British Parliament suffered lastingly as a result. It was also not generally realized that only because a very few full-timers like Morrison, Butler and Gaitskell kept the whole institution going, were so many others able to treat it as a part-time job. The experience also filled me with heartfelt amusement at the Conservative theory that a cut in income tax makes people work harder. The effect on me of a cut in income tax, throughout any part of life whenever I had a choice, was to say that thank heaven I don't need to write another article in order to pay the gas and electricity bills; and a rise in tax was equally a spur to effort.

In the 1950s, meanwhile, I found the centre of life shifting away from working hours to children, family and the West Country. By 1951, my elder son, Peter, was fourteen, Martin twelve, and the twins, Helen and Catherine, six. Happily they came to share the rock-climbing, surf-bathing, moor-walking pattern which my own youth had created, and our three weeks in the summer on Dartmoor and the North Cornish coast turned out to be even more precious than in my own first youth. Indeed at times it seemed to be the reality, and the rest of the year the illusion. The intense beauty of Dartmoor in particular, in its ever-changing variety of moods, colours, contours and horizons is still a revelation to those who know it most intimately. My growing but intermittent love of it in the 1920s and 1930s, became in the 1950s, because shared with the family, an unbreakable bond, strengthened by the enthusiasm of their response. In the earlier summer months – stimulated by a glorious evening at Winchester in June 1951 for an *Any Questions* session with Dick Crossman and Toby Low – I also formed a habit of a visit there every other Saturday or so, a picnic with Peter and Martin by the river, a wholly idle afternoon watching cricket, and a train journey home in the late summer evening over the Hampshire hills, in time for Sunday at the *Herald* next day.

Nevertheless the Opposition battle in the House had to be fought unrelentingly. The greater freedom and closer team spirit with political colleagues are some compensation for the loss of the immense expertise of the Civil Service. To be left suddenly without a private secretary of the highest ability and loyalty like Derek Mitchell feels, for a few days, almost like losing one's sight and the use of one's limbs. But in my case in October 1951 the opportunity for a more direct and daily partnership with Hugh Gaitskell made up for these losses. At first some of us ex-junior ministers, including Jim Callaghan and Kenneth Younger as well as myself, did not quite know how to behave in Opposition or where to sit in the House. Attlee soon settled this by saying that privy councillors sat on the front bench and others did not. In those days members could not move to and fro, as became the custom in the 1960s between front and back benches: so that in 1951 if you were a privy councillor you could only speak for the Government and not for instance make a constituency speech from back benches. Also there were no 'shadow' appointments (the expression, apart from 'Shadow Cabinet', only dated from 1954): and privy councillors on the front bench spoke on any subject when asked to by the Leadership. I became a privy councillor at the end of 1951, and I decided to make Treasury and Board of Trade affairs my province on the front bench. Jim Callaghan, on the other hand, did not become a privy councillor, but was from the very first and uninterruptedly elected to the Parliamentary Committee (Shadow Cabinet) of the Party. This after a time put him too on the front bench. But before this we together enjoyed one memorable Friday in the House on 23 November 1951, which opened our eyes to the glorious freedom of Opposition. I had been asked to look after the not very exalting topic of the 'Expiring Laws Continuance Bill'. Arthur Salter, now a Treasury Minister, incautiously remarked that 'great and grave' economies would have to be made in local authority spending. Callaghan and I leapt upon this in a thin Friday House and teased Salter most of the afternoon into more and more indiscretions.

From the end of 1951 onwards through thirteen years of Opposition I became a regular attender at Question Time. After thirty years' study of Question Time from all sides, I still believe that it is in general a most valuable, if not the most valuable, form of parliamentary procedure. Certainly it seldom enables the questioner to penetrate deep. But a great deal of information is extracted; and if the minister refuses to answer, it is made obvious that he is doing so. You have to listen to other parliaments attempting Question Time, or a substitute for it, to realize the merits of our own. In few or any other parliaments can thirty or forty subjects be raised in fifty-five minutes in full publicity. Question Time is also a genuine form of public 'accountability', and offers more drama and dialectical ebb and flow than any rival procedure. True, I notice a distinct worsening in brevity and precision in the 1960s and 1970s. In the late 1940s, some fifty or sixty questions were almost always completed in fifty-five minutes. In my last Question Time as a minister in 1967, I reached number ninety. But in the late 1960s and 1970s, due purely to verbosity in both question and answer, hardly half of the average of the 1950s was reached, and the PM had to have an artificial cut-off at 3.15. A return to the brevity of the 1940s would be a most valuable parliamentary reform; and another would be the lengthening of Question Time from fifty-five minutes to one and a half hours at the expense of general debate.

My main parliamentary job in these years was putting across the Labour Party's case in economic and financial debates. Hugh Gaitskell naturally became Chairman of the Parliamentary Labour Party Finance Group, and a strong, harmonious team was built up around him, including Roy Jenkins, Tony Crosland, Jack Diamond, Douglas Houghton, Dick Mitchison and, after some months and some gyrations, Harold Wilson. Mitchison, once in the 1930s a writer of revolutionary pamphlets, had now become our benevolent legal adviser and professional draftsman. As soon as the Finance Bill began its long battle in April, we met almost daily at 2 o'clock in a Committee Room to decide speakers and tactics in that day's debate; and usually before this conferred with the ever-affable Sir Charles McAndrew, Tory Deputy Speaker, and Chairman of Ways and Means, to let him know which amendment we hoped he would call. Out of these lunch-hour colloquies grew the practice, later formalized, of numbering amendments and listing those to be called in the 'No' lobby before the debate. Sir Charles was the best Deputy Speaker I remember; sharp, humorous, and genuinely impartial. He also offered sherry at the lunch-time rehearsals. Gaitskell conducted the 2 o'clock meetings in a fashion that pleased almost everybody, and normally made them enjoyable in themselves.

After the new Government's cuts in the food subsidies at the end of 1951, which we fiercely attacked as a flat contradiction of Woolton's election promises, there was less violent Party feeling in the later Budget debates. This was partly because Butler, our main antagonist as Chancellor, was able to reduce taxes in an easier situation due to falling world prices of food and materials after 1951, and partly, I believe, because he had privately

RAB'S EASTER EGG

Rab's Easter Egg – Gaitskell, Dalton and the author among the onlookers. Cartoon by Low, *Manchester Guardian*, 2 April 1953

much more sympathy with our arguments than with the old deflationary Tory policies of 1931. Butler himself once surprised us by talking of 'our social-democracy' in this country. For this reason, the *Economist* invented the term 'Mr Butskell' to describe the apparent concordat. But it pretty soon evaporated; and indeed the word itself first appeared in an *Economist* article headed 'The end of Mr Butskell'.

It is the job of an Opposition spokesman in Parliament to expose the weaknesses in the Government case and the strong points in his own. But he should stop short of appearing to rejoice in national misfortunes and failures. Once in this period (February 1953), after I had made some week-end speech, I was telephoning in the House when Churchill came lumbering past and as he saw me remarked with high jocularity: 'I see you take a very gloomy view,' and added, as he stalked off: 'I am sure you hope you're not right.' The danger for all parties which spend too long in Opposition is that they tend to think increasingly of making a case that will weaken the Government, and less and less ask themselves the question 'What would I really do if I were in office?' In 1952-3 almost all the Opposition jobs on the front bench in the economics debates fell to Gaitskell and me, because Harold Wilson, since his resignation in 1951, had placed himself on a back bench below the gangway. One evening in 1952 Gaitskell asked me whether I thought he should invite Wilson back on to the front bench for economic debates. (Wilson had not been elected to the Parliamentary Committee.) Gaitskell wondered whether this might tend to bridge the gap. I said off the cuff I did not see why we need, as Wilson had placed himself on the back benches and could let Gaitskell know if he wanted to return. Later, I think in 1953, Gaitskell mentioned the same possibility again and I said it seemed to me about time Wilson was persuaded to return. So Gaitskell asked him, and he came. In the 1951-4 period the Labour Opposition was in a particular difficulty. The rise in prices due to the Korean boom wore off in 1952, and for many months world prices were falling. It was the easiest and most favourable moment in our post-war economic fortunes. The sacrifices of 1945-51 were yielding their reward; and taxes could be reduced and rationing could go. Petrol and clothes rationing had indeed already gone under the Labour Government. But this made Opposition uphill work in 1951-4; and incidentally caught the Conservatives in a difficulty after 1954 when the balance of trade turned adverse again.

What made effective opposition in the House, however, even harder was the continuation even after 1951 of the 'Bevanite' feud. The name 'Bevanism' was itself illuminating because after 1951 the drive came from Bevan personally, and it was seldom clear what major issues were supposed to be at stake. The whole squabble seemed to me destructive and unnecessary, because I had never felt strongly either way about the original issues ostensibly in dispute. Also, remembering Harold Wilson's conduct in the 1949 devaluation crisis and Bevan's hysterical outburst to me in the passage when he heard of Gaitskell's appointment as Chancellor, I could not help suspecting what the real motives were, even if unconscious, for keeping it all going. Very soon 'Bevanism' became a notable case of what Thucydides, in his account of the civil war in Corfu calls 'stasis':[1] faction for faction's sake in which the protagonists know which side they are on, but usually cannot remember why it all started. Crossman blurted out this state of mind in a talk with Dalton,[2] who quotes him as saying 'The quarrel would go on and on. The Bevanites would never let it die. In the end Bevan would win.'[3] Dalton comments: 'All personal hatreds.... Just not adult.'

In any political party the local activists understandably tend to be zealots. They are much more interested in what they would like to do than what practically can be done. In the British Conservative Party the extremist few want to restore hanging and mangle the welfare state. In the Labour Party they would like to nationalize almost everything and cut defence spending to 50 per cent or so below wherever it stands at the moment. It is always open to any politician of scant scruple to mobilize support by purporting to agree with the extremes. Bevan, who had also a genuine impulse towards extremes, and usually did not like discussing serious policy soberly,[4] could not always resist the temptation, and his disciples followed suit. The trouble about such capitulation to the zealots is that it inevitably leads to crushing electoral defeat, for the simple reason that 98 per cent of the electorate are very different people from the Party extremists. It also puts the moderates in the Party in an awkward position because they are compelled either to keep silent or argue against the dogmas of the faithful. All this was forced to the surface by the Bevanite group in the 1950s. In addition almost all of the group, other than Bevan and Wilson, had not been ministers in the Attlee Government. This both generated in them some resentment against Attlee, and left them inexperienced in the practicabilities of government.

Very soon after the 1951 election the discovery that this group were holding regular Monday meetings and deciding tactics excited anger in the rest of the Parliamentary Labour Party. Already in March 1952 the traditional Standing Orders of the Parliamentary Party had to be introduced, after a Bevanite revolt in that spring's defence debate. The Bevanites, rather desperate for a justification of the continued meetings of their group, occasionally quoted XYZ as a precedent, and Michael Foot even does so in his excellent biography of Bevan.[5] This of course ignored a vital distinction. The Bevanite group was one of MPs discussing political tactics in the

---

[1] Thucydides, Book III, para. 80–85.
[2] Dalton, *High Tide and After*, p. 390.
[3] Dalton, p. 389.
[4] See Crossman's account quoted by M. Foot, *Aneurin Bevan*, vol. II, p. 374.
[5] Foot, vol. II, p. 359. Incidentally Michael Foot says XYZ was founded 'by Douglas Jay and a few others in the early 1940s'. In fact it was founded by Vaughan Berry and others in 1932, and I joined several years later. See Chapter 3 of this book.

House, such as how to vote at Party meetings, and reaching decisions. Foot himself says that after the 1951 election 'the Bevanites sought to organize themselves into a more effective parliamentary group. . . . It was agreed to elect a regular chairman and meet at a regular time in the parliamentary week.'[6] XYZ on the other hand was a dining and talking club which considered no parliamentary business, had no officers, reached no decisions, and after 1939 composed no papers. In the early 1950s many in the PLP felt with some reason that a group of the Party which regularly discussed policy and tactics and reached decisions amounted to a 'Party within a Party' and was likely to provoke retaliation. So the road to faction was opened up, to the deep but impotent regret of many of us who believed that such disunity would lead infallibly to defeat at the next election.

In August 1952, a month and a half before the Morecambe Party Conference, I enjoyed a Parisian interlude. William Hayter, then serving in the Paris Embassy, and his wife Iris – always a most endearing hostess – invited me and my son Peter, aged fifteen, to stay with them in Paris. For Peter it was a voyage of discovery which he seized with avid enthusiasm. We all visited Chartres, where Hayter and I had stayed in the school trip from Winchester just twenty-seven years before. One day Jean Monnet lunched with us in Hayter's flat, and expounded in fluent English his vision of, in effect, a federated Western Europe. Monnet's real basic argument, to which he always returned, was the need after repeated European wars for France and Germany to bury the hatchet. As a Catholic his strongest loyalty seemed to be to Christendom, not to France. All arguments concerned with a wider world than Catholic Europe, all mundane thoughts of the living standards of the common people, were swept aside. It became very apparent, if one listened carefully (with Monnet talking, you could only listen) that the French, Germans and Italians, in his view, desired some sort of federation because they had little confidence in, or loyalty to, their own fragile constitutions. Monnet talked as one whose country had been defeated in the war. It was a deeply instructive lesson to me.

Back at home in the autumn of 1952 a Labour Party Conference faced us, with the Bevanite issue unresolved. Though I had hoped in the early months of that year that the feud would fizzle out, I had to decide in September whether to stand as a candidate from my local Party to the National Executive. The Party rule in those days laid down that an MP candidate for the Executive must be the delegate of his local Party at the Conference. I knew that as a delegate I could not accept a 'mandate' from the Party to vote on policy contrary to my convictions. This my Party generously accepted; but a worse dilemma loomed. Was I to accept their 'mandate' also on the election of candidates to the National Executive? To do so might mean my

[6] Foot, vol. II, p. 358. In Dalton's words, The 'Bevanites met to decide their attitude and tactics at PLP meetings, hoping to win prestige victories on this or that issue' (Dalton, p. 386.

voting largely for people who, I believed, would damage the Party. But not to do so would disfranchise my local Party. No doubt the ballot was secret, and a local Party would not know how votes were cast. I soon decided, however, that I could not mislead them, and must therefore accept their 'mandate' on candidates. I next enquired of two leading members of the Party, who afterwards attained high positions in and out of Governments, and asked what they would do. They each replied: 'What is the difficulty? The ballot is secret.' Just before the Conference I asked Gaitskell, who was of course standing, what he would do. He replied that he had thought carefully about it, decided that he could not mislead his local Party, and would therefore, on NEC candidates, accept their 'mandate'. I did the same. Because of this dilemma, after my local Party GMC on 24 September, a few days before the Conference, I wrote in my diary that: 'I much regretted the decision to stand for the NEC and go as delegate. Never again.' I kept this vow.

The Morecambe Conference of 1952 was memorable as one of the most unpleasant experiences I ever suffered in the Labour Party. The town was ugly, the hotels forbidding, the weather bad, and the Conference, at its worst, hideous. The only day I enjoyed was a drive on Sunday to the Lakes with my wife and Shiela Grant Duff, who was living in a farm in Cumberland near by. During some debates at Morecambe an apparently organized claque of extremists yelled from the gallery in a chorus of combined hysteria and hatred such as I had never encountered and found acutely distressing, indeed alarming. The hatred had a totalitarian ring. I had never before, not being a football enthusiast, seen human beings transformed in the mass into screaming fanatics; and as I listened in the worst moments, I reflected that presumably this was the type of frenzy which Hitler and Goebbels excited and for all I knew, Mark Antony. The nastiest interlude came when Arthur Deakin, the no-nonsense champion of the TGWU, used his 'fraternal greetings' to hit back at the Bevanites. They had just contrived the election of Wilson and Crossman to the National Executive instead of Morrison and Dalton. Being frontally attacked, the claque in the gallery lost control altogether, and the ensuing howls of hatred left wounds in the Party which were not quickly healed. Deakin later, and not very fraternally, described those who tried to shout him down as 'howling dervishes'. Later that evening I remarked to Gaitskell in a private talk that the Conference was my idea not of democracy, but of 'mob rule'. I never intended this phrase to be repeated, least of all in public. But in a speech in the very next week at Stalybridge Gaitskell remarked that 'It is time to end the attempt at mob rule by a group of frustrated journalists.' I told him next time we met that I feared this language was a political blunder, and he answered that he now thought I was right. But six months later he said he had changed his mind; and that his speech (including especially 'mob rule') had established him with the really influential trade union leaders, Arthur Deakin, Will

Lawther and Tom Williamson, as a far more effective bulwark than Attlee against extremists, and so conferred on him growing political strength.

Even Morecambe, however, had its humorous moments. My colleague, the delegate from South Battersea, none other than the one later expelled from the Party,[7] used to confer with some cell of cloak-and-dagger collaborators outside my bedroom door after midnight. I had to tell them I did not mind what they said, but I hoped that they would say it more quietly or elsewhere. Secondly, one evening Harold Wilson joined a group of us drinking coffee in a hotel and met – I think, for the first time – a young Transport House secretary called Marcia Williams, who was with us. My memory, which may be at fault, is that I helped in the introduction. Thirdly, Dick Crossman supplied the great laugh of the Conference. Having been elected the day before to the National Executive, he went to the rostrum amid cheers in the foreign policy debate on 1 October. He started thus: (I wrote down the words at the time) 'I had prepared a fiery speech, but after yesterday think it wise to be more sober.' For three seconds, subdued laughter from Dick's old friends, including those like myself, who had known him for thirty years, and who saw the trap into which he was falling. For another few seconds, a second wave of laughter from a wider circle who by this time saw the joke. Then booing for ten seconds from the sharper-witted extremists present, who by now realized how Crossman had actually boasted that, being safely on the National Executive, he would henceforth moderate his views. Next loud and prolonged booing by the whole body of extremists who saw at last that those laughing were actually making light of a great betrayal. And finally renewed uncontrollable laughter from Crossman's old colleagues at the indignation aroused among the hysterics at what the former knew to be quite normal practice for him. It was a full minute before the speech could continue, and Crossman must have been almost the only person present who did not understand the tumult and counter-tumult around him. Sitting silent, and probably having known Dick longer than anyone else in the hall, I could not help appreciating the finer points of this unrehearsed human comedy. It was not his finest minute.

There were also some serious interludes at Morecambe. Noel-Baker and Jim Griffiths spoke splendidly in the same foreign policy debate as Crossman; and the Griffiths speech in particular re-inspired me by its living proof that the highest flights of Celtic oratorical fervour can be combined with common sense. Bevan himself surprised with a reasoned speech on unemployment on the first day of the Conference (29 September), and brought the house down with a ringing plea for 'Socialist planning at workshop level'. Everyone cheered this phrase to the echo, and nobody had the least idea what it meant. Gaitskell performed the remarkable feat of arguing in five minutes the extremely unpopular case for defence spending and won a quiet

[7] See p. 158.

hearing even from that audience. Thanks to him and to Attlee, an anti-re-armament resolution was defeated at the end of this debate. And the great success of the Conference was Herbert Morrison, who on Tuesday, 30 September, immediately after the announcement of his defeat for the Executive after twenty-five years, spoke seriously, unresentfully, and humorously, and received at the end what I recorded at the time as a 'deafening reception'.

But the feast of oratory was largely in vain, and it was the 'howling dervishes' who reverberated in delegates' minds as they went home. The majority of Labour MPs felt in particular that the removal of Morrison and Dalton from the Executive, in favour of what looked like an organized Bevanite ticket, was a mortal blow at the Party. So the faction-fight smouldered on through 1953, 1954 and 1955, periodically bursting into flame, and annihilating the efforts of some of the rest of us to restore the Party's reputation with the electorate, until the general elections of 1955 and 1959 had been predictably lost. The re-emergence after 1945 of a partisan press, with a large Conservative majority, would on the evidence have made it very difficult in any case for the Labour Party to win an election. The Bevanite 'stasis' made it impossible. Those in the Bevanite camp who kept the feud going were, apart possibly from Bevan himself, imbued much more with blindness than malice or ambition. They did not know what they were doing in electoral terms. Bevan himself saw the folly of it after 1955, when it led to electoral defeat and Gaitskell's election as Leader of the Party at the end of the year. But the more myopic of his disciples needed the second defeat of 1959 before they understood.

After Morecambe, the great majority of the Parliamentary Labour Party wanted the Bevanites disbanded as an organized 'Party within a Party'. Having found time to spend a glorious day with Peter at Salisbury Cathedral on one of his days off from school in early October 1952, which did much to restore my peace of mind, I wrote a leader in the *Herald* on 14 October urging the Bevanites to disband voluntarily and call off the conflict. At this moment a 'Keep Calm' group emerged, consisting of Strachey, Strauss and Stewart, which Dalton described as the 'Soft Centre'. The motion to disband organized groups was carried on 23 October in the PLP by the decisive majority of 188 to 51. In the division lobby that night, having stayed on speaking terms with Bevan since our dealings in the Attlee Government, I made some would-be friendly remark; to which he replied 'Herbert Morrison is a liar.' This reminded me of Ernie Bevin's famous gibe made – I have little doubt, though there is no conclusive proof – about Bevan. When someone said to Bevin that Bevan was 'his own worst enemy', Bevin replied: 'Not while I'm alive, he ain't.'[8]

However, in the election for the Deputy Leader a few days later, Morrison defeated Bevan by 194 votes to 82. Close on the heels of this,

[8] I could never discover direct evidence for this oft-told story.

H

came in November 1952 the vote for the Shadow Cabinet; and the majority of the Party insisted that the Bevanite device of voting for a ticket of six or eight individuals, while the rest of the Party normally distributed their votes widely on ground of personal merit, should be countered by the classical remedy of the Second Ballot. And of course the Bevanite 'list' this year provoked a counter-list from the majority. On the first ballot, Griffiths, Gaitskell, Chuter Ede, Callaghan, Dalton and Robens were elected outright, and Bevan came twelfth. Bevan behaved hysterically at the meeting on 19 November when this was announced, and Strachey became melodramatic, saying to me 'We will have to say farewell.' However Bevan duly calmed down, and on 27 November, in the second ballot, Soskice came top and Bevan twelfth out of the finally elected twelve. In the second ballot I voted for Bevan among others, as it seemed to me that he plainly should be *one* member of the Shadow Cabinet. So did Roy Jenkins, Tony Crosland and Austen Albu to my knowledge, for the same reason. Only a few days later Bevan most amiably asked me for material for his speech in a censure debate on the Government, and chatted genially across me with Attlee about the tactics for this debate.

A week or so before this in a Fabian Autumn Lecture on 25 November, I had tried to switch back a little attention to serious economic policy and to the long-term promise of the Cripps-Gaitskell national strategy by expounding the idea of a ten-year recovery plan for Britain. Dalton and Strachey lent me confidence by sitting on either side of me on the platform. My theme was the need for steady, long-term industrial investment and a 30 per cent rise in the volume of exports over ten years, mainly from engineering, steel and coal. (In those days we believed that a resumption of coal exports was possible, as it should have been.) In fact in the next few years UK exports – apart from coal – increased faster than I forecast. My plan was a modest success, and even received favourable comment from *The Times* and *Guardian*. Even the dismal science can be an antidote to a surfeit of emotional spasms. The *Economist* even described the plan as 'a possible bridge between Bevanites and non-Bevanites'. *Tribune* asked me to write an article; Harold Wilson invited me to speak in his constituency. Wonders, I felt, never cease.

Throughout 1953, the year of the Coronation, the Bevanite squabble flickered on. The Bevanite group did not of course really disband. But it turned itself into a smaller, private lunch discussion-group. Michael Foot recalls: 'So over the next few years a much attenuated Bevanite group – six members of the [Labour Party] Executive, Bevan himself, Crossman, Driberg, Mikardo, Wilson, plus . . . Jenny Lee, John Freeman, J. P. W. Mallalieu and myself – assembled every Tuesday lunch-time while Parliament was sitting, at Dick Crossman's house at 9 Vincent Square.'[9] In early February, *Tribune* revived the faction spirit by attacking Lincoln Evans,

[9] Foot, vol. II, pp. 390–91.

the leading iron and steel trade unionist of the day, for taking a knighthood. Percy Cudlipp, without consulting me, retaliated with a violent leader in the *Herald* denouncing *Tribune*; and warfare broke out all round. When the National Executive of the Party then rebuked everyone, the mood I encountered among parliamentary colleagues was markedly one of sorrow rather than of anger. But I wrote in early March: 'Party strife now so bad after the Lincoln Evans attack by *Tribune* and Executive's rebuke to *Herald* for attacking Bevanites that I almost despair of Party.'

In April of this transitional year I allowed myself a few days interlude at Königswinter on the Rhine attending the Anglo-German annual conference organized by the admirable Frau Milchsach, who devoted her life to fostering Anglo-German friendship. My efforts at No. 10 in the winter of 1945–6 to keep the Germans from outright starvation had apparently been reported to Frau Milchsach and I was pressed as a sort of champion of Anglo–German reconciliation to go to Königswinter. Crossman, always fascinated by Germans, was there with a motley company including Christopher Mayhew, Denis Healey, Vaughan Berry, Bob Boothby, Nicholas Kaldor, Kingsley Martin and the volatile Woodrow Wyatt. The hotel was uncomfortable, the Germans humourless, and the debates somewhat formal. At this period the serious issue was the future of German armed forces – the suggested 'European Defence Community' (killed by the French) and 'German Re-armament'. I had frankly begun to feel that by 1953 enough had been done to restore Anglo–German amity, and that a little lightheartedness might be permitted. Notes were normally passed to the chairman from would-be speakers. Once I could not resist passing up to the chairman (Boothby) a note saying 'Herr Martin Bormann wishes to speak', and planted on Nicholas Kaldor a coat label (which all but he could read) with the name 'Martin Bormann'; indiscretions which, I fear, provoked hilarity among the British and incomprehension among the Germans. Despite this, I was to my surprise asked again in later years.

Though we spent many days and nights in the spring and summer of 1953 toiling away at the Budget and Finance Bill, it was not an easy year for Opposition. At lunch on 16 July Gaitskell, Crosland and I reviewed the political and economic prospect and agreed that no major initiative seemed possible. Gaitskell was inclined to think Attlee too weak in handling the Bevanites; but I recorded: 'waiting policy inevitable; but I don't like it'. Then one of those curious incidents occurred out of the blue in August which make politics so unpredictable. I noticed on 8 August a sentence in the sixteen-nation UN Declaration on the Korean war which said that the war 'will in all probability be extended beyond Korea'. This prospect of extending the war into China struck me as wholly contrary to the UN principle of resisting territorial aggression against South Korea. On Sunday 9 August, I wrote a full leader for the *Daily Herald* the next day denouncing the idea, and agreed with Patrick Gordon-Walker a letter to *The Times* signed by each of us, which they published on 12 August. *The Times* wrote a leader approving this letter; other papers supported it and only the *Economist* disagreed. Churchill, whose health had worsened that summer, immediately returned to London, saw Salisbury, and issued a rather feeble Government reply. So I used my August freedom, following up the letter with a series of *Daily Herald* leaders condemning any intention of extending the war further. On 14 August the Labour Party made an official statement supporting the *Daily Herald* argument. The Bevanites then joined in with backing from an article in *Tribune* by Barbara Castle. At Postbridge, Dartmoor, in August, we were joined by Norman Robertson, Canadian High Commissioner in London and a very able and impressive Canadian civil servant, who shared my view that the Korean war had gone far enough. Eisenhower, Robertson said, had recently told him that he would 'probably get rid of Dulles within the year'. Unhappily he did not.

At the Party Conference that autumn, October 1953 at Margate, so mercifully sunnier than Morecambe or Blackpool, all passion seemed to be spent on the Bevanite front. A happy compromise was reached by which Morrison rejoined the National Executive ex-officio as Deputy Leader of the Party. Remembering the torments of Morecambe, I only attended for one day; but did hear Gaitskell in a brief but memorable speech on education propound the principle that 'it is better in education to build up rather than tear down'. In the Parliamentary Committee (Shadow Cabinet) election which followed the Conference later in October, Bevan came ninth and Harold Wilson missed election by one vote. On the announcement of these results, the Bevanites generated a new storm in a teacup. Bill (J.P.W.) Mallallieu wrote an article in *Tribune* in November 1953, in effect accusing unnamed MPs of voting one way in the Parliamentary Committee elections in the House, and telling their constituency parties they were voting another. Mallallieu had been a good friend of mine in City journalism in the 1930s, as well as an Oxford contemporary before that, and became one of my junior ministers at the Board of Trade after 1964. This waspish article of his seemed to me altogether out of character. It evoked almost equally childish recrimination and renewed resentment against Bevanism, before the armed truce was restored.

Then just before the end of 1953, news came to me like a thunderclap of a totally unforeseen upheaval in the *Herald*. I discussed leaders as usual with Percy Cudlipp at about 5 p.m. on the evening of Friday 27 November, and after writing them went home. At 8.15 someone on the *Time & Life* staff rang me to ask for comment on Cudlipp's resignation from the *Daily Herald* which, they said, had just been publicly announced. This left me, for a time, frankly unnerved. Cudlipp had become my main link and close friend at the *Herald*. The parliamentary salary had not been raised since 1946 – for seven years – and more than half my income came from the *Herald*. I had set myself never to work for a paper which did not support the Labour Party. Next day I spoke to Cudlipp. The truth was that the Odhams management had been constantly pressing him to produce plans for 'raising the circulation to four million', and he finally had the bravery to write a memorandum saying bluntly that this could not be done unless very large sums of money were spent. Odhams (Dunbar was still reigning) accepted Cudlipp's resignation and appointed a new editor whose abilities were simply not on the same level as Cudlipp's. I decided to carry on as if nothing had happened and just fight the battle out to the end. It would have been a wonderful solace that weekend if I had known that I would remain on the *Daily Herald* staff for another five and a half years.

Arriving, however, at the office on the next day, Sunday afternoon, I found it ironical to remember how fourteen years before Francis Williams had walked out of the office to be succeeded by Cudlipp; and how little I would have guessed at that moment that I should ever come to grieve at Cudlipp as suddenly departing. From this moment what organization had previously existed at the *Herald* slid into chaos. Editorial conferences were often incoherent. Responsibilities were blurred. Hugh Pilcher, a professional journalist and political writer, whose sanity throughout all this was a breath of fresh air, once remarked to me that the situation was now so bad that soon someone would be stabbed in the chest. After a few oscillations and brighter moments, circulation continued to fall. I found it intensely distressing to see a great organization treated in this way, let alone one that had once raised high political hopes and aspirations. Each day after 1953 I moved out with intense relief from the bear garden of Long Acre to the comparative order and sanity of Westminster, and longed for the day when I could afford to devote myself wholly to serious politics and the Labour Party. As a forlorn hope, I sometimes talked with Tom Williamson, General Secretary of the General and Municipal Workers' Union, and wrote at his request a private memorandum in August 1954 stating what the real facts were and how I believed the *Herald* could be saved. In agreement with Williamson, I sent this to the TUC directors and to Surrey Dane of Odhams, Vice-Chairman of the *Daily Herald* after Southwood's death. A talk with Dane did not much encourage me. He was a likeable man who understood Labour Party aspirations. But his favourite saying was: 'Sooner or later you come up against reality.'

The truth was, as one can see clearly in retrospect twenty-five years later, that the decline of the *Herald*, though aggravated by reckless Odhams' decisions, was just one part of the general decline of Fleet Street from the mid-1950s onwards. High costs, restrictive practices, excessive pay, falling standards and – finally – 'independent' TV competition for advertisements, made a cut-throat commercial scramble inevitable. I once asked Percy Cudlipp before his break with Odhams what he thought would happen if his younger brother, Hugh, joined the *Herald* and was given a free hand to raise the circulation by any method he liked. Hugh Cudlipp was then considered the chief Fleet Street wizard. Percy thought for a moment, and then replied that he believed the circulation would continue to fall. When he said this, neither of us knew that Hugh Cudlipp *would* be given precisely this chance a few years later when the *Daily Mirror* swallowed Odhams; that the circulation would still fall; that he would then blame this on the name *Herald* and the Labour Party link; and change this to the *Sun* – and that the great revival would still not occur until Rupert Murdoch took over the *Sun* and turned it into a Chinese copy of the *Mirror*.

For the obstinate fact was that no mass market existed after the 1950s for the *Daily Herald* in anything like the form we had all hoped to preserve. Percy Cudlipp told me one day his view that popular papers which tried to be serious would lose circulation and advertisements; that the mass papers would tend to degenerate into crime, scandal and sensation sheets with a touch of pornography; and that commercial competition would threaten anyone who resisted these forces. One manifestation of this slide was the increasingly prevalent Fleet Street doctrine that only bad news was news. Crime, disaster, violence, bombs, impending national 'bankruptcy', protests and demonstrations are news. But reports of success, a problem solved, a contented family, factory or housing estate, are not 'readable'. A leader applauding the Government is 'dull'; but one attacking it, or at least attacking somebody, may help sell the paper. Of course some sections of the press and TV still stood out against this disease. But I suspect that more of the nation's troubles in this period than are commonly realized – excessive national self-criticism, for instance – sprang from changes not in the hard facts themselves, but in Fleet Street policies generated by the circulation struggle.

Parliament, Percy Cudlipp also thought, would soon cease to be reported – unless there was a lurid scene – in any but the 'quality' papers. What he did not quite foresee was that the decline of Fleet Street would in turn damage Parliament and the political system because the mass public, seeing Parliament mainly through the distorting mirror of the press, would believe that Parliament had in some way changed. Yet though here again honourable exceptions in the press have survived, and the battle is not wholly lost, this is to a great extent the story of the 1960s and 1970s. If the mass newspaper reader, for whom we used to write in the *Herald*, no longer found a report of a serious political debate, but only of occasional uproars or outbursts, he would believe that serious debate had ceased and hysteria had taken its place. He would not know that he was being misled. Certainly radio and even TV have done something to retard the general slide (one of Trollope's newspaper editors was prophetically called 'Mr Slide'). But despite broadcasting efforts, it remains hard in these circumstances for those living and working outside Fleet Street or Parliament to know what is really happening.

To me working daily in both spheres in the 1950s the whole depressing downward spiral was increasingly plain. Ordinary Members of Parliament, specially on the back benches, found themselves hemmed in by a triple pressure. First their best efforts usually went unrewarded and unknown because unreported; secondly their low salary prevented them from paying a secretary or doing the job as they would have wished, or forced them to work outside; and thirdly they were publicly criticized for not doing the work they had been trying to do – and very often by the same people who were helping to make it impossible. I could only answer my constituency correspondence properly in the 1950s because the *Daily Herald* typists were allowed to help me with it. But others had not even this luck. They mostly could not hit back. Instead they spent rather more time in the Tea Room of the House and rather less in the Chamber. Hugh Gaitskell was seriously worried about these tendencies and strongly supported efforts to raise the parliamentary salary materially, which was not accomplished until the mid-1950s. This certainly averted a much worse deterioration; but it came just too late wholly to reverse the damage which morale had suffered. For a further twist in the downward spiral then set in. Public attack began to be made on the very failings, now partially real, which under-payment and the attitude of those making the attacks had done much to generate. Some sections of the press, having succeeded in damaging Parliament, were complacently able to announce that Parliament's reputation had fallen.[10] Of course the decline of Fleet Street was not the only causal factor at work; and a good deal was achieved after the 1950s to prevent under-payment becoming too damaging. But part of the harm done before the mid-fifties unhappily proved irreparable.

Such was the background against which some of us were facing the Tories on the one hand and the Bevanite faction on the other in these Opposition years; and against which I was still seeking to maintain some serious purpose in the *Daily Herald*. Early in 1954 the bone of contention was 'German re-armament'. The reality was the inevitability of a revived Germany possessing some armed forces; and the question was whether these would be independent national forces or somehow contained within a wider Western alliance. The catchword 'German re-armament' suggested that the British Government, or perhaps the Labour Party – by passing a resolution – could decide whether Germany was 'armed' or not, with the implication that only those who secretly sympathized with the Nazis would advocate any such proposal. The Bevanites seized on it avidly; and the crux came in February 1954. Attlee had laid down conditions for the Labour Party to support the proposed 'European Defence Community', and Gaitskell persuaded the Shadow Cabinet that the Party should explicitly approve this in the House. On 23 February Wilson moved a dissenting Motion opposing 'German re-armament' in the evening meeting of the Parliamentary Labour

[10] See a letter from George Strauss in *The Times* of 4 August 1978, recording how a *Times* leader of 1954 prevented a crucial rise in pay and the start of a pension.

Party, which I have described on page 134. If Wilson's motion had not been defeated (by 111 votes to 109), Attlee might have resigned the leadership of the Party.

Also in the uninviting cause of common sense on 'German re-armament', I went to Bristol that week-end with Tony Crosland to speak in his constituency in defence of the Party's unpopular policy. We returned this time to a new controversy on the annual Defence debate, traditionally a source of trouble in the Labour Party, as the pacifist wing is always straining to vote against Britain having almost any defence forces at all. This time, after the narrow escape on 'German re-armament', Attlee and Morrison, wisely I thought, decided that the Party could reasonably oppose the particular defence programme advocated by the Government. Gaitskell was not happy about this; and Crosland, Jenkins, Woodrow Wyatt and I met to argue out whether we ought to oppose Attlee and Morrison in the Party meeting. We decided not to, and afterwards felt we were right, as harmony was preserved, and the Party voted unitedly for a woolly motion which turned out in the debate on 2 March to be reasonably defensible. Next month, April 1954, even greater harmony seemed to be emerging when Attlee spoke to great applause in the Parliamentary Party meeting on the menace of the hydrogen bomb and proposed to launch a debate in the House also. A little earlier he had uttered one of his most celebrated dicta on the same subject. Harold Davies, an enthusiastically Celtic Labour Member, not lacking in verbal exuberance, had at a Party meeting described the horrors of the H-bomb with high emotion, but at such length that the clock had reached the lunch hour when he rose to the climax and predicted the total extinction of the human race unless the Party at once passed a resolution. Attlee stood up and commented: 'We'll watch it; meeting adjourned.'

In the debate on 5 April 1954, Attlee spoke moderately and realistically in a complete non-party spirit, described the facts of the H-bomb and called for international action. There was a general ovation from all sides. Churchill rose to follow and was expected to respond in the same non-party spirit, but for once the old man had completely misjudged the audience. He began with a party attack on Attlee for not having continued the wartime Atom Bomb Agreement. This caused resentment and uproar. It gradually became clear that Churchill had prepared a party speech, and not being capable of altering it spontaneously, was determined to plough on. As soon as the House realized this, resentment turned to embarrassed sadness. And the speech ended in painful silence. Edwin Plowden, who was sitting in the Civil Service box, supporting Churchill, told me afterwards that Churchill had hopelessly misjudged the occasion. But for Attlee and the Labour Party the debate was a major success; and the optimists, always with us, began to predict that the Bevanite trouble would now happily evaporate.

But this was not to be. Only a week later, on 13 April 1954, Bevan lost control again and virtually contradicted Attlee on the Front Bench at Question Time. I was sitting between them. Eden made a statement on Indo-China and South East Asia, suggesting the possibility of the SEATO Pact. Attlee was mildly critical of this; whereupon Bevan moved, muttering and gesticulating, across me to the Despatch Box and contradicted Attlee with a scathing attack on Eden. That afternoon most of the Parliamentary Labour Party reacted with exasperation against Bevan in greater strength than at any incident before. They complained that the whole recovery of the Party was being set back by an outburst of megalomania. Immediately Bevan was formally rebuked in the Parliamentary Committee ('Shadow Cabinet'), and announced at a Party meeting next day that he had resigned from that Committee. Till this I had always hoped and worked for a reconciliation between him and Gaitskell; but that evening wrote: 'From this moment I feel him to be impossible.' Ironically, the next consequence was Wilson's appearance on the Parliamentary Committee in succession to Bevan, provoking bitter feeling between Bevan and Wilson. More important and more lasting, the incident most probably made it certain that Bevan would never be Leader of the Party. The resentment had gone too deep.

The third consequence, however, was even longer lived. Attlee not unnaturally ruled from that moment formally that members of the Labour Party on the Front Bench should stick to defined subjects, and not trespass on their neighbours. This had previously been a mere gentlemen's agreement. Gaitskell backed the new arrangement strongly and later as Leader himself added the Convention that the Leader should assign responsibilities to other members of the Shadow Cabinet. He believed this would lead to more informed opposition speeches and more systematic study and research. Under Churchill and most previous régimes, opposition spokesmen had simply been asked *ad hoc* to speak in a particular debate. I never myself took the new régime too literally, and continued during Question Time to intervene on any Treasury or Board of Trade subject as I chose. But from this time onwards the Attlee/Gaitskell reform became accepted practice. People first began to talk of 'the Shadow Chancellor' and before long to announce 'appointments to' and 'resignations from' such 'Shadow portfolios'. This system largely dates from Bevan's outburst in April 1954.

After another long, hard grind on the Finance Bill in these again unpromising circumstances in May and June, I left for Brazil on 3 July with a Parliamentary Delegation, which included Lord Cromer of Barings, later Governor of the Bank of England and British Ambassador in Washington. It is conventional for Members of Parliament, particularly when in opposition to 'broaden their minds' periodically by foreign travel. I was slow to follow this practice, partly out of respect for the tax-payer's money, but after eight years in the House it seemed that the experiment should be tried. I chose Brazil for a start because of its tropical climate and its completely different economic, social and political scene from those familiar in Western

Europe. Here was a country with already sixty million people in 1954, a genuinely multi-racial society, with more national resources than perhaps any country in the world, with as large an area as the US, blessed with luridly beautiful scenery and equally beautiful women, but cursed with such inequality of income and wealth as to make genuine freedom and stability apparently impossible. The famous tropical beauty of Rio Harbour does not disappoint; but then one discovers the other city of half a million people living in primitive poverty or near it in shanty towns hanging from the mountainside.

My interest, amid the social functions and entertainments, was to study the causes of this poverty and the system of social services and taxation. The basic facts were indeed simple. Owing to lack of tax revenues, the Budget was hopelessly unbalanced, and the Government therefore borrowed the necessary funds from the Bank of Brazil, which created the cash required. Prices rose at the time of my visit by about 100 per cent a year. The then Minister of Finance unexpectedly invited me to give him my views on his Budget problems. I pointed out that if he raised only a fraction as much as we did in income-tax per head his budget problem would be solved. He said that was impossible because in his country the rich bribed the tax collectors. 'Then why not recruit honest tax-collectors?' I asked. 'In this country,' he replied, 'they do not exist.' This, I had to admit, made the problem distinctly more difficult. This conversation enabled me to understand more explicitly than ever before that in a modern state richly endowed with natural wealth, but without a progressive direct tax system, extreme poverty is bound to persist side by side with ostentatious affluence. If the millionaires, of whom there were plenty in Brazil, each escape taxation by bribery, then inequality and destitution on a large scale will prevail, however rich the nation as a whole may become. Rio, with its gorgeous luxury and its mountainside shanty city, was a living example of the *laissez-faire* state untempered by effective direct taxation or social services. I remarked to a colleague on the flight home that I would in future include the Inland Revenue with Shakespeare and Parliamentary Government as Britain's greatest contributions to the world.

In the course of our fortnight's stay our delegation visited the President, Getulio Vargas, who talked in most cultured English and claimed Roosevelt and Churchill as his friends. In the early 1920s, when Mussolini Fascism was in fashion, Vargas had installed himself as a Mussolini-type dictator and remained in power till 1945. At that time, as fashions changed, he introduced a democratic constitution on the American model, was elected the first President and still retained this office in 1954. At our meeting he asked us why the 1954 Conservative Government under Churchill had not reversed most of the reforms of the Attlee Government. We were all most impressed by the performance; but a fortnight after our delegation left, Vargas committed suicide.

In the winter of 1954–5 the Bevanite troubles again appeared to be simmering down and a faint hope revived that as a result Labour fortunes might recover in time to win the expected 1955 election. The Party Conference of 1954 at Scarborough passed off comparatively peacefully, but that autumn the Labour Party in Parliament had to face the issue of the 'Paris Agreements', intended to bring Germany into NATO. This was argued in a reasonably serious Party meeting on 11 and 12 November at which Bevan spoke more moderately and so more effectively than usual.

In the debate that followed in the House on 18 November Gaitskell made his first speech there on foreign affairs. It was a major success and started the further upsurge in his reputation which led to his emergence as Leader a year later. I was greatly cheered at listening to one of those really serious and convincing debates which periodically revive one's faith in parliamentary life. But at the end of the debate the extreme pacifists, including Emrys Hughes, Sydney Silverman and S. O. Davies, voted against the Party Whip. Twenty years later this would have been wisely ignored. But in the atmosphere of November 1954 furious resentment flared up among the majority of the Party against publicized disunity which was now clearly threatening Labour election prospects. The strength of this anger was shown at a Party meeting when a compromise motion merely rebuking Emrys Hughes, S. O. Davies and the rest was overwhelmingly defeated and the whip was withdrawn. I described this meeting in my own record at the time as a 'madhouse of a meeting' at which 'all the hysterics spoke'. But it was this gratuitous episode which began to make the success of the Conservatives in the 1955 election nearly inevitable. The essence of the tragedy throughout this period was Bevan's failure to realize in time the necessity for him to reach an understanding with Gaitskell. In the end he did. But it was just too late, and the last years of his life and his rare abilities, and those of Gaitskell, were restricted to Opposition and sadly wasted as a result.

For the moment, at the end of 1954, the pendulum swung temporarily back, with a powerful speech by Gaitskell in the House in December which pleased everybody on the Labour side, attacking the Government's whole economic policy. My thoughts, I admit, in December 1954 and January 1955 were concentrated even more on my son Peter's chance of achieving a scholarship to Oxford. On 12 January I came home from the daily ordeal at the *Herald* to find his brother and sisters waving a telegram announcing that Peter had won the senior open history scholarship at Christ Church. The happiness of the whole family was unrestrained.

In these early weeks of 1955 it was already being rumoured that Churchill would soon resign in favour of Eden and a general election be held. Hopes were encouraged in the Labour Party that faction-fighting would at last be held under the surface. But the Defence Debate on 2 March led to yet another disastrous eruption at this fatal moment by Bevan himself. He demanded somewhat menacingly an assurance from Attlee that a British H-bomb would never be used to repel a purelyc onventional aggression. It was a dramatic debate, as Churchill – who hardly ever spoke again in the Commons – rose to the surprise of all of us in the middle of Bevan's speech and admitted for the first time that he had been paralysed in the previous year. Some of us non-Bevanites, including Bob Mellish, Fred Peart and myself, discussed whether we should suggest to Attlee that he could give this assurance in his reply. In the course of the evening I did try to see Attlee. But as he was sitting on the bench, I consulted Herbert Morrison; who replied very firmly that Attlee had better be left to make up his own mind. At the end of Attlee's speech Bevan again demanded an answer, and being ostentatiously dissatisfied with Attlee's response refrained from voting for the Labour Party's Motion. Most of the usual sixty followed his lead and abstained (though Wilson, Crossman, John Freeman and some other Bevanites voted this time with the Party).

To large sections of the Party, this came as the final provocation, not because they agreed or disagreed on the issue, but because they felt that hostile questions put to the Leader of the Party in the House, followed by a mass abstention, and all this perpetrated just before a general election, were a mortal blow to the Party's election fortunes. If it had not been just one more in a whole series of outbursts it would not have generated so much indignation. The feeling against Bevan, as expressed to me at this time by my rank-and-file colleagues, was stronger than ever before. So the Parliamentary Committee recommended a motion to the Party for the withdrawal of the whip from Bevan: and this, together with a compromise motion merely condemning his conduct, were to come before a Party meeting on 16 March. I recorded on 15 March my own feelings as follows: 'I very much dislike this sort of thing and regret that it has to be done at all. But I am sure it is inevitable.' According to the account Gaitskell gave me privately on the day of the Committee meeting (7 March), both he himself, Attlee and Soskice had been opposed to pushing the matter to the length of expulsion from the Party, but favoured a final warning. Dalton tells us he himself voted against withdrawing the whip.[11] Naturally the Party was hopelessly split at the crucial meeting on 16 March; but the extent of the exasperation against Bevan was shown by the fact that the compromise motion was lost, though only by 138 votes to 124, and the official motion to withdraw the whip was carried by 141 to 112.

The next step according to the Labour Party's Constitution was for the National Executive Committee to decide for or against expulsion from the Party altogether. By this time most of the Parliamentary Committee, Gaitskell told me, favoured temporary expulsion. But not Attlee. He produced at the last moment a compromise plan by which Bevan should merely be rebuked and asked for assurances of reform: and it was carried in the NEC

[11] Dalton, p. 410.

by fourteen votes to thirteen. Attlee, who, I am sure, also disliked this sort of thing intensely himself, was almost certainly wise to achieve this last-minute compromise. For the election was upon us; and indeed on the very day of the NEC meeting, 23 March (my 48th birthday) rumours strengthened that Churchill would resign on April 5. The row with Bevan had very naturally pushed the Tory Leaders to the obvious conclusion – that now was the time for a new election under a new leader. But though the election result would have doubtless been even worse for the Labour Party if Bevan had actually been expelled, the whole unnecessary conflict of March made defeat inevitable. These incidents together ensured the victory of the Tories in the election and the choice of Gaitskell rather than Bevan as Leader of the Party later that year.

At the end of March Churchill, though now eighty, gave a dazzling display at Prime Minister's Questions, but resigned shortly afterwards. When Eden announced the general election in May, I was again attending the Königswinter Anglo-German Conference. Herbert Morrison was also there when he heard the news of the election; and as Attlee was also away from home, Morrison, Gordon-Walker and I composed a public statement for Morrison to make about the election news. It was an election I entered almost certain that Labour would lose. The Labour programme and manifesto of 1955 were less convincing than those of either 1951 or 1959. But it was at least better to perform the outdoor rituals in May rather than February or October weather; particularly as my local Party at this time believed enthusiastically in conducting continuous outdoor meetings in crowded shopping areas. At one outdoor meeting two strident females made vociferous attacks on the coloured residents of the area. They were only silenced when an older-style cockney male voice retaliated: 'If you're both so proud of being white, why do you spend so much time painting your faces?' I carried through these exercises to the full, even though after the election it usually turned out that whatever we did, the 'swing' in North and South Battersea was almost identical with those in other constituencies bordering ours. In the 1955 election the national Tory majority rose from seventeen to sixty seats. In Battersea, as in 1951 and as expected, we lost the South constituency and won the North, my own.

After the election, people began to ask whether Attlee now proposed to retire. Most Labour MPs hoped he would not. They did not want more conflict, this time over the succession. At the first Party meeting after the election he offered to go on, if the Party wished, to the end of one session only. There were cries for him to carry on. Bevan leapt to his feet, and urged him to carry on without any time limit. Attlee asked if that was the general wish, and loud cheers were the answer. 'Very well,' he said, and went on to the next business. There was much irony in this exchange. Bevan certainly knew he then had no chance of election as Leader after the controversies of March and April, but believed that he would do better later. But the decision finally knocked not merely the unlucky Herbert Morrison but Bevan himself out of the running. In the immediately following election for the Shadow Cabinet (Attlee and Morrison as Leader and Deputy Leader did not have to stand) the results were interesting: Griffiths 186, Gaitskell 184, Callaghan 148, Robens 148, Wilson 147, Summerskill 133, Bevan 118, Brown 101, Noel-Baker 100, Greenwood 95, Stokes 77, Mitchison 76. This in itself was an early signal that Bevan had not much chance against Gaitskell in an election for the Leadership. But in addition, contrary to expectation, the session went on to December, and by December Gaitskell's reputation in the Parliamentary Party had, as a result of his performance in the House in the meantime, become unassailable. The story of the leadership stakes in 1955 was another example of events turning out in a way which none of the participants foresaw, except perhaps Attlee. Nobody could criticize his attitude: he was willing to stay or go as requested by the Party. My own belief is that he would have preferred to go in May and even more strongly in December; but that he believed it was in the interests of the Party that Gaitskell should succeed him, and that this was most likely if the election was held at the end of the year.

I spent the first ten days of June on an exceedingly instructive visit to Moscow. William Hayter, now Ambassador in Moscow, and his wife Iris had invited me to stay in the Embassy there as their guests, and I seized on the chance to visit them in the two-week gap between the election and the meeting of Parliament. The British Embassy in Moscow commands a splendid view directly across the river towards the medieval red walls, eighteenth and nineteenth-century palaces and Byzantine cathedrals of the Kremlin. I was astonished indeed by its beauty and magnificence, seen from this angle on a late summer evening. Stalin in his last month of near-madness had ordered the removal of the British and American Embassies from central Moscow. The Americans moved; but the British hung on until his death, and were not again asked to leave till very many years later. By the time of my visit, two years after Stalin's death, Russia was enjoying the years of 'thaw', and of genuine 'collective government'. Malenkov had been replaced as Prime Minister in Febraury 1955 by Bulganin; but both of them, together with Khrushchev (now General Secretary of the Communist Party), Molotov (still Foreign Secretary till June 1956), Mikoyan and Kaganovich, were all prominent in the ruling praesidium. In these months, before the famous 20th Party Congress at which Khrushchev denounced Stalin, the iron bars were just beginning to be loosened, and Russian leaders were willing to meet foreign diplomats and even visitors for the first time. The Government had also begun to realize explicitly that the food supply and basic consumer goods were crucial and that heavy industry could no longer be treated as an over-riding priority.

Naturally I did not see the horrors of the prisons and labour camps. One never does see these things in a totalitarian régime; but one knows they are there. My most vivid impression was the vast if fascinating scale of the human and economic problem; over 200 million men, women and children just emerging from a cruel tyranny, and struggling by means of a still, stifling political system to convert in a few years some of the most primitive and war-stricken areas of the world into a modern industrial state. Sitting on the benches in the summer sunshine in Moscow's innumerable public gardens, I was usually surrounded by groups of ten to fifteen children under five shepherded by a grandmother (which in Russian is the same word as 'mother-in-law'). To my surprise the grandmothers were very willing to converse, even though I only knew half a dozen words of Russian, and greeted the information that I was British, and the father of twins, with hearty smiles. Certainly there was no basic hostility to foreigners among the common people. Occasionally an elderly bearded man walked by with the traditional Russian peasant look, appearing mildly bewildered at the placid times into which he had somehow survived. One could not help reflecting that he must have seen the Czarist years, the 1914 war, the revolution, the civil war, the purges and famines of the 1920s and thirties, the Nazi invasion of 1941-5 and the Stalin years thereafter. In the magnificently laid out Agricultural Exhibition in 1955 the crowds were being deafened by loudspeaker exhortations from Khrushchev, interspersed with mechanical music, glorifying his experiments in growing maize by 'the American method' and his gallant if rather desperate 'virgin-lands' programme for Southern Siberia.

In my evening talks with Chip Bohlen of the US and other Western Ambassadors, the main topics were the extent to which the 'thaw' would be allowed to go, and the final outcome of the rivalry between Malenkov and Khrushchev. It was then the general view of the Western observers that the concentration on agriculture, housing and consumer goods would continue; that the standard of living would rise; but that this would not be permitted to encroach far on defence spending. Almost all agreed, including Hayter, that if the West wanted to influence the Russians, contact was better than boycott. Had it not been for the Suez and Hungary disasters, this might well have proved true even sooner. About Khrushchev and Malenkov, however, the professional observers were almost all wrong. They mostly thought Malenkov would come out on top. This was partly no doubt, because he was highly intelligent, quick-witted, and apparently disposed towards much more humane internal policies. Nine months later I heard Malenkov in London most skilfully and effectively (with a translator) address a meeting of the Parliamentary Labour Party and answer questions from all comers. At a party with Hugh Gaitskell in Hampstead on this visit, he conversed pertinently and humorously on British affairs. Khrushchev, on the other hand, was at first sight an impulsive, aggressive, hard-drinking peasant, awkward and unpredictable. But though the ambassadors under-rated Khrushchev, they were right in believing that the worst horrors of Stalin's rule had gone.

They were in no doubt that in the two years or so since his death some millions of political prisoners had been released.

Mikoyan, to William Hayter's mild surprise, agreed to lunch with us in the Embassy on Tuesday, 7 June. John Morgan, Hayter's secretary and excellent translator made a long and frank conversation possible. Mikoyan, already an Armenian revolutionary in 1919, was by the 1950s well known to the British for his commercial agility and his astonishing political survival value. He had been a member of virtually every Soviet Government since 1919 and lived until 1978. The current joke in Moscow in 1955, retailed by taxi-drivers, was that if the Czar was restored, Mikoyan would be his Lord Chamberlain. He started at lunch by talking about Yugoslavia which he had just visited with Khrushchev, and said he thought they had over-concentrated on industry and neglected agriculture and food supplies. He admitted Russia had made the same mistake. He then asked me what I thought about Moscow. I said I admired the parks and gardens, and the way the children were cared for, but thought housing conditions for ordinary people still very bad. To my surprise he agreed, and said: 'Certainly we haven't done enough, but we're beginning now.' He next asked why the Attlee Government had pursued what he called an 'anti-Soviet policy' and formed a nuclear alliance with the US, in reply to which I boldly reminded him that the Korean war and the Berlin Blockade in particular, viewed by us as a country of less military power than Russia, were bound to be highly alarming. To my even greater surprise, he made no attempt to defend the Berlin Blockade, and described it as 'just an incident', virtually admitting that it had been a mistake. This was the first time I heard any Russian openly criticize Stalin's policies.

At this time, unknown to me of course, Khrushchev's speech to the 20th Party Congress was only six months away; and the process of de-Stalinization had evidently begun within the Government. On economic policy Mikoyan agreed that the Soviets had little grain to export; but when I suggested that before long with a growing population and industry they might be wise in the future, like ourselves, to buy wheat from Canada and the US, he would not explicitly agree, though I suspect he feared this might be true. I also told him I had been reading the Soviet press, and thought it a pity they were so misleading about Britain. When he said his press was one-sided, but so was ours, I reminded him that we did allow the *Daily Worker* to be published. As the lunch proceeded, Mikoyan became increasingly jocular and frank, telling before the end how he and Stalin (as Georgians and Armenians) used to 'drink damnation to all the Russians'.

That afternoon Nehru arrived in Moscow, and drove openly through the streets. It was a huge success. Crowds, perhaps officially mobilized, became spontaneously enthusiastic. Some Russians said this was the first time most ordinary Russians would ever have seen an Indian. Two days later (9 June) by coincidence came the traditional Queen's Birthday party in the garden of the British Embassy. Nehru came, and the Russian leaders seized the opportunity to visit the Embassy virtually for the first time. At other gatherings I had already met Molotov, as expected a portentous but very uncommunicative figure; Kosygin (then a deputy PM and regarded as a coming man by the ambassadors) much more talkative and very ready to discuss airports, seatbelts and the Russian weather; and Benedictov, Minister of Agriculture, a tall handsome man who said that the Russian public were 'ungrateful' for the large rise achieved in meat supplies. First to arrive at the Queen's birthday party was Marshal Zhukov, the first Marshal of the Soviet Union, a national hero, and commander-in-chief of the Russian armies that invaded Germany in 1945. Resplendent in a gorgeous uniform, muscular and self-confident, he certainly looked the part. Next arrived Bulganin and Mikoyan with a retinue. Bulganin, whose little Edwardian beard gave the impression, perhaps truly, that he was now anxious for a quiet life, presented me personally with a ticket for the grand reception to Nehru in the Kremlin that evening; and joined in a talk with a party of British trade unionists about working conditions in Britain.

I then fell in with Kuznetsov, a Foreign Office under-secretary, an intellectual and Tolstoy expert, who had worked some years in the US and spoke fluent English. He lunched with us in the Embassy again later in Moscow: I met him again in trade negotiations in 1965; and he still survives in the Soviet hierarchy in the late 1970s. At the 1955 Queen's Birthday party he was most anxious to understand the reasons for the Tory success in the May general election. I gave my honest opinion (that the Labour Party had been quarrelling) and took the chance again to criticize the Soviet press and suggest some gestures his Government might make if they really wanted friendlier relations. He showed special interest in Arthur Deakin. The Hayters then whisked me off to meet Nehru, who had with him his daughter, Mrs Gandhi. I asked whether he remembered my taking him for a walk on Hampstead Heath in 1935, and he did not. But when I mentioned Shiela Grant-Duff, his face lit up, and he answered 'She was my secretary for six months. Didn't she write a book about Czechoslovakia?'; and remembered that his daughter had stayed with her in Chelsea in the 1930s. Despite Nehru and Bulganin, however, the great success at this party was the 21-year-old youngest ballerina of the Bolshoi Company, who wore no lipstick or make-up of any kind, spoke only a few words of English, and was surrounded by most of the young British and American officers and diplomats at the party.

That evening we repaired to the Kremlin for dinner to Nehru, and ceremonial speeches. We shook hands as we entered St George's Hall in the Czarist Palace with Bulganin, Nehru, Mrs Gandhi, Khrushchev, Malenkov, Zhukov, Kaganovitch (who did not survive long), and Mikoyan (who did). More marshals were present, a splendid body of men indeed, now in their evening glory reminiscent of Byron's Assyrians 'gleaming in purple and gold'. Was this a class society? When I have since heard the catchphrases 'élite' or '*crème de la crème*', I think of those formidable, beaming magnificent marshals. But had they not helped to win the greatest military victory in modern times? Before dinner, an interlude of music, dancing and a puppet show gave one the chance to observe this interesting audience more closely. Bulganin smiled at all comers. Khrushchev chattered and grinned and looked exceedingly bear-like. Mikoyan attended to the performance and clapped his hands in excitement. Malenkov sat as impassive as a sphinx – much more dignified, the Western visitors felt, than the gesticulating Krushchev. The marshals beamed in perfect unison.

We then moved to the banqueting hall for dinner, and 300 or so first-class citizens, including myself, were allowed to sit. But the remaining 500 or so present had to eat their dinner standing. I championed individual freedom uncompromisingly by refusing flatly, despite extreme pressure, to drink a single drop of the horrible Russian alcohol. On one side of me a high Indian official spoke fluent English and was mainly interested in the reported climb of Kanchenjunga by an English party. Then Bulganin spoke, translated into English for the Indians, and stuck firmly to platitudes and pleasantries. Nehru replied with a few sentences in Hindustani, and continued for twenty minutes in English, translated by an Indian into Russian. It was a brave speech in which he said countries with huge military power had a special duty to preserve the peace.

As I flew home via Helsinki and Stockholm next day, I asked myself again: Was it right to meet and converse with these characters, who must have had some complicity in the crimes of Stalin? When I was in Moscow again fifteen months later, a story was going the rounds of the taxi-drivers and others, about Khrushchev's Phillippic against Stalin at the 20th Party Congress at the end of 1955. In the midst of his description of Stalin's atrocities the tension was so great that a voice called out: 'What were you all on the platform doing at the time?' Khrushchev paused, and said: 'Will the comrade who asked that question, please stand up and ask it again more clearly.' Fifteen seconds' deadly silence ensued, at the end of which Khrushchev said: 'That is what we were doing.' But the question remains: whether a totalitarian régime is more likely to be influenced by contact or by ostracism. My visits to Moscow convinced me, though with due scepticism, that contact is the better bet. But of course if this is true of Soviet Russia, it is also normally true of South Africa, Chile, Argentina, Cuba, China and any totalitarian regime Left or Right.

Gaitskell was a stronger believer than I in the virtue of foreign travel, and in particular getting to know the US. He persuaded me in the latter part of 1955, both to spend two months in the US and to attend one of the so-called 'Bilderberg' long week-end conferences in Germany. The Bilderberg Conference was this time at Garmisch, a beautiful Alpine village in Germany south of Munich. These conferences were curious affairs, presided over by Prince Bernhard of the Netherlands, and liberally sprinkled with the chairmen of famous multi-national companies. Substitute 'multi-national tycoons' for 'Party leaders', and I was constantly reminded of Gilbert's words:

> Party leaders you will meet
> In twos and threes in every street
> Maintaining with no little heat
> Their various opinions.

Many worthy characters were present at Garmisch: Paul Hoffman of Marshal Aid fame, Marjolin, the French planner, Van Zeeland, my hero of the Belgian devaluation of 1935, Geoffrey Crowther, Denis Healey, American Senators, and a few TUC delegates. Guy Mollet, instigator of Suez as French PM a year later, and Professor Hallstein, head of the German Civil Service and later of the Brussels Commission, were also there. I did not altogether like the atmosphere of well-heeled and rather unctuous good will. The subject was broadly 'uniting Europe' and the plan for a 'European Defence Community' which the French had just repudiated. Essentially, I believe, the Bilderberg Conferences were anti-Communist initiatives, which later became an engine of Common Market propaganda. My clearest memory of this Conference was of Hallstein making a remark about Germany reaching some defence agreement and reserving the right to reconsider it later. I was conscious of Anglo-Saxon eyebrows being quietly raised all around me. Did this mean Germany would sign an agreement and later repudiate it if inconvenient? This session petered out with five minutes to spare; and Prince Bernhard observed smoothly that Professor Hallstein's remark had aroused special interest, and perhaps he would elucidate it for a few minutes. Appearing to be puzzled by the need for this, the Professor improvised for a few minutes, at the end of which the Anglo-Saxon eyebrows were raised equally politely but even higher.

My tour of the US in October and November 1955 was organized at Gaitskell's suggestion, under the US Congress's so-called 'Smith–Mundt' legislation, which generously finances out of public funds visits by foreign 'leaders' who choose entirely of their own free will where they go, what they do, and whom they see. My first casual impressions of the US were mixed. First was the warm hospitality of Dean Rusk whom I had met at the Garmisch Conference and on the Atlantic flight. He invited me at once to dinner and an excellent theatre in New York. Next was my curious first night in Washington. With my companion, the Town Clerk of Coventry (who happened to be on a similar tour), I strolled after supper out of the Fairfax Hotel in Massachusetts Avenue for a few minutes. Twenty yards along the 'sidewalk' I felt a stinging blow on the side of my head, and became unconscious for four or five seconds. Regaining my senses, I saw the Town Clerk looking startled, blood streaming from my ear, my glasses on the pavement, and a coloured boy running away down a side road. I had never then heard of the word 'mugging'. When we staggered back to the hotel and rang the police, the officer said: 'It's going on all over the town to-night.' In the rest of my tour, when addressing numerous discussion groups and societies of various kinds, I was repeatedly asked to describe my recent experiences in Moscow. Was I followed, they always asked, in my solitary long walks round Moscow? Not as far as I know, I had to answer; but on my first night in Washington I was knocked unconscious in the street.

This, however, was bad luck: and there were more lasting lessons to be learnt about American life, as I found in the next seven weeks in Boston, Pittsburgh, Cleveland, Madison, Chicago, Denver, San Francisco, Los Angeles, Dallas, New Orleans and Atlanta. Of many impressions the strongest was perhaps the depths of the American people's attachment to genuine democracy – almost extreme democracy bordering on anarchy by British standards, with everyone from the President to local Judges and Attorney Generals elected by mass suffrage on a party ticket. Next, contrary to what I had always been taught, was the basic similarity, despite the obvious differences, between the US and Britain in habits of thought, political assumptions, basic education and view of the world. At its strongest, naturally, among Washington officials and Harvard academics, this similarity struck me as permeating far wider and deeper than I had been led to expect. Not merely at Harvard, where I met ex-Marshall Aid colleagues, and friends of Gaitskell like Milton Katz and Lincoln Gordon, but in Madison, Berkeley, Los Angeles and Atlanta, one felt one might have been visiting a British university. In its whole Federal and state system of taxation and social services, all research showed how much more progressive it was, and more akin to the British system, than those of the Latin countries. For that very reason democratic government was more secure.

What fascinated me most, made vividly explicit in Georgia, was the still dominating and acute problem of 'integrating' black and white in the Southern States. In 1954 the Supreme Court had delivered its famous judgement that 'equal but separate' provision for black and white did not satisfy the basic guarantee of human equality in the constitution; and had required all responsible institutions to end 'segregation' within a reasonable period of years. When I stayed in Atlanta in November 1955, schools and universities were still either for whites or blacks and were strictly segregated. Indeed I was requested by the conductor in a bus to move out of the seats provided for negroes, and in order to show I was not going to be pushed around told him that I was a negro. Most intelligent Americans I met in Georgia, white or black, said it would be exceedingly difficult to force de-segregation, particularly in schools and universities, after a century of deeply rooted tradition. Yet de-segregation was in fact virtually complete, so far as the law can make it, ten years later. It has never seemed to me that the US has been given enough credit for this fundamental and peaceful revolution.

Back in London at the end of November 1955, just in time to visit Peter during his last term at Winchester, I found everyone expecting Attlee to retire. Percy Cudlipp, now working for the *News Chronicle*, had called on him in the Chilterns and boldly asked him when he contemplated retirement. Attlee replied: 'As soon as possible.' I also found what I recorded at the time (6 December) as a 'landslide of opinion in favour of Gaitskell in the Parliamentary Labour Party', due to his superlative performance in the Finance Bill debates in October and November. Herbert Morrison had been given his chance in these weeks, but had failed badly. Attlee said to me privately later: 'He had his chance and he muffed it.' At the Party meeting on 7 December, Attlee rose at the start, said that speculation about the leadership was bad and so he was resigning forthwith. He thanked the Party and sat down. This took three minutes. Everyone present stood up and clapped for several minutes: and after listening to tributes from all round, he walked out. I could not help reflecting on the meeting I had attended twenty years before with Gaitskell and Durbin at which Attlee's unexpected election was announced. The last thing I conceived possible then was that he would be succeeded by Gaitskell. On the day after Attlee's announcement, I lunched with Gaitskell, as I was rejoining the Finance Bill team that afternoon. We discussed his prospects, and he and I estimated he might get 130 votes, which should be decisive. He remarked: 'Strangely enough I don't very greatly care,' which in retrospect may not sound serious, but by which I think he meant that he could very happily carry on, win or lose.

That afternoon, in the middle of the Finance Bill debate, we learnt that Bevan had put out a statement saying he would stand down in favour of Morrison if Gaitskell would do the same. At first thought I guessed this was a clever move, as there would be much sympathy for Morrison (which I shared) because of his twenty years' wait and his immense services to the Labour Party. Also Gaitskell might be represented as an impatient, ambitious young man trying to push out a revered Party Leader. But as soon as I went into the Tea Room for a little refreshment, I found I was quite wrong. Ordinary Labour Members, including some Bevanites, pressed me from all round to urge Gaitskell to stand firm; and I returned to the Front Bench and told him so. He said he felt himself that he would be letting down his numerous supporters if he drew back. I also advised him to respond to a message from the *Daily Herald* asking him to make a statement. A little later he went out and said to the press that he had the highest regard for Morrison, but it was for the Party to choose whom they wanted. As the debate ended at 9 p.m. Gaitskell left to consult Dalton, and

I had some supper with Roy Jenkins and John Strachey. The Party reaction by this time was quite contrary to what I expected. So far from sympathy with Bevan, or even Morrison, there was general anger at what was seen as a clumsy manoeuvre by both of them against Gaitskell. Not to be outdone in this act, Crossman provided light relief by suddenly announcing in the *Daily Mirror* that he would support Gaitskell.

Most Members cast their votes on the Monday morning, 12 December, and the result was to be announced on the Wednesday, two days later. The belief was strong in the Party on the Monday and Tuesday that Bevan and Morrison were working together, as would be perfectly understandable with Shinwell and others. This I cannot confirm. But I did record the following as definite at the time: Gaitskell had given full notice to Morrison as long ago as October, before the Butler autumn Budget, that he meant to stand. Secondly, Gaitskell told me that Attlee had let him know on 5 December of his decision to resign, and that Attlee had by then already informed the Queen and Prime Minister and a few others, including Arthur Moyle, his long-standing Parliamentary Private Secretary. Arthur Moyle assured me that Attlee had undoubtedly wanted to resign throughout 1955, and decided not to wait any longer when he believed a clear choice would be made. I have no doubt that this is true, and there is no evidence for the version propagated by Bevan and the *Tribune*[12] later that Attlee was pushed against his will. Moyle would have known his real feelings and Bevan would not. But it was certainly highly ironical that in May 1955 Gaitskell was inclined to think Attlee should retire then and that Bevan opposed it; whereas if Attlee had resigned in May, Morrison and not Gaitskell would almost certainly have been elected Leader. Later on the evening of 7 December I had heard Churchill say to Morrison in the passage: 'I very much hope so.' To which Morrison replied: 'That's very nice of you.' And Churchill added: 'But I won't say so. It might do you harm.' Churchill was evidently wishing him well in the contest, and speaking in his chivalrous and magnanimous mood in an effort to wipe out the old quarrel between them over their respective responsibility for the Lewisham bomb disaster of 1944. It was typical of him and plainly much appreciated by Morrison.

On Wednesday 14 December the result was announced as follows:

Gaitskell 157
Bevan 70
Morrison 40

This result was quietly received, since the blow to Morrison was keenly felt by all. The traditional Celtic seventy stuck to Bevan; but the Anglo-Saxons voted almost solidly for Gaitskell. Nevertheless the Party which so voted was astonished – like the electorate in 1945 – at the way in which

[12] And Foot, vol. II, p. 495.

it had itself polled; notably at the size of Gaitskell's vote and the smallness of Morrison's. Morrison then handed over the chair to Gaitskell, who thanked the Party, said that it was only age that divided him from Morrison and appealed to Morrison to continue as Deputy Leader. This clearly had the strong support of almost the whole Party; though Shinwell characteristically called out: 'Don't do it, Herbert.' Morrison then replied that he would resign the Deputy Leadership, because he must retain his 'self-respect', and that if he was too old for the Leadership, he was too old for the Deputy Leadership also. He could not face the 'gibes, jeers and scorn of the Tories in the Chamber'. He then walked out of the Palace of Westminster, and was not seen there again till after the Christmas recess.

It was (as I then recorded) a 'tense, sad scene', particularly for those of us who had worked with Morrison for twenty years or so, and knew how unflagging his services had been. If he had accepted then and there the pressing request of the meeting to stay on as Deputy Leader, he would have undoubtedly become the most popular man in the Party. But Shinwell was at this moment his evil genius. By persuading Bevan, as was generally believed, to make the disingenuous offer to stand down, Shinwell had damaged Morrison's vote; and he then completed the damage by urging him to resign the Deputy Leadership. The tragedy of Morrison's wrong decision impressed on me sharply at the time the truth of what Dalton often said privately: how few politicians finish their working lives serenely, and how many become disgruntled and embittered because, despite long service and major achievements, they just miss one further goal. Attlee stands out as one of the very few, who by his well-timed resignation in 1955, avoided this crevasse also.

Yet though Bevan's disruptive sorties over the previous twelve months had ensured Gaitskell's election, it was Gaitskell's own outstanding performance in the House in 1955 which won him such a surprisingly large majority on the first ballot, which a year earlier nobody would have predicted. It had become clear to those who feared a resumption of Bevan's excesses that a vote for Gaitskell was now the best way of holding the Party together. Though still under fifty, Gaitskell shared with Stafford Cripps one rare quality which was immensely valued by the solid core of Labour MPs. By calculated lucidity and unadorned rational argument, he in the end produced a more *emotional* conviction than rhetoric could achieve. Bevan's most splendid speeches entertained, impressed, even enthused. But when one inquired of his hearers next day what he had said they were often not at all sure. And they were even less sure what he might say next. But Gaitskell's *persuaded;* and left conviction where there had previously been doubt. When therefore members asked themselves whom they would prefer as leader, over the next five, perhaps ten years, and probably PM, the answer was plain. These qualities, which I had come to recognize in Gaitskell over the twenty years since I first addressed envelopes for him in Chatham in 1935, became apparent to his fellow MPs in the years between 1951 and 1955, and to the mass of the British public outside Westminster in the next seven years of his life.

In reply to my own personal letter of congratulation, Gaitskell replied on 27 December 1955, as follows:

In a way it seems absurd to write because, thank goodness, we see so much of each other and know each other so well. But all the same I feel I must say thank you in writing not only for your very nice letter written in the evening of the 14th but also for all the help and encouragement you have given me especially in these last four difficult years. The prospect *is* pretty formidable, but to me at least it makes an immense difference to know that we shall be in this together as we have been now for so many years. It's *quite* sure that in *our* case there will be 'friends at the top' as there have been all the way up.

Gaitskell's election as Leader opened up the wonderful prospect of a new Labour Government with him as Prime Minister while still in the prime of life. The year 1956, which ended so grimly, started full of hope for Labour supporters. My own belief was that Gaitskell and Bevan would see the common sense of working together; that they would make a powerful combination; and that Wilson would become a valuable lieutenant, no doubt as Chancellor of the Exchequer. Immediately, Jim Griffiths stood for the deputy leadership and defeated Bevan by 151 votes to 111. Griffiths possessed all the Welsh eloquence without the egotism. In my visits to the new Development Areas for the Board of Trade in 1944–5, I used to stay with him in Llanelly, and had drawn freely ever since on his abundant knowledge of South Wales, the social services and the coal industry. Gaitskell set out to defuse past quarrels by asking Bevan to take on the affairs of the Colonial Office, and Wilson of the Treasury, on the Opposition Front Bench. Amid these first attempts at harmony, my first private talk with Gaitskell, after his election as Leader, was a little sobering. The system of allocating Front Bench responsibilities had not yet fully hardened into public appointments to 'Shadow' posts. I had ever since 1951 spoken and asked questions on both Treasury and Board of Trade issues, and I had worked in both Departments. But I now assumed that Harold Wilson, as a member of the Shadow Cabinet, and for the sake of harmony, must take over the Treasury lead from Gaitskell, and I should concentrate mainly on the Board of Trade. Gaitskell tended to be very sensitive to the charge of harbouring personal allegiances and was determined to distribute responsibilities strictly for the good of the Party as a whole. For the moment I almost felt that my long friendship with him was going to prove a positive obstacle. We agreed, however, that, with Wilson taking the now so-called 'Shadow Chancellorship', the rest of the arrangement should not be too hard and fast. We also discussed the ever-nagging problem of the *Daily Herald* – and I was able, as it happened, to give the paper on the same day the news in advance of the public announcement that Butler was likely to leave the Treasury and be succeeded by Macmillan.

The Front Bench arrangement operated almost at once much more harmoniously than I had earlier feared. On Board of Trade subjects I was normally to take the lead, and on Treasury subjects to join in whenever I felt inclined. This worked perfectly well from early 1956 right on till the 1964 Government was formed. I do not remember ever having a serious dispute with Harold Wilson about the sharing of duties. That was partly because the new arrangement got an unexpectedly happy send-off on 21 February 1956. In this debate, I was asked to make the opening and Wilson the wind-up speech; and I devoted a great deal of pains to this beforehand – without of course in those days any 'research assistants' or such frills. Sometimes one could do too much preparation, and then be confronted with a frivolous House which did not want facts and figures. But I always judged it prudent to err on the side of solidity. That way one at least avoided major disasters, and I often found that ordinary Labour Members told me afterwards that they were grateful for the hard figures. Oddly enough, Emrys Hughes, Scottish pacifist, regarded usually in the House as an eccentric wag, used often to make such comments to me. Nevertheless even for the most experienced professionals, it was ever difficult to judge correctly beforehand the exact mood of the House – as witness Churchill himself on 5 April 1954.[1] In the February 1956 debate, I traced the worsening trade balance and mounting gold losses of 1955, against the background of a series of cheery quotations from R. A. Butler, as Chancellor, during that year. This exposed him as wholly unprepared for the economic slide of 1955 after the easy ride he had enjoyed in 1953 and 1954. He had even remarked at one stage that his financial policies would 'widen the human spirit'. So it chanced that this speech of mine luckily hit the right note; and Wilson's wind-up in the same spirit was equally applauded. Even Butler chortled merrily. Fleeting as these moods are in a human assembly, Labour Members in the corridors felt for the moment that things were on the mend, after the conflict of the Leadership election.

In his hatchet-burying mood, Gaitskell laboured very hard to get everyone, particularly Bevan, Wilson and Crossman, working harmoniously together. Rightly, he saw that what Crossman needed was a real hard practical job to do which would divert him from playing politics. So Gaitskell asked him to head a formal and expert Labour Party Committee to re-think the whole pensions and national insurance system in the light of the ten years' experience since the Beveridge Report and Jim Griffiths' National Insurance Act of 1946. I was to join the Committee. We also had the exceedingly valuable help of Richard Titmuss, Brian Abel-Smith and Peter Townsend. This was the best job Crossman ever did, and the most constructive Labour Party Committee on which I ever served when the Party was in opposition. The two central principles which in the course of the argument became unceasingly clear to us and in the end won unanimous

[1] See p. 232.

agreement, were these: first, that since the ordinary man or woman would rather pay £1 a week as an insurance contribution than as income tax, and so feel that he or she had earned their own pension, the contributory principle was right (contrary to what Bevan used to argue); and secondly, that since a single fixed contribution and pension for all must mean either too high a contribution for the lowest-paid, or too low a pension for the well-paid, it was inevitable that the contribution and pension must be earnings-related in future, if pensions were eventually to ensure a decent living standard in old age. The main snag was of course the growth of non-government pension schemes, and here the English compromise of 'contracting out' was agreed to be the most practical solution.

On these principles, the Report entitled 'National Superannuation' was evolved, and published in May 1957. It was generally well received. Far the greatest contribution had been made by Titmuss, Abel-Smith and Townsend. The whole plan, approved by the Party Conference in October 1957, was included as the major proposal in the Labour election manifesto in the 1959 election and again in 1964. In the interim John Boyd-Carpenter as Conservative Minister for National Insurance, largely accepted its principles by introducing his own more modest 'earnings-related' scheme. I more than once warned Crossman in the months before and after the 1964 lection that the job of turning our plan into legislation, and passing it through Parliament, was so demanding that we should hurry it forward as soon as the new Government was formed. Unfortunately this was not done; and after nearly six years of that Government, the legislation had been introduced but not fully enacted when the election of 1970 was held. It therefore fell in the end to Barbara Castle in the 1974 Labour Government to carry 'National Superannuation' into law. Thus did the 1956 National Superannuation Committee originally design the plan for what has now become a long-term social security scheme basically agreed by all Parties.

The spring of 1956 opened with the visit of Bulganin and Khrushchev to London. It was a period of high hopes for 'détente', though the word had not yet become fashionable. Two unprogrammed incidents stand out in my memory of the 'B & K' visit to London. When Bulganin and Khrushchev were being entertained to dinner by the Labour Party in the Harcourt Room of the House of Commons, I was winding up the Budget debate opposite Harold Macmillan in the Chamber, and could not attend. But strange rumours were whispered along the benches about a brawl breaking out between Khrushchev and George Brown at the dinner downstairs. The truth was that Khrushchev had made some remark about Britain conspiring with Hitler to invade Russia. George Brown called out, 'May God forgive you' or some such words; and Khrushchev, when this was translated, seemed surprised at being thus answered back. For once my sympathies were whole-heartedly with Brown. The second strange encounter in April 1956 was at Claridges. Asked to the party given by the Soviet Embassy to meet Bulganin and Khrushchev, I arrived to find a crush so great that some distinguished guests could hardly stand up, let alone move. William Hayter overheard Bulganin rebuke the Soviet Ambassador, Malik, for inviting so many guests and, when the poor Ambassador explained it was hard to leave people out, Bulganin applied a Russian word to him which meant roughly an illiterate peasant. Then the cameramen discovered that Charlie Chaplin was present. I have often noticed that cameramen are the undisputed masters at all modern public functions. Even kings and dictators meekly submit to them. At this party they seized Bulganin and Chaplin, planted them in a suitable spot for photography, and literally bundled not merely Khrushchev and R. A. Butler and the staff of Claridges, but also the Soviet security men, forcibly into any odd space remaining. Bulganin and Chaplin, impotent though not amused, meekly complied. A little later Hayter, with appropriate diplomatic tact, rescued Bulganin and Khrushchev and shepherded them to a private room with some British ministers, where I learnt afterwards, a rational conversation ensued.

Also in the early months of 1956 Gaitskell set out to strengthen the Labour Movement not merely in Parliament but, so far as he could, in the country outside. He regarded it as part of his job to ensure that the majority view of the Labour Party should get some sort of voice in the press. The contemporary picture was indeed distressing to those of us who in the 1930s and again in 1946 and 1947 had invested such faith and hope in a free popular press and the *Daily Herald* in particular as a major safeguard of social-democracy. The *Daily Herald* was now internally in turmoil and externally losing circulation. One evening the new editor suddenly and apparently without any consultation, wrote a leader advocating unilateral disarmament. Next day he was genuinely surprised at the outraged protests from Labour leaders. Naturally I was blamed by some of my colleagues in the House. At this period, *Reynolds News* offered some hope, but *Tribune* operated openly as a propaganda sheet for the Bevanite faction. With 80 per cent of the press in Conservative hands anyway, it was hard to see how the Labour Party could ever win a general election in these circumstances. So Gaitskell attempted a three-pronged campaign: to strengthen the *Daily Herald* by active co-operation with Surrey Dane, the Chairman; to introduce new writers into *Reynolds*; and more boldly to take over *Forward*, a bankrupt old-style Scottish publication (and once Ramsay Macdonald's voice), and launch it as a national Labour weekly in popular form.

With the *Daily Herald*, Gaitskell and I had little success. The economic forces described in the previous chapter were too strong; and after eighty years of universal free education the future lay ever more clearly with the *Daily Mirror* and its imitators. Surrey Dane, though an Odhams director, was more sympathetic to the Labour Party's aspirations than Southwood or Dunbar had ever been; but his disillusion with Fleet Street was now so deep that one felt his unspoken prayer for the *Daily Herald*, was: 'May it last my time.' With *Reynolds*, formally a Co-operative organ, more promising progress was made. The Editor, Bill Richardson, arranged with Gaitskell that Woodrow Wyatt and I should write regular diplomatic and economic articles respectively. I contracted to visit Moscow for a month again in the autumn of 1956, write a number of articles on internal Russian affairs, and then start a weekly economic column. This arrangement was financially welcome to me, since with four children approaching university age, and only one rise in parliamentary salary since 1946, my finances were distinctly close-hauled.

Forward was a more ambitious venture. It had been edited till recently by George Thomson, before he became a Dundee MP, and a young man, John Harris, who in 1956 operated from Glasgow. At first we compiled the paper over the telephone between London and Glasgow. But in September 1956, ironically on the eve of the Suez Crisis, we launched the new more up-to-date *Forward* from a very small office in Holborn. Francis Williams agreed at my suggestion and Gaitskell's invitation to become editor. George Thomson and John Harris were the salaried editorial staff; Jack Diamond and Alf Robens looked after finance and advertising; and I usually wrote a weekly article. It was a particularly happy and to me welcome group of colleagues; almost a working paradise compared with the *Daily Herald* of the fifties. I thus wrote every week from 1956 to 1959 for the *Daily Herald*, *Reynolds* and *Forward*; and this took quite a bit of fitting in with the calls of the whips, the Front Bench and my constituency. The idea of *Forward* was to try out whether a weekly Labour paper could pay its way without a political subsidy. With my sobering experience of the *Daily Herald*, now lasting over nineteen years, I did not myself believe it could. I often thought of Surrey Dane's dictum already quoted[2]: 'Sooner or later you come up against reality.' In the event we did not come up against realities for five years, and *Forward* survived till the 1960s.

In July of 1956 John Foster Dulles, the US Secretary of State, cancelled without warning the US contribution to the Egyptian Aswan Dam plan; and President Nasser retaliated by nationalizing the Suez Canal. The Suez crisis burst on this country and others with almost the suddenness and gathering momentum of the First World War in the late summer of 1914. From it Britain never fully recovered; but the part played by the Labour Party has not yet been fully understood. A legend was spread later that Gaitskell, for some dubious political reason, changed his mind between August and November. That is wholly untrue. What happened was this. In the last few days of July he talked privately with Eden, and was satisfied that the British Government had no intention whatever of using armed force. He told me he 'knew' from Eden that nothing of this sort was intended. He proposed, therefore, in the debate of 2 August to warn Nasser

[2] See p. 229.

against being too intransigent, but saw no real need to warn the British Government against the preposterous idea of resorting to arms. I had already heard at the *Daily Herald* office, however, from W. N. Ewer, who was still diplomatic correspondent, that he believed from his Foreign Office contacts that the Government were preparing a military expedition. I therefore, together with John Hynd MP, who had been a minister in the Attlee Government, saw Gaitskell at the House on 1 August, and persuaded him to include in his speech a warning to Eden against violating UN obligations by any sort of invasion of Egypt. Gaitskell at first thought this unnecessary, and had unfortunately been induced by his sympathies with Israel, and a visit from the Israeli Ambassador, to include some words in his speech about Hitler and Mussolini. But he agreed to our suggestion that he should also insert these words:[3]

I must, however, remind the House that we are members of the UN, that we are signatories to the UN Charter, and that for many years in British policy we have steadfastly avoided any international action which would be in breach of international law, or, indeed, contrary to the public opinion of the world. We must not, therefore, allow ourselves to get into a position where we might be denounced in the Security Council as aggressors or where the majority of the Assembly were against us.

Immediately after the debate I saw Ewer again that evening at the *Daily Herald* office; and Ewer told me positively that the Foreign Office were 'contemplating war'. (I recorded this conversation at the time.) I then rang up Gaitskell also that evening and repeated this to him. He replied that he frankly did not believe it, as he had seen Eden. At the time when he spoke in the House on 2 August, Gaitskell did not know of these much more positive statements by Ewer and the diplomatic correspondents. When, however, he saw the press generally on the morning of 3 August, he told me that he began to fear I was right, because of the strikingly similar tone of all the diplomatic correspondents.

In the conversation in the evening of 2 August, Gaitskell had agreed with my suggestion that I should write a letter to *The Times* warning the Government and arguing against any use of force. Next day I rang Denis Healey, as he was regarded as a foreign affairs specialist, and we drafted a letter together which appeared in *The Times* of 7 August, signed by both of us, as follows:

Sir – If the Government seriously mean to use military force over Suez, other than in self-defence, or in pursuance of our international obligations and the United Nations Charter, they will do so in defiance of very large sections of opinion in this country. The critical decisions now facing us must really be taken with a calm understanding of the realities, and not in a mood of impatience or anger.

What are the realities? In nationalizing the canal company Colonel Nasser has

[3] Hansard, 2 August 1956, cols. 1616–17.

acted in an exceedingly ill-judged, high-handed, and untrustworthy fashion. But, so far, as your Special Correspondent in the article 'Company and Canal' on 2 August points out, he has not 'violated the terms of any international treaty'. It is true that the offer of compensation so far made appears grossly unconvincing. But this is an issue to be settled in the cool atmosphere of the law, before the appropriate international forum. By no conceivable argument can it justify the use of force by one party.

Secondly, Colonel Nasser's whole conduct is certainly a threat to the far more important principle of the security and freedom of the canal, accepted by all the main Powers in the 1888 Convention. If he were to violate this, force would be justified; and we might well say so. But he has not yet done this (except in the sense of blockading the Israel tankers, which we have connived at for years past); and, as your Special Correspondent again points out, it does not follow that, because he has nationalized the company, he has closed or threatened to close the canal.

We were, therefore, shocked by your leading article of August 1, which says that 'quibbling over' the legal issues 'will delight the finicky and comfort the faint-hearted', and goes on to urge, apparently with no reference to our international obligations, that we should 'be ready from the start to use force if Nasser answers' a proposal for control 'with a refusal'.

These matters are not 'quibbles' in the eyes of most civilized nations. Such language could be used, with at least equal plausibility, by China to excuse an invasion of North Korea, Formosa, South Vietnam, or Hongkong, or by Russia to justify an attack on Finland or Persia. Action on these lines by Britain, not clearly in conformity with the UN Charter, would largely destroy in a day the moral and political force built up painfully since 1945 behind international law and order, for which we all fought in Korea, which has been the basis of United Kingdom foreign policy for eleven years, and which is the greatest single defence of Britain in a world which we can no longer dominate by military power. It would also array against us in the United Nations (where, do let us remember in good time, we as well as others can be arraigned as aggressors) not merely the Arab and Iron Curtain countries, but most of the East, several Commonwealth members, and many small nations.

Such a unilateral act of force would be a stupendous folly – unless and until Colonel Nasser resorts to force himself. If, therefore, he rejects the plan for international control which emerges from the coming conference, the nations concerned should forthwith apply all effective economic and diplomatic sanctions. Should, on the other hand, Colonel Nasser accept, the way would be open for new talks on economic development.

If we thus keep right scrupulously on our side, and act resolutely, we shall have far the best chance of vindicating the essential principles at stake.

Yours faithfully,
Denis Healey
Douglas Jay
House of Commons, August 5

This letter was given great prominence by *The Times*, and messages of support from all quarters reached us in large numbers. On 8 August, however, Eden made a hysterical broadcast denouncing Nasser in tones which further frightened a number of my colleagues. Gaitskell who had left after our conversation for a few days' holiday in Pembrokeshire, wrote to me thus on 9 August from Little Haven, Pembrokeshire:

Thanks for your note and for sending me the cutting from *The Times*. I thought your letter was very good. It coincides very much with my own view and should have some influence on the Government. I am a little worried about the continuing misrepresentation of my speech both from the extreme right and extreme left. How difficult it is to avoid this. But I am making a speech 18 August in Scotland and can perhaps make some retort then. . . . I hope you managed to get into touch with Jim Griffiths. I have told him I will gladly come up if he wants me . . . . I was glad you rang up. Do so again if you feel like it.

These interchanges make perfectly clear that Gaitskell was not adopting anything like Eden's threatening attitude at this time, and that he was already worried by the misrepresentations which were springing up. On 12 August, now thoroughly disturbed by the reports we were sending him (as Parliament was in recess, I was working full time on the *Daily Herald*), he returned to London and called a meeting of the Shadow Cabinet. He again saw Eden, who assured him most categorically that no use of force was intended. Convinced by this, and having issued a statement on behalf of the Shadow Cabinet in the sense of our letter to *The Times*, Gaitskell returned to Pembrokeshire. He took the view that Eden could not be deliberately deceiving him in confidential conversation as between Prime Minister and Leader of the Opposition. Partially reassured by this, I concluded for the moment that force had been contemplated, but that the public protest and Gaitskell's representations had induced Eden to draw back. I wrote at the time: 'Battle is thus won against use of force. I am sure Government originally intended to use it. US State Department said so.' The report about the State Department had reached me from Ewer. In this happier frame of mind I left on 25 August for our holiday in north Cornwall and Dartmoor. It was a strange three weeks that year, torn between the brilliance of the West Country and the black cloud of my doubts about Eden. Gaitskell wrote to me again on 5 September as follows: 'It is difficult to assess what the Government really intend. One gathers they are rather divided. I think it is most unlikely that, in the absence of any further action by Nasser, they could possibly go to war.' This again shows that Gaitskell did not believe force was contemplated. A few days later on 12 September I returned to London for a two-day second Suez debate requested by Gaitskell and the Opposition, and we were again all reassured by Eden that no bellicose action was planned. By this time even the hardiest sceptics in the Labour Party, including myself, were more or less convinced that nothing reckless was intended.

In this comforting atmosphere the Labour Party Conference was held at Blackpool. Bevan was elected Treasurer of the Party in succession to

Gaitskell. I left a week later on 10 October for three weeks in Leningrad and Moscow, expecting no international convulsions. Though William and Iris Hayter had again intvited me to stay in the Embassy, I was announcing myself to the Soviet authorities as a journalist and as a tourist on my own for the first week in Leningrad. With other tourists there, I spent much of my time with an official guide inspecting the magnificent line of carefully preserved imperial palaces. I noticed that there seemed more statues of Peter the Great than of Lenin, and very few of Stalin. Elsewhere my attempt to photograph squads of Russian children playing in the parks excited apparently much pleasure and amusement, but I was warned off photography when near the submarine yards at the mouth of the river. My uppermost thought on leaving Leningrad, and seeing the long line of Imperial palaces for the last time, was astonishment that the Czarist regime could have lasted right into the twentieth century.

On 15 October I started an intensive two weeks in Moscow of meetings with officials, and academics; visits to factories, schools, and shopping centres; and talks with Russian leaders at diplomatic parties; all greatly assisted by William Hayter's fluent Russian-speaking and extremely know-ledgeable assistant, Joe Dobbs. On the first evening we met Bulganin, Khrushchev and Mikoyan at an Afghan Embassy reception. Zukhov came with them, looking as splendid as ever. Bulganin, an ex-mayor of Moscow, showed knowledge and interest in London's satellite new-town policy, and said Moscow would have to do something like it. Mikoyan remarked that ballet girls were better diplomats than the professionals. The journalists present at this reception, however, surrounded Khrushchev and pestered him with questions about Suez – no doubt hoping for an indiscretion. This time he kept his head. Next day at lunch the French Ambassador told us he thought the Suez dispute would end in a negotiated settlement. On the even-ing of 18 October after a strenuous day we attended a memorable perfor-mance of Swan Lake at the Bolshoi, watched by Bulganin and Khrushchev in the Imperial Box; but next evening, 19 October, at a Kremlin party we noticed that only Malenkov and Shepilov (Soviet Foreign Minister) were present as hosts. We did not then know that Bulganin, Khrushchev and Mikoyan had flown to Warsaw to handle the uprising there which ended in the Gomulka régime. Malenkov, keeping off this topic, talked of his tour in Britain, which he said he had greatly enjoyed, and invited us to visit a Russian power station.

For the week-end of 20–21 October, Joe Dobbs and I left the capital for an interlude of real Russian life at Jaroslav, on the Volga, which we reached by a 400-mile train journey. In the evening at the hotel a violent controversy grew up between two young Russians drinking at the next table. One turned to us and protested that his neighbour was lying in pretending to have been an officer in the war, when anyone could see he 'was not fit to be an officer'. The hotel manager then ordered the two

I

protagonists out of the room on the ground that they were 'drunken hooligans molesting his distinguished English guests'. Next morning, we found the Ambassador's Rolls-Royce, which had come to fetch us back, surrounded by a huge crowd gazing with wonder at a phenomenon such as evidently they had never seen before. It was on this day, Sunday 21 October, that the anti-Stalinist Gomulka came to power in Poland tolerated by the Russians. On the drive home to Moscow we stopped at the religious city of Zagorsk, rich in superb mediaeval architecture, and watched a Greek orthodox service being intoned with plentiful gold ornamentation and swinging of incense. Returned to Moscow, after this flash-back into past centuries, we met a group of Soviet economists on Monday at the Academy of Science and argued the merits of their system and ours.

Next day, 23 October, on my way home I heard in Stockholm from the British Embassy officials there that fighting had broken out in Hungary between Russian troops and Hungarian insurgents. The British papers throughout the following week were naturally full of the uprisings in Poland and Hungary. So it was with a strong desire for a little peace and quiet that I arrived at the House of Commons on Monday 29 October. Within a few hours the news came through that Israel had invaded Egypt. We all still assumed – certainly Gaitskell did[4] – that there was no question of force being used by Britain or France. But next day, Tuesday 30 October, the crucial hinge of this gathering crisis, Guy Mollet, the French Prime Minister, was in London conferring with Eden; and a Tory MP remarked to me during Question Time: 'I hear we're going in.' I asked him what on earth he meant. He replied that we were to 'put troops into Egypt'. I simply did not believe this, but the news spread that Eden would make a statement at 4 p.m. He then announced that an ultimatum had been issued to Egypt (and nominally to Israel), and that British and French troops would be landed, ostensibly to separate the Egyptians and the Israelis. The House of Commons then spontaneously exploded in a way I never experienced before or since, and the next five days were much the most memorable of my thirty years in Parliament. Amid the general outburst of indignation, which overwhelmed the normal rules, Gaitskell could at first hardly get a hearing, but managed to demand audibly that there should be no troop movements until the House had debated Eden's ultimatum, and that the debate should be held later that day. The Speaker accepted this; and since in the resumed debate, Eden refused to give any undertaking, the Opposition voted solidly against the Government. And that very day, unknown to us in the debate in the House, the Soviet Government issued a conciliatory declaration on Hungary, in effect offering the anti-Stalinist Nagy Government, which had taken power, a sort of Dominion Status within the Communist Empire.[5]

[4] See his letter just quoted.
[5] William Hayter, *The Kremlin and the Embassy*, p. 142.

Next morning, Wednesday 31 October, a meeting of the Parliamentary Labour Party was hastily summoned, at which – surprisingly – Stanley Evans (known as 'Featherbed Evans' after his attack on 'feather-bedded farmers') argued that when British troops were involved, however mistakenly, the Party must support the Government. I replied that this was not the British constitution at all, and quoted Chatham and Burke during the American War of Independence and Lloyd George on the South African War. Gaitskell came down firmly on this side, and said simply that opposition would certainly be unpopular, but was clearly right. On the same day Edward Boyle and Anthony Nutting honourably resigned from the Government, and in effect ended their political careers. From that morning of 31 October right through to Saturday 3 November, the House debated Suez almost continuously, with repeated divisions, and unprecedented sittings throughout Friday and Saturday. The first climax came on the afternoon of Saturday 3 November, when, as Eden again refused to call off the invasion, the whole Opposition side of the House stood up and called on him to resign as he walked out. The indignation and uproar were spontaneous, and 'behind the Speaker's Chair' accusations of 'murderer' were thrown to and fro, and the two sides nearly came to blows – but not quite.

On Sunday 4 November I travelled to Taunton and back, for a public protest meeting which had been organized on the spur of the moment, but was attended by six hundred people. I spoke with a good deal of violence, because that was how I felt; and the meeting responded with an intensity of feeling which I had not met at any public meeting for years past. One of the strange manifestations of the Suez crisis was the series of instantly improvised, yet crowded, public meetings springing up in the most unlikely places. The dominant motive in my mind, which I believe the great majority of the Labour Party and many others shared, including high civil servants, was fear that the reputation of the country was being mutilated; and that the whole system of internatonal security and the UN for which the war had been fought was now being endangered. Looking back with hindsight twenty years later, I am inclined to think the damage was even greater than most of us then feared.

British troops landed in Egypt on Monday 5 November, and the Russians on the very same day issued their 'rocket rattling' threat to the world, offering to come to the help of Egypt. On the following day, the second climax of this crisis, Gaitskell called for another immediate debate, and made his most masterly speech of the whole crisis. He demanded an immediate cease-fire and total reversal of Eden's policy: and ended with these words:[6]

In his broadcast the Prime Minister said that what we want is to stop the forest fire from spreading. That fire is spreading with appalling rapidity. It has spread

[6] Hansard, 6 November 1956. Col. 39.

to Hungary. One spark was sufficient perhaps, to cause the Russian invasion of Hungary. . . . We must stand together with our allies . . . only one thing can achieve this object, and that is to get back to the principles we abandoned last week, to call off the fighting in Egypt, to obey at last and at this late moment the Cease-Fire Resolution of the UN, to withdraw our forces as soon as possible, to give up taking the law into our own hands, and to give our full support for the new international police force without quibble or conditions. Let us get back into line with our friends and allies, and save our reputation and the peace of the world.

This was on all counts one of the two most powerful speeches I heard in my thirty years in Parliament.[7] It was received in silence even by Conservatives, who clearly at heart could no longer contest the overwhelming logic of the argument, or the strength of Gaitskell's conviction that the country's whole future was being imperilled. It was one of those very rare speeches which left its hearers of all kinds with the certainty that the Government's policy simply could not be continued. Even Michael Foot, in his biography of Aneurin Bevan, which is persistently critical of Gaitskell, says this of the Suez debates:[8]

Bevan was also impressed, as who could not be, by the revelation of the iron in Gaitskell's character; somehow what formerly looked like obduracy was transmuted to shining courage.

Gaitskell's speech on 6 November was followed by R. A. Butler, who was generally believed in the House to be opposed to Eden's policy, or else characteristically unable to make up his mind whether he was or not. He took refuge in saying that he would convey Gaitskell's message to Eden; and later that evening Eden announced a cease-fire in deference to the UN Resolution which the United States, Canada, and almost all other Western nations had supported. An explosion of applause from the Labour side of the House greeted Eden's statement, and the minority of Conservatives still actively supporting him visibly collapsed. It was not of course solely the continuous demonstrations during the week in the Commons and Gaitskell's and Bevan's speeches (they were now united) which forced the Government to pull back from catastrophe. The condemnation of the Anglo-French move by the UN and in particular the US and the whole Commonwealth; the threat of withdrawal of US financial support; the damage likely from totally alienating the US and the Soviet Union together; all these played a part. But it was precisely these dangers which formed the burden of the case Gaitskell was arguing. Parliament on this occasion *did*, as memorably as in May 1940, by representing national opinion, change the Government's policy and the whole course of events at a moment of

---

[7] The other was Cripps's in August 1947. Gaitskell's finest speech of all, on the EEC, was made of course outside Parliament at the Brighton Party Conference in October 1962.
[8] Michael Foot, *Aneurin Bevan* (London, 1973), vol. 2, *1945–60*, p. 517.

supreme crisis and saved the country from even greater catastrophe. It has always surprised me, on reading academic or journalistic lamentations about the alleged decline of Parliament's ultimate authority over governments, to note how seldom these pessimists remember the Suez debates, and the climax of 6 November 1956, which prove the contrary.

Later that same evening Frank and Elizabeth Pakenham held a party fixed before the crisis broke; and as the debate was now over and the issue settled, I decided to go. Hugh Fraser, always a popular colleague in the House, but now a 'Suez-Grouper', or Eden supporter, was among the guests. Feeling was high, but civilities were happily preserved. Later still that evening Gaitskell arrived from a triumphal appearance at an Albert Hall anti-Suez demonstration to which he had given the news of the cease-fire. He had spent a considerable day, but was able duly to propose a toast to Elizabeth, a close friend since Oxford days – it was some sort of celebration – before it ended.

This narrative and Gaitskell's letters quoted will show that there was no truth whatever in the myth afterwards concocted by the Tory press that Gaitskell had changed his ground for some mysterious reason in the course of the Suez crisis. He was just as staggered and incredulous as the rest of us when on 30 October Eden announced the ultimatum and military expedition. Gaitskell remarked to me on the way home after one of that week's debates: 'I will never believe anything Eden says in public or private again.' The simple truth was that Gaitskell had no notion during the 2 August debate that any military action was intended; that he was extremely reluctant to believe the warnings I passed on to him; that he wholly accepted the reassurances Eden gave him then and in the September debate; and that the announcement of 30 October came as a thunderbolt. His fierce opposition in October to the use of force was wholly consistent with his attitude throughout the entire controversy.

In retrospect the grim question arises – even more fateful than the apparent 'collusion' between Israel, France and Britain[9] – whether the Russians would have honoured their conciliatory offer of 30 October to Hungary if the Eden ultimatum of the same day had not been delivered. The coincidence of dates is both extraordinary and tormenting. When the Russians decided on their conciliatory statement of 30 October, they could not have known of the Anglo-French ultimatum. When the British Cabinet approved the ultimatum, they did not know of the Russian declaration or the withdrawal of Russian troops from Budapest. The Russian declaration offered the removal of Soviet advisers and economic equality for Hungary, much as had been agreed with Poland. Hayter sent a telegram to the Foreign Office that day saying he thought this was to be believed.[10] On 3 November,

[9] Selwyn Lloyd's memoirs, published twenty years later, suggest that it was more a case of confusion than collusion. Selwyn Lloyd, *Suez 1956 – A Personal Account* (London, 1978).
[10] Hayter, p. 145.

four days *after* the Anglo-French ultimatum, the Russian Government decided to send their troops back to Budapest. On 4 November they did so, and fighting continued for several days. On 5 November – the day the Anglo-French landing occurred – Shepilov handed to Hayter in Moscow his 'rocket-rattling' note threatening reprisals against Britain and France. Hayter's considered opinion was that though the peace party in Moscow (Khrushchev and Mikoyan), did prevail on 30 October, two events intervened to swing back the majority on to the side of the hard-liners (Zukhov and Suslov). These events were: first, the rash decision of Nagy after 30 October to withdraw from the Warsaw Pact, and request the departure of all Russian troops from Hungary, instead of accepting the Russian offer; and secondly the Anglo–French ultimatum. Hayter's conclusion was that 'the Soviet decision to go all out in Hungary was caused by Nagy, and not by Suez, though the latter contributed something'; but Suez was 'a Godsend to Russia.'[11]

Whether, therefore, the final invasion of Budapest and suppression of Nagy would have occurred without the Anglo-French ultimatum, can never be determined beyond doubt. What is certain is that Suez enabled the Russians to suppress Nagy with far less international hostility than they would otherwise have faced; that the Soviet 'rocket-rattling' of 5 November convinced Middle Eastern and Asian countries, when the cease-fire was announced, that Britain and France had surrendered to Russian pressure; and that British influence and prestige suffered as a result enormous and lasting damage. Though the growth in the relative economic strength of other nations – the US, Russia and the Arab states – was bound gradually to erode British influence in these areas, the survival of it arising from the past and the two wars would in all probability have been longer-lived, if it had not been recklessly put to the test in this one fatal gamble.

How did Eden come to make such a colossal miscalculation, and how did the British Cabinet system fail to stop him? Part of the answer, I believe, was the persistence of that perennial political fault: fighting the last battle and avoiding the mistake made last time. Just as Baldwin and Chamberlain thought they were avoiding the mistakes made at Versailles; Eden when faced with Nasser, and John Foster Dulles when faced with North Vietnam, both imagined they were avoiding the mistakes made against Hitler, and so made equal and opposite blunders. Partly responsible also, no doubt, was Eden's personal character. One observer, an ex-civil servant, in conversation with me, predicted trouble from the start 'because we are in the hands of that dangerous phenomenon, a weak man who wants to prove he is strong'. Watching Eden myself in all his Commons appearances, at each stage of the long Suez tragedy, I was convinced that there was truth in this: that we were in the presence of a civilized but irresolute man, with a streak of hysteria, who was conscious that he was no Churchill, but

[11] Hayter, p. 153.

anxious to prove to the Conservative Party that he could act like one. For Eden the tragedy was bitter. If he had never become Prime Minister, he would have preserved his once great reputation. As W. N. Ewer remarked to me when it was all over, never were the words more true: '*Capax imperii nisi imperasset*' (Capable of ruling if he had not ruled).

The years 1957 and 1958 in British politics, after the emotional convulsion of Suez, were something between an interlude and a hangover. In repeated bye-elections the electorate were recording their condemnation of Suez by consistently voting favourably to the Labour Party. Gaitskell was working steadily to advance Labour Party policy by making public ownership plans more practical, and expansion of social services and public investment the key points in the programme. He and Bevan were now working tolerably well together, particularly since Bevan became 'Shadow Foreign Secretary' in 1957. Knowing that the next government, if any, would probably be his last, Bevan saw himself, I believe, and justifiably, as a future Foreign Secretary. Meanwhile, Harold Macmillan, who had taken over as Prime Minister rather than Butler after the Eden debacle, to everyone's surprise, was trying to exorcize the haunting ghost of Suez, while publicly pretending with some skill to be doing otherwise. In these months there seemed to some of us in the middle ranks of the Labour Party real promise for a constructive future; with Gaitskell and Bevan in co-operative harmony, and the prospect of less dogmatism on public ownership. To my surprise in the annual election for the Parliamentary Committee (Shadow Cabinet) in November 1956 in the aftermath of Suez, I found myself tying with Patrick Gordon-Walker at ninety-three votes and only three places short of the Committee. Frankly I always hated these personal rivalries, which were forced on one by the system. Roy Jenkins, who was politically a close friend and colleague in these years (and never used to stand himself), often told me I should be more pushing. Fairly clearly this time, it was the vehement speeches I had made on Suez which had attracted this vote. Also, early in 1957, our Opposition Front Bench responsibilities for economic debates were more tidily sorted out. Gaitskell arranged that Arthur Bottomley should take over the Admiralty and Commonwealth, Gordon-Walker should support Wilson on the Treasury, and I should stick to the Board of Trade but still keep my interest in the Treasury. From this moment Wilson showed himself particularly co-operative.

On the policy front also the prospect still seemed a good deal more cheerful in the summer and autumn of 1957. For some time I had been trying to propagate in internal Party counsels the idea of a more modern form of public ownership which eventually materialized – again nearly twenty years later – in the National Enterprise Board of the 1970s. My argument was that the old-fashioned State monopoly – popularly known as 'nationalization' – was suitable for physical monoplies like electricity and gas, but not suitable for manufacturing industry generally. A more suitable form of public ownership there, I suggested, would be some sort of national finance corporation which would own some of the shares of many firms, rather as the government had successfully owned half the shares of BP for half a century. The trouble was that the simpler souls in the Party had learnt the word 'nationalizaion' by heart, and believed that any movement away from 'nationalization' was a movement away from public ownership. It was largely due to this verbal confusion – such is politics – that it took nearly twenty years before the NEB conception became the conventional wisdom of the fundamentalists in the Party. In June 1957, however, Gaitskell came to see me, when I was still prostrate at home as it happened from a slipped disc, with the draft of a new Party policy paper on public ownership. This was the germ of 'Industry and Society', largely drafted by Peter Shore, then head of the Research Department at Transport House, and published a year later. In our talk I argued in favour of public 'participation' rather than 100 per cent ownership, and Gaitskell evidently sympathized. The approval by the 1957 Party Conference of 'Industry and Society' was certainly a major step in modernizing the Party, and Bevan himself had been a member of the Sub-Committee which had first approved the document.

Still more crucial and much more divisive, were the debates on disarmament and nuclear weapons which led up to the Party Conference of October 1957. It was in this year that the controversy over British nuclear weapons, and the demand that this country should unilaterally abandon them, began to arouse such fierce emotions. To me it was a false controversy. Having so long believed in the widest internationalism, the UN as the key organization, and general disarmament as the only way of avoiding eventual war, I regarded this sudden impulsive demand that Britain alone should disarm, as a sad debasement of the whole issue. The suggestion that this country should unilaterally act in this way meant either that the advocates of such a policy believed Russia and other countries would shamefacedly follow our moral example, or else that this country would certainly be relatively weakened. Faced in argument with this dilemma, the unilateralists in general took refuge in purporting to believe that the Russians would actually respond in the described manner. I remember Gaitskell relating to me a conversation he and Bevan and others in the Shadow Cabinet had held in this period with Bertrand Russell, who had been invited to come and state his views. Russell was foolish enough to argue that the Soviet leaders would thus meekly follow our humanitarian example. Bevan, according to Gaitskell, pounced on this even more emphatically than Gaitskell himself, and pointed out to Russell that in that case the disagreement was not a moral one at all, but a difference of opinion on the psychology and political motives of the Russian leaders. On this, Bevan said, he and Gaitskell were probably better judges than Russell. Bevan had evidently been touched on a very sensitive nerve by the suggestion that Russell's political judgement was more expert than his own.

To me this question of the practical effects of unilateral British disarmament was always the rational key to the controversy. But it naturally became swamped by a load of emotional confusion and was then organized into a pressure group by the Campaign for Nuclear Disarmament (CND). The great majority of CND supporters were genuine idealists, who fully believed they were serving the cause of peace, but were unable or unwilling to think out the practical issues. No doubt, however, there was a small minority who were not sorry to see this country weakened relatively to the Russians. Gaitskell of course believed above all in clear thinking, and as a result was perhaps occasionally too sharp with the honestly misguided idealists. But the controversy could only end in one way, as it did: the emergence of a consensus in Britain in favour of international control and limitation of nuclear weapons, accepted by the US, the Soviet Union and other nuclear powers. In the interval, however, between 1957 and 1964, much misled idealism in British politics was turned to waste and bitterness by the unilateralists.

In 1957 the controversy over 'the Bomb', as it became crudely known in Fleet Street, reached its emotional climax in Bevan's speech to the Labour Party Conference at Brighton that autumn. The issue arose in the form of a choice between one resolution calling for a unilateral end to manufacture of the H-bomb, and another from the National Executive Committee calling for a unilateral end to nuclear tests and a multilateral offer to end manufacture. Bevan, as Shadow Foreign Secretary, agreed to speak for the Executive resolution and against the unilateral alternative. He reached the decision to do so on his own, without consulting even his 'Bevanite' disciples. When he rose to speak in an intensely emotional atmosphere, his closest friends did not know – nobody really knew – what he would say. He first developed in a restrained manner a rational and powerful argument: that if this country renounced manufacture, it would either be simply relying on its nuclear allies to do what it professed to regard as immoral for itself; or else it would have to renounce for the sake of consistency all its alliances and commitments. At this point interruptions from Bevan's outraged adherents goaded the bellicose impulses he was striving to restrain. When some of his long-standing faithful supporters shouted at him, he shouted back. He then burst out into the declaration that the unilateral resolution would send a British Foreign Secretary 'naked into the conference chamber' (by which he in fact meant the absence of allies rather than the absence of the bomb), and that this was not statesmanship but an 'emotional spasm'.

The Conference rejected the 'unilateral' resolution by an overwhelming majority. But the Bevanites were shattered and heart-broken. Women among his previous supporters were seen weeping in the hall. To them indeed his speech was the unkindest cut of all. Jennie Lee nobly stood by him; but Michael Foot, Barbara Castle and Ian Mikardo were for the time alienated and baffled. The *Tribune*, for the first time ever, openly attacked Bevan and allowed its columns to be filled with letters hostile to him. Why did he act in this way, it was asked on all sides? The obvious cynical view – that Bevan simply changed his mind because he wished to be Foreign Secretary and the second most influential minister in a Gaitskell Government – was, I am sure, wide of the mark. Bevan was capable of egomania, but not of cynical dishonesty. Part of the reason, I believe as one who watched him throughout these years, was his growing maturity and waning aggressiveness. Another was the encounter with Bertrand Russell and other doctrinaires who professed to be better judges than Bevan of Khrushchev's psychology. For Bevan liked intellectuals, but disliked academics. Another reason, I noted at the time, was his series of conversations with Khrushchev himself in the summer of 1957 in Russia, during which Khrushchev expressed the hope that Britain would keep its nuclear weapons so as to soften the conflict between the US and the Soviet Union. Certainly Bevan now saw himself as Foreign Secretary in a Gaitskell Government, and must have believed (he was near sixty) that this was probably his own last chance of major office and of achieving the influence on world events to which he had always aspired. The truth probably was not that Bevan's views changed in order to attain office, but that when he regarded the surrounding world through the dispassionate eye of a man who might soon become Foreign Secretary, the facts looked very different to him. Could he in a British Labour Government really renounce not merely our nuclear weapons, but our nuclear allies? He was honest enough, in the final test, to admit that he could not. And so he felt rationally compelled to reach the same conclusion as Gaitskell had held all the time.

Nobody present could fail to see Bevan's speech – conversion, if you like – at Brighton in 1957 as a moving human drama as well as a political upheaval. I was thankful that Bevan and Gaitskell on the same dispassionate grounds had reached the same conclusion on the main issue, and that the myth could no longer be propagated that Bevan was standing for some great alternative policy. With 'Industry and Society' and 'National Superannuation' also approved at Brighton by a convincing vote, the prospect for the Labour Party seemed to be transformed. A celebration was even held to relaunch the *Daily Herald* under its new editor, and most of the Party leaders attended. It was now just twenty years since I had first joined the paper, and my once ardent hopes for it were not yet quite extinct. At this party I met for the first time Frank Cousins, the new General Secretary of the Transport and General Workers Union. True, Cousins had just spoken, rather confusedly, on the side of the unilateralists. But my immediate impression of him was that he seemed simple-minded and not really to have thought it all out. No doubt I was much too optimistic in writing at this time that Brighton 1957 'wipes out Morecambe. It is as good as Morecambe was bad. It means Nye has decided he wants to win the election. There will be no "party within the party".' For nobody could then have foreseen that by the time the next Labour Government was formed, both Bevan and Gaitskell would have died.

In the autumn of 1957, however, Bevan's performance at the Brighton Conference, which caused such consternation in the constituency parties, widened support for him in the Parliamentary Party. In the Shadow Cabinet election of November 1957 he moved up to third place. (Gaitskell and Griffiths as Leader and Deputy Leader did not now compete.) The order this year of those elected was: Wilson, Mitchison, Bevan, Soskice, Callaghan, Robens, Greenwood, Tom Fraser, Brown, Noel-Baker, Gordon-Walker, Bottomley; and of the also rans: Younger, Lee, Summerskill, Willey, Hall, Jay, Stewart, Ungoed-Thomas, Benn, Peart, Healey and eight others. In all the elections of this period Soskice and Mitchison, both lawyers, always polled very high votes because, quite apart from their views and debating talents, they were so unsparingly generous with personal advice to colleagues in the House on all manner of political, professional and other problems. In Soskice in particular, Gaitskell always had the greatest confidence.

In 1958 and 1959, with an apparently reunited Labour Party, and after seven years in opposition, the objective of winning the next election began to dominate our minds. I accordingly felt obliged to accept invitations for week-end speeches to local Labour Parties anywhere from Truro to Aberdeen, with too often long-drawn-out Sunday train journeys back to an evening on the *Daily Herald*. For many years I found these expeditions the most exhausting aspect of a politician's life: forty-eight hours spent, and two to three hundred miles travelled and a sleepless night endured, in order to address in a chilly school perhaps fifteen people, ten of whom were already converted. It was my ill-luck that in the 1950s Fleet Street discovered that there was no value in reporting most political speeches; so that one's finest efforts were not likely to be noticed beyond the fifteen persons actually present. True some, like John Strachey, hopefully sent out 'advances' to the press. Strachey told me he once felt bound, in order to keep faith with the press, to read out a learned discourse about the Chinese 'off-shore islands' of Quemoy and Matsu to an audience consisting solely of a few ladies making tea in a marquee on the outskirts of Dundee. One occupational risk in these trips was the food supply. At Newcastle once, after a full day's 'week-end school', I was invited to the home of a Party enthusiast at about 8 p.m. on the assumption, I thought, that I would at least get some supper. I was presented with the Sunday papers to read; 8 p.m. passed and 9 p.m.; and as 10 p.m. approached, I silently wondered at what hour hunger would overcome politeness. Could I have the face to say: may I have some supper? Not until 10.45 did I do so.

One hazard for which I soon became fully resigned was the habit of local Labour dignitaries, acting as chairman, of introducing me with some such words as these: 'It's a great pity there are so few people here tonight. Of course the meeting was fixed on the same evening as the Co-op dance' (looking at me as if this was my fault) 'but you people ought to have turned out in better numbers. Mr Jay will now speak if you think it's worthwhile.' To this I became so acclimatized that I used to bet Woodrow Wyatt (with whom I was paired in so-called 'brains trusts') on our outward journey that we would be greeted with the words, 'There won't be much of an audience tonight.' He was particularly scornful of my cynicism on one journey and took a large bet that nothing of the kind would happen. On our arrival a very gloomy individual said: 'You won't get much of an audience tonight.' Why not? I said, delighted at winning my bet and expecting the usual answer about the 'Co-op dance'. 'Because the lights are out,' he said. Woodrow joined in at this point and asked how long it normally took to get the lights put right. 'Three months,' the lugubrious official replied. So I was well prepared when I later travelled to Leeds to speak in the by-election in which Keith Joseph was first elected to Parliament. It was winter, snow was falling; and the meeting was at a school on the windswept northern heights of that city. After my four-hour train journey and taxi drive from the station, I was received (one could not say 'greeted') by a positively funereal character with the words: 'You won't have many people here tonight.' When I enquired why, he mournfully replied: 'We did put out 3000 leaflets: but they had the name of the wrong school.' I persisted boldly and asked whether somebody had been posted at the wrong school to tell any potential audience which was the right one; to which he crushingly retorted: 'Wouldn't be worthwhile.'

Nevertheless, though the thoughts of most of us on the Labour Front Bench were largely fixed in 1958 on the run-up to the next election, my week-ends were not wholly devoted to speech-making adventures. Peter and Martin were both at Oxford, following in Peter's case eighteen months' national service in the Navy including service in Malta and Cyprus, in the course of which he had been nearly involved in the Suez expedition. Both his previous housemaster and I independently wrote him a letter arguing that whatever he thought about the Suez policy, it was the duty of a member of the Armed Forces to obey orders. Our letters proved to have been wholly unnecessary. In February 1958 we ventured on a twenty-first birthday for Peter given in All Souls, to which we invited among others all our old friends with sons or daughters who were then undergraduates in Peter's generation at Oxford: notably, the Pakenhams, the Kaldors and the Callaghans. Jim Callaghan dined with me beforehand in College, and his daughter Margaret, who married Peter three years later, was among the guests, though they could not recall afterwards having met one another at this particular celebration.

These rejuvenating interludes, however, were brief, as in the winter of 1958-9 unemployment began to increase seriously for the first time since the war. The higher Bank Rate and credit squeeze introduced by Peter Thorneycroft as Chancellor in 1957 were having their effect. As a result, in January 1959 I was rather suddenly given a most arduous job by the Labour Party: to tour all the old depressed areas – the new Development Areas – where unemployment was again growing rapidly, and report to the Labour Party on what ought to be done. Dalton proposed this operation, on the pattern of his famous 'Commission' of 1936 which toured the old 'Special Areas' and produced a report which was one contribution to our Distribution of Industry Act of 1945. But Dalton in 1936 led a team, and I was supplied with one typist from Transport House. Stiff though the proposition was, we contrived in that very cold winter to visit in two weeks most of South Wales, Merseyside, industrial Scotland and the North-East Coast; and collected information from a fine variety of authorities and individuals in those areas. It was cheering, despite the discomforts of rapid travel in icy weather, to meet so many old friends and colleagues of the war-time Ministry of Supply days and the post-war industrial development effort.

But it was also distressing to see at first hand the extent to which the 1945 policy had been eroded and run down during the seven or eight years of Conservative Government since 1951. By 1959 the then Government had narrowed the original Development Area boundaries, leaving out some areas of high unemployment, and had virtually stopped many of the more crucial development programmes. I wrote forthwith my report in the form of a fifteen page pamphlet, which was published by the Labour Party at a Press Conference, under the title: 'Unemployment: the Douglas Jay Report'. It set out the current facts, and made a dozen practical proposals: the re-start of factory-building by the Government; an advance factory programme; a tightening up of Industrial Development Certificates in fully employed areas; more grants for roads, water supply, etc.; clearance of sites; rent rebates on government factories; re-opening of Board of Trade offices in Swansea and Dundee closed by the then Government; more government contracts for Development Areas; steering of new industry to Lancashire; wider Development Areas; easier loans through the Development Area legislation; and help for Northern Ireland.

This pamphlet was pretty widely noticed, and it prodded the Conservatives into new legislation after the 1959 election; though some of its ideas had to wait until I myself put them into action after 1964. But in these early weeks of 1959 much of the political effect of all these exertions was thrown away by the tactical dilatoriness of my own colleagues. There was naturally to be a parliamentary debate on my report; and I repeatedly pointed out to Gaitskell and the Shadow Cabinet that it should be held in February while unemployment was still high and not delayed till March when Ian McLeod, the Minister of Labour, would probably produce a lower figure. Week by week, however, the debate was postponed on one pretext or another; and was finally held on 18 March, by which time McLeod contrived by some slick ingenuity to secure, with a few hours to spare, the reduced March figure for his speech in the debate. McLeod was quite entitled to his improvisation; but not for nothing, I felt on this occasion, did he first make his reputation as a professional card player. My colleagues on the *Daily Herald* next morning improved on the occasion by suggesting that it was somehow due to me that the debate had been postponed.

By this time the situation on the *Daily Herald* had worsened again so far that it was plainly impossible to continue working there any longer. Circulation was still falling; the link with the Labour Party very tenuous; and the Fleet Street fashion of blaming all journalistic troubles on 'politics' had gained control. The only other paper for which I wished to work was *Reynolds,* and I arranged by mid-1959 to build up my financial articles there into a regular financial and investment column. I left one torrentially raining midsummer day in 1959 the *Daily Herald* Long Acre complex which I had entered with such sanguine optimism twenty-two years before; and made my way to an even smaller office in the *Reynolds* building at the northern end of Grays Inn Road. At least I could now devote the whole second half of the day, as I had always wished, to parliamentary life and work in the House of Commons. But there was one snag. I had long planned, having been without a car since 1942, to buy one in 1959 for use on holidays at any rate a year or two before the children got married and left home. But the *Reynolds* assignment (though in fact it survived till 1964) seemed to me so precarious that, rightly or wrongly, to the family's disappointment, I postponed the long-promised car for just one further year.

In the run-up to the general election of October 1959, the Labour Party was full of renewed optimism. Gaitskell, Bevan and Wilson were working amicably together in the Shadow Cabinet. Even Dick Crossman was co-operating wholeheartedly with Gaitskell. The Tory Government, or so we thought, was still suffering from the miasma of Suez, and the spectre of unemployment resurrected by the previous winter. Gaitskell in what looked like a clinching stroke, recruited Hugh Cudlipp of the *Daily Mirror* stable to translate Labour Party policies into a mass-produced illustrated election pamphlet. We were all delighted with this. In the campaign itself the opinion polls at first seemed promising; though I began to feel that the response from working people was not quite what it had been in 1950 and 1951. Somehow in the last week the feeling changed and the opinion polls narrowed; and in the event the Conservatives won. The Tory vote was actually down from 49·8 per cent to 44·3 per cent of the votes cast; but Labour went down from 46·3 per cent to 43·6 per cent. So the Conservative majority rose to 100. What went wrong? A legend grew up in subsequent weeks that the turning point was a speech by Gaitskell a week before polling day in which he suggested that Labour's proposed social reforms could be paid for by economic growth rather than higher rates of income tax. Gaitskell's argument was a perfectly respectable one, though doubtless, like any assumption about the future, unproven. But to suppose that its logical weaknesses were so immediately apparent to millions of electors, that they reacted with general scepticism and altered their voting intentions is from all my experience of electioneering, a completely unrealistic view of the voting public. This particular legend probably owed its currency to the fact that it was convenient both to Conservatives and to Bevanites.

The real reasons for the Conservative success in 1959 were, I believe, more deep-rooted. First, economic conditions in the world were relatively easy for Britain because prices of food and materials were low or falling and British governments up to the end of the 1950s followed the sensible policy of buying food and materials as cheaply as possible and limiting by quota the import of manufactured goods. This gave us gradually rising standards as well as the full employment established by the Attlee Government. And as long as this lasted, the electorate tended to vote for the government in power. Secondly, the steady build-up of Conservative Party propaganda in the press, which had been suspended in the years 1939–45, continued through the 1950s. Thirdly, the damage done by the Bevanite controversy in 1951 and 1955 had clearly not, as we had hoped after the 1957 reconciliation, been fully dissipated by 1959. Finally, in the shorter term, a boost to the economy since the grim winter of 1958–9 had brought down unemployment quickly.

Such was probably the truth about 1959. But at the time the election result was a deeply felt disappointment to all my closest friends and myself. The chance of serving at the prime of one's life with, and under, Hugh Gaitskell was indeed – literally – the chance of a lifetime. The mirage came so near, and vanished so far. For this was the ideal moment when, for the sake of the country's future, Labour should have won. The news on that Friday 9 October, was certainly the acutest political disappointment I ever suffered. I spent that afternoon in the Labour Committee rooms, at 177 Lavender Hill, Battersea, where we had worked for weeks, discussing with our indefatigable agent, Bert Amey, and numbers of other loyal Party workers what had happened and why. The first of their conclusions was that the younger generation of the 1950s had lost some of the idealism of the war and post-war years and were more materially-minded than their fathers. We had been appealing too late to a generation which had gone with the 1930s and 1940s. Bert Amey expressed it in this way: 'The young people of today aren't selfish, but they are self-centred.' Later that Friday I saw Martin, who had been working with Peter for our Party in the election, off to Oxford; and the genuineness with which he shared my disappointment was the greatest comfort to me on that day.

Then something very unexpected hit me: the aftermath of an article I wrote that weekend for *Forward* of the following week (16 October). This article, and the one on the Reichstag fire, which I contributed to the

Economist twenty-six years before, were the two which caused the greatest explosions of anything I ever wrote. Another myth in the Labour Party came to be built up out of it, which was a classic example of that common political phenomenon: an elaborate and sinister conspiracy being detected in what was really a series of accidents. The myth was this: that Gaitskell and I and a few fellow intellectuals had hatched a conspiracy (within hours, apparently, of the election result) to remove public ownership from future Labour policy, to sever the link between the Party and the trade unions, and alter the wording of 'Clause 4' in the Party's Constitution; that we had concocted this plan at a secret meeting in Hampstead in the week-end following the election result; and that I had launched the campaign by advocating all these propositions in my article.

The truth was this. I had formed the idea in our Battersea Committee rooms on the Friday afternoon (9 October) of writing an anonymous article in *Forward* recording the ideas of the ordinary Battersea Party workers, based on a month's canvassing experience, about defects in Labour propaganda, and the Labour 'image'. This I started to write in this spirit on the Saturday morning. On the Sunday morning Gaitskell asked some of us who were in reach to discuss the lessons of the election over some drinks at his house.[12] It was a chance group, far from an economists' clique, since Gaitskell's PPS, a trade unionist, and Herbert Bowden, the Party Chief Whip, happened to be there. We only sketchily discussed policy or public ownership; and I casually mentioned that I was recording for *Forward* the experience of my Party canvassers.[13] Gaitskell thought this worth doing. On Sunday afternoon, when finishing the article (which I meant to be anonymous), Eric Fletcher MP for an Islington constituency rang me up and said he thought, from his canvassing experience, that the misuse of the word 'nationalization' had lost us more votes than anything else. He was so emphatic on this, that though never having intended to mention public ownership, I inserted some paragraphs in the article arguing that the word caused confusion, and that it was public investment and enterprise we wanted, not more State monopolies. I was arguing for the solution which eventually became the National Enterprise Board.[14] Finally on Monday morning, when I handed the article to Francis Williams, he suggested that it would have more journalistic value if I signed it, and I weakly agreed. Here is the article (with only the detailed electoral figures and sub-headings omitted):

[12] He had by this time already rung up Bevan and asked him to stand as Deputy Leader if Jim Griffiths stood down. Bevan agreed. Foot, p. 629.

[13] Michael Foot gave some currency to the myth that this was some great council of war (p. 630) that 'a bold initiative was set in motion by the Right-wing of the Party, and it does appear that the lever which helped to let it loose was pulled at that Sunday meeting in Frognal Gardens and quite unpublicised of course at the time'. Naturally Foot did not know what had happened.

[14] For the sequel see pp. 332–3.

Let us think of the future. The election is over. But the country and the Labour Movement go on. The time to start winning the next election is now.

First, let us be clear about the facts. Illusions and dogmas are the worst enemies. There has been a persistent drift away from Labour towards the Tories ever since 1945. This has been apparent in almost all Western countries; and is doubtless due to the absence since 1945 of the violent slumps and unemployment which prevailed before 1939....

... So the question is this. Why was the swing against a discredited government so small? And why did it go partly to the Liberals rather than Labour?

A full answer to this can only be given after thorough study (which the Party should carry out) of the statistical results. But all of us who have canvassed for hours, and answered questions at dozens of meetings in this election are bound to have formed provisional conclusions.

Here are mine. We failed to attract the anti-Tory vote for three main reasons:

1 The better-off wage earners and numerous salary-earners are tending to regard the Labour Party as associated with a class to which they themselves don't belong.

Few of them – least of all the women – feel themselves to be members of a 'working class'. We are in danger of fighting under the label of a class which no longer exists.

If you doubt this, ask anyone who canvassed intensively in the last four weeks, particularly in the new housing estates.

We must have a wider, cross sectional appeal. What the public wants is a vigorous, radical, open-minded party.

2 The word 'nationalisation' has become damaging to the Labour Party. This is a fact; and it is no use denying it, even if you deplore it. We have allowed the word which properly applies only to public monopoly, to be associated with social ownership as a whole.

The myth that we intended to 'nationalise' anything and everything was very powerful in this election – any canvasser will agree. We must destroy this myth decisively; otherwise we may never win again.

3 Favourable economic circumstances for the Tories meant more, in terms of votes than any moral argument or propaganda vigour could counteract. True the old people, the unemployed and badly housed, were suffering badly.

But too many average wage-earning families, with TV and second-hand car, did not see (unless they were coal miners) so much wrong with Tory Britain. True, our national income ought to have been higher, and only lower import prices had enabled it to be as high as it was. But these facts seemed unreal and irrelevant.

From all this, I believe certain conclusions – like it or not – emerge pretty plain. We cannot fight indefinitely on the assumption that we only win in years of acute unemployment.

Such conditions are now most unlikely, unless the Tories behave with insensate folly (and ignore their expert advisers). Enough has been learnt about economic policy since 1932 to prevent violent slumps. What the private enterprise system cannot do unaided and unplanned is to achieve rapid expansion and any sort of social justice.

Therefore, if Labour is going to win, we must remove the first two fatal handicaps: the class 'image' and the myth of 'nationalisation'. We must modernise our-

selves quickly into a vigorous, radical, expansionist open-minded Party representing – and being seen to represent – everybody who wants reform and expansion.

As such we can win. But if we don't do this, there is a real danger of a long dog-
fight between Liberals and the Labour Party, which could keep the Tories in
power for forty years.

How do we do it? Least hard should be to kill that 'nationalisation' myth
decisively. This won't be done by just not talking about it. We must now make it
plain that we believe in social ownership through the Co-operative Movement,
municipal enterprise and public investment; but that we do not believe in the
extension of the public monopoly to manufacturing industry or distribution.

The public has shown that it approves the existing public boards in the public
utility industries, but does not want them extended further. We should say we
accept this decision of the electorate and would in future propose no further
'nationalisation'.

It would not damage the real basic aim of the Movement, if we agree to leave
steel outside the bounds of compulsory public ownership. The case is good. But
it is really not worth jettisoning the things for which we really stand – social justice,
a fair deal for the old, real equality of opportunity, peace and disarmament – for
the sake of a form of ownership in steel. To do so would be to betray the old, and
all the others who suffer so acutely from Tory rule.

How do we exorcise the popular feeling that we are tied to a dying class?

This is not so easy. Any 'arrangements' with the Liberal Party is out of the
question. The Liberals are unreliable, often reactionary, and have little to offer.
And the Trade Unions must remain an essential foundation of the Labour Party.
– But we must also purge out of our propaganda, speeches and writings the phrases
which have kept this damaging myth alive: 'The militant working class', 'working
class solidarity', and all the rest. Society has now changed; and the motor-workers
in the housing estates just don't feel that way any more than the salary-earners in
the suburbs.

Has the very name 'Labour' become a vote loser on balance? Obviously many
Tory newspapers think so, because a few months ago their papers started to talk
of the 'Labour Party' and not the 'Socialist Party' for the first time for thirty
years. May they be right – or will they be right five years hence?

It would be unthinkable to give up the name 'Labour', which holds the loyalty
of millions. But might there be a case for amending it to 'Labour and Radical', or
'Labour and Reform'?

Certainly we should urge radical reforms of the betting, licensing and Sunday
Observance laws – perhaps abolition of hanging and votes at eighteen also.

One practical change we should surely also make. We should again hold the
Party Conference in future in May and not October. This would stop giving the
public the impression that the political Labour Party simply endorses in the
autumn decisions taken by the Trade Unions' so called 'block vote' in the summer.
Though this is not true, it is a legend which can be easily spread. Far better, let
the political Party take decisions, and let the Unions and TUC hold their conference in the light of these in later months.

Next, a minor change in the Party constitution might help to prove to the public
that the Parliamentary leaders are free of pressure from any non-Parliamentary
body. Why not make the National Executive a truly federal body, with represen-

tatives as now of the Trade Unions, but otherwise of the Regions of the Party, and the Parliamentary Party.

Members of Parliament could then only be elected to the National Executive by the Parliamentary Party. This would prevent any apparent clash between the Parliamentary Party and the NEC, and would make full Parliamentary freedom plainer to the public.

And through all this, don't let's forget that we won in 1959 over twelve million votes, nearly forty-four per cent of those cast. It's not a revolution in ideas and principles we need.

It's a little more radicalism in bringing the statement of them up to date quickly, and accepting the actual society in which we live – and ourselves largely created – instead of pretending it is still the society of forty years ago.

With this spirit, I am certain we could win.

This article did not propose severance with the unions but said: 'the Trade Unions must remain an essential foundation of the Labour Party.' It did not propose relinquishing public ownership, but only the State monopoly and the word 'nationalization'. It did not propose jettisoning the word 'Labour' but possibly adding to it. It never mentioned 'Clause 4'. It was not inspired by Gaitskell or anyone else in Frognal Gardens, but by my Party workers at 177 Lavender Hill. But having handed the article to Francis Williams, I largely forgot about it, and we dined that evening in Chelsea with Frank and Elizabeth Pakenham, who always nobly organized a consolation party (they had done so in October 1951) when spirits were low. The Gaitskells were there, and also Hugh Cudlipp who had perfected the election pamphlet. Cudlipp in a highly festive spirit maintained the morale of the gathering by merrily proclaiming, as the evening proceeded. 'We all went down together. We all went down together.'

When I opened my *Evening Standard*, however, nearly a week later on the day when the article appeared, I was astonished by the furore it had excited. My reason for writing something immediately after the election result was the belief that, if the Party policy and propaganda were to be modernized in time for the next election, the controversy involved should be surmounted as early as possible. I made a mistake, however, in putting my name to the article, because my close association with Gaitskell led people to believe he had some responsibility for it, when in fact he had no idea I would mention public ownership, or indeed policy at all, or the name of the Party. But he wrote to me with characteristic friendship, on 20 October, in no way blaming me for this, but in the following words:

I hope you are not discouraged and dismayed by criticisms of your article. I do not agree with all of it – as you know; but it was a most courageous step whose value, I feel sure, will be felt in the future – however many faint-hearts there may be who are terrified by the sound of the breaking of glass cases! As you will understand I have, for the moment, to keep out of this public controversy myself – but I felt I must send you these words of friendship and appreciation – no need to reply.

This letter itself shows that Gaitskell did not agree with all I said. Tony Crosland wrote expressing almost entire agreement with the article, but surprise at my candour.

I had also probably been mistaken in writing the article in my normal *Daily Herald* style, which was unadorned by the qualifications and ambiguities which politicians learn to use. So the legend spread wider and became ever more lurid with each new rendering. To all these distortions, I replied firmly in another article in *Forward*, in a speech at an Oxford Union debate on 29 October arranged by Peter (in which Roy Harrod chivalrously and vigorously supported me) and in a short speech at the Party Conference at Blackpool at the end of November, which was itself an inquest on the election. After the Oxford speech, Gaitskell wrote to me (30 October) saying: 'I was glad you were able to stress last night that you were not opposed to further public ownership. There has been a great deal of confusion about this because of the misleading extracts published from your article.' In the Party Conference I repeated in the clearest possible language: 'We certainly need more public ownership, but public ownership of a kind suitably adapted to what we want to own.' But, as usual, the myth in these cases is seldom overtaken by the truth. Jim Callaghan, who on the whole regarded the whole thing as a political indiscretion, gave me most friendly and excellent advice at this time: notably to correct the misunderstanding on 'nationalization'; to speak at the Party Conference to avoid being accused of running away; and not to stand again for the Shadow Cabinet until the sound and fury had abated. Through the whole of this episode, incidentally, my own constituency and local party showed to me most endearing friendliness. Though many must have disagreed with what I was supposed to have said, not a single criticism from my own party supporters reached me, so far as I can recall.

It was in the spirit of Callaghan's advice not to run away that I made a brief Blackpool speech (four minutes to 3000 people), and it was received with incomprehension rather than assent or dissent. But the day of this speech on a showery, drenching, November morning was almost as horrific as Morecambe in 1952. Rising before 8 a.m. in order to be in time for the starting pistol, I looked out of the eastward-facing window of my grim Blackpool boarding house on to a tangle of wet roofs, dense cloud, and grey, rain-swept gutters and chimneys. Amid them glowed fiercely a lurid, fiery object. What, I asked myself, exactly was this non-conforming user amid the encircling gloom? It was in fact, as seen in Blackpool in November, the rising sun.

That spectacle, and not Gaitskell's or Bevan's speeches, let alone mine, remained for me the sharpest memory of Blackpool 1959. But to the outside world what mattered was the speech in which Gaitskell as leader of the Party made public his comments on the general election result. The legend was that this speech represented the supporting offensive in the campaign started by my *Forward* article:[15] that Gaitskell's reference to modernizing Clause 4 of the Party constitution was all part of the attack on 'nationalization'; and that Gaitskell and I and a few others had secretly concocted the whole exercise together. Again the truth was different. I knew nothing about Gaitskell's idea of mentioning Clause 4, or about any of the contents of his speech, until John Harris handed me a copy on the night before at Blackpool. When I read it, I was surprised at the idea of bringing in Clause 4, and told Harris when I returned the typescript that I thought this unwise. Harris then told me that Gaitskell had shown the speech to Bevan, and Bevan had read it and expressed no disagreement. Michael Foot in his biography of Bevan[16] leaves it doubtful whether Bevan had seen the full text of the speech. I have no doubt whatever that Harris told me categorically the speech had been shown to Bevan.

In the event, however, Bevan now elected Deputy Leader of the Party, played the game magnificently. Barbara Castle, Chairman of the Party that year, had put the fundamentalist case for public ownership; and Gaitskell had followed with the case for modernization. Bevan summed up by reminding the Party of Euclid's proposition that if two things are both equal to a third, they must be equal to one another. Both Gaitskell and Barbara Castle had expressed agreement with Bevan himself. 'They are both equal to me and therefore must be equal to one another.' So in the language of a desiccated calculating machine the great Welsh orator, in a way nobody else could have done, soothed the explosive passions which were simmering not far below the surface. Delegates laughed in heartfelt merriment at the unexpected alliance between Bevan and Euclid. It was, though none of us knew it, Bevan's last speech to a Labour Party Conference.

The argument about Clause 4, however, did not end there. Having originally thought this part of Gaitskell's speech a tactical mistake, I for a time in the latter weeks of 1959 came to wonder whether it might after all have been wise to suggest amending the constitution – the wording of the Creed, in this case – rather than the practical programme. But in the end the mention of Clause 4 turned out to be unwise. It was the very fact of laying hands on the Creed itself, not the suggested re-wording, which outraged the fundamentalists and Marxists. So, as so often, Callaghan came to the rescue with the suggestion that a New Testament should be *added* as a supplement to the Old. And all the time under the surface the battle was being won. For when we came to the 1964 Government, my central idea of a National Finance Corporation to finance industry had become orthodox, and by 1974 the full realization of this idea in the National Enterprise Board had even become the banner of the so-called Left.

[15] Foot, p. 639, very honestly admits that Gaitskell's speech did not accept much even of my *Forward* article.
[16] Foot, p. 640.

Somebody in 1959 had to start the transition from the Old Testament to the New.

Escaping meanwhile from Blackpool and the incessant rain, I encountered on Preston station Bob Boothby,[17] who told me that he too was absconding to London because he found he could no longer endure the appalling gloom. Fortified by Boothby's company, and a little refreshment, and a happy comradeship in our mutual depression, I enjoyed myself for the first time that week on the journey back to Euston.

My *Forward* article and the Clause 4 debate at Blackpool were not the only immediate aftermaths of the 1959 election result. Another was one of Crossman's extraordinary escapades, which left Gaitskell deeply disillusioned. Gaitskell had long insisted on thinking the best of Crossman and wishing to harness his talents and energy to some constructive purpose. With 'National Superannuation' he had succeeded. He told me a few days after the election that he had asked Crossman also to come and give his views, and that a casual conversation followed about, among other prospects, the allocation of Front-Bench Opposition duties. One idea mentioned was that Harold Wilson might be ready to change from the Treasury to Foreign Affairs. Crossman, however, without any warning and immediately after this talk, told Wilson (despite the latter's well-known tendency to believe in conspiracies) that Gaitskell was scheming to undermine his position. This story, as retold by Crossman, was grossly untrue. But some believed it, and Gaitskell had the unenviable job of convincing Wilson of its untruth. I know Gaitskell was staggered by this particular exploit of Crossman and suffered the same major disenchantment which so many others had experienced. Crossman's motive, I would surmise, was not so much malice, as reckless loquacity.

In the midwinter weeks of 1959–60 I reflected on the controversies of the previous six months, and wondered whether it was worthwhile rethinking the whole basic issue of the meaning of socialism and the relevance of public ownership. It was twenty-two years since my *Socialist Case* had been published, and much should indeed have been learnt since them. On the other hand the extra workload of writing a full-scale theoretical book in addition to Front-Bench labours, the call of the Division Lobby, the Constituency and *Reynolds*, was distinctly forbidding. Having also by this time shared every politician's experience of seeing selected sentences from speeches or writings taken out of context and perverted, I asked myself whether the game of serious writing was really worth the candle. By Easter 1960, I had decided to take the plunge – heartened perhaps by the fact that I had at last bought the family car after an eighteen-year wait! My aim in the book was to write something rather more philosophical and less purely economic, than Tony Crosland's illuminating *The Future of Socialism* of four years earlier. Crosland had touched only lightly on the basic question

[17] He was reporting the Conference for a London newspaper.

whether any moral virtue resides in the economic consequences of *laissez-faire* and the distribution of incomes generated by a free market.

My main thesis was that Marx had been misled by major errors in economics into treating public ownership virtually as an end, whereas it is really only a means; and that in the circumstances of the second half of the twentieth century, social ownership should mainly take the form of public investment and financing, and part-ownership of private industry rather than rigid State monopoly. In particular, the book argued for worker-participation and for a 'National Finance Corporation' as a State investing organization which 'would act on investment principles and normally select shares on these grounds' – the essence of the National Enterprise Board idea. As these were the years of continued controversy over the control of nuclear weapons, I also argued the case for strengthening the UN into a real World Authority, as the only serious long-term hope of avoiding nuclear war, rather than by unilateral disarmament or the formation of narrow regional blocs, political or economic. I felt sure however, that the irrelevance of 'unilateralism' would fairly soon emerge, and was disinclined to become deeply involved in this controversy myself. For this reason, I stayed away from the Party Conferences of 1960 and 1961 at which Gaitskell was first defeated on the unilateralist issue, and then a year later was triumphantly vindicated. Despite Bevan's tragic death in 1960, the memory of his 1957 Conference speech convinced most people that he would have stood on Gaitskell's side in the latter stages of the controversy.

The years 1960 and 1961 were also the last years at Oxford of both my sons Peter and Martin; and I allowed myself to spend rather more time there than since pre-1939 days, and so to push on with my new book in the more placid atmosphere of All Souls. In the spring and summer of 1960 Peter achieved the treble of passing first into the Civil Service, winning an excellent First in PPE, and being elected President of the Union. I was lucky enough to attend the 'Presidential debate' which led to his election, in which the chief outside speakers were Ted Heath and Jim Callaghan. Peter had by now become engaged to Callaghan's daughter, Margaret. In January 1961, having helped me with the book in his last months at Oxford, Peter took up his civil service option and started work in the Treasury. Norman Brook, still Secretary of the Cabinet, invited me as an old colleague for a private talk. He wanted to assure me that Peter would in no way suffer as a Treasury official under a Conservative Chancellor because of his family link with Callaghan and myself, and that he trusted Peter to treat all official confidences as absolute. I had no trouble in assuring Brook in return that Peter understood the British constitution as well as he or I, but I appreciated his friendly gesture. Reggie Maudling when Chancellor a little later (when Callaghan was Shadow Chancellor) insisted, as one would have expected, that normal confidences should in no way be withheld from Peter.

My book was published, under the title *Socialism in the New Society* in January 1962, and was received by a full first leader in *The Times*. I came in retrospect to hope that the book had perhaps helped in converting the Labour Movement from 'nationalization' as a dogma of earlier years to more experimental policies such as the NEB. It was, however, still written too early for me to face adequately the dilemma of incomes policy, which became the crucial economic issue of the 1970s. That (as with *The Socialist Case*) was its main defect.

The early months of 1961 saw the sad end to the story of the *Daily Herald* as a Labour Party newspaper with a political policy independent of the press combines. The *Daily Mirror* Group (International Publishing Company) made a take-over bid, which after negotiations was accepted for the whole of Odhams Press. Perversely, one main motive for this was the IPC desire to get hold of Odham's women's magazines because they were more profitable than their IPC rivals. The *Daily Herald* was thrown in as an appendage. Gaitskell on behalf of the Labour Party joined with Sir Christopher Chancellor, Chairman of Odhams, and Vincent Tewson of the TUC, in a strenuous but vain effort to save the *Herald*. At a meeting of the Parliamentary Labour Party Gaitskell promised anxious members that he would do all he could to preserve the Party's paper, and George Brown as Deputy Leader of the Party spoke inconclusively after him. Brown records in his memoirs[18] how in 1953 he agreed to act as an adviser to Mr Cecil King and the *Daily Mirror* in return for a small retaining fee, and this arrangement still prevailed at the time of the take-over struggle eight years later. Brown was fully entitled to make this arrangement. Indeed Michael Foot and I were on the *Daily Herald* payroll as writers for a time. I knew of Brown's assignment, and Brown could also reasonably assume, as I did, that Gaitskell knew also. But shortly afterwards, Gaitskell told me that he had not known and should have been told. It was an unfortunate misunderstanding. In the event, the IPC won the take-over struggle for largely financial reasons; and the *Herald* was later turned into the *Sun* and in the end sold to Rupert Murdoch with the results we all know.

In 1960 and 1961, while the *Daily Herald* was thus being lost to the Labour Movement, the Common Market controversy broke into British politics. On 14 November 1958, the French Government had vetoed Maudling's plan, which the Labour Party had supported, for linking this country and other West European countries with the EEC in a wider free trade area. This French action was strong confirmation that the exclusion[19] of the British Government by the French from the Schumann negotiations in 1950 was deliberate long-term French policy, and that the myth of British refusal to negotiate was a propaganda invention. On 31 July 1961

[18] George Brown, *In My Way*, pp. 61–2.
[19] See pp. 198–200.

however, Macmillan, beset by many difficulties, economic and political, suddenly announced his intention to seek entry to the EEC. My original scepticism about the EEC at this early stage sprang from my belief that much wider international organizations, not rival regional blocs, were in the world's best interest; that confinement in as narrow a trading bloc as the EEC could be harmful to the UK, 80 per cent of whose trade in natural conditions was outside it; that the high agricultural protectionism of the EEC would be particularly damaging to the UK as the world's greatest food importer; and that the EEC's supra-national constitution was undemocratic since binding legislation was enacted by unelected bodies. An industrial free trade area in Western Europe, however, linked with the EEC was for these reasons the best solution for the UK. The full conclusions, to which several years' more detailed study carried me, are set out later in this book.[20] But it was a speech of Reggie Maudling in the House as early as 12 February 1959 which first alerted me to the full economic dangers of British membership. He said this in words I never forgot and with his usual unanswerable clarity:[21]

We must recognize that to sign the Treaty of Rome would mean having common external tariffs, which in turn would mean the end of Commonwealth-free entry, and I cannot conceive that any government of this country would put forward a proposition which involved the abandonment of free entry. It would be wrong for us and for the whole free world to adopt a policy of new duties on foodstuffs and raw materials many of which come from under-developed countries at present entering a major market duty-free.

Together with Gaitskell, Maudling understood the whole issue better than anyone else in British politics; but I fear that in time he became so pummelled by the establishment as to lose the will to speak out unpopular truths. For many months in 1960 and 1961 I refrained from joining in the controversy myself because I feared it would both monopolize my energies and bring me into conflict with old friends and close colleagues. For the sake of both constructive reforms at home and liberal international policies, I fervently hoped the whole controversy would be avoided. But when Macmillan announced his initiative on 31 July 1961, I realized I must make up my mind. In the course of a week's family holiday in Brittany in August, I reluctantly decided that the battle must be fought if immense damage to this country was to be avoided.

Gaitskell also maintained publicly an open mind on the whole issue well into 1962. Anyone who cared as much as he did about this country's economic life, and also about the Commonwealth, must have intensely disliked the EEC's agricultural protectionism and dear food policy. But two particular lessons, I believe, finally brought his mind down against

[20] See Chapter 13.
[21] Hansard, 12 February 1959, col. 1381,.

membership with the force which stunned so many people at the 1962 Brighton Conference. The first was an XYZ dinner in April 1962 at which Roy Jenkins had invited Jean Monnet to meet Gaitskell and convert him to the Common Market faith. Monnet spoke long and fluently and repeated everything I heard him say when staying with William Hayter in Paris in 1952. Gaitskell listened. He then questioned Monnet persistently about the whole project, and in particular the extent to which the UK would have to erect trade barriers against Commonwealth countries. Monnet's answers were vague and evasive. Jenkins looked pained. But Gaitskell pursued his questions relentlessly, step by step, on and on, from one line of defence to another, for a space of over an hour without pause. Eventually Monnet, now looking pained himself, and unable to answer further, took refuge in saying: 'Well one must have faith.' To which Gaitskell replied: 'I don't believe in faith. I believe in reason: and there is little reason in anything you have been saying tonight.' It was from that moment, I believed at the time, that Gaitskell felt impelled to the conclusion that if even Monnet, the great apostle of the Market gospel, could not put up a better case than this, then the balance of a rational argument must be against British membership.

Even so he refrained from committing himself decisively in public until the autumn of 1962. I was with my family in north Cornwall at that time when Gaitskell announced on the Labour Party's behalf, after a Conference with Socialist Commonwealth leaders, that the Party would not accept membership unless free access to the UK for at least the primary products of the Commonwealth was guaranteed. It was the advice of two people, I learnt afterwards – Denis Healey, and Harry Lee, Prime Minister of Singapore – which finally decided him to speak out publicly. Healey had always been profoundly sceptical and scornful of the patently spurious arguments of the pro-Market propagandists, and particularly of their pretence that EFTA did not exist. Gaitskell was unusually well-informed about the economic realities of the Commonwealth, and British trade generally, about which public ignorance was becoming common. He cared about the Commonwealth deeply, having many family links with Burma. His brother also served in the Sudan Civil Service; so that Lee found Gaitskell exceptionally understanding. Thus the stage was set for the greatest speech he ever made: on the UK and the Common Market at the Brighton Party Conference in October 1962.

On the day before the full Common Market debate at that Conference, the Fabian Society had arranged a 'fringe meeting' in a nearby Brighton restaurant, where Roy Jenkins and I were to put the case for and against Market membership. Shirley Williams, then Fabian Society Secretary, was to preside. Unfortunately and unexpectedly, about 150 people turned up in a room designed to seat seventy to eighty. I noticed Kingsley Martin jammed against a wall, unable to move. Despite the tumult, however,

STRANGE BEDFELLOWS

Strange Bedfellows – cartoon by Low, *Guardian*, 16 October 1962. An early and perceptive view of the anti-ECC campaign

Roy Jenkins and I both managed to make fully argued, somewhat impassioned speeches. An impromptu debate ensued about the progress of the US Trade Relations Bill; and up-to-the-minute telegrams from Washington were produced by both sides.

My relations with Roy Jenkins, which had been very close in the 1950s, were still cordial at this time. But I was beginning to feel that his association with the Bonham-Carter family, arising out of his excellent book *Mr Balfour's Poodle* and his biographies of Charles Dilke, and later Asquith, was increasingly assimilating him to the Liberal way of life. Belief in the Common Market had a natural attraction for Liberals. First it could be represented as 'progressive' and 'new'; secondly it kept one away from sordid, backstairs subjects like housing, food prices and old-age pensions. It was a seductively drawing-room form of radicalism. I was at first surprised that Jenkins, with his South Wales mining background, should have been susceptible to these influences when Gaitskell was completely immune to them. More goodwill was extinguished when in a letter to the *New Statesman* at this time Jenkins used what he knew to be a misquotation in an effort to discredit my argument. In general, I must in honesty admit, I never found I could harbour warm sympathy with those who were deeply opposed to my convictions on fundamental issues such as appeasement, or the EEC, which affected the whole future of this country. To maintain amicable relations with people who disagree on minor arguable controversies, including some in other parties, is certainly a refreshing part of democratic life. But tolerance is one thing, and friendship another. It is hard in my experience to feel personal affection towards those who are actively working to destroy, however unconsciously, something for which one cares deeply. It is causes, not parties, which divide and unite.

On the day after my debate with Jenkins in the crowded restaurant, Gaitskell rose in the full Conference to argue that only if the five conditions laid down by the Party were satisfied should Britain join the EEC. He spoke for nearly one hour, and carried virtually every delegate in the Conference with him; and his speech remains today far the most penetrating and masterly analysis of the whole issue written or spoken by anyone. He started (no doubt mindful of Monnet) by appealing for rational argument and not prejudice. 'Are we "forced" to join? The answer to that is "No".' 'Would we necessarily, inevitably, be economically stronger if we go in, and weaker if we stay out? My answer to that is also – "No".' He quoted the economist Donald McDougall saying, 'There is really no compelling economic argument for Britain's joining unless it is thought that, without being exposed to the blast of competition from the Continent, she will never put her house in order.' If we join, 'The barriers go down between us and the six countries of Europe. But they go up between us and the Commonwealth.' 'We would gain in markets where we sell less than one-fifth of our exports, and lose in markets where we sell about half our exports.' 'Nobody who has ever glanced at the problem can really suppose that there is any advantage to be expected from the switch.' . . . 'It is an essential fact of the Common Market agricultural policy that we are obliged to import expensive food from the Continent of Europe in place of cheap food from the Commonwealth. Nor can it be denied for one moment . . . that food prices at home are certain to rise. . . .' The CAP was 'one of the most devastating pieces of protection ever invented'. 'We sell to the world, not just to Europe.' Gaitskell then showed that so far from Commonwealth markets declining, they were growing fast, but that we were failing to maintain our proportionate share of them. He mentioned Maudling's speech of 12 February 1959, already quoted above.[22] He was evidently

[22] See page 281.

trying to restrain the contempt he felt for these economic arguments. 'If I have spoken strongly about these economic arguments let me say . . . that it is not because I start with a prejudice, but because I am sick and tired of the nonsense and rubbish that is being written and spoken on this subject.' . . . 'If we were presented today with a tremendous choice, whether to go into a world federation under a world government . . . there is not one of us who would say "No." But it is not wise or necessary to join *any* group. If it were proposed that we should join the USA, I do not think it would be universally popular.' . . . 'It is not a matter of just any union; it is a matter of what are the effects of this union.'

Gaitskell then turned to explain with brilliant clarity what the torrent of pro-Market propaganda was seeking to dissemble: that if a political federation was intended, that was something utterly different from a customs union, and we had better be clear what it meant. 'It means that powers are taken from national governments and handed over to federal governments and federal Parliaments. It means . . . that if we are going into this, we are to be no more than a State (as it were) in the United States of Europe, such as Texas and California. . . . It does mean, if this is the idea, the end of Britain as an independent State. I make no apology for repeating it. It means the end of a thousand years of history. You may say "Let it end"; but, my goodness, it is a decision that needs a little care and thought. If on the other hand, we could "build a bridge" between the Commonwealth and Europe, this would be a fine ideal . . . but you cannot do that if at the beginning you sell the Commonwealth down the river.' He then set out the five conditions: the safeguarding of EFTA; guarantees for the new as well as old Commonwealth; freedom to control our own economy; guarantees for our agricultural policy and food supply: and freedom to pursue our own foreign policy. Above all Gaitskell made clear that we must negotiate with the determination, if our terms were not accepted, to remain outside. 'What is the alternative. It is not a disastrous one at all. If we are obliged to say: "Well we cannot accept these terms" and to suspend the talks for the moment, we are not going to face economic disaster. There is much that can be done – a conference with EFTA and the Commonwealth to enlarge the trade between us.' Next he demanded that the electorate and not just the Government or even Parliament should take the final decision. 'We are now being told that the British people are not capable of judging this issue – the top people are the only people who understand it. This is the classic argument of every tyranny in history. It begins as a refined intellectual argument and it moves into a one-man dictatorship. We did not win the political battles of the nineteenth and twentieth centuries to have this reactionary nonsense thrust upon us again.'

The speech finished with the following words, which should have – and would have, if Gaitskell had lived – set the theme of British national policy for the rest of this century:

After all if we could carry the Commonwealth with us, safeguarded, flourishing, prosperous: and if we could safeguard our agriculture, and our EFTA friends were all in it: and if we were secure in our employment policy, and if we were able to maintain our independent foreign policy, and yet have this wider and looser association with Europe, it would indeed be a great ideal. But if this should not prove to be possible: if the Six will not give it to us, if the British Government will not ask for it, then we must stand firm by what we believe, for the sake of Britain, and the Commonwealth and the world: and we shall not flinch from our duty when that moment comes.

The effect of this speech on the crowded, fascinated audience was devastating. It was unique among all the political speeches I ever heard; not merely the finest, but in a different class, even from Gaitskell's Suez speeches. It can only be described as an intellectual massacre. Nobody had anything else to say. For its uniqueness rested in its ring of truth. It was conviction Gaitskell inspired, not just emotion. Everyone in the hall capable of recognizing the truth knew that this was the essential truth about the future of this country. The next words of the official Conference Report were not inapt. They record the Chairman, Harold Wilson, as saying: 'After that speech and that unparallelled ovation any words from the Chairman would be otiose.' He proposed and the Conference instantly agreed that 'This historic speech' should be printed and forthwith made available to the whole country. Even an elderly Conservative, and fervent Churchillian, spontaneously affirmed to me as we emerged from the hall that it was the finest political speech he had ever heard or hoped to hear. Naturally none of us knew, any more than we did after Bevan's in 1959, that it was Gaitskell's last great speech. When all was over I drove home to London feeling such immense relief that I decided to take a whole day off in the country next day. My deep thankfulness sprang mainly from my confidence that the country would henceforth be set on the right track; but partly also from the firm belief that though Gaitskell's speech would remain my political creed for the rest of my life, I could now largely contract out of this dreadful controversy, and leave it to him.

In November and December of 1962 unemployment began to rise steeply again, as a result of the Selwyn Lloyd credit squeeze in the summer of 1961 which had ended the post-1959 election boom. By December 1962 unemployment had reached alarming levels for the second time since the war. The winter of 1962–3 also proved as cold as 1959 and nearly as cold as 1947. Gaitskell formed the idea that he and I together should carry out another tour in January of the unemployment areas to ascertain the up-to-date facts on the spot, and launch a major demand for action when Parliament reassembled in late January. I was delighted with this project because in spite of the exhausting experience of the 1959 tour, Gaitskell's presence as Leader would greatly enhance the value of the exercise, and I could contribute a rather greater knowledge of the areas in detail than he could. We would be working together more closely than ever. On the final day of Parliament before Christmas he told me we should be starting from London in the second week of January. It was the last time I saw him.

I heard before Christmas that he was in the Manor House Hospital, Hampstead, with flu; and a few days later he returned home. Just before we were due to start in the New Year, I learnt that he had returned to hospital, and that he wanted George Brown, as Deputy Leader of the Party, to join me on the tour instead. So George Brown and I set out together from Euston on 15 January for the North-West; after which we were to go on to Clydeside and then to Newcastle and the North-East. We started our first day in Liverpool at 7.30 a.m. in the docks, and drove in the afternoon to North-East Lancashire; and in the midst of a Conference at Burnley we heard that Gaitskell was now seriously ill. At the end of the day's work I suggested to Brown that we should drive back to Manchester airport together, and try to decide whether we should continue the tour or return to London. Brown, to my surprise, insisted on travelling to Manchester in a separate car, and I had to face the dilemma alone. At first I thought one could not in these circumstances carry on with the tour; but then I wondered whether this would not disappoint and let down the Labour Party in Scotland and the North-East, where they had made elaborate arrangements.

At Manchester Airport Brown was still disinclined for a private talk to decide our next move, but proceeded instead to give his views about Gaitskell to a number of journalists and others who gathered round. This was one of the most painful half hours I have ever spent. In the course of it, Brown announced he was returning to London. I decided to continue; and when I reached Glasgow, was at least thankful to find that the Labour Party members and officials there were greatly relieved I had done so. So the crowded programme of the tour went ahead in bleakly cold weather for several days in the Glasgow and Newcastle areas, which by now I knew so well; with news of Gaitskell's worsening condition reaching us every few hours. At a Labour Party meeting at Sunderland on 18 January, Fred Willey, MP for that area and a good friend of mine, told us that Gaitskell had died. He was then only fifty-six and died of a rare disease, hard to diagnose or cure.

Gaitskell's death at this moment was, I believed that night, and am even more certain in the retrospect of over fifteen years, not merely an inexpressible tragedy for his friends and the Labour Movement, but a catastrophe for the nation. For he not merely possessed the pre-eminent straightforwardness, common sense and moral authority of Attlee, but a wider intelligence and a deeper understanding of the economic and social issues of the age than any of his contemporaries in British politics. And to these qualities he added a capacity for loyalty to friends and causes, and a power of determination which, as John Strachey once remarked, deserved Matthew Arnold's phrase: 'Will like a dividing spear'. If he had lived, the future of this country would, for three reasons, have been far different and far happier. First he would, as the public were beginning to realize in the last year of his life, have exercised, like Attlee and Cripps, a moral influence over his Party and British politics generally in the 1960s and 1970s, which was sorely needed and sadly lacking. Secondly, he would have based his long-term policy on upholding above all the welfare and influence of this country and the Commonwealth, which he believed we could lead, founded on the widest possible trading freedom, and the closest possible political alliance with – but not submergence in – both the EFTA and EEC groups in Western Europe. Thirdly, he would have pursued these long-term aims with a persistence and sureness of purpose more like that of the Churchill Government of 1940 and the Attlee Government of 1945.

I was driven back that evening of 18 January 1963, from Sunderland to Newcastle, realizing all too well that the whole future had become grim and unpredictable. Indeed I wondered whether it was any good staying in politics at all. For want of advice and comfort from somebody, I later asked Herbert Bowden, Labour Chief Whip, a colleague respected by all of us, and a most loyal friend and admirer of Gaitskell, what he meant to do. 'I shall carry on,' Bowden said, 'so far as is humanly possible.'

Consternation was the mood of the Parliamentary Labour Party after Gaitskell's death as it assembled at Westminster on 22 January 1963, for the resumed Session. It had been believed that the Party's internal conflicts were over under his undisputed leadership, and that its fortunes were set fair for the next election. But the immediate election of a new leader was now unavoidable. George Brown, as Deputy-Leader, was naturally and justifiably a candidate, and was regarded by some as representing the trade union core of the Party. Wilson, however, arrived back hotfoot from New York, and became a candidate, with the backing of all the ex-Bevanites. Though the de Gaulle veto on UK membership of the EEC, in the same week as Gaitskell's death, had switched off the Common Market controversy for the time, anti-Market feeling in the Party was very strong. Wilson gave a number of anti-Market Labour Members to understand that he shared their views. Will Blyton, in particular, Durham miner, MP, and strong anti-Federalist, told me later that he had canvassed for Wilson on these grounds.

I did not myself favour either of these candidates as prospective Party Leaders or Prime Ministers. Together with Jack Diamond, George Strauss and others, I took part in persuading Jim Callaghan to stand, though he was reluctant and clearly did not expect to win. Those of us supporting him met in Jack Diamond's flat in Westminster, and found that there were more votes for Callaghan among senior members of the Party than among back-benchers generally. Those longest in the House knew the candidates best. I had no doubt myself that Callaghan would make both the best election-winner and Prime Minister. But he probably suffered from not having been a senior minister in the Attlee Government, whereas both Wilson and Brown had been, though Callaghan had been elected to every Shadow Cabinet since 1951. In the event the result was:

Wilson   115
Brown   88
Callaghan   41
K

In the second ballot Wilson won by 144 to Brown's 103. Undoubtedly Wilson gained by adding the anti-Market to the ex-Bevanite and Celtic vote. But the result was finally determined, I believe, by Members' assessment of the two men rather than by ideology. One colleague said to me gloomily: 'We have to choose between a man we don't like, and a man we don't trust.' Wilson's performance in the House in Opposition had often been excellent and Brown was unpredictable. According to one tea-room story current at the time Brown had thrown away half a dozen Welsh votes in three minutes by an unprovoked tea-room tirade. This was gossip, for which I have no first-hand evidence, but it was widely repeated. By a fairly narrow margin the Party felt it was safer with Wilson.

So by the twist of fortune, Wilson's election, following Gaitskell's death, brought me on to the Shadow Cabinet. I was the runner-up at the election in the autumn of 1962 (having regained my place as the *Forward* article of 1959 was forgotten and the EEC came to the fore), and so moved on to the Committee instead of Wilson, since the Leader counts as an ex-officio member. Here I remained right up to the formation of the 1964 general election. Members of the 1962–3 Shadow Cabinet, apart from Wilson and Brown were, in order of election: Callaghan, Soskice, Houghton, Fraser, Gordon-Walker, Mitchison, Stewart, Healey, Gunter, Willey, Lee. Crossman, Crosland and Jenkins were never elected to the Committee before 1964, mainly because their attendances in the House were infrequent and Crosland and Jenkins had the reputation of being 'aloof'. Life in a Shadow Cabinet, at least in a Labour one, is rather less awe-inspiring than the public might suppose. It normally meets only once a week, on a Wednesday afternoon, to discuss the business for the following parliamentary week, and to decide who speaks for the Party about what. Systematic general discussion of major policy tends to be infrequent at Shadow Cabinets; and the information and briefing is vastly inferior to what the Civil Service provides for a real Cabinet. Nevertheless Shadow Cabinets do sometimes get a little beyond 'Next Week's Business' and at least debate unexpected issues which suddenly crop up. Their greatest value, I found, was to enable Front Bench speakers in the Party, before speaking in the House, to discover what their colleagues, including their Leader, were thinking. By 1963, on the Labour side, the division of 'Shadow' jobs had hardened under Gaitskell's influence; but I stuck to my Board of Trade plus Treasury general remit. Callaghan, as the only member elected every year since 1951, and also as an ex-Inland Revenue official, took the 'Shadow Chancellorship'.

In the 1963 Shadow Cabinet we all consciously made a sustained effort to avoid the quarrels of the Bevanite past and to co-operate with Wilson. In this we were moderately successful. We were much helped by the gathering misfortunes of the Macmillan Government, which was beset by rising unemployment, confused economic policies, and a series of scandals including the exposure of the spy Vassall and eventually the bizarre Profumo affair. Macmillan's Government never really recovered from the 'night of the long knives' of July 1962, when Macmillan himself panicked and sacked six senior Cabinet ministers, including the luckless Selwyn Lloyd, the Chancellor. Next day in Parliament at Question Time, the unhappy Macmillan was being challenged on the massacre, and one devoted supporter, trying to help, asked whether he should not be congratulated because he 'had kept his head, when all about were losing theirs'. This provoked the longest spontaneous laugh I ever heard in the House. At the interview in which Selwyn Lloyd was dropped, Macmillan had suggested that the dismissal be explained on grounds of Selwyn Lloyd's age; but Selwyn Lloyd advised against this, as Macmillan was several years older. Selwyn Lloyd had ill-luck, as a lawyer, to be pitchforked into the Foreign Office and Treasury where he was never at home. For the same reason he made an admirable Speaker in the 1970s.

In May of 1963 John Strachey, George Thomson and I visited India and Pakistan for two weeks as a delegation from the British Labour Party and as guests of the Indian and Pakistan Governments. The tour was first suggested by Gaitskell late in 1962, and sprang from his wish to maintain an active link between the Labour Party and the Nehru Government. John Strachey and George Thomson, both close friends of mine, were most agreeable companions, and well-informed about Indian affairs. India was one of Strachey's favourite subjects: and to balance Warren Hastings (an indirect ancestor of mine) he had a grandfather who had been Governor of Bengal. We visited Delhi, Calcutta, Dacca, Kashmir, Lahore, Rawalpindi and Karachi. Our time in India had to be balanced by time in Pakistan. In Rawalpindi Field-Marshal Ayub Khan, then autocratic ruler of Pakistan, talked to us for an hour in rapid-fire Sandhurst slang, and was exceedingly candid about the state of his country. He described parliamentary democracy with phrases such as 'what-you-call-it', and in appearance precisely resembled Field-Marshal Alexander of Tunis. But we all found him a much more impressive character than we had perhaps expected: sagacious, human, well-intentioned, ready to learn, but somehow bewildered by the magnitude of his country's problems. Our only trouble in Pakistan was a joke we had made in the corridor of the splendid Parliament building in Delhi; to the effect that we wished we had conditions like this in Westminster in which to work. This was repeated in the Pakistan press as a proposal from us that the 'capital of the Commonwealth should be transferred to Delhi'.

Nehru, who was then at the height of his authority, gave us the friendliest possible lunch in his home in Delhi, and was anxious for all the latest information about the Labour Party and the British Government. He was more disposed to listen than Ayub. But after we had ranged over India's food, trade, population (it was then only 444 million) and employment problems, he evidently enjoyed reminiscing about his early years in England, and the India League days of the 1930s when I had first met him. Among other ministers we called on Moraji Desai, an austere and laconic figure, who resembled Stafford Cripps not merely in character and philosophy but even in appearance. I was not surprised when later, in the 1970s he became Prime Minister at the age of over eighty. Our conclusions about the Indian economy were, first, that they should concentrate on strengthening their food production, and secondly that they would be wise to conciliate the international oil companies in the search for oil and gas. In the first we proved right; but in the second results have been disappointing.

On Nehru's advice we spent a few days at Srinagar in Indian Kashmir, where we dined with Mr Panikkar, ex-Indian Ambassador to Peking, a great historical scholar. We questioned him throughout a fascinating evening about the history of central Asia for centuries back. He related how recently the Chinese had built a road across Indian territory in the Kara Koram area, and how the Indians never heard of it till he was invited to a celebration of its opening in Peking. Next day finding myself in sight of the Himalayas for probably the only time in my life, I was determined to gratify my mountain-climbing impulse by at least ascending a 600 foot rocky pinnacle prominent in the middle of Strinagar, though in rock-climber's terms it was an ascent and not a climb. Thomson and I strongly pressed Strachey not to follow, as he had trouble with his leg. Strachey insisted, but eventually agreed to go slow and rest if he felt weak. When we returned from the summit, with its view of 20,000 foot snow peaks, we found Strachey near the foot and beset with aches and pains. He recovered sufficiently, however, to make the journey home to England in fair comfort. After a broken night's sleep in the plane between Karachi and Beirut, Strachey and I fell into a several hours' intimate conversation, half way as it were between sleeping and waking, Asia and Europe, night and day, continuing all the way to London, in which we explored each other's views on personal as well as political life.

When he saw his doctors on his return, Strachey was advised to have an operation on his back to cure the trouble. A week or two afterwards he suffered a sailing accident with his son Charles off the Essex coast; and was forced to swim ashore, and developed heart weakness. Despite this he decided in July, not much later, to go ahead with the operation, and died a few days afterwards. He was only sixty-one. The news was a bitter shock to George Thomson and me. Naturally we wondered whether we could have more forcibly resisted his efforts to climb the rock pinnacle; but it was typical of Strachey to leap at a chance of climbing, sailing, cricket or tennis, almost as avidly as at a new idea. His death was another serious loss to the Labour Party. Bevan, Gaitskell and Strachey all died within three years. I believe that the social-democratic side of Strachey's mind had in the post-war years finally triumphed over his Marxist leanings, and that his knowledge of defence issues could have been of real value to the 1964 Labour Government. I increasingly admired Strachey's open-mindedness; and despite the frequent long essays, found him a cooperative as well as ever-stimulating colleague.

In October of 1963, Harold Wilson made his first speech as Party Leader at the Scarborough Labour Party Conference, and unveiled the 'white heat of the technological revolution' as the salvation of the country. I was not much impressed myself with the technological revolution. But his speech was well received: and I suppose it was his method of steering away from more 'nationalization' plans on the old model. (He had told me after my *Forward* article in 1959 that if I hadn't written the article, we should have achieved my aims sooner.) Only a week later, as the Tory Conference opened at Llandudno, Harold Macmillan, struck down by illness, announced his resignation as Prime Minister. After several days of Conservative turmoil, and to the amazement of most people – and certainly mine – he was succeeded by Alec Home. This strange news reached me at Brighton when my wife and I were installing our twin daughters, Helen and Catherine, now eighteen, in their first term in Sussex University. Though the choice of a Conservative leader was not my business, the cold-shouldering of Butler for the second time struck me as a typical Macmillan contrivance. This was the era when the Conservative Leader still 'emerged', as it were, from fasting and prayer. On parliamentary form since 1951, Butler certainly had much the stronger claim. No doubt the chasm over appeasement and Munich still yawned; and Churchill, Salisbury and Macmillan had even now not forgiven Butler for his support of Chamberlain. Had they forgotten, however, that Alec Home went to Munich with Chamberlain as his PPS? I would have expected Macmillan to be more magnamimous at this late stage, even though I had held a cool opinion of him ever since reviewing one of his books *Reconstruction* in my *Economist* days in the 1930s. Nor is it a very notable claim to fame to have shared responsibility for both Suez and Brussels. But Macmillan's most illuminating memoirs at least show that there was a good deal behind the mask that he had previously been unwilling or unable to display. If he was misjudged, his own histrionics were largely to blame.

Alec Home was pitchforked into No. 10 Downing Street, no doubt much to his own surprise, with only one year to go before a general election became compulsory. Despite his hereditary title and his being Foreign Secretary while still in the Lords, he was popular in the Commons because he was frank and friendly and avoided Macmillan's efforts at showmanship. I once complimented him in a Commons passage on the brevity of a speech of his, and he surprised me by replying: 'It's a classical education.' He made a gallant effort in his bare twelve months, to restore Conservative electoral fortunes from the low level to which they had finally sunk under Macmillan. Inevitably 1964 became largely a run-up to the election. The

Labour Party had been in opposition for thirteen years, and some of us felt that if we did not win this time, Britain would be in danger of becoming a one-Party State.

From March 1964 onwards, and for most of the spring and summer, I was locked in the most unpromising subject of Resale Price Maintenance – or RPM – by which is meant the right of a manufacturer to control the price charged by distributors of his product. Ted Heath, now rather grandiloquently called 'Secretary of State for Trade, Industry and Regional Development', had introduced a major Bill, which raised many passions, particularly from small shopkeepers. The whole episode was very revealing of Ted Heath. He represented his Bill as a great radical reform. It was my job as Labour Party spokesman on these issues to manage the opposition to it in the House; and my own personal view was that it made only a small difference to the economic life of the country. Heath, characteristically, having seized on the idea, was determined to push it through at all costs, and was unwilling to listen to any arguments. We frequently pointed out that if the aim was to get rid of RPM, this could be done by simply repealing Clause Twenty-Five of Peter Thorneycroft's Act,[1] which made 'individual RPM' enforceable in law, rather than by a major Bill with dozens of clauses. Heath never answered this. This Act may have been one cause of the subsequent decline of the small local shop.

However, the real importance of the debates on the Bill, as I thought, was that they kept the *Daily Express* in an anti-Tory mood in the months running up to the election. My lifetime theory has already been mentioned in this book that you cannot win a general election – or referendum – with the whole press against you; and here was the *Daily Express*, as a champion of the small shopkeeper, in full cry against Heath. Since a number of Tories supported the *Daily Express* line, we were able to keep the debate – and the *Express* – in full spate for many weeks right into the summer. As the Tories had a normal majority of 100, it was hard actually to defeat them on a vote. But twice we nearly did. First, our team, after weeks of argument, had reduced Heath to such a lame reply to an amendment that we were evidently going to win if the vote was taken at once. At this late hour Harold Lever came in, having been absent all day and having just put some guests in the public gallery. I wrote him a note beseeching him not to speak when Heath sat down, so that we could vote. When Heath finished, Lever rose and talked for long enough for the crisis to pass and Heath to rally his forces. Secondly a little later on by great efforts we again got many Tory dissidents angry and on our side and were fairly sure of winning. I suspected (rightly) that the chance of defeating a government in these circumstances would not recur in my parliamentary life. We lost by only one vote; and some time later Roy Jenkins, I read in the *Economist*, boasted that on this occasion he had been sitting in the Library and did not bother

[1] Restrictive Practices Act 1956.

to vote because he thought the Bill such a bore. But despite these outbursts of private enterprise, the hostility of the *Daily Express* to the Government was, I believe, one of the influences which prevented a recovery of the Tory vote in the October election.

In the months running up to the 1964 election, I made one other major effort, which failed, to persuade Harold Wilson to refrain from a rash experiment which caused immense trouble for the 1964 Government: the creation of a Department of Economic Affairs alongside the Treasury. This plan, which was simply a repetition of the discredited muddle of 1945-7, was bound to fail for reasons set out elsewhere in this story.[2] Having direct experience of 1945-7 myself, I arranged for both Norman Brook and Edwin Plowden (now both outside the government machine) to give their views to Wilson. They together knew more about the higher government machinery for managing the economy under several governments than anybody else; and they agreed with me that the DEA would be a disruptive experiment. I invited Norman Brook and Harold Wilson to lunch with me at the House and argue over the whole project. Brook was forthright as ever; Wilson listened politely. But it became pretty clear to me that he had promised George Brown to put him at the head of the DEA. This was a prime example of creating bad organization in order to appease pesonalities – a classical recipe for trouble. Wilson, I am sure, knew the scheme was ill-judged, but for some reason put personal appeasement first.

The 1964 election was very hard fought: and there was a 'Now or Never' spirit in the Labour Party. The Gaitskellite wing of the Party, which had never wanted Wilson as Leader, scrupulously refrained from making the same trouble for him, or causing the same dissension, as the Bevanites had under Gaitskell and Attlee. For that reason a much greater appearance of unity was preserved. This is the real element of truth in the notion that Wilson was specially successful in uniting the Labour Party. In previous general elections, I had gone on speaking tours round the country. In the crucial 1964 contest I decided to stay in London and work with my local Party. In Battersea, since my constituency (North) was more easily winnable than South, the normal strategy was that workers from both should concentrate on the marginal one: South. So I spent the greater part of my time laboriously canvassing in streets outside my own constituency; which of course led to complaints in my own that I 'hadn't been round'. Towards the end of this time, therefore, I returned to my own area, where I was one of the very few canvassers: an interesting experiment, which again appeared to show that canvassing has little effect, because there was still no discernible difference in the results.

The most memorable event in this election in Battersea was a speech by Attlee. He was now close on eighty. When asked by Transport House whether he wished to speak at this election time, he was reported to have

[2] See p. 166.

replied: 'Owing to age I can only do two meetings each night.' One evening he was due for his second speech at a crowded meeting in South Battersea where the other candidate and I had for some time been answering noisy questions from all comers. On arrival Attlee's tiny frame was more or less carried through the throng and up to the platform. When we lifted him on to the platform the barracking had not ceased; but when he began to speak, just audibly, it did. He said only this: 'I have seen many elections. I have lived through two Great Wars, and a lot of governments, good and bad. I am a very old man. I shan't live much longer. But I hope to live till Friday. And if on Friday I hear that a Labour Government has been elected, I shall die happy.' He sank back into his chair, to thunderous cheers from all sides.

For honour's sake I continued my loud-speaker and canvassing operations right through until 9 p.m. on 15 October, when the poll closed. At that hour I was stopped in the rain in a gloomy road near Clapham Junction by a stranger who informed me that Khrushchev had resigned. Bemused by this incongrous news, and exhausted with electioneering, I drove straight across a red light on my way back to Labour HQ. No harm came of it. At the Battersea Party HQ this time there was a feeling of victory. Later in the evening we heard we had won all the four Wandsworth constituencies: North and South Battersea, Putney and Tooting. The main reason for this, I was fairly sure, was the full effect of the Conservative Rent Act of 1957, suspended until after the 1959 election, which had forced up rents of middle-class homes threefold or fourfold throughout London, and alienated many thousands of lifelong Conservative voters. This probably won the 1964 election for Labour at least in London. Next day, working my last day at *Reynolds* (and indeed my last day ever in a newspaper office), I heard after lunch that Labour had won the crucial seat in Meriden (at 2.47 p.m.) and so now had a clear majority. The actual final figures were Labour 317; all other parties 313; and so we were back in the situation of 1950, with a majority of four soon to become three.

Totally exhausted that evening, I turned my mind to the prospective Labour Government. It is a characteristic of our system that a senior minister takes on the job of running a great department and trying to govern the country when he is twenty-four hours away from utter physical exhaustion. The outlook was not improved by the fact that, as in 1950-1, our tiny majority would mean constant attendance in the House. On the other hand, it was very apparent to me that, yet once again in my life, fortune had just swung my way. By the narrowest margin both percentagewise and in the total vote, and at the last election at which I would be the right age, Labour had won by the skin of its teeth, and I should join the Cabinet – for about six months, I privately guessed. How much better it would have been if we had won in 1959.

In any case, even Saturday 17 October was hardly a respite. I was rung after breakfast by Derek Mitchell the Prime Minister's Private Secretary, and my own of thirteen years before at the Treasury – the call was somewhat delayed by my twin daughters' constant use of the telephone – and saw Wilson in the early afternoon. He offered me the Board of Trade, and I got it confirmed that Distribution of Industry policy, about which I cared most, would remain with the Board of Trade. I then walked straight from No. 10 to the Board of Trade at 1 Victoria Street, and was met at the entrance by the Permanent Secetary, Sir Richard Powell, and the Principal Private Secretary, Peter Carey. Powell I hardly knew till this day, but soon found an excellent colleague; brisk, friendly and decisive. Peter Carey, whom I had never met before, was highly experienced, having served Maudling, Erroll and Heath, and proved invaluable to me until he was promoted in December. Not many years later he became himself Permanent Secretary of the Department of Industry. These two introduced me to the others in the Private Office, including one of the junior private secretaries, Mary Thomas (Heath had not really approved of women secretaries); but that afternoon I was more impressed by the splendid view of Westminster Abbey from my own office window.

Powell, Carey and I then settled down to discuss policy. What were my views? I firmly disagree with Dalton's emphatic doctrine that a minister must immediately 'assert' authority over his officials, however senior, by aggressive behaviour. Having served as both a minister and an official, this did not suit me. My way was to achieve a friendly relation by rational discussion: and I think we succeeded from the start. My main interest, I made clear at once, would be in reviving and re-invigorating the flagging Development Area policy; but I believed our maximum energies must be devoted to promoting a world-wide export drive by all practical methods on a wider front than ever before. My other main priorities would be to encourage freer trade in Europe based on EFTA and in the wider world under the GATT Kennedy Round which was already being negotiated. Powell told me at once that we were facing a balance of payments deficit estimated by the Treasury at £800 million for 1964, and economies on imports had to be made quickly. I was not surprised. Back to old times, and memories of 1947, 1949 and 1951. And though I well knew the Treasury's natural impulse to overpaint bad news, (the *current* payments deficit, the normal criteria in the 1940s and again in the 1970s, was nearer £400 million), I realized that we must act at once. Later that same Saturday afternoon I moved on with Powell to a meeting with Jim Callaghan, George Brown and senior officials to discuss alternative policies.

It was at this point that the 1964 Government went grievously wrong. It made two primary mistakes in economic policy in its first week. One was to restrain manufactured imports by an internationally illegal import 'surcharge' rather than a legal quota; the other was the formation of the DEA, which as in 1945-7 caused persistent overlapping between departments and consequent indecision. Since 1964, perhaps in an effort to obscure these errors, a myth has been propagated that the then Government's prime mistake was the failure to devalue the pound in that first week-end in October 1964. This is, I believe, false reading, based on hindsight and disregard of the alternatives open to us in 1964. Quite apart from economic policy, a government cannot morally, in my judgement, declare or imply throughout an election that it will not devalue the currency (as it must so imply), and then turn round almost the next day and proceed to do so, and glibly put the blame on its predecessors. This would be indefensible morally, and would generate far more cynicism than is inevitable anyway about politics and politicians. Nor can a British Government suddenly announce to overseas holders of sterling that its value has been deliberately depreciated without reasonable proof (as in 1949) that this was unavoidable. If I had been asked, I would have ruled out devaluation on moral grounds. But in any event in 1964 the economic case for it was far from demonstrable. The figures of comparative export prices simply did not show what they showed in 1949. The 1964 current deficit of about £400 million was not beyond the power of a quota to correct; and the capital outflow could have been checked by more effective exchange control. The right course would have been to restrain less essential imports by an internationally legal method for a fair period; and if after a time this proved plainly ineffective, to let the exchange value of the currency float freely.

Wilson, Callaghan and Brown were therefore right, as I judged then and judge now, to decide on Saturday morning, 17 October, as emerged later, against instant devaluation.[3] The real mistake came immediately afterwards. Two alternatives for limiting imports were presented to us at the meeting already mentioned later on the Saturday afternoon which I attended with Callaghan, Brown, William Armstrong and Denis Rickett of the Treasury, Tony Crosland, a junior Minister at the DEA, Eric Roll of the DEA, Richard Powell, Bill Hughes from the Board of Trade and Alec Cairncross, head of the Economic Section. These were nearly all old friends and colleagues of mine from one period or another. The two alternatives were to limit manufactured imports either by quota or by a 15 per cent surcharge. The surcharge was illegal under both GATT and EFTA; whereas quota limitation was explicitly legal under both the GATT and EFTA Treaties. I therefore argued strongly for quotas on the ground that legality was the key point; that if we acted illegally we should be forced to desist and be plunged back into crisis; and that our freer trading policy was based on EFTA, whose members would be particularly affronted by the surcharge. To my surprise and disappointment, I found myself, in this company, in a minority of one. It was soon clear that the officials had decided a quota system would be too much trouble, and the economists

[3] Harold Wilson, *The Labour Government of 1964–70* (London, 1971), p. 7.

were influenced by the academic fashion veering at that moment in favour of taxes rather than physical controls. Brown and Callaghan fairly evidently had little view of their own, but had been persuaded. They all made light of the illegality of the surcharge, to an extent which I found astonishing. Tony Crosland even told us that he had met some anonymous Norwegian the night before who had told him Norway would not worry at all over our surcharge. Ironically, in the sequel, it was the Norwegian reaction which was the most violent. Two clinching arguments were used by the officials advocating the surcharge; the first was a telegram from Eddie Cohen our Ambassador to EFTA in Geneva saying that in his view there would be only mild protests from EFTA. Who was I, a mere ignorant politician, to argue against the Ambassador on the spot? The second argument was the assertion that the surcharge could be imposed in a week or two whereas quotas would take much longer. Yet when I inquired a little later from the head of the Board of Trade department responsible, I was told quotas would not have taken materially longer to impose than the surcharge.

Next morning, Sunday 18 October, we met at No. 10, with Wilson and Burke Trend (Secretary to the Cabinet) added to the group. The argument was the same; and I recorded the following note of it myself at the time: 'I opposed the surcharge as strongly as I could, predicted that it would cause endless trouble with EFTA, and queried all the arguments on the other side. Again I had no support, not even from the PM whose previous views might have led me to expect he would agree. To be quite certain that I had done my best, and got my views firmly on record, I formally and strongly opposed the surcharge at the first meeting of the new Cabinet on Thursday 22 October – again with no support.' Wilson is thus quite mistaken in saying that 'there was no disposition to argue' on the new surcharge.[4] I took good care to oppose it strongly, and Gerald Gardiner (Lord Gardiner, then Lord Chancellor) recognized this by telling me a few months later, that in view of the sequel, he now thought I was right. He was the only colleague who did (apart from Crossman alter).[5] So the fatal decision was taken; and my immediate task for many months ahead became the public defence of a policy which I deeply regretted. Had we accepted the quota system instead, we should have avoided the disastrous controversy with our best friends in EFTA; we could have kept it in force, with modifications, for as long as needed, as was done throughout the years 1945–59; and we might well have escaped the worst of the exchange crises of 1966 and 1967 which accompanied the enforced removal of the surcharge.

The creation of the DEA was the 1964 Government's second major blunder, as was generally recognized by its abolition three years later. It was founded on a fallacy: the naive belief that you need a rival Department to press for reflation while the Treasury presses for deflation. Not merely

[4] Wilson, p. 19.
[5] Richard Crossman, *The Names of a Cabinet Minister*, vol. 1, p. 116

was this bound to produce muddle and friction. But it ignored a fundamental economic fact: that the Treasury must accept responsibility if and
when the pound falls and the gold and dollar reserves flow out; and that
it cannot do this unless it controls economic policy.[6] Unhappily also, in
the event, the trouble caused by the DEA – though as a department it
included many admirable officials doing their best in an impossible
position – was further aggravated for two other reasons. First Wilson
gratuitously gave way to a request from Brown for a vague DEA mandate
over international economic policy, which Wilson himself later admitted
was a mistake when writing[7] that Brown 'added – I now think I was wrong
to agree – responsibility for the main issues of overseas economic policy
[to his other functions]. This caused endless problems with the Board of
Trade and to some extent abutted on to Treasury responsibilities in the
field of overseas finance.' Secondly, the DEA tended increasingly to become
a mere pressure group within the Government – before long in favour of
Common Market membership – and a source of gossip in the press directed
at other departments with whom it was having a dispute. These activities
were pushed to a point quite unknown in Whitehall under the Churchill
Government during the war or the Attlee Government thereafter.

George Brown and the DEA did one good job for which they should be
given credit: persuasion of the TUC and FBI to join in a declaration of
restraint on pay and prices in December of 1964. This certainly contributed
to the whole economic effort in the Government's first two years. It was
a great pity the DEA, so long as it existed, did not confine itself to these
general inter-ministerial tasks. Just two instances of its less helpful
initiatives can be given as examples of how co-ordination between government departments should *not* be conducted. One of my first tasks in
Development Area policy was to re-schedule wider areas as Development
Areas under the existing legislative powers dating back to my original
Distribution of Industry Act of 1945. This could be done at once; after
which a new Bill giving much wider powers could be introduced. But the
DEA obstructed because it could not grasp that much essential re-scheduling could be carried through at once, without waiting for the new legislation.[8] Secondly one of my main initiatives in export promotion was to set
up a government-supported national company which would assist smaller
firms in the marketing and transport problems of exporting. I got little or
no support in this from the DEA. Some years afterwards when I privately
asked a prominent ex-official of the DEA why his department had spent
so much effort attacking the Board of Trade, he replied: because the Board
of Trade failed to set up a national export company.

Having wrestled unsuccessfully with the Whitehall establishment over

[6] See again p. 166.
[7] Wilson, p. 5.
[8] See p. 308.

the week-end of 17–19 October on the surcharge, I found my next job was a public speech on Tuesday evening, 20 October, to the International Chamber of Commerce, attended by a galaxy of company chairmen and distinguished foreign visitors, including Dr Luns, then Dutch Foreign Minister, and later Director-General of NATO. I caused some trepidation in my department by saying that I dictated my own speeches. My theme this time was that the Government intended to promote vigorously the Kennedy round of world tariff cuts; and that at home we believed in both public and private enterprise, but that Parliament was the proper authority to draw the line between the two. To this dinner both Ted Heath and I had been invited during the election; so that whoever was President of the Board of Trade on the night could speak, and his 'shadow' attend as an honoured guest. As we assembled before dinner in our white ties, Ted Heath walked straight up to me, said 'Congratulations' with a stony stare, as I attempted to smile, and promptly moved off. However, the speech was widely reported – not mainly because of its merits but because the Government was enjoying its first honeymoon weeks – and Lord Aldington (Toby Low, previously a Conservative in the House, and now a banker and close friend of Heath) wrote me a very friendly letter expressing something near to City goodwill for the new Government.

Next assignation in this crowded month, I found, was a visit starting in ten days on 30 October via Moscow to open a major British industrial exhibition in Peking. Welcome as this was as a move in the export campaign, it started with a comic interlude. I told my officials that I did not want to fly to Peking unless it was perfectly clear that the Chinese Government had invited me; and on being asked by my office the Chinese Chargé d'Affaires in London replied that he knew nothing of any such invitation. However a week later, the same dignitary returned smiling to say that all was in order and that his Government had forgotten to tell him. Before leaving I just had time to set in motion the export promotion review and plans for an 'advance factory' building programme in the existing limited Development Areas. On 26 October Callaghan and Brown publicly announced the Government's decision on the import surcharge at a press conference. This gave the Conservative Opposition a great chance to attack the choice of the illegal surcharge as opposed to the legal quota. But they missed this almost entirely because Reggie Maudling in his first speech virtually admitted that he would have preferred the surcharge. I met the assembled EFTA Ambassadors at 9.30 a.m. on the morning of Monday 26 October, and explained all our proposals and the reasons for them. Naturally, they concentrated in protest against the illegality, to which we had no real answer; so that we were forced back on emphasizing the £800 million deficit left us by the previous Government, which (as was foreseen) was not helpful to the exchange value of the pound. The Ambassadors were stiff and frosty, but not quite yet as vehement as I feared.

Evidently they personally understood our difficulties; and it was the later pressure from the business interests affected which compelled their Ministers to raise such a storm. To me, as a fervent believer in EFTA as the invaluable basis for British trading interests in Europe, it was particularly distressing to be forced to start by thus unnecessarily souring our relations with our best friends.

On 30 October I duly left for Moscow and Peking, seen off at Heathrow by my wife and twin daughters, and accompanied by the indispensable Peter Carey, and Tony Welch of the Board of Trade, whom I had known in New College days. Stopping briefly at Copenhagen on the way, I met the Danish Trade Minister and tried to smooth his feelings about the surcharge controversy which was now warming up. To do this I explained to him confidentially our plan for 'unilateral acceleration' of the tariff cuts by ourselves within EFTA, which is described later in this chapter, which would have largely solved the EFTA crisis, and which was sabotaged by the French. We had one night and day in Moscow, where Humphrey Trevelyan was now Ambassador. He told us of his belief that Khrushchev had been removed, not because of any differences on policy, but because of his dictatorial and intolerant attitude to his colleagues. It had been arranged, we found next morning, that I should meet Kosygin as well as the Soviet Trade Minister. Kosygin had taken office as Prime Minister and Head of the Government, though not of the Party, on Thursday 15 October, and our Government on Friday 16 October; so that we could at least exchange compliments on being both a fortnight old. (As I write fourteen years later, Kosygin is still there.)

My day in Moscow (31 October) I recorded at the time as follows:

Next morning we drove to the Kremlin through the main gate from the Red Square, and were conducted to Kosygin's office by an extremely smart, extremely handsome pale blue-eyed young officer, who struck me as coming from the world of Congress dances and Vienna in 1815. Kosygin's room was far more austere than this, with the conventional desk at one end, and a long table with about ten chairs on each side. Kosygin and the Deputy Trade Minister, Kuzmin, received us (The Trade Minister Patolichev was in Paris), and four or five officials accompanied them. I was supported by the Ambassador, Tony Welch, Peter Carey and our interpreter. We sat opposite one another across the table, and began congratulating one another on the formation of the two new Governments. I at once formed the view that Kosygin was more cordial than he needed to be and he went out of his way to say – not just formally, but convincingly – that Russua wanted good relations with Britain and the new Government. Trevelyan confirmed to me afterwards that Kosygin showed more than conventional cordiality. Had it been Khrushchev, he might well have remembered the famous Labour Party dinner in the House of Commons in 1956 when he claimed to have been insulted by George Brown. Kosygin struck me as a typical Scotsman – 'dour' was the word which kept occurring to one – meticulous, well-informed, argumentative, perceptive, but suddenly dissolving into a joke or smile when one was just inclined to believe that prickliness was his main characteristic. We discussed economics and Anglo-Russian trade. I argued the need for greater purchases by the Soviet of British goods to narrow the UK deficit in trade, as had been promised by Patolichev to Heath in the previous April. He trotted out accurately all the set Soviet excuses, but promised that Soviet purchases would increase – as indeed they did, though not fast enough. We naturally took down all his concrete points, such as complaints against British firms setting up plants in Russia, including Courtaulds, and gave a documented reply a few weeks later. We left after about forty-five minutes, and went on for a longer talk with Kuzmin in his own office in the wedding-cake Foreign Office building.

Kuzmin was a rather pig-like Khrushchev, pugnacious, and given to aggressive jokes. We pursued the question of the trade gap, demanded chapter and verse for Soviet complaints, and I explained that Soviet purchase of Australian and Malayan raw materials did not help the UK balance of payments. I don't think either Kosygin or Kuzmin really believed it did. The truth was obvious enough to us; that the Soviet were deliberately creating an export surplus with the UK, in order to buy sterling area wheat and raw materials. After this thorough talk and promises of better Soviet purchases in the UK, we all had lunch, and I noticed that the atmosphere was far more jovial and friendly than it had been in 1956 when I was last in Moscow. The Ministers and officials present were also more openly bourgeois and more obviously living much as their counterparts would have done in a western city. I noticed the far greater expanses of flats built since 1956, the far better appearance of the people, and the great increase in motor traffic.

As we left this lunch, I was asked to say a word over Moscow radio. I said I would, and was approached by a Russian who thrust a microphone before me and said in English 'Mr Jay, did you have a satisfactory talk with Chairman Khrushchev this morning?' Looking puzzled, I replied 'Don't you mean Chairman Kosygin?' 'Yes, yes, of course,' said the Russian. I assumed that these remarks were not live, and that he had the chance to cut this part of the conversation.

And so on to Peking that evening in a Russian jet via Omsk and Irkutsk. I was intensely curious to see Siberia and Central Asia: but daylight did not emerge until Irkutsk. The most enjoyable part of the journey was chess with Peter Carey before Omsk, and least enjoyable the descent at 4 a.m. Moscow-time to Irkutsk, since the plane was inadequately pressurized and this gave me violent pains in the head. Hoping to warm ourselves by walking briskly from the plane to the restaurant at Irkutsk airport, we were warned to slow down because of ice. At this point we were happily mistaken for a Cuban trade delegation and given VIP treatment which meant (I desperately wanted very hot coffee) cold tea for breakfast. This, I thought, shivering, is one of what are called the 'fruits' or 'perks' of office. More alluring was the view of Lake Baykal surmounted by forests, and great stretches of Mongolian mountains as we flew the remaining 800 miles to Peking.

At Peking Airport we found that the King of Afghanistan was landing almost simultaneously and the troops and bands were lined up for him, not us. He was, after all, a king. We were at least greeted, however, by charming Chinese girls with gifts of flowers as well as by the sterner Trade Minister, Dr Yeh Chi Chuang, a distinctly elderly veteran, reputed to have kept his job because he endured the 'Long March' with Mao in 1947–8, like a hero of Marathon in fifth-century Athens. While we were still walking across the airport, the Trade Minister asked whether Britain would be willing to sell China a number of VC10s. He seemed to want twenty or twenty-five, with perhaps more to follow. On the spur of this inopportune moment, I tried to be encouraging, though adding that there might be difficulties. I realized at once that this might be a major chance for the British aircraft industry, and the Minister pressed his request throughout the visit.

China was evidently the only country in the world which could not buy American jets and which did not want to buy from the hated Russians. But we were clearly not able to accept categorically without Cabinet authority. This, as it turned out, was the major real issue of the visit. On my return, I backed the proposal, as also of course did the British aircraft industry, as hard as I could for six months, through all the appropriate intricacies of the government machine. It was stubbornly opposed by the Foreign Office, on the ground that the Americans did not like it, and by the Commonwealth Office on the ground that the Indians thought the Chinese might use VC10s to drop atom bombs on India. As a result of opposition from those two departments it was defeated; and of course before very many years the Chinese were buying American jets like anyone else. This was a tragically missed chance for the British aircraft industry. It was also a classic example of a flaw in the British government machine which I have often noticed: the habit of overseas departments notably the Foreign Office, of acting in the Cabinet and in Whitehall as in effect an advocate of the views of a foreign government. In 1965 in this case the FO vetoed the VC10 sales and dealt a heavy blow to a major British export industry.

My main formal jobs in Peking were to negotiate two-way trade opportunities of many kinds with Trade ministers, to open the ambitious British Industrial Exhibition intended – as gradually it did – to increase British exports, and to see how far senior Chinese ministers were prepared for more normal relations between the two Governments. At this time we exchanged only Chargés d'Affaires and not Ambassadors because of the Chinese grievance over our attitude to Taiwan (Formosa) and Chiang Kai-Shek. The following is my account made at the time of this week in Peking:

I discussed quite amicably with Mr Yeh, the Trade Minister, the possibilities of our buying more Chinese materials and selling her more capital goods, and even some consumer goods. At the time of these talks trade between the UK and China was at the ridiculously low level of about £20 million each way.

Next and rather more impressive Minister was the younger Deputy Trade Minister, Mr Lu Hsu Chang, who had travelled in Europe, including the UK, and seemed altogether more up-to-date and aware of the facts of life in the outside world. A charming and conscientious university girl student acted as interpreter for me throughout the trip.

After the first dinner ceremonies and opening of the Exhibition, it was arranged that I should meet the Economic overlord and Deputy Prime Minister, Mr Li Hsien Nien, a very different character. He had been a guerilla war leader for twenty years, with a peculiarly savage reputation. I had some doubt about the purpose and wisdom of such talks, since I could not see what they could achieve, but was strongly pressed to hold them by the Chargé d'Affaires, and by the FO member of our party, Mr Maclehose. My self-assurance was not increased, on arriving at the resplendent new Government buildings (sited on the side of the imitation of the Red Square called the Square of the Revolution), to find that these talks were to be held not in a small room with half a dozen people, as one might have expected by Western, Moscow or Indian standards, but in a vast hall with thirty or forty people present. We sat in semi-circle armchairs with myself and Mr Li facing one another, as it were, at the keystone of the arch. I started, as advised by the FO corps, by expressing a desire for less distant relations between the two countries, and asking his views on such subjects as the UN, disarmament, etc. It was our Government's policy to sound out the possibilities of China joining disarmament talks at Geneva. Mr Li was intransigent, peremptory, and dogmatic. There was no attempt to admit that the other man's point of view might have something in it. He laid it down that his Government should take their seat in the UN Security Council, that Taiwan should be handed over to Peking and the Chiang Kai-Shek regime liquidated, and that the Americans should sithdraw wholly from Vietnam and South East Asia. China could not have any conversations with anyone who did not accept these doctrines at the start. I kept up the conversation for about forty-five minutes, including translation. I just managed to end on a note which, if not affable, at least avoided acerbity, by saying that at any rate the British had one factor in common with the Chinese, and that was their belief that they were absolutely right about everything and everyone else was wrong. When this was translated, I saw for the first time just the flicker of a smile on Mr Li's stony and hitherto grimly inscrutable face.

A few days later I met Chou En-lai, the Prime Minister, and ex-Foreign Minister. He was of course far more polished and urbane than Mr Li, having lived in Paris in his university days in the 1920s, and attended conferences all over the world. But in substance he was equally intransigent. He trotted out the same dogmas on Taiwan and Vietnam. Trying in vain to get away from these unpromising subjects (we were again sitting at the apex of a semi-circle addressing an audience of about forty in a huge hall), I said that at least he would not oppose the British Government's wish to see his Government take its place on the UN Security Council. That, he replied, was not the wish or the policy of the British Government. I suggested that perhaps, on its own wishes and policies, if on nothing else, the British Government might be a better authority than he. Not in the least, he said. As long as Britain retained a consulate on Taiwan and did not recognize Taiwan as part of Communist China, then it was not Communist China which we wished to see seated on the UN Security Council, but something else.

To escape from this topic, I asked Chou En-lai what he thought (the FO brigade wanted this question put) of the change of Government in Moscow from

Khrushchev to Kosygin. He replied by asking what I thought. I said I had supposed that he would be better informed than we; but that if he wanted to know our guess, it was that Mr Khrushchev had become so intolerant and aggressive towards his colleagues that they had finally got fed up and pushed him out. This successfully elicited what I think was Chou En-lai's genuine view. Not at all, he said; Khrushchev had been thrown out because he had refused to accept China's policies and views, and had picked a quarrel with Peking. The proof of this, said Chou En-lai, was that 'Khrushchev is a very remarkable man, and only the will of the Soviet people as a whole could have pushed him out.' I found this a charming example of a very clever man, deceiving himself as naively as the most simpleminded. Chou En-lai was determined to have an explanation which fitted in with his own Government's prejudices. The new Soviet Government, he said, would work closely with China. He visited Moscow himself for the October Revolution ceremonies about a week later, and was much less cordially received than he had expected.

Chou En-lai naturally attacked the new Labour Government for not dissociating itself from United States foreign policy, imperialism, etc., etc. I said that we stood by the alliance with US but reserved the right to criticize US policy when we chose. And we, replied Chou En-lai, stand by our alliance with Russia and reserve the right to criticize their policy when we chose. Here he showed himself agreeably more flexible than Mr Li; and I finished by thanking him for his Government's co-operation in supplying water to Hong Kong. We ended by being photographed in a posed and amicable group. The Peking Exhibition itself, where I spent a great deal of exhausting time and visited every stand, was in all appearance successful. It was visited by tens of thousands of Chinese technical experts who came by special ticket; and a large number of prominent British firms, from aircraft to electrical equipment, TV and scientific instruments, were represented.

On the Sunday of my week in Peking, we were allowed a day off – my first since the start of the general election – in which Mr Lu, the Deputy Trade Minister, took me and the rest of the party on the normal tourist expedition to the Ming Tombs and Ming Sculpture and to a section of the Great Wall, where I allowed myself the relaxation of ascending a 600-feet slope at my own pace. This was the part of the trip which interested the British press, though the *Daily Express* representative was the last member of the party to reach the top. My main impression of China, with all allowance made for the shortness of the time and the limited area visited, was the contrast with India and Pakistan. In the cities of the Indian sub-continent, the existence is all too apparent of very large numbers of men and women with no fixed occupation or working life. In Peking, the impression was one of busy, hurried, organized activity, and innumerable projects, constructional, industrial, agricultural, being pushed forward by a hard working, purposeful, disciplined – no doubt over-disciplined – labour force. Here was a working nation of over 700 million being steadily industrialized, nearly able to feed itself (importing a little wheat but exporting rice) and already armed with atomic weapons. Later events did not alter the opinion I then formed that the deep underlying suspicion between the Chinese and Soviet Governments was likely to be a major influence on the world's political future.

Back in Moscow on the way home, I was surprised and delighted to learn that the British Government had already adopted and announced my plan for control of office development in London. The telegram shown to me in the Moscow Embassy added a comic postscript. 'Her Majesty's Government,' the telegram quoted from the Queen's Speech, 'attach particular importance to the control of tents.' My mind turned to a conversation I had had with a Peking historian about Genghis Khan. But 'tents' turned out to be a misprint for 'rents'. On return to London I arranged to report to Harold Wilson on Moscow and Peking, and was surprisingly invited to his house in Golders Green. One might have thought the new Cabinet would have wished for a report from one of its members who had met Kosygin and Chou En-lai in the first month of its existence; but these records are traditionally covered by telegram in the Whitehall system. The only mention I heard of our Peking telegrams was from the Queen at a party given in the Palace on the evening of my return, in which she showed that she followed details of the official papers much more closely than I had realized. My talk à deux with Harold Wilson was amiably straightforward and cordial, and even raised hopes that my resolve to establish a firm working relationship would be fruitful. But it was the only time I ever entered his Golders Green home.

Before attending my first EFTA Council in Geneva in mid-November, only about ten days were left me to speed up the export promotion plans which we intended to announce in December, to launch our new Development Area drive, and to announce these intentions in the House in the Debate on the Address. For the Development Areas, since the DEA was beginning to create the difficulties and delays already mentioned, I decided to go ahead at once with my programme of 'advance factories' in the areas of worst unemployment in the existing Development Areas. This I knew had been one of the chief successes of the 1945-51 period. It could be done reasonably quickly; and the intervening Tory Government had drastically cut down these programmes. It gave me the greatest personal pleasure to announce this first programme on the day I left for Geneva, 18 November. This proved in fact to be the beginning of a continuing series of advance factory programmes which we expanded throughout my years at the Board of Trade until 1967, and it was maintained as a rolling programme by all Governments thereafter.[9] These factories probably did more than any other means, apart from entirely new industrial estates and one or two spectacular projects by major firms like Ford or BP, to maintain employment in the

[9] Curtailed but not cancelled by even the 1979 Conservative Government.

worst threatened areas in the 1970s. Between 1964 and 1968 nearly four million square feet of factory space in advance factories were built in Development Areas, representing employment for up to 50,000 people. But the delay in rescheduling new areas for nine months, caused by the DEA, sadly limited action in 1965, particularly in South Wales. Indeed in South Wales the previous Government had de-scheduled the areas containing all the main industrial estates: Swansea, Bridgend, Hirwaun and even Treforest. In the Development Areas generally, however, the advance factory programmes of 1965 and 1966 prevented a much more acute rise in unemployment when major coal-mining closures occurred in the late 1960s.

At the EFTA Conference of 18–21 November at Geneva, I expected irony, but not the melodrama which occurred. The irony was two-fold. First Patrick Gordon-Walker, who attended as Foreign Secretary though he had lost his parliamentary seat at Smethwick, and I were strong believers in the closest possible co-operation with EFTA, but were forced by the Cabinet decision on the import surcharge into a violent dispute with our friends. Secondly, being myself the one member of the Cabinet, who had stubbornly opposed the surcharge, I now found myself as the chief spokesman with the job of publicly defending it. The situation could have been saved, had it not been for a deliberate wrecking act by the French which was one of the most illuminating incidents of these years. An ingenious escape from our dilemma had been suggested by the chief Board of Trade official concerned with international trade, Bill Hughes. This was known as 'unilateral acceleration', and meant that Britain would reduce her normal tariff in advance of the other countries within EFTA, while imposing the surcharge at the same time. This would preserve the 'non-discriminating' character of the surcharge generally, and in practice avoid a breach of the EFTA Treaties. It was this which I mentioned confidentially to the Danish Minister in Copenhagen on my way to Moscow and some thought it was through this display of 'open government' by the Danes that it leaked to the French. While I was away, the French seized on a meeting of the 'Group of Ten' in Paris, who were discussing a temporary loan to sustain the pound, and refused to co-operate in the loan unless 'unilateral acceleration' by us in EFTA was abandoned.

This was an act of pure hypocrisy and hostility by the French: hypocrisy because 'unilateral acceleration' had already been practised in the EEC, and hostility because the blocking of EFTA unilateral acceleration did no good to France, but merely damaged EFTA, and the UK in particular. It never should have been accepted, and I believe would not have been if we in the Board of Trade had been told of the French manoeuvre. The Americans were exceedingly helpful throughout. Since there was no special need for French inclusion in the loan, the French should have been told they could stand out if they wished, but that the unilateral acceleration would go forward. But unhappily when Denis Rickett of the Treasury phoned the Foreign Office from Paris, the FO official spoke directly to Gordon-Walker in a telephone box in Birmingham, without ever telephoning Richard Powell of the Board of Trade, who I believe, would have objected. Telephoned in these conditions without proper explanation of what was involved, Gordon-Walker reluctantly accepted the French demands. Thus a crucial decision was taken in an improvised telephone conversation. In its calculated hostility, the action by the French was reminiscent of their manoeuvre in 1950 excluding the UK from the talks on the Schumann Coal and Steel plans, and then proclaiming afterwards that we had refused to join them. Harold Caccia, in 1964 Permanent Secretary at the Foreign Office, was so incensed by the French Government's conduct over 'unilateral accelaration' that he remarked to Gordon-Walker that we must never forget it. I did not; but everyone else did.[10]

This story, which seems never to have been published before, had one outstanding moral for those of us who knew the real facts: that in time of real need American Governments are basically friendly to this country, and that the French for whatever reason seldom are. For if the Hughes 'acceleration' compromise had been accepted (and nobody but the French opposed it), the quarrel with EFTA could have been avoided; the surcharge could have been kept in force much longer; and our balance of payments position greatly eased in 1965-7.

In the event, however, Gordon-Walker and I arrived in Geneva on 18 November with our escape route blocked. On top of this, it was the British turn to take the chair, and I accordingly had to act as chairman of a major international conference for the first time in my life. All began well with a pleasant dinner for Gordon-Walker and me by Frank Figgures (later Sir Frank), Secretary-General of EFTA, a British civil servant and admirably helpful colleague, whom I had known slightly since New College days.[11] Next day the conference began in the hotel on the shores of the Lake of Geneva, and with Figgures's help all went reasonably smoothly. The surcharge was not discussed at length. In the evening the traditional 'working dinner' was held, after which we foregathered round a table for general discussion. The party included not a few picturesque and basically friendly characters whom I later came to know well, all of whom would have remained stoutly pro-British but for the surcharge: Gunnar Lange mild, courteous and scholarly, the very pattern of a Swedish Social-Democrat; Hakkerup of Denmark who could sing drinking songs in five languages; Kreisky, Austrian Trade Minister, and later Chancellor; and Hans Schaffner, Swiss Economic Minister and later President of the Swiss Federation. Schaffner was a formidably able man, a master of fluent

[10] Not mentioned in Wilson, or in Crossman.
[11] At which time because of Figgures's sturdy build, Maurice Bowra in one of his notorious witticisms had called him 'Lord Figgures of Fun'.

English, with a remarkable flair for economics, and for the British economic problem in particular, a profound believer in EFTA, and much the most forceful, eloquent and penetrating critic of the EEC and all its works whom I ever met. Schaffner turned out to be yet another of those colleagues whom I first encountered as fierce antagonists and came greatly to respect. However, at this first after-dinner session, without any warning, the Swiss announced that they had agreed with the other leading EFTA countries to move at the Conference next day that, in view of the illegality of the British surcharge, the rest of them should impose a retaliatory surcharge on British exports unless and until we removed ours. This, they said, they would do next day unless we that evening agreed to remove the British surcharge forthwith.

Quite apart from the lack of notice, I had never been confronted by a situation quite like this. The economic and political dangers were obvious to us. If EFTA imposed a 15 per cent surcharge on British goods, Commonwealth, EEC and other countries would probably do the same; and the whole of our Government's strategy for restoring the balance of payments would be in ruins. This was the absurdly weak position in which the surcharge blunder had placed us. Also I felt little doubt that news of the imposition of a surcharge by EFTA would provoke a possibly violent run on the pound (and this was shown to be correct by the fact that even though EFTA retaliation was in the end avoided, a dangerous run did occur later that month). The argument was not made much easier by the chance that I was both chairman and chief British advocate, and that we sat informally round a table and more than one protagonist spoke at once. I was supported by Gordon-Walker, who did not show marked stomach for the fight, Bill Hughes of the Board of Trade and Marjoribanks of the FO. Eddy Cohen (who had advised that EFTA would not mind the surcharge) and Figgures, who had to be impartial, were both there. For the first few hours up to midnight we British simply argued that in the name of common sense and the spirit of EFTA, the other members should refrain from retaliation until we all had time to consult our Governmens. They flatly refused, and Schaffner grew ever more aggressive in his colourful oratory. I became quietly convinced that we were in for a trial of strength, more akin to an all-night sitting and that if necessary we would keep them up throughout the night till the Conference met next morning.

Making the happy suggestion of a half-time pause for drinks at midnight, we repaired for a private British review of the state of play. Gordon-Walker was inclined to say: to hell with them; let them go ahead and retaliate if they are so unreasonable. I argued that if we kept them up all night, we might save the day. The officials supported me, and we resumed with the repeated argument that the surcharge was temporary. As the small hours wore on, I found myself faced more and more by a non-stop dialogue with Schaffner. 'What did "temporary" mean?' 'A matter of months rather than years,' I said. The phrase was dissected till about 3 a.m. when we reached happy agreement on a Schaffner proposition that a 'matter of months' meant a shorter time than 'a matter of months rather than years'. Gordon-Walker and I then got Harold Wilson's agreement by telephone to the shorter phrase. About twenty times between 3 a.m. and 4.30 a.m. Schaffner said 'No' to my appeal for a concordat based on this phrase. But at 4.30 a.m. I got his silent assent (most of the others were asleep or at least silent), to my suggestion that he and his colleagues would withdraw their proposed retaliation if we undertook next day to end the surcharge 'in a matter of months'.

This was not quite the last act at Geneva, because though the extremely friendly Austrian Social-Democrat, Kreisky, had agreed to the concordat, his Catholic colleague next day at the formal Conference again questioned it. Our hearts sank. I risked saying that we had reached agreement on the night before and the matter was settled. He remained silent and that was the end of it. The officials in the British delegation agreed that evening that we had had no alternative course other than to sit it out, and that we had had a narrow shave. But I then, due to inexperience, made a mistake. It was the custom of leaders of delegations to give a press conference, and I innocently gave a straightforward account of what had happened. But most of the other delegations, particularly the Swiss, gave a highly doctored one, slanted to their own point of view; in this case that they had forced the British to abandon the surcharge by keeping us up all night. The real truth was that we had induced them to abandon retaliation by keeping them up all night. But it is a commonplace of politics that the story which gets in first usually gains currency. I also first noticed that week the tendency of the British press to do what other countries' press seldom do: to swallow the view of almost any country but their own. However, the essential result was the avoidance of a 'surcharge war'.

On the final evening at Geneva I dined, much more agreeably, in Cohen's minor castle on the shore of the Lake, and had a fascinating talk with Gunnar Lange (who turned out to be a Shakespeare enthusiast) about EFTA, our two Governments' social-democratic policies and the future of Western Europe generally. It left me with an even deeper recognition of the wealth of political accord, practical co-operation and understanding which Britain could have achieved with the EFTA countries – most of them strongly social-democratic – which we had temporarily marred by the surcharge, and later tragically smashed by the terms on which we joined the Common Market. That was the first long-term moral of the November Geneva meeting. The second was the economic tight-rope on which we were walking, as was shown by the sterling crisis at the end of the month. Flying home from Geneva that week-end, with these thoughts in my mind, I felt that the five weeks since polling day in October had been something of a baptism of fire; what with Kosygin, Chou En-lai and Schaffner, not to mention the DEA. But events did not slow down in this '100 days'. Already by the week-end of 21–2 November violent pressure on sterling developed, and Callaghan and Wilson asked Gordon-Walker and me whether we thought Bank Rate should be raised at once. We both thought it essential to consult the American Government, and this was done before the Governor of the Bank announced the rise on Monday 23 November. But the pressure continued until Wednesday 25 November, when the Governor, Lord Cromer announced a $3000 million loan from the Federal Reserve Board in Washington. The crisis was over, and Wilson asked the economic ministers for a drink in celebration at No. 10. Cromer, I felt, deserved every congratulation for this rescue act, even though he may have advocated all sorts of impossibly reactionary policies in the previous few days. But again the outstanding moral was the helpfulness of the Americans in a real crisis.

Callaghan – never before a Treasury minister during an exchange crisis – faced all this much more staunchly than I expected. He was shaken, but not seriously. He was notably calm and lucid in discussion. He did tell me several times that he didn't expect to stay in the job much longer, and doubted whether any of us would be there a year later. Having myself gone through 1949 and 1951, and the lesser horrors of 1947, I replied that this was much exaggerated; and we had better get used to an exchange flutter every six months or so (also an exaggeration). But Callaghan learnt from the experience, as he always learnt from hard facts; and learnt in this case that people who criticize 'the Treasury' for caution or obsession with the balance of payments do not have to find the gold and dollars when the reserves are running out. His own confidence grew from this moment. I soon felt greater respect for him, and trust in him, than for most of my other colleagues. There was more than one opinion why sterling suffered an attack at this particular moment. The Opposition, rushing to pin the blame on the Government, seized on the November Budget and tax proposals. (Maudling could not blame the surcharge, as he had himself supported it; so he blamed 'the inept handling of' the surcharge.) Some blamed the EFTA meeting; though this was equivalent to blaming the original surcharge decision which had made the EFTA protest inevitable. Probably the main single reason was the £800 million payments deficit and the publicity the Government was forced to give to this in order to justify the surcharge. (It would have been better to quote only the *current* deficit of about £400 million.) A subsidiary reason may well have been misunderstanding on the Continent of the November Budget, in particular the decision to raise old-age pensions. This was of course an election pledge, and had to be carried out.

As it happened, I was not very enthusiastic myself about all the November Budget proposals. Early in November, just after I had got back from Peking and Moscow, Callaghan asked me to discuss his forthcoming autumn Budget, due in a month's time. I was disturbed to discover that he proposed to introduce a Corporation Tax instead of Profits Tax, and to announce in November that he would launch it in April. I was wholly in favour of a Capital Gains Tax, but was unconvinced of the need for the upheaval of changing over from Profits Tax to Corporation Tax. I tried to persuade him to postpone the announcement. But he said he could not change now. The Government was, I feared, being influenced by a desire for at least the appearance of rapid action. The Corporation Tax was urged on Callaghan with the best of intentions in the first few weeks of the Government's life by Kaldor and Robert Neild, who had in the previous year been members of a Labour Party Advisory Committee with Douglas Houghton, Crosland and Jenkins. I had refrained from joining this Committee because I wanted to concentrate on another concerned with Development Areas. The advocates of Corporation Tax seemed to me to ignore the fact that the existing Profits Tax enabled taxation on companies to be varied anyway without varying the tax on individuals, and vice versa. I became even more sceptical when supporters of Corporation Tax, who originally criticized Profits Tax because it encouraged company saving, now began to argue that this was one object of Corporation Tax. Looking at this change in retrospect, I doubt whether enough was achieved by the changeover to justify the turmoil it caused. Gratuitious as this controversy was, however, it could not be blamed as a major cause of the sterling crisis of late November 1964, when compared with the payments deficit left to us.

After the November crisis and throughout December my time was largely devoted to bringing to birth our ambitious new export promotion package. The Board of Trade officials responsible, together with the Export Credit Guarantee Department (ECGD), and the British National Export Council created by Ted Heath, which I welcomed – all tackled this with great enthusiasm. But before the package was completed, several interludes occurred in December which were also a relief after the November crises. First, George Brown's Declaration of Intent on Pay and Price Restraint was publicly signed by the TUC and FBI. For this all credit should be given to him and the DEA – it was indeed Brown's finest hour. Next, in the second week-end of December an abbreviated Labour Party Conference was held in Brighton at which I had little to do other than attend a Cabinet meeting in the hotel, but had the chance to see my twin daughters who were in their second year at Sussex University. The Conference was a victory rally, and few worried about the fearful exchange crisis of two weeks before. John Strachey once said to me: 'All Party Conferences do harm: but some do more harm than others.' This did less than most.

Thirdly, I returned just before Christmas from an exceedingly heartening visit to my old battle-ground, the North-East Coast. Sadler-Forster, now Chairman of English Industrial Estates at Team Valley, with whom I had launched the whole policy in 1944-5, was still in charge; and I met for the first time Ronald Wood, the new Board of Trade Regional Controller in Newcastle. Both of them did an immense amount to maintain industry and employment in the North-East when the coal industry was contracting rapidly in the 1960s. Few people in their working lives can have had more satisfaction than I had in these two days in seeing the industrial estates we had launched in 1945 now hugely extended and employing thousands: for instance, Aycliffe, Hartlepool, Spennymoor, Sunderland, Jarrow and of course the greatly enlarged Team Valley. We were able to end the trip by announcing in a press conference at Hartlepool a number of new industrial expansion schemes for the North-East.

By early January 1965 we were nearly ready to publish the export promotion package, on which my Department had been working strenuously since October. But it was held up at the last minute by an attempt on George Brown's part to take it over and make it himself, or compromise by leaving it to the Prime Minister. This was an example of the conflict caused by setting up a superfluous department like the DEA. One trouble was that Brown had committed himself to a week of talks with 'industrial correspondents', and as he often had nothing much to say, this was in danger of degenerating into a source of gossip and rumour. I always intensely disliked 'demarcation disputes' and had no wish to engage in one with Brown. But the Board of Trade officials and ECGD, who had done all the work, were incensed at this sort of mishandling of the government machine; and indeed nothing discourages people more than to have all recognition of their work snatched away without a word of thanks. So to maintain their morale I had to insist on a Board of Trade announcement. The Prime Minister hesitated; and before he could make up his mind, Sir Winston Churchill fell dangerously ill. It was then thought we could not hold a press conference at such a moment. After Churchill's death it was decided to wait till the funeral was over; whereupon the Bank of England advised that it was not possible to prevent a leak on the whole package in the City. So with Wilson's approval, I made the full statement at a press conference on 26 January 1965.

We had planned the export package on the assumption that a faster rise in export volume was far the best way out of the country's economic difficulties; and we built it mainly round the ECGD and British National Export Council (BNEC). I had always regarded the ECGD as a powerful instrument in the modern economic world. The BNEC had grown from Cripp's original Dollar Export Council and the later European Export Council, and had recruited a large array of leading industrialists and City figures, backed by the FBI (later CBI), who gave their time voluntarily to export promotion. Outstanding among these were Sir William McFadzean of British Insulated Callenders Cables, Sir Alexander Glen of H. Clarkson and Shipping Industrial Holdings and Sir Derek Pritchard of Allied Breweries. One particular pleasure to me was to work again with my old war-time colleague Norman Kipping, now still Director-General of the FBI. The BNEC did revive some of the close co-operation between private industry and the Government which I had known in wartime. Formally the export package consisted of: a whole range of new export credit facilities including a cut in interest rate to $5\frac{1}{2}$ per cent for long-term export deals and much easier long-term guarantees generally; the enlargement of the BNEC to include a Commonwealth Export Council; and a new offer of 50 per cent government grants for export and import missions organized by the BNEC; government grants for British export exhibitions and 'British Weeks', all over the world; a major enlargement of this programme; government grants for export research; the strengthening of the commercial section of diplomatic posts abroad to assist British exporters; and an expert study of my plan for an export marketing company to revitalize small firms.

This was not the sort of stuff which excites lurid headings in the popular press or wild enthusiasm among MPs. But it was welcomed as a solid contribution to our real national struggle with the balance of payments, and a sensible partnership between public and private enterprise. It was the Government's most positive effort that winter to escape from the trade deficit with which we had been left; and one which I felt morally had to be made, simultaneously with the import surcharge, before falling back on devaluation. Throughout 1965 and 1966 we steadily extended the export programme, and British Weeks and export exhibitions were held all over the world, including particularly ambitious ones in Tokyo and Moscow as well as Milan, Lyons and Amsterdam. Fortunately also in January 1965 we were able to announce some much improved export figures: not to be attributed, as I explained, except in very small degree to new promotion efforts since October; but showing nevertheless what was possible. Contrary to mild discouragement from Board of Trade officials, I coupled a public congratulation to British industry with the figures.

It was something of a relief in the early weeks of 1965, after excessive overseas travels before Christmas, to settle down to my real ministerial job in the Department and in the House. The sheer work load on a senior minister, I found, had become even greater by 1965 than in 1944-51. A few senior ministers, including the Chancellor, Foreign Secretary, Minister of Defence and President of the Board of Trade, had not merely a large number of meetings to get through in the day, but an enormous volume of paper work at night. This was largely because 'co-ordination', which was sadly lacking between departments in the early years of the war, and had been carried to a fine art in about the 1944-50 period, had been seriously overdone by the 1960s. What took three hours to decide in 1944, and three days in 1950, too often took three months in 1965. There was always one more committee to placate. My ordinary working day started in the Department or Cabinet Office or No. 10 at 9.30 or 10 a.m. (Cabinet meetings filled almost every Monday and Thursday morning), and continued in the House and Department till about 8 p.m. Then at about 10 p.m. two or three Red Boxes were landed on me which usually took me, either at home or in the House (except on Saturday and Sunday nights), till 2 or 3 a.m. to finish. The quickest way was to work in bed at home from 10 p.m. onwards. By this means every decision wanted by the Department at the end of the day was delivered to them next morning in writing when they go tto the office.

I was well aware that it is always good advice to delegate, and I had excellent junior Ministers: Roy Mason, George Darling and Ted Redhead. But in practice I was always faced with the dilemma at, say, 1 a.m. that if I gave ten minutes to a problem, I could probably save at least forty-eight hours in achieving a decision. To hesitate was to stop the whole vast machine. Secondly though in theory high policy should be decided at the top, and particular applications delegated, in politics the things which arouse passion are very often not the general but the particular: the closure of this factory, or the protest of this MP. So despite the hour I often felt conscientiously bound to do it myself. I seldom found it hard to make up my mind; but when in doubt liked to meet the main protagonists in the debate and argue it out. Long continuation of these hours left me, I found, physically strained, but not physically or mentally over-tired. Sometimes for the first time in my life it was hard to stay awake in the afternoon and evening in the House. But only once in three years did I fall asleep at 2 a.m. with the light switched on and official papers spread around me.

In February and March 1965 the Government was recovering from the fearful shock of Gordon-Walker's defeat by 200 votes in a 'safe Labour seat' at Leyton. This was a tragic piece of ill-luck for Gordon-Walker, since it nearly ended his public career, and only the exploitation of the race issue at Smethwick had forced him into Leyton. Though Wilson neatly reacted by making Michael Stewart Foreign Secretary and Tony Crosland Secretary of State for Education, some of my senior colleagues, including Wilson, were behind the scenes seriously perturbed, and there was talk of another early general election or even a change of economic policy. This never seemed to me sense. It was far wiser, now that we had secured the dollar loan and launched the export package, to give time for recovery to develop; and this view soon prevailed. I still had hopes at this time of reasonably harmonious relations within the Government. Indeed at this moment Callaghan and Brown seemed to have achieved a working relationship in spite of the absurdity of having two conflicting Departments. Though Brown's methods were at times already causing surprise, the rest of us hoped for the best. Once Brown arrived half an hour late for a meeting of the Government Economic Development Committee, of which he was

Chairman, and insisted on re-debating a civil aviation issue which had already been discussed and decided. Even Roy Jenkins, supposed to be a close ally of Brown, was exasperated.

I remained philosophical, therefore, if not jubilant, when Wilson ruled that Brown and not Michael Stewart as Foreign Secretary would be my partner at the next EFTA Council meeting on 23 February also at Geneva. Cynics remarked that someone else turned up when there was a concession to make, and whereas it had been left to me to defend the Government against violent attacks on a policy I did not like anyway. For we had now decided to offer a cut in the surcharge from 15 per cent to 10 per cent on 26 April, and we were authorized to disclose this to the EFTA Ministers at the same time as it was announced by Callaghan in the House of Commons. My argument had been that we should thus get the political advantage of announcing this gesture as early as February, though not incurring the cost of the extra imports till after the end of April. Unfortunately when I arrived in Geneva, I was told by my officials that there had been trouble at a press conference, and that both British and foreign journalists were ruffled. My own press officer used what I hoped were needlessly strong expressions in describing this encounter. I asked to meet aggrieved press men during the evening and calm them down. This I did as best I could, explaining that British ministers, including myself, were in the habit of using good plain English. The British journalists, however, entirely refrained this time, for patriotic reasons, from making all the trouble which they easily could have out of this incident.

That evening, before the Conference next day, another ministerial 'working dinner' was in the programme, and I naturally did not approach it with great enthusiasm. Schaffner of Switzerland and Lange of Sweden were present. At this gathering Brown, without any warning to me, put on a remarkable performance. For about two hours he kept up a Delphic monologue, interspersed with rhetorical questions about the surcharge, at the end of which he revealed – most confidentially – that with their agreement we could next day offer the cut from 15 to 10 per cent. The idea presumably was to ensure their welcome before we made the final announcement, and Brown evidently regarded the whole exhibition as a triumph of diplomatic subtlety. I did not like these histrionics myself, preferring a straight statement of what we had to say. I also feared that able and distinguished men like Schaffner and Lang might feel they were being treated as wayward children. However in the event, the news was received by EFTA with gratitude if not with enthusiasm. To give Brown his due, no visible harm was done by the theatricals, though no visible good either.

Much of March 1965 and the following weeks I spent steering our two Board of Trade Bills of this session through the Standing Committee of the House. These were the Office Development Bill, authorizing the Office Development Permits, and the Monopolies and Mergers Bill. The latter greatly strengthened the Monopolies Commission's powers, as we had promised, with the support of the Liberal Party; and also for the first time gave the Board of Trade power to stop a merger, including a newspaper merger in particular. This latter proposal sprang from an idea I had propounded off my own bat in the debate on the ICI take-over bid for Courtaulds during the previous Parliament, and it had been accepted by the Labour Party. These mornings in standing Committee – three hours, two days a week on top of everything else – were extremely laborious. Invaluable help was given in this and all Board of Trade Bills by George Darling, as Parliamentary Secretary, who was always able to take over when I was obliged to attend the Cabinet, EFTA or some other unavoidable job. George Darling seemed actually to enjoy – a remarkable taste – answering for the Government in a Standing Committee. The golden rule for a minister conducting a Bill through Parliament, I always said, is to be brief, dull and friendly. Many junior ministers do not discover this for some time. Darling understood it to perfection. On the Monopolies and Mergers Bill in Committee we had a nominal majority of fourteen to thirteen; but somehow, with some changes, it got through.

Throughout the early months of 1965 the Government was involved in various major controversies and decisions outside my departmental sphere. Wilson did valuable work in heading off the well-meant American plan for a 'multi-national' naval force, and reaching an agreement on Polaris submarines, which effectively lasted for many years, and put to sleep the smouldering conflict within the Labour Party about the British nuclear deterrent. Long and difficult arguments continued throughout the winter on the question whether to continue the Concorde and the military TSR2 plane. On Concorde, provided it was technically sound, I judged that on balance, since the project had proceeded so far already, and since termination meant breach of a Treaty at huge expense (another elaborate French contrivance), then we had better continue. On the TSR2, about which controversy raged right up to the end of March 1965, the issue seemed to me far more difficult. To cancel a major British project and buy American military planes at great cost was repellent at first sight. In this particular controversy, I found Roy Jenkins's attitude surprising and disappointing. As Minister of Aviation, his first ministerial job, he had a clear responsibility, and indeed the TSR2 was the major decision facing him in these months. I often could not discover whether Jenkins was in favour of cancellation or not. In the end the Government continued Concorde and cancelled the TSR2 (on 31 March). In the case of Concorde, I still have little doubt that we were right, in the light of the technical success in the 1970s of the London to Washington, London to New York, and London to Singapore services. It was the last time Britain was likely to hold a clear lead over the US in a major high-technology project.

On the April Budget, introducing the Capital Gains and Corporation

Taxes, which devoured so much parliamentary time and nerves that summer, I had much clearer ideas, though I kept them to myself. I still doubted whether the Corporation Tax was worth all the time and trouble. On one evening when the Finance Bill was in its Committee Stage in the full House, and I was in Wilson's room with Brown and William Armstrong, Wilson's PPS Ernest Fernyhough came in after a division to say there had been a tie at 186 all, and the Opposition were calling for the PM to appear. Wilson decided to go into the Chamber, and then – probably wisely – decided not to. A few minutes later he was asking Armstrong whether it would really matter if we gave up the Corporation Tax altogether. Curiously enough the amendment, on which the Government majority had been reduced to a tie, turned out to be one (affecting unit trusts) which the Chancellor could easily accept, and which the Board of Trade had actually been supporting within the Government.

In the first week of March 1965 I was at last able to visit the South Wales Development Area and see for myself once again how far the Industrial Estates and other projects, which I had helped to launch in 1945, had now progressed. It was on this trip that I found the full extent to which the Conservative Government in the early 1960s had let the whole Development Area effort in South Wales run down. That Government had so contracted the legal Development Area boundaries that new government factory-building and the development of estates had almost come to a stop. Not merely were the main estates still all outside the Development Area boundary; but the Steel Company of Wales (as it then was) proposed reducing its labour force by something like 5000. It also seemed inevitable that employment in coal would greatly contract in the 1960s.

As soon as I got back to London, I set about a determined push to get all the main previous South Wales Development Areas rescheduled; but still encountered stubborn opposition both from the DEA and even some of my own officials in the Board of Trade. Owing to the great success of the Development Area policy in the first ten years after the war, some officials held the view that the Welsh problem was virtually solved. They had not grasped the extent of the coming drop in the coal-mining labour force. It was not till September 1965 that I overcame all this opposition, and got the essential areas, including the four leading South Wales Estates, re-scheduled. Due to this delay, the new round of factory-building had been postponed for nearly a year, and was not completed in time for the first big releases of labour from the coal industry. During 1966, owing to this lost time, unemployment in South Wales was higher than in the North-East Coast or Scotland. For my new Industrial Development Act, which rescheduled virtually the whole of Scotland and Wales, did not become law until August 1966. If we had waited for this, the recovery in South Wales would have been delayed another twelve months. After the passing of the 1966 Act, however, and the usual time lag, the excess of unemployment in South Wales over the North-East and Scotland began to disappear.

The spring and summer of 1965, though they seemed turbulent at the time, with problems such as Vietnam, the TSR2, and the Budget nagging persistently in the background, were nevertheless, seen in retrospect, the most successful and even harmonious of this Government. There was tension between Brown and Callaghan, and curiosity about the activities of George Wigg and others at No. 10; but the Common Market controversy had not yet divided the Government. My own days and nights were so heavily loaded in these months with export promotion, the revitalizing of the Development Area policy, and pushing the Board of Trade's Bills through Parliament, and compulsory visits overseas, that I had little time or taste for general conversation with colleagues. Next overseas visit after Geneva in February was to India and Pakistan in April. I was always very conscious that ministerial visits half-way round the world cost a lot of public money, and should only be carried out if they really achieved something worthwhile. They were always exhausting and often damaging to health. But it was a plain duty to visit India and Pakistan in 1965. Our trade with both countries was still lagging far behind what past contact should have made possible; and the Indians, still very hostile to China at this point, would have been much offended if a British Trade Minister, having visited Peking at the end of 1964, did not appear in India reasonably soon afterwards.

After being stranded for three or four hours on an airport bench in Karachi in the middle of the night while the aircraft was repaired, we were restored by John Freeman's admirable hospitality in the High Commissioner's home and garden in Delhi. At a whole day's meeting with the Indian Trade Minister and business men, I was at least able to convince them that we as a Government were anxious for much greater trade. But the basic difficulty with India and Pakistan always emerges: that they are too poor to buy much from us, and that we cannot buy on a large scale the textiles they would like to sell. After a day at the Taj Mahal, which nearly fulfilled my expectations, but did not somehow for me touch quite the same chord as had St Peter's, Chartres, or Salisbury Cathedral, we flew on to Calcutta. The drive from Calcutta airport was ghastly: eighteen miles of unbroken slums and shacks, with human beings drifting around among occasional goats and cattle, and pools here and there of presumably polluted water. It was as infinitely oppressive to the spirit, as was the burning air to the body. I was not much cheered to find my bedroom even at the British Deputy High Commissioner's house barricaded with shutters and fans to keep the hot air out; and during the night, I could not get the phrase 'Black Hole of Calcutta' out of my head. Next morning I was to receive 150 guests at a cocktail party; but after half an hour could no longer stand up, and had to sit on the grass. The following day I spent miserably in bed, and escaped the day after to Karachi where it was possible to recover in a deck chair in a temperature of only about ninety.

My next overseas venture, in mid-May, was far more enjoyable: to Amsterdam with my wife for an export promotion 'British Week'. By pure chance my son Martin happened to be in Amsterdam that week on behalf of BP. I found Amsterdam as endearing as Calcutta was repellent. Certainly Amsterdam could teach London something about architecture, tidiness, cleanliness and good order. Tremendous efforts had been put into this British Week by the export promotion staff, and we all worked extremely hard at every form of publicity for British goods. Dr Luns, still Dutch Foreign Minister, excelled himself in after-dinner speeches; and Princess Margaret performed every ritual to the satisfaction of all. True the Princess's aide, Lady Elizabeth Cavendish, at dinner in the Royal Yacht, kept asking me, in the hearing of Queen Juliana, why the Government did not at once press on with the Wolfenden Report's proposals. 'What is the Wolfenden Report?' Queen Juliana asked me, and I referred her to Lady Elizabeth. It was impossible, certainly, throughout the export campaign, though we tried, to estimate statistically the value of each form of promotion. Basically I had no doubt that what mattered most was to make exporting profitable. Other things being equal, however, direct promotion must help.

In May 1965 came a much more ambitious venture; a conference in Vienna with Wilson and all the other EFTA Prime Ministers to try out the idea of some sort of 'bridge-building' association between EFTA and the EEC. The surcharge controversy was now quiescent, and Wilson, under pressure from propaganda about 'European unity', conceived the idea of some sort of looser association involving freer trade between 'the Six', and 'the Seven'. This was of course the right solution economically, and because right economically would have imposed no lasting political strains, and would have been beneficial to Britain. I had always been a strong supporter of this solution, and of closer association and freer trade in Western Europe, short of sacrifice of the political independence of the UK or the abandonment of our traditional policy of free import of food and materials. No practical or technical objection existed whatever to a solution by which industrial free trade could prevail between all EFTA and EEC countries, but in which each member of the EFTA group would retain its own appropriate agricultural and food policies and the same political independence as a member of the OECD or NATO. Indeed this was precisely the solution which was adopted by all the EFTA countries except the UK and Denmark after those two joined the EEC. All this Wilson well understood; and his conversation with me on the Trident on the way to Vienna on Sunday 23 May 1965, implied that this was his settled objective. He even remarked that he had taken care to preserve an anti-Market majority in the Cabinet. The most natural and logical form of 'bridge-building', and one of which Wilson often spoke at this time would have been for the EEC Six to have joined EFTA as one member. This alternative was then known as the 'Munchmeyer Plan'.

L

Though basically this was the right solution, I was deeply sceptical on our way to Vienna whether the Brussels fraternity would have the honesty to accept it. If they genuinely wished for the maximum political harmony in Western Europe, and if the French were genuinely not intent on weakening the 'Anglo-Saxons', they would accept it enthusiastically. Germany, Holland, Belgium and Italy would on their own, I believe, have done so. If on the other hand the Brussels ideologues really cared not about unity, but about federation, and if the French had other aims, they would refuse. In this sense the bridge-building venture was a test. Whether Wilson really believed the offer would be accepted, I could not guess. Certainly hard-headed EFTA ministers like Schaffner, Lange and Kreisky understood the Brussels mentality only too well, and expressed privately their belief that the offer would be refused or at least obstructed. They wanted to 'strengthen EFTA', but they saw no harm in the offer being unitedly made, if only to test the sincerity of the EEC. There was accordingly complete harmony among the EFTA prime ministers, and no opposition to Wilson's initiative. As a result of the Vienna meeting (24 May 1965), a final invitation was sent after the next EFTA meeting at Copenhagen on behalf of seven Western European Governments to the EEC to work out a closer association on these lines.[12] In the event not merely was it not accepted. No reply was ever received. Here is a crucial chapter in the history of the EEC which should never be forgotten.

By June of 1965 signs were growing clearer that the UK balance of payments was still in trouble, and that more action would be necessary. Before these came to a head, I had the far more rewarding interlude of several more days on the North-East Coast, checking up with our officials on all the industrial schemes coming forward. On this visit I opened on 18 June the major new Teesside Industrial Estate, which soon proved a marked success. But as governments learnt so often and painfully in the post-war world, it was easier to build new factories than to prevent outflows of gold and speculation against sterling. By the summer of 1965 I had become convinced that we were maintaining so strong a flow of demand at home that exports were being held back and imports excessively encouraged. Unemployment was down to 1.2 per cent. No sensible expansionist and advocate of full employment has ever denied that there must be some level of money demand which is excessive, which will force up prices and upset the trade balance by swelling imports and checking exports. Unfortunately, this simple piece of economic sense was somewhat at a discount in 1965, partly because of the natural human impulse to pair off into two sides – 'left' and 'right', 'expansionists' and 'deflationists' etc. – and partly because the DEA had come to regard itself as the professional expansionist against a deflationist Treasury. George Brown saw himself in this picture-esque light, and appeared to be in favour of more expansion in any

[12] The communiqué following the Vienna agreement is set out in Wilson, p. 106.

circumstances. Another illusion bemused the minds of the non-economist ministers in the Government in this period: the belief that something exists called 'planning' which is distinct from physical planning on the one hand, and economic policy on the other, but which, if only you could hit on it, would overcome all tiresome difficulties. This illusion stalks for instance through Crossman's diaries, which imply that somehow if only Brown would quickly devise a plan, all the troublesome dilemmas presented by the Treasury would fade away. But unhappily there is no such animal.

In the last few days of May 1965 and the first few days of June up to 3 June, when Bank Rate was reduced from 7 to 6 per cent, Wilson had the idea of simultaneously reducing Bank Rate and moderately tightening hire-purchase restrictions. The purpose of this was to ease the credit squeeze in force since November, but at the same time curb any further rise in consumer spending and imports. It was a sensible if not very dramatic plan, and Callaghan as Chancellor supported it. But Brown opposed it with great vehemence. One evening at this time Wilson very reasonably gathered at No. 10 for a general talk with himself Callaghan, Brown, myself, and the three Permanent Secretaries, William Armstrong, Eric Roll and Richard Powell. The meeting lasted till after midnight, largely because Brown marched up and down the room in eloquent dissent, and finally remarked that the scene would not look well in either his or Wilson's memoirs. I could not fathom the motive for this demonstration, at what should have been a careful assessment of just what measures were needed. In the end, Wilson's proposals were agreed; the Cabinet confirmed them; and they were generally well received.

By early July, however, it was clear that more had to be done. Reserves were again being lost and the pound was falling. Home demand was excessive, and exports being held back. We also had to face a lower import surcharge from October. Denis Rickett spoke to me in this sense, after one meeting, saying he devoutly hoped something would be done. I already agreed with him, but was anxious that action should be moderate and selective – not a blind deflationary swing. This was the origin of the July 1965 measures of restraint; which were intelligently prepared, skilfully carried out, and successful in correcting the trade balance without markedly increasing unemployment. They were indeed the most successful act of economic policy in the whole of this Government's life. The reason for their success was simply that they were rationally prepared by the small group of ministers most concerned, together with their senior officials, and that Brown on this occasion finally co-operated with his colleagues. Those concerned were Wilson, Callaghan, Brown, myself and the four corresponding chief officials. We met five or six times at No. 10 from Sunday 11 July, to Sunday 18 July 1965. This was the nearest approach I knew in the Wilson Government to the smooth and effective method of reaching decisions which prevailed under Attlee and Cripps. The resulting

July 1965 package mainly consisted of the postponement of a number of public investment schemes, with complete exemption for projects in Development Areas and for house-building, schools, hospitals, and factories everywhere. Building licences were introduced for other schemes, and IDC's and HP restrictions tightened. Another big ECGD concession was made to help exports. I had argued strongly from the beginning for exemption of Development Areas, housing and industrial buildings. The package was announced by Callaghan in the House on 27 July, and coincided with the Conservative crisis over the selection of a leader in succession to Alec Douglas-Home.

A short time after Heath's totally unexpected election as Tory Leader in preference to Maudling had been announced on 28 July, I met Maudling in the House, and quite candidly expressed my regret, adding that I was much surprised. 'So was I,' he also candidly replied. Maudling always struck me in the 1950s as far the best economic debater on the Tory side, and indeed far the best economic mind, together with Gaitskell, in the House of Commons in the thiry years I was a Member. He was no fanatic on the Common Market or anything else. He was as subtle and sensitive to economic realities as Heath was often wooden and doctrinaire. He understood the crucial value to this country of EFTA and of free imports of food and raw materials. Had he become Tory leader, I do not believe the country would ever have joined the EEC so hastily, and therefore on such damaging terms. But by only seventeen votes Heath won. This must have been a cruel shock to Maudling, and in later years, I came to feel, he never fully recovered his self-confidence or strength of purpose. His early death in 1979 was a sharp loss to Parliament as well as a personal tragedy.

On 11 August, only a fortnight after Callaghan's July statement, I was at last able to announce some all-time record export figures. These were of course in no way due to the July measures. But the sustained recovery in the trade balance in the second half of 1965 showed that those measures did enable the export campaign and import surcharge to take effect. This success is best measured by the figures of import and export volume for the whole years 1963, 1964 and 1965:[13]

Volume (1961 = 100)

	1963	1964	1965
Imports	107	119	120
Exports	108	111	117

During 1965 the volume of exports was markedly increased and the volume of imports hardly at all. As a result the current balance of payments deficit was eventually cut from £375 millions in 1964 to only £45 millions in 1965. To achieve this, and hold unemployment below 2 per cent at the

[13] *Annual Abstract of Statistics*, 1970.

same time, gave one even then some sober satisfaction; but by the standards of the 1970s it was almost miraculous. For me, therefore, the working year ended unexpectedly pleasantly with a visit to Oxford a few days after the publication of the trade figures, a dinner at New College, speeches on the export record, and an evening with William and Iris Hayter in the Warden's lodgings. Next day, I drove to Southampton and with Richard Powell toured the Board of Trade shipping establishments there and at Calshot Castle before spending the night at Winchester on the way to join the family in Cornwall for three weeks.

Back at work in September my first and welcome job was again to visit the South Wales Development Area and announce the re-scheduling of much wider areas. I had now, after nine months' argument, overcome the DEA resistance, and got it agreed that as a first instalment we should reschedule the crucial areas including the main industrial estates, and then as the second round, as soon as the new Industrial Development Bill were enacted, reschedule even more widely – as it turned out most of Wales. This was very good news for Wales, and it was just in time to avoid disastrous unemployment. On this trip I opened a new municipal industrial estate at Merthyr – welcome local enterprise – and gave the signal for a major new factory-building programme at Treforest, Bridgend, Hirwaun, and Swansea, now all brought again within the Development Area.

On 12 September, Wilson organized an all-day meeting of ministers at Chequers, at which we were to review the whole situation, sit back and think, etc. This is certainly a very necessary exercise. The only trouble is that events not wholly foreseen in the grand strategic plan tend to arise within a few weeks and knock you over. However, in this case legislative projects were at least pushed forward, particularly the Industrial Development Bill about which I cared most, as well as my Companies Bill and Trades Descriptions Bill. All these were to be included in the Queen's Speech. But the centrepiece of 'strategic planning' at this moment was George Brown's 'National Plan'. It was a noble effort, and professionally most competently prepared by Sir Donald McDougall, an Oxford economist then working in the DEA. Its defect was the assumption described earlier here that one could put into effect a paper plan which evaded the necessity for the country to balance its overseas accounts and presumed that there would be no major strikes. The 1948 Cripps Plan succeeded because we retained the power to control the level of our imports, as well as many other controls. The Brown Plan of 1965 collapsed in face of reality because we had failed to re-introduce quotas on manufactured imports in 1964 and were forced by the illegality of the surcharge to withdraw the latter in 1966. However, the Plan was published with all due solemnity on 13 September 1965. But Brown's opposition to import quotas in October 1964 had in fact predoomed his own well-meant Plan to early death.

The crowded six months from September 1965 to March 1966 were still a pleasantly constructive period in this Government's life; as the Common Market issue had not yet been dragged in to cause conflict. My first export enterprise in this period was a full-scale British industrial exhibition in Tokyo for which I left by air on 14 September. Exhausting as are these trips, they occasionally yield precious moments. We flew in the September evening over the Arctic to our first stop at Anchorage in Alaska; and the Northern tip of Greenland, which I had somehow expected to be grey, cloudy and blurred, in fact shone brilliant in sunset colours. Huge snow ranges, glaciers, frozen fjords and black rock cliffs thousands of feet high were sharply visible in the clear light; and it was strange to think that no human eye had ever seen this unworldly spectacle from this angle in any previous age. In Tokyo itself the opening of the exhibition and trade talks with the Japanese ministers swallowed up most of a strenuous week. Nearly half a million people visited the Exhibition itself, and the Rolls-Royce was usually drawing much the biggest crows. The whole display was nearly ruined by a typhoon which threatened, and then moved off at the last moment. I woke up in the night and felt the whole Embassy shake in what I took to be the typhoon; but was told in the morning it was a minor earth-quake. Observation of the Tokyo scene, meanwhile, with the naked eye strengthened my scepticism about international comparisons of real incomes. The statisticians might prove that Japanese real incomes per head approached the Western standards; but housing conditions in Tokyo would certainly not have been tolerated by any section of the British public.

Back from Tokyo, I was able to attend a ministerial meeting on 23 September to settle finally the Queen's Speech and legislative programme. My main interest in the Queen's Speech was to press on with the Industrial Development Bill, now bogged down in a controversy within the Government over the plan to give 'investment grants' to induce industry generally to invest.

Despite these delays, however, I did manage in the few days between these London meetings and the Blackpool Labour Conference, to visit Dundee, Edinburgh and Glasgow and review factory building progress with the authorities there. National Cash Registers at Dundee asked for another advance factory and we clinched this immediately. Dundee, previously a jute city, had been a special care of mine ever since Ministry of Supply days when we had poured munitions work into the area. In the first Development Area expansion in 1945–6, National Cash Register had started up on the new estate there, and by September 1965, was employing 4000. NCR were a spectacular example of the great American firms which seized on the facilities offered by our Development Area policy after 1945, and generated employment of many tens of thousands particularly in Scotland thereafter. Honeywell, Caterpillar and IBM were others. So far from the 'multi-nationals' having damaged the British economy, they in fact saved Scotland from near industrial collapse in the post-war world. Had these firms not been steered by London to Scotland, much of Scotland would have been industrially destitute in the thirty years after 1945. The Scottish Nationalist myth that London rule deprived Scotland of employment is precisely the reverse of the truth. For remarkably few purely Scottish arms expanded substantially in these years, and many (e.g. North British Locomotive and Fairfields) collapsed.

After this Scottish week I drove, as an act of piety, to the Blackpool Party Conference, where I happily had nothing to do, and so seized on the chance to confer in Liverpool with the Corporation about persistent delays in getting new ventures started on Merseyside. In 1945 the Liverpool Corporation had insisted on managing the Kirkby Royal Ordnance Factory (which I then wanted to develop in the same way as Aycliffe and Bridgend) as their own industrial estate; but after several years' delays they handed it over to the Board of Trade. In 1964-5, there were greater delays in starting the Merseyside share of our November 1964 advance factory programme than in any other area. I hoped that if the President of the Board of Trade, as the senior Minister responsible, drove over for a day to meet the Corporation in Liverpool, with the chief Board of Trade officials, the Corporation might respond, and more progress be made at last. Our enthusiasms for helping Merseyside to help itself was this time not encouraged by our being kept waiting for nearly half an hour in a side office by the Leader of the Council and Town Clerk; but in the end we persuaded them to sell us the only available site. Later in the year other Lancashire authorities intervened and caused further delays.

Next move in the export campaign was a full-scale 'British Week' in Milan that autumn, with massed British goods in the shops, and cultural activities and general publicity to coincide. For me it proved an unexpectedly romantic interlude. Composing very late at night a few days before a speech for the opening ceremony, I thought I might risk mentioning the impact of the Italian Renaissance on the English Elizabethan age, and since Verona is not too far from Milan, the influence on Shakespeare at the time *Romeo and Juliet* was written, of the Italian scholar, Signor Florio, who was then living in Lord Southampton's household. Checking my reference to *Romeo and Juliet* set me reading long passages, and I flew to Milan with line after line running in my head. After my speech, an Italian dignitary remarked to me: 'That was a very apt reference to *Romeo and Juliet*'; and when I asked why, remarked: 'because we are going to a full performance at the Scala this evening, with Margot Fonteyn and Nureyev, of the ballet *Romeo and Juliet*.' The lines still ran in my head; and the performance, before what seemed like all the youth and beauty of Milan, was superb, worthy of Shakespeare, and the most marvellous unison of drama, dancing poetry, music and colour I have ever witnessed. I was wholly converted to this method of displaying British achievements. And the week more prosaically turned out, in addition, a proved export success.

Immediately after this venture, I had to face up, as I had long known I must, to the troubles of the British textile industry, always a thorn in the side of the Board of Trade. A long weekend visit both to Bradford for wool and Harrogate for a cotton conference was next in the October programme. To any honest President of the Board of Trade the problem of textile imports must present an acute moral dilemma. On the one hand the poorer countries of the world cannot develop unless the richer buy goods like textiles which the former can produce, and Britain has a special obligation to Commonwealth countries such as India, Bangladesh and Hong Kong. On the other hand textile spinning and weaving employment is, or was, very heavily concentrated geographically in the UK in East Lancashire and the West Riding of Yorkshire. It was also unfair that the UK should bear the whole burden while countries like France excluded Asian textiles almost entirely. My difficulties had been made greater by George Brown's tendency before the 1964 election to promise the textile unions that a Labour Government would give to the industry itself power to control imports. With some effort I had got the wording of this pledge watered down; but an ambiguous impression was created. My basic solution was to limit cheap imports to a very gradual growth, to encourage the creation at home of a modern multi-fibre industry, and to press through the GATT so-called 'generalized preferences scheme' (an idea of Ted Heath's which I heartily supported) for larger textile imports into the Continental advanced countries. This solution was in the end adopted, with fair success, and as a step towards it in 1965–6 I introduced the first 'global quota' on virtually all textile imports from low-cost countries.

In October 1965, however, we were still seeking to formulate these policies in consultation with the employers and unions in the industry. At Bradford the wool men's grievances fortunately concentrated on the export rebate the government was then paying, and which was not helping the wool industry as much as was intended. I was able to get this put right fairly quickly. Harrogate was more formidable, with the most celebrated textile magnates mobilized: Frank Kearton of Courtaulds, Joe Hyman of Viyella, and Billy Winterbottom an old cotton stalwart of the Lancashire Cotton Corporation, now on the Courtaulds Board. At dinner I found myself between Kearton and Hyman, neither of whom I had met before. I was much impressed and highly entertained. With the benefit of their ideas, and the equally valuable help of Ord-Johnstone, the Board of Trade official responsible, I composed only that evening a speech explaining what we hoped to do, and in it mentioned the 'global quota'. To my considerable surprise, it was most amicably received. Billy Winterbottom even rose to say it was the most positive help the textile industry had had from the Board of Trade for a very long time. A few days later, Tony Barber, who was then the official Tory Front Bench critic of the Board of Trade, told me candidly that he saw my speech had gone down well, 'much too well from my point of view'. Barber I always found, whatever one thought of his policies, a generous, and indeed personally friendly, colleague and antagonist in the House.

In the last few days of October the next regular EFTA Conference of Ministers was held at Copenhagen. This time my companion was not George Brown but Michael Stewart, now Foreign Secretary, who could be relied on to stay coldly rational; so that no trouble need be feared. All went well. We reached sensible compromises on such issues as export rebates and 'drawback', and the tranquillity was only ruffled by a new Norwegian Minister, Mr Willoch, who at first felt it his job to say 'no' to everything. The ever-witty Hans Schaffner of Switzerland called him 'Mr Will-Not'. This was the EFTA Conference which sent the formal invitation on behalf of seven countries to the EEC for a 'bridge-building' experiment, which was never even answered.

By 8 November the Board of Trade's export promotion plan had reached a stage when I was able to hold another press conference and announce Package No. 2 of new measures, including still better credit facilities (the ECGD remained a strong card) grants for joint market research, advertising and so forth. Lord (Wilfred) Brown had by this time joined us as Minister of State for exports. With his long business experience, he was most valuable in export promotion; even though Wilson had the odd habit of shuffling junior ministers about without consulting the senior ministers concerned. I could not help noting that despite all these solid efforts, unexplained press criticism of the Board of Trade continued. I had not brought myself at this stage to believe that other ministers in the Government could be collaborating with the press in criticizing their fellows. I had some idea of inviting a previous colleague such as Clem Leslie or John Harris to join us on press work; but after a discussion with a press officer on the plane on the flight back from Tokyo, and with Richard Powell thereafter, we decided to give the job to an existing Board of Trade official who was popular with the press. My whole inclination was to believe that one should concentrate on the job, and let the results speak for themselves.

A fortnight after the Copenhagen Conference, the impossible Mr Ian Smith declared his UDI in Rhodesia. Wilson had made laudable and strenuous efforts over a long period to restrain him. But the Cabinet was now presented with the unsought but inescapable dilemma: what should the British Government do? There were really only three possible courses: first to embark on a military expedition against a rebel Government; secondly to organize economic sanctions with UN authority; and thirdly to do nothing. No military advice available to the Cabinet offered any hope that military action would succeed at all quickly. The lines of communication were too long, and our forces were too strained. The danger of getting involved in a Vietnam type of war was not inviting; though some African countries demanded the use of force – by us. Unfortunately if you run down your defences and bases too far, you cannot enforce your admirable political policies. This time, however, complete inaction in response to direct defiance of the law, and in face of African and home opinion, was judged to be impossible; and the second recourse of economic sanctions was therefore adopted. The Government immediately took the dispute to the UN Security Council. I believed at this time that this was the right decision, even though I had little hope that sanctions would end this wretched dispute at all quickly. The settlement of 1979–80 seems to me to have justified the 1965 decision. Very little disagreement showed itself in the Cabinet at the time.

My next assignment was the OECD[14] in Paris with Jim Callaghan and Tony Crosland, in late November. The OECD was by now a far more formal, if still useful, organization than in its first creative OEEC phase in 1948–50. Our main aim was to push forward the generalized preference scheme by which all the richer countries would admit more exports from the poorer. It looked to me in Paris as if it would be strangled by French legalism, though in the end it survived. M. Wormser, the notorious French negotiator in the original Heath negotiations with the EEC, was busy in a sub-Committee spinning and weaving words around the infant project. We were also addressed in full session by M. Couve de Murville, then Foreign Minister, a chilling experience. A grey man, intoning even greyer words, he left one feeling that this was to him a tiresome demagogic chore made necessary by an impending French election. Far more engaging was the young Giscard d'Estaing, then French Finance Minister, who approached me on the steps outside whatever palace we were occupying, and asked searching questions in perfect English about our British economic policies. Had not we gone too far in raising the old-age pension so quickly? Was the Budget really balanced? I pointed out that we had also raised taxation; and he looked a little shocked – taxing the rich! Giscard was clearly a highly cultured, genuinely liberal-minded man, on close telephone terms incidentally with Callaghan, as I knew from the latter; and he understood my feelings about the French system of taxing the poor by indirect taxes as well as I understood his feelings about our preference for direct taxes. He reminded me curiously of Christopher Hinton – tall, wiry, intellectual, high-principled and sardonic, and in Giscard's case, it seemed, willing to wound the plutocratic establishment, but still afraid to strike a blow. I got the impression that he was both interested and attracted by British social ideas but feared they would never survive in France.

In December 1965 one genuine, if not spectacular, constructive effort of the Wilson Government was safely brought to fruition. We signed a

[14] Organization for Economic Co-operation and Development, successor to the Organization for European Economic Cooperation formed to administer Marshall Aid in 1945.

free-trade area agreement with Eire. I was always enthusiastic about this venture, as the erection of a tariff barrier between North and South Ireland had long seemed to me one of the more grotesque economic follies (before the Common Agricultural Policy was invented) of the present century. Officials in 1965 had been working on the free-trade-area plan for months, and the Eire Prime Minister, Mr Lemass, came to London in December to reach and sign a formal agreement. For national honour's sake Fred Peart, Arthur Bottomley and I held a final haggling session at Lancaster House, which was expected to last till the small hours, though everyone knew we should reach a compromise at some hour – and one leaning towards the Irish, as always in Anglo-Irish negotiations. Suddenly just before midnight Harold Wilson arrived. His account of this night[15] records his arrival at a moment of 'crisis'; which was broken by Lemass and himself adjourning and a last-minute British concesssion on lamb. My own record, written shortly afterwards, was only slightly different:

H. W. arrived just before midnight and turned the proceedings into something of a Dutch auction, with the two delegations periodically dropping into different rooms. We settled about 2 in the morning with much good will and good humour. I read stories later in the press how Wilson had heroically arrived and saved the negotiations from breakdown.

However, Wilson's statement that 'good sense, good will and lamb quota and thirst' finally produced agreement fully accords with my memory. We ceremoniously signed the Anglo-Irish Free Trade Area Agreement at No. 10 next day, 14 December. When putting my signature to it, I was fascinated to find that the previous Anglo-Irish Trade Agreement had been signed in 1938 by Lemass (as Trade Minister) for the Irish and Neville Chamberlain for the British. To have extinguished the tariff barrier across Ireland in 1965 was a genuine if minor achievement.

Even in these months family life went on, though with a normal working day from 9.30 a.m. till 2 a.m. or 3 a.m. next morning, I did not see a great deal of it. In early December after a short illness my mother died, three months short of her ninetieth birthday, and ten weeks after the birth of her first great-grandchild, Peter's daughter, Tamsin. My mother retained her deep religious convictions and Christian standards throughout her life, and lovingly collected all records of her children's and grandchildren's fortunes. Her fidelity to her own principles will long be remembered by her children and grandchildren. When nearly ninety she told me she had first voted Labour at the age of seventy-five, and that what persuaded her was listening to the conversation of Conservative ladies in Hampstead. She had always been an ardent devotee of Christmas as a family festival, and Christmas 1965 was, after sixty years, our first without her. We spent the afternoon of Boxing Day that year with the Callaghans and Peter and

15 Wilson, p. 185.

Margaret at No. 11 Downing Street.

A few days after Christmas, I celebrated the return to work of Mary Thomas of my private office, who had been hurt in a motor accident, by asking her to lunch. She had done a great deal to smooth the wheels of office life in the previous fifteen months, for which I felt much gratitude. As soon as the Christmas break was over, the conflict over Investment Grants and my Industrial Development Bill heated up to a final crisis. I was exasperated by this time at the intolerable delay to a Development Area Bill by the stupid wrangling over Investment Grants. I discovered one day when lunching with Jack Diamond and Douglas Houghton in the House that we were all three privately opposed to the proposed grants and thought the 'Free Depreciation' favoured by industry and preferred by the Treasury and Inland Revenue would be much better – plus of ' course outright grants in Development Areas. We then found that Callaghan sympathized with us. As it was my Bill, I wrote a Minute to the PM suggesting a revision of the whole scheme. The PM called a meeting at No. 10 including Callaghan and myself. Only George Brown whole-heartedly supported Investment Grants. It was decided to refer the dilemma back for the last time to a working group of officials who were given ten days to report. Meanwhile Callaghan and I examined the arguments again with William Armstrong, now heading the Treasury, David Serpell of the Board of Trade, a highly intelligent official (who incidentally shared my enthusiasm for Dartmoor) and Alec Johnston, now Chairman of the Inland Revenue. Opinion at this talk seemed to be moving clearly in favour of Free Depreciation. But ten days later the officials – I never quite new why – came down in favour of Investment Grants at a resumed meeting at No. 10 in January, and it was decided to go ahead. By this time, after a year's argument, I hardly cared, as long as we could move forward with the Bill and with the new Development Area powers. At least the Investment Grant was to be 40 per cent in Development Areas and 20 per cent elsewhere. We announced these plans with a White paper and press conference on 17 January 1966. Here is another lesson for those who want Parliament to spend even more months minutely examining Government Bills. The wonder is in many cases that they ever get intro-duced into Parliament at all. Ironically in this particular case after the next two Governments had deliberated yet again, policy settled down in the end to Investment Grants in Development Areas and Free Depreciation outside. Later experience convinced me that Investment Grants had proved more valuable than I expected.

One of the 'spin-offs' from the controversy over Investment Grants was the formation of the Industrial Re-Organization Corporation, announced a little later and headed by Frank Kearton. Following on my sugges-tion in my book *Socialism and the New Society* in 1962 that the modern method of public ownership and industrial finance was to set up a National

Finance Corporation, I launched this idea at one of the No. 10 talks on Investment Grants. It was remitted to the Departments, and was somewhat mauled in the DEA and Ministry of Technology into a corporation mainly to be engaged in promoting mergers. This was not what I intended, and I do not believe that all the mergers (e.g. British Leyland) promoted were justified by greater efficiency. However, after the whirligig of time and fashion, and the abolition of the IRC by the Heath Government, the Labour Government of 1974 adopted what was essentially my idea in the National Enterprise Board: which was to invest in industry, own shares, provide capital, and build up what would in effect be a public holding company. So finally after sixteen years most of us came round to the modernized idea of public ownership which I had propounded in *Forward* in 1959.[16] What was then denounced in the Labour Party as wildly reactionary, had now become accepted orthodoxy; and the process was consummated when in 1978 (after nineteen years), Norman Atkinson, MP, Treasurer of the Labour Party, and regarded as a 'left-wing' spokesman, used these words:[17]

steel, shipbuilding and aerospace were probably the last manufacturing industries any Labour Government would want to take over in the form of a single-produce, single-management structure. The future prime industrial and commercial candidates for public ownership do not lend themselves to that sort of organization. The whole Labour Movement should now carefully re-examine its current thinking in regard to managerial concepts. Straight orthodox nationalization should be replaced by forward-looking systems of co-operative self-management.

This basically was what I argued in the *Forward* article nineteen years earlier. The National Enterprise Board is, I believe, the better solution, because it meets a need, avoids compulsion, and operates entirely with willing partners.

Another remarkable incident at this time, which also illustrated the necessity in modern conditions for an authority like the NEB, was the sudden collapse of Fairfields, the Clydeside shipbuilders. One Tuesday morning at the end of 1965, the Chairman and Managing Director of Fairfields, one of the oldest and best-known shipbuilding firms in the country, called on me to report that they were financially unable to pay wages after Friday of the same week. Unless the Board of Trade, which was the sponsoring department for shipbuilding, put up approximately £1 million within a week, the whole firm would have to close down. Already since 1964 Roy Mason for the Board of Trade had produced a thorough report on the shipbuilding industry, and we had set up a Shipbuilding Industry Board and provided finance to strengthen the industry. I naturally asked when the Fairfields Board had discovered the facts they reported, and was told that they were not aware of it until a day or two before. I often

---

[16] See page 272.
[17] *The Times*, 30 May 1978.

recalled this interview when I heard in later months and years denunciations of Labour Governments for 'interfering' in private enterprise.

At the time, I told my officials that we could not allow a major Clydeside shipyard to collapse, and some rescue plan must be devised. In the event we found the money within a few days. The yard was saved; and we avoided the dismissal into unemployment of several thousand men on Clydeside. I was surprised, however, to learn from the Board of Trade legal advisers that we could spend the £1 million without prior parliamentary authority, according to the doctrine that the Crown could do anything which it was not specifically precluded from doing by Parliament, provided it legitimized it afterwards. At this point, in the effort to preserve the yard, George Brown joined in. His idea of inviting Iain Stewart, a progressive Scottish industrialist, to be chairman, with a new constitution for the company and full employee participation, was a happy one. So we reached a firm decision in January 1966, and the yard – 'Govan Yard' – survived through the vicissitudes of Upper Clyde Shipbuilders to become part eventually of the publicly owned shipbuilding industry – and then be threatened with closure once again by the Conservative Government of 1979.

By January 1966 active if informal talks were being held among senior ministers about launching a general election in March or May. In November I had noticed signs that Wilson and Callaghan were contemplating holding one in December. It seemed to me that the country would not want another upheaval only fourteen months after October 1964. For once I wrote a considered non-departmental minute to the PM advising against December. I argued that if the public resented an unnecessary election they might vote against us and concluded thus: 'The country, I believe, having elected a Parliament, normally expects that Parliament to carry on and develop its policies without provoking the disturbance of another election.'

Wilson, rightly decided against the December election. But by January I got the impression that he and Callaghan were disposed towards a March election on the ground that we really could not go on much longer, and in particular face the spring Budget exercise, with a majority of three. I no longer by the spring felt clearly opposed; and as it happened, Wilson announced the election on 28 February for polling on 31 March. His guess turned out right, as the overall majority rose to ninety-seven. The Government had a fair record. It had both cut down the balance of payments deficit and preserved full employment. Experience of 1964–6 and of 1974 suggests that the electorate is sympathetic to a Government with a tiny majority which asks for support after a reasonable time.

Early in February, to my great surprise, having been gifted for most of my life with exceptional good health, I fell ill. I first noticed symptoms at a week-end discussion on general policy at Chequers on 6 February between the Cabinet and the Labour Party National Executive Committee. At this incidentally I first met and was much impressed by Jack Jones of the

TGWU, who asked penetrating questions about the export drive. Being determined to make the opening speech a few days later in the final debate on the Investment Grants White Paper and coming Industrial Development Bill, I kept working; but arranged to retire to bed in the middle of the debate, leaving the ever-competent George Darling to wind up. I wrote a note to Tony Barber, the main Opposition speaker explaining this, and he responded with both a cordial note and a friendly explanation of my absence in his own speech. For me it was a strange interlude; after two years' intense activity, now resting in bed, with a telephone and red boxes beside me, plenty of flowers, and constant visitors ranging from Shiela Sokolov-Grant, faithful since Oxford days, to Mary Thomas of my private office. The truth was that eighteen months of almost uninterrupted work, and repeated overseas travels and jet ordeals, had taken their toll, and I needed two quiet weeks to regain strength. While I was recuperating, George Darling also moved the Second Reading of our Companies Bill, which was now moving forward after a long trial in Whitehall.

Back in good health for the election, and convinced that we had chosen the right moment and would win, I resolved firmly not to wear myself to the bone as in the 1950s and 1964. So I limited my expeditions round the country to a few (including one in Lancashire to proclaim our 'global quota' on textile imports); and kept my street appearances in Battersea within reason, and my other speeches to neighbouring constituencies. The most memorable event in this election was Harold Wilson's speech at Bristol on 18 March on the Common Market. He denounced in the strongest language the proposal to join the Common Market on terms involving acceptance of the Rome Treaty and Common Agricultural Policy: 'Nothing could be worse,' he said, 'if vital British and Commonwealth interests are to be safeguarded, than to enter these negotiations, as we did before, cap in hand, and if we were to state, as our opponents now state, that we shall accept whatever conditions are offered to us. . . . We shall go in if the conditions are right. And those conditions require that we must be free to go on buying food, and raw materials, as we have for a hundred years, in the cheapest markets in Canada, Australia, New Zealand and other Commonwealth countries – and not have this trade wrecked by the levies the Tories are so keen to impose. . . . We reject any idea of supra-national control over Britain's foreign and defence policies.'

I was frankly overjoyed when I read these words. I thought it inconceivable that even Wilson could go back on such categorical pledges, at least for two or three years, though he had characteristically included some weasel words about 'going in if the conditions are right'. In his book Wilson records the latter words but not those quoted in my previous paragraph.[18] If this country was to be 'free to go on buying food and raw materials, as

[18] Wilson p. 218.

we have for a hundred years, in the cheapest markets', and if we rejected 'supra-national control of political policies, I should have felt very differently about our joining the Common Market. It seemed for a moment as though the whole horrid threat of the Government's being split over the Market, and myself forced into unwelcome conflict with close colleagues, had now been avoided. On the same day, as I had to make an election speech, I drafted one, in almost identical words with Wilson's, and had a full 'advance' prepared. At this moment a message arrived from No. 10 saying that Wilson hoped other ministers would leave this subject alone – and in effect, not say what the PM was saying. I presumed that George Brown had protested, and somehow pressurized Wilson into sending this message. I decided on balance, perhaps wrongly, to alter my speech, as I might merely give Brown a handle for criticism, and it might well be better that Wilson's speech should speak of itself. In the event Labour won the election and Wilson made few ministerial changes. He rang me next morning and asked me to stay at the Board of Trade.

Up to this point the Wilson Government had a defensible, indeed creditable, record. The damaging consequences of the original mistake on the import surcharge had not yet emerged, because we had not yet been obliged to remove it. The morale of the Government had not yet been soured by too many suspected leaks from No. 10 or other ministers; and the Common Market had not yet been allowed seriously to divide the Cabinet. Some of the older ministers such as Soskice and Frank Longford, preserved the older standards. Callaghan I also found a most reliable, co-operative and competent colleague. He impressed me by exhibiting some of Gaitskell's talent for always doing a more difficult task much better than one expected. Though economic policy was not his previous first love, he was in committees almost invariably lucid, good-humoured and brief. His essential talent, I believe, ever carefully cultivated, was for learning: learning quickly a new atmosphere, a new subject, a new technique Michael Stewart, as Foreign Secretary, though he did not stir the blood, was equally rational and lucid, and at this time a straightforward supporter of the EFTA free trade area and Commonwealth policies and a sceptic about supra-national adventures. Among my main colleagues as economic ministers, Ray Gunter usually said nothing in Cabinet, but upheld the union connection and seemed equally at home in Whitehall and in Parliament. He wholeheartedly supported the Board of Trade's Development Area plans.

Frank Cousins has often been under-rated as a Minister. His Ministry of Technology could not carry out the grandiose plans worked out by Wilson for transforming British industry in a few years; but it did at least save the computer industry from collapse as effectively as the Board of Trade shored up the shipbuilding and textile industries. Cousins was sedulous, hard-working and well-informed in Cabinet Committees. He had read the papers more carefully than many colleagues. But he spoiled his initial reputation by obstinately and foolishly treating the House of Commons with a sort of blustering superiority. He simply refused to learn its habits or even its language; and while Bevin had done likewise, Cousins unfortunately did not possess Bevin's commanding ability or irresistible sense of humour. On incomes policy, which finally led to his resignation, Cousins was stubbornly doctrinaire. Crossman, now known to me for over forty years, was all over the place, but fortunately not impinging too much on economic policy. He could claim credit for his 'option mortgage scheme' to help poorer house purchasers, and for a general increase in new house-building. But he must bear some responsibility for the ill-considered plunge into 'high-rise' building of flats, which was launched in this period, and which proved one of the worst mistakes of post-war housing policy. To be fair, nobody else seems to have criticized it at the time. The experts unhappily forgot to ask the ordinary public whether they wanted to live in these fifteen-storey technical marvels. The question was also beginning to be raised among Crossman's colleagues at this stage whether his prime working object was to carry out the Government's policies or to collect material for his diaries. The more critical interpretation gained ground when in one discussion, Crossman was challenged about these activities, and replied that if anyone objected he would resign from the Government and continue the diary. Indeed he describes himself at one point in the diaries rather too accurately as an 'outside observer on the inside'.

Healey, as Minister of Defence, did not cross my path, and as he shared – and had indeed strengthened – my views on the Common Market, I regarded him as an ally. It was once said of him at this time that he dominated the Cabinet without convincing it. But his energy and capacity were undeniable. In retrospect, I believe he pushed the dismantling of British defence forces, particularly naval, too far and too fast, encouraged by what at times seemed to me the complacency with which some, like Crossman and Jenkins, regarded any diminution of British influence. But the hardest colleague with whom to deal was George Brown. In the 1950s I had long valued working with him, as one who resisted the Bevanite extravagances, and stood for a strong British defence policy and no unilateral disarmament. But suddenly before 1964 he announced one day that he regarded it as, in his opinion, economically beneficial for the UK to join the EEC. I frankly doubted whether George had thought out the economic arguments, or made any serious estimate of the balance of payments consequences. However, despite this, after 1964, I recognized and praised his successes on the incomes policy front. But there were early shocks: for instance, a meeting with some recalcitrant shipbuilding employers, which I took at his request in his room and had coaxed with great difficulty into a reasonable compromise, when Brown walked in late and delivered some distinctly uncalled-for observations. I was greatly relieved that such incidents never percolated through to the press. Brown's method of argument was once aptly described to me by someone who had experienced it as 'bulldozing rather than reasoning'. However, somehow up to 1966 an uneasy peace was maintained between him and the rest of the Government.

Wilson himself at this stage had allayed some of the fears of those who had been critical of him during the Bevanite troubles. He had held the balance reasonably fairly and amicably between ex-Bevanites and ex-anti-Bevanites in the Cabinet. His versatility, fluency, and knowledge of the details of Government were not in dispute. But he did not inspire trust. Suspicion about his 'kitchen Cabinet' and persistent leaks from No. 10 had not at this stage become serious, however. On the other hand Wilson interfered too often in other departments and was not a good chairman. He talked much too much, and in discussion ignored the standards of Attlee and Cripps, though he had direct experience of them. He allowed ministers to repeat what was already in the papers before the meeting, and too often himself made a comment on each intervention from others. Business took much longer than it would have done under Attlee. Nevertheless these were faults which could be borne, and most colleagues in March 1966 were only too glad to give him the benefit of the doubt for having survived the test so far.

A few days after the election, now recovered from my illness, but still somewhat weary, I drove down to Cornwall, with my wife and son Martin for a welcome Easter. Between Exeter and Okehampton the rain was so heavy, and the traffic so dense, and the glare of headlights in the dark so distracting, that for the first time in my life I had to hand over the driving to Martin. Arriving at the Crackington farm on the cliff, with eighteen months' work, an illness and two general elections safely behind me, I sank thankfully, contentedly and comfortably on to my bed; whereupon the leg collapsed and the bed sagged to the floor.

After the 1966 election, just when most members of the Wilson Cabinet began to feel moderately thankful that they had survived eighteen months and decisively won an election, everything began to go wrong with the Government. First was the conflict and mistrust caused by the efforts of Wilson and Brown to break away from Gaitskell's policy over the Common Market and embark on approaches for entry. Second was the original mistake, made in 1964 over the import surcharge, now coming inevitably home to roost. Third was the growing abandonment by some ministers of the Attlee standards in dealing with the press. Immediately in April 1966, however, a Budget had to be introduced. The general lines of the Budget had been rather boldly, but I think rightly, forecast by Callaghan before the election, so as to avoid the charge that he had during the election concealed his plans. In April, about two weeks before the Budget, Callaghan called me to a very private meeting at the Treasury with himself and high officials from the Treasury, Ministry of Labour, and the then Ministry of Pensions and National Insurance. Kaldor was present. I was surprised to learn that the Treasury, needing more revenue, were proposing to introduce a sort of pay-roll tax falling discriminatingly on services as opposed to manufacturing industry. It was to be called 'Selective Employment Tax'. The idea partly derived from Kaldor's current theory that countries with expanding manufacturing industries showed growth while others did not. This seemed to me possibly to smack of the *post hoc, propter hoc* fallacy, in that the manufacturing expansion might be due to the growth and not vice versa. There was of course one strong argument for the SET. Since manufacturing industry would be exempted, most exports – though unfortunately by no means all – would be assisted. But to be asked to give a view on this at five minutes' notice was distinctly daunting: and all I could say off the cuff was that the proposed tax would be widely unpopular (e.g. with the Co-ops), and that if we did impose it, there must be exemption for non-manufacturing industry in the Development Areas. At the time I recorded my immediate reaction in these words:

I said I was neither for nor against this on merits; but I was not convinced that it had been sufficiently thought out to justify introduction at short notice; even though it was technically practicable. I thought it would be better to postpone the thing for some months of argument in preparation for another Budget. By the standard with which we prepared tax changes in Stafford Cripps's day this proposal was ill-digested.

Callaghan, though a much wiser Chancellor than I had once expected, was perhaps a little apt to seize on patent remedies, particularly if put forward with great ingenuity by distinguished academics like Kaldor; and events proved him right in arguing that he had to find the revenues somehow.

So the Kaldor brain-child went forward with Callaghan's recommendation to a bewildered Cabinet on 2 May, the day before the Budget. It had of course long been a conventional complaint of other ministers in Budget Cabinets that they were being presented with *faits accomplis* and could not argue. This traditional grumble was duly advanced on this occasion, and is even re-echoed once again in Crossman's diary.[1] But unhappy experience over many years has shown that a longer period than twenty-four hours (under Cripps it tended to be the morning of Budget day) generated discreditable leaks; and the 1966 Cabinet was not one of the least leaky yet known. On this particular day, I made it clear for the record that I did not think there had been time to prepare the SET adequately; but added, in support of the Chancellor, what I had already told him privately, that if anything I thought he was not increasing taxation enough; that we were heading for a midsummer boom which would upset the balance of payments; and that if we did not act toughly now there would be trouble later.

These warnings were brushed aside. Ministers other than the Chancellor are always willing to accept any easement by a Chancellor and to question any higher charges; so that the luckless Chancellor is apt to be in a minority of one. But as it was too late for change, this Budget went ahead with the SET and inadequate tax revenue in total. In the following months the SET proved highly unpopular, annoyed the Co-ops, and gave the Tories a free run of opposition.

The other decision reached immediately on the economic front was more wisely planned. Early in April we had to decide when to end the notorious EFTA surcharge (now cut to 10 per cent), as we had promised. Wilson, Callaghan, Brown and I met in Wilson's room in the House to discuss this. It was pretty clear again that if we announced the end well before the date when it took effect, we should win the political goodwill at once and postpone the economic burden of the extra imports. Callaghan's suggestion that we end the surcharge in November 1966, and announce it at once, was accepted by all. But disagreement sprang up later in April about the time of the announcement. I was due at the end of April to open a British export 'Week', at Oslo, where the surcharge was most unpopular.

[1] Richard Crossman, *The Diaries of a Cabinet Minister*, vol. 2, p. 510.

The Budget was on 3 May, and Brown and I had to attend an EFTA Conference in Bergen in late May. The right course was evidently to announce the end of the surcharge, which was a tax, in the Budget speech, and simultaneously in Oslo in the latter part of the British Week. This offered the extra attraction that our gesture to EFTA could be proclaimed by the Duke of Edinburgh in Oslo at the same moment as the Budget Speech.

But Brown wanted to announce the change himself at the EFTA meeting in Bergen in May. This had every disadvantage, including forcing the Duke of Edinburgh to share with us ministers the burden of defending the surcharge in Oslo. Wilson, Callaghan and I all opposed this, and Brown was overruled. As a result I spent the first few days at Oslo again defending the surcharge which I had so vehemently opposed, and which was soon to disappear, and the Duke of Edinburgh two days later triumphantly announced its disappearance – a very happy arrangement. For other reasons as well, the Oslo Week was highly successful. A few days earlier a lunatic had burnt down one building in the British industrial exhibition in a protest against the surcharge. But the opening ceremony, the brevity of the speeches, the cordiality of the Norwegian King, and the splendid affability of Sir Alexander Glen, all turned the tide in our favour. Beneath all this however, one could feel that it was the instinctive sympathy between British and Norwegian political convictions, and memories of the war, that mattered most.

I again learnt one other sobering lesson at Oslo; the remarkable difference between the British press and that of most other countries. The Norwegians were mildly cheating against the spirit of the EFTA Treaty by charging a 'revenue' duty on cars which in fact wiped out the preference which in EFTA they should have been giving to British over German cars. I had been fighting hard on behalf of the British car industry to get this corrected. At a press conference in Oslo, one or two Norwegian journalists attacked the surcharge, and I amazed everyone by defending the British and criticizing the Norwegian Government for the car duty. The Norwegian papers all loyally, and patriotically, defended the indefensible car duty. But the British press, so far from defending the import surcharge, criticized me for daring to criticize the Norwegians. In country after country I noticed this antithesis, which is seldom understood by British newspaper readers who normally do not see the overseas papers. The press of almost every country in the world normally backs up its own country, right or wrong. But much of the British press, because of the Fleet Street doctrine that grumbling sells a paper, almost as normally attacks its own country, right or wrong. This does real and unnecessary harm. In my export campaign travels, I sometimes felt growing sympathy with the cynic who said: 'There is nothing wrong with Britain except Fleet Street.'

My next export-promotion venture was to Canada at the end of May, where our main object was to persuade the Canadians to be more restrained in imposing anti-dumping duties on British goods. This they accepted in the Kennedy Round settlement some months later. In meeting most of the Canadian ministers in Ottawa, I was struck (while making due allowance for the courtesy of my hosts) by how much more British and less American the whole atmosphere was than one could have guessed from London. Lester Pearson, the Prime Minister, who had been a Rhodes Scholar at Oxford a year or two before Gaitskell's time and mine, was a warm personal friend of Gaitskell, and wanted to talk mainly about the decision of *The Times* to print news on the front page, which he said had changed his whole world. At dinner Paul Mart n, the Foreign Minister, Bob Winter the Trade Minister, and Mitchell Sharp, the Finance Minister (then expected to succeed Pearson), found the issue of Lord Moran publishing a book about Churchill's medical record more absorbing than any other. Bob Winter, previously a colleague of British industrialists on the Board of Rio-Tinto-Zinc, and a keen admirer of the then Chairman, Val Duncan, always impressed me as one of the few most intelligent, friendly and generally liberal-minded ministers with a wide outlook on the world, of any country with whom I had to do business. He unhappily died suddenly and still young. One of the follies of these later years was the fashion by which British Governments, instead of building on the immense reserves of goodwill towards Britain in the Commonwealth, underrated them, and so largely threw them away.

By the spring of 1966, however, within weeks of the election victory, the first black cloud appeared preceding the industrial storm which by the end of that summer had rolled back the economic recovery achieved in 1965. On 19 May a seamen's strike began in support of the demand for a 6 per cent pay rise, and some other fringe benefits – at that time a steep increase. The most the Government could legitimately offer within our then successful incomes policy was $4\frac{1}{2}$ per cent. The seamen had a strong historical case; but it was made no more convincing by the presence among them of an extremist group headed by Communists – Wilson's 'tightly-knit group of politically motivated men'. Callaghan, Bill Rodgers (then at the Ministry of Labour) and I met in mid-May to decide whether the Government could bless a rise beyond $4\frac{1}{2}$ per cent. The Board of Trade was responsible for shipping. None of us thought it possible to go beyond $4\frac{1}{2}$ per cent without inviting a flood of other pay claims. We recommended accordingly to the Cabinet, and there was no dissent. I summed up the dilemma at the time in these words: 'If we had given way, the whole wages line would have crumbled, and on all rational calculations, the balance of payments would have slid back into deficit. By bravely refusing, we provoked a strike, which ruined two months' exports and produced the same result.' Were we right? It is perfectly possible that the balance of payments would have suffered either way. But, in retrospect, by a narrow margin, I am inclined to believe we were wrong.

Despite repeated and heroic efforts at conciliation and compromise by Ray Gunter as Minister of Labour and a Court of Inquiry, the strike continued obstinately till the end of June. The whole recovery of exports and the balance of payments, which we had patiently achieved since October 1964, was disrupted. Exports suffered sooner than imports because ships carrying imports came into port before being laid up, whereas those carrying exports simply did not sail. The export figures thus dropped severely in May, and disastrously by £70 million or about one fifth in June. These figures I had to announce in mid-July. Imports had not yet fallen correspondingly. I explained to a press conference of financial journalists in mid-July that the figures were misleading and temporary, and these experts in general reported this faithfully. But the figures in themselves provoked a flight of funds from sterling, and in turn the largely psychological crisis of July, which the Government had to meet in order to protect the reserves. Figures published later in 1967 showed that in the second half of 1966 we actually achieved a current balance of payments surplus of £48 million, despite the ending of the import surcharge in November. The disinflationary 'measures' taken in July no doubt helped this. But it still looks very much as if even the strike could have been survived without crisis measures, had not the 'hot money' flow been added to the halt in exports. Certainly if the strike had not occurred, recovery of exports and the balance of payments would have continued fairly steadily throughout 1966.

Was there another psychological contribution to the flight of funds which did so much damage in July 1966? Wilson[2] says most illuminatingly that in the July crisis the Governor of the Bank of England (Leslie O'Brien) 'became a regular part of the Downing Street pattern. . . . I would judge from his remarks that he felt we might have to devalue if and when we joined the Common Market, but unilaterally and out of the blue: no.' Trouble in the exchange market was also caused during M. Pompidou's visit to London in early July by rumours that the French thought sterling would have to be devalued if Britain joined the Common Market.[3] Crossman tells us in his diaries[4] that Roy Jenkins also was saying privately that joining the Market would probably mean devaluation of the pound. I was very conscious at the time that this was the pro-Marketeers' real belief. But it is fascinating that those who were urging us to join, and claimed some knowledge of economics, were privately admitting that joining would damage the balance of payments and the pound – particularly as they were publicly advocating entry on the grounds of the benefits of it to the British economy. I would judge myself that the effect of the seamen's strike on the export figures would in itself have caused a flight of hot money, even with-

[2] Harold Wilson, *The Labour Government 1964-70* (London, 1971), p. 252.
[3] Wilson, p. 250.
[4] Crossman, vol. 2, p. 574.

out the threat of Common Market entry. But the latter doubtless intensified it: and the honest attitude of the Governor of the Bank remains an instructive comment on the motives of the political pro-Marketeers.

Meanwhile a more constructive diversion for me was a visit to Moscow on 6 July to open a major British industrial exhibition there. The weather was brilliant, warmer than in London, and three or four members of the Praesidium turned up for the opening ceremony in the open air amid the silver birch trees. I risked in my opening speech putting in a sentence congratulating the Mayor of Moscow on providing such splendid weather; and to my surprise this, being translated, provoked general mirth. In talks with Patolichev, the Russian Trade Minister, we pressed extremely hard again for bigger Russian purchases to match our own. But I had to stop short of threatening not to buy their timber, because the considered view in London was that we should only have to pay more for timber elsewhere. Nevertheless this exhibition was followed by somewhat bigger Russian orders. Reggie Maudling was representing the Dunlop Company at the exhibition and celebrations; and I boldly predicted in an after-dinner speech that Patolichev would remain in office longer than Maudling or myself. This at least proved true. Wilson visited the exhibition with Kosygin a few days later. It was during this trip that Wilson was alleged to have suspected a conspiracy against him in London. I saw no evidence of it.

Returning myself to London, I found that the exchange crisis, however caused, was all too real and had to be checked. Even before the seamen's strike I had believed that the economy was overheated. The rational remedy, as successfully applied in July 1965, would have been a moderate disinflationary dose. But publication on 4 July of the gold losses in June turned the general nervousness into a crisis even before the trade figures were announced on 13 July. From the end of June onwards I advocated moderate measures; an intensified version of the July 1965 curbs, which would have enabled the promising export recovery to be resumed, and the temporary effects of the seamen's strike, now ended, to be overcome. I therefore asked repeatedly in June and early July, for a series of meetings, similar to those in July 1965, of Wilson, Callaghan, Brown and myself, with the four senior officials involved, to work out precisely the extent of the restraints. In response partly to my requests, such meetings were fixed four or five times to be held at No. 10, and each time cancelled an hour or so beforehand. I pressed for an explanation of this chaos in the government machine, and was told that Brown was unwilling to attend such a meeting. He apparently felt too strongly about it.[5] Only general discussion was possible at Cabinet on 12 and 14 July. On 13 July, the day the trade figures showed the effect of the seamen's strike, I was due to visit Sussex University and see my daughters Helen and Catherine receive their degrees in the

[5] Crossman, vol. 1, p. 574.

Pavilion; and Wilson was there to give formal thanks for an honorary degree. Almost as soon as I had been photographed with the twins outside the Dome, I was asked by the press and BBC to comment on the trade figures. At this stage my explanation of the temporary effect of the seamen's strike on the export figures naturally had little effect. Wilson and I got back to Victoria at about 5 p.m. to attend at 5.30 p.m. a meeting at No. 10 at last fixed to reach clear decisions on the action required. It was cancelled at 5.15 p.m. and for the same reason. (Wilson says[6] that 'a difficult situation had arisen'.) I then strongly suggested to No. 10 that if Brown was unwilling to talk, the rest of us should meet without him; but nothing happened.

Ministers thus moved into the final stage of the crisis with no proper discussion, one senior participant lurking in his tent, the Treasury preparing an unnecessarily severe package and a pro-Marketeer minority clouding the issue by urging devaluation for irrelevant reasons. Wilson returned from Moscow on the morning of 19 July to face a meeting that day which would be forced to take final decisions. The Treasury papers before us, making precise proposals and not offering alternatives, had only been in ministers' hands for about thirty hours. This was a mockery of sensible government, and I had never seen anything like it in the eleven years which by that time I had worked in the government machine. As a result, the disinflationary measures overshot the mark substantially, caused unnecessary unemployment and undermined the Government's reputation. For instance, an HP down-payment on cars of 40 per cent was introduced, which was bound to mean a violent recession in the motor industry; whereas a moderate change would have pushed cars, as desired, into the export market. Unhappily, for several reasons, the argument declined not into an assessment of just how much restraint was needed, but into a doctrinal debate as between the alleged crude alternatives of 'deflation' and 'Tory policy', etc., on the one hand; and devaluation, expansion, 'planning' or even the 'Socialist alternative' on the other.

As a result, the excessive Treasury figures, and most of their detailed proposals, were reluctantly accepted. First reason for this was the shortness of time and the crisis atmosphere made inevitable by the failure to hold earlier preparatory meetings between those who best understood the issues. Second was the presence of a majority of non-economic ministers who could not be expected at this short notice to realize that the real question was quantitative and not doctrinal. The third was pressure from a curious minority of those like Jenkins who wanted devaluation to ward off the damage of entering the Common Market, supported by Crossman, who, though simple-minded on economic policy, greedily picked up from the academic economists expressions like 'expansionism', 'deflation', 'planning', etc. Confronted with these condusions, I could only say that I thought the proposed disinflation was too great in total, but would prefer even

[6] Wilson, p. 252.

this to either doing nothing or outright devaluation. I did not believe the case for devaluation was as yet made out. In answer to a question from Wilson I agreed that there was no case, on grounds of 'purchasing power parity', for devaluation. The fact that devaluation was being urged by pro-Marketeers for reasons they dared not admit naturally did not incline me to support it.

In the division lobby of the House on the evening of 19 July, amid these discussions, I could not help observing Jenkins, Crosland and Crossman behaving conspiratorially and pressing undecided members of the Cabinet to support devaluation. I normally abstained from these sort of methods, but this time decided that they must be countered. I urged Frank Pakenham and Douglas Houghton to stand firm on the other side in the final decision next morning, and they did not need much persuasion. Throughout the two days' debate between ministers, Brown remained almost completely silent, apparently dissociating himself from the whole proceedings. He still seemed to take the simple view of 'either expansion or deflation', and not unnaturally regretted what he regarded as the death of his 'National Plan'. By objecting to *any* restraint, he made it almost inevitable that the whole Treasury package would be accepted. And so the Cabinet approved about 95 per cent of it, including a six months' pay and prices freeze, and Wilson announced the result with considerable skill in the House on 20 July.

I left the final meeting disillusioned, but in the end relieved. My opinion of the way the whole issue had been handled was expressed by some words I wrote at the time: 'I no longer expected or hoped for the right decision, but merely sought to prevent disastrous blunders.' It would have been a worse blunder either to do nothing or to devalue at that moment. Compared with this, an overshoot of £200 million in disinflation seemed almost a minor error; though it was enough in employment terms to conceal most of what we had done to restore employment in the Development Areas, which was just beginning to show results. At least a new Steering Committee on Economic Policy was now set up, under Wilson, later including Crossman as well as the economic ministers, and first met on 11 August. After 20 July 1966 a legend grew that we could and should have devalued in that month. With all the benefit of hindsight, I still believe this view is wrong. It can be argued at almost any time in any country that devaluation will help exports. But one of the defects of a regime of fixed exchanges is that the government of a major country must have a far stronger case than this for choosing a given moment for a cold-blooded devaluation. In July 1966, as stated above, little case existed on grounds of comparative prices. Secondly with unemployment well below 1·5 per cent, the economy was as near as it could be to overheating, and it was common sense to believe that mild restraint would right the balance of payments without sacrificing full employment. Thirdly the balance of trade and payments would improve when the temporary effects of the seamen's strike, ended in June, wore off.

And the advocates of devaluation seemed to forget that the Government had as recently as May publicly given the improvement in the balance of payments as the reason for ending the import surcharge. To announce only a few weeks later that the balance was so bad that we had to devalue would have exposed the Government to ridicule. The advocates of devaluation could have argued with some reason, though they did not, that the enforced removal of the surcharge in November would upset the balance of payments again. So far as this had substance, it was another condemnation of the decision to prefer the surcharge to quotas in October 1964, since quotas could have been maintained. Some, with benefit of hindsight, have also argued that the devaluation of November 1967 shows the chance should have been seized in July 1966. But this disregards the intervening events which made the 1967 devaluation inevitable: the closure of the Suez Canal, the application to enter the EEC, and finally the Liverpool dock strike in the autumn of 1967.

It was not these economic controversies, however, which filled the public mind after 20 July, but rather the growing unemployment which followed the Treasury package 'overshoot', and the shock to the Labour Party of what seemed like a sudden abandonment of the 'National Plan'. July 1966 was something of a turning point in British economic history. For ten years thereafter, partly of course for international reasons, unemployment never fell so low again, and total employment in manufacturing industry scarcely regained the 1966 level. It was also a turning point in the Wilson Government's fortunes. The honeymoon was over, as it was for the Attlee Government after August 1947. For the confusion and excessive disinflation of July 1966, however, the main responsibility must rest on Brown for his share in preventing coherent discussion between ministers. Wilson must bear some also for not insisting that if Brown would not attend meetings, they should be held without him. And perhaps the most unhappy result of all from July 1966 was Brown's transfer to the Foreign Office. On 20 and 21 July we were told in the House that Brown was offering and withdrawing his resignation at intervals. The story was added, though some questioned its accuracy, that he only withdrew it because Bill Rodgers, then a junior Minister, had collected about a hundred signatures in one evening in the House to a petition requesting him to remain. I had no direct experience of this petition; but a few days later Wilson made the strange decision to move Michael Stewart from the Foreign Office to the DEA and replace him by Brown. There was certainly nemesis in this unlucky decision. For the Wilson Government never recovered from July 1966. And the main reason for this was the conflict and gratuitously added economic strain, which both sprang from the futile attempt to join the Market in 1966 and 1967.

The story of the Common Market controversy after July 1966 does not make much sense unless one analyses first the real issues which were at stake for the future of the country. Each of us must here decide for himself whether he believes the preservation and strengthening of British influence in the world are something worth striving for or not. With those who believe they are not, I cannot argue. To see no value, and take no pride, in a nation which has preserved democratic Government unbroken by vilent upheavals for 300 years, which has increasingly upheld human rights and civil liberties, and which has pioneered the struggle for greater social justice – to ignore all this and much else is to abandon rational judgement. But for those who are not blind to this record, the practical question is this: how best can we preserve in the new world of the later twentieth century, and the next century, the strength of this country and its capacity to defend the institutions and values in which we believe? In the post-1945 world British economic and military power were bound to decline *relatively* to that of certain other countries and the rest of the world as a whole. All this could be, and was, predicted. For instance the decline of British manufactured exports *as a percentage of world exports* after 1945 was predicted by the British Treasury in 1947–8. (What is not so widely known is that the absolute volume[7] of British exports rose enormously after those years.) But the certainty that British power and wealth would decline relatively was a reason, not for mere lamenting, or for encouraging a still further decline, but for fostering and preserving the precious assets, moral and material, which we still possessed and on which we could most effectively build in the future.

If these are the right objectives, and if this country has world-wide and not just sectional or regional values to offer the world, we need the widest practicable contacts – human, cultural, political and economic – with other countries and continents. In trade we should not impose barriers on imports of food or raw materials. We should remain members of inter-national and multi-national organizations, regardless of colour, creed, geography or wealth, from the UN and its agencies to the Commonwealth which we had also ourselves created by exporting much of our own popu-lation to new British countries overseas. Having also ourselves promoted a world-wide system of trading, which was the foundation of our nineteenth-century strength, it should have been clear common sense to foster these assets in the present century. In addition, in the post-1945 world, since Soviet military resources must greatly exceed our own, security demanded that we should join with the US and the largest possible group of Western and other nations in a defensive military alliance. In all these spheres, of politics, trade and defence, it thus remains a prime British interest to avoid too narrow or regional an outlook.

Secondly, national policy must be founded on the clear recognition that political strength in the modern world depends partly on military strength, and military strength depends largely on economic and industrial strength.

[7] Some facts and figures are given in the Epilogue to this book.

The history of the US, the Soviet Union, China and Japan over the last thirty years proves this yet again. Their political strength has grown with their economic strength. Perhaps we ourselves could have enforced our political will in Rhodesia if we had not curtailed our military capacity so fast. But, however that may be, the prime object of policy should have been, and should be, to build up our economic capacity. And though there is no space here to scrutinize the full story of the British post-war economic effort, one or two facts stand out indisputably clear. First, it is a crucial British economic interest to buy our essential imports – food and materials – at as low a cost as possible, and secondly to practise some restraint in importing manufactured consumer goods. To put it crudely, the British interest is free trade in food and materials and some curb on imports of manufactures. This policy we largely pursued till the end of the 1950s, and in these years our balance of payments was more often in surplus than in deficit, and our real living standards were rising. Support for the balance of payments by these policies was all the more vital because the most persistent reasons in these years for our low growth and investment were the repeated Government-imposed deflations forced on us by threatened payments deficits. It remains true that the stronger the balance of payments, the easier it is to promote growth, real investment and full employment.

The key to British post-war policy should, therefore, have been preservation of the political and economic assets that history had bequeathed us, notably in the Commonwealth and sterling area; free trade in food and materials (with direct Budget support for farming) and some limit on manufactured imports; and close political and military accord with the United States. With this policy, pursued as resolutely and intelligently as for instance the Soviet Union and France have pursued their own interests, we could have retained and still could retain, very substantial and lasting influence in the world.

Our first serious mistake at the end of the 1950s was to abandon, too soon, the quota limitations on imports of manufactured goods which had stayed in force since 1945. In 1950 manufactured imports represented 18 per cent of our total imports, 33 per cent in 1960, 51 per cent in 1970, and 61 per cent in 1978. This improvidence had already worsened our position in the 1960s; but we still enjoyed great advantages gained from past policies. The Commonwealth preference system enabled us to buy a huge proportion of our imported food and materials at low cost, and gave our exports a substantial preference in the large and growing markets of Canada, Australia, New Zealand, South Africa and elsewhere. Our free trade association in EFTA with Sweden, Norway, Finland, Denmark, Austria, Switzerland and Portugal both guaranteed free entry for our manufactured exports to all these countries, *and* left us free to import food and materials as we pleased. In these circumstances of largely free trade with EFTA and the Commonwealth, and moderate tariffs sanctioned by

GATT with the US, and the rest of Western Europe, our free trade flowed naturally as to about 30 per cent with the Commonwealth, 20 per cent with the EEC, and nearly 20 per cent with EFTA. The reasons for this were mainly physical and climatic, based on geography and the international division of labour. It was a rare piece of good fortune for Britain that the countries from whom we could most cheaply buy what we essentially needed were those with whom we enjoyed the closest human and political links. Because these were the lowest-cost and most efficient producers, we bought wheat largely from Canada and Australia; mutton, lamb, butter and cheese from Australia and New Zealand; beef from Australia and Argentina; and maize, our principal feeding-stuff, from the US. From Western Europe, we bought remarkably few essential imports, except timber from Scandinavia, and bacon and butter from Denmark – all from EFTA countries.

All these supplying countries enjoyed high standards of living, and were able through efficiency and geographical good fortune, to supply us cheaply and at reasonable profit to themselves. The idea sometimes propagated in these years that we in Britain were exploiting poor overseas producers by buying 'cheap food' was an illusion based on ignorance. New Zealand's exports to this country of the most cheaply and efficiently produced lamb and dairy products in the world were a classic case of the benefits of international trade: highly valuable to both countries, and pre-eminently to the British consumer. And it so happened that New Zealand had maintained their supplies at low cost throughout the war, and the immediate post-war years of world food shortage, out of political loyalty to Britain. Thus it followed that the combination of EFTA with the Commonwealth partial free trade area was of great value to all the countries concerned, but most of all to ourselves because it gave us both export markets and low-cost imports; and at the same time it assured us of political friends, without calling in question anybody's ultimate political independence. Had we not made the mistake of admitting excessive manufactured imports after the late 1950s, our trade and payments would have been as manageable after 1960 as before.

The Common Market, on the other hand, was based on entirely different principles from EFTA and the Commonwealth, and on economic policies which were bound to be exceptionally damaging to Britain. It forced us to *buy food at artificially high prices and admit unrestricted manufactured imports*: precisely the reverse in each case of our prime national interest. EEC entry for us was thus bound to mean, first a steep rise in the price of most of our very large food imports, and an abolition of all tariffs on imports of just those manufactured goods (e.g. cars) of which we were already importing far too much. The reasons for this were historical, and not anybody's fault. Thanks to history the Continental political as well as social and economic system had been founded since the nineteenth century on high agricultural protection. In Britain, on the other hand, the Repeal of the Corn Laws in 1846, great liberating decision, had progressively benefited the mass of the people at the expense of grain-growing land-owners, and kept down our industrial costs by enabling a higher real wage to be earned by a lower money payment than would otherwise have been needed. The full beneficial effect for us was only fully felt in the 1880s and 1890s when as the United States re-established peace after the Civil War, great quantities of low-cost North American grain flowed into Western Europe. Britain bought it freely; and in the later stage after the 1947 Agricultural Act, home farming prosperity and efficiency were added to low consumer prices by the device of direct 'deficiency payments' to farmers out of the Budget. The Continental countries, however, in the 1880s and 1890s, reacted by imposing high tariffs designed to exclude North American grain and protect their own high-cost farmers. Entrenched agricultural protectionism on the Continent thus long preceded the Rome Treaty. What the Common Market did was to convert high protectionism into extreme protectionism, which excluded imports of many essential foodstuffs altogether. The EEC 'intervention' system, which ensured that even intensive home production could not bring prices down, was the final turn of the screw against the consumer.

Thus at least a generation before the Treaty of Rome the three Conservative-Catholic parties of France, Germany and Italy had acquired for themselves a rocklike vested interest in high agricultural protection. This vested interest was virtually immovable for two reasons: first because these Conservative parties regarded themselves as dependent on the votes of peasant farmers who cared more about keeping prices up than anything else; and secondly because if the ruling groups in these three countries – especially France – had resorted to the British deficiency payments system to support agriculture, they could not have continued to avoid a proper level of direct taxation on the higher incomes.[8] These were the rocks on which so many attempts to 'reform' the Common Agricultural Policy subsequently broke; and it was the failure to understand these Continental realities which misled many well-meaning but narrow-visioned British observers into believing you could break down the CAP 'from inside'.

[8] Repeated statistical inquiries have shown that the percentage of public revenue raised by direct taxation in France and Italy is barely half that in the US, Scandinavia and the UK. The following figures are taken from OECD Revene figures for 1975-6:
Direct taxation as a percentage of total revenue 1976

Denmark	62
Australia	58
US	57
UK	55
Sweden	52
Germany	40
France	27
Italy	26

Every attempt to do so since has proved its impracticability over again, and the suggestion of such reform always meets with the objection from the Continental countries that a deficiency payments system 'could not be afforded'. That is why the choice between extreme agricultural protectionism on the one hand, and the deficiency payments system on the other, is crucial not just to the economic future of Britain, but in principle to the distribution of income and wealth in all the great democracies of Western Europe. This in turn may help the puzzled observer to understand why entry to the EEC and adoption of the CAP were so eagerly welcomed by many of those in Britain whose property (particularly agricultural property) and incomes were well above the average.

The Common Market was thus based on extreme agricultural protectionism, supplemented by two other forces: a drive for *laissez-faire* economics and for political federation or outright union of hitherto independent countries. It was designed by the founding fathers, Spaak, Monnet, Schumann, Adenauer and the rest, to gain the support simultaneously of the agricultural vested interests, the great multi-national industrial companies, and the political federalists. The flat contradiction between *laissez-faire* economics and agricultural protectionism was blithely ignored because it suited the main countries to ignore it. Agriculture was different! Of course the whole enterprise had many worthy objectives, was supported by many idealists, and was likely to be beneficial economically to Germany, France and Italy. If a country which has long practised agricultural protectionism continues it, and joins an industrial customs union in addition, it will unquestionably benefit. For the food and agricultural situation will not change; but gains from industrial division of labour and wider exchange will be set against it. This is what happened to Germany, France, Italy and probably Belgium in the early years of the EEC. But the effect will be completely different in a country like Britain, which has based its economy on largely free imports of food for over a century.

If these were the real economic issues which the country faced when pressure to join the Common Market mounted in the 1960s and 1970s, what choice should we have made? The wisest course would have been (as Gaitskell argued in his 1962 speech) to opt for the wider alternative and avoid the strait-jacket of narrow regional nationalism. This meant in practice, building on the open trade system of EFTA and the Commonwealth, and extending it through GATT negotiations and the most liberal arrangement with the Common Market compatible with our own successful food and agricultural policies. The fact that such an arrangement would almost certainly have succeded is demonstrated by the ease with which all the EFTA countries which chose not to join the Market (Sweden, Norway, Finland, Austria and Switzerland) negotiated industrial free trade area agreements with the Common Market. Norway, by staying outside, won free entry for industrial exports into the EEC, retained control of its internal affairs including food and agriculture, and secured a 200-mile-wide exclusive fishing zone. Britain by joining was forced into the damaging CAP, had to submit to bureaucratic legislation, lost the 200-mile exclusive fishing zone we would otherwise have enjoyed, and gained in return exactly the same free access for industrial export as Norway and the rest secured without any of these sacrifices. The British attitude, if properly thought out, should have been this: 'We are loyal and active members of the UN and its agencies, of NATO, of the OECD, EFTA and other European authorities; and we favour a liberal system of international trade, generally, both industrial and agricultural. We are therefore willing to join any European customs union for industrial trade, provided that it involves no new or steeper restrictions against trade with the outside world, no disruption of our own food and agricultural policies, and no interference in our internal political and social affairs; i.e. no acceptance of the Treaty of Rome or the CAP in their present forms. When the Common Market is willing to accept these terms, we are willing to join. Until and unless this is accepted, we are determined to maintain all present political links throughout NATO, the OECD, etc., to attempt to widen the EFTA and Commonwealth preference systems, and to reach a liberal trade agreement with the Common Market.

Had we made an offer of this kind, we should have been bound, either way, to fare better than if out of failure to understand the consequences we accepted terms bound to be economically damaging. Either we should have preserved, without joining, all the advantages of the EFTA and Commonwealth systems (covering 50 per cent of our trade); or if the offer was accepted, we should have gained, in addition without economic loss, such political advantages as allegedly derived from membership. We could thus afford to wait. Our bargaining position was in fact strong, because the French wished to sell us expensive food we did not want, and the Germans wanted to sell us industrial goods we did not need. All this the French well understood. But our own Foreign Office did not.

If, however, we rejected this common sense course, and were deluded into thinking that membership was somehow good in itself, and any terms had to be accepted in order to secure it quickly; then all sorts of disastrous implications followed. First, in tactical terms, the French (whose objective was always to weaken the 'Anglo-Saxons' as well as strengthen themselves) merely had to declare such and such terms to be final, and we were bound to accept them. The Foreign Office in these years got itself repeatedly into the ludicrous position of arguing, not that the terms were beneficial to Britain's future, but that these were the only terms we could get. Secondly, and more fundamentally, the long-term economic consequences of capitulation were bound to be profoundly damaging. The result of substantial acceptance of the CAP was almost certain to be in any normal year a steep

M

rise in the import price, as compared with what we should otherwise have paid, for our main foods and feeding stuffs; which together represented a massive import bill, and a major element in our living standards. The price of food under the CAP was bound in any normal year to be much higher than the world price, both because for climatic and physical reasons grain can be produced at a lower real cost in North America, meat in Australia and South America, and dairy produce in Australia and New Zealand, than in Western Europe; and secondly because despite this, the CAP was founded on the economically absurd principle of raising agricultural incomes every year as fast as industrial incomes.

Therefore the imposition of the CAP strait-jacket of artificially high prices, import levies of up to 100 per cent, or more, and 'intervention' buying for stocks, in place of the previously open British system was bound to set off in the UK a series of damaging consequences. The extra cost of food imports added a new and gratuitous load on our balance of payments. Next the higher price of food handed on to the consumer meant either a lowering of the real standard of living particularly of all those on low incomes; or alternatively a rise in the money incomes of wage-earners, salary-earners and pensioners – probably a little of each. But a rise in pay rates throughout industry inevitably raises the labour costs of exports. The spectacular success of the Repeal of the Corn Laws and of the free import of grain in the nineteenth century was based on the truth that lower prices of food enabled rising real wages to be paid and export costs kept down at the same time. Even in the 1960s the British wage-earner and his family still spent nearly 25 per cent of their income on food. The artificial raising of food prices by the CAP after 1972 was, together with the indirect effects of the Arab oil cartel, one of the main causes of the pay inflation of the 1970s.

But the immediate injury to living standards through dearer imports was only the beginning of the damage. Next major effort would be on exports. Two influences would be at work. First we should lose free entry and preference for our exports throughout the Commonwealth Preference Area; and a high proportion of our exports enjoyed this in Canada, Australia, New Zealand and South Africa, all large markets (the last being a member of the Preference Area but not the Commonwealth). Indeed the total of our exports enjoying this free entry or preference in the 1950s and 1960s was greater than our total exports to the Common Market countries. Secondly the rise in labour costs due to higher food prices would further reduce our exports. (This was the fact which I found almost all industrialists forgot, except for a very discerning few.) And this handicap would affect all our exports to all parts of the world. Against that, of course, had to be set an increase in exports to the Common Market Six due to the removal of their tariffs on our goods. This was the famous 'market of 200 millions'. But unhappily, like so many propaganda slogans, it embodied a glaring fallacy. The gain in our exports to the Common Market would be set off against the loss to the Preference Area. But unfortunately the rise in our *imports from the Market* would also have to be set off against the gain in our exports to it; leaving inevitably a net swing towards deficit in general trade additional to the extra cost of food.

Though the quantities were of course not easy to estimate, a simple exercise in logic could demonstrate that the UK must suffer a net trading loss in balance of payments terms. The effect on goods other than food can be regarded separately, first in trade with the world outside the Market Six, and secondly with the Six themselves. Outside the Six all the effects would be adverse: loss of preference and higher export costs. Within the Market, trade with the original Six (not the Eight, because Denmark and Eire were already in an industrial free trade relation with us) was at issue. And here two forces would work against us in the trade balance, if we joined. First, as our industrial tariffs were in the main higher than those of the Six, the latter would gain more than we by a reciprocal cut to zero. Secondly our industrial costs would be forced up by the rise in food prices and theirs would not. The balance of trade between the Six and the UK in manufactured goods must accordingly swing against us. Therefore since the effect in the world outside the Six (in goods other than food) was wholly adverse, and within the Six must be adverse on balance, the total world effect must also be adverse.

In addition to this, the third major item in the profit and loss account was the net Budget payment which the UK would have to make to the Brussels organizations. This payment had of course to be made across the exchanges and was therefore a burden on our precarious balance of payments as well as on our Budget.

These were the main adverse economic effects likely from entry: higher food prices, a less favourable balance in manufactured goods, and a Budget payment.[9] They were not the end of the damage: because full acceptance of the Treaty of Rome and Brussels regime must also mean total abandonment of exchange control on capital outflows by this country for the first time since September 1939. In practice the UK did not submit to this folly until 1979. The effect of it could be very large; but since capital movements are notoriously difficult to calculate, I always assumed it in my estimates to be small. One major consequence, however, could be easily foreseen. As long as the UK belonged to EFTA and the Commonwealth Preference Area, a multi-national company contemplating real investment in Western Europe, would be wise to place one factory in the Common Market and one in the UK; thus enabling its exports to enter into the Market, EFTA *and* the Preference Area on favourable terms. But if the UK joined the Market and left the Preference Area, and if EFTA

[9] For the actual outcome, see pp. 491-3 and following.

formed a Customs Union with the Market (as it did), then a multi-national company would have no reason to locate any new factory in the UK rather than in the centre of the Continental Market countries. On balance the change in capital movements, though hard to quantify, and possibly not large, was therefore likely to be adverse. Statistics for the late 1970s show that it has been.

Such were the realistically assessed economic consequences of joining, as examined in the 1960s, and as they were also assumed in Gaitskell's Brighton speech in 1962. It also seemed to me in those years, the main duty of anyone who took the problem seriously to try to estimate the magnitude of these consequences, hard though this was – I did my best both within the 1964 Government and later outside it, and put the total net burden on the current UK balance of payments at between £500 million and £1000 million a year in the money values of the mid-1960s. In my book *After the Common Market* published in 1968 (where the economic argument is set out in much greater detail), I estimated the next extra burden on our current balance of payments very modestly as at least £500 million. I put the increase in imports from the Six at £200 million, which turned out to be a ludicrous under-estimate. Two years later in February 1970 (by when money values had of course fallen) in a paper[10] for the Manchester Statistical Society I revised my estimate of the total extra burden to over £1000 million on the current balance of payments. Not very dissimilar estimates were published in official Whitehall Papers in 1967 and 1969, but showing wider margins between the most optimistic and most pessimistic forecasts.[11]

These were the alternatives facing the Wilson Government, as a drive for membership suddenly began to show itself in Whitehall in the summer of 1966. The detailed figures and analysis merely proved the already manifest truth that if we both raised the price of food imports, and admitted a much greater import of consumer goods, our payments balance was bound to suffer. The advocates of entry, no longer able to deny this indisputable fact, fell back on the assertion that despite these certain losses, some mysterious 'dynamic' gains would emerge some time later. This was to lower the debate to the realm of mysticism. For while a strong exporting economy, by stimulating home investment, can generate a cumulative process in its own favour, an economy faced with an excess of imports will as surely suffer a descending spiral – low profits, low investment, low employment. The magic 'dynamic' gains were a fiction.

There was also, however, a political side to the debate. In Harold Macmillan's day pro-Marketeers argued that we must sacrifice some national independence and sovereignty in order to gain the economic prize of

[10] Douglas Jay, *The European Economic Community* (Manchester Statistical Society, 11 February 1970).
[11] For the actual outcome see pp. 491–3 and following.

the great 'home market'. In 1966 and 1967 the pro-Marketeers, forced to admit that joining would economically mean a loss – now called a 'price' – turned the argument on its head, and asserted that 'the argument is political'. In this they usually meant either that their argument was irrational, or else that their previous economic argument was unsound. But of course a serious political issue was involved. For we were being asked to join, not an international but a supra-national organization. Under the Rome Treaty laws (called 'regulations', 'decisions' and 'directives') could be made by the central oganization which had binding force on the people of tbe member countries. Many of these (regulations and decisions) were directly binding without any need for the approval of the national Parliaments. No such power existed in the UN, or any of its agencies, the IMF, NATO, the OECD, EFTA or with any of the international organizations sometimes glibly compared with the Market. Adherence of Britain to such a constitution meant that for the first time for centuries laws binding on the British public could be made by an *external* authority not elected by the British public. This would be, if accepted, the most fundamental constitutional change made in the British constitution since at any rate the seventeenth century.

It involved a further revolution, however, in addition to the imposition of external legislation. The Common Market laws were enacted not by an elected body at all, but either by a meeting of ministers, or worse still by a Commission of appointed officials. Secondly, instead of legislation by public debate and public voting, basic to the British system at least since 1689, Common Market legislation was discussed and enacted in secret. To adopt such a constitution was not merely a massive abandonment of independence by the UK as such. It was also to abandon the principle maintained in this country for generations, that the individual citizen shall only be bound by legislation publicly enacted by a body they themselves had some part in electing. This was the ultimate principle of parliamentary democracy, as I had always believed, for which this country fought in two Great Wars. The spectacle of so many eminent and ostensibly educated persons, not merely in political life but in the academic and professional world, being ready to throw away, apparently without a qualm, the principle of government by democratic consent which they had professed as an article of faith for generations past, was to me even more profoundly shocking than the rush of the establishment to back appeasement in 1938 and 1939. Had they really never believed it? Or did they just not understand?

Advocates of entry could, of course, have argued a wholly different case. They could have said that they stuck to the principle of legislation only by a fully elected Parliament, but they wished this to be a Parliament of a new federal or unitary Western European State, which would extinguish the independence of the existing national states. As William Pickles of the LSE pointed out in one of the rare lucid contributions to the debate in these years,[12] that the supra-national character of the Common Market imposed a dilemma inescapable in the end: either you abandoned the ultimate democratic principle of legislation by an elected body; or else you surrendered Britain's independence and merged this country in either a federal or unitary state. Formally the Rome Treaty provided for a unitary and not even a federal state. The national Parliaments and Governments do not figure in the constitution, as the State authorities do in that of the US; and the EEC Council, Commission, Assembly and Court of Justice are single and central. Whether, however, the new EEC State was to be unitary or federal; the dilemma equally remained. Those joining must sacrifice the essentials of either Parliamentary government or national independence.

It was of course open for anyone who wished it to argue frankly and publicly for either of these courses. But in that case two implications followed. First if a country is to be asked to make the most revolutionary choice for several centuries, the nature of the choice it was facing should be made abundantly clear to all. This was one of the central themes of Gaitskell's 1962 speech. But it was *not* made abundantly clear to all. Pro-Market propaganda, from the time when M. Spaak urged the foundation of the Market quickly before the public realized what was happening, consisted largely of an attempt to conceal the fact that membership involved the sacrifice of national independence and the creation of the 'United States of Europe'. Hence the proliferation of disingenuous double-speak such as 'political union' and 'Europe'. Those, however, who despised these solecisms, and believed openly and honestly, as some did, that the formation of a Western European Federal State was desirable, still had two basic questions which required an answer. Should Britain join any such union? And if so, which particular group was it most desirable we should choose?

The answer to the first question must depend on the balance of all the economic and political arguments set out here. But the main weakness of the case for submerging Britain in some larger unit lies in the simple fact that it was recommended on the grounds that the economic gains justified the political sacrifice, when the economic analysis showed that a loss and not a gain would result. But the second question remains: Why submerge, if we are going to submerge, in this particular unit? If a country with an unbroken record of Parliamentary government and civil liberties maintained for centuries were to put all this at risk by merging with a larger group, the first criterion should have been to choose a group with a similar record of stability stretching back, if not so long, at least till its

---

[12] See William Pickles, *Not with Europe*, Fabian Society pamphlet. Pickles was one of the honourable exceptions to the intellectual rot which set in; as were Arthur Bryant, Roy Harrod, Nicholas Kaldor and John Winnifrith.

foundation as a state. It is not obvious that Germany and Italy were the leading claimants to this distinction. Either the Scandinavian democracies or the Commonwealth countries practising genuine Parliamentary government had a markedly stronger claim. No pressing necessity, however, for joining any such an association was apparent in the circumstances of the 1960s and 1970s, in addition to the close contacts prevailing, with the international organizations of which we were already members.

Moreover the case for the federal or unitary state had been entirely outdated by the 1960s. As originally developed, and as I heard it expounded by M. Monnet himself in Paris in 1952, it was intended to prevent a further war between France and Germany. But after the rise of Soviet power since 1945, this was no longer a serious possibility. The aim of creating a politically federated Germany and France, so as to prevent another European war, had lost meaning and point by the 1960s. The threat, if any, was now from the Soviet Union. Times had changed, and France and Germany would no longer wish, or dare, to fight one another. At this point in the debate, a wholly different argument was advanced by the advocates of membership. Western Europe, it was said, was now faced by a totalitarian Soviet Union, armed with superior 'conventional' military weapons, and a huge nuclear arsenal as well. This could only be resisted by the formation of a new super-state of equal political and military strength in Western Europe. Certainly much of the drive for something usually and vaguely called 'political union' sprang from this confused belief, and no doubt a great deal of the huge financial resources of propagandist bodies like the European Movement, sprang likewise from the motive of preserving a *laissez-faire* economic system. But this belief was founded on more than one major historisal fallacy.

The first major weakness was this. If fear of the military strength of the Soviet Union was the decisive factor, then only the nuclear power of the United States could in the last resort counter it. The possibility of a Soviet nuclear threat cannot safely, at least to my mind, be taken lightly; but the more you believe in it, the more inexorably must you accept the fact that only the US nuclear capacity can act as a counter deterrent, until such time as all the great powers are rational enough to dismantle simultaneously their nuclear armaments. In addition, NATO already exists, and has existed since the late 1940s, pioneered by the British, and including the US and Canada, precisely to counter any Soviet military agression. The notion that you could improve the ultimate security this gives to Western Europe by excluding the United States is simply, in defence terms, laughable. If NATO does not work, nothing will. Instead it well might prove that the attempt to create a sort of half-hearted rival to NATO, would blur NATO's defence responsibilities and so risk confusing and weakening its effectiveness. Indeed the whole argument that Britain has to adopt a damaging food, agricultural and trade policy in order to achieve an effective deterrent to any Soviet threat has only to be stated to be seen as ludicrous.

This conclusion indeed is made even more conclusive by the briefest examination of cost. If we are relying on the US nuclear strength to deter the ultimate Soviet threat, then NATO is far the most practicable instrument. If we are not, then the putative United States of Europe has to build up, almost from scratch, a nuclear armoury approaching that of the Soviet Union and the US. The cost of this would be enormous; for Britain it would be additional to the economic costs already analysed here; and it would end up, not in nuclear disarmament, but in the creation of a fourth would-be nuclear super-power, to be added to the US, the Soviet Union and before long China. Can anyone rationally believe that this would promote world peace, nuclear disarmament, or even the security of Western Europe? An attempt by Western Europe by itself to match the nuclear power of the Soviet Union might indeed make things worse by weakening the US will to defend Western Europe. It is also all too clear from the late 1970s that Soviet expansionism is not likely to be confined to Eastern Europe, but is ominously spreading to Africa, the Middle East and the Indian Ocean. If the military cost of defending these areas, in addition to full nuclear rearmament, were really to fall on Western Europe, unsupported by the US, Western Europe would be economically crippled.

Those who sincerely believe that the foundation of another super-power is desirable in itself, should ask themselves a broader question. Is the creation of a fourth super-power, rather than the strengthening of genuine international institutions, really likely to promote peace and stability? History suggests the contrary. The unification of Germany in the Bismarck era of the 1860s, which with its customs union led to political centralization, is the closest analogy and to some extent the prototype of the EEC. But that nineteenth-century unification led, oronically enough, to *three* Great Wars. German 'unity' was the condition, if not the cause, of the wars of 1870, 1914 and 1939. Without a German super-state, these wars would not have occurred. This record also shows the hollowness of the facile assumption that the creation of a fourth super-state would enhance the security of Western Europe or anywhere else.

Thus when the whole issue was seriously thought out, the over-riding conclusion emerged that for the UK to join the Common Market on terms involving wholesale acceptance of the Treaty of Rome and the CAP, was to sacrifice the substance of our national future for a shadow. The economic and constitutional sacrifices were certain, substantial and immediate. The 'political' gains were hypothetical, distant and vague. In fact the economic loss was bound to mean a political loss in the medium and long term, just because the political strength of a modern nation depends on its economic potential. Far the safer course, therefore, was to adopt the widest international, rather than narrow, regional alternative. That was the conclusion of the broad general argument. To me personally, in addition, to swallow the Rome Treaty and the CAP, food taxes and all, would be to abandon my lifelong belief in redistribution of wealth by progressive taxes from the rich to the poor; in free imports of food; in law-making as well as government by elected authorities; and in international organization rather than regional blocs. To sacrifice all this would be to go back on 1689 and 1832 as well as 1846 and 1945. So for me the die was cast.

Yet after the 1966 election, for no solid economic or practical reason, organized pressure began to mount. Why, and from where it came, is better answered later on in this narrative.[13] As early as June 1965, because even then there were signs that the DEA was tending to convert itself into a pro-Market pressure group, I set out a formal and considered analysis of the economic consequences of joining on any terms which then seemed probable. I had been asked at a ministerial meeting on 25 March to circulate such a paper. I sent it formally to the PM on 15 June 1965, saying that it had been composed with the help of the Minister of Agriculture (Fred Peart).

In this paper I argued the basic free-trade case against entry involving the acceptance of the CAP. I explained that membership would mean 'the imposition of a new series of levies and other import barriers against a large proportion of our imports of food and temperate agricultural products, and some materials, which now enter duty-free and quota-free'; that this would cause 'a switch of our food supplies from cheaper Commonwealth and other non-EEC sources partly to dearer suppliers from within the Six and partly to dearer home production' and so 'a rise in the average price of our food imports as a whole', and a resulting 'large and permanent damage to the balance of payments'. In the light of the Ministry of Agriculture figures I suggested – very modestly as it turned out – that retail food prices would be gratuitously raised by £600 million or £700 million (in 1965 money values) or about 14 per cent. With similar understatement I estimated that the effect on the rest of our trade with Western Europe would be 'neutral', i.e., that the much publicized increase in our exports to the EEC could be at least balanced by an increase in imports. My conclusion was that 'economically the application of the EEC's agricultural and levy system to the UK would be heavily disadvantageous to us on balance in the long run as well as the short.'

This was the only serious analysis of entry which surfaced among ministers – or so far as I know was made – in Whitehall in 1965. Neither the DEA nor the Foreign Office attempted any reasoned answer. At this stage Michael Stewart, as Foreign Secretary, and his Permanent Secretary, Harold Caccia, were expressing general support for our policy of strengthening EFTA and the Commonwealth links, which was in 1965, gradually improving our balance of payments. In the debate on foreign affairs at the

[13] See chapter 15.

Labour Party Conference of October 1965, Stewart spoke of 'technological co-operation, work to reduce tariffs and greater cultural contacts', and concluded: 'It is more sense to go on with these things than to talk in an airy fashion of "joining with Europe" without defining what you really mean.' Yet after the 1966 election a 'Ministerial Committee on Europe' of the Cabinet was set up by Wilson, which included himself as Chairman, Stewart, Brown, Callaghan, Healey, Peart, Thomson, Bowden and myself. Other ministers appeared at times. At an EFTA Conference in May 1966 in Bergen, in a sort of mediaeval Viking castle, melodrama was avoided; and I was able to talk with George Thomson, a friend of mine since *Forward* days, about the whole Market issue, and set out the hard facts about the CAP and our balance of payments. He admitted to no views of his own. In the Committee itself in May 1966, as I recorded at the time, 'there was a majority clearly against any overt move, and in favour of building up EFTA and concentrating on our own balance of payments problem.' Stewart expressed views in this sense, and Peart and Crossman supported him. Only Brown wanted to forge straight ahead with EEC membership, despite our own looming balance of payments difficulties.

After my visit to Canada in May 1966 already recorded, I decided to circulate to the Committee a more formal paper setting out the damage to our balance of payments likely to follow from acceptance of the CAP. Before circulating this paper to other ministers in July, I gathered comments on it from all those concerned at the Board of Trade. It was wholly concerned with the economic consequences, short-term and long-term, of member-ship or association with the EEC. Though there were of course differing estimates of the various balance of payments loss involved, the only explicit disagreement I encountered in my own Department with the general expectation of some substantial loss was from my Permanent Secretary, Sir Richard Powell. He minimized the losses due to higher food prices, and argued that given reasonable transitional arrangements and adequate economic management the effects could be contained, and the improvement in productivity that would come from exposure to stiffer competition would be a countervailing gain. This was a fair statement of the intelligent pro-Market case, though it omitted any criticism of my statistical estimates. I thought it at the time just as much a piece of wishful thinking as it appears in the late 1970s after a good few years of 'exposure to stiffer competition'. Apart from this in my three years at the Board of Trade, Sir Richard and I hardly ever had a major disagreement, and at all other times I had the greatest confidence in his open-mindedness and the greatest respect for his abilities. Possibly, however, in the case of the EEC I should have ensured more positively that my view was maintained firmly throughout Whitehall as being those of the Board of Trade.

Both before and after my amended paper was circulated in July to ministers, there was still a clear majority in favour of not pushing Market approaches any further. Healey and Peart were on my side in the relevant Committee; Stewart and Callaghan were somewhat wobbly, and Wilson oracular, not to say incoherent. Peart wrote to me on 10 June saying he was 'very much in sympathy with your general line of argument, and in particular with the conclusion that we should be in no hurry to start bargaining with the EEC or probing in a way which might slide into negotiation before we have properly assessed the economic implications'. George Thomson had to deny on 28 June that he had said at a Western European Union meeting that we were to 'seek entry' to the EEC. Crossman joined in on 4 July with a minute to Stewart (still Foreign Secretary) protesting about the conflict between the current FO 'guidance' telegrams and the PM's Bristol speech during the election campaign, and declaring himself 'alarmed' that changes of policy seemed to be contemplated. I sent a short minute to Stewart on the following day 5 July in these words:

I have seen Crossman's minute to you of 4 July on our attitude to the EEC. I should like to say, in advance of the French PM's visit here this week that I agree strongly with the general argument of his minute. The PM's speech at Bristol seemed to me a fair summary of the Government's policy, and I am not aware of any decision to change it since. In particular I disagree with the implication in the brief for the French visit . . . that the UK might in certain circumstances be prepared to accept the CAP.

Michael Stewart replied to both of these minutes by saying that the FO briefs did not conflict with the PM's speech in the Debate on the Address in April, and that he had no 'wish to pre-judge the decisions which will have to be taken in the light of' the various studies which were supposed to be going on. Meanwhile Brown alone was overtly pressing for some gratuitous move. It only emerged in November that 'during 1966' Brown and Thomson had been holding 'exploratory discussions' with European countries.

A few days after the announcement of the 20 July economic measures, however, Wilson – as already related here – transferred Brown to the Foreign Office. Nobody, least of all Brown or Stewart, had expected this. Had Brown been allowed to resign on 20 July, the application to join the Market would probably never have been made. Why did Wilson make this decision? He says himself:[14] 'We seemed to be drawing near to the point where we would have to take a decision about Europe.' (Wilson seemed, by the time this book was written, to have himself fallen into the verbal confusion between Europe and the Common Market.) 'George Brown seemed to me the appropriate leader for the task that lay ahead.' But this only made sense if Wilson wanted to join the Market; and this would have been in violent contradiction with his Bristol speech only four months earlier. With more reason he may have feared that great trouble would have been caused by Brown, as head of an economic department,

[14] Wilson, p. 272

leading an almost open campaign of opposition within the Government against the Chancellor's economic policy now accepted by the Cabinet; and that there seemed nowhere else to put him except the FO.

In early September of 1966 I left for a fortnight's speech-making tour of Australia, which had two aims: the first to promote British exports; and secondly to assure the Australian Government and public that Britain would abide by its defence commitments with Australia, and that if we ever joined the Common Market, Australia's essential trade with us would be effectively safeguarded. I repeated these assurances in good faith throughout Australia; as they had been explicitly agreed with the other senior ministers concerned in London. Both the Board of Trade and Commonwealth Relations Office were very anxious that I should make this trip. But I felt deeply in the following year that these assurances were not being honoured; and this was one main reason for my growing disillusion with my own Government. Before I left for Australia, Sir Alexander Downer, the Australian High Commssioner in London came to see me, and urged me with great persuasiveness and feeling to do whatever I could to prevent the two countries drifting apart. He impressed me immensely. At this time all the fashionable media talk was about 'weakening' of the Commonwealth link and waning of pro-British sentiment in Australia. Downer believed all this to be superficial; he greatly valued the association between the two countries; and he was deeply anxious for much more determined efforts to preserve it. The memory of my talk with him, and many others in Australia, again made painfully manifest to me what a wealth of goodwill and influence this country gratuitously threw away in countries like Australia by failing to champion our own interests and their own in the negotiations with Brussels.

The Australian tour itself was extremely strenuous. Since Australians tended to complain that British ministers seldom visited them, I kept assignments at Brisbane, Canberra, Sydney, Hobart, Melbourne, Adelaide and Perth; attended a Cabinet meeting and Question Time – more informal than ours – in Canberra; met a host of Australians from the Conservative PM, Mr Holt, and future Labour Leader, Gough Whitlam, to Don Bradman. The ablest political leader seemed to me to be Jack ('Black Jack') McEwan who had converted the Country Party to an industrial outlook. Outside the conference rooms and hotels I was pleasantly surprised, due in part to unfamiliarity, by the colour, warmth and variety of the semi-tropical Australian scene; Hobart in particular, more unspoilt than Sydney, rivalled Rio and San Francisco in spectacular beauty. This was the most rewarding as well as exhausting of all the journeys I made for the Board of Trade, basically because the common institutions and the common interests of the two countries were so plain. Australia could sell us great quantities of grain, meat and dairy products – the staple foods of the British public – at the lowest prices in the world, and offer free entry or a preference to most of our exports in return. I was foolish enough in these two weeks to believe that such manifest advantages for us must be obvious to all sane people in my own country.

Back in England in October this seemed rather more doubtful. I learnt that there was to be a meeting at Chequers on Saturday 22 October, to discuss yet again our attitude to the Common Market; and anxieties began again to mount. The Chequers gathering was a meeting of Cabinet ministers and not a formal Cabinet; and leading officials were present. These included William Armstrong from the Treasury, Burke Trend, Douglas Allen of the DEA (head of the Treasury in later years), Con O'Neill from the Foreign Office and Tommy Balogh from No. 10. The plan was for ministers to listen to and question officials in the morning and then themselves as ministers express their own views in the afternoon. The difficulty about the morning session was to know whether officials were expressing their own unbiassed personal views, or supposed to be making factual statements or trying to represent their ministers' views. This led to some trouble in the afternoon because ministers were alleged to be unfairly quoting other ministers' officials on their side. Most notable contribution came from William Armstrong, an essentially honest man. He said in effect that the British economy could not for eighteen months or two years stand such an adventure as joining the Market. He spoke with restraint, but powerfully as ever. It was fairly clear, though he did not say so explicitly, that he thought an approach to the Market would force devaluation of sterling. Brown and Con O'Neill were evidently furious at Armstrong's telling the truth. But the weight of official evidence was against any abrupt move, and I went into lunch feeling that if Armstrong and Balogh agreed they could hardly be wrong.

After the amicable lunch, every member of the Cabinet assembled for the afternoon session. My record made at the time of this gathering was as follows:

In favour of a move towards the EEC were George Brown, of course, Jenkins, Crosland, Gardiner, Gunter, Pakenham, Houghton, Gordon-Walker, and Cledwyn-Hughes. Against were Healey, most powerfully, Peart, Bowden, Marsh, Ross, Castle, Greenwood and myself. Wobbling carefully were Callaghan and Stewart, and wobbling frivolously Dick Crossman – who said in effect that the whole thing was futile and undesirable, but that as he knew it would not succeed, he favoured other people making themselves ridiculous by trying. This was counted as a vote at this solemn assembly in favour of our joining the EEC. Harold summed up at the end, saying on the one hand and on the other, etc, and suddenly producing a plan out of his hat for him and George Brown doing a joint 'probe' round the Six to see if the conditions existed for favourable negotiations. We were assured that alternatives would be explored, so that we would not be left like the Tories with no policy if we failed; that we would not accept surrender terms like Heath; and that the negotiations would not be allowed just to drag on. Harold Wilson said the team would be balanced because Brown in the past had been pro-EEC and HW against. He tried to convey the impression to the anti-Marketeers that he was still sceptical.

I said that I presumed we were taking no formal decision on a proposal we had only heard verbally a few moments before, and Wilson agreed.

Nearly half the Cabinet were at this stage against any application to join; and if Callaghan and Crossman had been so counted, more than half. Some of the others, I thought, supported it more out of the belief that Wilson wanted this, than for any other reason. (Douglas Evans in his book, *While Britain Slept*[15] gives, with no authority quoted: Jay, Peart, Castle, Marsh, Crossman and Benn as 'either opposed outright or deeply sceptical'. My memory is that Benn was somewhat ambiguously in favour.) Even I found Crossman's frivolity on this occasion breath-taking. An issue which would drastically affect the living standards and political constitution of this country for a generation was to be handled as little more than a parlour game. Crosland I also found sadly disappointing. He had long professed to be impartial and uninterested in the issue. On this afternoon he asked me why, if the economic arguments were so adverse, most industrialists favoured joining. But he knew as well as I did that if you asked industrialists what effect they estimated higher food prices would have on their labour costs, most of them did not understand the question. The truth was that few industrialists had thought it out, as was proved later by the huge swing in the trade balance in manufactures against this country which virtually none of them foresaw.

It was pretty clear to me at the end of the afternoon on 22 October that Wilson had thought of his probe idea well before the meeting, concerted it with George Brown and waited till the end to introduce it as a compromise. This indeed he admits in his own account.[16] If he had proposed an immediate application then, a majority of the Cabinet, including Healey, would have been against it. In addition, as Healey frequently insisted, de Gaulle would veto it. At the time of the Chequers talk Healey and Peart told me they were uncertain what Wilson was contriving. Some colleagues thought he intended the probe as a device to prove to the Tories that real negotiation was not possible. But by this time I had little doubt that Wilson had devised this strategem, so as to appear to be suggesting a middle course, but that he really intended it to lead on to a surrender. Peart a little later told me that he was not sure that Wilson was not now intending an application. Naturally it was not easy for any member of the Cabinet to oppose outright what was represented as a compromise method of testing out the ground, with no commitments; and so the decision was taken on 9 November, and announced in Parliament on 10 November, to conduct a 'probe' of the Common Market capitals. In this announcement Wilson said that the probe did not amount to acceptance of the CAP or even to an

[15] Douglas Evans, *While Britain Slept : The Selling of the Common Market* (London, 1975).
[16] Wilson, pp. 293–4.

application for membership. But by this time general distrust of Wilson's intentions was spreading among his colleagues. By inserting the words 'We mean business' in this statement, Wilson in my view went beyond the spirit of the ministers' agreement at Chequers. In retrospect it became clear that the object of the probe was not primarily to find out the facts, but to allow time for a major reversal of policy not to look too glaring.

The question remains, and must now be asked, why Wilson suddenly embarked on this U-turn at this moment. He himself says:[17] 'The case for applying to join the EEC had been strengthened in my mind.' But he does not say why. He merely remarks[18] that a number of Labour Members in the 1966 Parliament were pro-EEC; but this could hardly have impressed him so much and so quickly. Nor had there been any change in the real facts, or the fundamental merits of the argument, since Wilson's Bristol speech in March. Why then did he change his view between March and October? An intelligent man does not, on rational grounds, alter his entire view on a fundamental issue affecting the whole future of his country in six or seven months, when the facts have not changed. There was no visible sign of Wilson's somersault until Brown arrived at the FO at the end of July. Nor is there any dispute that Brown, wanting a new venture after the eclipse of his own DEA on 20 July, put heavy pressure on Wilson from that moment to move towards joining the Market. He found a willing accomplice at the FO in Con O'Neill, who had become something of a Euro-fanatic in the course of his spell as Ambassador to the EEC in Brussels, if not before.

Why, however, did Wilson capitulate to this pressure? Surely a mere desire to stop Brown pestering him on this subject cannot be the whole explanation. Since motives are not capable of proof, I can only state the opinion I formed at the time, and have found confirmed by much evidence since. Wilson tended to be obsessed by the press, and in particular what it said about him. Just as Attlee almost totally ignored it, and cared nothing for what it said; so Wilson could not get it out of his mind. Brown had long been a friend of Cecil King, Chairman of the *Daily Mirror* Group, and had quite openly and legitimately worked for this group before 1964, as recorded earlier here. King, like many in the City at the time, had become a pro-Market extremist, and was plainly urging Brown and Wilson to push on with an application. King's own diaries make all too candidly clear, what was unknown to most of Wilson's colleagues at the time, that King was frequently indulging in private conversations with Wilson.[19] (Indeed he was actually offered a post as a junior Minister at the Board of Trade, which was happily averted by the grace of God and his own refusal.)[20]

[17] Wilson, p. 293.
[18] Wilson, p. 224.
[19] *The Cecil King Diary 1965-70* (London, 1972).
[20] King describes himself frankly as knowing 'nothing of exports' (King, entry for August 1965).

Wilson would have been extremely sensitive to any threat of a press campaign by the *Mirror* Group denouncing him as unfit to be PM; and the fact that such a campaign was eventually launched by King shows that it was no idle threat; even though, with a rich irony, it ended in the eclipse not of Wilson, but of the egregious Mr King. No doubt many influences were playing on Wilson; but I see no convincing explanations of his sudden and unexplained change of front between March and October of 1966 other than the threat held over him of a hostile press campaign from the *Mirror* Group, and the belief that this could be skilfully averted by at least the appearance of an approach to Brussels. I wrote at the time that I felt sure 'George Brown and ultimately Cecil King had pushed HW into all this.'

Some may question whether such a man as King would have tried to pressurize Wilson on his EEC policies, or presume to interfere with his selection of Ministers. I would invite such doubters to study the evidence advanced by King himself: in particular the following entries in his published diaries:

11 February 1966: Wilson is planning to take the country into the Common Market. George [Brown] is scared of announcing this now, as it might split the Party.

20 March 1966: As I have mentioned earlier in this diary, I was told by George Brown that Wilson intends to join the Common Market.

19 April 1966: Had an hour with PM. Was asked for the first time to go in through the Cabinet Office in Whitehall. . . . About Europe, he said he thought we should be in in two to three years. The negotiations would be done by Thomson and not by George Brown.

26 June 1966: My dear Harold . . . The Common Market. This is not the best British foreign policy. It is the only one.

5 July 1966: My lunch with Wilson lasted one and a half hours, and was a deep disappointment . . . I said I should have thought it better to dismiss Cousins rather than wait for him to resign. [One can imagine the reply that Attlee would have given to this advice.]

24 July 1966: Had lunch at Much Hadham with Mark Norman. Among other guests was Louis Franck, Chairman of Samuel Montagu, and regarded as one of the ablest of the merchant bankers. . . . He seemed to know a lot about me, and said that some future Government would have to have a large business element. In such a Government he foresaw prominent places for Robens and myself.

8 November 1966: George [Brown] thinks he will screw up Wilson to make a joint statement with him about joining the Common Market.

10 November 1966: Wilson has come out this afternoon with a pretty definite declaration of his intention to join the Common Market. Hugh Cudlipp was summoned at 2.30 p.m. to 10 Downing Street to be told the glad news . . . Hugh was quick to point out to me – undoubtedly correctly – that Wilson is in trouble with Rhodesia and in a mess at home and this is, in part, a gigantic red herring to distract attention.

Cecil King speaks for himself. But whatever precise weight you assign to his prodding of such a man as Wilson, it was after 22 October 1966 that the fatal slide began. Within a few days of the Chequers meeting of that day, and before the statement in the House on 10 November, the normal three-monthly meeting of EFTA ministers was held at Lisbon on 26-9 October. The other EFTA countries, notably Sweden, Switzerland, and Portugal, were extremely anxious that the UK should not break away and join the Common Market. Only Denmark was hesitant. The rest preferred strongly, as did I, 'strengthening' and if possible enlarging EFTA. They wished to retain their political imdependence, and control of internal economic policy, and were confident that EFTA could (as it did) reach an industrial free-trade agreement with the Market. But our own FO was embarking on a manoeuvre to extract ourselves from the London Declaration, rightly agreed by Maudling earlier, which Gaitskell strongly backed, that no EFTA country would secede to the Market unless all did together.

The FO policy of trying to creep out of this undertaking was another example, together with the treatment of our Commonwealth colleagues, of the alienation of the goodwill of our best friends by eroding our obligations to them, which was involved in a hasty rush into the Market. Fortunately Michael Stewart, though now First Secretary at the DEA and not Foreign Secretary, came with me to Lisbon; so that we were spared any theatricals. Indeed, in the course of the argument over the 'London Declaration', Stewart actually proposed adding words to the communiqué which would strengthen the binding force of that Declaration. He was thoroughly straightforward in reporting back to London the strong opposition of our EFTA partners to any secession to the Market. We agreed, together with George Thomson and the officials on our delegation, to send a telegram to colleagues at home in this sense. Schaffner, of Switzerland added pointedly that de Gaulle would undoubtedly veto British membership, as he did. Indeed, just before we left Lisbon, de Gaulle made an uncompromising statement opposing British membership. This made me feel a good deal happier than for some time; and I gratefully enjoyed the genuine gaiety of the final dinner and dance in a superb royal palace. The contrast nevertheless was a little too glaring between this faded eighteenth century splendour and the visible poverty in the Lisbon streets. The Salazar regime was still in power.

On Monday 5 December, the heads of government of the EFTA countries – Sweden, Norway, Denmark, Switzerland, Finland, Austria and Portugal – were assembled at our invitation in Lancaster House to be told about the forthcoming 'probe'. They were also, as the FO hoped, to be induced to acquiesce in our abandoning our obligations under the London Declaration. It was, I felt throughout, a thoroughly discreditable proceeding. Here were the Prime Ministers of six friendly countries, who wished to continue an association beneficial to us all, and to whom we were bound by Treaty; and we proposed to tell them that we intended to slide out of our undertakings. In the morning Herr Schaffner, now President of the Swiss Federation, made a passionate speech in colourful, almost Shakespearian, English denouncing the whole manoeuvre. He recalled how the ancestors of the Swiss, the Helvetii, decided to emigrate to Gaul in 58 BC, and before leaving, burnt their villages and their fruit trees to ensure that no laggards hung back. But in the Rhone Valley they encountered Julius Caesar at the start of his famous marauding expedition into Gaul and Britain; and the Swiss army was massacred, leaving a miserable remainder to return to a derelict country. This was a historic warning, he said, against burning one's boats or one's homes. Switzerland would stand by EFTA. Schaffner was eloquent, powerful and unanswerable; the delegates dispersed for lunch with his oration ringing in their ears.

After lunch, however, when these six distinguished PMs led by Herr Krag of Sweden, were to have re-assembled in the Conference room at the due hour, George Brown failed to reappear. After some minutes, it was reported that he was drafting what he called a communiqué in the lunch room. He called for a typist, and after a further pause, Wilson arrived and invited Brown to re-join the Conference; to which Brown replied in the hearing of several EFTA ministers: 'I call for a typist: and all I get is a prime minister.' Wilson then went for a walk in Lancaster House garden, and we all waited another twenty minutes or so for the British Foreign Secretary to reappear in the Conference. I could never understand the motives of the two chief actors in this comedy; but I did not feel it greatly enhanced the reputation of the British Government – or sadly the country – for dignity or wisdom. Whether it much softened the resentment felt by the visiting ministers at the British desertion of EFTA, only Hans Schaffner could adequately relate. Perhaps this is why Wilson himself, in his detailed account in *The Labour Government 1964–70* never mentions the meeting of 5 December 1966, at Lancaster House; but merely comments as follows on the dinner to EFTA ministers at Chequers the night before: 'What a relief it was to meet with serious heads of Government who knew what they wanted and meant what they said.'[21] This I can unreservedly applaud. On the day after the Lancaster House meeting Brown informed his ministerial colleagues that the Probe met with the unanimous support of the EFTA countries.

After the EFTA meeting in December the Probe duly began and continued throughout the early months of 1967. It was no more than a charade from the start. The realities were that de Gaulle would not agree to British entry; that great economic damage would be done to us on any terms remotely possible; that the French knew this very well; that the EFTA countries passionately wanted us to stand by EFTA; and that the EEC

[21] Wilson, p. 317.

countries apart from France were not deeply interested. The myth was that Wilson and Brown were discovering the terms on which entry might be possible. So throughout the winter the two of them strutted and fretted their hour upon the stage. They went to Rome and Paris in January 1967, and Brussels, Bonn and Hague in February. The performance was accompanied by a vast outpouring of telegrams by the FO, the ritual official entertainments, much dialogue by the leading actors, and no doubt a major expenditure of public money. But nothing material was learnt which we did not know before. None of the telegrams dared discuss what really mattered: the extra cost of the burden which the CAP and EEC budget would impose on our balance of payments. Wilson reported expansively to his ministerial colleagues on the state of the game. After the Paris visit, for instance, he explained that de Gaulle had been greatly impressed to learn how much grain was now produced annually in Britain. Asked by Healey how de Gaulle had expressed his interest in this, Wilson answered that he had said little. 'Perhaps he was bored,' replied Healey.

The French did show, however, how well they understood the real facts, and how unlikely they then thought that we would surrender on the CAP. M. Pompidou, the PM, is quoted by Wilson[22] as saying that 'there might be great difficulty in absorbing' Britain's world-wide Commonwealth interests 'within a Community which was more restricted in terms of its geographical horizons and more protectionist in terms of its economic policies'. De Gaulle himself then made an observation which, if followed up, would have been worth more than all the play-acting of that winter. He asked whether 'some other means of British participation' could be found . . . 'an agreement between Britain and the Six' . . . 'something entirely new'.[23] This was evidently the seed of the offer[24] again made by the General in February 1969 and so fatally rebuffed by the FO. It could have offered a settlement acceptable to all, which would have avoided all the damage to this country. The General understood it all clearly enough. Further evidence that some settlement of this kind could have been reached if the British Government had pressed hard enough for it, comes from a telegram sent by Patrick Reilly, our Ambassador in Paris, a little earlier (11 June 1966) recording a conversation of his with M. Couve de Murville, then Foreign Secretary. Couve de Murville said he saw three possibilities: (1) The UK might accept the CAP. (2) The UK might enter the EEC without participation in the CAP. (3) The EEC might decide to scrap the CAP and re-negotiate. Reilly added: 'I asked M. Couve whether he thought the second and third possibilities, which seemed to me the most interesting, were really likely to be politically acceptable to the Six. He replied that he thought that politically they would be very difficult indeed. Nevertheless he thought

[22] Wilson, pp. 339-40.
[23] Wilson, pp. 340-1: reported to the Cabinet on 26 January.
[24] See pages ooo and ooo.

that if they were of interest to the UK they should be discussed, and that it would be wrong to evade them.' So these alternatives were not totally ruled out from the start by the de Gaulle regime.

Amidst all this I lunched on 29 November with John Silkin, then Government Chief Whip, who turned out to be strongly sympathetic to my views on the Common Market. Since Government Chief Whips normally sit silent, looking wise, in Cabinet itself, it was a pleasure to hear his candid views. He thought I should acquire a second Parliamentary Private Secretary, because he said pro-Market ministers were indulging in pro-Market propaganda in the Parliamentary Labour Party, and it should be countered. I told him that my PPS, Dan Jones of Burnley, had all the Celtic virtues, even though he was once accused by my private office (no doubt falsely) of pairing himself for a crucial vote and failing to pair me. Official private secretaries believe that the prime function of a PPS is to pair their ministers when necessary, remembering no doubt W. S. Gilbert's classic definition of the function of a PPS:

> . . . The privilege and pleasure
> Which we treasure beyond measure
> Is to run on little errands
> For the Ministers of State.

John Silkin most helpfully suggested a Labour Member, whom I little knew, as a supplementary PPS; and as my private office wanted a special 'pairing PPS', and Silkin pressed his candidate, I agreed. It was a mistake. The new PPS exhibited a tendency towards innocent indiscretions of which I knew nothing, but which were then attributed to me by those with suspicious and guilty minds.

By December 1966 the monthly trade figures, which had become by this time the thermometer of the Government's success or failure began to improve. Our export promotion efforts, now that the effect of the seamen's strike had worn off, were beginning to tell, assisted by the 1966 deflation. I found the December figures good enough for me to return to the charge in the relevant Cabinet Committee on the July measures, and argue that there should be some relaxation. In December meetings of his ministerial committee, I argued for an easing of the HP restrictions in the depressed car industry and for a continued advance factory programme in the Development Areas. The first was opposed by my colleagues, but the latter accepted. I was reasonably pleased with this half loaf, because it impinged on the greatest area of need. As unemployment had already by December 1966 risen above the level contemplated by the July measures, I took care to announce a new advance factory programme in the House. Also in December came an even more pleasant interlude: another tour of the North-East Coast areas, to see new factories and estates now being built. With Sadler Forster and the equally zealous Board of Trade Regional

Controller Ronald Wood, I visited Team Valley, Sunderland, Billingham, Consett and elsewhere in a day and a half. This strenuous trip ended with a brief but vivid flash-back to my past – and future – life in the form of lunch at the Northumberland home of John Pumphrey, a close friend in my sixth year at Winchester, now Deputy-Chairman of the Northern Area of the National Coal Board, with Christine Bicknell who had fought with me for the Distribution of Industry Bill in 1944–5, and my secretary, Mary Thomas.

In January 1967 still more encouraging trade returns were published. Imports had dropped in November, because of the impending end of the surcharge, from about £500 million to £437 million; and the rebound of these postponed imports might have been expected to push up the total in December to about £570 million. In fact it was only £507 million, against exports of £423 million. These seemed to the Board of Trade statisticians to be the best trade returns for two years, and presaged a possible actual visible surplus if no strike or other misfortune intervened. In the Ministerial Steering Committee on Economic Policy – despite my fear that an EEC application might blight all these hopes – I pressed for some more cautious relaxation. The Committee now consisted of Wilson, Callaghan, Brown, Stewart, Gunter, Crossman, Healey, Houghton and myself. Others of course attended.

The 'Probe' and our attitude to the EEC were also discussed in this Committee on 9 January. Briefs for the probe had been produced by the FO, which were characteristically weak and woolly on the economic issues, and seemed to me to be beginning to imply capitulation on the CAP. I had therefore circulated a paper of my own, arguing that as we were engaged in a Probe and not negotiations, the briefs should be taken as implying no decisions on policy. I expected to be in a minority, though counting on support from Healey, Peart and Bowden, whom I had seen beforehand, and was prepared for a showdown. Wilson started by saying that no decisions were implied one way or the other by the briefs, and called on me for comment. I said I merely wanted to be sure we were making no new decisions, but wondered afterwards whether I should have said more. That day I lunched with Peart. He left me with the belief that if I was going to resign on this issue, I should resign virtually alone.

The Steering Committee met again on 13 January to review the employment prospects and the consequences of the July measure. Contrary to the advice of my Department and Callaghan, I had put in a paper arguing that unemployment had gone far enough and advocating lower interest rates and a relaxation of HP curbs, particularly on cars. Unemployment had now reached 2·6 per cent. Before the meeting I had a private talk with Callaghan, and came nearer to serious disagreement with him than ever before. HP regulations were formally my responsibility. However, I agreed to leave out from my paper mention of interest rates, since Callaghan feared garrulity about this on the part of Crossman. At the Committee I only got audible support for any relaxation from Frank Longford. Wilson and Callaghan argued that any relief should come in the Budget. The debate that day was on a higher level than usual, despite dark hints from Brown and Crossman about floating rates. I fully supported a paper from Callaghan advocating a long-term policy of keeping unemployment under 2 per cent and Callaghan on this morning was particularly friendly. The good trade returns mentioned above had been published the day before. Wilson to my surprise actually said 'the President of the Board of Trade has raised exports 20 per cent above the equivalent month of 1964'.

An effort next day to take a free relaxed Saturday evening off with my wife at the Carlton cinema had an unexpected sequel. Walking back along Pall Mall afterwards, who should we meet but George Brown and his wife doing precisely the same thing. He invited us to a drink in the FO residence in Carlton House Terrace, and proved to be in a highly sentimental mood. I summoned up all my remaining fraternal spirit for the sake of harmony among colleagues. But George then plunged into a heartfelt lament about a malicious press campaign against him based apparently on some alleged indiscreet repartee with a lady at an Embassy dinner. The *New York Times* was the main target of his complaint. Since I had been marvelling for months at the restraint of the press in not reporting some other colourful incidents, I could hardly believe my ears. Satan rebuking sin is odd enough; but Falstaff complaining that he gets a bad press seemed to me even odder.

In the second half of January, however, the Common Market controversy was warming up in the House as well as within the Government. For Wilson and Brown were due to embark on their trip to Paris on 24 and 25 January. It became clear at this time that pro-Market propaganda from the European Movement and the EEC Commission itself was being brought to bear on a massive financial scale on the press, universities, Parliament and industry. As contacts were clearly being maintained by these pressure lobbies with ministers like Jenkins in the Government, the rest of us were compelled to forge similar contacts. William Pickles of the LSE, a life-long expert on France, understood better than almost anybody what was going on, and remained a valuable adviser, as I had found him in 1961 and 1962. On 20 January an excellent letter was published in *The Times* from Pickles, Roy Harrod, Richard Kahn of Kings College, Cambridge, and others warning us of the economic and political trap into which we were being led. On the day before I had been asked to speak on 'Britain's Trade and the EEC' to a London Labour Party gathering in Committee Room 14 in the House. To my surprise 250 people turned up to what I had expected to be a private meeting, for which I had no written text. I spoke first of the success of the export campaign, and secondly gave a formal economic analysis of the effects of joining the Market on various conditions, without arguing for or against membership, and quoting only the figures used by Wilson in his March 1966 speech. Not a single word leaked from this virtually public meeting to the press.

Wilson and Brown reported to ministers on 26 January their meeting with de Gaulle in the previous two days. It was at this meeting – or rather in the course of a friendly lunch – that de Gaulle was reported to have spoken oracularly about 'something entirely new' and specially designed to suit this country. I only intervened to say that this was precisely the sort of arrangement I was advocating, and that it should be strenuously pursued. Both Callaghan and Crossman smiled at me sympathetically at this point; but I doubted whether many others present grasped the nature of the crucial opportunity we were being offered. It was also at this meeting that Brown challenged Crossman about reports that he was composing a diary record of Government transactions for later verbatim publication. Crossman replied that if his colleagues did not like this, he would resign and continue the diary outside. I could not help wondering whether Wilson and Brown were not prolonging this trivial squabble in order to divert ministers from discussing the crucial offer which de Gaulle had made. One or two of those present seemed for the moment more interested in the future of Crossman's diary than the future of the country.

Attlee at this moment sent a public message to Shinwell congratulating him on his anti-Market stand, and saying there was no need to be 'hustled into' the EEC. Several colleagues commented to me that a view held by both Attlee and Gaiskell did deserve to be taken rather seriously. In the same week Will Blyton, the well-known Durham Miners' MP, told me that an anti-Market group of Labour MPs had been re-formed with Alfred Morris, Peart's PPS, as secretary. He said one hundred MPs had promised support. By this time I had become nearly convinced that Wilson meant to capitulate, and offer membership on any terms, and that I should have to resign in the spring.

Two other temporary diversions from the strains of this controversy occurred in February 1967. First Crossman introduced a wonderful reforming plan for the House of Commons to sit in the morning; and secondly Kosygin and his Trade Minister, Patolichev, visited London. The great Crossman reform ended in a fiasco. The real abiding reason why Parliament cannot normally meet in the morning is that secretaries nowadays will not work after 8 p.m.; and the only way for a Member to handle his constituency correspondence properly is to work on this in the morning, and attend the House and its committees in the latter half of the day. So on 1 February at the first morning session so few people turned up that votes could not be taken, and had to be postponed till the afternoon. The sitting, however, continued till 3 a.m. next day, and the Government's crucial Consolidated Fund Bill was counted out and lost. Crossman tried to get it re-introduced next day, but was ruled out of order by the Speaker. So ended this experiment in modernizing Parliamentary procedure.

Kosygin's visit to London for a week from Monday 6 February, also began with a comedy. Callaghan, Brown, Benn and I were all lined up in Downing Street to travel to Gatwick, when fog diverted the plane to Heathrow. So we were all turned round, and the official drivers managed the eighteen miles from Downing Street to the appropriate Heathrow runway in eighteen minutes. At dinner that evening the number two in the Soviet Embassy in London, Vaseev, was very frank in conversation with me about the Chinese. They were in his view, primitive and crude; did not know how to manage a Communist state, let alone a great industrial society; and were conducting a 'peasant' or *petit bourgeois* revolution. Much of the Kosygin visit was taken up with frantic, if worthy efforts behind the scenes by Wilson and Kosygin to patch up a truce on the Vietnam war, which came to nothing, as Wilson relates.[25] On Tuesday morning in the official session at No. 10 – backed by an unaccustomed second row of advisers and translators – we discussed trade. I was asked to start with our standing complaint about the trade balance, knowing very well the Russian arguments. I proposed pressing on with a number of practical industrial deals, including one with Courtaulds, which was signed next day.

Kosygin, having recited the usual excuses, proposed a long-term agreement by which we could each plan ahead in the light of each other's industrial needs. This fitted in with Wilson's ideas of grand mutual planning arrangements and the Ministry of Technology. Though I was somewhat sceptical, we naturally welcomed the idea as a better chance for British exports. But when Trade Minister, Patolichev, visited London a little later ostensibly to work out concrete details of this, he took a thoroughly *laissez-faire* view, saying in effect that the Russians would buy goods as and when they wanted them. When we gently reminded him that Kosygin, his own Prime Minister, had suggested the whole idea, he seemed quite unmoved. He remarked – implying to me that Russian politics were in some ways not so unlike British – that there was no point in making forecasts because they only led to accusations that they were wrong and had not been carried out. Much the most useful method of trade negotiation with the Russians, I found, was to put their officials in direct touch with British firms that had goods to sell which the Russians wanted to buy.

Kosygin himself at the end of the first Downing Street session recorded his standard grievance about the 'COCOM' list of strategic goods banned from export to Russia, and enlivened it with a story that he had been heckled by Soviet workers in the Vladivostock area who were protesting about this sinister list. He accompanied this absurd picture with one of his rare, frosty smiles, which made it pretty clear he did not intend us to believe it. He thought it a good joke. In the following afternoon session I

[25] Wilson, pp. 350–65.

asked for greater facilities for BOAC and BEA – as they were then – in access to Leningrad and trans-Soviet flights to Japan, and quoted the Soviet agreement with Japan Air Lines. (The Board of Trade had by this time taken over civil aviation.) Kosygin, as ever full of information, contradicted flatly the account the Japanese had given us of their arrangement; but he was evidently willing for a deal. He agreed to the possibility being mentioned in the communiqué, and progress was made later on this front at least. At the end of that week, after such heavy mouthfuls of both the Common Market and Kosygin, I was not at all sorry to spend the week-end at All Souls, and dictate a full-dress speech on my coming Companies Bill for the Second Reading on Tuesday 14 February, in the House. For the moment even Company law seemed a more attractive subject than the Common Market.

After this peaceful Oxford interlude came a curious, chequered week in my ministerial life. First on 14 February, the same day as the Company Bill debate, I was able to publish a record monthly export figure of £472 million. This showed that our prolonged export promotion efforts were bearing fruit, but also that the disinflation of July 1966 was, as intended, helping exports. Unfortunately imports were also a record; partly thanks to the ending of the surcharge. On the next day I was due to talk with the Economic Group of the Parliamentary Labour Party. I was conscious that in the terrific pressure of Board of Trade work, I had not kept nearly as closely in touch with the Parliamentary Party as I wished, and therefore welcomed the meeting. The whole incident was, as it turned out, an excellent example of the conspiracy theory of politics – or rather the falsity of that theory. The Party authorities had without my knowledge fixed the meeting for this day with my private office; but the press afterwards concocted the fable that I had selected this date because Wilson and Brown would be on their travels in Bonn. Another theory, invented by the *Sunday Times*, was that I had acted in deep collusion with Wilson, in order to provide him with a makeweight in the Cabinet against Brown. In fact I arrived at the meeting armed with only very rough notes on several subjects such as the balance of payments, balance of trade and economics of joining the Common Market. Only four or five people were present (later about twenty), and when I enquired what subject they preferred, the vote went for the Common Market. It might just as easily have gone the other way. I then sketched out three or four different assumptions, and some estimates of the consequences, good and bad, for imports, exports, etc., but I repeated that I was reaching no conclusion. The rise in food prices, I said, was hard to estimate, and might on some assumptions be higher than a previous official estimate of $2\frac{1}{2}$–$3\frac{1}{2}$ per cent a year, perhaps up to 4 per cent. I had said much the same to the less confidential meeting (already recorded here[26]) of not twenty, but 200 or so, in the House only a few weeks before.

[26] On p. 374.

Next morning, however, I was astonished to see lead stories in *The Times* and other papers treating this casual talk as a considered statement of policy. Crossman rang me in apparent excitement at breakfast. Someone must have gone straight from the meeting to the papers concerned and given them a circumstantial but garbled report. The negligible differences between estimated rises of 3 or 4 per cent in the cost of living became a great 'split' in the Government. Some answer of mine about periodic flights of capital became 'a crisis every few years'. I never knew who it was that gave this report to the press; or whether his motive was a misguided belief that he was warning people of the dangers of joining the EEC, sheer garrulity or an attempt to be clever. But Wilson and Brown fairly evidently, if characteristically, believed it was the work of my new PPS acting with my connivance. Fortunately I had specifically told my PPS not to give any report to the press, and he assured me he had not done so. Since I detested leaks, whether disguised as 'open government' or otherwise, and seldom if ever spoke to the press, the whole incident would have been merely trivial, had there not existed in Downing Street at this time a tendency to believe in conspiracies. Wilson quite reasonably asked me to come and give an account of what really happened, and this I did, complete with my illegible notes. This meeting was mainly taken up, not, as was reported in the press, with discussion of my 'speech', but with my assurances that I frequently told my PPSs that they must observe the rules. Wilson admitted that my talk did not contravene Government policy. And that would have been the end of it, but for the misguided efforts of the staff at No. 10. It had been agreed between us that our meeting there should not be reported and that, in order to avoid more publicity, I should, as is often done, enter and leave No. 10 by way of the Cabinet offices and not through the front entrance. Next day the press reported that the meeting had occurred, and that I had entered and left by a back entrance.

This incident, thoroughly trivial in itself, aggravated, I found, a mistrust of the No. 10 regime which had been growing. In my first two years at the Board of Trade I disregarded warnings that sensitive information given to No. 10 might find its way into the press. But by 1967 a belief had spread in other private offices, including my own (whose standards were extremely high), that information, however confidential, given to No. 10 might find its way somehow to the press staff, who seemed to be a law unto themselves. Other ministers and Whitehall generally had become uneasy about the alleged existence of a 'kitchen cabinet' at No. 10. Up to 1967 I disregarded this as mere gossip. But Crossman's diaries, not to mention those of Marcia Williams (*Inside No. 10*) and Cecil King (*The Cecil King Diary 1965–70*) show that the cynics were not wholly wrong. Crossman records[27] Crosland saying in August 1966, after a protest by Wilson about leaks: 'Of course we don't mind that kind of thing being said by the PM, but

[27] Crossman, vol. 1, p. 603.

we all know that most of the information goes to the press either from No. 10 or from the environs of the DEA.' This way of running a government does not generate trust.

We in the Board of Trade in 1966-7 were particularly nervous about giving early information to No. 10 on the monthly trade figures, which of course were prepared initially by our Statistical Department. In these years Stock Exchange prices tended to jump sharply one way or the other on the publication of these figures, just as if they had been a Budget announcement. Any premature leak would have provoked a scandal which, in a hostile press, might have grown to the proportions of the Dalton catastrophe of 1947. To help in avoiding this, I had decided on the sensible advice of Gordon Newton, editor of the *Financial Times*, to state publicly at the start of the year the dates and times at which the figures would be made public every month. This responsibility was plainly mine. But No. 10 constantly asked for the figures twenty-four hours or even forty-eight hours before publication. After the 'Back Door' incident described above, I gave instructions that the trade figures, if asked for by No. 10, were only to be given personally and verbally by myself to the PM at his request. By this rather drastic means we averted a disaster.

A week after my impromptu talk to the Party Economic Group, I was due to speak formally on 23 February to the Commonwealth Producers Organization about Commonwealth trade. I therefore at the meeting with Wilson asked whether he thought I should speak there confidentially, or from a formal text given to the press. Rightly, I thought, he chose the latter, and reasonably asked to see the text first. Since lavishly financed pro-Market propaganda was trying to belittle Commonwealth trade, and since in fact in reasonably free and fair conditions 30 per cent of our trade was still with the Commonwealth Preference Area, and only 20 per cent with the Common Market, it seemed worthwhile simply to set out the bare facts; particularly as Wilson had long been an apostle of Commonwealth trade and had enthusiastically pressed for the extension of the British National Export Council to the Commonwealth, which I had carried through in 1964. The only comments, besides the figures, which I put in this speech were taken from Wilson's own speeches. He therefore agreed to the whole draft except for one sentence; and as I did not like his redraft of this, I omitted it altogether.

On the evening after this speech, I travelled to South Wales, actually this time to open two new industrial estates and speak in Swansea about our whole factory development and employment policy there. Two days before I had met the Scottish group of Labour MPs in the House and explained out plans for Scotland in detail. There was naturally renewed worry about unemployment in both Scotland and Wales. Since June, unemployment had risen in the country as a whole from under 1·5 to 2·6 per cent; and coalmine closures were threatened on a large scale. In Wales I started by opening a minor new estate at Pontadawe in the Swansea Valley, announced a new project there, and drove on to the Rhondda municipal offices to check progress on all practicable building sites in the Rhondda with the municipal, Board of Trade and Welsh Industrial Estate officials. We found that for every site except one, a definite project was planned. And so on to an extremely heartening afternoon at Talbot Green, Llantrisant. Here a new estate of seventy acres was launched, the biggest since Bridgend, Hirwaun and Swansea, with which I had been so closely involved in 1945. Llantrisant, was a nearly ideal site, being within easy daily travelling distance of the Rhondda, having plenty of space, and being the nucleus of an expanded town. Under the previous Heath regime at the Board of Trade, it would have been outside the Development Area, and so all government help would have been impossible. I was able to announce that building work on roads and new factories would start in two weeks. Not long afterwards, the Government was persuaded to move the Mint from near the Tower of London to Llantrisant; and this sealed the success of the whole project, both estate and town.

In the sharpest possible contrast with this cheering interlude, came next week the normal three-monthly EFTA Council Meeting, this time at Stockholm. In the circumstances, of course, it was dogged by general suspicion and regret at Britain's effort to join the Common Market on terms which the EFTA countries knew must turn out to be both damaging and humiliating. I could not relieve these anxieties, because I did not know either what Wilson intended, or what the Cabinet might decide. I flew to Stockholm with Michael Stewart, now First Secretary; and all we could expect to do was to temporize while expressing our own deep personal goodwill towards the EFTA countries and their ministers, particularly Lange of Sweden, Schaffner of Switzerland and Kreisky of Austria. At this conference, the individual declarations of faith in EFTA and respect for this country made to me personally by these ministers left me now inclined to believe I would have to resign if my own Government unilaterally applied to join the EEC. Schaffner again told me privately he believed that if an application were made to join the EEC, it would fail. On our first working day, Thursday 2 March, Brown arrived and appeared at the end of the traditional 'working dinner'. There was little pressing business, and ministers and high officials – about twenty altogether – were informally gathered round several tables in the conference hotel for general talk when Brown walked in. Lange of Sweden, as Chairman of the EFTA Council, was proposing that he also should tour the Six Common Market capitals, and explore the possibility of some EFTA–EEC association. This seemed to me a harmless, if futile exercise; but I treated it seriously, as Lange was a very distinguished social-democrat and political leader.

Brown, however, bluntly turned it down, in front of all present. At this point Schaffner said affably that he hoped Brown would listen to what he,

Schaffner, had to say; to which Brown replied in effect that he would not. Trying to keep the temperature down, I interposed that Brown was speaking for himself, and that I would like to hear Schaffner's views. Brown then turned upon me, professed to take the phrase 'speaking for himself' as a disagreement on high policy, and demanded that one or the other of us should return to London forthwith. I stayed silent; presuming these observations to be just a display of exuberant high spirits. The ensuing silence was painful. In the end it was broken by some tactful contribution from, I think, the Austrian delegate. Naturally, as there were half a dozen journalists waiting outside the door, most of us feared a blazing press story the following morning of violent disagreement on the EEC between Brown and me. By the grace of God, and the good sense of the British and EFTA officials present, nothing whatever appeared, though my secretary and I went to bed in very great gloom, only slightly relieved for me by his assurance that he was certain I was right to say nothing whatever. Next morning Schaffner remarked to me privately: 'I admired your dignity last night: it reminded me of the dignity of a Roman Senator.' I said this was over-praise, and inquired whether he meant the Senator whose beard was pulled by an intruding barbarian. 'That,' he said, 'is exactly what I meant.'

On Tuesday of the following week I met Denis Healey in his room in the House and told him the full story of the EFTA Conference; in particular that no minister there believed an application at this time could possibly end in anything but failure. Healey wholeheartedly agreed. He favoured arguing in the Cabinet that no application should be made until the Kennedy Round of negotiations on world tariff cuts had been completed, until there was a prospect of reasonable terms, and until our own economy was stronger. It was reassuring to hear at least one senior minister talking common sense in contrast to the stream of nonsense now pouring out of the FO. On the day before I had also talked with Peart who seemed to have more fight in him than I had feared, though he now believed that Wilson had given in and intended to force an early application if he could.

I therefore arranged to see Callaghan, with whom I could talk easily and frankly, on the Thursday of this week (9 March) after Cabinet. At this Cabinet Wilson had announced that a sixty-page document would be circulated on the outcome of the talks with the Six and 'recommendations' would later be put by Wilson and Brown to the Cabinet. This convinced most members of the Cabinet that Wilson definitely meant to propose an application. With Callaghan alone after the Cabinet, I first discussed the Budget. The economic prospect was now much better, with exports 10 per cent up on the previous year, and the 1964 deficit overcome. We both thought a fairly neutral Budget, with higher spending reflating the economy gradually, was the right next move. On the Common Market, I tried to get Callaghan to understand the huge burden on our precarious balance of payments which the CAP would impose in the long term as well as the short. At this period people who had no special economic flair, or knowledge of French politics, genuinely did not understand that this was the central issue.

Callaghan did not seem even now to want to take this seriously. Instead he asked me whether I would resign, and added that he did not think Healey or Peart would. I said that I might, but that my future was less important than the future of the country. He only replied that Brown had told him Wilson was 'so playing things that there would be only one resignation'. This talk greatly disappointed me, as I had more faith in Callaghan's common sense and seriousness than in most members of that Cabinet. It also depressed me, since it was further evidence that Wilson meant to press on without seriously examining the real issues. Later that evening I dined with Roy Harrod, who was full of scorn for those who ignored the damage that membership would inflict on the balance of payments. I decided that before making up my mind whether to resign I would circulate to the Cabinet a considered paper on the balance of payments consequences of entry. Of course, the Treasury should have done this – and in Cripps' and Gaitskell's time would have done so. But I soon found the FO was pulling every possible wire to prevent any such paper being circulated.

In the following few days, therefore, I set out to compose such a paper myself, with both official and unofficial help. So far no official estimate of the total effect on the future balance of payments – what really mattered – had been allowed to appear before ministers at all. There had merely been separate and unrelated estimates of, e.g., effects on food prices, size of levies; with plenty of relevant and irrelevant detail which prevented most ministers from seeing the wood for the trees. No estimates whatever had emerged of the effect on British exports to the whole world of higher labour costs due to higher food prices, or of the loss of our preference in the Commonwealth and EFTA, or even of the swing of the trade balance in manufactured goods against us with the EEC Six itself. A great deal of ingenuity somewhere in Whitehall must have been devoted to suppressing these topics entirely. Indeed the very fact that so much trouble was taken to suppress them showed that in the FO view they would turn out to be arguments against entry. However, I decided to circulate my paper even if the whole of the rest of the Cabinet, and Whitehall and the rest of my Department were against me. What is the good of being a minister otherwise?

On Sunday 12 March I discussed the draft in detail at home with young Michael Stewart, an economist at London University and Oxford friend of my son Peter, and with Peter himself who had served six years in the Treasury and was now leaving to join The Times. Both of them were better economists than I. In the following few days, so as to act with the full knowledge of my Department, I asked John Heath, the chief economist, and Jack Stafford, chief statistician, to comment on the paper and correct the figures to the best of their ability; though of course I took full responsibility for the arguments. This they did with the greatest care; and Richard Powell, my Permanent Secretary, quite legitimately expressed his disagreement with the conclusion. Having dictated the paper in final form, and warned Burke Trend, Secretary of the Cabinet, that I would soon wish to circulate it, I received a message from Trend just after the week-end of 18–19 March, saying it would be best not to circulate the paper till after Easter (26 March). I took this as implied agreement that my paper would be circulated after Easter; since the PM would surely not otherwise have asked me to postpone it.

As a result of the postponement, however, ministers began, on 21 March, their detailed debates on the issues supposed to be involved in entry without any estimates of the effect on the balance of payments before them. In this way ministers' minds were diverted still longer from the crucial issue. Wilson also split the first discussion up into a number of topics, so that I could not make the general speech I had intended. In spite of this, Healey, Bowden and Willie Ross, as well as Peart and myself argued for postponement of any application; and Dick Marsh, Barbara Castle and Tony Greenwood were on our side. Wilson was closely questioned whether the German Government had not advised postponement, and the FO here had gone to the length of trying to conceal from other members of the Cabinet a letter written by Frank Roberts, our Ambassador in Bonn, to Con O'Neill at the FO making it plain that the Germans were advising us to delay the application until the autumn. When I first asked the FO formally for this letter, they said they knew of no such advice being given, and I only finally gouged Roberts's letter out of them after Easter on 29 March. I circulated this, together with a similar telegram from Roberts to other colleagues who had requested them. They should have received both from the FO.

Roberts's letter was dated 9 March, and in it he reported the German spokesman, Lahr, as saying he 'frankly did not like the idea of a formal British application next month since this would give the French an opportunity, and indeed might almost force them into a position of acting negatively'. He preferred a 'declaration of intent' and a statement that the problems of entry 'still required further bilateral examination.' Similar advice came from Hallstein, President of the EEC Commission. In a letter to Con O'Neill at the FO on 3 March, Marjoribanks, FO representative in Brussels, reported a conversation with Hallstein, in which Hallstein said he disagreed 'with Jean Monnet's advice that the negotiations should be as short as possible and confined only to the main questions, leaving details to be settled later. This, he affirmed, was simply not possible.' In further ministerial discussions on 21 and 22 March, major changes in the CAP as a condition of entry were promised.

In the midst of these conflicts, Easter intervened, and on 23 March, the day before Good Friday, and also incidentally my sixtieth birthday, I left with Peter for the Isle of Wight where most of my family and Peter's were spending Easter. But I had heard by phone during the week-end from my office that Trend said efforts were being made to suppress my paper. On returning to the office early in the post-Easter week, I learnt that Wilson was definitely trying to prevent its circulation. This seemed to me carrying the process of suppressing rational discussion too far. I had always believed, and still believe, that any member of the Cabinet has the right to circulate a paper to his colleagues however much they may disagree with it. I therefore completed the paper, spoke to Trend and agreed with him that I would talk to the PM, which I did on Thursday 30 March. He raised difficulties about circulation of papers which were not inter-departmentally agreed; but I insisted that I was forwarding my paper with a formal request that it should be circulated. I did so next day. My secretary then received a note from No. 10 dated 30 March, saying: that 'this morning' the PM had suggested 'that a decision on whether papers on any aspect of entry to the Communities should be circulated to Cabinet, and if so what form they should take, ought to be left for the Cabinet to decide when they resumed their discussion on Thursday next. The PM would of course be happy to see a private copy of the paper before then.' On 3 April another minute arrived from No. 10, reporting the PM as ruling that my paper 'should be held over . . . until we decide at the next or a subsequent Cabinet what papers we shall need'.

I had some further talks with Healey, Bowden and Peart before the next Cabinet on 6 April, which was wholly devoted to the EEC, and particularly to regional policy and capital movements. It was now becoming clear that, quite apart from food and the balance of payments, even Development Area policy and Industrial Development Certificates would be undermined if exchange controls were to be weakened. More than half the Cabinet were by now sceptical about the whole exercise. Even Crossman seemed to be wobbling back to the anti-Market side, if this could be inferred from the fact that he had no difficulty in puncturing the arguments coming from Jenkins and Brown. But Wilson again appeared to be set on the application, for reasons which he did not justify by argument. At the start of this latest discussion, since the balance of payments had still been hardly mentioned, I formally raised the issue of my paper, and got some support. Wilson then trotted out the argument that such papers should be 'inter-departmentally agreed'. I replied that this was acceptable, if time could be allowed for such agreement, and received specific confirmation from Trend later that there would be. On 9 April yet another minute arrived from No. 10 tortuously explaining why my paper could not yet be circulated. This time the doctrine was that 'it would be desirable that ministers' papers should not be circulated until after the Cabinet had completed their consideration of the necessary studies of officials'.

The following week began with a Budget Cabinet on Monday 10 April, and the Budget itself on Tuesday. I was thankful to be in general harmony with Callaghan at least, and to have induced him to make some small concession to the motor industry, though I still thought, and said, that unemployment was being allowed to rise too high. Thursday 13 April was a black day, with a Cabinet on the EEC and a Greater London election, in which Labour lost control of London for the first time since Herbert Morrison's victory in 1934 (and in which my wife lost her Battersea seat there after many years' service with the LCC and GLC). In the EEC discussion, it was agreed at last that the balance of payments should be discussed on 27 April, which I took to mean my paper in some shape or form. That evening also I talked with Peart, and he came nearer than any time yet to promising to resign, on the understanding that I would, if an application were made. I also had to speak on Monday in the Budget debate. On the Saturday morning I received a typed letter without signature or address but with a London suburban postmark saying that the FO had instructed the Paris Embassy not to mention in general telegrams special letters to the FO which might be embarrassing to it, since these were leading to demands from Home Departments to see the special letters. This typed letter might have been a pointless hoax; but a close colleague told me he knew of an FO official living in the relevant suburb. Instead of a signature it ended with the words: 'None dare call it treason'.

In the following week the EEC argument continued on Tuesday and Thursday. We were still, even now, precluded from discussing the balance of payments; and the argument had assumed something of a set pattern. Regional policy, 'agriculture' and the legal and constitutional issues were debated; and the substance and logic came from the critics. Jenkins and Crosland made debating replies and were echoed by Stewart, who had veered right round the compass since a year before. The critics were precise. The replies were vague and woolly, decked out with cliches such as 'wider markets' or 'technological progress'. In the course of this week I agreed not to circulate my balance of payments paper, because the official group of economists and statisticians (including Kaldor, Balogh, Robert Neild and Alec Cairncross) had agreed on their own paper. It seemed to me that this impartial estimate was by now likely to carry more weight than mine. But it was now nearly two months since I had sought to circulate my estimate to my Cabinet colleagues. The entire resources of the FO, No. 10 Downing Street, and the Cabinet offices had to be mobilized to prevent this. Yet Wilson in his account of these deliberations pronounced[28] that: 'Individual ministers who wanted to circulate their own papers were not precluded from doing so.' Some may think this a little misleading.

But the clinching irony was this. Whereas I in my paper, with the help of the Board of Trade statistician, had estimated the probable loss on the

[28] Wilson, p. 387.

N

balance of payments due to EEC membership at between £450 million and £820 million a year; the official experts in their paper put it between £400 million and £920 million (all, of course, in 1967 money values). Their estimate of the maximum probable damage was therefore even greater than my own. In the nature of the case such forecasts can only be opinions within a range of probabilities. To suppose they can be exactly estimated is a fallacy. But it is an even more dangerous fallacy to think that because something cannot be exactly estimated, it therefore does not exist. A serious contribution to the main issue had been made a little earlier by Wilfred Beckerman, then economics fellow at Balliol, in a letter to *The Times* on 20 February. His estimate of 'the total adverse effect on the current balance' was that 'it might be in the region of £800 million a year' – as against my more modest £450 million to £820 million. I had deliberately set the figures rather below what my real conviction suggested, because my less informed colleagues seemed so drugged by propaganda that the real truth was likely to strike them as past credence. But of course in the event, in the light of experience in the late 1970s, as is recorded later in this story, all these guesses turned out to be marked under-estimates of the damage: particularly in the case of two items, the Budget burden and the deficit in manufactured goods with the Six.[29]

Though, however, I under-estimated the damage, at least my persistent efforts to circulate a paper had produced a serious official assessment which, though hopelessly belated, could not be wholly ignored. An extra payments burden of even £600 million, would be a disastrous set-back to this country's long struggle for economic recovery. The trouble, and the tragedy, was that Brown, Wilson, Jenkins, and others mainly in the FO, reached conclusions before they had made any serious effort to estimate the economic consequences at all. That was indeed the basic truth in the whole tangled story of Britain's plunge into EEC membership. The pro-Marketeers were now too committed to admit that they were wrong. Their considerable exertions were therefore now concentrated on discrediting the figures, or diverting attention from them.

Nor was I helped at this stage of the controversy by also having to conduct full-scale trade talks with the Canadians, the Australians, and the Russians in the two weeks before and after 23 April. In the midst of the talks with Patolichev, already mentioned,[30] I received one morning a verbal message from No. 10, asking whether I knew how an allegedly most unfair report of a speech by George Brown on the EEC to the Parliamentary Labour Party, had found its way into the *Guardian*, and whether I or my PPS had spoken to the *Guardian*. I sent a verbal message back that I was not present at the PLP meeting, had no idea what Brown said, had not read the *Guardian* and had not seen the PPS in question for several days.

[29] See chapter 17.
[30] See p. 376.

It was not till Saturday morning, 29 April, that the Cabinet actually discussed the effect of EEC entry on the balance of payments in the light of the official estimates. By then the press was predicting that the decision was virtually a *fait accompli*, and ministers were learning more of the PM's intentions from the press than from him. But there was some discussion, and thanks to the official paper not altogether a worthless one. Callaghan, courageously, admitted that the CAP would add a load of about £600 million to the balance of payments, but then less courageously said this might be 'manageable'. I wondered what Chancellor since 1945 had advised his colleagues that a load of £600 million on the balance of payments (particularly a gratuitious one, springing from a policy earlier recommended for its economic benefits) would prove 'manageable'. I made my main contribution asking whether it could really be sense deliberately to weaken the UKs basic economic strength when political and military power in the modern world depended for the foreseeable future on economic and industrial power. Crosland followed trying to minimize the whole issue by casting doubt on the figures. His case and that of Jenkins consisted in effect of reviving the argument that since the economic damage could be not exactly estimated, it therefore did not exist. Jenkins admittedly had committed himself for so long that he could hardly admit himself to be in doubt. But Crosland, though I knew Jenkins had pressurized him for years, was fully as able to understand the economic consequences as Gaitskell, Harrod, Beckerman, Kaldor or Richard Kahn; and seemed to me not to be doing justice to his own economic intelligence. He must have known as well as I that the arguments being used by Brown and others were, as Gaitskell had called them in October 1962, less than five years before, 'nonsense and rubbish'. Nothing basic had changed since that speech of Gaitskell, except that the CAP had been made deliberately much more oppressive to the UK. Nevertheless I was saddened to be forced thus into conflict with Jenkins and Crosland, since I had been such close friends and colleagues with both for so long in the 1950s. In this final week of argument, Stewart and Gordon-Walker had sunk into the pro-Market camp without trace. Peart, Healey, Bowden, and Barbara Castle emphatically upheld my own argument, and Ross, Marsh and Greenwood firmly if less explicitly. Callaghan I recorded at the time as in the middle, though 'wobbling', and Crossman as 'intermittently on our side'.

The debate continued at Chequers at 10.30 a.m. next morning, 30 April, a beautiful day. This was strictly not a Cabinet meeting, but an off-the-record debate. It was expected, however, to be the final decisive clash, and decisions whether or not to resign would have to be taken very soon. We appeared to be working to a pre-ordained time-table, laid down by the PM, the reasons for which had not been disclosed. The balance of payments issue was to be discussed; but Crossman introduced a diversion. He was against all the arguments for joining, but favoured the application nonetheless. He now said that devaluation would be a necessary consequence of an application, and his case appeared to be that as he wanted devaluation, he favoured anything which would provoke it. I had never before since 1945 heard a senior minister argue for a policy which he considered economically damaging on the ground that it would force devaluation. Callaghan naturally had to follow with a declaration of faith against devaluation as such; and much valuable time was then wasted. In the middle of the morning I joined in, and replied in particular to Crosland's argument that a £600 million burden on the balance of payments 'did not matter'; and asked why, in that case, must this country abandon its whole military and political influence 'East of Suez', as he and most of the pro-Marketeers were urging, on the ground that we 'could not afford it'? It cost less than £600 million on the balance of payments. If we could not 'afford' that, we could not afford the CAP. If we could afford the CAP, we must more easily afford our presence East of Suez. Nobody else tried much longer to belittle the balance of payments burden. By the end of the morning, Healey, Peart, Bowden, Castle, Ross, Marsh and Greenwood were clearly on my side; and Wilson, Brown, Stewart, Callaghan, Gardiner, Gordon-Walker, Longford, Gunter, Jenkins, Crosland and perhaps Crossman on the other. This left Benn and Cledwyn Hughes uncertain, and the balance of payments debate now closed, with the force of that argument clearly on our side.

In the afternoon the agenda was a straight paper by Wilson and Brown proposing an immediate application. So anyone who opposed this was challenging the PM as well as the Foreign Secretary. Brown's opening speech was largely devoted to typical FO short-term guesswork: discrediting the argument that Germans advised postponement and that it was better to complete the Kennedy Round first. Healey then made one of the most forceful contributions in the whole controversy, maintaining first that an application was almost bound to fail, secondly that no case for it had been made out on merits anyway. By this time Wilson and the pro-Marketeers were admitting that there was no positive economic case. Dick Marsh came out flat and firm against any application. Callaghan was in favour, though his reasons were still shadowy. Crossman was in favour because he hoped and believed the application would fail. This was counted as a vote in favour. Benn disappointed me by acquiescing in an application on obscure, if fashionable, grounds of technology (another Yes vote). Barbara Castle sent me notes saying I should speak after Crossman; but, probably wrongly I waited till the end. I argued as Healey had that there was no point in an application until we could get acceptable terms, and there was no prospect of them at the moment. I did not realize till afterwards that though speaking last – as in the House of Commons – immediately before a vote is considered an advantage, in this peculiar procedure at Chequers the speeches *were* votes, and consequently the last speaker was the only one who could not influence anyone else. I did at least, however, succeed in extracting the clear admission from Gerald Gardiner that full acceptance of the Rome Treaty meant surrendering for the first time for centuries the sole authority of the British Parliament to legislate for the British people. This, I argued, neither Cabinet nor even Parliament, without a mandate from the electorate, had any right to do. Wilson summed up by saying that the 'drift' of the debate was in favour of an application, and that he would draft a statement to be made in Parliament for examination in a formal Cabinet on Tuesday.

I asked some friendly colleagues afterwards whether they thought the 'drift' was in favour of an application, and they replied that formally it came to thirteen to eight in favour. This of course counted Crossman, Benn and Callaghan in favour, as well as Wilson and Brown themselves. Had Crossman and Benn (neither of whom at most times favoured entry) and Callaghan voted the other way, the balance would have been eleven to ten against, even after counting Wilson and Brown with the 'Yes' group. Those against were: Healey, Marsh, Bowden, Ross, Castle, Peart, Greenwood, Jay; those in favour: Wilson, Brown, Callaghan, Crossman, Benn, Gardiner, Cledwyn Hughes, Longford, Gunter, Crosland, Jenkins, Stewart and Gordon-Walker. So narrow was the margin by which the 1967 Government took this fateful plunge. Certainly no clear majority in the Cabinet was strongly in favour of entry. The issue was decided by those who, having no firm views of their own, voted with the PM, plus on this occasion Crossman and Benn. In modern conditions, where the PM has the sole power of appointment and dismissal, and where few Labour ministers or potential ministers have independent means of support like the nineteenth-century aristocrats, this is probably unavoidable. Election of ministers by MPs, as in the Australian Labour Party, would perhaps be worse. Nevertheless the present British system does place very great, and probably excessive, authority in the PM's hands to swing the whole boat by switching the 'Don't Knows', or 'Daren't says' this way or that.

Driving home from Chequers that evening with Frank Longford, I realized that I must decide within two days whether or not to resign before the proposed statement was made in the House. Frank was wonderfully friendly and helpful, though he took the opposite view on the Market. One could not have wished for a better confidant at such a moment. He strongly advised me not to resign, on the ground that only an application was intended, that the terms were still to be decided, and that the application might well fail. I said the absolute minimum must be the re-affirmation of the safeguards and conditions in the 1966 election manifesto and Queen's Speech; and added that I felt extremely inclined to resign and put the real facts before Parliament and the country which I could not now do. I felt no disillusion towards Frank Longford as a pro-Marketeer. He was a devout Catholic, and I noticed that to many such the Common Market tended to be equated with Christendom and Eastern Europe with anti-Christ. This perfectly sincere attitude was even more common among Continental Catholics; including indeed the founding fathers of the Market: Monnet, Spaak, Adenauer and Schumann. But though I understood and respected it, I could not agree that this particular vision of Christendom justified a system of crushingly high taxes on the staple foods of the common people. To me that was a principle also. I also felt that any application without firm safeguards for the Commonwealth would be a breach of the undertakings I had been authorized to give in Australia in September 1966. Bowden told me later that he felt this latter point strongly. As I went to bed that night, I had decided that I must insist on some formula about safeguards and conditions being inserted in the statement.

Next morning, Monday, Bowden told me he had heard from Wilson that a promise of safeguards would be included several times in the statement. I talked with Bowden separately, because he was very fastidious about not appearing to gang up against the PM. My reply was that Wilson was clearly conferring with Brown anyway, and we had a perfect right to do the same. At 9.45 p.m. in my room in the House, I met Healey, Peart, Barbara Castle and Willie Ross; and they were all in favour of insisting on references to safeguards comparable with those in the Queen's Speech. On this there was unanimity. But nobody offered to resign on the issue of the application as such, though I was willing to if it were done collectively. I believe if it had been, subsequent events might have been very different. However, it was clear that evening that if the promise of safeguards was included, I would have to resign alone or not at all. That evening, by agreement with the others, I dictated and sent the following letter to Wilson:

CONFIDENTIAL   1st May, 1967

Dear Harold,

I have not yet seen the draft statement, to be circulated, which you propose to make on the EEC in the House.

Since this is to replace, as I understand it, any conditions to be attached to the application itself, it may be worthwhile my mentioning now two conditions which seem to me vital.

First, I believe we should include words – either 'conditions' or 'safeguards' – identical with, or equivalent to, the phrases used in our Election Manifesto, the Queen's speech, and your 10 November statement. The essential words were 'provided essential British and Commonwealth interests were safeguarded' or 'if our essential British and Commonwealth interests can be safeguarded'. It does not seem to me enough to say that there are, e.g. problems to be solved or matters to be discussed.

Secondly, I trust that in the statement we do *not* specify particular or detailed interests or issues on which safeguards are necessary. It seems to me that if we do this, we weaken our bargaining position seriously by implying in advance that any other safeguards not specified will not be necessary.

I very much hope the draft may be able to meet these two essential points.

Yours sincerely,

At the Cabinet on Tuesday morning the draft statement was discussed. One of the more grotesque oddities of the whole proceeding was that the Cabinet neither then, or at any time, decided to accept the Treaty of Rome or the CAP. If it had been asked to, it would amost certainly have refused. It merely approved a Statement; and in effect decided to make an application, conditional on safeguards. The key words in the Statement, on which we insisted, were these. First on the Budget: 'The financial arrangements, which have been devised to meet the requirements of the Community's agricultural policy as it exists today would, if applied to Britain as they now stand, involve an inequitable sharing of the financial cost and impose on our balance of payments an additional burden, which we should not in fairness be asked to carry.' On agriculture: 'This will require suitable arrangements, including an adequate transitional period, to enable the necessary adjustments to be made.' On the Commonwealth: 'There are also highly important Commonwealth interests, mainly in the field of agriculture, for which it is our duty to seek safeguards in the negotiations. These include in particular, the special problem of New Zealand and of Commonwealth sugar-producing countries, whose needs are at present safeguarded by the Commonwealth Sugar Agreement.' Only twenty minutes was allowed at the start for study of this document, which had not been circulated before. The discussion concentrated on the wording of the references to safeguards. I proposed and managed to carry three or four amendments strengthening those phrases; including 'suitable arrangements' as well as a transitional period for agriculture; as only this would enable me to continue the fight afterwards. The Statement at least finished up better than I had expected. At the end of the morning Wilson asked if the Statement was agreed. He proposed to make it in the House that very afternoon; so that an atmosphere of *fait accompli* had been created.

To my surprise Dick Marsh, who had scarcely spoken, said flatly that he was opposed to the whole proposition. Barbara Castle said, So was she. I had always understood from Norman Brook and other authorities that opposition in Cabinet to a majority decision was equivalent to resignation; but this doctrine does not seem to be unanimously accepted. So, not wishing to appear in any way less firm than Marsh and Castle, I added that I wholly agreed with them, and was only like others regarding the Statement as a compromise accepted by a minority as the majority view. So this meeting ended, and Wilson made his amended Statement in the afternoon.

I then had to decide whether to resign that day. If I did so, it was clear I would be alone. I received almost universal advice not to. An acute dilemma is always involved here for any minister in any Government. For there are so many issues to be faced, and so many jobs to be done. I grieved at the thought of abandoning the Development Area drive, which I knew would slacken without me. Secondly it is always hard to say at what point in time one should resign. Decisions come in a series, not (except perhaps for a declaration of war) in one fell swoop, with no before and after. Duff Cooper resigned after the announcement of the Munich Agreement, but not while a series of previous surrenders were being made. He was probably right. Nye Bevan hesitated after the 1951 Budget, and then chose a rather irrelevant moment. In the case of May 1967, it was most forcibly argued by Healey and others, that it was the terms and safeguards of entry which counted, not a mere formal application before any negotiation. Indeed this was substantially true. What mattered was not whether we became formal members of the EEC, but whether we accepted the Treaty of Rome and the CAP. The Cabinet had not done so. Moreover in this case, as Healey so confidently affirmed, the application would probably be turned down by de Gaulle, and anyone who resigned would not merely abandon the struggle, and all his other work, but would look extremely silly when the veto came. And of course it did come in November. These arguments clearly convinced those of my colleagues who agreed with me on the main issue (though Bowden, as I learnt later, had told Wilson he must quietly leave the Government if the application went ahead). But I was still not convinced on the afternoon of 2 May. I believed Wilson and Brown, after the decision and statement, would presume that the Treaty of Rome and the CAP had been accepted in substance, and that questioning of them might now be ruled out.

In these circumstances, one is inevitably affected by those whom one trusts most and who understand the issue. I found that all the anti-Marketeers whom I met in the Parliamentary Party were strongly in favour of my staying in the Government, and, as they put it, carrying on the fight. Michael Foot explicitly urged this with a force which impressed me. So did many back-bench Members of the Party. Continue the resistance, they said, and let the Prime Minister declare himself by dropping you if he chooses. On 1 May, Monday, I had dined with my son Peter, who had written on this day in *The Times Business News*, which he had just joined, a full anonymous article putting my economic case against membership. This analysis attracted a lot of notice. But Peter also argued strongly to me that this was the wrong moment for resignation, and that one must continue the struggle. Those working in my own Private Office tactfully made me conscious that they also hoped I would stay. This was, no doubt, partly politeness and partly professional loyalty. But it is human to be a little influenced by those who have for months on end worked devotedly with one and for one. The only individual voice which privately and forcefully recommended resignation to me at this moment was Nicky Kaldor, who said simply that the application would prove a catastrophic mistake[31] and it could not be right even to seem to condone it. With only a few hours to make up my own mind, I came to the conclusion that as the principles at stake were the Rome Treaty and the CAP, and as the Government had not accepted these, it was best to continue the fight within the Government; and either to win the argument, or else, if and when the Cabinet had plainly sacrificed the principle, to resign unless the PM declared himself by dropping me from the Government first. So later that day I told my private office that I had decided not to resign for the moment, and I could not help being affected by their evident relief.

I now believe, however, that I was partly wrong and that there was a better way of achieving the same end: i.e., forcing the real issue. I was remaining in the Government on the assumption that the references to 'safeguards' and 'arrangements' which we had secured in the statement would enable us thereafter to argue against the evils of the CAP and the unprecedented surrender of the sole right of the UK Parliament to legislate for the UK. But Wilson and Brown had of course so worded the statement that it might arguably mean, or not mean, this. It was only some years afterwards that I remembered in this context the means by which Dalton secured the Distribution of Industry Bill in 1945, and so saw clearly what I should have done that weekend.[32] Dalton wrote a letter to Attlee saying that he could not remain in the Government if it did not approve and push on with this Bill. He proposed to publish this letter if the assurance was not given. I should have written similarly to Wilson asking whether the application implied acceptance of the Treaty of Rome and the essentials of the Common Agricultural Policy. If the answer was 'Yes' or (more likely) ambiguous waffle, I should have resigned and published both letters, thereby recording that these were the issues of principle. Why did this solution not occur to me at the time, when I had worked so intimately with Dalton in his dilemma? I can only say that it did not. In fact when Wilson dropped me from the Government in August that year, everyone assumed rightly that this was due to my continued firm attitude on the Common Market right up till then, and so my decision in May made little practical difference. And when de Gaulle unsheathed his veto in November, the whole elaborate application proved to be futile.

These issues of principle and deep feelings were then superseded by some Wilsonian comedy. In the debate on the EEC application in May, the combination of the Tories, now mainly pro-Market, the Labour 'Payroll Vote' (ministers and whips must vote with the Government or resign), and a group of Labour pro-Marketeers, ensured a majority for the Government.

[31] Nicholas Davenport in his autobiography says he gave the same advice at a lunch at the Athenaeum. But this was on 18 May, by which time, the opportunity had, for the moment passed.

[32] See chapter 6.

A Three-line Whip from both the two main Parties is bound to do this for almost any proposition; but eighty-two Members voted against, probably the largest vote ever recorded against a combined Government and Opposition Three-line Whip. I was happily not included among the array of Government speakers, though the unfortunate Bowden and Peart were so conscripted. Peart very bravely expounded many of the horrors of the CAP, the rise in living costs which would follow, and the general economic burden on the country. This speech justifiably attracted more notice than anything else in the debate. I attended such of these speeches as occured when I had no pressing appointment. But at the time of Wilson's own contribution, I had a long-standing appointment with Sir Ashton Roskill, a distinguished lawyer and public servant, at the time Chairman of the Monopolies Commission. It was my normal rule to attend debates in the House if my Department was involved, or if I had no other working engagement at the time. I had attended other periods of the debate, and saw no reason to vary this rule in order to hear Wilson's speech; but he took this as a public manifestation of opposition for the Government's policies. Callaghan told me after the Cabinet on Thursday of the same week that Wilson was much annoyed about this. The issues themselves seemed to me worth more emotion than the presence of this or that minister at this or that moment on the bench. Callaghan was, however, extremely friendly and advised me to make a speech showing I was not dissociating myself from the Government. Wilson told me the same day that all the PPSs who had abstained on the Common Market division, including one of mine, must resign. I told him I was only too glad, as I had been repeatedly accused of instigating activities by a PPS, of which I knew nothing, and would have myself terminated the arrangement some months before, had not Brown at the crucial moment demanded that I should. It was a vast relief at the end of this week to spend a tennis-playing Whitsun week-end in Suffolk, with the family of Shiela Sokolov-Grant, and with Christopher Cox (now Sir Christopher), of the Commonwealth Office, whom I had known continuously since New College days.

After this week-end, a further brief respite from the Common Market struggle intervened, but not before in the next few days I had spent much of a visit to the North-East Coast negotiating with Wilson about a speech I was to make to the Commonwealth Press Association in the following week. And then, lo and behold, on 16 May de Gaulle delivered a press conference bombshell making it perfectly clear to any but the deaf that he would not accept British membership of the EEC except on surrender terms. Any reasonably sensible British Government would, at least, have then postponed the whole venture. The opinion polls at this moment showed massive opposition in the country to pushing on in these circumstances. But the FO reaction was in effect that if surrender was necessary, then we must surrender. Meanwhile my visit to the North-East was, as usual, a refreshing return to reality. Our factory-building efforts, revivified since 1964, were now expanding on a major scale. I opened a number of factories in the course of two days, and also our new Investment Grant office in the Billingham New Town on North Teesside. The Board of Trade had achieved a marked success in rapidly organizing the new offices needed and locating them in areas of unemployment, including Billingham. It was one of the mistakes of the subsequent Heath Government first to cancel investment grants entirely, and then when the whole machine had been dismantled, to reinstate them in Development Areas. This, together with the abolition both by the Heath Government and the following Wilson 1974 Government of the previous administration's prices and pay authorities, were the salient examples in the post-war years, of carrying party government too far.

This record would be misleading if it suggested that the Common Market controversy was dominating our whole time, and whole thoughts in these months. It was merely added to the stream of necessary administrative activities, and to several other explosive conflicts. For it is also a characteristic of ministerial life that things come up and hit one which one had neither intended, hoped for, nor even expected. Three may be recorded here which were erupting fairly actively in 1967: the Egypt–Israel war, the controversy over the Third Airport; and the troubles of the cotton industry, as it was still then called. The Israel–Egypt war hit the Cabinet on 23 May only a week or two after the Common Market debate. Since there has been some dispute about what happened in the ministerial discussions, I summarize my own account made at the time. Brown explained verbally without previous warning that Nasser had requested U Thant of the UN to remove forces from the Gulf of Aqaba, and that U Thant had complied. Brown, as I and most of my colleagues understood him, wanted to join with the US in an immediate declaration that day that we and the US would 'assert' by naval action if necessary maritime rights in the Gulf of Aqaba. The purpose of this apparently was to satisfy Israel about the safety of her shipping in the Gulf of Aqaba, and so restrain her from starting military action on her own. Wilson appeared to support this. To many of us the whole proposal seemed much too precipitate. Callaghan questioned the wisdom of any action until we knew what the facts were, what the Americans would do, what forces we had, and what were the probable consequences. I started by resolving to keep quiet, as I was no expert on the Gulf of Aqaba. Healey, however, as Minister of Defence, supported Callaghan, though he was willing to embark on a contingency plan.

At this point I asked a number of questions: notably what forces we had in the area. As Brown dismissed these as 'technicalities', I argued that we should not commit ourselves to use force where no clear British interest was involved, unless some over-riding reason had been demonstrated. There was much backing for this view from other colleagues, including

Frank Longford, Jenkins and Crosland, with all of whom I was heartily glad to agree for a change. Callaghan pointed out that Egypt would have the sympathy of all the Arab states. The occasion ended with a clear majority against any immediate action other than the exploration of contingency plans. After the meeting Callaghan and others expressed to me strong agreement with what I had said. It was particularly ironic that some who, like Brown, had favoured reducing our defence strength 'East of Suez' should now contemplate naval conflict in the Red Sea. Callaghan asked me a few days later whether his recollection could really be right that we had been asked to agree to a threat of force – an 'assertion' – before we knew the full facts. I said that was my recollection which the minutes appeared to confirm. At a further meeting on 25 May it became clear that the peace party was winning, and nothing more bellicose was agreed than an effort to secure a general declaration of maritime rights. My memory and record of this episode support the view of those who regard it as an example of the power which the Cabinet still has, if it chooses to exercise it emphatically enough, to reject a proposal from the prime minister as well as the foreign secretary and thereby, as in this case, prevent a rash adventure. A prime minister holds a lot of cards, as argued earlier in this chapter, but not all of them.

The Third Airport, though a lesser issue, was nevertheless tediously long-running. After the 1966 general election, Wilson indulged his disposition frequently to re-shuffle both ministers and departmental responsibilities. He carried this impulse, in my judgement, too far: and it was perhaps a confirmation of the criticism once made of him that he mistook activity for action. One instance of this was his transfer of responsibility for the engineering and shipbuilding industries away from the Board of Trade to his own creature the Ministry of Technology, and the handing of civil aviation, as it were in exchange, to the Board of Trade. Soon after this transfer of responsibilities in 1966 the aviation experts – notably the Department itself and the British Airports Authority – came forward with a proposal for the expansion of Stansted as the Third London Airport (after Heathrow and Gatwick) to cater for the growth of passenger traffic expected by the mid and later 1970s. I was told, however, that a public enquiry had been held, under the local planning legislation, separately from either aviation policy or Board of Trade responsibility for industry and employment, at which the Stansted expansion had been rejected.

Since Crossman was responsible, as Minister of Housing and Local Government, for planning legislation, I conferred with him over the whole problem. He was at this stage consistently helpful and we were in entire agreement. The trouble about the planning inquiry was that it simply considered the proposed Stansted project and no alternatives. Naturally many people in the area opposed the scheme, as they would have done anywhere. If we proceeded in this way, a succession of inquiries would say: 'No, not here'; there would be no airport; and Heathrow and Gatwick would seize up in the 1970s or 1980s. The need was to choose the best site after assessing all relevant issues; and these included environment, civil aviation, safety, defence, transport to London and elsewhere, noise, housing and employment. Crossman and I therefore agreed to set up a working group of officials at under-secretary level from all the departments concerned and gave them six to nine months to examine all the alternatives in the light of all these issues, and recommend the best solution. This they did, and reported unanimously in early 1967 in favour of some expansion of Stansted as well as at Heathrow and Gatwick. I had no doubt then, and have none now, that this was broadly the right solution. It was at the same as that accepted by Julian Amery in the previous Conservative Government; and in 1967 the relevant Cabinet Committees approved it almost without argument. I announced it in the House in May 1967, the same month as the Common Market debate. And there was virtually no opposition there either.

The main issues in this controversy were reasonably simple. First, since this country has traditionally drawn a large contribution to its balance of payments from shipping, and since shipping is likely to be largely superseded except for heavy freight by air transport in the future, it is a major national interest, that we should remain in the forefront of the civil aviation as well as tourist industries. Modern airport capacity is therefore essential. This country has in fact built up Heathrow since the war, despite its faults, into the busiest airport outside the United States; and the French were already in the 1960s building the Charles de Gaulle Airport to try to capture this primacy in the next generation. Secondly, and unhappily, 80 per cent of air travellers landing at or leaving present London airports have destinations or starting points in the south-east of England. If a London airport is sited too far from London, neither passengers nor airlines can be forced to use it. Many airlines can use Paris or elsewhere instead. Thirdly since a jet liner makes most noise after take-off, and since the wind is westerly or south-westerly for 80 per cent of the year in the south-east of England, the population suffering most from the noise are those living west or south-west of the main runways; from which it follows both that an airport on the east coast would cause much of its noise over land, and not over sea, and that Gatwick and Stansted, and to some extent even Heathrow, are fortunately not so badly sited as at first appears. From the aircraft noise point of view the Maplin area on the Essex Coast was a worse alternative than Stansted, since the population of the Southend area not far south-west of Maplin is about three times that to the south-west of Stansted. In any case, unless civil aviation is to be abandoned, the cure for aircraft noise had to be found in quieter engines rather than fewer flights.

Fourthly, since Gatwick and Stansted were both already in existence in the 1960s, the cost of moderate expansion at either of these was under £100 million in the late 1960s when a start could have been made; whereas the Maplin plan, including means of transport would have cost many hundreds of millions, even excluding the proposed seaport and close on £1000 million if that were included. Finally transport to Gatwick already existed, and could be brought cheaply to Stansted both from the M11 motorway and the electrified railway line at Bishops Stortford. But Maplin would have required both a new high-speed railway right into London, and a full-scale new motorway, involving serious noise and disruption of housing in east London.

There was no need for a series of Royal Commissions or public inquiries to establish these facts, though there may have been a need for some independent investigation to convince the public that every possibility had been explored. The only genuine fault in the advice given me was an under-estimate of the time it would take for Heathrow and Gatwick to be hopelessly overloaded. The official statisticians and air traffic experts in 1966 put this at 1974 or 1975. In fact it proved to be nearer 1980, thanks partly to the wild inflation of oil prices in 1974 which nobody could have foreseen in 1966. The error did not mainly consist of failing to realize that aircraft would soon be much larger. We took this explicitly into account in 1966–7.

The whole airport problem was debated for a full day on 29 June 1967 in the House, I set out the full facts and the full case for some expansion at Stansted in the opening speech. The Liberal spokesman, and Roger Cooke among the Tories, and several others told me privately afterwards they had found it most persuasive. Tony Greenwood wound up very effectively for the Government, and very little opposition was expressed. Peter Kirk, the MP for the Stansted area, unwisely told me later that he could 'call off' the opposition campaign against use of Stansted any time he wished. After the debate we could have issued, as I wanted, the necessary order for approval by both Houses, and the whole 'Third Airport' issue would probably have been settled. Lord (Lewis) Silkin, the first Minister of Town and Country Planning in the Attlee Government, and Lord Soskice, had promised to support the order in the Lords. However, other ministers hesitated, and at this moment a liberally financed campaign against the Stansted expansion, organized by residents in the area, erupted into the press. One newspaper after another, suddenly discovered all sorts of objections to the project, and it was not till later that I learnt fully how it was organized. Naturally there was local anxiety; but the determined opposition came largely from the wealthy minority. The Harlow and Stansted Trades Council favoured the plan on employment grounds. One local landowner, however, who happened to be an old friend of mine approached me privately, and I had to reply that the merits of the argument were overwhelmingly against him. Another landowner, a lady, vociferous in the campaign, was trying privately at the same time to sell her land to the British Airports Authority. Of the letters received at the Board of Trade opposing the scheme, a very high proportion came from W1 or SW3 postmarks. Those supporting it were mainly from Harlow and Stansted. A sum variously estimated at between £23,000 and £40,000 was spent by the objectors altogether on the public inquiry and the later campaign.

A most illuminating description of the whole episode emerged later in a BBC television broadcast on the airport controversy on 20 March 1969, in the form of comments by Mr David Lomax, one of the moving spirits of the opposition campaign. 'Among the larger houses around Stansted,' he recorded, 'there was already an elaborate network of charitable bring and buy sales and coffee mornings' . . . 'The response was staggering: the fund soared not to £25,000 but eventually to £40,000.' 'At one meeting three people gave £500 each, and they would have given more if the organisers had not been so worried about the bad publicity of a millionaire image.' A debate was then organized in the House of Lords, and the nobility of the East Anglia establishment were mobilized on a war footing. Mr Lomax tells us: 'We had the House of Lords Clerks lined up . . . they were very helpful . . . At least thirty noble lords were down to speak: almost all of them against the Stansted site, and many admitting a strong local interest. There was Lord Butler, a former Foreign Secretary and Essex MP, now Master of Trinity College Cambridge . . . Lord Dilhorne former Lord High Chancellor . . . Lord Plowden . . . Lord Goodman . . . Lord Jellicoe.' Lord Dilhorne himself explained in this broadcast: 'I came to be involved because Lord Plowden approached me and asked if I would take an active part in relation to Stansted. I said at that time: "I know nothing about it." . . . I did satisfy myself that the case put forward by the preservation society was a very good one.' Lord Butler excelled himself in the debate: 'Since 1929,' he said, 'I have known the district thoroughly. I know every village, every church, every road, every lane, every inn, every hamlet and every pub. . . .' This picture of Lord Butler making merry in 'every pub' in the wilds of Essex is one which I still find most endearing.

Nobody of course could complain about Essex residents organizing a protest campaign, and no doubt many of them acted for public-spirited motives. But there were two unfortunate aspects of this sectional outburst which did great damage to the chance of achieving a nationally desirable solution. First, large sections of the press, in one of its most irresponsible moods ever, swallowed the whole public-relations story with almost total disregard for the real issues. Secondly, and unknown to me at the time, some of my own Cabinet colleagues were privately encouraging the opposition. Roy Jenkins at least made clear his disagreement in ministerial discussions. But the expansive Mr Lomax also tells us: 'Some ministers went out of their way to make it plain they didn't approve of the decision, and if we could find some way of re-opening the case they would back us. Crosland was one of them before he became President of the Board of Trade. . . . We were at the same college at Oxford at about the same time, and I'd known him for twenty years, and he didn't ever conceal what his own view was from either Stan Newens [MP for the area] or myself.'

The Cabinet missed its chance to settle the whole matter by issuing the necessary Order in July and getting parliamentary approval for it. Then after I left the Government in August, it suddenly decided to do nothing. Why? Part of the reason was no doubt Crosland's hesitation, but also, according to the information reaching me at the time, another startling change of front by Crossman. He had been a staunch supporter of the Stansted solution for many months. But according to this account, which struck me as characteristic, though I cannot directly confirm it, he had now devised his great scheme for reforming the House of Lords, and he feared that the Stansted Order would offend their lordships.[33] So he persuaded the Cabinet to abandon the Order. In the end, of course, the House of Lords reform plan came to nothing, and the only lasting effect of this gyration was the loss of the Stansted Order. This was straight political cowardice; and it brought the normal consequences of political cowardice: indecision, delay, and an eventual return to the abandoned proposal.

After some months, in February 1968, Crosland appointed the Roskill Commission to survey again the whole Third Airport problem and make its own recommendation. It included many distinguished experts, including Sir Colin Buchanan, and carried through a vast number of detailed statistical inquiries into all the alternatives. Unfortunately, however, the Commission omitted Stansted from their short list of possible sites at the very start. The British Airports Authority were told that Stansted was bound to be in the short list, and therefore made no formal application to have it included. The Board of Trade also assumed it would be on the list. Why was it omitted? The Times (4 March 1969) said its inclusion would have been 'emotive', and the Financial Times said its omission was 'diplomatic'. The Commission itself said that if it had been included, it would have been rejected, and examined instead Nuthampstead, only a few miles away. Crosland stated in the House that the Government had not exerted pressure on the Commission to exclude it. Certainly the British establishment moves in a mysterious way.

The Roskill Commission after profound deliberation lasting two years and costing large sums of public money, recommended a solution which almost nobody had previously suggested: Cublington in Bedfordshire. But Sir Colin Buchanan (who was also urging the building of Inner London motorways, and seemed to me to have a remarkable capacity for being

[33] Crossman, vol. 2, p. 684.

wrong) dissented and came down in favour of a mammoth airport, seaport and New Town project at Foulness, soon re-christened 'Maplin', which no aviation authority had ever contemplated, and which almost everyone except Buchanan on the Roskill Commission had decisively turned down. A commercial consortium then sprang up (headed by an ex-Chairman of the National Union of Conservative and Unionist Associations who lived in Bedfordshire, according to *The Times*, 5 April 1971), which persuaded the Southend Corporation to invest public money in the project. Maplin was probably, together with the Inner London Motorways, the most hair-brained project advocated in this country since 1945. The arguments against Maplin were overwhelming.[34] It would cost ten or twenty times the original plan for expansion of Gatwick and Stansted. It might inflict as much noise on many people in the Southend area as Stansted would at the other end of Essex. It was so far from London, and the journey would have taken so long, that neither British Airways, the British Airports Authority nor foreign airlines wished to use it. And on top of all this, it was far from certain that another 'North Sea Surge', which has now to be expected one day, would not obliterate the airport if not the whole complex.

By this time, however, Mr Heath had appeared on the scene as Prime Minister, and contrary to the clear advice of almost every informed person, he decided in favour of Maplin; and the luckless Mr John Davies, as Secretary of State for Trade, was put up to announce this in the House on 26 April 1971. Why did Heath thus ignore all the expert advice? Unkind critics alleged that it was because his so-called 'Europeanism' had become a sort of superstition or intellectual disease which prevented him deciding any move on its merits as opposed to its 'European dimension'. Since Maplin faced the coast of 'Europe' – by which was meant the Continent – it was the right place for an airport, seaport and New Town. This, I would judge, is a crude explanation, unfair to Heath. Much more probably he was attracted by the 'prestige project' psychology of the South American type: build a huge, visible, spectacular, memorable, reminder of Heath's premier-ship, and damn the cost. So legislation was pushed through, a public board was set up, and large sums were spent on surveys and preparatory work.

Yet in time under the British political system common sense tends to raise its head. By the return of a Labour Government to power in February 1974, only millions, not hundreds of millions, had been spent on Maplin. Crosland had condemned it outright when it was announced in April 1971, and he deserves much credit for ensuring the cancellation of Maplin when he was back in office. Crosland's weakness was that he did not seem to be in favour of *any* site, but nonetheless admitted that new airport capacity was essential. And so, in the summer of 1978, the Callaghan Government

[34] The case against Maplin was powerfully stated not merely by the Roskill Commission but by Sir Peter Masefield, an ex-Chairman of the British Airports Authority, in letters to *The Times* on 2 February and 25 June 1973.

completed the full circle, and returned as quietly as it could to the 1967 plan: moderate expansion at Heathrow, Gatwick and Stansted. And in December 1979, the then Conservative Government, after further expert reviews, adopted the same solution.

It is charitable to regard the story of the Third Airport as just another example of British Cabinets muddling through. Certainly we got more or less *through* in the end to the point where we started. But a few more solid morals may be drawn from this sobering tale. I blame myself on two counts. First I should have pressed on more vigorously with the necessary Order in July 1967, after Cabinet and parliamentary approval for the policy had been won. I was diverted by the assumption that it would go through in the autumn anyway and by sheer pressure of other work. Secondly I should, in theory at any rate, have made a greater propaganda effort to explain the real issues outside of Parliament; though in fact full copies of my speech in the House on 29 June were very widely circulated. Here again the sheer time is not available for this sort of exercise, unless every department is to keep a full-blown propaganda section of their own (as only the FO does); and this I do not favour. But the more substantial lessons are these: the unwisdom of short-term political tricks; the dangers of delay and indecision; the vice of the Party system carried too far, by which each Government tends to reverse its predecessor's decisions; and the risk of pushing public 'participation' to the point where nothing is ever decided. During these twelve years the French built the Charles de Gaulle Airport (though too far from Paris); and it was due only to the success of Heathrow and Gatwick that we did not lose our primacy in air traffic. Frequently throughout this long story I used to remember the wartime meeting[35] when we decided in forty minutes on the site of Heathrow.

The transfer of civil aviation to the Board of Trade in 1966 had forced the unwelcome Third Airport controversy on me. But it had also brought with it a much more constructive and inviting responsibility: the strengthening of the British civil aviation, aircraft, and aero-engine industries. This was a job far more congenial to me. The aim was to re-equip British European Airways (as it was then) with improved Trident planes, to promote the BAC111 aircraft and above all to develop the Rolls-Royce RB 211 engine. With these objectives I held regular fortnightly meetings with Tony Millward of BEA, Denning Pearson of Rolls-Royce, the Ministry of Technology (then represented by John Stonehouse) and others involved. In this way the facts of a very complex problem were elucidated, and successful steps taken which, in time, resulted in the RB 211 engine being included in the Lockheed Tristar, and so eventually in the late 1970s in a major new Boeing jet liner. The Board of Trade used our overseas commercial staff to the limit in support of Rolls-Royce, who were as

[35] See p. 106.

technically brilliant as they were at that time financially amateurish. This was a notable case where the stakes were so high, and the finance required so huge, that any government would have been bound to give support – as John Davies found to his embarrassment in a Tory Government a few years later.

Another problem which sprang up and hit one in these summer months of 1967 was the persistent struggle of the cotton industry, now rapidly becoming a multi-fibre textile industry, to survive. My firstm ajor step to support it was to institute in 1965-6 the 'global quota' on cotton textile imports from all low-cost countries described in an earlier chapter.[3] The other crucial need, if the textile industries were to be saved, was the emergence of stronger firms and the large-scale modernization of plant and equipment: in effect the creation of a new highly mechanized multi-fibre industry. From the meeting at Harrogate in September 1965 onwards, I was convinced that this part of the job could best be done, with some help from the Government by Courtaulds, Viyella, ICI and one or two other firms. In the outcome this also was the method adopted; and in the years 1967-70 the capital expenditure of Courtaulds alone was running at £70 million a year, and a number of new textile factories were built in Development Areas. But unluckily before this programme was fully launched, an intense textile recession set in during the winter of 1966-7. This was part of the chronic world textile cycle; but it was also intensified this time in the UK by the excessive deflation of July 1966. I sought some solution which would check the fall in demand, without abandoning outright our re-affirmed obligation to the poorer Commonwealth countries. I proposed to Wilson in July 1967 that Purchase Tax on textiles should be lowered for six months, and that other help should be given. Wilson simply referred this to Callaghan; and action was blocked. I was, therefore, somewhat surprised later to learn that when Wilson received complaints about the textile recession at No. 10 from the unions in August, he never passed them to me or showed me his reply. On Saturday 12 August, a public meeting was held in Manchester by the textile interests to demand a virtual stoppage of all imports; and as this coincided with my long-awaited West Country holiday, it was arranged that Tony Greenwood, a Lancashire MP, should very nobly speak there for the Government this time. Here in retrospect, I probably made a mistake in not cancelling this part of the holiday. But there comes a time, in a summer like 1967, when one says: I am just going to take a few days off in the country.

For in June and July of 1967 the normal intense pressure of parliamentary life had reached a crescendo. On 19 July, for instance, I spent the morning at a Cabinet trying to control Government expenditure, spoke at a City lunch on our Companies Bill, and answered Board of Trade Questions for the full period from 2.35 p.m. to 3.30 p.m. On this afternoon, incidentally, we reached Question ninety-six – a score hardly if ever recorded in

[36] See p. 328.

the 1970s, as verbosity has steadily encroached on information. Immediately after this Question Time, I conducted, with the always invaluable help of George Darling, the debate on the final stages of the Companies Bill from 3.30 p.m. until 6.30 a.m. next morning. Quite a day; and the only debate I remember, when in reply to about the fiftieth amendment to the Bill at 6 a.m. or so, I was driven once or twice to reading my brief without being wholly sure I understood it. Next day I was told I must wind up an economic debate on the following Monday (24 July) in reply to Heath, with Mcleod and Callaghan as the opening speakers. But this time we had some good results to report. Record monthly export figures showing an actual visible trade surplus were published in mid-August. The preparatory week-end before this debate had been spent at our new rented cottage at Britwell Salome, near Watlington, Oxfordshire, in remote country on the edge of the Chilterns and fifteen miles from Oxford and All Souls. From this cottage, together with other members of the family, I derived immeasurable blessings of refreshment and tranquillity over the next thirteen years.

Despite all these diversions, however, my main efforts in June and July 1967 were devoted, first, to securing some relaxation of the excessive deflationary measures of July 1966, and secondly to insisting on the fulfilment of the promise that adequate safeguards for British interests would be included in any settlement with the Common Market. The rise in unemployment at home had confirmed my opinion that, for instance, hire purchase restrictions on car sales must be eased, and that if the measures needed to achieve full employment would result in devaluation, devaluation must now be accepted. Alternatively I was prepared to advocate import quotas on manufactured goods (which we should have adopted in October 1964) if this was necessary to avoid both unemployment and devaluation. I was distressed that my pressure for reflation was now antagonizing Callaghan as well as Wilson. But I was at least able in early June, after receiving a *cri de coeur* from BMC and Fords, to announce a Government relaxation in the HP restrictions on car sales. I next circulated a paper to the relevant Cabinet Committee for discussion later in the same week as the Economic Debate, explicitly proposing further relaxation in HP controls on consumer durables, furniture and carpets as well as cars.

Wilson wanted this deferred for security reasons to a private meeting of Callaghan, Stewart, himself and me; and I understood him to agree that this must be held in the next ten days. The minutes, however, relegated this meeting till September. I wrote in my diary in late July that, in view of the rising unemployment, I must 'keep up the fight, though I realized that I was antagonizing H.W. still further and he might retaliate in some reshuffle in the autumn.' On 2 August Wilson's secretary, Michael Halls, called on me to say that Wilson wanted to announce the HP relaxations himself in August. My last official meeting before leaving for Cornwall on

11 August was with my Permanent Secretary, Richard Powell, and others on 9 August, where we set in train, subject only to Wilson's and Callaghan's agreement, a major relaxation on the car and consumer durable front. It was now agreed I should telephone Callaghan about the timing of it a week or two later from Devon. I left for Cornwall believing that this battle was nearly won, even if it meant devaluation or import quotas.

Meanwhile the struggle over the Common Market terms had been rejoined. On 16 May, as mentioned above, de Gaulle virtually rejected the UK application in advance; and this strengthened the case of those like Healey who maintained that de Gaulle would block the whole project anyway, and that therefore there was no reason to be too pessimistic, let alone to resign. As, however, I had determined to fight the issue of the negotiation terms, I wrote a formal minute to my Permanent Secretary immediately after the May Commons debate laying it down as my view and Board of Trade policy that any quotas, levies or tariffs on imports of food – grain, meat and dairy produce in particular – into this country must be opposed. Bowden and Peart agreed to act similarly. I was pleased to be told that the *Daily Mirror*, which I did not read, had written a leader arguing that my continued presence in the Cabinet would throw doubt on the sincerity of the application. The so-called 'European Committee' of the Cabinet, set up to argue over the terms, met on 5 June with George Brown as Chairman. Wilson had included Callaghan, Peart, Bowden, and Ross as well as Jenkins, Stewart, Chalfont and myself on this Committee.

At this first meeting Peart, Bowden and Ross, though they agreed with me, were less firm than I had expected in supporting my principle of no restrictions on food imports. It now became ominously clear that the pro-Marketeers, having evaded any discussion on the terms – the realities – in the Cabinet itself, were now prepared for a virtually complete surrender to the EEC on both the CAP and the renunciation of parliamentary authority. Since Peart and Bowden were not willing to go the whole way in supporting complete free entry for food products, I decided to coalesce with them in pushing for as near an approach to this as they would accept, and meanwhile to write a formal letter to Brown recording my view. At the next meeting of the Committee, the issue came to a head. After I had repeated my view on food imports, Jenkins interrupted in an arrogant and hectoring manner which did not suit him, saying that all this had been decided in the Cabinet and could not be raised again. I replied that it had not been discussed, let alone decided, at the Cabinet; and that the May decision had been accepted on the basis of the promised safeguards. Chalfont, a junior Minister who was presiding in place of Brown, tried to smooth things down, but was fairly obviously drugged with pro-Market propaganda. On 13 June I wrote a formal letter to George Brown recording my view on food imports.

After another meeting of the Committee on 20 June, however, I received the following minute from the PM dated 27 June:

> I note from the minutes of the first meeting on 5 June of the Ministerial Committee on the Approach to Europe and from your letter to the Foreign Secretary of 13 June that you hold the view, and regard this as consistent with the Cabinet's decision to seek membership of the EEC, that our initial negotiating position *vis-à-vis* the Community should be for long term rather than for purely transitional duty free entry for cereals, meat and dairy produce.
>
> I do not regard this view as consistent with the decisions reached by the Cabinet and particularly with the terms of the statement of Government policy of 2 May, as agreed by the Cabinet. I do not therefore consider that this matter should be raised further, nor that it would be appropriate for you to circulate a paper on the subject, whether now or at a later stage.
>
> I am sending copies of this minute to the Members of the Ministerial Committee on the Approach to Europe and to Sir Burke Trend.
>
> H.W.

This was, frankly, a direct double-cross, which crudely exposed the whole manoeuvre. The Cabinet had never decided anything about the terms of entry as affecting what was the reality of the whole project: i.e., the food supply of the UK and its crucial influence on our living standards and economic future. Indeed the whole debate had been so stage-managed as to prevent this being discussed; and the Cabinet would never have approved a straight acceptance of the CAP. So far from the Cabinet having accepted the CAP on 2 May, all previous discussions had assumed that substantial and lasting safeguards would be essential. For instance, Wilson had said, when summing up at the meeting on 9 November 1966, as the minutes made clear, that we should need to negotiate certain permanent adaptations in the arrangements under the Treaty of Rome as well as suitable transitional provisions. In reporting on his famous 'Probe' tour of the EEC capitals as late as 21 March 1967, Wilson had also said, according to the official record, that we should need to negotiate a substantial change of the levy system under the protocol of accession, since in the present terms it would have severely damaging and inequitable consequences for us . . . and had assured his colleagues that at no point had it been said during the 'Probe' that all our problems could be solved by the concession of nothing more than transitional periods. Even later on 18 April 1967, Wilson recalled that the Foreign Secretary in the course of the 'Probe' had reserved our freedom to seek adjustments in the case of agriculture going beyond transitional arrangements, particularly as affecting the payment of import levies across the exchanges. It was also agreed at the end of this 18 April meeting that it would be necessary for us to reach adjustments to the CAP other than transitional periods notably with a view to lightening the burden of the CAP on our balance of payments. The Statement to the House on 2 May, the only document actually agreed by the Cabinet, included the assurances already quoted.[37] Finally Wilson in his own speech in the House on 8 May had himself spoken of possible solutions in the case of New Zealand including 'levy-free or reduced levy quotas for agricultural products . . . and promised that, whatever the method, the problem is one where we have the bounden duty to seek the necessary safeguards.'

In the light of these quotations, it was plain nonsense to argue that even discussion of levy-free entry for grain, meat and feeding stuffs, had been ruled out by the Cabinet approval of the 2 May Statement. All too clearly, Wilson had capitulated, for whatever reason to further pressure by Brown and others. Should I, therefore, reply by citing the quotations given above, and repeat that I could not accept this interpretation of the Cabinet decision? My private office, with the 100 per cent helpfulness and loyalty they showed in this difficult period, mustered all the relevant Cabinet and parliamentary quotations which were damning to Wilson's latest 'posture'. On the other hand all my ministerial colleagues were not merely convinced that de Gaulle would soon veto the whole exercise, but were also, by this time, heartily sick of the entire controversy. Only on 20 June, in a discussion of a report by Wilson on his conversation with de Gaulle on the previous day, Callaghan had remarked that the whole EEC project might be proving futile, and we should leave ourselves a way out. Heroic attitudes would evidently have evoked no sympathy even from my friends. I decided not to reply to Wilson's minute, but to continue the argument, and to leave it to him to drop me from the Government if he wished. Indeed by the time I read Wilson's minute I was so disenchanted with the whole Government that I was not sure whether it was best to continue the argument within it or outside. I recalled Herbert Bowden's remark to me when Wilson was first elected Leader of the Party: 'I shall co-operate so far as is humanly possible.' My aim for several years had been the same; but I now doubted whether it was humanly possible any longer. And that was the state of the controversy when the Cabinet dispersed for the recess in early August.

Throughout the next two weeks in north Cornwall I was telephoning to Richard Powell at the Board of Trade about the HP relaxations to ensure that they went forward. On 25 August, I had a telephone talk from Dartmoor with Callaghan in which he assured me that the relaxations were fully agreed; and the same evening I was asked to meet Wilson at Plymouth the next day. He then told me he was dropping me from the Government, because he was instituting an unwritten principle that all ministers should retire at sixty, and I had passsed this watershed by six months. I asked if he had any complaint about my record at the Board of Trade, and he said: 'None,' adding that it all had nothing to do with the Common Market, or what he called the 'press campaigns' against me. This I no more believed than did anyone else. I spoke to Callaghan next day, and he said later that

[37] See p. 391.

Wilson had discussed the re-shuffle with him, but had withheld from him some of the changes to which he would have objected. Bowden also left the Government. He told me afterwards that he felt, after the undertakings given to Commonwealth Governments about safeguards, that he no longer could stay in the Government; but was willing not to cause trouble by resigning publicly. He became Chairman of the ITA.

A more plausible account of the re-shuffle than the sixty-retirement age was later given to me by one of the other senior ministers involved. Wilson's original intention was to bring in Gordon-Walker, whom everybody wanted to see included, as Commonwealth Secretary instead of Bowden. But Brown intervened arguing that his own rush into the EEC would be impeded if I remained at the Board of Trade and an ex-Foreign Secretary, Gordon-Walker, was installed to argue the Commonwealth case at the Commonwealth Office. He would prefer George Thomson, whom he regarded as pliant, as Commonwealth Secretary.[38] The idea thus emerged that Gordon-Walker should go to the Ministry of Education (where he would not cause Brown trouble), instead of Tony Crosland, and Crosland should succeed me at the Board of Trade. Thus two possible obstacles to EEC entry could be avoided. This, I believe, was the substantial truth about the re-shuffle, and the general public belief that my attitude on the EEC made it impossible for me to remain in this Government was basically correct. One other minor excuse mentioned by Wilson to Callaghan was particularly strange: my differences with the textile unions. For in fact I had been urging, as mentioned above, concessions to the textile industry which had been constantly blocked by Wilson. Attlee's comment on this re-shuffle was: 'Wilson's no judge of character.' On 29 August Wilson announced on his own the HP relaxations which I had been proposing for the previous three months.

But that was not quite the end of this story. On 27 November de Gaulle declared his formal veto on our EEC application. And on 15 March 1968, George Brown, after a final explosive clash with his colleagues, resigned from the Government.

---

[38] Wilson himself gives a somewhat, but not very, different version (p. 427).

To find oneself suddenly bereft without warning, as I did on Sunday 27 August 1967, of one's current job, and cherished projects, one's office and one's trusted colleagues, is a strange experience. It combines a sense of freedom with a sense of loss. In Britain today almost nobody can be deprived of their job without a right of appeal, trade union support, compensation or a period of notice, or all of these, except a Minister of the Crown or Member of Parliament. With me on that Sunday on Dartmoor, however, the sense of freedom predominated; freedom to say uncompromisingly what I thought about the folly of the Government's Common Market application. On that Sunday my daughters, joined us for two shining summer days amid the Dartmoor rivers. But the sense of loss remained for working colleagues who had shared the past three years' exertions, in which so many public-spirited industrialists as well as officials had lent their support to. Within ten days of the announcement of the Government changes, I received over 200 personal letters from such friends and colleagues as these, in politics, the civil service and industry, sending good wishes and regretting my leaving the job. Naturally at such moments people write friendly letters; but most of these were kinder than I expected. Particularly heartening were letters from David Serpell, Second Permanent Secretary at the Board of Trade, who shared my love of Dartmoor, and from Richard Powell, the Permanent Secretary throughout these three years, from both of whom I gained the impression (though perhaps it was an illusion), that we had all of us achieved rather more than I had previously imagined.

The more mundane form of loss, however, which bore speedily in upon me was the sudden absence of a secretary, an office, or even a typewriter. For the past thirty years, I had possessed an office of my own and someone to whom I could dictate; and for thirty-eight years since joining *The Times* I had had some office to go to. For a moment I felt almost blind and deaf. But Mary Thomas, who herself had the rare knack of both surmounting and foreseeing practical difficulties, most nobly in the midst of her holiday joined us at Postbridge for several days, during which we answered almost all the 200 letters. Back in London, she undertook, until some new regime could be improvised, to handle in the evenings after a full day's work with my successor, at the Board of Trade, the invitations now pouring in to me to accept responsibilities of all kinds. By the end of two weeks I was certain that my chief aim from now on must be to explain to all capable of understanding it the harm which the narrow Common Market obsession must, if pushed too far, do to this country, and the vastly better long-term future offered to us by the wider, more liberal, alternative.

The comparative failure of the 1964 Wilson Government, by contrast with the Attlee Government of 1945–51, is startling. They both remained in office for about the same time: six years. Yet look at the brief summary of the achievements of the Attlee Government on pages 213–14 of this book, and try to reckon up a similar score for 1964–70. In social reform, as against the splendid record of 1945–51, the Wilson Government failed to pass legislation for the national superannuation plan, but made some progress with redundancy payments, children's allowances, and the ever disputed issue of comprehensive schools. It strove vigorously, and with some success to improve race relations, and to build more houses; and it set up the Law Commission and the Open University. But it failed completely with its 'In Place of Strife' reform of trade union practice, with Crossman's so-called parliamentary reform, and of course with the EEC application. On the economic front the Kennedy Round negotiations, affecting far more trade than all that of the EEC, and liberating far more trade than the CAP restricted, were successfully completed, and we achieved a Free Trade Area Agreement with Eire. Callaghan also rightly introduced a Capital Gains Tax. True, under the Wilson–Jenkins regime the Sterling Area system and British influence East of Suez were also largely dismantled; though whether this benefited anyone other than the long-term enemies of this country and of parliamentary democracy was always, in my view, highly doubtful.

The Wilson Government and Jenkins in particular could at least claim that, having inherited a large payments deficit in 1964, it handed over a £1000 million a year surplus in 1970–1 to the Conservatives, who again had completely dissipated this before the oil crisis of late 1973. Labour's favourable record here was partly due to the success of export promotion, but also to the 1967 devaluation. The strongest claim, however, of the 1964 Government to real national achievement, judged in the light of later history, was probably the sustained and in the end reasonably effective prices and incomes policy. For this at least George Brown deserves much credit. The abolition of the Prices and Incomes Board by the subsequent Heath Government was one of the worst mistakes in our internal post-war history. The 1964 Government also passed much meritorious second-line legislation: in my own sphere, most important, the Industrial Development Act, which in effect revived and widened Development Area policy to an extent which could not be reversed in later years; the Companies Act 1967 providing for much more disclosure of facts and ending some insurance scandals: a Monopolies and Mergers Act; the Trade Descriptions Act; and a Shipbuilding Bill to aid and reorganize that most vulnerable industry. But the contrast with the Attlee Government remains glaring.

Not merely was it a contrast of record, but also one of spirit. The Wilson Government was an unhappy one, in which unease and suspicion festered, in contrast to the sense of purpose and achievement which buoyed us up even in the most arduous moments in 1945–51. Much of course of the Wilson Government's failures were admittedly due to major mistakes of policy: the creation of the DEA; the choice of the surcharge; and above all the EEC application which fiercely divided the Cabinet and the Party, diverted huge reserves of administrative energy from the really crucial job of economic recovery, and finally ended in the veto. But the greatest single cause of the comparative failure of the Wilson Government was, I believe, the mistrust which some leading members of the Cabinet inspired among their colleagues; and above all their habit of private, unauthorized and biassed communications – alternatively known as leaks or 'briefs' – with unnamed journalists. Ministers who found themselves attacked in the press and traced the fingerprints back to No. 10 and the DEA, felt under pressure to retaliate. Before long it was suspected that an even more odious traffic was developing: a minister presenting an illicit scoop to a press man on the tacit understanding that the newspaper concerned reported that he was a most successful minister. One could almost identify some of the leaks by noting which ministers were paraded as outstanding successes, and sometimes the choice was extraordinary. Those who want to pursue this murky subject will find chapter and verse in Wilson's *The Labour Government 1964–70* and Crossman's *Diaries*.[1] Such insidious practices probably did more than anything else to sour the morale of the 1964 Cabinet. I possibly went too far the other way in avoiding journalists. In extenuation of these practices, it should perhaps be conceded that some of those who resorted to them, not having been members of the Attlee Government, had no other standards. Had Hugh Gaitskell lived to head this Government, all this would certainly have been different.

The Wilson Government can rightly claim that had it not been for the seamen's strike of 1966 and the Merseyside dock-strike of 1967, the dramatic improvement in the balance of payments would have occurred much sooner. Up to the first half of 1967, before the dock strike, the record was good. For the whole of the twelve months ending in June 1967 (which included part of the 1966 seamen's strike), our current balance of

---

[1] For instance Harold Wilson, *The Labour Government 1964–70*, pp. 473–6, and Richard Crossman, *The Diaries of a Cabinet Minister*, vol. 1, p. 551.

payments, visible and invisible, including Government expenditure over-seas, was only £67 million in deficit – compared with over £400 million in 1964. Revised figures, only corrected after I left the Government, showed that in these years UK exports were materially higher than we knew. Probably the fairest way of assessing the effect of our own export promotion drive at the Board of Trade in 1964–70 is to set down the simple figures of export *volume* in the 1960s:

UK export volume index (1961 = 100)	
1963	108
1964	111
1965	116
1966	121
1967	119
1968	136

The rise in export volume in 1965 and 1966 was a reasonably creditable performance. But the dock strike in the second half of 1967 then shattered the export effort for the time, and together with the end of the import surcharge, pushed us into devaluation in November 1967. In turn, devalu-ation exerted an electrifying effect on export volume during 1968 – and presented the fortunate new Chancellor, Jenkins, with an easy balance of payments prospect in 1969 and 1970. The whole experience does accord-ingly suggest that export promotion effort by Government as well as industry can pay off, and that it achieved a moderate success in these years.

The other campaign to which I devoted most time was the regeneration of the old areas of unemployment. For this the basic argument for me had always been not the human need alone, but the economic case for raising the productivity of the whole nation by offering productive work to those who could in practice only accept it if it was reasonably near to their homes. The whole effort had been lamentably weakened before 1964, and could not be fully regenerated until the Industrial Development Act of 1966 was passed; but here fortunately one can measure the results. I always believed myself that success would primarily depend on the volume of new factory space actually built rather than any indirect assistance by way of taxation, subsidies, road-building, etc. If one selects the figures for appro-vals of all government factory-building in the wider areas classed as Development Areas under the 1966 Act, the record is as shown opposite. These figures represent government-financed factories only, and private development would be additional. Within the total of government-financed factories, the total of advance factories approved had fallen to only 176,000 sq. ft in all in 1963–4. This rose to 745,000 sq. ft in 1964–5, 862,000 sq. ft in 1966–7, and 950,000 sq. ft in 1968–9. And the policy of regular advance factory programmes has continued ever since.

	Number of factories or extensions	Area in sq. ft (000)
1962–3	53	1652
1963–4	85	1667
1964–5	130	3273
1965–6	114	3148
1966–7	118	3074
1967–8	101	2572
1968–9	132	3015

The effect of the whole effort on unemployment in the Development Areas can also be measured. Here a popular fallacy often raises its head. Comparisons are made between the crude unemployment figures in Development Areas at different dates. But of course unemployment in Wales or Scotland and the North-East Coast is always substantially affected by the level in the UK as a whole. Distribution of Industry policy affects not the general level of unemployment, but the ratio of unemployment in the Development (or wider 'assisted') Areas to the average for Great Britain as a whole. On this crucial test the record of the 1960s is as follows:

Unemployment rate in Development Areas as percentage of Great Britain rate	
June 1962	200
June 1963	205
June 1964	221
June 1965	208
June 1966	200
June 1967	180
June 1968	168

Unemployment in Development Areas in 1964 was twice that in Great Britain as a whole, and rising; while by 1968, it had fallen to only 68 per cent greater. There is no doubt that deliberate Government policy in these years markedly reduced this ratio. Indeed by the 1970s the success had become so pronounced, and dispersal of industry from London and the Midlands had gone so far, that genuine doubts arose whether it should be pushed any further. The same broad conclusion was reached in a full statistical analysis in the Bulletin of the Cambridge Department of Applied Economics of March 1973 by Barry Moore and John Rhodes. They say: 'Over the period 1963–70 the cumulative employment generated directly by the stronger regional policy in Development Area manufacturing industries (excluding shipbuilding and metal manufacture) was about 150,000.' For my part, if I wished for any political epitaph, it would be these modest figures.

Though regretting that these major jobs were only three-quarters finished when I left the Government, I found that in the freedom of the back benches new activities crowded in on me. Within twenty-four hours of the Cabinet changes being announced, I was asked by Alistair Hetherington, Editor of the *Guardian*, to write three full-length articles for that paper explaining the damage that would be done by joining the Common Market on surrender terms. These appeared in the middle of September just before the Labour Party Conference at Scarborough. Before leaving Dartmoor, I had also agreed with the Editor of the *New Statesman* to write a 5000 word article for them on the whole Common Market–Commonwealth issue. The substance of the *New Statesman* article was later published under the title 'The Truth about the Common Market', and re-published by the Common Market Safeguards Campaign. In the next week Frank Kearton of Courtaulds offered me a job as a part-time director of Courtaulds, which – having ascertained from a friendly Richard Powell that there were no moral or constitutional objections – I accepted. At least this gave me an office to work in, shared part-time with my old antagonist David Eccles, now Lord Eccles, and R. A. Butler who, however, seldom turned up. I welcomed greatly the opportunity of joining Courtaulds. For if there was anything lacking in my experience it was direct knowledge of industry from the business side; I was a great admirer of Kearton's remarkable capacities; and if the textile industries were to be rapidly modernized, I had no doubt that Courtaulds were better able to do it than the Board of Trade.

Just before the Courtaulds announcement was made, I spoke at the first Labour Party anti-Market 'fringe meeting' at the end of September in Scarborough. Michael Foot advised me to do this; and the other speakers were Shinwell, Will Blyton (the Durham MP), Foot himself, Jim Mortimer a trade unionist,[2] and a most effective young speaker, Ron Leighton, whom I had not met before. This meeting was widely reported in the press next day, and established the existence of a strong anti-Market movement in the Labour Party. I also worked at this Conference with the young Alf Morris MP, a devoted anti-Marketeer, and Frank Cousins, who was moving a sceptical motion at the Conference. Though this motion was lost on the vote, we had certainly put our case fairly cogently.

My articles in the *New Statesman* appeared on 9 November; and were, I felt, the fullest statement of the case I had made. As soon as the House re-assembled, I took my first chance in the Debate on the Address on 2 November to make what was in effect my resignation speech. I took great trouble over this, and was listened to intently, even though it was all fact and argument and no rhetoric. The only interruption came from Eric Heffer, later a good friend, but then a pro-Marketeer whom I knew little. He asked why if I thought all this, I had not resigned sooner. I privately sympathized with him. But to complete the cycle, Heffer after a few more years' experience of the facts, became a convinced, indeed passionate,

[2] Later Chairman of ACAS (Arbitration and Conciliation Advisory Service).

anti-Marketeer himself, and resigned from the next Labour Government over this very issue.

In these autumn weeks I also arranged, with the help of Clem Leslie, a personal friend ever since Treasury days, and now another strong Commonwealth supporter, to write a full-scale Penguin by the end of the year. I duly delivered the typescript on 29 December, and it was published under the title *After the Common Market* advocating the wider and more liberal free-trade area solution. By 1 December we had formed a new Labour anti-Market Committee,[3] of which I became Chairman and Ron Leighton Secretary, which held its first public meeting in Liverpool on 1 December and continued its activity right up to the 1975 Referendum. Those who announced the launching of this Committee as founder members were Michael Foot, Alf Morris, William Pickles, Ron Leighton and myself. Many Labour MPs joined, but Frank Cousins could not make up his mind. Our purpose in this Committee was to convert the majority of the PLP and Labour Conference to support the basic conditions laid down for membership in Gaitskell's speech of October 1962; and in this eventually we succeeded.

On the same day, 1 December, I joined Sir Alexander Glen's H. Clarkson group of shipping, insurance and transport companies, and acquired an office of my own in Little Trinity Lane in the City, with Mary Thomas as part-time secretary to me and part-time employee of the Clarkson group. So after three months' turmoil I again had my own office to work, in (few MPs had any at Westminster even in 1967), and felt I could operate efficiently once more. It was just twenty-seven years since in 1940, I had left the City for the Ministry of Supply, and I felt almost pleased to be working there once more. Having also since September visited several of Courtaulds main factories, and re-joined the board of the Trades Union Unit Trust and another investment trust, I felt as I delivered my Penguin book to the publishers at the end of the year that I had not been idle in these rather breathless three months.

In the New Year, 1968, I decided to concentrate on two major political campaigns. There is no point in being a politician unless one is fighting for a cause. More than two campaigns I knew would risk dissipation of effort and failure in them all. To concentrate on one only would offend the principle of spreading the risk. But with two there was a reasonable chance of success in one. As it happened the two immediately selected themselves: first the Common Market, and the case for a wider trade system. Secondly I discovered at about this time that my constituency of North Battersea, and much of residential London, were threatened by what appeared a recklessly destructive and extravagant project for building four mammoth double-carriageway motorways round Inner and Outer London. As

[3] The Labour Common Market Safeguards Committee.

soon as I had studied these motorway plans, which were much more damaging than I first supposed, particularly to Battersea and Hampstead, I made up my mind that they had to be stopped.

The threat of the motorway proposals to any prospect of better housing in London first became known to me before 1964 when the then Leader of the Labour Group on the Wandsworth Borough Council, also Chairman of my own Battersea Labour Party, told me that an acutely needed new Council housing project was blocked because the LCC (as it then was) proposed to build 'some road' alongside Clapham Junction. On inquiring about this I discovered it to be the tip of a mysteriously much larger iceberg. On behalf of Battersea I expressed to the LCC our immediate opposition to the whole project. At the end of 1967 I learnt that the then Conservative GLC plan was on a far more massive scale than all but a few had realized. The GLC proposed to construct within and around London *four* full-scale six-lane or eight-lane motorways, overhead for more than half their length, and to continue the existing radial motorways (M1, M4, etc.) into London to meet them. Ringway 1, the innermost circle, was to run on the line: Shepherds Bush, Chelsea Worlds End, Battersea, Clapham, Camberwell, Deptford, the East End, Hackney, Islington, Camden Town, Hampstead, Willesden and so back to Shepherds Bush. Ringway 2 would have replaced the North Circular and embryonic South Circular roads; and Ringways 3 and 4 would have been constructed further out. The total cost of the whole monstrous project would have been at least £2000 million in 1970 values; or nearly as much as the British share of the Concorde, Channel Tunnel and Maplin Airport all combined. Houses and flats for a minimum of 60,000 people would have been destroyed, even on the estimates of the promoters of the scheme; and almost certainly for nearer 100,000 people in fact, and in areas of acute and long-term housing shortage.

Large parts of Battersea would have been laid waste by intersecting overhead motorway viaducts; and dwellings for 5000 people would have been lost in Battersea alone. At the same time the four Ringways would have contributed, even on the evidence of their promoters, almost nothing to the London rush-hour problem, the real cause of congestion, because the peak-hour travellers are very largely moving radially between the centre and homes in the outskirts. A first scrutiny of the figures also revealed that by simply omitting Ringway 1 and 2 from the plan, some £1500 million could be saved from the total £2000 million, and 90 per cent of the housing loss avoided.

It may now seem incredible that so hare-brained a scheme could have been propounded, let alone approved, by informed people. Yet it was strongly backed by the British Road Federation, by Sir Colin Buchanan's firm Colin Buchanan and Partners, then popularly regarded as omniscient on such matters, by the road engineers' profession generally, grudgingly by the pre-1967 Labour majority on the LCC (though they at least decided to build the outer Ringways first), and enthusiastically by their Conservative successors. On a sober view this must be explained as an alarming example (comparable with Maplin and the 'high-rise' flats of this epoch) of engineers' and technologists' meglomania, backed by vested interests, being given a free run almost without regard to what the ordinary public actually wanted. It embodied both the two basic errors of making a major moral judgement about comparative human needs without admitting it, and failing to measure the magnitude of the need against the magnitude of the cost. One attraction of the whole campaign to me was that it was a classic case of a struggle between the comon people and the technocrats in which the common people were right. For such opinion polls as were conducted in the relevant years showed that housing was always regarded as among the first few acutest needs, and more motorways at the end of the list.

In March 1968 I received a letter from Ben Whittaker, then Labour MP for Hampstead, suggesting that I should organize an all-Party group of local societies to resist the motorways on an all-London scale. Thus encouraged, I invited all the organizations of which we knew, including the Battersea Society and the London Amenity and Transport Association (LATA) to a meeting in the Grand Committee Room in Westminster Hall. This meeting was virtually unanimous in wishing to form such a central group forthwith, and I was elected Chairman and Mary Thomas became the working Secretary. We decided to call it the London Motorway Action Group. Duncan Sandys became deputy-Chairman, to maintain the all-party character of the Group. He was also Chairman of the Civic Trust, and his own constituency of Streatham was threatened by the motorways. Very soon eleven other London MPs and later over fifty other local societies had joined as members. The MPs were: Michael Barnes, Stanley Clinton Davies, Ben Whittaker (after the 1970 election, Geoffrey Finsberg), Bill Hamling, Hugh Jenkins, Marcus Lipton, Roland Moyle, Laurie Pavitt, Ernest Perry, Nigel Spearing and Robert Taylor. Societies representing almost every area in London threatened by the motorways were recruited: notably Barnes, Battersea, Camden Town, Chiswick, Hackney, Hampstead, Lewisham, New Eltham, Norbury, Peckham, Putney, Roding Valley, Streatham Vale, and Woolwich. With LATA came a most valuable expert Michael Thomson, a transport economist at the LSE, who believed that even on purely transport grounds, city motorways were not the right solution.

The London Motorway Action Group (LMAG) agreed initially, as a basic principle, that all these societies should join together to oppose the Inner Ringways as such, instead of each arguing that the nuisance should be transferred elsewhere. In fact the only major area and society which took the purely sectional view was Chelsea, whose spokesmen tended to argue that all traffic should be pushed into Battersea. Throughout the

o

controversy the promoters of the Inner Ringways, persisted in regarding almost any working-class areas as 'derelict' or 'obsolete' property, which could conveniently be demolished. Battersea and Hampstead became the prime movers in the whole enterprise, and Hampstead generously contributed much of the finance needed. The Working Committee of LMAG included up to two representatives from each member society, and any MP who wished to attend. It met monthly in a committee room of the House of Commons right through from 1968 till the effective end of the controversy in the spring of 1973. Its basic aims were agreed as these: that Ringways 1 and 2 should be abandoned; that radial motorways should not penetrate into London further than Ringway 3; and that the real traffic problems should be tackled by a combination of better public transport, 'traffic management' schemes (one-ways, etc.), and parking restrictions. The LMAG did not oppose the two outer Ringways, 3 and 4, but agreed that a motorway ring well outside the main London built-up area would be in most people's interest; and this was broadly the solution finally adopted.

Operations began with a series of public meetings in the threatened areas, and an approach to the minister responsible to request that a full-scale public inquiry should be held, at which we could deploy our full case. The first public meeting in Battersea to explain the threat and arouse opposition was held in February 1968, and scored a huge success. Deputations to ministers began with a visit to Richard Marsh, then Transport Minister on 2 May, at which he promised that no major schemes would go ahead without a public enquiry. A fortnight afterwards we expounded our case formally in a discussion with the leaders of the GLC. At a later 1968 meeting on the motorways, at Streatham Baths, with Michael Thomson, I was astonished on arrival to find that more than 1000 people had turned up, more than I had seen at even general election meetings for some years past. It was clear that we had stumbled on a cause which aroused immense popular feeling. At another meeting that year in the Westminster Hall Committee Room, John Betjeman, the Bishop of Southwark and Duncan Sandys made anti-motorway speeches to another crowded audience from all round London. A little later, February 1969, Roy Jenkins, now Chancellor, suggested to me a private talk about the Inner Ringways, and I saw him à deux at the Treasury. He was very sympathetic and evidently much impressed by the enormous cost of what the GLC were proposing.

The most important next move, as it turned out later however, was a lunch at the Anchor pub on the South Bank in the City in July 1969 with Reg Goodwin, leader of the Labour Opposition on the GLC. Since the GLC was the proponent of the whole scheme, which would collapse without it, I had always thought the best hope of defeating it was to convince the Labour Group on the GLC. Reg Goodwin assured me at this lunch that it was now firm Labour policy to oppose the 'North and South Cross

Routes', the major sections of Ringway 1, and he was pretty confident that the pro-motorway faction in the Labour GLC, led by Ted Castle at this time, would be defeated at the annual Regional Conference on 13 September. I promised to come and help. I felt sure I could count on Reg Goodwin – whose straightforwardness reminded me of Attlee – from that moment onwards. At the Regional Conference the efforts of Ted Castle to get Ringway 1 re-inserted in the Labour programme was heavily defeated. His own speech was nearly shouted down, and did more than my own, I felt, to promote our case.

Meanwhile the London Motorway Action Group itself, together with LATA, had launched a Study Group, headed by Michael Thomson, to prepare the formal and detailed case which we would present to the public inquiry when it was set up. Michael Thomson completed this not merely with great expertise, but much greater speed than the Government showed in settling what type of public inquiry should be held. So we decided to publish his report, on the authority of LATA, as a short book entitled *Motorways in London*, in the autumn of 1969. It did much to counter the incessant and liberally financed propaganda of the British Road Federation and GLC. Next step was a visit with Duncan Sandys to Tony Crosland, now Secretary of State for the Environment, to press our all-party argument for a really thorough public inquiry. Crosland promised a fairly early announcement. In the first week of December 1969 we therefore handed to the Minister of Housing our now fully documented case, and gave it to the press immediately afterwards. Since it happily coincided with a very critical statement on the GLC's plans by the Royal Institute of British Architects, quite independent of our own, the impact on the London press was unusually good. On 10 December Crosland announced in the House an Independent Inquiry, under Mr Frank Layfield QC, supported by assessors from outside the Government, and with Government financial help for the Inquiry Panel (though not for the objectors) with the cost of their own research. Strictly, it was an inquiry into the whole Greater London Development Plan, and not just into roads and motorways.

Nevertheless a formidable prospect confronted us independent objectors. The lawyers had fastened their grip on the Layfield Inquiry. It was to be 'adversarial'. I saw their point; all this guaranteed a fair hearing to everyone (if they could pay). But it also meant all the paraphernalia of learned counsel, witnesses, 'proofs of evidence', cross-examinations etc.; and more still, it meant huge expense over months and perhaps years. The principal promoters, the GLC, had their rate revenue behind them, and could spend virtually what they liked on legal representation; and they were backed by the British Road Federation (who managed to appear as 'objectors' on the ground that the plan was not grandiose enough), not to mention the road engineers' professional establishment; none of whom were short of money. Though we could not match a fraction of the GLC and road lobby's funds, we decided having asked for the Inquiry, to take it seriously, and raise what money we could. In all this we were greatly strengthened by two other members of the Group, David Hunter, a barrister, from the Camden Motorway Action Group, who with the help of solicitors found us Lord Colville as our chief advocate; and Stephen Plowden, a transport economist and consultant. During the whole period 1968–73 we raised nearly £20,000 which was just enough to pay our legal expenses and leave some modest fee for the professional transport economists. The biggest contributors to this, apart from the Hampstead Motorway Action Group, were the Camden and Lambeth Borough Councils who generously gave £1000 each. All the rest came from voluntary donations from members of the fifty or more local societies. Lord Colville proved a brilliant ally who astonished some of us by mastering, after a few sessions with Michael Thomson, not merely all the latter's economic technicalities and statistics, but even his algebra.

Owing to the long delay in launching the Inquiry, we decided at the end of 1969 that we must re-state the whole case; and a new document called *Transport Strategy in London* was composed by a specialist group under Michael Thomson's inspiration. Meanwhile a political interlude intervened in the shape of the GLC elections of April 1970. It seemed at last probable that if a Labour majority succeeded the Conservatives at County Hall, enthusiasm for the Ringways there would markedly diminish. At this stage, however, the Labour Party attitude was sceptical, but a little ambiguous; and as a result a breakaway group of anti-motorway enthusiasts calling themselves 'Homes Before Roads', put up candidates in the GLC elections. Their motives were excellent; but as so often happens with political amateurs, their candidates polled very few votes, probably at the expense mainly of the Labour Party, and the Conservatives remained in power at County Hall.

The Layfield Inquiry did not actually open at County Hall until 9 October 1970, and did not reach the transport issues till December. We duly presented *Transport Strategy in London* to the Inquiry in February 1971. It now amounted to a full-scale book of 300 pages, complete with Appendices A to Z (literally). Most important, however, it thoroughly and expertly argued the main issues at stake, and expounded our alternative and much less expensive practical strategy. Just in case the public, the press, and even the learned Panel, did not follow all the algebraic subtleties, I inserted a preface of thirteen pages of comparatively plain English summarizing what we proposed. My private opinion was that our case rested mainly, not on the mathematics, but on the manifest absurdity of destroying 30,000 houses, and ploughing up much of London, in the midst of a housing shortage, and at a cost of £2000 million. But it was essential to back this with a thoroughly expert demonstration that the motorways did not make sense even on transport grounds. *Transport Strategy in*

London was simultaneously handed to the press, and circulated to all the main government departments concerned. At the end of March, Thomson and I gave our so-called 'evidence', and for a day or so answered questions from Colville and the GLC lawyers.

The LMAG and LATA were the chief, but by no means the only objectors to the Inner Ringways. We encouraged our own member societies and others to lodge their objections, and a great many did so, including Wandsworth Borough Council; though none of them produced as professional a document as *Transport Strategy in London*. For instance, the Battersea Labour Party appeared on its own, with some ordinary members of the Party urging the extremely strong Battersea case. The Hampstead Motorway Action Group put up a notable performance, punctuated by much laughter and applause, which attracted so large a crowd that the Inquiry had to move to Church House, Westminster. Leslie Ginsburg, a planning and transport consultant, was the hero of this particular evening. And while the gladiatorial and forensic displays by Ginsburg, Colville, Thomson, Plowden and the GLC experts and advocates continued through 1971 and much of 1972; public meetings sprang up spontaneously all over London, for which we in the LMAG supplied speakers and propaganda ammunition.

Next major round in the struggle was a separate inquiry into the West Cross Route – the section of Ringway 1 from Shepherds Bush to the Chelsea Embankment – which was to cost £34 million *a mile* (in 1972 money values). The GLC wanted to start this section separately and in advance of the Layfield Report, and a separate public inquiry was held in Fulham Town Hall opening on 28 March 1972. The West Cross Route was a particularly mortal threat to Battersea, because it was almost bound to lead to a new motorway bridge across the Thames at Lots Road and so an inevitable overhead motorway of some kind through residential Battersea. Both the LMAG, and again the Battersea Labour Party, arranged to appear as objectors before it. A few days before the West Cross Route Inquiry opened, an anti-motorway meeting at Brixton, at which I spoke, was attended by 800 people. At the Inquiry, the GLC officials were clearly unprepared for such vigorous opposition. A few months later the 'Inspector' (i.e. the presiding officer at the Inquiry) reported to the Secretary of State against the West Cross Route, and fully accepted our argument that this bit of road could not be justified on its own independently of Ringway 1 as a whole. This was our first major victory.

In the end, after years of controversy, the whole London motorway dispute ended with dramatic suddenness. In the early weeks of 1973, five years after the LMAG had been launched, the issue was still undecided. The Layfield Report had been presented to the Government, but not published. So on 22 January we held an enthusiastic public meeting at Central Hall, Westminster, addressed by Geoffrey Finsberg, Conservative

MP for Hampstead as well as Michael Thomson and myself, demanding that the Report be published and the Inner Ringways abandoned. On 19 February, the Government published the Report, which to our astonishment recommended in favour of the most controversial Ringway 1 and one outer Ringway; and Geoffrey Rippon, the Minister, announced that the Government accepted this solution. At this moment, after five years of propaganda effort, we found ourselves almost totally defeated, with both the Report of the Inquiry and the Government against us on the main issue. How the Panel reached a conclusion which nobody had before proposed, I never knew. One rumour was that its members got short of time, and entrusted the whole transport section of the Report to the road engineer on the Panel.

However, we resolved to fight the last battle and went into action quickly. By chance the LMAG Working Committee met next day (20 February) and I had typed ready for signature a letter to *The Times* denouncing the Government's decision. It was signed by over twenty members representing a number of London societies, delivered to *The Times* an hour later, and appeared prominently on 22 February. I had also written a few weeks earlier congratulating Reg Goodwin Labour Leader on the GLC, on an emphatic anti-motorway speech; and he had replied that he had 'chanced his arm', but was now sure the Party would support him. This the London Labour Party did at a Regional Meeting I attended on Sunday 18 February. We were much helped at this moment by the news that the West Cross Route Inspector had indeed reported against the GLC's plans. The LMAG thereafter decided to restrain other bodies from putting up purely anti-motorway candidates in the GLC elections, and to run itself an all-out-anti-motorway campaign right through till polling day on 12 April. The slogan was to be: 'Stop Ringway 1', as the Government had cancelled Ringway 2 already. A very young recruit, Helene Middleweek, aged twenty-three, an ex-President of the Cambridge Union – later Helene Hayman, Labour MP – was appointed to organize a short, sharp, sloganized publicity campaign from her Chalk Farm flat, to synchronize with the GLC elections. She did it splendidly, staunchly backed in particular by Mark Bass of the Hampstead Motorway Action Group, one of the hardest workers in the whole London movement. It was a non-party campaign, sponsored by the LMAG, and it appealed to non-party anti-motorway opinion all over London. But its message coincided with Labour's election policy, and certainly a large number of normally floating but anti-motorway voters supported Labour. To back it from Parliament itself, on 20 March in the middle of the election campaign, I moved from the Labour Front Bench in the House, a motion critical of excessive road expenditure and deploring the London motorways. Nobody except the MP for Chelsea spoke against the motion, and the Government's majority fell to eleven when the vote was taken. On the evening of polling day in the GLC election itself, 12 April, it soon became clear that Labour had decisively won. Next day, Reg Goodwin, as leader of the new GLC, publicly pledged himself to abandon all the motorways except the relatively non-controversial Ringway 4. By July of that year the legal ban which sterilized the Inner Motorway routes was cancelled, and housing development began to go forward.

So those of us who fought this battle found ourselves faced after four years' and ten months' effort with total defeat, but after five years with total victory. The final cancellation of all the Ringways except no. 4 gave us even more than we had asked for. We were truly astonished by our own good fortune; for it is not often granted to any politician or group to achieve such complete success – still less to snatch it out of the jaws of failure. As I read Reg Goodwin's statement in the evening paper on 13 April on the pavement in Parliament Square, I could hardly believe it. Seen in retrospect, the success of the LMAG was due first to the willingness of its members from all areas and groups to join without too much dissension in a united effort; secondly to our concentration on hard work rather than hooligan activities at public inquiries, thirdly, to the fact that we enjoyed real press support, for instance from Simon Jenkins in the *Evening Standard* as well as many local papers; but above all because we had an unanswerable case. Most gratifying to me was the practical demonstration that all the experts had proved wrong: the engineers, the consultants, Colin Buchanan, even the well-meaning Layfield Panel, and the Department of Transport; and that the despised ordinary electors of London and the Battersea Labour Party had proved right. And thank heavens for a political system in which the electors were not merely proved right, but by the exercise of their vote decided the issue.

For if the Layfield–Rippon decision to embark on Ringway 1 had actually gone ahead, an almost unprecedented fiasco would have resulted. Just when petrol prices were nearly trebled in 1974, and when all government expenditure had to be pruned, London would have been left in the next year or two with half-finished concrete monstrosities, costing hundreds of millions to complete, in the midst of dismembered and derelict residential areas. From all this we were saved by the voters. Being human, the LMAG and Scrap Ringway 1 groups gathered a few weeks later for a brief celebration, at which they generously presented me with the complete works of Macaulay, who once lived in Battersea himself. I think he would have been on our side, and I never valued any gift more.

Compared with the issue of Britain's joining or not joining the Common Market, the London Motorways were no doubt almost a parish pump controversy; though the size of the proposed expenditure made it a pretty substantial pump. I never thought it at all likely that both battles could be won. Clearly if I could have chosen which of the two was to succeed, I would have chosen the Market. But it always seemed to me imperative that, whatever the outcome, the case against membership must be forcibly put, and that one of two fundamental objectives would thus be secured; either a national decision in favour of the wider and more liberal solution based on EFTA and the Commonwealth; or failing this, the negotiation of terms which limited so far as possible the inevitable damage due to membership. But I was never under any illusion about the immense forces, and above all financial backing, likely to be mobilized on the pro-Market side, nor the impossibility of any but surrender terms being obtainable in any rushed negotiations.

Why, however, one is bound to ask at this point, did almost the whole British establishment – the government machine, the City and the press – suddenly during the 1960s turn a simultaneous somersault, and embrace a policy which was bound to burden heavily our balance of payments, lower our living standards, weaken our international influence, alienate our best friends overseas and damage the control of our own Parliament over our own affairs? The near unanimity and the disastrous consequences were both reminiscent of 1938 to anyone who lived through both.[1] And from where did the massive political and financial pressure come, which engineered this wholly unpredicted volte-face? Details of the battle over British membership, and of the forces, personalities, and propaganda methods employed on both sides have been set out by Douglas Evans (*While Britain Slept*)[2] for the anti-Marketeers, and by Uwe Kitzinger (*Diplomacy and Persuasion*)[3] from the pro-Market point of view, and

[1] See pp. 71–2 for this comparison.
[2] Douglas Evans: *While Britain Slept : The Selling of the Common Market* (London, 1975).
[3] Uwe Kitzinger, *Diplomacy and Persuasion* (London, 1973).

need not be repeated. But some conclusions and morals can be drawn from what still remains in some respects an obscure story.

The first reason conventionally put forward for the establishment's volte-face was the loss of Empire, and the belief that some compensation for this loss had to be found somewhere. Having lost much of our international influence in one way, we must look for a substitute strategy – so runs the theory. But this argument is really too manifestly weak to have stimulated a major change of front by supposedly responsible people. For the question clearly arose, whether the new and freer Commonwealth might not be as great a source of strength; and if not whether there were other alternatives; and indeed whether membership of the Market would leave us stronger or weaker. It would be over-cynical to suppose that the alternative of using our political links with the newly independent Commonwealth countries for our own economic benefit as well as theirs (as the French did with their ex-Colonies), never occurred to the Tory mind at all. A rational debate on these questions would have produced various opinions, not an almost Gadarene rush for one panacea. The change of Empire into Commonwealth cannot therefore have been the major motive.

Secondly, it is suggested that the economic difficulties and alleged failure of the British economy led some to the conclusion: here is something new; let us try it. Again it is hard to believe that many serious people could have been influenced by this logic, which is the equivalent of saying: I am suffering from pneumonia, and not recovering; I will try going for a walk in the snow. The rational inference from economic difficulties was to examine the probable economic consequences of alternative policies, not to pretend that this particular one would magically put everything right. A third motive, mentioned earlier in this book,[4] which had been cogent before 1950, but was completely outdated by the mid-1960s and 1970s, was the long-standing desire of Jean Monnet and many others to prevent the historic Franco–German feud erupting into another European war. More realistic, certainly, was the fear of Soviet military power and the wish to build up the defences of Western Europe against it. From my attendance, already described, at the so-called Bilderberg Conferences, and from reading their literature, I have no doubt that this was one genuine motive and one source of the huge funds available to the European Movement. But again, since NATO by the 1960s had long been in existence; and since the US was a member of it, and Russian nuclear strength could only be deterred by US power, why should the British intelligentsia suddenly jump to the conclusion that NATO had to be bolstered up by another organization, in itself harmful to the UK and excluding the US? Another motive doubtless at work was a vague sentimental internationalism which regarded the EEC as just another international organization, when in fact it was an attempt to build either a new regional bloc or a new Federal State. This naive strand

4 See pp. 359–60.

of the movement corresponded to the Lansbury pacifism of the 1930s, but hardly could have dominated the City or the Foreign Office.

A further professed motive among pro-Marketeers in high places was the belief that the 'cold bath' of industrial competition would somehow miraculously enhance the productivity of British industry. This 'cold bath' theory, if pushed to these lengths, was at best sheer nonsense, but at worst a dangerous delusion. Experience unhappily shows – it was staring us in the face from the record of the textile, steel, and ship-building industries in this country in the 1930s – that unless industry is efficient already, fierce competition does not necessarily regenerate: it often kills. But this delusion was fervently propagated in the early Macmillan period by some leading civil servants, and swallowed later by the economic amateurs in the FO. It was of course largely a propaganda argument invented to justify a policy adopted on other grounds. It proved almost wholly false in practice, as witness the British motor industry in the 1970s. But in the 1960s it was hard for industrialists publicly to deny it, because this would seem to admit their own lack of efficiency.

A far greater part, however, was certainly played in converting the establishment by two economic motives which were powerful in the Conservative Party, the City and wider business circles. The first was the age-long desire of the British Conservative Party to halt and reverse the redistribution of incomes, and to achieve this by reducing progressive direct taxation and thrusting the tax burden back on to the consumer on the Continental model; and above all to bring back food taxes and a general sales tax. Ever since the classic defeat of the stern unbending Tories and grain-growing interests by the Repeal of the Corn Laws in 1846 and the removal of other taxes on necessities – a landmark in the conversion of Britain into a more progressive democracy – the Tory Party had hankered after a return of food taxes. Their efforts decisively failed in 1906 and 1923. Now the Tory Party in the 1960s suddenly saw the godsent chance to reintroduce food and other indirect taxes under the guise of 'European Unity' Not surprisingly the whole landowning hierarchy and much of the agricultural interest leapt at the chance. Within five years of our EEC entry food prices had doubled; and land values had risen five-fold – faster than for a century. Second attraction, I believe, to the wielders of great wealth, particularly in the City, was the promise of the uncontrolled movement of capital and the freeing of *laissez-faire* market forces apparently promised by the Treaty of Rome. It was genuinely believed in some business circles that competition would 'discipline the trade unions', put an end to strikes and restore the bargaining power of the employers. Wage-earners would be effectively caught between rising food prices and firm ceilings on money wages. Unfortunately for this theory, if employees refuse to be disciplined, the blast of competition produces not stability, but industrial conflict, depression and unemployment.

These in my judgement were the two really most important, but un-avowed motives for the sudden stampede into the pro-Market camp of the main Conservative, City and landowning interests. But the miraculous conversion of the Foreign Office has still to be explained. It was the almost frenzied passion of the FO after 1966 for joining the EEC at any cost which must bear a great share of the blame for the disasters which followed. In the era of Attlee and Cripps, economic policy, domestic and overseas – for they cannot be separated – was fairly in the hands of the Treasury which understood it. It was one of the major governmental blunders of post-war British history that in the 1960s the FO was allowed first to meddle in and in the end largely to determine, overseas economic policy. For the FO's assumption throughout these years was in effect that the balance of payments did not matter. As a result the country was saddled indefinitely with major gratuitous balance of payments burdens, earlier for the upkeep of British Forces in Germany and later for the huge cost of the EEC. The FO attitude is well, if quaintly, expressed by a remark of Lord Greenhill in this period, when he was official head of the FO, quoted by Douglas Evans: 'We tried to equip ourselves in dealing with the economic as well as the political arguments.'[5] The Treasury's attitude to the EEC, William Armstrong's for instance, was far more realistic.

But the positive obsession of the FO with the EEC, which led it to brush aside the economic realities has to be accounted for. And here one main motive would seem to be that characteristic bureaucratic urge: departmental empire-building. The FO chiefs would have replied if asked, that since a great new political power was being built up on the Continent, we had better join it. What they largely meant, consciously or not, was that the FO itself could gain a huge accession of influence – not to mention jobs, incomes, hospitality, etc. – if both political decisions and legislative power were transferred from the British Cabinet and Parliament to a bureaucracy in Brussels in which the FO would be heavily represented. The whole process of development in this country since the 1832 Reform Bill of transferring power from the executive to the electorate could then be conveniently reversed. This sudden prospect of greatly enhanced departmental influence helps to explain, I believe, the almost unanimous conversion of the FO in the mid-1960s, and the emotional intensity with which it pursued the aim of membership at any cost. The issue of parliamentary sovereignty and the rights of the electorate seems to have meant almost nothing to the FO at all.

Why, however, it may be asked, did this obsession begin to show itself so abruptly in the course of a few months in 1966. Up to that time under Harold Caccia as official head, the FO had remained reasonably level-headed, and scrupulous in its methods, believing broadly in the Atlantic

[5] Evans, p. 98.

Alliance, close co-operation with the US and friendly relations with both the Commonwealth and Western Europe. Caccia spoke in the most scathing terms in 1964 about the French wrecking of the 'unilateral acceleration' plans which would have solved our difficulty over the surcharge. The timing of the FO conversion must probably be attributed to personal accidents and in the main the return of Con O'Neill to the office in 1965 from a period as Ambassador to the EEC in Brussels. I had known O'Neill as a colleague at All Souls in the late thirties. He possessed all the capacities of the O'Neill family, but he was always stronger on emotional commitment (as his courageous resignation over Munich showed) than economic understanding. His sojourn before 1965 in Brussels may well have influenced his views. (It is notable that another great FO Euro-enthusiast, Michael Palliser, later Private Secretary to Wilson, was married to the daughter of Spaak himself.) At any rate early in 1966 O'Neill wrote the first documents which concentrated the FO's pro-Market impulses into a campaign, and seems very quickly to have converted Michael Stewart, then Foreign Secretary. Not long afterwards a 'European Integration Department' was set up in the FO, years before Parliament or any Cabinet had approved membership of the EEC. These moves would seem to have been more responsible than any other single cause for transforming the FO from a *bona fide* government department into a would-be government of its own, fighting for its own policies, and dispensing political propaganda throughout Whitehall and outside.

Yet another all-too genuine reason for the success of pro-Market propaganda was ignorance. Throughout the long debate I constantly noticed, particularly among the younger generation, a surprising ignorance of the hard facts of British trade. To give only one example: numerous people did not know that this country in free trade conditions imports its food mainly from countries with a higher living standard than ourselves: i.e., the US, Canada, Australia and New Zealand. I often met the argument, that raising our import prices for food would help producers in poor countries. But in fact of the few major foods bought from poor countries – tea, coffee and sugar – tea and coffee were not affected by joining the EEC, and the sugar-producing countries were if anything damaged.

These were, from my observation, the main motives which generated the change of front by the establishment in the 1960s. Some of them, however, such as loss of Empire, or a wish for a new economic policy, may explain a desire for change, but not for this particular change. Nor do they explain the source of the immense sums of money which were used to brainwash the misinformed general public. Where did the money come from? The first answer is: a great deal from abroad. Much of it was spent by the EEC Commission itself. The expenditure on propaganda, disguised or otherwise, of the European Communities Information Services (ECIS) was about £1 million a year in 1964, and had risen to over £3 million by the time of the debate on British entry in 1971 and to £7 million by 1975, the year of the Referendum. According to Mr Douglas Evans,[6] about one third of this was spent in the UK; so that sums of the order of £1 million to £2 million a year were being spent in this country on political propaganda from overseas in these years. Never before had such sums been spent here systematically on political propaganda over a long period; still less sums of public money, raised and organized from overseas. In any earlier period it would have been denounced as grossly improper that large scale political propaganda in the UK should be financed by public authorities overseas. These sums were spent not merely on innumerable pamphlets, leaflets, newsheets and media hand-outs, but lavishly on hospitality, visits, tours, and free holidays to British politicians, journalists, officials, industrialists, trade unionists, and anyone regarded in Brussels as an 'opinion-former'. High-ranking British journalists were among those subjected to this form of persuasion. In 1965 a very distinguished and level-headed EFTA Trade Minister, who afterwards was Head of State in his own country, told me that in addition to all this, the ECIS were paying secret 'retaining fees' to selected individuals in the EEC and other countries (including the UK) in politics, journalism and business. Challenged to produce evidence of this, he said I would never be able to prove or disprove it. He was a most reliable authority, and subsequent experience never convinced me he was wrong.

Supporting the ECIS was that strange hybrid body, the 'European Movement' – which deserved the name of 'The Establishment' if anything ever did – not a government, but always liberally supplied with funds; not a charity, but able to harbour charities in the same office building; not a political party, but at once dispensing often vitriolic political propaganda, and flaunting the names of all the parliamentary leaders on its notepaper. Starting in the 1950s with a group of visionaries, it recruited in the 1960s many of the key City figures of the day and gathered subscriptions from leading British banks and industrial companies. The attraction to the City of free capital movements overseas was naturally very great. A major portion of the almost limitless finance available was also no doubt derived from Continental business sources and the major multi-nationals. In seven months of 1971 £40,000 was spent by the European Movement on press advertisements alone.[7] Some £20,000 was raised at one dinner by 'Britain in Europe', one of the Movement's para-military allies. Before its most lucrative dinner at the Guildhall in 1969[8] (attended by the Leader of the Opposition and the Prime Minister), at which over £300,000 was raised, some of us in Parliament learnt that the Archbishop of Canterbury had been led into giving his blessing to this operation. Together with Robin

[6] Evans, pp. 101–2.
[7] Evans, p. 108. Mr Evans gives many further details of such expenditure.
[8] 28 July 1969.

Turton and Neil Marten, I called on the Archbishop to explain that this was not a charity occasion but political propaganda, much resented by large sections of the British public, including many within the fold of the Church of England. He had plainly been misled. As time went on, the FO and government machine, particularly under the Heath Government became more than ever mixed up with the European Movement. At the 'media breakfasts' at the Connaught Hotel in 1971, organized by the pro-Marketeers, it was hard to know whether the European Movement, the Foreign Office, the EEC Commission in Kensington Palace Gardens, or the Conservative Party were speaking.[9,10] At an earlier date, in the 1971 pro-Market campaign, Uwe Kitzinger states[11] 'In collaboration with the European Movement, the liaison with some leading figures in the media became in the end a very close two-way process. All in all it was probably one of the most massive and most expensive domestic government campaigns since the war.' Such was the hydra-headed publicity monster which faced those of us who set out in 1967 to ensure that British interests were defended.

Whence, however, came the central drive which energized and conducted this pro-Market publicity chorus? One major source was naturally the Brussels Commission itself, which claimed both the privilege of an international civil service, and the power to raise taxes, and the right to indulge in political propaganda. The adherence of Britain would greatly increase the revenues, the number of jobs and the scope and prestige of the Commission generally. Therefore they were in favour of it, and the use of EEC influence and political propaganda in Britain seemed perfectly natural to the continental mind. But another equally powerful force, much less appreciated, was the persistent hostility of French Governments to this country in the post-war years. Antagonism towards the 'Anglo-Saxons' remained one of the deepest, perhaps *the* deepest, element in de Gaulle's own political philosophy. It stemmed most probably from de Gaulle's own natural resentment of Roosevelt's fatal war-time flirtation with Pétain, which was largely foisted on him, and his Secretary of State Sumner Wells, by their Irish-American adviser, Robert Murphy, and by Admiral Leahy.[12] A major aim of French policy under Gaullist Governments – though the French Government and newspapers were usually too polite to mention this – was not merely to aggrandize France, but to weaken the 'Anglo-Saxons'. In dealings with the French in both the Atlee and Wilson Governments, I was often made reluctantly conscious of this.[13] Later examples

[9] Evans, pp. 110–11.
[10] Kitzinger, pp. 202–5
[11] Kitzinger, p. 157.
[12] As is very vividly recorded by Oliver Harvey, wartime secretary to Anthony Eden in his Diaries *The War Diaries of Oliver Harvey 1941–45*, ed. J. Harvey (London, 1968).)
[13] As for instance in the cases already recorded of the diplomatic manoeuvres over the Schumann Plan in 1950 and the EFTA 'Unilateral Acceleration' in 1964. See pp. 198–200 and 308–9.

were the cystallization of the CAP and the rushing through of the Common Fisheries Policy before British entry to the EEC. The Common Fisheries Policy harmed Britain even more than it benefited France.

Surely, however, it will be said, the French objective, as shown by the two de Gaulle vetoes, was to keep Britain out of the Market, not to drag her in? The question is natural, but reveals the extent of misunderstanding in this country of the French mind. There were always two schools of thought in France. One was to keep Britain out, and build a great new Federal State dominated by France; and de Gaulle at first came down on this side. The other more subtle, which Pompidou gradually accepted, was to undermine British influence by allowing her in on terms involving the abandonment of Commonwealth Preference and the Sterling Area (of which the French were jealous), the destruction of her industrial competitive power by the imposition on her of the Common Agricultural Policy and the major rise in labour costs which this would enforce. As Couve de Murville, a hard-line Gaullist, once said, British membership must mean either the end of the Commonwealth or the end of the Common Market. De Gaulle, who understood British interests far better than most leaders of British opinion by the 1960s, believed that this country would never accept uicidal terms.

In this spirit de Gaulle in February 1969 made a new and wonderfully far-sighted offer to Britain, whose rejection by a muddled Government was as catastrophic a blunder as Chamberlain's rejection of Roosevelt's offer in 1938. The parallel is tragically striking, and in neither case did the British public understand what was happening. Christopher Soames, our new Ambassador in Paris, lunched with de Gaulle on 4 February 1969, and later, in a telegram whose accuracy he had first confirmed with the French Foreign Office, reported to the FO what the General had said. Harold Wilson[14] summarizes de Gaulle's reported statements as follows: The General 'personally foresaw it [the Common Market] changing and would like to see it change, into a looser form of free trade area with arrangements by each country to exchange agricultural produce. He would be quite prepared to discuss with us what should take the place of the Common Market as an enlarged European Economic Association. He went on to suggest bilateral talks with Britain initially in conditions of great secrecy, on a wide range of economic, monetary, political and defence matters to see whether we could resolve our differences. He would like to see a gesture by the British Government proposing that such talks should take place, which he would then welcome.' Couve de Murville, who as PM was present at the lunch, gives an essentially similar account:[15] 'For de Gaulle, if Britain with her followers entered the Community, the latter would be radically transformed and become a free trade area with arrangements for

[14] H. Wilson, *The Labour Government 1964-70*, p. 610.
[15] Quoted by Kitzinger, p. 46.

trade in farm products. That might not nevertheless be such a bad thing. The two Governments could talk about it but on condition that they also discussed the resulting political association, in which the four principal partners, France, Britain, Germany and Italy would necessarily play a key role.'

This was an epoch-making offer from de Gaulle. True it was only made verbally; and it was not precisely defined. But in essence it offered this country a golden, almost unique, opportunity to secure almost all that our long-term political and economic interests required: an industrial free trade area in Western Europe, without any artificial raising of the cost of food or restrictions on Commonwealth trade; continued mutually close relations with the EFTA as well as EEC countries; and no loss of basic parliamentary sovereignty or unwarranted interference by the Brussels authorities in British legislative and internal affairs. It would also have removed most of the regrettable tensions and disputes between this country and France which spring from the attempt to force an identical agricultural policy on both of us. It might not have been possible to achieve all this in negotiation. But any sensible government would have followed up this offer as ardently and enthusiastically as Chamberlain should have followed that of Roosevelt in 1938. It may of course be said that de Gaulle did not really mean it, but was only thinking about it. But he had also at other times, for instance at the Elysée in January 1967, talked of 'alternatives', 'something entirely new', or 'an agreement – an association'.[16] The evidence suggests to me that de Gaulle in these moments was rising above the normal petty Gaullist hostility to the 'Anglo-Saxons' and was genuinely seeking solutions which would have reversed the causes of Anglo-French tension and benefited Western Europe as a whole.

Did the British Government, however, seize this priceless opportunity? The answer is that they either bungled or wrecked it. As in 1938, it was never explicitly brought to the Cabinet in the early stages. Wilson's reaction, as he describes it, was not unfriendly to the offer. But the FO immediately discovered all sorts of snags. The idea of a 'directorate' of Britain, France, Germany and Italy (though this was not the heart of the offer), would annoy the other EEC members. We must inform the Germans and others in order to avoid being accused of a secret deal with the French. Michael Stewart, according to Kitzinger,[17] took a sadly doctrinaire view. He was now 'a convinced supporter of British entry into the EEC, and was not prepared to look at any substitute'. So in the FO, the policy which British interests demanded, was regarded as a 'substitute' for joining the EEC! Wilson, when he heard of all this on 11 February, 'had to leave within minutes' for Bonn, and was doubtful whether to recount the story to the German Chancellor, Kiesinger, or not. Telegrams from the FO

[16] Wilson, p. 610.
[17] Kitzinger, p. 50.

pursued him at Bonn and induced him, seemingly against his better judgement, to tell Kiesinger the facts 'in a few simple sentences'.[18] On return to London Wilson found that the FO had sent a full account of the de Gaulle statement to a number of Embassies, for which they had no authority from the PM or Cabinet. The French then discovered this, and regarded the FO version of de Gaulle's suggestion as distorted in such a way as to stir up prejudice against France. Both de Gaulle and the luckless Soames felt their confidence had been exploited by the British Government; and when the FO published its own version (without the authority of the Cabinet, and only grudging consent from the PM)[19] a violent anti-British campaign broke out in the French press. The crucial offer to Britain was never made again, and all the British public – and it seems from Crossman's diaries some of the Cabinet – knew of the whole story was that something had occurred which was called the 'Soames Affair'.

Even Wilson fairly clearly blames the FO during this episode, if not of actually misleading him, then of gross bungling. He said he was 'furious' at the note sent to him in Bonn. Certainly muddle and misunderstanding were all too real. But at a moment such as this the FO should have strained every nerve to avoid muddle, and should have whole-heartedly welcomed and pursued this precious initiative in order at least to see if it was genuine. Instead of which the PM was pushed into fatal errors, and the facts were largely concealed from the Cabinet until the publication of the document by the FO had irrevocably destroyed the chance of constructive talks with de Gaulle. It is hard to resist the conclusion that the FO, having decided to push for EEC entry for the motives set out earlier in this chapter, was determined, regardless of the PM or Cabinet, to wreck any alternative policy as being a 'substitute'. If so, the FO did an incalculable disservice to this country. Seen dispassionately in restrospect, the wrecking of this offer without even further discussion was a more calamitous error, because it may well prove irrevocable, than Munich or Suez. From Munich we eventually recovered, at vast cost; and Suez arguably only hastened the inevitable. But the blunder of February 1969 probably extinguished our best hope for the future.

The parallel[20] between the mistakes of Chamberlain in 1938 and the FO in 1969 was only one of the grisly resemblances, for those of us who lived through both, between the controversy over appeasement and that over the Common Market. In both cases one encountered a stifling orthodoxy; mysterious unanimity in the press (worse in the later case); a closing of the ranks by the City, the publicity industry and the Conservative Party; a stampede of trimmers and wobblers onto the side of intellectual fashion;

[18] Wilson, p. 611.
[19] If Richard Crossman, *The Diaries of a Cabinet Minister*, vol. 3, entry for 13 February 1969 is to be accepted.
[20] See pp. 73–4 for the comparison.

and a strong distaste by the big battalions for rational argument. The great difficulty of getting the minority view expressed in the press, TV or radio in 1962–75 was grimly reminiscent of 1938–9. The particular line-up was also quaintly similar. On the Conservative side, the massive majority who on balance in 1938 were more influenced by their dislike of an alliance with the Soviet Union than loyalty to Britain; and in the 1960s and 1970s were more eager to undermine a progressive tax system and 'discipline the trade unions', than to preserve the political and economic liberties and independence of this country. But also on the Conservative side, a genuine patriotic, if small, minority who in the 1930s fought Munich, and in the 1960s and 1970s a similarly small and genuinely patriotic minority who took a wider view of their national loyalties. So on the Labour side, a dwindling minority of starry-eyed internationalists who in the 1930s believed Hitler could be stopped by voting against the Defence Estimates; and in the 1960s and 1970s as sincerely believed that the EEC was an exercise in Socialist brotherhood. And a growing majority in each period in the Labour Movement who grasped the hard realities. The most marked difference was the huge injection in the later chapter of financial resources from abroad into the internal British propaganda debate. Ribbentrop's efforts were puny by comparison.

Soon after the rejection of the de Gaulle offer in 1969, the General himself was succeeded by Pompidou, who by now evidently believed that the British could be induced to accept surrender terms. If they were really willing to buy large quantities of surplus French farm products at high prices, and accept the whole Rome Treaty constitution, why should France resist? So he was very ready to see the Brussels ECIS machine used to undermine British negotiating power by strengthening inside this country the forces which were willing to accept a settlement on *any* terms. It was a great help to the French Government to know that whatever terms might be demanded, a loud propaganda voice would be raised in Britain itself to demand that these should be accepted. One particular theme in the Fifth Column propaganda barrage must be mentioned here. The public were constantly told, even in the early stages of the controversy before 1970, that the UK real standard of living had fallen below that of various Continental neighbours. This was misleading as a statement of fact, quite apart from the false implication that if we adopted their policy of agricultural protection our real incomes would rise. The propaganda trick consisted in repeating figures of money incomes and implying – and often actually stating – that these represented 'standards of living'. The price levels of the different countries, and purchasing power of the currencies, were virtually never brought into the comparison at all. Figures for instance of comparative pensions and other social payments in money terms were quoted without any mention of the fact that food prices on the Continent were twice as high. Yet it is a simple platitude that if countries A and B have the same real income per head, and prices (at the prevailing exchange rates) are twice as high in B as in A, then money incomes in B will have to be twice as high as the level of A. If you then quote the figures of money incomes, and treat them as real incomes, you will have 'proved' that country B's real incomes are twice as high as A's, when your calculation started by assuming they were the same! Throughout much of the pro-Market propaganda of the sixties and seventies, this simple deception was practised.

In fact during the years before entry to the EEC, British food prices were in many cases not more than half those in the Continental EEC, and living costs generally were very substantially lower. Figures of real consumption of all sorts of products – from butter and meat to telephones and TV sets – showed that real incomes were not far different from those of say, Belgium, Holland and France. In these years the only thorough-going research into comparative living standards by a reputable international authority was made by the UN and published in 1975 under the forbidding title of 'A System of International Comparisons of Gross Product and Purchasing Power by the Statistical Office of the UN, the World Bank, and the industrial Comparison Units of the University of Pennsylvania'. It was summarized in the *Financial Times* on 2 December 1975, but otherwise almost completely ignored by the British press. It showed that, when purchasing power was taken into account, real consumption per head in the UK, before entry into the EEC, was not far different from that of Belgium, Holland and France; or even of West Germany, and substantially above Italy. The actual figures of real consumption per head in 1970, shown as a percentage of US real consumption were as follows:

US	France	W. Germany	Holland	Italy	UK
100	67·9	61·2	62·9	46·0	62·2

This comparative level of actual consumption was admittedly partly due to the UK consuming (together with the US) a larger percentage of our real Gross Domestic Product than France or Germany. But our high living standard was also substantially due to our much lower prices, particularly of food. In 1978 the same UN authority re-calculated the figures for 1973, the first year of EEC membership. These showed real consumption per head, as a percentage of US real consumption, as follows:

US	France	W. Germany	Holland	Italy	UK
100	67·9	63·9	60·3	47·4	62·2

The statistical fallacy of misrepresenting money incomes as real incomes was virtually never exposed – apart from *Financial Times* articles on 2 December 1975 and 13 March 1979 – by the British press in these years.

It was bolstered up in the public consciousness by another muddle. This was the confusion between a different rate of growth in real incomes among several countries over the same years, and a different level of real incomes in the same year. It was true that real incomes in the UK *rose less fast* in the 1960s than those in certain Continental countries (though in the EEC they rose less fast after the Rome Treaty was signed than before). But it does not follow from this, and was not true, that in the late 1960s before our entry into the EEC, our *real living standards were lower* than those countries. The question why the Continental countries, both in EFTA and the EEC showed greater real growth in the 1960s than the UK is another issue; and was probably due in part to a slow-down in the UK's growth after we abandoned our quotas on manufactured imports in 1958–9. But the simple fact remained that if we gratuitously sacrificed our main advantage – low-priced imports of staple food – our real income in the future would be less than if we did not.

Continuous propaganda, however, based on this statistical falsehood, markedly undermined this country's self-confidence and bargaining strength. We were 'poorer' than these countries, therefore we 'could not afford' to stay 'isolated'. As soon as Pompidou had grasped that the British might actually capitulate to the substance of the CAP, it naturally served his purpose very well that this propaganda should be widely disseminated in Britain and financed if necessary by the ECIS itself. France's surplus of farm products, caused by excessively high prices, which higher direct taxpayers in France were not willing to finance themselves out of tax revenue, had to be sold somehow; and if the UK were outside the EEC, this would have to be sold to the UK and others at knock-down, subsidized world prices. But if the UK came in, and accepted the CAP, then it could be unloaded on us (as has largely happened) at twice to three times world prices. It was therefore wholly in the French national interest, and indeed of that of Continental agriculture generally, that British resistance to acceptance of the CAP should be weakened by internal propaganda alleging that we must accept any terms. It very soon became clear that the pro-Market organizations in this country would call for immediate acceptance, whatever terms were proposed. If this country had declined to join until the CAP had been fundamentally relaxed, or until we had been exempted from it, then the EEC might in time have been induced – as indeed de Gaulle offered – to accept this. The cost of subsidized exports would at some point have been too high for the Six to bear. But the existence of a propaganda machine within the UK, which advocated both haste, and acceptance of any terms, made serious negotiations in the genuine interest of the British people increasingly impossible.

Such were the formidable propaganda and financial forces facing those of us who, after the rejection of the de Gaulle 1969 offer, wished to resist any settlement with the Common Market which would weaken this country's future economic strength. But this seemed to me no more reason for giving up than in 1938 and 1939. Throughout 1968 and 1969, with the de Gaulle veto in force, it was my aim, having formed with others the Labour Committee for Safeguards on the Common Market,[21] to work within the Labour Movement to ensure a firm British attitude if negotiation should be resumed at any time. Even though George Brown had disappeared in March 1968 from the FO, and Con O'Neill had ironically resigned a few days earlier after a quarrel with Brown, the French interest in our joining on French terms seemed to me too clear to assume that the danger had passed. By early 1968 several organizations had already been founded to back the general idea of a more outward-looking trade policy for this country based on a much wider spread of countries than the Common Market.

Early in that year a number of us from all parties formed a regular but informal parliamentary group, whose aim was to study and propagate these ideas as an alternative to joining the EEC, and in particular to watch opportunities in Parliament for arguing for more liberal policies. This became known as the Study Group, or at times the North Atlantic Free Trade Area (NAFTA) group. Robin Turton, a Conservative ex-minister, and later Father of the House, was the first Chairman: and Neil Marten, Derek Walker-Smith and Hugh Fraser from the Conservative side, and Alf Morris and myself from the Labour side, were early members. The Study Group, though always small, developed remarkable stability and longevity, throughout the various long twists and turns of the controversy. It consisted entirely of back-benchers; so that Labour members of the Government could not join. Its personnel varied, but it continued to meet almost weekly during parliamentary sessions throughout the 1970s. From the start in 1968 it also organized talks in the House on an all-Party basis by non-political speakers, including economists, industrialists, ex-civil servants and others. Outside Parliament a non-Party organization, the Atlantic Trade Study, pioneered by Sir Michael Wright, a previous Ambassador to Norway, and supported by economists as well-known as Roy Harrod, James Meade and Harry Johnson of the LSE, had already published a pamphlet: *The Free Trade Area Option* whose conclusions were similar to those of my Penguin: *After the Common Market*. The central aim of those who formed these groups, in Parliament and outside, was not any rigid scheme, but a widening industrial free-trade area, without extreme agricultural protection, based initially on the UK, EFTA, and some Commonwealth countries, but open for any nation to join which wished. As this wide association was conceived, there would have been nothing to prevent either the US or the EEC in time joining if and when they wished; and the latter would indeed have been the neatest solution of all.

These ideas attracted much interest. As early as February 1968 I was

[21] See page 415.

asked to attend an Anglo–American–Canadian Conference in New York University by the Centre for International Studies at that University. This conference was sponsored by Senator Javitts and Nelson Rockefeller; and Frank Cousins, Roy Harrod, Harry Johnson, Hugh Fraser and Alfred Morris came from London as well as myself. The idea was here evolved, and had much support from academic opinion and some US industrialists, of a possible Anglo–American–Canadian free trade area; and from this the name NAFTA gained currency. Few regarded it as immediately practical politics, but with more political will it might have progressed further. Also in February 1968, as I had been asked to give a lecture in Brussels University I explained why so many British people found it hard for this country to join the existing EEC. Both M. Spaak and M. Jean Rey, President of the Commission (with whom I had negotiated most happily in the Kennedy Round) were present. M. Spaak said I did not understand the 'Community spirit'. But as he had just had a stand-up row on the platform with M. Capitant, a French Gaullist, I could not help replying that M. Capitant did not seem to understand it either. In May I debated at the Fontainbleau 'European Institute of Business Studies' with M. Lecanuet, a centre French politician and ex-Presidential candidate, a motion advocating the immediate 'unification of Europe'. M. Lecanuet was a most affable character with a Kennedy smile, but so small that he spoke sitting down to disguise his shortness. On my way home via Paris, it emerged that the air-traffic controllers were on strike as part of the wave of strikes which had followed the battle between police and students in the Paris streets. Our BEA Trident crept home at only 1000 ft over France without the help of the air-traffic-controllers, and the unification of Europe was brought no nearer.

Most ambitious venture, however, for publicizing the free-trade-area case, was that organized by Sir Maxwell Stamp, then working in the City, and the Atlantic Trade Study at Church House Westminster on 1 July and 2 July. Edward du Cann, Eric Wyndham White, the General Secretary of GATT, Fred Catherwood, Professor Ted English of Toronto University and Congressman Long of Maryland were among the speakers. I noticed Richard Powell of the Board of Trade, Roger Makins, and Con O'Neill in the audience. At a dinner afterwards a letter to *The Times* setting out these ideas was composed and signed by most of the speakers, British, American and Canadian, and published on 5 July. After one of a series of dinners that month given by Sir Michael Wright, Jim Callaghan advised the Atlantic Trade Study to be more active, since he favoured anything which discouraged US isolation. In October the ATS itself held a two-day conference in London elaborating the wider free-trade-area idea and inviting comments. This time Harold Watkinson, Tory ex-Minister and now in the City, Reggie Maudling, John Winnifrith, till recently Permanent Secretary of the Ministry of Agriculture, Peter Runge of the CBI, Harry

Johnson, Paul Streeten, economist from Sussex University, and Sir Alexander Glen, all contributed.

Watkinson spoke most effectively, showing his scepticism about the 'EEC only' attitude; but far the best speech came from John Winnifrith. He gave a straightforward and convincing account of British food and agricultural policies since the repeal of the Corn Laws, contrasted with the agricultural protectionism of the Continent, and drew unanswerable conclusions. Intellectually this was the best speech I had heard in the whole controversy since Gaitskell's in 1962. Reggie Maudling delivered at lunch some agreeable fence-sitting comments. Harold Caccia, former Permament Secretary at the FO acted as Chairman during this ATS Conference. Caccia was no Euro-fanatic, but shied away from expressing firm opinions either way. It was one of the oddities of the whole controversy – just like 1938 again – that if you were pro-Market, you said so dogmatically, but if you weren't, you maintained a diplomatic silence.

During the autumn of 1968, I also met privately some of my ex-colleagues in the Wilson Government and learnt something of their troubles. At a private lunch with Fred Peart early in November I enquired, now that we outside were promoting so much debate on alternatives to the Market, whether someone like himself in the Cabinet might not do a little more to resist the FO's obsessions. Peart's heart was in the right place; but the impression was plain that, once Wilson had capitulated, he had no stomach for the fight. Michael Stewart he regarded sadly as 100 per cent brainwashed by the FO and Healey as weakened by his failure to preserve British influence East of Suez. On the previous re-shuffle of the Government in August 1967, Peart thought Wilson had picked on me because I had not sat on the bench during Wilson's May speech in the House. At dinner with Jim Callaghan a few days earlier at my house, I asked whether he ought not to become Deputy Leader of the Labour Party, now that George Brown had noisily left the Government. I found Callaghan, as ever, as I recorded at the time, 'charming but elusive'. But he was unreceptive to the idea of standing as Deputy Leader, or of any great exertion to wean the Government away from Euromania – though he didn't share it. I still, as I had in 1963, believed that Callaghan was the best hope for the future of the Labour Party. But someone had called him a 'non-issue-motivated' man. To me the cause was everything. To him, I felt, the men and women were the realities, and the issues by comparison were the transient and embarrassed phantoms.

My third heart-to-heart talk in the autumn of 1968 was with Ray Gunter, Minister of Labour throughout my three years at the Board of Trade. He had now left the Government in protest at his treatment by the PM. He accused Wilson of having stimulated back-bench Labour MPs to sign a motion in the previous December opposing a Cabinet decision over arms sales to South Africa. The breaking point with Gunter had come over his transfer from the Ministry of Labour to the Ministry of Power. Wilson had first wanted to move Barbara Castle to the DEA, but Jenkins objected; so he hit on the Ministry of Labour instead. But he refused to tell Gunter who would succeed him at the Ministry of Labour; and Gunter had only read in the press later that it was Barbara Castle. In the early months of 1969 the Government was too embroiled with its internal struggles over Barbara Castle's 'In Place of Strife' proposals for trade union reform to make any move towards either the EEC or NAFTA policies. In meetings of the Parliamentary Labour Party I spoke against 'In Place of Strife', on the ground that, whether or not reforms might succeed, it was folly for a Labour Government to pick a fierce public quarrel with both the trade unions and the Parliamentary Labour Party. This view, strongly backed by Douglas Houghton, of course prevailed. Callaghan in a lunch with me on 8 May 1969 was in a bellicose anti-Wilson mood, and used strong language about the methods by which Wilson had sought to push 'In Place of Strife' through the Cabinet. Jenkins and Barbara Castle were apparently, apart from Wilson, its only strong supporters.

It was shortly before this, however, at the end of April 1969, that de Gaulle so perversely and unnecessarily resigned, and the prospect of another British application for membership reappeared on the horizon, and with it the need to fight this uphill battle for the third time. So we anti-Marketeers redoubled our propaganda effort in the summer of 1969, concentrating on the dangers to the UK if we accepted the CAP, whose madness was now becoming even plainer, thanks partly to most illuminating articles by Mark Arnold-Forster in the *Guardian*.[22] Robin Turton, Neil Marten and others in our group decided at this stage to put down a motion opposing any hurried new application to join the Market, and to try to get this argued on 25 July in the annual debate on the summer adjournment. Many signatures were added to this motion within a few days, and Turton, Marten and I all took part in the debate. Whether due to this or to a *Sunday Express* article in early August explaining the likely effect of Market membership on British food prices. I received a large volume of letters in these weeks from the public opposing membership. Neil Marten wrote to me at the same time suggesting that we formed a national all-Party, anti-Market organization outside Parliament as well as within. Opinion polls were moving against entry. In early September Enoch Powell made a long speech virtually retracting his earlier pro-Market attitude and supporting the anti-Market case. I was delighted to have his powerful advocacy on our side, but as it was now just eight years since I embarked on the campaign, I did wonder why he had not thought of it before.

In September also, on return from holiday in the West Country, I learnt from Norman Willis, Jack Jones's extremely able personal assistant at the

[22] e.g. on 4 July 1969.

TGWU, that Jack Jones meant to support at the Labour Party Conference that month a motion very much on the lines of what we in the Labour Safeguards Committee had drafted insisting in effect on Gaitskell's conditions for EEC entry. This was a long step forward, and the start of a long alliance with Jack Jones, who proved as staunch, reliable and highly intelligent a political associate throughout the next six years as one would wish. On Sunday 28 September, our Labour Safeguards Committee held a pre-Conference anti-Market meeting in the Brighton Pavilion, addressed by Michael Foot and Shinwell, before an audience of 300 to 400, at which we urged support for Jack Jones's motion. At the Conference the National Executive accepted his motion but also a statement of its own. But we had certainly come a long way since 1967 towards our goal of committing the Party to the Gaitskell safeguards. Like most Labour Party Conferences, Brighton 1969 had its interludes of light relief. After the EEC debate, I was due to join George Brown (still Deputy Leader of the Party), in a TV discussion in a room in the Conference Hall. Turning up on time, I was told that George Brown was still in a nearby hotel but refusing to move. Just as zero hour arrived, he was escorted into the studio by a retinue of aides, but protested he would not bandy statistics with me at any price. So I was offered seven minutes by myself, and expounded the relevant facts and figures without interruption.

In October 1969 at a Commonwealth Parliamentary Association Conference in Trinidad, and later in Washington, I discussed alternative ideas for wider Commonwealth and Atlantic free trade. At the CPA Conference in Port of Spain, the British delegation were bombarded with demands from Africans to declare war on Mr Smith's Rhodesia regime, and what with that, and the heat, we tended in the tropical evenings to repair to the hotel swimming pool among resting air hostesses, the most decorative of whom told me that she lived, not as we had vaguely surmised in Honolulu or some South Pacific coral island, but in the Fulham Road. In Washington, I stayed with my son Peter, now *Times* correspondent there, and with his help met Carl Gilbert, the US Federal Trade Representative, Nat Samuels, the Under Secretary for Economic Affairs, and Congressmen Henry Reuss and Clarence Long. The Americans were sympathetic as ever to British ideas, but evidently few of them had yet grasped the threat of the EEC to US farm exports or the economic consequences of membership to the UK.

Back in London at the end of October, the General Management Committee of my own Battersea Labour Party staged without much notice – as GMCs do – a debate on Common Market membership. I did not join in, following my settled policy of non-interference. They voted against membership by sixteen to nine, and this spontaneous decision stood unchanged throughout the remaining years of the controversy. In the later months of 1969, with de Gaulle replaced by Pompidou, the European Movement resumed its propaganda drive for UK membership; and the feeling grew in the Labour Party as well as among anti-Marketeers generally that some united, all-Party organization was sorely needed to counter the European Movement. Up till then Labour MPs of the purest orthodoxy like Michael Foot and Manny Shinwell, who were also strongly anti-Market, believed that pressure must be exerted wholly through the Labour Movement. By late 1969, confronted by the massive if mysterious financial resources of the pro-Marketeers, and their all-Party front, even these purists became convinced that an all-Party counterweight was needed quickly.This was the crucial signal to me and my fellow activists in the Labour Committee.

As early as November, I started talks with Neil Marten from the Conservatives in Parliament, and Sir Robin Williams, director of the Anti-Common Market League (ACML) and personally a member of Lloyds and also a Conservative. These two became close colleagues of mine for ten years thereafter. Neil Marten was an excellent parliamentarian, always good-humoured, active, well-informed, courageous, and straightforward in dealings with all comers; and Robin Williams an efficient organizer, and a skilled writer of pamphlets and leaflets. The ACML was in 1969 the longest serving anti-Market organization, having been born in September 1961. Lord Hinchinbrooke, and Robin Williams were also prominent members right through till 1969. On the Labour side Richard Briginshaw (later Lord Briginshaw) of NATSOPA[23] had set up in 1961-2 the Forward Britain Movement, which had published pamphlets of mine. Finally a rather more shadowy organization, called 'Keep Britain Out' (KBO), had been founded in the 1960s by S. W. Alexander, a traditional free-trader and strong believer in free food imports, who had earlier been secretary to Beaverbrook and a rival City editor of mine (in the *Evening Standard*) in the far-off 1930s. He was joined in KBO by Christopher Frere-Smith, a solicitor, and Sir Ian McTaggart, a property company director. It is no easy job to weld or coax a number of existing and competing voluntary bodies into one effective whole. I found it a good deal harder in this case than with the LMAG. Most of December 1969 and January 1970 were spent on these exertions, interspersed with more pleasurable preparations for my daughter Catherine's wedding in January. Early in December Callaghan told me at a lunch that Wilson was now lukewarm about EEC entry and that the only enthusiasts left were Jenkins and Stewart. Apparently after Callaghan, in a speech on the Debate on the Address in the autumn of 1969, had contrasted low living costs in the UK, with much higher costs on the Continent, Stewart had written him an angry letter. Here was the FO again indignantly objecting to the truth being told.

Thanks largely to Neil Marten and Robin Williams, the union of anti-Market groups was eventually clinched at a meeting on 12 January 1970 at the Wig and Pen in Fleet Street between Neil Marten and myself on one side and Robin Williams, Hinchinbrooke and Ian McTaggart of the ACML

[23] National Society of Printing Operatives.

and KBO. It was agreed that the previous organizations should remain formally in existence, but should operate if possible from one office, and should combine in one effective working Committee. The membership of the Committee of course interlocked with the Parliamentary Study Group and the purely party bodies. We gave the new organization the name Common Market Safeguards Campaign (CMSC), to show that it had positive and not just negative aims, and launched it at a press conference on 4 February 1970. At last we had one organization, an office in Park Lane, generously offered by McTaggart, and one whole-time organizer, Ron Leighton, who had been secretary of the Labour Safeguards Committee since 1967. The support for the CMSC was widespread, despite the pervasive pro-Market campaign. Arthur Bryant, the historian, became President, with Shinwell, Robin Turton and later Sir Ian Bowater, as Vice-Presidents, myself as Chairman and Neil Marten, Vice-Chairman.

To counter the efforts of the European Movement to insinuate that no anti-Marketeers were quite respectable, the CMSC steadily recruited a number of patrons from politics and outside, including seventy-five Members of Parliament. These came from different Parties – from Labour for instance: Eric Deakins, Michael Foot, Reg Freeson, John Gilbert, Richard Marsh, Jack Mendelson, Alfred Morris, Stanley Orme, Fred Peart, Reg Prentice, Peter Shore, John Silkin and David Stoddart: and from the Conservatives: Ronald Bell, Richard Body, Eric Bullus, John Farr, Michael Clark-Hutchison, John Jennings, Toby Jessel, Donald Kaberry, Stephen McAdden, Roger Moate, Harmar Nicholls, Ronald Russell, and Derek Walker-Smith. The industrialists included Sir John Hunter, Sir George Dowty, Sir George Bolton, previously of the Bank of England, and Lord Campbell; and the trade unionists Jack Jones, Richard Briginshaw, Laurence Daly, Albert Hazell of the farmworkers, Dan McGarvey and many others. For those from the professions and universities, room could be found only for a few on the Campaign's notepaper; but these soon included Lord Bowden of Chesterfield, Sir Roy Harrod, Sir Alan Herbert, Sir Fred Hoyle, Lord Kaldor, Lord Kahn, Peter Oppenheimer, William Pickles, Richard Titmuss, Sir John Winnifrith, Lord Francis Williams, and Lord Woolley, previously President of the National Farmers Union.

From February 1970 right through till the 1975 Referendum the organizing Committee of the CMSC met regularly and the most frequent attenders were Neil Marten, Robin Williams, Richard Kitzinger (the Treasurer), Ian McTaggart, Frere Smith, Leighton and myself. Of these Marten, Williams and Kitzinger best understood the need for political movements of this kind to hold together. It was probably a weakness of the Campaign that the constituent parts almost all remained formally in existence. There was some case for this: for instance, separate Labour and Conservative groups provided a haven for those who would in no circumstances work with individuals from other parties. But the total stength of the Campaign would have been greater if rather less rugged individualism and rather more political experience had prevailed. Immediately following the first press conference, however, subscriptions and donations were received from many thousands of individual supporters to supplement the few more substantial donations with which the Campaign started. We always relied on individual enthusiasts and not, like the European Movement, on wealthy corporations; and all the Campaign's activities were maintained over the next few years on a budget of between £10,000 and £20,000 a year.

The date of the initial press conference was well chosen. For only a few days later the Government published its own White Paper estimating the balance of payments cost of membership: and this was debated for two days in the House on 23 and 24 February. By chance also my paper to the Manchester Statistical Society already mentioned[24] was read on 11 February, estimating the curent balance of payments cost at over £1000 million a year. As the White Paper took refuge in a large margin between the possible minimum and maximum, but put the maximum at £1100 million, my estimates had to be treated seriously. We therefore took full advantage of the two-day debate in the House to ask what was the sense of gratuitously loading the country with this burden. Harold Wilson's own speech in this debate reminded me of Lloyd George's classic remark about John Simon: 'He has sat on the fence so long that the iron has entered into his soul'. At the end of March Peter Shore, still a junior member of this dying Government, surprised us all by a major speech pouring the coldest water on the whole idea of the EEC, and declaring that the electorate not the politicians must decide.

A few weeks later in April the Campaign held its first big public meeting at the Caxton Hall, Westminster, with Walker-Smith, Arthur Bryant, Reg Prentice and Michael Foot as the speakers. This was one of the best, most valuable and effective public meetings I have ever attended; but was of course scarcely reported in the press, except in the *Daily Express* – the one anti-Market voice at the time – and the *Financial Times*. Otherwise, a silent censorship, as in 1938–9, had set in. Another excellent meeting was held by the Campaign at this time at Newcastle, when Sir John Hunter, Chairman of Swan Hunter and Dan McGarvey, General Secretary of the Boilermakers Union – two pillars of Tyneside industry – spoke together on the same platform for almost the first time in their lives, in harmonious opposition to Market membership, supported by Will Blyton, ex-Durham miner, and Robin Turton who lived in a castle in North Yorkshire. John Hunter stood out from his fellow industrialists in having the courage to voice his convictions. But later, after the June general election, he told me that he was compelled to withdraw from the Campaign because he had

[24] See p. 356.

already been dropped by the Government from the Board of British Rail, and his own fellow directors felt that Swan Hunter itself might be deprived of government help if he continued to express his views. This was in itself an instructive example of the way the Heath Government sought to suppress any anti-Market views. On 3 June the Safeguard Campaign published an up-dated version of my earlier pamphlet now called *The Truth about the Common Market 1970*, summarizing the whole of our case; but by this time the general election of June 1970 was in full swing.

Till only a few weeks earlier, Labour's chances had seemed hopeless. But suddenly the opinion polls swung, and Wilson decided to take the plunge. And by a week before polling day, 18 June, virtually everyone believed Labour would win. Ted Heath had included in his Party manifesto the notorious phrase, in asking for a mandate on the Common Market, 'Our sole commitment is to negotiate; no more, and no less.' At the time this was universally taken to mean that before he actually signed a Treaty or proposed legislation on such an overriding constitutional issue, he would be morally bound to seek a new mandate from the electorate. It was in May 1970 also that Heath affirmed that we should never enter the Market without the 'full-hearted consent of Parliament and people'. On the evening of 15 June, perhaps due to excessive loud-speaker exertions in the street on top of so many other activities, I for once fell ill and had to rest at home all next day. On Wednesday, 17 June, the *Evening Standard* Opinion Poll predicted a Tory win by 1 per cent. Apparently something had changed. Throughout my life up to 1955 I had predicted all general election results, after much statistical thought, and got them all wrong. From then onwards, I made my guess after the poll closed, solely in the light of the feel of my constituency throughout the last day; and have since got them right. After 10 p.m. on 18 July 1970, I told Mary Thomas, who had canvassed with me throughout the day, that I doubted whether we had won; and next day we knew that Heath had a majority of forty-three over the Labour Party. So now we were landed with the most devout Euro-fanatic of the lot as PM. But against this he faced the Labour Party in Opposition, and more likely to be influenced by the anti-Market case now that its leaders would no longer be daily brainwashed by the FO.

By June 1970 I felt able to devote almost my whole time to straight politics, as I had parted company with Courtaulds only a few months before the election. From my three years with Courtaulds since 1967 I learnt a great deal. It was most refreshing to be taking some modest part in carrying through a major modernization programme in a big industry. In these years, as a part-time non-executive director, I spent two mornings a week at Courtaulds' head office in Hanover Square studying the company's affairs on paper, lunched with my fellow directors there several days a week, and visited a large number of new and old factories throughout the country.

Courtaulds' job in the 1960s was to create a British multi-fibre industry, stretching from cotton, wool and nylon to the whole range of synthetic fibres, working on a shift system, equipped with modern machinery, employing men as well as women, and building a fair share of its new plants in Development Areas sorely needing employment. It was a special joy to me to visit the new plants in the very areas which I had got scheduled as Development Areas in 1945 and again in 1965–6 and in many cases on the industrial estates I had launched: for instance in Swansea, Merthyr Tydfil, Workington, Carlisle, Merseyside, Carrickfergus (Northern Ireland), and Wrexham, as well as long-established plants elsewhere. The great new weaving plant at Skelmersdale between Liverpool and Wigan was one of the few failures, not mainly in my opinion due to faults of management. But though in these years the nature of the fibres produced was always changing, the world textile cycle lived on, with a sharp recession at least every three or four years; and while total profits of the group before tax rose in my first years in Hanover Square from around £30 million to £50 million, the shareholders could have complained – but seldom did – that the return on capital was pretty meagre for such massive capital expenditure.

Frank Kearton was by common consent the intellectual power house of the whole enterprise. The great merit of private enterprise is its ability to operate as a temporary, licensed, dictatorship; and provided this is temporary, and licensed by watchful colleagues, it offers immense benefits in quick decision. The Chairman and full-time executive directors of Courtaulds worked in the same corridor, usually with their doors open, and frequently lunched there together. Kearton's knowledge of the business – scientific, financial, organizational, and statistical – was remarkable, and his soliloquies thereon almost invariably fascinating. I found that though board meetings tended, like Cabinet meetings under Harold Wilson, towards being monologues by the Chairman, Kearton's monologues were normally both more illuminating and more entertaining than Wilson's. In these years Kearton was also of course Chairman of the Industrial Reorganization Corporation. Next in brain power came Arthur Knight, the financial director and later Chairman, a London School of Economics product, and a *laissez-faire* economist and accountant by nature, who left me in no doubt that the finances were handled with puritanical rectitude which would have delighted the conscience of the founder, Samuel Courtauld II. When Lord (R.A.B.) Butler, now almost the patron saint of the firm, attended and occasionally inquired where the money would come from for these vast plans, Knight assured him that it would be found. And it was. Deputy Chairman, however, and most long-serving member was Reg Mathys, whom I had met as a patent expert when I was at the Board of Trade. He was sometimes suspicious of all these modern ideas, and particularly disliked 'do-gooders', but was omniscient about the industry. I was not exactly exhilarated to hear in April 1968 that George Brown was to become a 'productivity counsellor' at Court-aulds; but he was not to be a director and providentially our paths did not cross.

There was no serious dispute on the Courtaulds board about the wisdom, indeed the national necessity, of the technical modernization of the industry. More disputable perhaps was the parallel process, beloved by Kearton. known as 'verticalization' by which wholesaling and distributive firms were absorbed into the group. Beyond a point, it could be criticized by austere economists as no more than the creation of a captive market to ensure the success of the great manufacturing plants. So many powerful forces, however, not least low-cost imports, threatened the British textile indus-try at this time, and the maintenance of employment and of Courtaulds large and growing exports were so crucial, that some measures of self-defence seemed to me justified. More doubtful was the acquisition of still further competing plants in the spinning, weaving and knitting industries. Unfortunately Courtaulds' relations with the Board of Trade were not at their best in this period, because the directors with some reason thought the Monopolies Commission Report (which I originally authorized) on Courtaulds was unfair; and Crosland, then at the Board of Trade, could not make up his mind what to do about this Report.

At the end of 1969 the much publicized Joe Hyman – once regarded as twin saviour of the industry with Kearton – suddenly disappeared from the board of Viyella after a boardroom row, whose details were unknown to us. The prospect of ICI taking over Viyella revived talk, both in public and private, of some sort of co-operation or deal between ICI and Courtaulds. It so happened that Kearton was on occasion seeing Michael Clapham, Deputy Chairman of ICI, to discuss carbon fibres at this period. A minority view surfaced within Courtaulds which for a time favoured some link-up with ICI. This even took a humorous form in lunch-time talk of a possible Courtaulds bid for ICI. Another plan slightly less in the realms of fantasy was for the formation of a joint Fibre Corporation to manufature the fibres previously produced by both firms. Courtaulds and ICI had jointly set up British Nylon Spinners in 1945 and built the full-scale factory at Pontypool, which I had promoted from the Board of Trade Development Area side, but which had been sold to ICI before 1967. In all these talks, humorous or otherwise, I was opposed to any plan for a deal, merger, take-over, exchange of shares or any other association with ICI which would mean in practice less competition between the two. I was never in any case a believer in the huge industrial mergers, which were fashionable in 1968 and 1969 with the creation of the Ministry of Technology. I had seven years earlier argued from the Opposition Front Bench in the House against the take-over of Courtaulds by ICI, and I would certainly have felt bound to resign if any merger plan were approved. This was the majority view in Courtaulds, and it prevailed.

In early 1970, however, a new idea took shape in Kearton's ever-fertile mind: the take-over of a major British pulp-producing and publishing combine, which could launch Courtaulds into almost wholly new territory. This evidently appealed to the Chairman's unflaggingly constructive and expansionist spirit; and nobody could have painted the new vision in more brilliant colours. But I was unconvinced, despite at least one long discussion which might be described as a monologue à deux, on the day before a decision had to be made. Meditating overnight, I realized Kearton would be deeply upset if the Board did not accept this new advance into unknown country, but that I could not honestly recommend it. The 'leisure and communications industry', as he called it, was not one in which Courtaulds had any expertise. The attempted bid would in any case probably fail, and make Courtaulds appear clumsy as well as grasping; and if it looked like succeeding, Parliament and press would ask what interest a textile group had, apart from pulp, in plunging into the political arena. David Eccles, I found, wholly shared these doubts. Next day the council of war took the form of a rousing oration from the commander-in-chief, and a series of short sharp 'yes' or 'no' votes with a time limit, from the subordinate officers.

The younger spirits cried 'Forward' almost without exception, even if with no great warmth. Almost the only open doubters were the more senior Mathys and Knight. I learnt some time afterwards that ministers had already been told of the plan, and were opposed to it. At the Board meeting, not knowing this, I still felt bound to say that I was not in favour. David Eccles described the plan as 'marrying a prostitute', which was taken not to be a vote in favour. Altogether the scene reminded me somewhat of Alexander the Great's confrontation with his own army at its point of furthest eastward penetration beyond the Indus. The King of Kings ordered yet one more advance to find new worlds to conquer; the higher commanders pleaded for restraint; and the troops simply refused to move. The outcome in Hanover Square was very similar: acceptance of the inevitable, and strategic retreat, announced even more abruptly than the call to battle.

Soon afterwards, however, Eccles and I were given to understand that – presumably in view of the disagreement – we were no longer invited to stay on the Board beyond the end of the year. This we naturally agreed to accept. Throughout this controversy I found myself entirely at one with Eccles, who was helpful, candid and perspicacious. He believed, as I did, that the proposed political battle would end either in costly defeat for Courtaulds or prolonged conflict. It would be good neither for Courtaulds nor the nation. As it happened, Eccles had just received another offer (to be Minister of Arts in the possible Heath Government); and as I was sixty-three, the job had only two years to run anyway. Nevertheless, these latter events did seem to reveal an odd streak which fitted strangely into

Kearton's remarkable range of outstanding capacities. For what is the good of having part-time non-executive directors in a great modern company if they are never allowed to disagree with the chairman? If the chief merit of private enterprise lies in the power of a licensed temporary dictatorship to act quickly and move mountains, then it must not become unlicensed. Somebody on the Board must be ready to challenge any tendency, however human, towards megalomania. Secondly, if part-time directors have any value, it is surely their willingness if necessary to oppose the chairman, since their whole livelihood does not depend on their job. What, however, would have actually happened if Alexander had marched bravely on to the uncharted East, nobody will ever know.

P

Mr Heath: the Treaty and the Bill

Seen in sober retrospect, the process by which the Heath Government between June 1970 and January 1973 manoeuvred this country unwillingly into the Market still seems to me a thoroughly shabby episode. During the 1970–1 so-called negotiations virtually every major safeguard for British and Commonwealth interests was surrendered, with no mitigation of the crippling CAP, except a 'transitional' period; and the entire constitution of the Rome Treaty was swallowed, including the transfer of legislative sovereignty from the British Parliament to overseas unelected bodies for the first time for centuries; while the ministers responsible explained to the public, with the help of a lavishly financed propaganda campaign, that nothing of the kind was happening. The Treaty of Accession embodying all this was never directly debated or ratified by Parliament; and the legislation which purported to legalize the whole constitutional revolution, consisted of a few sweeping clauses and was passed under a guillotine, without any amendments or any Report Stage in the Commons, and by repeated majorities in single figures on crucial constitutional issues. The whole operation violated the spirit, if not the letter, of parliamentary practice, and deprived the results, in my judgement, of any moral respect or authority.

The Foreign Office method of conducting the negotiations made it clear from the start that virtually unconditional surrender would result. Having decided that entry was somehow desirable in itself, the FO naturally did not believe the terms mattered, but only the speed with which the deal could be fixed. Heath fell in admirably with this by wanting everything to be settled by a certain date – well before the next election; and as this became well-known to the French, the British negotiators started on hopelessly weak ground. For as the cut-off date approached, they were bound to accept whatever was then on offer. Heath in the words of Uwe Kitzinger, was 'determined that there should be no delay on the British side.'[1] By contrast with this, the French had insisted on the CAP being signed, sealed and delivered *before* any negotiation with the UK: 'comple-

[1] Uwe Kitzinger, *Diplomacy and Persuasion*, p. 92.

tion' before 'enlargement'; thus demonstrating again that, for France, the CAP *was* the EEC. The FO's normal procedure, as I learnt to my cost before 1967, was this: first to discover what the French would or would not accept, and then persuade British ministers not to ask for what the French would refuse. The French – or other EEC members – accordingly only had to let it be known that such and such was not negotiable, and the result of the deal was already determined. This was the reason why the Rome Treaty and CAP were swallowed virtually without amendment. Indeed the whole Rome Treaty and the legislation involved, were accepted in Barber's opening speech without this ever having been approved by Parliament or the electorate. The real issue at stake for the future of this country – whether we accepted the CAP or the transfer of sovereignty – was almost certainly never debated and approved as such by the Wilson Cabinet. It never came explicitly before that Cabinet while I was a member, and I have been assured by others that it did not thereafter. Instead the FO prepared a 'negotiating brief' during the 1970 election for unloading on which ever Party won, and the Conservativet Cabine accepted it on Heath's enthusiastic endorsement.

Happily the Labour Opposition was now far better equipped to expose the whole negotiating performance which lasted from the late summer of 1970 until the signing of the Treaty on 22 January 1972. The resignation of the Labour Government had freed Peter Shore, John Silkin and Fred Peart to join the rest of us and voice their real opinions about the Market in the House. An unofficial anti-Market group of Labour MPs was formed, known as the Peart Group, because it met in Peart's room; which included: Peart, Shore, Foot, Silkin, Will Blyton, Alf Morris, John Mendelson, Stan Orme and myself. Some very vigorous young anti-Market Labour MPs had also entered the House in 1970; of whom Eric Deakins, John Gilbert, Nigel Spearing and Stanley Clinton-Davies, were the most active. Contrary to what the press tried to pretend, most of these were not of a 'Tribune' type, but from the Centre or Right Centre of the Party. Soon after the election, on 29 June, I also lunched with Jim Callaghan and again tried to persuade him to stand as Deputy Leader of the Party (now that Brown had lost his seat). This was justified in any case and would have avoided the arch pro-Marketeer, Roy Jenkins, being elected. But Callaghan declined, saying the Deputy Leadership meant nothing real, and he was as Party Treasurer a member of the National Executive anyway. A few weeks later Peter Shore told me he was deeply opposed to EEC membership and wanted to fight this battle to the limit. In mid-July with the support of both the Peart Group and the all-Party Study Group two similar 'Early Day Motions' (one Labour and one Conservative) were launched calling for strong safeguards in any Common Market settlement. This time we secured eighty-five Labour and forty-three Conservative signatories.

In the weeks after the election, since Heath's mandate was to 'negotiate,

P*

no more and no less', I decided that there was a sound case for arguing that either a referendum or a general election should be held before any Treaty with the EEC was signed or legislation passed. My contention was that while on all other than basic constitutional issues, Parliament rather than the electorate should ultimately decide, nevertheless where the constitution and the powers of Parliament itself were being altered, there was unique justification for a referendum *or* election. Though the argument was often misrepresented as simply a call for a referendum, my essential case was for decision by the electorate. I supported it with quotations from G. M. Trevelyan's *British History in the Nineteenth Century and After*, where he comments as follows on Lord Grey's decision to hold an election in 1831 over the then government's Reform Bill: Lord Grey 'established the fundamental principle of the new constitution, namely that in the last resort the opinion of the nation is to count for more than the opinion of the legislators'. On 1 August 1970, *The Times* published a signed article of mine setting out this argument, which I intended to be the start of a long struggle for a referendum. The immediate response exceeded my hopes, with letters of support from all sides: in *The Times* itself from William Pickles, Arthur Bryant, Clem Leslie and Neil Marten. Nicholas Kaldor, with characteristic kindheartedness sent a postcard from France warmly praising – in fact over-praising – my article; and another postcard reached me on holiday in Cornwall expressing support for the referendum from Tony Benn, hitherto a slightly reluctant pro-Marketeer. It was the Year of Conversion; and the idea of the referendum had been born.

Also in this August Thames TV held a fifty-minute programme in which Neil Marten and I put the straight case against EEC membership and Duncan Sandys and Dick Taverne in favour. This was almost the only occasion throughout the eight years from 1967 to 1975, when I had the chance to state the case in more than a few seconds on any broadcast programme; and very nearly the only instance before the 1975 Referendum when an unfettered *straight* TV debate was held at all. The BBC and other authorities staged many programmes 'covering' the EEC, but all too often they preferred an 'angled' type of discussion. So all credit to Thames TV. But the rarity otherwise of straight and unfettered debate on TV throughout these years was a sad commentary on the system; and the extent of pressure by the European Movement on the BBC and other authorities is well documented by both Uwe Kitzinger and by Douglas Evans ('media breakfasts', etc.).[2] At the Labour Party Conference of 1970 our Labour Safeguards Committee fringe meeting was more crowded than ever, and I had recruited as speakers: Dan McGarvey of the Boilermakers, Peter Shore, Stan Orme, Shinwell and Reg Prentice. We urged support for a TGWU anti-Market motion and some of us in the next few days canvassed

[2] Kitzinger, pp. 204–5, and Evans, pp. 110–14.

sedulously for this among the main unions. In the course of this I met Hugh Scanlon for the first time and found him extremely friendly, but with far less grasp than Jack Jones of the Market issue. In the Conference itself the TGWU motion was only lost by 2,950,000 votes to just over 3,000,000. We had come nearer to our long-standing goal of converting the Labour Party.

By 29 October Heath's negotiator, Geoffrey Rippon made a statement in the House which was taken, at least by those who understood it, to mean that the Government was determined to join on almost any terms. A fortnight after this our all-Party Study Group was more formally constituted as the 'Common Market Study Group', with Sir Robin Turton remaining an admirably hard-working Chairman, and membership including Walker-Smith and Neil Marten on the Conservative side, and Shore, Silkin, Alf Morris, Moyle, Clinton-Davies and Orme on our own. Most of the work of weekly scrutiny of EEC affairs fell to this Group. Another new convert, Eric Heffer, spoke publicly against membership also in this November, and Benn published a letter to his constituents calling for a referendum. Throughout this period the Safeguards Campaign was issuing pamphlets and organizing meetings (e.g. at the Beaver Hall in the City in early December, with speakers from Sweden, Norway, New Zealand and Eire, as well as Peter Shore). Some 200,000 copies of a 'Question and Answer' pamphlet I had composed on the Common Market were printed, and 150,000 of these distributed by Easter 1971. In December 1970 *Daily Telegraph* opinion polls showed 16 per cent in favour of EEC membership and 66 per cent against. Tactics for the campaign within the Labour Party began to materialize around Christmas 1970. In a talk with Crossman, currently Editor of the *New Statesman*, I found him now professing strong anti-Market views. He thought Wilson was in a fix, fearing to be accused of changing his mind again. Crossman favoured a drive for a decisive vote at the Labour Party Conference. A few days later in the House, Benn expounded to me his tactical plans, which I thought sensible: a Party motion in the House demanding a new election before any decision and a Labour promise in the election manifesto to hold a referendum. Benn still purported to be in favour of membership on 'technological' grounds; but when I told him this was nonsense, he did not reply with much conviction.

By January 1971 the threat of a 95 per cent sell-out by Rippon and Heath was becoming so obvious that all possible time and energy had now clearly to be devoted to countering it. A four-hour high level talk-in at the Grand Committee Room in Westminster Hall was organized by the Safeguards Campaign, in which Sir John Winnifrith (not long retired from the Ministry of Agriculture, Fisheries and Food), Kaldor, Walker-Smith and Benn expounded a massive economic and constitutional case against the surrender terms which Rippon was contemplating. Next day, 21

January, in a two-day debate in the House I tried to set out the full economic consequences of the terms contemplated, predicting an extra £1000
million burden on the balance of payments: and Enoch Powell delivered
the first of his passionate Philippics on the theme of national independence.
This was one of the best speeches I ever heard in the House, nearly
comparable with those of Cripps and Gaitskell. It inspired conviction and
conversion. In the same week the Tribune Group launched a motion
condemning the Rippon terms outright, and within two weeks it collected
121 signatures. David Wood of *The Times* even told me that 50 per cent
of the then Tory Cabinet were strong sceptics (probably including Maudling
Whitelaw, Walker and Hogg). The New Zealand and Australian Governments disappointed us by not saying loudly and clearly at this time what
we knew they wanted. Dining with Keith Holyoake, the New Zealand
Prime Minister in April, I tried to convince him he would be wise to do so,
since the British public were wholly on his side. But the FO tactics,
particularly twisted as it seemed to me, were first to tell these friendly
ministers in private that we should get better terms for them if they kept
quiet, and then tell the British public that the ministers in question must
be satisfied because they had said nothing to the contrary. Being more
gentlemanly than the FO, the Commonwealth ministers were tricked, and
the public misled.

In the spring of 1971, alerted no doubt by the evidence of growing
anti-Market feeling, and expecting a crucial parliamentary vote later in
the year, the European Movement decided to step up its propaganda
machine into top gear by the easy method open to it, but not to us: huge
spending of money. The expenditure of the European Movement alone
(which was of course additional to that of the European Communities
Information Services) rose from £41,006 in 1969–70, to £105,658 in
1970–1, and to £644,734 in 1971–2.[3] Of the latter enormous sum, £270,000
went on 'advertising and public relations'. The income of the Movement
in 1971–2 was £915,904. The European Movement's huge income was
drawn both from big firms and banks, and from a few wealthy individuals,
one of whom was reported to have given £500,000.[4] He was later knighted,
but was apparently not the largest individual donor. Against this £915,904
on the pro-Market side, the Safeguards Campaign had barely £20,000
to spend in 1971. We could not hold out the hope of knighthoods to
individual donors; though the number of small subscriptions was very
large. Thus on into the summer and autumn of 1971 MPs and the public
were drenched with pro-Market propaganda.[5] Altogether 6½ million items
of literature were distributed by the European Movement and allies in
these months of 1971. On 11 May a full-page advertisement appeared in

[3] For these and further details see Kitzinger, pp. 210–12.
[4] Kitzinger, p. 212.
[5] Kitzinger, p. 221 and following pages.

The Times, organized by Roy Jenkins, and purporting to be signed by 100 Labour MPs, apparently favouring almost any terms for EEC membership. Some of the names turned out to be not fully authenticated. We therefore organized a counter-advertisement in *The Times* with over 100 MPs names from all parties, to synchronize with Heath's May visit to Paris; but in the effort somewhat strained our finances.

The pro-Market propaganda campaign of the summer of 1971 was timed to coincide with the crunch in the Franco–British dispute. Pompidou was evidently not yet convinced that even Heath was really willing to surrender 95 per cent of British and Commonwealth interests. Soames therefore arranged in secret for Heath to visit Paris and assure Pompidou that in fact he was, and that he was in a hurry to do it. So Heath flew to Paris on 19 May, and in two days' private talks with Pompidou and an interpreter convinced him that the British Government was indeed prepared to give in – apart from a few cosmetics – on the Rome Treaty, the CAP, the Commonwealth and the sterling area. Pompidou was convinced, and in June in Luxembourg the main lines of the settlement, on issues other than fishing were agreed. On sugar, source of the last major dispute, the British aim had always been to protect the impoverished Commonwealth sugar producers in the West Indies and elsewhere, either by insisting that the Commonwealth Sugar Agreement, which had greatly benefited these countries and the UK consumer ever since 1950, must be maintained, or that the EEC must undertake to buy 1,400,000 tons of Commonwealth cane sugar annually at a reasonable price. In the end, even if this latter point had been gained the EEC could easily evade it by buying the Commonwealth sugar, and selling a corresponding amount of beet sugar on world markets thus depressing the price – as it did in the 1970s. But Rippon did not even secure this assurance; all he got was a pledge that the Market '*aura à coeur*' the interests of the Commonwealth producers, which was translated officially as 'will have as its firm purpose'. The truth was that poor Rippon was up against Heath's political time-table. He could not argue any longer. But, even apart from sugar, the extent of the surrender of basic British interests in the whole agreement had already been mercilessly exposed in questions to Rippon in the House after his statements on 17 May and on 24 June.

At this moment, by another odd twist of political fortune, I had to appear before a Selection Conference of my local party, because the constituency boundaries had been changed, and my colleague, Ernest Perry, of South Battersea was therefore entitled to offer himself as candidate for North Battersea, although I could not offer myself in the other constituency. On 30 June, after a little speech from each of us, I was re-elected by twenty-seven votes to seven. However confident one feels of support, any politician must be glad when this sort of experience is over.

By mid-summer the scene of the EEC controversy shifted to the Labour

Party and to a prospective first crucial vote in the Commons in the autumn on the substance of the agreement. My efforts, and those of my immediate Party colleagues, Peter Shore, Alf Morris, John Silkin and Ron Leighton were devoted towards the special Labour Party Conference, promised by Wilson, to be held in July on the proposed Rippon–Heath settlement. Our close ally in this was Norman Willis,[6] Jack Jones's personal assistant in the TGWU. He fully carried out all his undertakings that the TGWU would oppose the Rippon terms at the July Labour Party Conference, at the TUC Conference, and the full Party Conference at the end of September. Another firm ally was Jim Callaghan, who was being advised privately by Terry Pitt of the Labour Party Research Department and my son Peter, then Economics Editor of *The Times*, on the details of the controversy. They backed the idea of re-negotiation, and a referendum pledge. Callaghan told me at a talk I had with him on 29 June that he could not force an apparent change of mind on Wilson as early as the 17 July Conference, but would guarantee a satisfactory National Executive Committee statement at the end of the month. It seemed to me odd that Wilson's conscience could be appeased by the lapse of a fortnight; but if so, then so be it. As a result of this Wilson–Callaghan compromise, the 17 July Conference in the Central Hall, Westminster, did not take the formal decision; but did make it inevitable. Speakers in the Central Hall were rather oddly called on a strictly 'Yes' and 'No' alternative basis, though this far from represented the balance in the Conference. Michael Stewart was called to speak – or rather shout – from the gallery, *for* the Rippon agreements and I myself against them. Stewart astonished me by asserting that the Labour Government would have accepted these terms. For in fact the Cabinet never approved anything like them. But the best speeches for and against, also from the lofty gallery, were made for the anti-Marketeers by Peter Shore, who made his political name in those five minutes; and for the pro-Marketeers by John Mackintosh. Wilson in the end made such an anti-Market speech that it was the anti-Marketeers who went home happy at the end of that day.

Next day to my great surprise, Hugh Cudlipp, who had been abusing anti-Marketeers in the *Daily Mirror* for years past, rang me up personally and asked me for 1000 words as a signed article for the *Mirror* stating our case. He published it at once and unchanged. On 28 July the National Executive, as Callaghan had promised, approved by sixteen votes to six a statement condemning the Rippon terms outright. Wilson's conscience was salved. But the rest of us had achieved after four years the first objective we had set ourselves in 1967; we had converted the Labour Party. At the end of a Parliamentary Labour Party meeting on the EEC on 19 July, however, Roy Jenkins made an extraordinarily bitter and frustrated speech. He became vehemently emotional and attacked the

[6] Afterwards Deputy General Secretary of the TUC.

Australians with such violence as almost to suggest that he was imbued not so much with infatuation for the EEC as impatience with all things British. Many of those present walked out, and feeling erupted all round at the close. One Member after another told me later that Jenkins had now gone too far altogether.

The conversion of the Labour Party against Market membership on surrender terms was signed and sealed at the normal annual Conference of the Party at Brighton in October. Callaghan, in a speech at Bradford in September pledged a future Labour Government to 're-negotiate' the Heath terms. This was the first public promise of re-negotiation. By the time of the Party Conference in October, the opinion polls, which had been swung by the torrent of pro-Market propaganda in the summer nearer to the fifty-fifty mark, had now turned back our way, and stood at about 50 per cent against and 30 per cent in favour of membership. It was remarkable that public opinion had resisted the expenditure of nearly £1 million on propaganda in a few months. A week before the Brighton Conference it was decided at our Labour Safeguards Committee (Foot, Shore, Peart and Mendelson being present), that we should avoid extreme resolutions, which might be defeated – a common Conference trap – and urge everyone to vote for the National Executive's own motion straightforwardly opposing entry on the Heath terms. This was the message of our annual 'fringe' meeting on the pre-Conference Sunday (3 October) in the Brighton Pavilion. Michael Foot, Stan Orme, Brian Walden, Laurence Daly of the miners, Barbara Castle, the President of the New Zealand Labour Party and myself were the speakers. Afterwards I offered Shinwell, the Chairman, a lift home to his hotel, but he preferred to walk. He was then only eighty-six. The vote opposing the Heath settlement, after a powerful speech by Callaghan and firm pledge to scrap the settlement, was carried by five to one in the Conference.

So after nine years we had returned to the point where Hugh Gaitskell had carried the Party in his ever-memorable speech at Brighton in 1962. It was a more sweeping victory than most of us had expected. I could not help sitting on the beach for half an hour, recalling 1967, and reflecting that the whirligig of time does bring in his revenges. But the struggle would now shift back to Parliament. At Brighton the pro-Marketeers characteristically, having failed in the straight democratic vote, immediately attempted to find a devious way round. While I was philosophizing on the beach, Bill Rodgers, apparently now the pro-Marketeers' self-appointed chief organizer, no doubt hoping to divert attention from the five-to-one defeat, hinted to the press that very evening that twenty to seventy pro-Market Labour MPs might vote in the House in favour of Heath; and even that Wilson might have approved some deal by which they would be forgiven for voting against the Labour Party at the end of October, if they supported the Party throughout the legislation which followed. Wilson flatly denied that there was any such deal; and I do not believe myself on the evidence that these rumours were more than what the pro-Marketeers would have liked to believe and an attempt to divert attention from their defeat at the Conference. Their decision to spread such rumours, however, was the first sign of the extreme lengths they were prepared to go in defiance of Labour Party rules, traditions and loyalties.

Meanwhile the Safeguards Campaign, also in preparation for the Commons vote on 28 October, had been organizing, in addition to meetings all over the country (I spoke at Slough, Skegness, Highgate and Edinburgh in the second half of September alone), for a grand finale in Trafalgar Square in October. Since this clearly had to be as all-Party as possible, it involved some of the most exhausting negotiations I ever endured. At times I was again reminded of Dalton's already quoted dictum: 'Once a Communist, always a crook'. The Ministry of Works had rather absurdly allocated the most suitable day for Trafalgar Square, Sunday 24 October, to an extremist group. However we eventually succeeded in regaining 24 October, and forming a Trafalgar Square Committee, including among others Bob Wright of the AUEW, who was consistently helpful and firm. After various extremists had been suggested as speakers, we agreed on Walker-Smith, Michael Foot, Judith Hart, Bob Wright, Lord Woolley, and Teddy Taylor, Scottish Tory MP who had just resigned from Heath's Government in protest against the settlement.

In announcing this at a press conference, we also gave the news that a batch of writers – J. B. Priestley, Robert Conquest, John Osborne and Kingsley Amis – had become Patrons of the Campaign as well as the Labour MPs George Thomas (later Speaker), Willie Ross and Barbara Castle. Sunday 24 October turned out as fine a demonstration as we could have wished. Many thousands, thanks partly to trade union support, marched in bright sunshine from Hyde Park to Trafalgar Square and filled the Square. Lord Woolley, Cheshire farmer and veteran ex-President of the NFU, showed a fine talent for knockabout oratory to a mass audience. Teddy Taylor was excellent. When a man has just resigned from a government, he usually says what he really thinks. Next day *The Times* published a full-length photo on its front page of the crowded square.

Our Trafalgar Square rally came in the middle of the crucial debate, which was to last six days and end on 28 October. The Conservatives had at this late moment announced a 'free vote' for their Party. But this was only a manoeuvre. They knew that forty or so hard-line Conservative anti-Marketeers would vote against the motion anyway, and everybody on their 'payroll vote' – ministers, whips, and parliamentary private secretaries – were given to understand that they were of course expected to support the Government. It was hoped that the gesture might delude the Labour Party into imposing no formal Whip. But this failed. In the Parliamentary Labour Party meeting on 19 October before the debate, a motion to oppose Heath's terms was approved by 159 votes to 89, and the proposal for a 'free vote' rejected by 140 to 111. So a three-line Whip was duly imposed, and by all the rules and traditions of the Party the alternative for Party members was either to vote with it or abstain. As the debate wore on feverish calculations were being made by various self-appointed whips about the result. Norman St John Stevas was supposed to be concocting mysterious lists for the Euro-fanatic Tories, Bill Rodgers for their equivalents in the Labour Party and John Silkin for the confirmed Labour anti-Marketeers. The general assumption was that sixty or seventy Labour pro-Marketeers would abstain, and the Government would have a majority of fifty or sixty. It is possible that the anti-Marketeers made a mistake here in spending too much time on rational argument, and not pressurizing individual pin-pointed doubters by the same rather cloak and dagger methods as St John Stevas and Rodgers. But unless this had begun much earlier, it could not have affected the result. To my surprise I was asked, though not a member of the Shadow Cabinet, to make the wind-up speech for the Party on Monday 26 October. This was apparently due to a friendly suggestion from Jim Callaghan.

It was my first Front Bench speech for four years. I decided to argue the fundamental case against this country throwing away its one great advantage of low-cost food imports and low industrial costs and being submerged in high agricultural protectionism. Clearly many Members still did not realize that this was what we were doing. Though one is quite used after twenty years in the House to a little late-night frivolity even on serious debates, I was, I must admit, genuinely shocked by the routine post-prandial light-headedness with which the Tory lobby-fodder were treating even this debate. Drama and tension were, however, certainly there on the last day, 28 October. But somehow I felt the tension to be slightly unreal, compared with the Suez debates. On the evening of 27 October Douglas Houghton, who played an odd role, announced that he would vote with the Conservatives and not abstain. Some said this was part of a deep-laid plot, and a signal to the Labour pro-Marketeers to vote rather than abstain, and it was put about, probably falsely, that it was done with Wilson's connivance. I was not fully convinced myself that the bulk of the Labour pro-Marketeers would actually vote against the Party on a three-line Whip, until the Tory anti-Marketeer Hugh Fraser told me so in a lobby in the mid-afternoon of 28 October. In the event sixty-nine pro-Marketeers supported Heath, and thirty-nine Conservative anti-Marketeers voted against him and with the Labour Opposition. Some twenty Labour MPs abstained. This gave a majority of 112, more than any of us expected, for the motion accepting the Heath settlement. Heath was visibly delighted, many of the Tory doubters shame-faced, and the Labour anti-Market majority furious at the behaviour of the rebels. Feelings were so high that few went home for hours afterwards, and I talked much too late with Peter

Shore and Judith Hart in the latter's room about the next rounds in the battle.

Enormous pressure had been concentrated by the Tory Party machine, not merely in the House but more insidiously in their constituencies, on Tory doubters. On almost all issues a minority in either Party can be found who have no very strong views on one particular point, and it is pressure by the whips on them which often detemines the result. In the Conservative Party this herd-instinct is usually stronger than in the Labour Party, and all the more credit must therefore go to the thirty-nine Tory anti-Marketeers for standing firm. Had the sixty-nine Labour rebels simply abstained, as according to Party rules they should have, Heath would still have won. Had they, however, voted strictly in accordance with decisions of the Party Conference and Parliamentary Labour Party, Heath would have been defeated; his Government would probably have resigned; and this country would probably not have entered the Market. Wilson was perfectly justified in saying a few days later that, in deciding to vote with Heath they had kept the Conservative Government in power. The truth was that, by this time, with extremists like Jenkins and Rodgers, the pro-Market doctrine had become a religion, transcending all other loyalties.

Also, according to strict Labour Party rules, rebels who voted against a three-line Whip should have had the Whip withdrawn, and might have been expelled from the Party. This was the doctrine applied to the Bevanites in the fifties. But where pro-Market fanaticism was involved, all normal rules and moral scruples were waived. Ironically also, it was the antics of the Bevanites and later the Tribune Group, and the more tolerant attitude of John Silkin as Chief Whip towards them, which made it easier for the sixty-nine pro-Marketeers in October 1971 to defy all established rules. And by a further irony, which the sixty-nine did not foresee, their action in doing so enabled in future the Tribune Group and other minorities in the Party, including on occasion the anti-Marketeers, to defy two-line, three-line or any other sort of Party decisions with impunity.

The vote of 28 October, however, had no legal effect. The Treaty of Accession with the Market had not yet been drafted, let alone signed or ratified. Legislation by the British Parliament was still to come. For the moment even this seemed in doubt, as it was rumoured that the Government might commit the final constitutional enormity of presuming that the 28 October vote had itself given the force of law in this country to all EEC legislation. I raised this with Wilson in a Party meeting, and questioned Heath about it in the House without getting at first a convincing answer. Another discouraging consequence of the 28 October vote was Sir Max Aitken's surprise announcement in the *Express* on Saturday, 30 October, that he could not continue the paper's anti-Market campaign because of the vote in Parliament. One had never noticed before that the *Express* changed its policy overnight because of an adverse vote in Parliament. It

was assumed by most people that though Max Aitken had felt bound hitherto by his father's philosophy, the establishment – no doubt in the person
of Ted Heath – had got at him too. Up till now one newspaper out of a
dozen or so was on the anti-Market side; henceforward none unless you
counted the *Morning Star*. By chance the immediately following week-end,
30–1 October, was for me the date of the All Souls annual gaudy and
election of two new prize fellows, for which I was functioning as a part-time
examiner for the first time since 1935. I had been generously re-elected by
the College in 1968 as a 'distinguished senior fellow', a small group of ten
which at this time also included Hailsham, Wilberforce and Keith Joseph.

Although Rippon may have seemed already to have sacrificed almost
every essential British interest by June 1971, there was one more surrender
to come; the British fishing industry. Seeing that Heath and Rippon were
prepared to swallow virtually anything, the French during 1971 rushed
through a 'Common Fisheries Policy', designed to do as much additional
damage as possible to Britain, and incidentally benefit most of the other
EEC members who had exhausted much of their own reserves of fish, and
wanted to move in on our much more ample stocks. Rippon shocked the
House of Commons by announcing the extent of the capitulation on 13
December of 1971. In the case of fishing, the background to the struggle
with the EEC was this. The world as a whole was moving from a twelve-
mile to a 200-mile exclusive fishing zone round the coasts of each country:
and as this country was thereby pushed out of a 200-mile zone round
Iceland, we could only be compensated by a 200-mile zone round the UK.
This 200-mile zone would be particularly valuable to us, particularly in the
North, because of our coastline; and Norway obtained it by the simple
expedient of staying out of the Market. If however, we entered the EEC,
then the other member States of the Market would share our 200-mile zone
with us; and as 60 per cent of the total stocks in the entire EEC 200-mile
zone came from the British area, the other member countries would clearly
gain enormously and we should lose. If was therefore vital, if we joined,
to secure at least a fifty-mile exclusive zone with the new EEC-shared
200 miles. The British fishing industry, debarred from Icelandic waters,
regarded this as the absolute minimum.

Heath and Rippon, however, did not even ask for this. They asked for
only the out-dated twelve-mile limit and failed to get it. What Rippon
announced was a mere *six-mile zone* limited exclusively to British vessels,
extended only to twelve miles in certain parts of Scotland, the North East
and South West of England, and part of Northern Ireland. In all other
areas the water between six miles and twelve miles was to be shared with
other EEC countries. But even this was not the full extent of the surrender.
For this concession was not a permanent arrangement at all, but a mere
'derogation' to last until 31 December 1982, 'after which all British waters
would be open to all Common Market vessels'. Rippon was so ashamed

here of his capitulation as to indulge on 20 December in out-right mis-representation. Both he and Lady Tweedsmuir in the Lords told Parliament this was 'not just a transitional arrangement which automatically lapses at the end of a fixed period', but that before the end of 1982 there would be a review to 'determine conditions thereafter'; which meant, as Lady Tweedsmuir assured the Lords, that the veto would be in British hands to ensure that the concession continued 'thereafter'. But when the Treaty which Rippon had accepted was published in January, this proved to be untrue. The French had carefully insisted on the following words in describing the review: 'provisions which could follow the derogation in force until 31 December 1982'. This meant of course that the concession ceased then, and any new arrangement was liable to the veto of any EEC member. The French could veto the continuance of the 'derogation'; but we could not veto its cancellation.

While Rippon and Heath gave in to this further French victory, the Norwegians stuck out for precisely the conditions for which we had been fighting with them, and secured a 'continuing' arrangement after 1982. But the most remarkable part of the whole story was that not merely did Rippon abandon the Norwegians in his hurry to give way, but that Heath even sent a secret message to the Norwegian PM before Christmas 1971 urging him to hurry up and give way also. This was the famous message which, when leaked, was found to contain the sentence: 'It is very important for us that we present this question in a manner that will appear satisfactory to fishing interests.' The Norwegians were pressed to capitulate so that our fishermen would not see how much worse they were being treated than the Norwegians. But Norway refused and won her point.

There followed what always seemed to me constitutionally the most deplorable part of the whole proceeding. The vote of 28 October had been taken without of course the fishing agreement being known, but also without the Treaty of Accession being published. It became apparent in January 1972 that Heath proposed to sign the Treaty of Accession on behalf of the British Government before it had been even published, let alone debated in Parliament. In defence of this it was argued that Treaties had traditionally been signed by the Crown and later formally ratified after approval by Parliament. But there had never before in modern times been a Treaty which transferred legislative power over British subjects from the British Parliament to unelected bodies outside this country. Nor had the Heath Government any shred of mandate from the electorate for a constitutional revolution.

So some of us persuaded the Labour Opposition to put down a vote of censure on the Government for proposing to sign the Treaty before Parliament had even read it. This motion was debated on 20 January, and Peter Shore who was becoming with Michael Foot the main Front Bench critic of the whole proceedings, made a powerful attack; and I was able later, if briefly, to show that the fishing industry had been tricked, because the veto was in French hands and not ours. To this no answer was given. But Heath went ahead and signed the Treaty on 22 January, and as a result neither it nor the Treaty of Rome were ever specifically debated or approved by the British Parliament at all. They were merely supposed to have been given formal legal force by an obscure formula in the European Communities Bill, published soon afterwards, which formula appeared to be little understood by many of Heath's well-drilled supporters who voted for it. But as soon as the Treaty of Accession did see the light of day, it was clear that virtually none of the long-promised essential safeguards for British and Commonwealth interests had been secured. All UK food imports after a mere five years transition would be subject to the often prohibitive EEC levies. Canadian wheat (a staple British import) as well as US wheat and maize would bear them; and Canadian cheese would in effect be excluded altogether. No concessions whatever were obtained for Australian butter, cheese or beef, which were soon almost totally excluded or for Australian wheat. This was a straight breach of the assurances I had been authorized to give Australian ministers in 1966. In the case of New Zealand, mutton and lamb were to bear for the first time a 20 per cent import tariff after the transitional period. Cheese imports from New Zealand were allowed levy-free entry on a descending scale from 68,580 tons in 1973 to 15,280 in 1977; but 'after December 1977 the exceptional arrangements laid down for imports of cheese may no longer be retained'.

Only for New Zealand butter was the supply allowed to continue, but at a gradually diminishing rate: from 165,811 tons in 1973 to 138,176 tons in 1977: after which 'appropriate arrangements' were to be 'determined by the Council, acting unanimously on a proposal from the Commission'. Again any future arrangements after 1977 could be vetoed by the French. Yet a New Zealand Minister had been given assurances by the Heath Government which enabled him to say publicly in July 1971: 'It would be a breach of faith for the concept of unanimity to be re-introduced.' But the Treaty re-introduced it. On sugar, Heath had to be content with the phrase 'aura à cœur', which was legally without meaning. On the budget contribution, the UK was bound to pay across the exchanges a sum much greater proportionately than the ratio of her GNP to that of the whole EEC; and likely to grow from £500 million towards £1000 million a year. Throughout the Treaty it should be noted, French interests were tightly secured by precise legal language: 'the derogation in force until 31 December 1982 (fish)'; 'After December 1977 the exceptional arrangements laid down for imports of cheese may no longer be retained'; arrangements after December 1977 'to be determined by the Council acting unanimously . . .'. But when it came to British interests, the Treaty takes refuge in woolly expressions of intent such as 'aura à cœur', 'appropriate arrangements,' etc.

Why, however, did Heath and Rippon carry surrender thus to extremes on nearly every vital point? The answer is two-fold. The first was the hurry already described. The European Communities Bill had to be passed in the 1972 session if the deed was to be done before the next general election; and so even if there were a guillotine, no amendments, no Report Stage, and nothing but a perfunctory glance at this great constitutional revolution, by that staunch watchdog of the Constitution, the House of Lords, the Bill must be introduced in February 1972. When, therefore, Rippon reported on fish or anything else in December 1971 that if he said, 'No,' there would be no agreement, Heath had to authorize him to say, 'Yes.' The French knew this fully as well as Heath and Rippon; and so all they had to do to gain any crucial point was to say, 'No.' Such is the fatal folly of negotiating against a publicly known time-table. The second reason was the existence of a fifth-colum propaganda machine in this country. Heath knew – and the French knew, since through the ECIS they were partly financing the operation – that, whatever the terms, however damaging to Britain, the European Movement propaganda machine, and most of the British press would leap into action and say that the settlement was wonderful. So the Treaty was signed in January 1972, to almost unanimous applause in the press, like the Munich Agreement. The French were perfectly entitled in all this to defend their national self-interest with ruthless efficiency. The tragedy was that Heath and Rippon, in their self-imposed hurry, almost wholly surrendered ours.

On the day of the signature of the Treaty of Accession, the Safeguards Campaign and the various other anti-Market groups held a combined meeting at the Central Hall, Westminster. Peter Shore and Derek Walker-Smith spoke first in a public session; and a private session followed, with all of 300 people free to give their views on how the anti-Market campaign should be run. Most of those present urged complete amalgamation of all anti-Market groups. I privately agreed with them. By this time hardened leaders of the old Anti-Common Market League like Victor Montagu (the former Lord Hinchinbrooke) also supported amalgamation, though they had earlier wanted to preserve the League's independence. It would of course have been sensible to pool all resources. In voluntary movements, however, you cannot give orders. But the Conference at least recommended the 'maximum co-ordination'.

At this same crucial moment in January 1972, Callaghan was unhappily debarred by illness from the Common Market debates. I visited him early in that month in Lambeth Hospital near the Elephant & Castle, where he had just had a prostate operation. He was astonishingly active, and thoroughly cheered at the thought of five or six weeks' rest from work.

A few days after 22 January the long awaited European Communities Bill was published. There was to be no specific debate on the Treaty of Accession at all because Heath's time-table did not allow it; and the Second

Reading of the Bill was set for 17 February. From the Bill it now emerged that the most revolutionary change in the British constitution for 300 years was to be achieved by a legal conjuring trick. Instead of amending all British laws conflicting with Common Market Law by the approved parliamentary method, which would have required a 'Bill of 1000 clauses', the European Communities Bill laid down in twelve clauses that all past, and future EEC legislation and Treaties (including the Treaty of Rome and Treaty of Accession) were to have the force of law in this country. The anti-Market majority in the Labour Party naturally now decided to oppose this Bill by all possible parliamentary means. The Parliamentary Party, as well as the Conference were opposed to the Heath settlement, and a normal Whip would be imposed. Even on the so-called 'Houghton doctrine' of voting one way on 28 October 1971, and the other way on the Bill in 1972, it was clear that if all or nearly all the PLP followed the Whip, and all or nearly all the thirty-nine Tory anti-Marketeers stuck to their principles, the Bill could be defeated and the whole damage to the country avoided.

Naturally we did not know how many of the Tory thirty-nine could still be depended on. At this stage the informal Peart Group became the official Opposition nucleus opposing the Bill, led on the Front Bench by Foot, Shore and Peart, and most actively supported by Eric Deakins, John Gilbert, Nigel Spearing, Ronald King-Murray a first-rate Scottish lawyer, Brynmor John and Denzil Davies (two lawyers from Wales), Stanley Orme, Eric Heffer, Jack Mendelson and myself. Most of these normally attended the Group's private meetings. It was a great joy to be working together with an official group of the Party and with these younger members, in a cause which one whole-heartedly supported – almost like being back in the fifties with Gaitskell. We kept in touch with the Tory anti-Marketeers through the Study Group. Neil Marten, Walker-Smith, Richard Body and Roger Moate were the Tory nucleus of this Group. Enoch Powell did not join the Study Group until after the passing of the Bill. Robin Turton had resigned as Chairman of the Group from the moment when the Labour Party went into formal opposition to the Treaty and the Bill. He was a man of scrupulous – some would have said old-fashioned – standards and his way of putting it was that he was willing to work with Douglas Jay but not with Harold Wilson. So I became Chairman thereafter (the Group was still active in 1978–9). There were over ninety divisions in the Commons on the Bill, in every single one of which I voted.

The Second Reading debate lasted throughout 15, 16 and 17 February, with the division on the night of 17 February. It was, as I recorded at the time, an exceptionally good debate, more worthy of the issue than any yet. Neil Marten made the best speech I ever heard from him, brilliant and sparkling, and attacking Heath for every sort of bad faith. Walker-Smith was very powerful, and Powell as good as ever. Large numbers came into the House to listen to Marten and Powell. Teddy Taylor, having voted

'No' on 28 October, now announced he was supporting the Bill. Nobody knew what the result would be. Virtually the whole Labour Party, on a three-line Whip, were now voting against the Bill, and some Tories would vote against it also. But every conceivable pressure had been put on wobbling Tories by the PM and the Whips. Heath told them the Government would resign if it was defeated. The result was a vote for the Second Reading by only 309 votes to 301. So this constitutional revolution was imposed on us by eight votes in 600. Of the thirty-nine Conservatives who voted 'No' on 28 October, only thirteen did so on 17 February, with two abstaining. Those who voted against, despite all pressure, included Walker-Smith, Marten, Turton, Bell, Moate, Powell and Body, together with Hooson from the Liberals, and Molyneaux from the Ulster Unionists. If only half the thirty-nine of 28 October had stuck to their guns, the Bill would have been defeated. The defectors from the thirty-nine had not in the main been persuaded by arguments about the merits of joining the Community, but merely by the specious claim that 28 October somehow established a *fait accompli* – which it had not. At the same time seven Labour pro-Marketeers abstained or were 'unavoidably' absent on 17 February. If they had voted with their Party, the Bill would have had a majority of one.

This was to me the most tragic moment in the whole story. So much vast effort had been made for so long by the opponents of the Bill to defeat it at this stage; and despite the huge propaganda resources, and all the influence of the Government ranged against them, they had only failed by this tiny margin of eight votes. Feeling – genuine, deep and almost uncontrolled – erupted all round the Chamber, and particularly on the Labour benches near me, when the figures were announced. It was the fiercest moment in the House since Suez. Labour Members suddenly realized that the small group of six or seven Liberals sitting in the midst of us had all (apart from Hooson) voted with Heath, and that if they had voted the other way, the Bill would have been defeated. In the heat of the moment the Liberals were waved across the floor by the surrounding Labour Members, and a furious Labour Whip took Jeremy Thorpe by the arm and urged him to cross over. Thorpe, not knowing whether this was mockery or aggression, stood up and sat down by turns. My emotion, I fear, equalled my powers of restraining it; and in order to avoid seizing the miserable Liberals immediately in front of me by the throat, I tore up all the paper within erach and showered it on their befuddled heads. Some of the press next day reported all this as a 'scuffle'. It was not. It was merely very strong feelings just under control.

On 22 February the Ways and Means Resolution, which in effect transferred major powers to tax British subjects away from Parliament for the first time for centuries, was debated for a whole day and voted against. The Government made an effort to start the Committee Stage on 29 February;

but the Chairman of Committees, Wing-Commander Grant Ferris, produced the extraordinary ruling that the Bill merely supplied the 'nuts and bolts' for carrying out a decision already reached on 28 October (when the Treaty had not been signed, let alone published), and therefore that hosts of amendments put down, including amendments to the Treaties which the Bill was supposed to endorse, were out of order. He ruled fifty-seven of the first sixty-nine amendments to be out of order. Our confidence in this ruling was not strengthened by the discovery that it had taken three weeks for the learned clerks to make up their minds on this point. The Chairman's announcement provoked uproar from all sides, lasting for several hours and the debate was abandoned. This was followed by a discussion in the House next day (1 March) on a motion censoring the Chairman's conduct, and after 10 p.m. that evening, by a series of points of order which again prevented the Committee Stage being started, and lasted till 7.15 a.m.

The closure cannot be moved on points of order! The Chairman, Grant-Ferris, was remarkably patient; for never before, or after, in my thirty yeasr in the House can I recall a series of points of order being continued throughout the whole night. After yet another vote of censure (this time on the Government, for drafting the Bill so as to prevent proper discussion), the Committee Stage proper was not started till 7 March. In the censure debate on the Government Willie Whitelaw made a peculiarly poor speech, which I described as deplorable; when he met me afterwards in a passage he characteristically commented: 'You were quite right. It was deplorable.' From 7 March onwards ever-increasing pressure was exerted by Heath and the Conservative Chief Whip to bully or brainwash the Tory wobblers back into their normal status as pliant lobby fodder. Among other devices the Tory Central Office again organized opposition to anti-Market Tory MPs in their own constituencies. The votes developed into a series of desperately narrow escapes for the Government, in which one amendment carried would have necessitated a Report Stage and upset Heath's precious time-table; but in which the Government were never actually defeated.

In the Labour Group opposing the Bill, and in the all-Party Study group, we then decided to concentrate on amendments requiring a consultative referendum to be held in this country before the Bill came into operation. We based ourselves on Heath's argument that 'full-hearted consent of Parliament *and people*' was necessary. It was now nearly two years since my article in The Times of 1 August 1970 calling for a referendum, and the demand for it, systematically backed by the Safeguards Campaign, had made great headway. But we had to secure the official blessing of the Labour Shadow Cabinet (of which Foot, Shore and Benn were members) if this amendment was to be supported by an official Whip. First, on 15 March, the Shadow Cabinet rejected it. But then Pompidou came to our rescue by announcing that a referendum would be held in France on British entry; and so after a vote on the Labour National Executive on 22 March in favour of a referendum, the Shadow Cabinet supported our amendment.

As a result, in April immediately after the Easter Recess, Roy Jenkins, George Thomson and Harold Lever resigned from the Shadow Cabinet – and Jenkins from his Deputy Leadership of the Party. The response to this of many Labour MPs was that they were glad to be rid of these three, who were clearly out of sympathy with the Party and obsessed by the Common Market. Their resignation was a tacit admission that the British public did not agree with them anyway; and it seemed particularly grotesque (as Jenkins had voted against the Second Reading) to treat as a matter of sacred principle the undesirability of consulting the British electorate on an issue of basic constitutional change. Their decision in fact ended Jenkins's and Thomson's association with the Labour Party; which I still personally regretted, as they had been for years two of my closest friends. Jenkins and Lever, however, still voted with the Party against the Third Reading. On 12 April, the Parliamentary Party meeting decided to support the referendum amendment by 129 votes to ninety-six in a debate in which Jenkins spoke not very effectively in reply to Shore. Michael Foot wound up brilliantly this time on the high emotional note which suits him so well. The debate in the House itself on 18 April on this amendment was impressive on both sides. I rehearsed the full historical arguments, the precedents of 1832 and 1910, and the verdicts of G. M. Trevelyan and Churchill. But the motion was of course lost in the House, since the Jenkinsites abstained. It was now increasingly suspected that there was secret collusion between the Jenkinsites and the Tory Whips.

On 19 April I moved an amendment in favour of closer relations with EFTA, which was only lost by eight votes. At this point the Government introduced a guillotine which only a few months earlier would have been regarded as unthinkable on a constitutional Bill. The Liberal Party since 1918 had virtually never voted for a guillotine. But again, when the Common Market was at stake, all normal scruples were swept away, and with the help of the Liberals and a few extreme Jenkinsites, the Government won by eleven. On 3 May the majority in successive votes was nine, six, four and eight. Michael Foot revealed at a Party meeting next day that in each of these divisions more Labour members were absent unpaired than the total of the Government majority. This strengthened almost to certainty the belief among Labour members as a whole that Jenkinsites were secretly in collusion with the Tory Chief Whip before each division to ensure the number of abstentions necessary to rescue the Government and the Bill. It is so arithmetically improbable that the Government's majority should so often have been in single figures without their losing a single vote that I was myself forced to the conclusion that this must be true. The resentment in the Labour Party grew to be red hot. Neil Kinnock a young Member whom I scarcely knew before, voiced these suspicions at a Party meeting, and explicitly asked whether such collusion was operating. He got no answer. He flatly accused the pro-Marketeers of organizing the defeat of their own Party.[7] Kitzinger mentions Thomson, Stewart, Taverne, Albu, Carol Johnson, Lawson, Mayhew and Barnes as abstainers at one stage or another. No doubt it could have been argued that if we anti-Marketeers co-operated with the Tory anti-Marketeers, surely Labour pro-Marketeers were entitled to do the same. From the point of view of the Labour Party, however, there is some difference between persuading individual Conservatives to vote with the Labour Party and agreeing oneself to vote with a Conservative Government.

The mysterious narrow majorities continued without ever falling below four. On 24 May the majority fell to five; on 8 June to six and ten; on 20 June to nine, five, eleven and eight; on 21 June to eleven; and on 22 June on the Common Agricultural Policy again to five. Also on 14 June, the most crucial of all votes after the Second Reading, on the key Clause Two which made EEC laws applicable in this country, the majority was eight. Many had thought it extraordinary that any proposition should be laid before the British Parliament by any Government declaring that laws not approved by the British Parliament should be enforceable in this country. Certainly fifteen years earlier it would have been unthinkable. On 14 June 1972 there were still some Conservatives left who could not stomach it. Some seventeen voted with the Opposition. But five Liberals, supported even this, and according to the Labour Chief Whip, at least nine Labour MPs abstained unpaired (including Albu, Strauss, Thomson, Carol Johnson, Freda Corbett and Lawson). The belief that deliberate collusion prevailed now became irresistible. In further Committee Stage debates on 27 and 28 June, the hairsbreadth escapes by narrow majorities still continued. On 27 June the majorities were eight, ten, ten and nine. In one of these June divisions when the Government's majority was five, Michael Foot reported that ten Labour Members were absent unpaired. Altogether he said the Government could have been defeated twelve times on the Bill but for Labour abstentions; and this would have meant the end of the Government as well as the end of the Bill.

Some years earlier, in these circumstances, the persistent abstainers would almost certainly have been expelled from the Labour Party. Quaintly however, the very fact that so many ex-Bevanites, including Foot, had been rebels themselves in the past, made this unacceptable. The right course, I believe, in fairness to Labour MPs who were honestly paired, would have been for the Labour Whips to publish the names of those absent unpaired; for only the Whips know for certain who is paired. This was more than once proposed by myself and others, but only occasionally carried out. The last two days of the Committee stage were 2 and 4 July; and since the Government were still undefeated, they were just able to

[7] Kitzinger, p. 388 and 395. Hansard of course does not show whether a Member, if absent, is paired or unpaired.

hold to their time-table and move on to the Third Reading on 13 July. Wilson urged at the previous Party meeting that there should be no abstentions. The majority on Third Reading was seventeen, with sixteen Tories voting against the Bill. The Labour Members absent unpaired were Strauss, Stewart, Thomson, Albu, Barnes, Corbett, Crawshaw, Hannan, Carol Johnson, Lawson, Mayhew, Rankin, and Taverne. If they and the Liberals had voted against the Government, the Bill would have had a majority of one. So the Bill passed the Commons, and was greeted by that historic defender of the British Constitution, the House of Lords, with platitudes in plenty but not a single amendment.

In that hectic summer of 1972, and the long, weary struggle on the European Communities Bill, almost the only respite was the Whitsun week-end. On Saturday 27 May, having been divorced a few months earlier, I was married to Mary Thomas at Wheatley near our Oxfordshire cottage. I had now worked continuously with Mary for eight years, and daily for five years; and we worked happily ever after.

In the struggle over the Common Market, now that the Act was passed, the next aim was to commit the Labour Party to include in its coming election manifesto a commitment for a re-negotiation and referendum, with an understanding that if the country voted 'No', Britain would withdraw from the Market. At a meeting of the Peart Group on 10 May 1972 attended by Peart, Foot, Shore, Morris, Barbara Castle, Mendelson and myself, we agreed that it was best at the October Party Conference formally to propose re-negotiation and a referendum. I had already drafted a resolution whose keywords were: 'This Conference rejects the terms negotiated by the Tories for entering the EEC, and calls upon a future Labour Government to reverse any decision to enter unless new terms have been negotiated, consistent with British interests, and the assent of the electorate has been given to them.' This motion was duly circulated to friendly local parties by the Labour Committee for Safeguards, and versions of it duly appeared on the Conference Agenda. On 20 July I had a long private talk with Callaghan about the next steps. He had more or less led the successful demand in the previous summer for renegotiation and a referendum. Now I found him enigmatic. I wanted him to agree that during re-negotiation the UK should suspend EEC membership and stop paying subscriptions.

In the same week Neil Marten and I signed a letter to all Safeguard Campaign supporters, saying we intended to continue the fight and demand re-negotiation and a referendum. In August the Safeguards Campaign agreed to work with the strong anti-Market Movement in Norway and Denmark, and I arranged to speak in Copenhagen in September. This turned out to be a vast outdoor rally, attended by 6000 people, with bands singing and circus turns, interspersed with short speeches, organized by the 'People's Campaign Against the Common Market'. Any attack in any language against Brussels was warmly applauded. Someone said it was the largest political meeting in Denmark since 1945; but I was told that, as in Britain, almost the whole press and TV had somehow been muzzled by Brussels pressure.

Final preparations for the Labour Party Conference of 1972 at Blackpool were laid at a joint meeting in Peart's room of his Parliamentary Group and the Labour Committee for Safeguards on 25 September. The aim was to get our motion in favour of re-negotiation and a referendum passed, and avoid being manoeuvred by the extremists into losing a motion for outright withdrawal from the EEC. At this meeting Bob Wright of the AUEW, Marsden of the AUEW Constructional Engineering Section, and some other union extremists attended, as well as Foot, Shore, Peart, Mendelson, Barbara Castle and Orme. We agreed a compromise – or so we thought from Bob Wright's helpful summing up – by which we would advise support for the AUEW 'withdrawal' motion, and they would vote for ours as well as their own. We got our motion 'composited' in the desired form, and Dan McGarvey of the Boilermakers agreed to move it. He asked me at the last moment to dictate a speech for him; and was touchingly profuse with his thanks. We had already duly urged support for both motions at our 'Labour Committee' fringe meeting on Sunday 1 October, which was most enthusiastic, with Shinwell, now eighty-seven, still briskly presiding.

Later that evening our Committee met again and learnt that the National Executive Committee had agreed to accept our composite 'Boilermakers' resolution, but were also moving a motion of their own which at any rate included the demand for re-negotiation and a referendum. Then Bob Wright told us to our astonishment that the AUEW had decided to vote *against* our resolution. This was not the fault of Wright, who acted fairly and squarely in all dealings I had with him. It was evidently a typical double-cross by the Communists in the AUEW – John Mendelson described it to me as 'wilful sabotage by the Communists' – who apparently wanted to see both their own extremist motion and our effective one defeated. So they decided to vote against ours on the ground that it only offered 95 per cent of what was required! In the event at the Conference itself, both the NEC Statement and the Boilermakers' resolution were approved, and the AUEW 'withdrawal' resolution rejected. The substantial result of the Conference – and Labour Party Conferences do count when Labour is in Opposition – was therefore that the Party was now hard-and-fast committed to re-negotiation and a referendum. Our main object had thus been achieved.

In the autumn session of 1972 it soon appeared that the anti-Market troops in the country generally had not been too disheartened by the passing of the European Communities Act in the summer, and that the Conference Resolution had restored a fighting spirit. On 22 November Callaghan carried a compromise in the Shadow Cabinet by which any decision on attending the EEC Assembly at Strasbourg was put off for a year. This was directly in line with the Boilermakers' motion carried at the Conference, and it was later accepted by a vote of 140 to 50, by the Parliamentary Party. Also on 22 November, the House itself threw out by thirty-five votes (with forty Conservatives abstaining) a Government Immigration Order which would have given EEC immigrants a preference over Commonwealth immigrants. After so many narrow reverses in the House that year this result was greeted with one of the loudest shouts for a very long time. Since Heath was organizing a so-called 'Fanfare' for January 1973 to herald British membership of the EEC, the Safeguards Campaign decided to hold a counter-meeting at the Central Hall on the evening of 30 December. We risked music from the Musicians Union and a torchlight procession over Westminster Bridge. It is always a nice question whether such histrionic gestures will provoke enthusiasm or ridicule. But this time it all turned out highly successful. Dr Mansholt, EEC Farm Commissioner, remarked a few days later at a Hampton Court celebration of British membership that the EEC 'had failed to improve the condition of the mass of the people generally'. I sent him a telegram of congratulation.

Many of us had feared that with membership a legal *fait accompli*, opposition would die away. But this did not happen. As food prices rose, and the balance of payments moved against us, even *before the rise in world oil prices* at the end of 1973, resentment against Brussels policies increased rather than decreased. The Safeguard Campaign therefore published a pamphlet, which I had written, *The Common Market and Dear Food*. My wife, now working for Richard Body's Open Seas Forum, had been researching into the figures, and with the help of these and the pamphlet, I made an all-out attack on the CAP in the House on 18 July 1973. Everyone really knew, I said, that the object of the CAP was to raise food prices. Why else impose levies and exclude imports? But when Ted Short, now Deputy Leader of the Labour Party quoted my figures in the debate, from the front Opposition bench, Heath tried to challenge this; and after an exchange of letters between him and Short, I set out the full case in a letter to *The Times* which was not contraverted. More dramatically, anti-Marketeers and animal lovers together carried on 12 July by twenty-three votes a motion against the export of live animals to the Continent for slaughter, which was almost certainly contrary to EEC regulations. In early August Sam Brittan wrote an article in the *Financial Times* very frankly and honestly recanting his pro-Market views of the 1971 period under the heading: 'Why I was wrong on the Common Market'. All credit to the *Financial Times* and Sam Brittan for its appearance. At the 1973 Labour autumn Conference at Blackpool, a resolution which I had agreed with Harry Urwin and Alex Kitson of the TGWU, re-affirmed the Party's promise to consult the electorate, was carried by a five-to-one vote. Any tricks by the AUEW were averted this time with the help of Stan Orme and Hugh Scanlon; and Commissioner George Thomson imported from Brussels to promote the pro-Market cause, did just the opposite by undiplomatically driving about Blackpool in an ostentatious American car. In early November, when Parliament reassembled, Roy Jenkins stood again as a candidate for the Shadow Cabinet, thus in effect accepting the Party policy on the referendum. I heard from a colleague that at the first meeting of the new Shadow Cabinet, Jenkins had proposed a general playing down of the EEC issue, but that this had been decisively rejected by Foot and the majority. On 10 November – just before the oil price explosion broke on the world – at a major Safeguards Campaign rally in the Central Hall in Westminster, I was able to read a letter from Wilson firmly promising a referendum or election on the Market issue. He told me afterwards for the first time that he meant the referendum to be decisive and not just consultative. The best speech at this meeting came from John Winnifrith tearing the CAP coolly to pieces with all the authority of an ex-Permanent Secretary of the Ministry of Agriculture.

Some people now forget that this country after a year in the EEC had already fallen into acute balance of payments deficit at the end of 1973, *before* the new Arab–Israeli war and oil price explosion of December 1973 shook the world into the OPEC era and oil boom of the 1970s. On 13 November of 1973 the Heath Government had to announce a visible trade deficit of £373 million for October alone. Membership of the EEC had already, by raising the price of food imports and increasing the flow of manufactured imports from the Continent, contributed to building up a new huge payments deficit. It was already running at between £1000 million and £2000 million a year at the end of 1973. The other major cause of this was the extraordinary 'Barber' credit inflation of 1971–3, which nearly doubled the quantity of money in two and a half years. Naturally this led to rising imports. There was much irony also in the fact that the Labour Government in 1964 was handed a large payments deficit, that it returned to the Conservatives a £1000 million surplus in 1970, and that this had been turned to an over £1000 million deficit again by the end of 1973. Then the oil cartel struck and more than doubled this deficit in 1974. The real moral of this record was that we entered the EEC at the worst possible moment, just as the cost of oil imports was bound anyway to push us into the red.

January 1974 was a lurid month, which reminded me of February 1947 and the Shinwell Fuel Crisis. The miners seized on the situation to enforce an overtime ban; industry was squeezed on to a three-day week; oil prices rose steeply; and rumours of an impending general election came and went. Heath was certainly right in his basic attempt to maintain a firm incomes policy, though his own action in raising food prices made it much more difficult. His mistake was in failing to see that coal-producers' incomes must (with oil prices soaring) be given a special increase. He was offered a way out by the TUC, who undertook not to quote an exceptional rise for the miners as a pretext for other all-round rises; but his whole political future was thrown away because of his obstinate failure to seize on this precious and perfectly justifiable line of escape. Jack Jones and Hugh Scanlon were making conciliatory gestures. Yet Heath chose an election instead. His stubborness was characteristic. As with Resale Price Maintenance and the EEC, once he had embraced an idea, he stuck to it with all the obstinate blindness of Neville Chamberlain.

Throughout most of the February 1974 election it looked as if Heath would win, as the Tories clearly expected. Their scare story was that the trade unions were being seized by dangerous left-wing extremists, and Heath was saving the country from their grip. The Labour Party's more moderate election theme was the Party's greater ability to avoid industrial conflicts, of which certainly the public were heartily sick. I concentrated on steady canvassing in North Battersea. We finished with a surprisingly enthusiastic meeting in Wandsworth Town Hall, with Wilson addressing 2000 people. His pledges on the Market were now reasonably clear. I repeated them to make them even clearer. On the final day (28 February), I told my wife between the close of the poll and the count that I felt the two main parties were dead level. She said she thought Labour was slightly ahead.

My own majority was declared about midnight as 10,400, rather better than 1970; and still later at ITV headquarters in Wells Street, it emerged that Labour was just winning. The final result was Labour 301; Conservatives 296. This somewhat further confirmed my pet theory that elections in a modern two-Party State tend towards a photo-finish, because if both sides contend equally skilfully for centre opinion, that is the most likely result. In the case of February 1974, however, I have little doubt that the balance was partly tipped by the belief that a Labour Government would grant a referendum on the Market, and that they would at least try to re-negotiate for better terms. Enoch Powell undoubtedly strengthened this belief by advising people to vote Labour for this reason. On Friday 1 March, the day after polling day, I joined a TV programme with Robin Day, Reggie Maudling, Jack Jones, Joe Gormley and Michael Clapham of the CBI, while Heath was making desperate but futile efforts to patch up a coalition with the Liberals. I argued that, having lost a majority in the Commons, Heath ought to resign and leave it to the Queen to look after the next Government. On Saturday he did; and we repaired to a gloriously restful week-end at the Bristwell Cottage amid spring sunshine. It was now seven years since I left the Government in 1967, and we at last had a Labour Government pledged to re-negotiation and a referendum.

After the February 1974 election the anti-Marketeers' new job was to ensure that the Labour Government carried out its long promised re-negotiation. I knew that Callaghan genuinely wanted to do so. But knowing also the FO too well, I could see all too clearly what might happen. They would warn him persistently of the danger of acting in any way not strictly legal within the Treaty of Accession. They would argue seductively that if the re-negotiation could leave the Treaty of Accession unaltered, every-thing would be so much easier. We anti-Marketeers on the other hand must fight for drastic changes in the CAP and parliamentary control of legislation, whether Treaties had to be amended or not; and if possible on non-compliance during the negotiation period. On 14 March, after I had spoken in a debate in the House on food prices and re-negotiation, Callaghan asked me to a private talk in his room at the FO. Despite much friendliness, I noticed signs already that he was slipping under FO pressure. He doubted whether we could prevent the food price increases due under Heath's Treaty going ahead in April. I pointed out the danger, if we accepted this, of drifting further and further into a corner from which it would be harder and harder to escape. He had evidently not squarely faced the dilemma: that if the letter of Heath's settlement were to be strictly followed, then basic changes in the CAP would be impracticable. This first talk disquieted me; as did reports reaching me at the same time of chaos at No. 10 due to the reassembly there of Wilson's 'kitchen cabinet'. However, we set about re-creating the all-Party Study Group in the House to monitor the re-negotiation; and Marten recruited representatives of the SNP and Ulster Unionists to join us. The Parliamentary Labour Group was also re-formed with Nigel Spearing as one of the most active members, now that Peter Shore, Deakins and other had joined the new Government. Shore was very ready, however, to maintain informal contact during the re-negotiation.

At the end of this March I left for Washington and Williamsburg, Virginia, for the annual Anglo-American Parliamentary Conference. Henry Kissinger, who was leaving for Moscow that evening, received our whole party on arrival for refreshments in his own room at the State Department. He was most fothcoming, pleased with Callaghan's pro-American first speech as Foreign Secretary, and evidently anxious for friends. Just a week later, back in London, while working at mid-day in my office at Westminster, I received a desperate phone call from the US Embassy, asking if I could get two tickets for Kissinger's twelve and four-teen-year-old son and daughter for Prime Minister's Question Time in the House. Kissinger, on his way back from Moscow, was spending half a day in London at the British Government's invitation; but the Sergeant-at-Arms and Speaker's Office had turned down his request for two tickets on the ground that they had none. It took me an immediate dash to the Sergeant-at-Arms, twenty minutes' argument, an appeal to the Chief Whips of both parties, and an offer to accept all the blame myself, to get the necessary tickets with five minutes to spare.

Callaghan again raised hopes with his first speech on re-negotiation at Luxembourg on 1 April, which reproduced verbally much of the Labour election manifesto. The Safeguards Campaign in mid-April held a press conference to publicise another pamphlet I had written, entitled *The Common Market; The Way Out*, which argued that if re-negotiation was not successful, the next stop must be for the UK to amend the European Communities Act and re-join EFTA. At this conference I read a letter to me from Harold Wilson of 5 November 1973, promising that a referendum would 'almost certainly' be held. This letter was written before Wilson became PM. But the press seized on it as a firm promise of a referendum by the Prime Minister, and gave it surprising publicity. I began to fear at this stage that we might be moving towards a Referendum in which anti-Marketeers generally could be compelled to reject terms which Callaghan as well as Wilson would be recommending. I therefore still fervently hoped that the re-negotiation would be serious and not the cosmetic exercise, confined mainly to the EEC budget, which the FO was plainly concocting. Shore warned me at the time that the 'mood was changing': i.e. weaker ministers, under constant prodding from the FO, were turning soft. The FO was evidently scared of the argument for re-joining EFTA, and it started to put out stories that this was somehow impossible: in which of course there was not a shred of truth. *The Times* published a plausible story on 28 May that the Cabinet a few days before had turned down proposals for a fundamental re-negotiation, and that only cosmetics – 'within the rules of the Community' – were now intended.

On 5 June I again spoke in Copenhagen to an enormously enthusiastic out-door rally of 5000 again by the Danish 'People's Movement Against the Common Market'. The leaders again told me that in Denmark the common people were dead against joining the Common Market, but almost all the 'top people' were in favour. They suspected what some called hospitality, and others bribery, but could not prove it. On the day before,

Callaghan had spoken again about re-negotiation in Brussels, and most people at Westminster found this markedly weaker than his speech of 1 April. On 6 June Callaghan asked Neil Marten and myself to meet him and talk. Since Marten was not available, Roger Moate, who as a young Tory showed much courage throughout these years in maintaining firm views on the Market, came with me instead. Naturally Callaghan maintained that he had not weakened since 1 April. He intended, he said, to fight on the CAP, and the budget contribution, and was he opposed to 'political and monetary union'. We pointed out that if there were no changes in the Treaties, the economic burden of the CAP could not be materially reduced. Callaghan was at least entirely firm on the referendum. But I was not much reassured by this whole conversation, as Callaghan was so clearly retreating gradually. Since he had amicably volunteered this conversation, I blamed myself afterwards for not arranging then and there for us to have regular talks while the re-negotiation continued. At least this might have been some antidote to the official pressure. From this moment onwards the liaison I had maintained on the Market with Callaghan ever since 1971 began to fade.

On the same day as the meeting with Callaghan, Peter Shore gave me a depressing account of discussions within the Government. He and Judith Hart had secured some gains on trade and aid; the Treasury had shown some life; but Fred Peart on the CAP had collapsed. He was now only asking for 'slaughter premiums' on beef, which were most desirable in themselves but only one part of the whole food issue. Shore said the anti-Marketeers in the Cabinet would stand together and reserve the right to attack the final settlement when it was reached. Slightly more cheering was a letter I received from Wilson promising 'fair treatment' for both main points of view in the referendum. I had written on behalf of the Safeguards Campaign observing that Labour, Liberal and Conservative would no longer be the main protagonists, and arguing that normal rules about broadcast time, money, etc., should apply to the 'Yes' and 'No' groups instead. Wilson's letter of 21 June said: 'I understand and sympathize with the point you make, and I accept the principle of fair treatment for the main points of view.' I asked whether this principle would be embodied in legislation, and he replied (1 August): 'A referendum raises a new situation, and I will see that the matter is looked at in the preparation of any legislation.' So the referendum was now at least an accepted fact. We had come some way in the four years since I had first advocated it in July and August of 1970.

At this time, believing that it was crucial for Parliament to scrutinize EEC legislation as long as we were members, I joined the Scrutiny Committee, a Select Committee of the Commons set up to tackle this job. Throughout the whole controversy some of us had tried to get MPs and the public generally to understand that the EEC was a matter not just of negotiation but of *legislation*. 'Regulations', 'decisions' (both claiming direct legal force without any 'enactment' by the British Parliament) and 'directives' were now pouring out of Brussels from the Council and Commission together at the rate of several thousand a year. All the Scrutiny Committee could do was to pick out a few as important, and recommend the House to debate them for at least one and a half hours. John Davies, ex-industrialist and Conservative MP, proved a most fair-minded Chairman of this very laborious Committee, though his views on the EEC were the opposite of mine. I had found him an engaging colleague when I was President of the Board of Trade and he was Director General of the CBI, and Committee work suited him. But he was neither a natural politician nor parliamentary speaker. Unfortunately the whole work of the Scrutiny Committee rested on the assumption that the Government would wait for a recommended debate in the House before assenting to legislation in Brussels. In a debate in the House on 11 June 1974, therefore, I asked Roy Hattersley, then an FO Minister, whether he could promise for the Government that no minister would thus assent to legislation until the recommended debate had been held. 'Yes certainly,' he replied. 'Any other arrangement would be intolerable.' And Callaghan, sitting beside him, nodded his head in ready agreement. It is a sad reflection on the whole Common Market controversy that some of us tried continuously over the next four years to get this modest undertaking at least embodied in a Parliamentary Resolution. Yet in July of 1978 Michael Foot was forced by his ministerial colleagues to go back on a promise he had given to do so.

By August of 1974 it was clear that events were shaping for a referendum in 1975, and to me regrettable but probable that anti-Marketeers would find themselves aligned on one side and the Government with the European Movement on the other. At this moment Clive Jenkins of ASTMS approached me and suggested a 'Fighting Fund' and a united anti-Market organization. I wholly agreed with him, but I was under no illusion about the enormous weight of finance, and propaganda which the establishment – one can only call it that as it embraced the government, Whitehall, the European Movement, the press and the City – would array against us. In reply we could mobilize a better case, a majority of so far unbrainwashed public opinion, two years' actual experience of the Market, many thousands of enthusiastic amateurs, and the great mass of the trade unions and Labour Movement. What was needed to make this alliance effective was united organization; and this was precisely what the Safeguards Campaign had been created to provide. Neil Marten, like Clive Jenkins, wholeheartedly favoured an all-Party movement, and we jointly consulted leaders of other anti-Market organizations. We had promises of co-operation from people as diverse as Jack Jones and Harry Urwin of the TGWU, Sir Robin Williams, Air Marshal Bennett and Christopher Frere-Smith, before we dispersed in August for a few weeks' respite.

But we had not yet fully reckoned with the psychological, as opposed to the physical and financial problems. In September on returning to London, and meeting Frere-Smith and Tory MP Richard Body at the Reform Club, we found to our surprise and concern that Frere-Smith had apparently again veered off into a phase of wishing to run 'Get Britain Out' as a rival army to the Safeguards Campaign. A major split at this late stage was a bleak prospect. Frere-Smith was a passionately sincere anti-Marketeer, had much energy and some organizing capacity; but at crucial moments his distaste for working in a team got the better of him. He did not seem to understand that a political crusade is either a team, or it is nothing. The Safeguards Campaign up to now had been remarkably free from the petty factions that normally beset voluntary movements; but now the balance tipped. Strangely enough, party-political differences had virtually nothing to do with this. I have never worked more smoothly with anyone than with Neil Marten and Robin Williams, both Conservatives.

Before these difficulties were overcome, however, the second 1974 election was announced in September; and the signs were that Labour would win, making the referendum a certainty. Indeed the fact of re-negotiation and the promise of the referendum strengthened the Labour appeal to floating voters. Peter Shore, in a talk with me on 20 September, specially welcomed the Labour manifesto pledge of a popular vote 'within twelve months'. He said Peart was now a lost cause (the retirement of Winnifrith as Permanent Secretary had removed his backbone): Prentice and John Morris had gone soft; and only Foot, Benn, Barbara Castle, and Ross were completely firm besides himself. The Safeguards Campaign sent a questionnaire to candidates during the October election, and I added a *Spectator* article backing the referendum. When the result of the election at Battersea was announced, my majority had risen from 10,400 to over 11,000, and I knew that Labour must have won with an increased majority, and that the referendum must come within twelve months.

This was equally clear, however, to the European Movement, who were evidently already building up a vast propaganda onslaught on the scale of a major party's general election campaign. It was urgent that anti-Marketeers should get themselves equally organized and united; but unhappily, despite great efforts, by Neil Marten in particular, completion of these arrangements was still held up for personal reasons throughout November and into December. More than one meeting had to be held either at the House or the *Spectator* office, nobly lent by Harry Creighton, (a strong anti-Marketeer and then owner of the *Spectator*), at which Neil Marten, Robin Williams, Frere-Smith, Clive Jenkins and either Jack Jones or Alex Kitson for the TGWU, Ian McTaggart, Crichton, Patrick Cosgrave, and myself normally attended. Having no desire to be chairman of the new organization, I suggested Neil Marten, as most likely to provide harmony. George Wigg emerged from the shadows at one point with some far-fetched rumour and then subsided again.

Eventually on 17 December, Jack Jones, who was offering to subscribe money as well as manpower, put his foot down to our great relief. He proposed the name 'National Referendum Campaign', which was not ideal; but anything was better than indecision. Neil Marten became Chairman of what was in effect a co-ordinating 'umbrella' for all existing anti-Market bodies; and Jack Jones, Frere-Smith and I became Vice-Chairmen, with Ron Leighton and one of Jack Jones's assistant, a New Zealander, Bob Harrison, who proved extremely valuable, as more or less full-time organizers. By January we had therefore an office in the Strand, a name, notepaper and a tiny nucleus of staff. Undoubtedly we suffered throughout the whole campaign from the delays and obstructiveness which had previously held back progress, and prevented a united propaganda effort being mounted throughout November and December. We were just in time, however, in January to present ourselves to the Government for the referendum legislation as a representative central body. As an experiment in harnessing together quickly a fairly numerous group of enthusiasts, prima donnas, and crusaders, none of whom will accept orders, it was in the end much more successful than for a time looked likely. The main credit for bringing it off should go to Neil Marten and Jack Jones, without whom there would have been no anti-Market 'umbrella' organization to steer the campaign, and to accept public money for this purpose. On 7 January the first NRC press conference was held with Neil Marten in the chair. On 23 January Harold Wilson announced that the referendum would be in June, and that dissident ministers could be allowed to campaign on the 'No' side if they wished.

In this January opinion polls still showed a majority opposed to EEC membership; and it was an open question whether the limitless financial and propaganda ammunition available to the European Movement – now called 'Britain in Europe' – could overturn the natural balance. Launched at this crucial moment, the NRC supplemented but did not supersede the Safeguards Campaign, Anti-Common Market League and Get Britain Out. The job of the dozen or so enthusiasts working at 422 The Strand was to link and service the local 'No' groups springing up all over the country, to supply them with speakers and propaganda 'literature', to publish the necessary national leaflets and pamphlets, to negotiate with the Government on finance and the broadcasting authorities on programmes, to organize the special TV and radio programmes allocated, to answer the press, to hold national press conferences and to produce the crucial 'No' pamphlet that the Government was to distribute to every voter at national expense. It was, in effect, to carry out the work of the headquarters of the political parties during a general election. All this was done, with very slender resources and the inevitable stops and starts, within little more than two months from the birth of the NRC.

As early as 10 February, Marten and I, as representing the official 'No' organization, were negotiating with Ted Short, then Leader of the House, on fair treatment for both sides in the legislation. As part of a referendum this was, of course, a complete innovation in the British political system. But Short was exceedingly helpful, and the legislation which had been very controversial went through remarkably smoothly. A day later Marten, Frere-Smith, Bob Harrison of the TGWU and I called on Sir Michael Swann, Chairman of the BBC, to ensure fair treatment for both sides on radio and TV; and a day or two after this on Lord Bowden (previously Herbert Bowden), Chairman of the IBA. Bowden was fully as co-operative as Swann. Indeed as he had, like myself, left the Government in 1967 on account of his views on the Common Market, he was doubtless personally not unsympathetic to us. By February the NRC had formed an 'Operations Committee', which met weekly and carried on right through to June. At this stage we were joined by John Mills, a young man of great capacity, who ran a successful business, and was then Labour Chairman of Camden Council Housing Committee, and with Harrison added just the straight organizing talent which was needed. He moved mountains in distributing vast piles of 'literature' all over the country in a very short time.

On 10–11 March, the final Summit Meeting was held in Dublin of the British and EEC ministers conducting the re-negotiation. Wilson joined in at the last moment, realizing apparently that if the amendments related solely to the budget and the whole of the CAP was untouched, and New Zealand and other Commonwealth trade unprotected, the whole operation could hardly be presented as even cosmetic. As it was now clear that the Government would announce the results, and its own recommendations, in a week or so, we set about via Labour Party channels planning a counter-demonstration for the dissident ministers who were to be allowed to declare their views. I was in touch throughout the 15–16 March weekend with Tony Benn and Peter Shore. The plan was for us to hold a meeting for Labour MPs in the Grand Committee Room, Westminster Hall, when the dissident Cabinet ministers would speak; a motion would be signed by all opposing the settlement as inadequate; a press conference held; and the motion placed on the Order Paper of the House. Invitations to 130 MPs to attend this meeting had been delivered by this time. Wilson rose on 18 March in the House to announce the re-negotiated terms and to add that the Government regarded the re-negotiation as a success and recommended the country to support the new settlement. At 6 p.m. that day our unofficial meeting assembled in the Grand Committee Room, and about seventy Labour Members turned up. Shore, Foot, Benn, John Silkin, Barbara Castle and Judith Hart attended from the Cabinet, and sat on the platform. I was voted into the chair. The ministers declared their opposition to the re-negotiated terms, and our prepared motion re-affirming this was signed at the meeting by about seventy of those present. At 7 p.m. that day Roy Hughes, as Chairman of the so-called 'Europe Committee' of the PLP and I met the press lobby correspondents and handed them the motion. By next morning it had attracted 118 signatures, and by two days later 138.

The Government's White Paper setting out the full 're-negotiated' settlement was published on 18 March. In substance it affected nothing but New Zealand butter and the prospective EEC Budget contribution. The Paper claimed credit for 'beef slaughter premiums', a species of deficiency payment, which were most welcome but could probably have been secured anyway without re-negotiation. In the case of New Zealand, there were no concessions on lamb or on cheese (which latter was still to be totally excluded from the UK); and on butter the period of exceptional imports on a descending scale was simply extended from the end of 1977 to 1980. After that year it became merely a 'derogation' which cannot legally continue if vetoed by any other EEC country. No concessions were obtained for Australian wheat, lamb, butter or cheese or for Canadian wheat or dairy produce. On the budget a highly complex formula for re-calculating the UK's future contribution was included, which was ingenious and obscure. It promised a 'refund' of part of the UK contribution if a number of conditions were simultaneously fulfilled. It was very unlikely that they could all be at the same time. The *Economist* (not an anti-Market paper) said that the new budget terms were likely to make the prospect worse than the EEC Commission itself had proposed. An even more conclusive comment was the actual consequence. By 1979 Britain had got virtually no benefit from the re-negotiated budget terms, and our net contribution had risen to £780 million, and was soon to be £1000 million.

By ill-fortune these intense efforts on the Common Market front were at this time for me superimposed on long, laborious and contentious sittings of the Commons' Wealth Tax Select Committee, of which I was Chairman. The more vociferous Conservative members of this conclave and the one vociferous Liberal (Pardoe) could not always resist showing the Party flag; and as many of my Labour colleagues were sparse in attendance, I found myself at times operating as simultaneously Chairman, Minister and Chief Whip for my own side (rather like being batsman, wicket-keeper and umpire at once); and the experience convinced me that Parliamentary Select Committees are often very fallible instruments, which should be used as little as possible. Their conclusions all too often represent the chance view of a chance group of individuals and depend on who happens to be attending when votes are taken. However that may be, for me in March 1975 the effort to keep all these balls in the air proved a bit too much. On the evening of 20 March, just after the convulsions over the Re-negotiation White Paper, and a fractious meeting of the Wealth

Tax Committee, I attended a constituency function at Wandsworth Town Hall and absurdly, for the first time in my life, fainted. As my daughter, Helen, was to be married to David Kennard of BBC TV in the Commons crypt two days later, I judged it wise to spend the next day in bed. The wedding, despite plaster on my forehead and a strike by the Commons restaurant staff settled in the nick of time, lived up to expectations. Jim Callaghan attended the reception, and was characteristically jovial on the subject of re-negotiation. At an unconventional party in the evening, also at the Palace of Westminster, a much above-average feast of oratory was served to us by J. K. Galbraith, Robin Day, my son Peter and the bridegroom. I was nervous of fainting at any moment and encouraged myself with the thought that this marriage at least proved how re-negotiation *can* succeed.

The House itself debated the re-negotiated terms on 7, 8, and 9 April. By now the Speaker was very generous in calling me on this issue, and I followed Callaghan, Margaret Thatcher and Jeremy Thorpe on the first day, all of whom of course supported the new terms – though the Conservatives had previously said the old ones could not be improved. I simply showed that the changes affected virtually nothing but New Zealand butter and the Budget, and even here were extremely tenuous. Very few others in the debate discussed the new agreement at all but instead returned to the old generalities. Since the Government had on its side the 'payroll vote' of Ministers and Whips other than the staunch dissenters, as well as almost the whole Tory Party and the Labour pro-Marketeers, they were bound to win the vote. But 144 Labour Members voted against the Government's motion, including Foot, Shore, Benn, Castle, John Silkin and Hart from the Cabinet. Even Walter Harrison, Labour Deputy Chief Whip, a Yorkshireman of strong opinions, voted against it. Michael Cocks, then Labour 'pairing Whip', later Chief Whip, who was not very well known to me at the time, in talking to me that week used some of the most violent language I have ever heard about the Common Market.

From early April on till the Referendum vote in June, the few of us most responsible for the National Referendum Campaign spent the day working at the Strand Office, speaking at meetings in the evening or giving regular press conferences. We started on 12 April with a public meeting in the Conway Hall, Red Lion Square, addressed by a Danish anti-Marketeer from the Strasbourg Parliament, Mr Maigaard, and John Winnifrith, Peter Shore and Neil Marten. At the start some storm-trooper elements from the National Front, who had arrived in protest against their exclusion from the NRC, tried to disrupt the meeting and intimidate the platform by barking like animals for some minutes on end. We had refused to accept the National Front or Communist Party as members of the NRC. Being Chairman at this meeting, I had to remain patient until they had yelled themselves hoarse rather than have them thrown out by the police, as they no doubt hoped. My distaste for these types deepened a lot further at that meeting. After they had trooped out, some of the best speeches I heard in the whole campaign were made by Winnifrith, Shore, Marten and the Dane. The latter gave a brilliant virtuoso performance, in a language not his own, full of wit, passion and argument.

At a meeting a fornight later at the Central Hall Westminster, to be addressed by purely Labour speakers, including Jack Jones and Benn, the police were worried that there might be simlar trouble. But this time no thugs of any kind were seen or heard. Next day, 26 April, the Special Labour Party Conference was held in the Sobell Sports Centre, Islington, to pass judgement on the re-negotiated terms. It was expected to reject them, and did so by a two-to-one vote; thus confirming our long struggle in the Party. But it was a strange conference in more ways than one. Wilson and Callaghan spoke, knowing they would be defeated on a major item of policy by their own Party. Jenkins sounded as if he was addressing any Party but his own. Strangest of all was the result of the Conference's decision. A Labour Party Conference cannot dictate to a Government which is responsible to Parliament. Nor can it even dictate any more than any non-parliamentary body can, to the Parliamentary Labour Party; and Gaitskell fought rightly for this latter principle. But it can dictate by the constitution of the Labour Party to Transport House and the Labour Party machine. Most of us in the Party had assumed that if the Party Conference rejected the re-negotiated terms, the Party machine would promote Party propaganda to that effect in the Referendum. It should have done. But at a meeting of the National Executive, following the Conference, the decision was taken in effect that Transport House should be neutral, and leave every local Party to do what it liked. No clear explanation was ever offered why or how the NEC reached this odd conclusion, which was contrary to what its members assured me they expected.

The effect of it, however, was both to intensify the glaring inequality between the forces ranged on both sides in the Referendum, and to load an even greater task and responsibility on the NRC. For the Government, the European Movement, the EEC Commission's 'Information Services', the Tory Party and Liberal Party machines were to campaign for a 'Yes' vote. But the Labour Party, which had formally and constitutionally decided in favour of a 'No' vote, was to be in practice neutral. We in the NRC were then in effect fighting a general election with a staff of a dozen or so, with a small number of others within the Safeguards Campaign, Anti-Common Market League, GBO, etc., against two political parties, the Government and the whole witches' brew of the European Movement and its plentiful progeny.

However, we set about it, even though some felt it was rather like the Hungarians in Budapest resisting Russian tanks with their bare fists. We next issued a pamphlet by John Winnifrith demonstrating beyond dispute that the imposition of the CAP on this country was bound substantially to raise the price of food. This, I believed, we should have made the central if not the only, theme of the whole campaign. It was true. It was overwhelmingly important for the whole nation. And the public both understood and believed it. Of course the separate issue of democratic and parliamentary sovereignty was equally important; and it was also true that a flood of imported manufactured imports from the Continent would, if we stayed in the EEC, increase unemployment. But some perfectly sincere and indeed fervent anti-Marketeers had not the propaganda sense to see that in public sentiment the cost of food was the dominant and decisive issue. And so since the NRC was a spontaneous gathering of all sorts of clans, the propaganda impact was probably dispersed and weakened. If there had been only one national newspaper on the 'No' side, and food had been the concentrated propaganda theme, I believe the impact would have been much greater. But in view of the huge disparity of propaganda forces, it probably would not have been decisive.

In the last weeks of the campaign, in the intervals of speech-making all over the country we concentrated at NRC HQ on getting out the leaflets, organizing the allotted TV programmes, and holding daily press conferences. Despite our tiny staff, ten million leaflets and pamphlets were distributed, besides of course the publicly delivered 'No' leaflet itself. For the TV and radio programmes a choice offered itself. Should we put on the air well-known characters like Michael Foot, Barbara Castle, Jack Jones or Neil Marten, whom many would recognize, but whose talks might savour of the old-fashioned 'political programmes'? Or should the actual job be done by TV and publicity professionals who would excel in contemporary technique and expound the general theme agreed by the NRC 'Operations Committee'? Rightly or wrongly we chose the latter, and had valuable help from Patrick Cosgrave, Paul Johnson, Ken Little of the BBC, and George Gale, flamboyant ex-editor of the *Spectator*. Main spokesmen on the TV programmes were Patrick Cosgrave and Paul Johnson. To the 'No' pamplet we devoted great pains. Since committee drafting is always clumsy, Enoch Powell and I alone produced first attempts, and these were polished by the two of us and George Gale. The finished product was not wholly satisfactory; but it was brief, simple and done on time, and at least as good as its opposite number.

At the daily press conferences, which were at the end of May moved from 55 Park Lane, the Safeguards Campaign office, to the Waldorf Hotel, Aldwych, to suit the journalists, and held in an appropriately less lavish hall there than those of 'Britain in Europe', we varied the personnel and the subject from day to day. Non-politicians joined in, such as William Pickles on the constitutional issues, and on the legal, Leo Price QC, and Patrick Neill QC, another barrister and later Warden of All Souls. For the last press conference on 3 June we mobilized Foot, Shore, Powell, Jack

Q

Jones, Barbara Castle, Neil Marten and a Norwegian anti-Marketeer who described how extremely well Norway was faring outside the Market.

The most serious and sustained argument however, on the real issue which I encountered outside the Commons in the entire campaign was a TV debate well-organized by Granada on 2 June. It followed the procedures of a Commons Standing Committee. Miss Harvie Anderson a Scottish Conservative MP acted admirably as Chairman. Speakers for the 'No' party were Shore, Marten, Powell, Judith Hart, Douglas Henderson of the SNP and myself; and for the 'Yes': Heath, Roy Jenkins, Maudling, Steel and Hattersley. Reasonable time was given, and the speeches were spontaneous back and forth as in a Commons Committee, with a five-minute limit on each. Shore and Powell were the strongest on our side and Jenkins for the opposition. We ourselves were thoroughly pleased with the programme, believing (as is doubtless human) that we had the best of it. By polling day, 5 June, the opinion polls had shown a consistent two-to-one majority on the 'Yes' side, and I did not believe we could win. All 5 June I spent in my own constituency with a loud-speaker. Next day we arrived at Earls Court for the count, and by the afternoon it was clear that the vote was following pretty closely the two-to-one ratio recorded by the polls. Later in the afternoon those who had worked themselves to exhaustion in the NRC enterprise since January, and other supporters, gathered in the House for a final farewell party given generously by Neil Marten.

The result of the Referendum was a historical tragedy. From it will flow,

The Common Market: British public opinion 1966-75

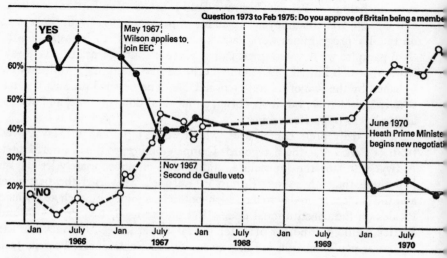

and are already flowing, a long series of national reverses, conflicts, and ever-growing economic burdens which will increasingly weaken this country. Had the 'No' votes won, it would have been the greatest triumph for genuine popular democracy, for the common people over the rich and selfish, in modern British history. But at least it was established by the Referendum that the British electorate had the constitutional and legal right, if they wished, to leave the Common Market. For everyone in the Campaign admitted that this would happen if the electorate voted 'No'. All speakers agreed that if Parliament could pass the European Communities Act, it could also repeal it. The Government's own pamphlet, delivered to every household, contained the memorable statement that our membership 'depends on the continued assent of Parliament'. On that assurance the country voted. The same Government pamphlet repeatedly affirmed that parliamentary authority must and would be maintained. No sanction whatever was given in the Referendum for moves towards a Federal EEC, or for steps towards Federation such as direct elections to an EEC Assembly or for economic and monetary union. None of these were advocated in either the Government pamphlet or that of 'Britain in Europe'.[1] The Safeguard Britain Campaign, which after the Referendum succeeded the Common Market Safeguards Campaign, was founded on the Referendum principle of the 'continuing assent of Parliament'.

One major puzzle, however, concerning the 1975 Referendum remains.

[1] Indeed economic and monetary union was explicitly repudiated in the Government pamphlet.

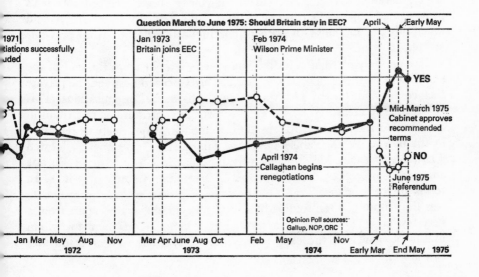

Why was it that public opinion, which according to all the evidence had for some years been generally opposed on balance to EEC membership, suddenly swung round and favoured it only for the few months in which the vote was taken? The graph on pages 486–7 taken from the *Sunday Times* of 8 June 1975, records that for seven years before 1975 as the nature of the EEC became increasingly understood, public opinion was almost continuously adverse to membership, with only short periods in early 1972 and late 1974 showing equality or a slight majority in favour. In the years after the Referendum the majority opposed to membership reasserted itself and was pronounced in 1977, 1978 and 1979. The broad explanation seems to be that as soon as the Referendum became a certainty, the European Movement and its allies demonstrated that by spending enough money on propaganda carried to the saturation point, votes could be bought. And they succeeded.

First, quite apart from money privately collected, three – not two – leaflets were distributed to every household in the country at public expense: two recommending a 'Yes' vote and one recommending 'No'. For though the National Referendum Campaign and Britain in Europe provided the 'No' and 'Yes' leaflets respectively for public distribution, the Government itself added a third, recommending 'Yes'. It was perhaps not wholly surprising that with leaflets nationally distributed in the ratio of two to one, the vote should have been in the ratio of two to one. This was an indefensible decision of the Government. Under the Attlee Government, and under previous British Governments, the guiding principle had always been that (apart from accepted uses such as ministers' speeches and White Papers) public money should not be used for publicity purposes, except on non-controversial issues such as public health and safety, national savings, etc. Heath, of course, first breached this with propaganda leaflets distributed to Post Offices in 1971 and 1972, and unhappily the Labour Government continued this decline from previous standards.

The publicly circulated leaflets, however, were far from the end of the story. On top of this, a vastly greater disparity existed between the private finance available to the pro-Market and anti-Market organizations. This is most easily measured by the total of private contributions to Britain in Europe and the National Referendum Campaign respectively as recorded in the official White Paper[2] published later. The Government allocated £125,000 to each side. But by private subscription Britain in Europe amassed £996,508, and the National Referendum Campaign £8611. In terms of total finance available the ratio in favour of 'Yes' propaganda was thus more like ten to one. The White Paper shows that apart from a very few large donations from very wealthy men, the payment to Britain in Europe came from the leading firms in the City and the largest companies

[2] Cmnd 6251.

in British industry. The roll-call includes almost every major firm on the Stock Exchange, and most of the joint stock and other banks. But in yet further additions to the expenditure of Britain In Europe and the Government, the European Communities Information Service also joined in with large but unpublished propaganda spending in the referendum. This must surely have been the first time in British history that a foreign governmental organization, using public money, was allowed to finance massive one-sided propaganda during an appeal to the electorate. Mr Douglas Evans records[3] that ECIS's budget for 'public relations' rose in 1975 to the colossal figure of £7 million annually, a very large proportion of which was to be spent by their London, Cardiff and Edinburgh offices. Since in the 1960s about one-third of the ECIS propaganda budget was spent in Britain, the ECIS probably spent nearer £2 million than £1 million on the Referendum campaign – additionally of course to Britain in Europe and the Government.

As against a more than ten to one financial advantage for the pro-Marketeers, the ratio of public meetings held was estimated at about four to one in their favour by BBC representatives at a discussion organized by the Media Society in a Commons Committee Room on 17 June 1975. No estimate of the ratio in leaflets distributed at non-Government expense is available to me; but I would guess it was at least four to one. And in addition to all this, of course, virtually the whole press, as well as the Government machine and the two political parties which were active, joined in on the pro-Market side. Only a few papers like the *Financial Times* and the *Guardian* included signed articles from each side. In all these circumstances, and on a dispassionate view it is remarkable that 8,470,000 people voted 'No', and that the 'Yes' ratio was not far greater than two to one. Indeed it is strong evidence that if the propaganda flow had been equal each way, the electorate would have voted 'No'; a conclusion again confirmed by the fact that when the deafening propaganda barrage was largely withdrawn, it was only a matter of months before the opinion polls again showed an anti-Market majority.

Though this must be the broad conclusion, nevertheless when the dates are closely examined, one further question about the Referendum demands an answer. As the chart shows (pages 486–7), the 'No' majority in the country began to decline gradually in early 1974, and the two lines were virtually level at the turn of the year. By March the 'Yes' vote was well ahead; and by April it had reached the two to one ratio shown in the final result. Indeed in the last few weeks up to 5 June, the 'Yes' vote was receding and the 'No' vote rising again. Yet the main pro-Market propaganda chorus did not reach full blast, and the leaflets did not descend, till April and May. Why did the figures move so sharply in January and February of 1975? David Butler in an article adjoining the *Sunday Times* graph of

[3] D. Evans, *While Britain Slept : The Selling of the Common Market* (London, 1975), p. 101.

8 June 1975 called this the 'mid-winter switch'. The only rational explanation I can see for this early switch would be that constant press and radio reports in the winter months of 'success' in the re-negotiation, culminating in the final public recommendation of the settlement by the Government in March 1975, before the public could clearly understand the facts, carried as much weight with the voters as the whole subsequent propaganda barrage. Since a third of the Cabinet publicly opposed the settlement, this is to assume a remarkably high degree of public trust in the word of Wilson and Callaghan. It is, however, consistent with the recorded fact that the balance swung towards the 'Yes' side at the time of Heath's alleged success in reaching agreement in January 1972, and again when Callaghan started to re-negotiate in the summer of 1974. It would also be consistent with the later disillusion shown by the electorate, when the failure of re-negotiation to alter the CAP or the Common Fisheries Policy or the Rome Treaty became apparent to all. But to any would-be objective historian of these events the precise timing of the crucial 'mid-winter switch' must still present something of a puzzle.

Such was the story of the Referendum in its national perspective. To me personally the disappointment of such a travesty of free democratic choice was a little tempered by the fact that since the early months of the year I had privately believed the result to be inevitable. I also derived some melancholy satisfaction at least from the confirmation of my belief, held since schooldays, that you cannot win a major battle for the minds of the electorate if the whole British press is against you. In earlier battles – against appeasement, for full employment, for the Development Areas, against Marxism, and for a drastic redistribution of wealth – fortune had been on my side. In June 1975, however, as one looked forward rather than backward, the most saddening thought was of national misfortunes to come. By the late 1970s some of the consequences had become clear for all to see. The economic effects had proved more damaging than most of us pessimists and sceptics had foretold. All the promises held out by the pro-Marketeers that there would be no major difference in food prices inside and outside the EEC have been proved to be sheer nonsense. The 'Yes' pamphlet, issued by Britain in Europe for the Referendum (under the name of Roy Jenkins, Edward Heath and Jo Grimond) said this: 'If anything, the Community has saved us money on food in the past few years. . . . The days when big surpluses of cheap food could be bought around the world have gone, and almost certainly gone for good. Sometimes Community prices may be a little above world prices, and sometimes a little lower.' This was the most cynical deception of ignorant people, in the whole murky story.

The reality has been this. By 1977 and 1978 the price of grain in the EEC (including feeding stuffs), the basis of most foods, was double the world price; and of other standard foods more than double. The levies on food imported by the EEC were themselves as great or greater than the world price itself: a more vicious level of food taxation than was ever imposed by our own Corn Laws between 1818 and 1846. Best authority for this is the EEC Commission itself. In its agricultural report for 1977,[4] it said this: 'By the beginning of 1977–8 the import levies for all the major cereals were greater than the world market prices for the cereal itself: i.e., the world market prices were less than half the Community threshold prices.' The EEC Commission's own Report[5] for 1977 gives the average price of wheat as 116 per cent above the world price, barley 106 per cent above, maize 103 per cent above, beef and veal 96 per cent above and butter 288 per cent above. So far from there being no 'big surpluses of cheap food' in the world, by 1977–8 the United States was again restricting grain output because it could not be sold; Australia was destroying beef herds because of the exclusion of beef from the EEC; and the EEC's own huge 'surpluses' were being sold abroad to Russia and other countries outside at half or less of the world price.

The imposition of the CAP on this country, only temporarily and partially alleviated, has therefore indisputably raised the price of food to the British family far above what they would have paid outside. And it has raised the price not merely of the half of our food which is imported, but of the home-produced half also, because this is the essence of the CAP. But in the attempt to minimize the effect on the retail price paid by the consumer, pro-Market propaganda has indulged in two statistical tricks, which ought to be exposed. First in the price of 'food', as quoted, all foods like tea and coffee, unaffected by membership of the EEC, have been included. The rise in the price of those foods which *have* been affected by the CAP is of course much larger. Secondly, no allowance has been made for the fact that distribution margins are normally calculated by traders as a percentage. This means as a matter of arithmetic that if distributive costs are half the final retail price, and if the farm gate price rises from 100 to 200, the final price to the consumer will rise from 200, not to 300 but to 400. If this is allowed for in the calculation, the rise in the retail price to the British consumer caused by EEC membership of foods affected by the CAP, though not precisely calculable, must (in view of the figures quoted above from the EEC Commission) be nearer 50 per cent than the 10 or 12 per cent often quoted.

Such is the record of membership in terms of food prices. But the main economic damage to Britain, partly due to this, was bound to be the unnecessary load on the balance of payments, the equally unnecessary rise in the cost of living, the resulting loss of real income, and the industrial conflicts the latter would naturally provoke. The burden on the balance of payments consists of three main parts: the higher price of food imports,

[4] *The Agricultural Situation in the Community*, 1977 Report.
[5] Pp. 202 and 203. In 1979 these percentages were very similar.

the net Budget payment, and the increased visible deficit in trade in manufactures with the old EEC Six. In my estimates in the late 1960s and early 1970s of the net balance of payments loss, I put the total as of the order of £500 million or £1000 million a year in the money values of those years, which would have meant a figure somewhere between £1000 million and £2000 million in the money values of the late 1970s. The most authoritative estimates in these later years, and broadly accepted by the Government's statisticians, has been that of Messrs Richard Bacon, Wynne Godley and Alister McFarquhar in the *Bulletin of the Cambridge University Department of Applied Economics* of March 1979. Counting only two elements in the payments burden – the Budget contribution and dearer food – these Cambridge statisticians put the 'direct cost to the balance of payments' in 1978 at £1137 million.

To this, however, has to be added the increased deficit in trade in manufactures with the EEC Six. The relevant figure here is our trade balance, not with the remaining eight members of the EEC, but with the original Six, because we had already by 1972 established free trade in industrial products with Denmark and Ireland, and this would have continued anyway had we not joined the EEC. It is our trade with the Six which was changed by membership. One must also exclude trade in food and oil from the comparison, as food is covered in the Cambridge estimate, and the rise in the price of oil imports would have occurred anyway whether we joined the EEC or not. If, therefore, trade in goods other than food and oil with the EEC Six is examined, the record is as follows. In 1978, before the UK joined the EEC, we achieved a small surplus of £195 millon in trade in goods other than food and oil with the EEC Six. By 1979 this had changed to a deficit of £3800 million.[6] This is a far greater deficit than any of the pessimists predicted before entry. (My own forecast was less than £200 million). In face of these figures, some have argued that the UK has also moved into deficit in trade with the rest of the world as well as the EEC in these years. But this is the reverse of the truth. Our trade balance with the rest of the world in goods other than food and oil greatly *improved* in these years. It rose from a surplus of £1186 million in 1970 to a surplus of £2800 million in 1978.

It can secondly be argued that though we suffered a huge swing into deficit after membership in our trade in manufactured goods with the EEC, this may not have been wholly due to membership. But two facts suggest strongly that a very large part of the deficit was due to membership. First, membership involved *both* lowering our tariffs to zero on manufactures imported from very strong industrial exporters, particularly Germany, *and* a rise in our industrial labour costs relatively to these competitors, due to the artificial raising of our food prices. These two factors were bound to swing the balance against us; and it was only the extent of the swing which

[6] For these figures see Hansard *Annual Statement of Trade, Overseas Trade Statistics*.

serious forecasters all underestimated. If, however, one concludes that only *half* the increased deficit incurred in trade in manufactures since joining (I am sure an underestimate) was due to joining, then a further load of about £1900 million on this account has to be added to the £1137 million estimated by the Cambridge analysis for 1978. Thus in trade with the EEC (even if food is omitted) the 'great home market of 200 millions', which was publicized *ad nauseam* in pro-Market propaganda has turned out in reality to be a great UK deficit of at least £1900 million. Yet Heath's White Paper of July 1971 had said this: 'The Government do not believe that the overall response of British industry to membership can be quantified in terms of its effect on the balance of trade. They are confident, however, that this effect will be positive and substantial, as it has been for the Community.' In addition, an added deficit in manufactured trade of the order of £1000 million means increased unemployment of 200,000 or 300,000.

The final assessment must therefore be that EEC membership had added a wholly unnecessary and lasting burden of something like £3000 million to the UK balance of payments by the late 1970s. This cancels out much of the extra balance of payments' advantage of North Sea Oil in these years. It also means that, if the Cambridge statisticians are right in judging that an extra £1000 million loss on the balance of payments involves a £3000 million loss in GNP (due to the deflation necessitated), then the real loss in GNP has been at least twice that figure. Nor is the final balance sheet complete without mentioning the damage to the fishing industry which, though not quantifiable, was heavy and lasting.[7]

The intelligent pro-Marketeer will not deny the economic damage done to Britain; nor will he attempt to pretend that these are merely short-term losses to be outweighed by mysterious 'dynamic' economic gains, because the absurdity of this has been too clearly demonstrated. He will argue that the economic loss is somehow outweighed by 'political' gains; by 'unity', harmony, inter-dependence, or what you will. But is it? In reality all the fields of reasonable international co-operation as already pointed out,[8] were open to us without joining, as members of the UN, IMF, World Bank, NATO, the Commonwealth, EFTA and the OECD. Also perfectly practicable was technological co-operation with or without the EEC, as the Concorde (started long before we joined), the use of Rolls-Royce engines in US aircraft, and weapon-sharing with NATO, and many other projects testify. What did the EEC, politically, add? Here one moves from the partially quantifiable economic gains and losses to regions of pure conjecture. But it is at least arguable that British membership of the EEC has generated as much political conflict in Western Europe as it has averted – if not more. It has enforced an unnatural attempt at uniformity

[7] See p. 461.
[8] See chapter 14.

or conformity in policies where it is better for each country to act differently. On agriculture, on food, on fisheries, on monetary policy, and numerous minor issues, there would be far less conflict and sporadic bitterness, if, for instance, Britain and France both pursued the policies that suit them best, and desisted from trying to force the other to conform. Our political relations with many countries outside the EEC are much better than with France, just because we are not, in the case of our non-EEC friends, trying to force each other to do things which we do not wish to do. The 'political gains', to put it very modestly, are a matter of opinion. The economic losses are lasting, severe and indisputable.

In the first days after Hugh Gaitskell's death in January 1963 I began to fear that these blunders would be committed and these consequences brought down on the country. It seemed to me then that the Conservative Party's deep passion for indirect taxes, and food taxes especially, as a substitute for direct taxation, the City's longing for *laissez-faire* economic policies and freedom from exchange control and high taxes, and the age-long hankering of the farming and landowning interests for high agricultural protection, could only be resisted in the end by somebody with Gaitskell's resolution and force of character. His basic loyalty – and any who doubts this should read his October 1962 speech – was to this country, and to the US connection, to NATO and the Commonwealth, as being in the last resort the most trustworthy defences of the welfare of the British people. Had his policies been followed, this country would in any case have experienced a relative loss of economic and military strength, compared with the US, the Soviet Union and probably Germany. But we would have remained, not the head, but the centre of a liberal Commonwealth trading system, the centre of a possibly expanding EFTA, the closest ally of the United States, and a pre-eminent champion of human rights and genuine parliamentary democracy. Gaitskell would, I am sure, have grasped with both hands de Gaulle's offer of February 1969, just as Bevin grasped General Marshall's offer of June 1947.

Such is the might-have-been. Instead of it, we have had imposed on us for the time a second-best which is crippling, but not fatal, to this country. The wisest course for us now, having come as far as we have, would be for Parliament so to amend the European Communities Act as to restore to us economic and trading freedom in a wider world, exempt us from the CAP and Common Fisheries Policy, and provide that no legislation binds the British public unless and until it is approved by the British Parliament. If this were considered equivalent to leaving the Community, so be it. Until these basic reforms are achieved, the aim must be to moderate by all practicable means the harm being inflicted on our constitution and economic life, and in time to transform the EEC into a larger and looser association of all democratic nations willing to join, without excessive barriers against the rest of the world, and without supra-national institutions.

Nevertheless, though some of what has been thrown away can still be thus regained, the damage already done has been immense and enduring; and it will be a long time, if ever, before this country regains the strength and influence which it would have retained if less narrow-minded policies had been followed. We were offered the better alternative in 1969, and as in 1938 we rejected it. Those were the two prime blunders, and tragedies, of these years.

Epilogue

At the end of a narrative like this, it is possible only to assert, not fully to argue, the personal conclusions on some of the major questions to which these years have led one. Unhappily in the case of the UK the unnecessary controversy over the EEC has diverted far too much time, and therefore space in this record, from what should have been the most important issues of this century. Some of these are common to the whole free world, or the entire world; and others special to this country. Of those which appear to affect most of the non-Communist world, one of the more sobering for those of us who remember the 1920s and 1930s remains what must reluctantly be admitted to be a widespread fall in intellectual and moral standards since those years. Making all allowances for the natural human tendency to idealize the past, and for the uncertainty of the evidence, and having for a long time myself hoped to regard the change as a liberating and civilizing process, I concede partial defeat when confronted, in this country and elsewhere, with lower standards in education and the press, disrespect for the law, vandalism, drug-taking, crime, pornography, terrorism, and all the rest. While so much has improved, something has also been lost. The permissive society *can* become a demoralized society.

No doubt these historical swings – from austere standards to licence and back again – have long been familiar from Greece and Rome to the Puritan era, the Restoration, the Regency and the Victorian Age. But they have usually had a perceptible cause, and I have often asked myself, what is the cause in our century? It is no good offering as an explanation something peculiar to Britain, since the change is plainly far more wide-ranging. If I had to guess at the answer, my guess would be that the decline of dogmatic religion has not yet in the twentieth century been replaced by any clear ethical standards or teaching, and an intellectual void has thus been created. And so false gods such as Marxism and Fascism have found the field open. It is also hard to resist the conclusion that the spread of the commercial motive in the press, TV and the cinema, and the doctrine of giving the public what it wants, almost without limit, must bear some of the blame for the growth of crime and violence, throughout much of the

Western world. My generation, which did more to dismantle the religious dogmas than to replace them, must also accept some responsibility for not fully foreseeing the consequences. We were too afraid of being accused of moralizing and preaching. But if we did not ourselves believe in any ethical standards, for what reason did we fight against Hitler? And if we did, should we not have the courage to assert them?

Another conclusion from the experience of these years, which applies throughout the non-Communist world, and which I would offer with much more assurance, is this. Genuine free institutions and parliamentary government cannot easily, if at all, be preserved without a major measure of redistribution of income and wealth by the state. For one reasonably clear truth seems to me to emerge from the long economic controversy started by Adam Smith. Market forces are often a good way of producing goods and services, but a bad way of distributing income or property. Public control is a bad way of producing goods but a good way of distributing income. So both the *laissez-faire* economists and the traditional socialists were half wrong and half right. There is no moral defence for the grossly unequal distribution of income which unrestricted market forces normally generate; and the richer a country gets, the more grotesque the inequalities would become under pure *laissez-faire*. The crude market economy means, not one man one vote, but one pound one vote. And when private inheritance is added to uncontrolled market forces, the distribution of property becomes ludicrous. Yet it has proved perfectly practicable in the most advanced industrial democracies, notably Scandinavia, for far-reaching re-distribution of national income and private wealth to be carried through by the democratic state, while production in industry and agriculture is in general left to private ownership and market forces. Nor can it be a coincidence that the countries where this has been substantially achieved – in Northern Europe, the US, Canada, Australia, New Zealand and a few others – are those where human rights and democratic institutions are also most stable and secure. In others where re-distribution has either not been attempted or has so far failed – Brazil, Argentina, much of South and Central America, some Mediterranean countries, Iran and others in Asia – democratic government is precarious or non-existent, while the privileged and unprivileged fight it out. In southern Europe – Spain, Portugal, Italy and Greece – the issue hangs in the balance.

If, therefore, we genuinely want to preserve free institutions, the first necessity is to correct by democratic decision the share-out of wealth which sheer market competition would throw up. Of course it is possible to push the correction too far and disrupt the output of wealth which we are seeking to distribute. In my book *Socialism in the New Society* I argued that the optimum point could only be discovered by experience. For what it is worth, my own opinion is that in Britain in the late 1970s, having achieved so many of the reforms which some of us have advocated since the 1930s, we may have for the moment gone far enough in the case of earned incomes after tax, but not of great inherited private fortunes. Meanwhile new and gratuitous inequalities have been introduced by the CAP and food taxes, by extravagant tax privileges for owner-occupier's of houses, and by the 1979 Tory Government's assault on most forms of social spending. We must, above all, therefore, guard against those who attack progressive direct taxation as such and who urge a huge switch back to taxes on food and necessities, in disregard of the disastrous threat this would mount in time to the democratic process. To those who blame all human ills on high progressive taxation, I would answer: consider Sweden, which maintains as high direct taxation as any country in the world, and also not merely a stable democracy but the highest real standard of living ever achieved. Would you rather live in Sweden or Argentina?

The above reflections put into perspective, I believe, the traditional debate throughout the Western world over public and private ownership. It is the distribution of income and property, not the ownership of productive assets, which primarily matters. The obsession with ownership really dates from the years when Marx grew up, and when ownership of land had been for generations the principal source of wealth. Decisions on forms of ownership should be made out not on doctrinal but on technical, and practical grounds. Almost the only safe generalization is that 100 per cent public ownership is unsuitable for manufacturing industry, except probably where the immense appetite for capital of advanced industries, such as steel, aircraft, shipbuilding and nuclear power, is too great for private enterprise to meet. It would be a great gain for rationality if the frontiers of public and private ownership ceased to be an issue of violent party controversy. But one other truth does, to my mind, stand out clearly. Those industrial processes which remain in private ownership must be left with the reasonable freedom and reasonable level of profit, without which private business cannot operate effectively. Where we have private enterprise, let the state help not hinder it. Probably in the 1970s in Britain the squeezing of private business profits, and the hampering of its room for manoeuvre by all sorts of restrictions and obligations, have gone far enough, if not a little too far.

A further baffling dilemma has dominated economic debate in the industrial democracies in the 1970s. This again has affected, not just the UK, but almost all industrial democracies in the 1970s. Even in the US, consumer prices were rising in 1978–9 at 9 or 10 per cent and the President was forced to introduce a full-scale voluntary 'incomes policy'. The dilemma is this. Do we restrain rising prices, and falling money values (wrongly called 'inflation'), by a deliberate governmental 'incomes policy', or by remote control of the quantity of money (wrongly called the 'money supply') and the Budget? Here, basically, the answer seems to me plain. Trade union power has in many industrial countries in the 1970s reached a point at which reliance on remote control must mean *either* ever-rising prices, or more probably chronic unemployment and stagnation in output and in real living standards. The great achievement of Keynes and those of us who argued against deflation in the 1930s was to concentrate attention on the flow of money incomes and spending rather than the crude quantity or stock of money; and to establish that in any period when pay rates were not actually reduced, the annual flow of money incomes and spending must rise as fast as productive capacity if full employment was to be maintained.

It was thus established – and this was the great advance – that the Great Depression, the historic trade cycle and cyclical unemployment were a monetary, not technological phenomenon. It was this Keynsian revolution which gave us the full employment and world economic progress of the first twenty-five post-war years. But confusion returned when attention was switched back to the quantity rather than the flow of money. For the quantity can only affect prices by its influence on the flow. Naturally the quantity after a point does influence the flow; but every economist since the French Revolution has known that. Keynes, himself, and those of us who had a hand in compiling the 'Employment Policy' White Paper of 1944 never thought that demand could simply be pushed up and up and full employment thus easily maintained, if pay rates were forced up faster than the increase in output of goods and services. This is shown by the following crucial sentence in the 1944 White Paper which was approved by Keynes and James Meade as well as others: 'Action taken by the Government to maintain expenditure will be fruitless unless wages and prices are kept reasonably stable.'

It is an arithmetical truism, and not a new discovery of the 1970s, that if pay rates and therefore money incomes are increased faster than the supply of goods and services, then the general price level must rise. This follows from the fact that the total value of all goods and services sold must equal the total of money spent on them. On analysis, therefore, the debate between so-called Keynesians and so-called monetarists is largely a false controversy. In actual history from 1945 to the late 1960s pay rates in the advanced industrial democracies were not forced up much faster than productive capacity. So prices only rose slowly, and in the United States and Germany at times hardly at all. But by 1970 steeper pay rises began to be demanded and granted in most industrial countries, and prices began to rise faster. Though the huge rise in oil prices aggravated this, it cannot have been the sole cause, because the accelerated rise started several years before the end of 1973, when the explosion in oil prices began. In Britain pay rises of 20 to 25 per cent were being asked for and granted in 1969 and 1970. The only explanation which seems to me to fit the facts of the story is that trade unions, which had the power from the start of the full employment epoch in 1945 thus to force up rates, did not fully realize that they had this power till their knowledge, sophistication and resources had grown over the next twenty or twenty-five years. When they did realize it, the conditions of the 1944 White Paper were no longer fulfilled, and a new problem and threat to full employment emerged. The reason for the growing unemployment and so-called 'world-recession' of the 1970s was the excessive pay claims enforced by strike threats in these years, aggravated by the oil cartel.

The new circumstances forced those trying to manage the modern economies into a new dilemma. As pay and price rises accelerated (in the UK in 1974-5 for instance) the authorities could either let the money available rise fast enough for all to be employed at the high rates; in which case prices would rise still faster. Or else if they restricted the money available, unemployment must rise. Most governments decided, I believe rightly, that public opinion would not tolerate prices rising at 50 or 100 per cent a year. Therefore the money available was restricted through banking and budgetary measures; and unemployment increased rapidly. The only way out of this dilemma is for the government to limit directly the rate of rise in pay rates. That is the case for an incomes policy: which is, I reluctantly believe, the greatest single necessity for economic management, and in some countries the only road back to full employment, in an age when organized labour (usually the 'shop floor' and not the union bureaucracies) have discovered that in our highly capitalized modern economy they have the power to enforce pay increases which are bound to push up prices generally.

The only alternative policies are either to allow the 'inflation' to accelerate, or to restrict the total rise in money incomes by the remote control of limiting the quantity of money created by the banks. The latter method (adopted by the UK Conservative Government of 1979) is the expedient allegedly advocated by extreme monetarists. But to limit pay increases by this very remote control is rather like trying to steer a car from the back seat with two pieces of string tied to the wheel. You could only do it if you went painfully slowly, and even then for not very long. In practice, except possibly in the US and German economies, such monetary control without any direct incomes policy would mean prolonged deflation, high unemployment, no growth, and a very low level of investment. It would in fact, particularly in the UK, produce precisely the effects which economic policy should seek to avoid; and it would relegate this country rapidly to a far weaker comparative political and military situation in the world. It would also involve rigid restraint on pay in the public sector, and none in the private, which would generate intolerable political strains.

Far better, because it affords reasonable hope of high employment, growth and rising real incomes, is a balanced combination of monetary, budgetary, and a direct income restraint. Direct restraint of incomes is for obvious reasons exceedingly difficult; but it is not impossible. It has been achieved over periods of years in various advanced countries; and it was in g achieved with growing success by the Prices and Incomes Board set up by the 1964 Labour Government, and so unwisely abolished by Heath. Such control cannot be statutory, because the law cannot be enforced against determined strikers. But what it can do is to mobilize public opinion; so that the cases where all restraint is defied are reduced to the minimum. Two stages are involved in this type of policy; first a political decision, if possible agreed with unions and employers, that x per cent must be the non-inflationary pay norm for the year in question; and secondly some last-resort independent tribunal to decide, around the average, what the award should be in particular disputes which cannot be settled by ordinary collective bargaining.[1] Such an umpire cannot in my view be a Government or Parliament, since these are not suited to adjudicate on individual cases; but an authority much more on the lines of the Prices and Incomes Board or in some respects of a court of law. Certainly it is possible that some recalcitrant group will sooner or later strike against the umpire as well as the democratic government's incomes policy. But if that is going to happen in these circumstances, it will happen anyway, and no human contrivance – except perhaps long-term education – can stop it. The solution suggested here is not an infallible remedy. But I put it forward as, for Britain anyway, worth trying and the best hope we have. I believe we shall come to it in the end. Perhaps, one obstacle would be removed if trade unions moderated their obsession with 'collective bargaining', and came increasingly to look after the interests of their members in other ways.

One problem, however, has been rightly regarded as special to the UK; low industrial productivity and a slower rise from year to year in real output. But the nature of the problem has also been misunderstood. First it is not true that the UK economy in real terms did worse after 1939 than in previous periods. It did better. Secondly it is not true that real living standards per head were lower in the UK before entry into the EEC and the oil price explosion than in our Continental neighbours (with the possible exception of Germany and the Scandinavian countries). On the first comparison – with previous periods – the best criteria is the rise or fall in the volume of UK exports. If this is taken as 100 in 1900, it was 120 in 1921, 86 in 1932, 98 in 1946 and 504 in 1977. Our exports may have not risen fast enough since 1945; but they have risen faster in volume than at any previous period in this century, even though they have fallen as a percentage of world exports. The mistake has arguably been that we have imported too much, not exported too little. Secondly up to 1970 our real standard of living per head (as opposed to real Gross National Product per head) was not far different from most of our Continental neighbours. That has been demonstrated by a UN analysis published in 1975 and revised in 1978, and already quoted in this book.[2] This, the only reliable assessment

[1] These proposals are set out in much greater detail by James Meade in *The Fixing of Money Rates of Pay*, (Department of Applied Economics, University of Cambridge).

of comparative real-incomes and consumption made by a responsible international authority since the war, shows that UK real consumption per head was about the same in 1970 and 1973 as those of Germany, Holland, Belgium and France, and higher than Italy's; partly due, certainly, to our consuming too much of our total income, but also largely due to the low level of prices of necessities, mainly food, in the UK. What did actually depress UK real standards after 1973 was the five-fold rise in oil prices and the imposition on us of the CAP. But the rise in oil prices affected other countries also. It is the CAP which has unnecessarily and avoidably lowered our standards.

When these two persistent distortions are removed, the real problem can be seen in perspective. It is certainly true that we have consumed too much of our total income, and that our real output, productivity and therefore real incomes, have after a rapid rise from 1946 to 1951, risen more slowly than in most of the industrial countries – though not notably so than in the US. But here another confusion intervenes. For though real output has risen more slowly here in these years than in some other countries, it nevertheless has *risen substantially* and faster than in most previous periods. As a US economist[3] accurately summed it up in an article in the *Sunday Times* of 30 September 1978: 'In the first thirty years after the Second World War Britain enjoyed the fastest rate of economic growth in its recorded history and it has transformed the living standards of ordinary people.'[4] Between the accession of Elizabeth II in 1952 and the Jubilee in 1977, real incomes rose about 80 per cent; and the standard of living *was* doubled, if not in twenty-five years, then approximately in thirty. Whether you take the test of housing, educational opportunity, diet, holidays, health, infant mortality, the number of cars, telephones, etc., not to mention TV sets; by any of the critieria normally used, real incomes had nearly doubled in these years, and were rising again up to 1978 after a drop of a few per cent in 1976–7. Few would deny that many non-quantifiable satisfactions had improved at least as fast.

Nevertheless, productivity certainly remained comparatively low in this country and was rising more slowly. It is true of course that the UK's *percentage* of world production and trade was bound to decline in the second half of the twentieth century both because its nineteenth century lead was temporary, and because the recovery from the war of Russia, Germany, Italy, Japan and China was bound to depress our *proportion*. This would not, however, explain absolute low productivity. It is also true that in the 1950s and 1960s, the defeated nations, Germany and Japan, did best; and the victorious nations, the US and Britain, did comparatively worse. The losers, very probably, worked harder because at first they had more to

[2] See Chapter 16.
[3] Bernard Nossiter, 'The Leisurely British', *Sunday Times*, 30 September 1978.
[4] David Watt in the *Financial Times* (3 June 1977) gives figures substantiating this.

recover. But in the case of British manufacturing industry, the evidence seems very strong that the removal in two stages of restraints on manufactured imports (of quotas at the end of the 1950s and tariffs through EEC entry) has had a major effect in slowing down both production and growth of capital. But beneath all this, is there some deeper psychological or institutional cause which has held back British industrial progress?

This I still find hard to answer. I can think of three influences special to this country which *may* have been partly responsible. First, the persistent leaning of our educational system – and perhaps of the British character itself – towards the humanities and the professions rather than industry and business; secondly our tendency to be better at making inventions than exploiting them, which did not matter from 1750 to 1850, when few others exploited them, but did matter in the twentieth century (e.g. the jet engine and nuclear power); and third, the devotion of our trade unions and Labour Movement generally towards employment rather than production, and the restrictive practices that this generates. Our economic performance has not been bad. But it has not been as good as it should be. If I had to guess, and it is only a guess, I would single out as mainly responsible the obstinate devotion of our highly educated minority to the humanities, leisure and the pursuit of happiness; the extension among policy-makers of a free trade doctrine from food and materials, where it helps us, to manufactured goods where it does not; and the long-surviving bitterness and fear of unemployment among the working population left by the depressions of the pre-Keynesian era.

But however these controversies may be resolved, economic arguments are in the last resort only about means. When one turns from these to assess the ends for which these instruments exist, I find that what I value most after these fifty years are reason, toleration in the widest sense, and the institutions which have proved necessary to protect human liberty. It is the fanatics, maniacs and men of violence who do most harm. On the plane of reason you can agree; on that of unreason you will almost always conflict. So in the light of history let us defend without compromise human rights, personal freedom, civil liberties, call them what you will; and the institutions which preserve them: representative government, the ability of the people not merely to criticize but change their rulers, freedom of speech, freedom to form new parties or any other non-violent political movement, and the rule of democratically created law. These are easy to enumerate, very hard to create, and extremely easy to destroy. Hitler only took a few weeks after seizing power to smash all the defences of a sophisticated modern democracy. The lesson is far from new, but is all the more compelling in our age when the apparatus of tyranny and the weapons of destruction are so much more hideous and more efficient than ever before. Excuses for tyranny and oppression have of course always been plentiful: in this century from Mussolini, who was making the trains punctual, and

Franco who was preserving religion, to the 'One-Paty State', with one man, one vote, and one candidate. The pretexts are different; but their falsehood is always the same. Those who become impatient with the frailties and failures of democratic politics, and still think violence might be a newer and better method, should read Gibbon, or any truthful account of Nazism, or essentials without which liberty is merningless. The Communists and Khrushchev's memoirs on the last years of Stalin. Government by consent, with all its glaring faults, is better in the end than authoritarianism, just because experience shows clever men to be no less selfish than fools.

If it is also true as argued here, that a reasonable measure of social justice is in the modern world one condition of political freedom, then it follows that excessive inequality – greater than is economically unavoidable – is not merely a great evil in itself, but is also an enemy of freedom. Freedom and a measure of equality are not alternatives but are necessary to one another. In the Communist world there is no genuine equality because a tiny elite enjoy political liberty and the rest do not. There is no equality in the Soviet Union between the imprisoned dissident and the General Secretary of the Communist Party. And in the extreme liberal *laissez-faire* state large numbers are deprived by excessive inequality of the essentials without which liberty is meaningless. The Communists and *laissez-faire* liberals in a sense make the same mistake, since both think that you can have either liberty or equality without the other. So I remain an even more firmly convinced Social-Democrat than when I joined the Labour Party forty-five years ago.

Indeed in the age-long rivalry between the virtues of freedom, toleration and humanity on the one hand, and order, justice and fortitude on the other (the ultimate issue of all politics, and the only real meaning concealed by the muddled phrases 'left' and 'right', or if you like the contrasted values of Athens and Sparta), my allegiance, though any rational man must respect both, has inclined ever more strongly with the years towards the kindlier virtues. It may seem paradoxical to add that for that very reason my admiration for the spirit and institutions of this country grew incomparably stronger in the years 1939 and 1940, when I suppose the British showed the greatest fidelity in their history to the Spartan virtues. But in those years the British people also seemed to me to believe that they had something precious to defend, and wished to establish something even more civilized thereafter. What other country after all, has preserved an unbroken record of constitutional government for nearly 300 years, and fought right through the two Great Wars, without attacking anyone else or being first attacked themselves, to eventual victory? In a morass of transient controversies, let us not forget that. It is one reason why I can conceive of no better fortune, when the time comes to cultivate private rather than public aspirations, than to live, love, garden and die, deep in the English country.

Index